To
Warren Cole
with Best wishes

Shannon Point

Portland Oregon
May 1, 2005

D1405713

Business Valuation and Taxes

Business Valuation and Taxes

Procedure, Law, and Perspective

David Laro
Judge, U.S. Tax Court

Shannon P. Pratt
CFA, FASA, MCBA, CM&A, MCBC

John Wiley & Sons, Inc.

This book is printed on acid-free paper. ∞

Copyright © 2005 by John Wiley & Sons, Inc., Hoboken, New Jersey. All rights reserved.

Published simultaneously in Canada

No part of this publication may be reproduced, stored in a retrieval system, or transmitted in any form or by any means, electronic, mechanical, photocopying, recording, scanning, or otherwise, except as permitted under Section 107 or 108 of the 1976 United States Copyright Act, without either the prior written permission of the Publisher, or authorization through payment of the appropriate per-copy fee to the Copyright Clearance Center, Inc., 222 Rosewood Drive, Danvers, MA 01923, 978-750-8400, fax 978-646-8600, or on the Web at www.copyright.com. Requests to the Publisher for permission should be addressed to the Permissions Department, John Wiley & Sons, Inc., 111 River Street, Hoboken, NJ 07030, 201-748-6011, fax 201-748-6008.

Limit of Liability/Disclaimer of Warranty: While the publisher and author have used their best efforts in preparing this book, they make no representations or warranties with respect to the accuracy or completeness of the contents of this book and specifically disclaim any implied warranties of merchantability or fitness for a particular purpose. No warranty may be created or extended by sales representatives or written sales materials. The advice and strategies contained herein may not be suitable for your situation. You should consult with a professional where appropriate. Neither the publisher nor author shall be liable for any loss of profit or any other commercial damages, including but not limited to special, incidental, consequential, or other damages.

For general information on our other products and services, or technical support, please contact our Customer Care Department within the United States at 800-762-2974, outside the United States at 317-572-3993 or fax 317-572-4002.

Wiley also publishes its books in a variety of electronic formats. Some content that appears in print may not be available in electronic books.

For more information about Wiley products, visit our Web site at www.wiley.com.

Library of Congress Cataloging-in-Publication Data:

Laro, David, 1942–

    Business valuation and taxes : procedure, law & perspective /
David Laro, Shannon P. Pratt.

      p.   cm.

    Includes bibliographical references and index.

    ISBN-13 978-0-4716-9437-3 (cloth)

    ISBN-10 0-471-69437-1 (cloth)

    1. Business enterprises—Valuation—United States.   2. Business
enterprises—Taxation—Law and legislation—United States.   I. Pratt,
Shannon P. II. Title.

    HF5681.V3L37 2005

    346.73'065—dc22

                        2004013842

Printed in the United States of America

10 9 8 7 6 5 4 3 2 1

Dedication by David Laro

To my wife, Nancy,
and our family—
Rachel, David, and their children, Sophie and Asher
Marlene, Andrew, and their sons, Alexander and Benjamin

Dedication by Shannon Pratt

To my wife, Millie,
and our family—
Mike, Barb, and their sons, Randall and Kenny
Georgia, Tom, and their children, Elisa, Katie, and Graham
Susie, Tim, and their children, John, Calvin, and Meg
Steve, Jenny, and their children, Addy and Zeph

About the Authors

The Honorable David Laro was appointed by President George H. W. Bush to the United States Tax Court, confirmed by the Senate, and invested as a federal judge in November 1992. He formerly practiced law in Michigan for 24 years, specializing in tax law.

Judge Laro is a graduate of the New York University School of Law (LLM in Taxation, 1970), the University of Illinois Law School (JD, 1967), and the University of Michigan (BA, 1964).

Before joining the U.S. Tax Court, Judge Laro was chairman and CEO of a publicly traded international company. In 1985, he co-founded Republic Bancorp, a Michigan bank holding company that was rated recently by *Fortune* magazine as the fifth-best corporation in America at which to work. He was the founder and chairman of the board of directors of Republic Bank Ann Arbor, a position he held until he became a federal judge. Judge Laro has also held several public offices, including a Regent of the University of Michigan, a member of the State Board of Education in Michigan, and chairman of the State Tenure Commission in Michigan. He formerly served as director of the Ann Arbor Art Association and as a member of the Holocaust Foundation in Ann Arbor.

As adjunct professor of law at Georgetown University Law Center, Judge Laro teaches a class in business planning. He is also a visiting professor at the University of San Diego School of Law, where he teaches business valuation and tax litigation. He lectures on tax policy at Stanford Law School and is a member of the National Advisory Committee for New York University School of Law.

A frequent guest speaker, Judge Laro lectures for the American Bar Association, the American Society of Appraisers, the American Institute for Certified Public Accountants, and other professional organizations and associations. In addition, he has authored numerous articles on taxation printed in the American Bar Association *Journal*, the *University of Illinois Law Review*, and other publications. He is a fellow of the American College of Tax Counsel.

At the request of the American Bar Association and the Central Eastern European Law Initiative, Judge Laro contributed written comments on the Draft Laws of Ukraine, Kazakhstan, Uzbekistan, Slovenia, and the Republic of Macedonia, and on the creation of specialized courts in eastern Europe. As a consultant for the Harvard Institute for International Development and Georgia State University, Judge Laro lectured in Moscow to Russian judges on tax reform and litigation procedures. Judge Laro has also lectured to judges and tax officials in Azerbaijan on tax reform.

Judge Laro's noteworthy tax decisions include *Simon* (depreciation of antique musical instrument), *Mandelbaum* (lack of marketability discount), *Wal-Mart* (inventory shrinkage), *ACM Partnership* (corporate tax shelter), *Lychuk* (capitalization issues), and *Bank One* (valuation of financial derivatives).

Judge Laro's family shares his interest in tax law. His wife is a certified public accountant. Both of his daughters and one son-in-law are tax attorneys. For variety, his other son-in-law is a urologist. Judge Laro enjoys spending time with his family, especially his grandchildren, Sophie, Alexander, Benjamin, and Asher.

Shannon Pratt's reputation for knowledge and experience in the field of business valuation is legendary and unparalleled. He is the best-known authority in the field of business valuation and has written numerous books that articulate many of the concepts used in modern business valuation around the world.

He is chairman and chief executive officer of Shannon Pratt Valuations, LLC; Publisher Emeritus for Business Valuation Resources, LLC; and a member of the board of directors of Paulson Capital Corp., an investment banking firm specializing in small-firm IPOs and secondary offerings.[1]

Dr. Pratt holds an undergraduate degree in business administration from the University of Washington and a doctorate in business administration, majoring in finance, from Indiana University. He is a Fellow of the American Society of Appraisers, a master certified business appraiser, a chartered financial analyst, a master certified business counselor, and a certified mergers and acquisitions advisor.

His professional recognitions include being designated a life member of the American Society of Appraisers and also a life member of the Business Valuation Committee of the American Society of Appraisers, past chairman and a life member of the ESOP Association Advisory Committee on Valuation, a life member of the Institute of Business Appraisers, the recipient of the magna cum laude in business appraisal award from the National Association of Certified Valuation Analysts, and the recipient of the Distinguished Achievement Award from the Portland Society of Financial Analysts. He served two three-year terms (the maximum) as a trustee-at-large of The Appraisal Foundation.

Besides lecturing, writing, and teaching courses for such organizations as the American Society of Appraisers, the Alliance of Merger & Acquisition Advisors, the American Bar Association, and several state bars, Dr. Pratt is author of the following books published by John Wiley & Sons, Inc.: *Business Valuation Discounts and Premiums*; *Business Valuation Body of Knowledge: Exam Review and Professional Reference*, 2nd edition; *Business Valuation Body of Knowledge Workbook*; *Cost of Capital: Estimation and Applications*, 2nd edition; *Cost of Capital Workbook*; and *The Market Approach to Valuing Businesses*. He is also the author of *The Lawyer's Business Valuation Handbook*, published by the American Bar Association. He is coauthor of *Valuing a Business: The Analysis and Appraisal of Closely Held Companies*, 4th edition, and *Valuing Small Businesses and Professional Practices*, 3rd edition (both published by McGraw-Hill), *Guide to Business Valuations*, 14th edition (published by Practitioners Publishing Company), and *Guide to Canadian Business Valuations*.

He was a founder of Willamette Management Associates, and served as a managing director of that firm through December 2003. For more than 35 years, Dr. Pratt has performed val-

---

[1]Due to judicial ethical considerations, Judge Laro is not able to and therefore does not endorse, promote, or recommend any commercial or business services Shannon Pratt or others have created or with which they are involved, some references to which are included in this book for informational purposes only.

uation engagements for mergers and acquisitions, employee stock ownership plans (ESOPs), fairness opinions, gift and estate taxes, incentive stock options, buy-sell agreements, corporate and partnership dissolutions, dissenting stockholder actions, damages, and marital dissolutions, to name a few. He has testified in a wide variety of federal and state courts across the country and frequently participates in arbitration and mediation proceedings. Beginning in 2004, he practices valuation with Shannon Pratt & Associates.

Dr. Pratt develops and teaches business valuation courses for the American Society of Appraisers, the American Institute of Certified Public Accountants, and the Association of Mergers & Acquisitions Advisors, and frequently speaks on business valuation at national legal, professional, and trade association meetings. He has also developed a seminar on business valuation for judges and lawyers.

Besides life with his wife Millie, Dr. Pratt enjoys his model railroad, the ever-growing collection of glasses and mugs from many places he's visited, fine wines, and frequent visits from their four children and ten grandchildren.

Table of Contents

Table of Contents

Foreword

LEGAL PRACTITIONER'S PERSPECTIVE

Judge David Laro and Dr. Shannon Pratt have many years of experience looking at business data. Dr. Pratt looks at the data and its interrelationships for the purpose of evaluating the usefulness of the data in predicting or emulating the behavior of the marketplace. In that role, he has become well-known for his common-sense explanations of the tools of the appraisal profession and has become both the master teacher and the dean of the profession. The books he has authored and co-authored have become indispensable references for business amateurs—like most lawyers—who routinely encounter valuation issues.

Judge Laro looks at business data in the context of the cases that we advocates present to him. We cannot hire him like many of us have engaged Dr. Pratt over the years, but all of us, as citizens, have hired him to objectively ask whether the data and analysis laid before him makes sense and whether we advocates have used the principles developed by Dr. Pratt and others in a manner that advances the integrity of the tax system. Even when the resolution of issues is controversial, Judge Laro's name on an opinion signals thoughtfulness, thoroughness, and an effort to be helpful to the reading public as well as fair to the litigants in the particular case.

Thus, it is refreshing to see these two close observers of valuation issues collaborate on this intriguing volume. What the reader gets is something like a mural—depicting the life of a business appraisal from conception to preparation to the occasional ultimate use by a trier of fact. The coverage ranges from factors that precede but influence valuation, such as the choice of business entity (Chapter 7), to factors that shape the end use, such as the burden of proof (Chapter 5) and penalties (Chapter 6). The respective sections of the mural are drawn with great care and clarity and are a wonderful addition to the scholarship in this area. The reader's opportunity to appreciate the whole panorama, however, is priceless.

The authors have not tiptoed around subjects that have been controversial. The discussions of "the *General Utilities* doctrine" in Chapter 17 and discounts for lack of marketability in Chapter 18 address areas in which the interaction of courts and appraisers has been most lively in recent years. The lawyer whose practice encounters such issues can use these discussions to navigate around the pitfalls that both business practice and tax controversies can place in the way.

Nor have the authors avoided areas just because they are tough. Chapter 8, dealing with the special challenges of valuing S corporations and other pass-through entities, confronts some of the most complex and sometimes inscrutable current topics in the evolution of valuation law. That chapter is at once the most eclectic and the most meticulous discussion of these challenges I have seen to date.

Whether the reader practices before the Tax Court or not, and whether the reader handles valuation matters routinely or only occasionally, this volume will be a most valuable resource.

Ronald D. Aucutt, Esq.
McGuire Woods, LLP

Foreword

LAW PROFESSOR'S PERSPECTIVE

To write about valuation is a humbling task. No matter how ambitious and dedicated an author may be, eventually he or she is forced to acknowledge that even a lifetime of work would leave some aspects of the subject untouched. This offering from Judge David Laro and Dr. Shannon Pratt fills in some persistent gaps in the business valuation literature, as well as provides a surprisingly fresh treatment of perennial themes.

The range of the book is impressive. It covers such basics as the definition of fair market value for federal tax purposes and the features that distinguish it from fair value and intrinsic value. But it also digs into practical and procedural questions that many other valuation treatises leave out. And it analyzes several important evolving issues, such as valuing S corporation stock and selected international problems (transfer pricing and customs valuation), which require close attention from seasoned professionals and novices alike.

Business valuation experts often find themselves talking about *synergies*, and this work defines the term by example. Take the chapter on expert witnesses. Judge Laro's discussion of the relationship of the valuation professional to the litigation process provides a wealth of insight, from his unique and invaluable vantage point. But the chapter does not stop there. In its appendix, it is backed up by the Pratt organization's excellent directories of the many professional designations for appraisers and the associations that issue them. The reader gets both a guiding narrative from the judge, and hard data to help put his counsel into practice—the treasure map and the decoder ring in one package, as it were.

The chapter on the lack-of-marketability discount is another dynamic combination. Here one finds not only a summary of the traditional rationales for the discount and the studies on which its amount can be based, but also a thorough summary of the classic tax valuation cases in which it has been applied. The blend of appraisal theory with tax scholarship is impressive and useful.

Too often the best practitioners of a craft are so busy that they lack the time to pass their knowledge on. Some are stingy with their wisdom, and others are not very good at teaching. When the authors of this book sit down to write, however, the results are a thing of beauty. Enjoy, and learn from, every page.

John A. Bogdanski
Professor of Law
Lewis & Clark Law School

Foreword

BUSINESS APPRAISER'S PERSPECTIVE

I am honored that I was asked to write a foreword for a book written by two people who I believe are among the most prolific people in our industry, the Honorable Judge David Laro and Dr. Shannon Pratt.

I remember meeting the Honorable Judge Laro, almost a decade ago now, while he was teaching a valuation course at the National Judicial College. Prior to that, all I had ever done was read many of his opinions. I still remember walking into the classroom that day and seeing his name tent on a desk in the front row of the room. Almost immediately my stress level rose when I realized that I would be citing many of his opinions during my program that day. All I could think about was what would happen if I misrepresented or misstated something. I found his Honor to be extremely respectful, personable, open-minded, and eager to learn, as well as understand, as a judge.

Over time, I came to learn more about the judge and the person. I believe he sets a phenomenal example for us, as successful or ambitious experts, with regard to certain standards of professionalism, credibility, and character traits. His Honor really has a way of putting things in perspective. I believe this has never been embodied more succinctly and poignantly than in his Honor's own words as he answered the following question that was posed to him from the audience at a recent AICPA Annual Valuation Conference: "Your Honor, do you believe that this is the greatest job that anyone or you could have?" To this his Honor responded, "I surely have a wonderful job and career, but it is not the greatest. The greatest job I have is being a husband, father, and grandfather!" I commend you for your work as a person and a professional and thank you for your guidance and friendship through the years, and the opportunity to be a little part of it all.

Then there is Dr. Pratt. He needs little if any discussion in the valuation industry. I have often referred to him in my presentations as the "godfather" of valuations. Dr. Pratt has traveled the country helping so many of us in our careers. He has provided us guidance throughout the years through his writings, speeches, and subscriptions. I doubt that the industry would be at the maturity level it is without his works. He has always forced us to challenge our conventional wisdom and thoughts to find the better way to do things. He too has set an example to many of us without asking us for much in return. (Okay, maybe just putting up with some of his unbridled salesmanship.) He has formalized many of the processes and theories that we currently apply in our practices. He took positions at times when others would not—a true pioneer!

This book, like its two authors, is a unique work that provides practical sense and guidance in our profession. It is the first of its kind that presents methodology issues of valuation, as well as procedural issues and what I would call the environmental factors (i.e., court, audit, appeal, etc.) of a valuation matter from the perspective of both the court and the expert. Many valuators get involved in a project from the perspective of completing the valuation engagement and it is separate and detached from the consideration of procedural and planning factors that gave rise to the project in the first place. Additionally, many valuators may not consider the impact of their work on further developments such as audit, appeals, and trial. It is clear from the writing herein, and I have stated this in many of my presentations around the country, that these aspects are not separate and, quite to the contrary, they are pivotal to the proper documentation, understanding, and support of a conclusion in a valuation matter. From a legal perspective it is important to understand the theories that are to be advanced by the valuation expert, as well as to understand, from a valuation perspective, the theories that are to be advanced by the planners, implementers, and legal counsel that set up the case. It is these folks who typically bring us into the case, yet it is we, as experts, who have a material impact on the success of the plans from a tax-planning perspective, as well as the court case, if it is contested.

This book is the bridge that connects the legal assumptions and legal issues with the valuation theories that valuators apply to those assumptions and issues to get to an appropriately supportable conclusion in a matter. It provides a view from the bridge of the procedural environment. With this information and knowledge, experienced and fledgling valuators alike are much better prepared to embark on the journey. Thank you both again for all of your guidance through the years and all of the hard work you have put into this manuscript, which will prove invaluable for us in the industry!

Mel H. Abraham
CPA, CVA, ABV, ASA
Abraham Valuation Advisors

Preface

Valuation issues permeate the Internal Revenue Code. Some people have estimated that there are several hundred sections in the Internal Revenue Code, as well as thousands of references in the Federal Tax Regulations, that deal with fair market valuation. Each year, taxpayers report on their tax returns millions of transactions that require estimates of value. Billions of tax dollars are at stake in valuations and, naturally, the Internal Revenue Service is interested in collecting the amount properly due the Government. Given the multitude of transactions and the significant amount of tax revenue at stake, there are frequent controversies over the issues related to correct valuation.

A book on the relationship between federal taxes and business valuation is therefore not only appropriate, but also timely. This book focuses on the law, procedure, and perspective of business valuation, exploring not just the rules, but also the policy or administrative reasons for implementing them. This is not a book on how to litigate before any particular court. There are many fine litigation treatises available, and one interested in learning more about federal litigation should consult them as the need occurs. In this book, the authors have drawn upon almost 75 years of combined practical experience in the areas of taxes and business valuation, to provide the reader with a comprehensive resource for education and practice.

The reader who is looking for a discussion of some of the very latest tax cases may have to look elsewhere. For ethical considerations, Judge Laro must decline to comment on any tax case that is not beyond the appeal period or is in appeals. However, there is also another reason why such a discussion is not included here. This book endeavors to help the reader understand the law, procedure and perspective of business valuations, and as such is not dependent on any one case. As the reader will observe, case law on this subject is highly fact-specific; therefore, while a particular case may be interesting, it often is not precedential for the next case. The authors, therefore, have chosen to concentrate on providing the reader with the tools to analyze a proper business valuation, with the hope that grasping the essentials will be infinitely more helpful than studying a past case with limited application.

ORIGIN OF THE BOOK

The idea for writing this book came about when both authors appeared together a few years ago on a business valuation continuing education program. In addition to being a sitting judge on the U.S. Tax Court, David Laro also teaches business valuation to law students. Shannon Pratt, a well-known educator of long standing, has previously authored several books on valuation. Over an enjoyable lunch, we discussed the need for clear and helpful educational materials on valuation, and concluded that we could provide this—and more. We felt that a book that combines basic valuation techniques with the unique perspectives of the two authors would be helpful not only to students, but also to valuation practitioners, attorneys, accountants, bankers, and financial analysts, among others.

AUTHORS PROVIDE OWN PERSPECTIVES

By combining essential valuation basics with more exotic valuation procedures, this book endeavors to offer a wide range of valuation knowledge. At every opportunity, the authors provide valuable first-hand experience, as well as each author's unique perspective. It should be noted that Judge Laro's views are his own, and they may or may not be harmonious with those of his colleagues on the U.S. Tax Court, for whom he does not speak.

This book is the product of two authors, with selected contributions by L. Richard Walton, Esq., Alina Niculita, Nancy J. Fannon, Roger J. Grabowski, Z. Christopher Mercer, Chris D. Treharne, and Daniel R. Van Vleet. Shannon Pratt is responsible for the chapters addressing valuation approaches, techniques, finance-related issues, and other technical matters. David Laro is responsible for the chapters relating to tax and legal issues, such as experts and subsequent events. Although some effort was made to reconcile the writing differences between the two authors, there still remain some stylistic and substantive differences. We are grateful to L. Richard Walton, Esq., and to Alina Niculita for their contributions.

The contributed chapters do not necessarily reflect the views of either Judge Laro or Dr. Pratt, and are included for the sake of completeness.

TOPICS COVERED

This book combines basic information with important perspectives on current issues. The following topics are included to give the reader an understanding of the basic knowledge needed to appreciate business valuation in the context of the law governing fair market value for federal tax purposes:

- Standards of business valuation
- Subsequent events
- Business valuation experts
- Sources of law and choice of courts
- Burden of proof in valuation controversies
- Penalties and sanctions
- Valuation and choice of entity
- IRS positions

Next, this book addresses the techniques and procedures of performing a business valuation, with topics such as:

- Adjustments to financial statements
- Comparative financial statement analysis

- The income approach
- The market approach
- The asset-based approach
- Entity-level discounts
- Weighting of approaches

This book also addresses more complex subjects, such as:

- Valuation of interests in S corporations and "pass-through" entities
- Valuation of international transactions
- Discounts for lack of marketability
- Other shareholder-level discounts
- Valuation of options

Topics that especially concern the valuation practitioner and the attorney include:

- Economic and industry analysis
- Site visits and interviews
- Questions to ask business valuation experts
- Business appraisal reports

This book is an attempt to author, in one volume, a concise presentation of issues related to current tax-valuation practice. Both authors believe in the importance of quality business valuations, and one of our objectives is to promote high-quality business valuations in general. We hope it contributes to the knowledge of students and professionals alike—and that you enjoy reading it as much as we enjoyed writing it.

David Laro
Judge, U.S. Tax Court
Washington, DC

Shannon Pratt
DBA (Finance) CFA, FASA, MCBA, CBC, CM&A
Portland, OR
shannon@shannonpratt.com

Acknowledgments

Such a substantial undertaking does not, of course, happen without much assistance and insight from others. This book has benefited immeasurably from peer review by a dedicated group of professionals who provided valuable input and commentary.

We thank the following individuals who have reviewed the manuscript and provided suggestions for this book. We believe this volume truly represents a consensus of a broad cross-section of practitioners from all facets of the business valuation community.

Mel Abraham
Abraham Valuation Advisors

Ron Aucutt
McGuireWoods LLP

Dennis Belcher
McGuireWoods LLP

Jay Fishman
Kroll Zolfo Cooper

Roger Grabowski
Standard & Poor's division of the
    McGraw-Hill Companies, Inc.

Curt Kimball
Willamette Management Associates

Marlene Laro, Esq.
Frank Nolan, Esq.

James Rigby
Financial Valuation Group

Jeff Tarbell
Willamette Management Associates

Rachel Waimon, Esq.

Lewis R. Walton, Esq.

Richard Wise
Wise, Blackman

Portions of the manuscript were also reviewed by the following individuals:

Prof. Michael Devitt
University of San Diego School of Law

David Waimon, Esq.
Ernst & Young, LLP
Chicago, IL

The authors also thank the following individuals for providing their methods and views for inclusion in the controversial chapter on valuing S corporations and other pass-through entities, as well as for their assistance in pulling them together: Nancy J. Fannon, CPA, ABV, MCBA; Roger J. Grabowski, ASA; Z. Christopher Mercer, ASA, CFA; Chris D. Treharne, ASA, MCBA; and Daniel R. Van Vleet, ASA, CBA.

The authors are grateful to L. Richard Walton, Esq., for writing the International and Options chapters, as well as other valuable assistance. We also appreciate the contribution of several employees of Business Valuation Resources, including: Alina Niculita, CFA, Managing Editor of *Shannon Pratt's Business Valuation Update* and *The Economic Outlook Update*, for the case studies in the appendixes to The Income Approach and The Market Approach chapters; Angie McKedy, Financial Research Analyst, who assisted Alina and also prepared the bibliography to the Economic and Industry Analysis chapter; Doug Twitchell, Director of Financial Research, for his help with exhibits; Melanie Walker, Editor, for updating the Professional Accreditation Criteria exhibit; and Travis Bryan, Legal and Court Case Editor, for legal research.

We also acknowledge the valuable work of Janet Marcley, the project manager for this undertaking. She was the liaison among the authors, the publisher, and the outside reviewers. In addition, she typed Shannon's chapters, compiled the bibliography, and was responsible for obtaining permission to use material reprinted in this book from other sources. This book would simply not have been completed without Janet's dedication and able management.

We also thank Editor John DeRemigis, Associate Editor Judy Howarth, and Senior Production Editor Jennifer Hanley at John Wiley & Sons for their assistance and patience with this project. We also thank Missy Garnett of Cape Cod Compositors, who was responsible for the layout and typesetting of this book.

We thank Jeff Hamrick and Kevin Jacobs, who performed cite checking.

For permission to use material previously published, we especially thank the following:

American Bar Association
American Institute of Certified Public Accountants
American Society of Appraisers
Aspen Publishers
BIZCOMPS
Business Valuation Resources, LLC
CCH Incorporated
Emory Business Advisors, LLC
Nancy Fannon
FMV Opinions, Inc.
Roger Grabowski
Indiana University School of Law
Integra Information
John Wiley & Sons, Inc.
McGraw-Hill
Z. Christopher Mercer
NASDAQ
Peabody Publishing, LP
Practitioners Publishing Company
The Appraisal Foundation

Chris D. Treharne
Valuation Advisors
Daniel R. Van Vleet
Willamette Management Associates

We express our gratitude to all of the people mentioned above, as well as to all those who have had discussions with us about many conceptual and technical points in the book.

Standards of Business Valuation

SUMMARY

To determine the value of a business, one first must define the meaning of *value*. Although there are various definitions of value, the exclusive definition for federal tax purposes is found in the term *fair market value*. For nonfederal tax purposes, other standards for business value include fair value, investment value, and intrinsic value.

Fair market value is defined by the U.S. Department of the Treasury ("the Treasury") and involves a consideration of all relevant factors to determine value. It assumes an arms-length transaction between a willing buyer and seller performing a transaction, without any compulsion to buy or sell. The buyers and sellers are hypothetical, as is the market in which the transaction takes place. Although individual characteristics of the actual transaction may occasionally be considered, they usually are not. The buyer and seller are presumed to have knowledge of reasonable, relevant facts relating to the hypothetical transaction as of a specific valuation date.

Fair value is defined by state statutes and separately by the Financial Accounting Standards Board (FASB) for financial accounting purposes. Fair value is analogous to, but distinct from, fair market value. For state law purposes, fair value is used to determine value for dissenting or oppressed shareholders and occasionally in marital dissolution.

Another use of fair value is found in generally accepted accounting principles (GAAP) used by the accounting profession in the preparation of financial statements. There are at least two significant differences between fair value as used for GAAP and fair market value.

Investment value is a subjective concept, determining value from the perspective of the individual investor and thus taking into account individual characteristics.

Intrinsic value is the value of securities or a business from the perspective of a security analyst.

INTRODUCTION

Like beauty, value is in the eye of the beholder. What is value to one may be inconsequential to another. In this regard, value is mere subjective perception. Unlike beauty, however, the economic value of a business interest involves more than mere subjective perception. Valuation of a business interest involves a multitude of factors ranging from financial matters to historical perspectives.

Business interests are valued in a variety of contexts and for a variety of purposes. Governments use events and circumstances relating to business as opportunities to tax businesses and their owners. For instance, when businesses are sold, pay dividends in kind, or are the subject of a taxable estate, the government asserts a tax and the business interest must be valued. Lending institutions value businesses when money is lent, or when properties are foreclosed. Estates and gifts of property also must be valued to determine whether such interests are taxed.

To value a business interest, we must have a standard or definition of value. We use *standard of value* synonymously with *definition of value*. Stated concisely, business value must be measured and defined by a definition of value that is relevant, predictable, and reliable. Recognizing that the same business interest may have different values if more than one standard of value is used, value becomes largely a matter of definition.

Consider the various definitions of value throughout the life cycle of a diamond. In one sense, the diamond is nothing more than carbon, an inert mineral found in the earth's layers. In this regard, the diamond, except for some limited commercial uses, has little inherent value. If we define the diamond's value based on its raw mineral content, we have an object of fairly low value. We cannot eat it, drive it to work, or use it to take shelter when it rains; the diamond has a value equal to the sum of its carbon content.

Change the definition of value. Instead of measuring the diamond's value strictly by the economic value of carbon, we instead define the diamond's value by a standard that measures carats, clarity, cut, and color. We also value the diamond as a perceived commodity, a fiction due in large part to the millions of dollars poured into advertisements convincing the public that the diamond has special economic value as an object of beauty. Except for some limited enhancement created by cutting and polishing, the diamond is still just inert carbon; if we continue to value the diamond by its pure mineral status, it has limited economic value. When we value the diamond by a standard that puts a premium on beauty and permanence, however, we increase its value considerably. The emphasis of value has changed, and so has the value to the average consumer.

Now let us suppose that our diamond is purchased from a retail store for $1,000 and given to a young woman as an engagement gift. The diamond has a transaction value equal to its purchase price, but, in the hands of the woman, the diamond now takes on a new value measured by her sentiment; she would likely refuse an offer from someone to buy her diamond, even if the amount offered were significantly more than its original purchase price.

Assume further that the diamond is insured and, regrettably, is stolen. The insurance policy provides that the diamond is insured for its actual cash value. Alternatively, some insurance policies may replace the diamond at today's cost. Either way, the diamond's value is determined by the terms of a contract.

Finally, suppose that the diamond ends up in an estate that must value it for federal estate-tax purposes. Fair market value is now the standard, as determined by Treasury regulations.

As this example illustrates, there are a variety of different standards of value that can be used, ranging from intrinsic value to contractual value. Similarly, business valuation is also subject to varying standards of valuation. Our first task is thus to define the appropriate standard of value.

Among the various standards used to define business value are fair market value, fair value, intrinsic value, and investment value. It is possible, indeed likely, that the same business interest could have different values, depending on which standard of value we use. For federal tax purposes the standard is fair market value. We therefore emphasize fair market value, and its nuances, in this chapter.

SOURCES FOR DEFINING VALUE

Statutes

One should always consult statutes in the specific subject area that is being valued, as federal or state statutes often define the relevant standard of value. For instance, the Employee Retirement Income Security Act (ERISA) and the federal securities laws address valuation issues. There are many sections in the Internal Revenue Code ("the Code") that refer to fair market value.[1] Given the frequent usage of *fair market value* in the Code, it is somewhat surprising that none of these sections actually defines the term. As we shall see, the definition of fair market value is left to the Treasury Regulations ("the Regs" or "the Regulations").

States also have statutes that define value in the context of mergers, dissenters' rights, marital dissolutions, and family issues. If the business value issue arises in the context of a state law controversy or nonfederal valuation, one should heed the definition of value found in the state's statute. However, if the valuation involves federal taxes, state law does not control the definition of value and one should follow the Code and Treasury Regulations.

Treasury Regulations

As noted, the Code does not define the term *fair market value*, but the Regulations do. It is common for Congress to enact a statute and then delegate to the Treasury the responsibility of providing the detailed rules necessary to carry out congressional intent. Like statutes, Treasury Regulations have the full force of law.

---

[1]Also, there are thousands of sections of the Regulations that refer to *fair market value*.

Regulation section 20.2031-1(b) defines fair market value as:

The price at which the property would change hands between a willing buyer and a willing seller when the former is not under any compulsion to buy and the latter is not under any compulsion to sell, both parties having reasonable knowledge of relevant facts.

This definition is critical to all issues involving federal tax valuation, and we will discuss it more fully later in this chapter.

Case Law

In addition to statutes and the regulations interpreting them, definitions of value are influenced by case law that applies statutory definitions to the facts of individual cases. Cases thus offer perspectives that affect the definition of value.

Accordingly, one should always consult the relevant case law to understand how the court applies a given definition of value to a particular set of facts. Unfortunately, there are some shortcomings in the use of case law as a means to define and elaborate on business value. Five specific concerns are considered here:

1. *Fact-specific cases.* Valuation cases tend to be factually voluminous and very specific to those facts. Although there might be similarities in the factual patterns of one case compared to another, there are always differences. Lawyers are taught at an early stage in law school how to minimize the importance of these factual differences when they want to use a case as favorable precedent, and to highlight the importance of these differences when they want to discourage the use of a case as precedent. Valuation case law is almost always instructive, but is not necessarily precedential because of the specific nature of the facts of each case.

2. *Inconsistencies and confusion.* The reader of valuation case law can easily become confused when trying to arrive at clear valuation principles from the case law. This is so, at least in part, due to inconsistencies among the cases. For instance, one case may combine discounts to arrive at a valuation amount, while another clearly separates each discount as a distinct item. One case may weigh factors used in arriving at fair market value while another avoids weighing the same factors. Which is right? Why are they inconsistent?

   We rely on case law as an essential element of our jurisprudence. Our common law inheritance defines fairness and justice as treating people the same when their legal circumstances are the same. Accordingly, two valuation cases should theoretically reach the same result if the circumstances and facts of the two cases are the same. It does not always work out that way in practice for several reasons.

   Case law is the product of many variables:

   - The facts of each case likely will be unique.
   - Lawyers present their cases based on their own strategy and theory of the case. The lawyers' strategies and theories will vary from case to case, as lawyers see things differently.
   - Witnesses may present themselves differently. Some witnesses may be credible, while others lack sincerity. If a witness lacks credibility, the evidence that the witness testifies to may also lack credibility.

- The introduction and admissibility of evidence often varies from one valuation case to another. The trier of fact can decide a case based only on the trial record. If evidence does not get into the record because it was not offered, or was not admitted because of some objection, the record evidence in one trial may be different from that of another trial in which such evidence was admitted.
- Experts often disagree with one another about the proper valuation. The trier of fact may choose to accept or reject expert testimony in whole or in part. Sometimes, experts testify one way and then testify another in a different case. Inconsistent expert testimony often produces inconsistent results among cases.
- The trier of fact, whether it be a judge or jury, will vary in terms of sophistication, experience, perception, and judgment when it comes to valuation decisions.
- For all of these reasons, it is not surprising that valuation cases can seem inconsistent with prior cases, even where many of the facts look similar.

3. *Terminology.* One must be careful when reading cases for valuation guidance to make sure that, even though a particular standard of valuation is utilized, the standard has been correctly defined and implemented. For instance, some cases will say that they are using fair market value. We know that fair market value has a specific meaning and definition under the Regulations. Even though a case may state that it is using the fair market value standard, one must ensure that the components of fair market value, as defined by the Regulations, are actually present and an integral part of the valuation analysis. Unfortunately, not all case law reveals a uniform and consistent application of valuation standards, even though the terms used look correct.

4. *Differences among circuits.* Federal valuation cases are first tried by a federal trial court. These courts are the federal district courts, the U.S. Tax Court, the Court of Federal Claims, and the U.S. Bankruptcy Courts. These cases are then appealable to the appellate courts. Cases from the Claims Court are appealed to the Federal Circuit. Cases in the district courts are appealable to the various circuit courts that govern their geographic area. Tax Court cases are appealed to the various circuit courts in which the taxpayer resides. Sometimes, the circuit courts will arrive at conflicting results with one another, and, when they do, the conflict may be resolved by one last appeal to the U.S. Supreme Court. Remember that a precedent in one circuit may not be the same as that in another circuit. For instance, the application of subsequent events in one circuit may not be precisely the same in another.

5. *Federal versus state.* Federal case law interpreting the Treasury definition of fair market value is directly relevant in determining value for federal tax purposes. On the other hand, state courts that interpret state definitions of value may not be at all helpful when trying to argue a federal tax case. A sophisticated reader of case law must appreciate all these nuances to fully understand the impact of case law on valuation.

Contracts and Agreements

Another source for definitions of value may be found in contractual agreements of the parties. Parties to a contract are free to bargain for their own definition of value to meet their special situation. We note, however, that the Internal Revenue Service (also called the Service in this book) is not bound by the parties' determination of business value, especially if the parties are not bargaining at arm's length. Values (and the definitions of value) arrived at between family members are often suspect to the Service and to the courts.

Examples of contractual definitions of value are the following:

- Parties to buy-sell agreements often determine value by specific terms and conditions in contracts, which may or may not conform to any accepted definition of value in any general legal context. Some of these contracts may provide that the value of a business is defined by its book value, or by a multiple of earnings. Other contracts may indicate that the value of the business is defined by earnings before interest, taxes, depreciation, and amortization. Contractual measures of value are limited only by the creativity of the parties to the contract.

- Insurance contracts provide for specific values as a basis for their coverage. The insurance contract may limit coverage to the actual cash value of an insured item, less its accumulated depreciation. If so, that contract provides the definition of value. Business interruption insurance agreements provide specific definitions of just what values they will cover if a business is interrupted due to various insured causes.

- A corporation's articles of incorporation, its bylaws, or its board resolutions may contain business valuation terms. Such terms are common for buy-out or buy-in clauses and define their conditions as well as shareholder value.

- Lawyers commonly prepare pre-incorporation agreements to address issues such as the value of property that will be part of the opening balance sheet of a corporation.

- A prenuptial agreement is a contract where the intent of the parties is clearly to control the division and assign value of marital assets.

- Lawyers negotiate the value and nature of certain structured settlements to resolve complex litigation.

Revenue Rulings and Other Treasury Pronouncements[2]

The Treasury will issue Revenue Rulings (Rev. Rul.) and Revenue Procedures (Rev. Proc.), which are announced positions of the Service. Some of these rulings are directly related to establishing business value. For instance, Rev. Rul. 59-60 provides detailed methodology relating to the valuation of closely held corporate stock and other business interests. It lists eight factors to consider, as a minimum, when determining the valuation of closely held business interests. Rev. Rul. 93-12, relates to minority discounts in the context of family-owned businesses.

Revenue Rulings and other Treasury pronouncements, unlike statutes and Regulations, do not carry the force of law. Nevertheless, these are important standards that directly relate to valuation, and one is well advised to consult the published rulings of the government for guidance on valuation issues.

---

[2]See Chapter 22.

Professional Associations

Professional associations frequently define standards of value. An example is the Financial Accounting Standards Board (FASB), a professional organization primarily responsible for establishing financial reporting standards in the United States. The FASB's standards are known as generally accepted accounting principles (GAAP). GAAP uses predominantly transaction-based valuation—that is, valuation established in an actual exchange or transaction by the reporting entity. Accountants view values established in arm's-length exchanges as less subjective and more easily verified than values produced without an exchange.

A number of FASB releases pertain to fair value of various assets. For instance, Statement of Financial Accounting Standards (SFAS) No. 133 requires certain financial instruments to be reported on the balance sheet at fair value, with gains and losses included in current earnings. Whereas SFAS No. 133 does not prescribe specific methods for arriving at fair value, it does describe in general terms possible methods for determining fair value. These standards, while not law, certainly have an important influence on the definition of fair value for financial statement purposes. (Fair value in this context is quite different from fair value in the context of state statutes governing dissenting shareholder rights and partnership/corporate dissolution rights).

DEFINITIONS OF VALUE

With all of these potential sources for standards of value, it is essential that all persons engaged in trying to determine value understand and agree, at the outset, on the proper definition of value.

Fair Market Value

We emphasize the Code's fair market value over the other nonfederal standards of value because fair market value permeates all of the valuations done for federal tax matters. It is estimated that there are several hundred sections in the Code that involve fair market value in one manner or another. As noted earlier, the Regulations define fair market value as:

> *the price at which the property would change hands between a willing buyer and a willing seller, neither being under any compulsion to buy or sell and both having reasonable knowledge of relevant facts.*

History of Fair Market Value

We trace the first use of the term *fair market value* to *United States v. Fourteen Packages of Pins.*[3] In that case, the issue was whether the manufacturer shipped pins from England to the United States with a "false valuation" on the invoice; if it did, the shipment was illegal. In deciding that issue, the court ruled that fair market value, market value, current value, true

---

[3]H. Rept. 767, 65th Cong., 2d Sess. (1918), 1939-1 C.B. (Part 2), 86, 88.

value, and actual value all require the same inquiry: namely, what is the true value of the item in question?

Although the court in that case effectively held that *fair market value* was synonymous with other like terms, today we know that the term *fair market value* has been given a precise meaning separate and apart from other valuation terms.

The term *fair market value* appears to have been used in the revenue law as part of the 1918 Revenue Act. Section 202(b) of that Act stated that for purposes of determining gain or loss on the exchange of property, the value of any property received equals the cash value of its *fair market value*. The law offered no further explanation of the term *fair market value*, and the committee reports underlying the Act were equally unhelpful, utilizing the term without explaining it.

In 1919, the Advisory Tax Board (ATB) recommended an interpretation of the term.[4] There, the ATB stated that the term *fair market value* refers to a fair and reasonable price that both a buyer and a seller—who are acting freely and not under compulsion, and who are reasonably knowledgeable about all material facts—would agree to in a market of potential buyers.

Subsequently, in 1925, the Board of Tax Appeals (predecessor to the modern-day tax court) stated that the buyer is considered to be a "willing" buyer and that the seller is considered to be a "willing" seller. The Board also stated that fair market value must be determined without regard to any event that occurs after the date of valuation.[5]

Two years later, the Board of Tax Appeals adopted the ATB's recommendation that fair market value be determined by viewing neither the willing buyer nor the willing seller as being under a compulsion to buy the item subject to valuation.[6] The Board observed in another case that neither the willing buyer nor the willing seller is an actual person; instead, they are viewed as hypothetical persons who are mindful of all relevant facts. Specifically, the fair market value of an item is determined from a hypothetical transaction between a "hypothetical willing seller and buyer, who are by judicial decree always dickering for price in the light of all of the facts [and] cannot be credited with knowing what the future will yield."[7]

Finally, in 1936, the U.S. Supreme Court mandated that for federal income tax purposes, fair market value is determined by viewing the item under consideration on the basis of its best use. In the same case, the Supreme Court held that two adjacent pieces of land should be valued at the same value per square foot, regardless of the fact that one was being used in its highest and best use while the other was not being used at all.[8]

---

[4]T.B.R. 57, 1 C.B. 40 (April–December 1919).

[5]*Appeals of Charles P. Hewes*, 2 B.T.A. 1279, 1282 (1925).

[6]*Hudson River Woolen Mills v. Comm'r*, 9 B.T.A. 862, 868 (1927).

[7]*National Water Main Cleaning Co. v. Comm'r*, 16 B.T.A. 223 (1929).

[8]*St. Joseph Stock Yards Co. v. United States*, 298 U.S. 38, 60 (1936). The notion of "highest and best use" has also been recognized by Congress as a requirement of fair market value. H. Conf. Rept. 94-1380, at 5, 1976-3 C.B. (Vol. 3) 735.

Determining Fair Market Value Today

Today, determination of fair market value is a inquiry in which the trier of fact must weigh all relevant evidence of value and draw appropriate inferences.[9] An arm's-length sale of property close to a valuation date is indicative of its fair market value. If actual arm's-length sales are not available, fair market value represents the price that a hypothetical willing buyer would pay a hypothetical willing seller, both persons having reasonable knowledge of all relevant facts, with neither person compelled to buy or sell.[10]

The views of both hypothetical persons must be taken into account, and the characteristics of each hypothetical person may differ from the personal characteristics of the actual seller or a particular buyer.[11] Focusing too much on the view of one hypothetical person to the neglect of the view of the other is contrary to a determination of fair market value.[12]

Over the years, federal courts have developed a firmly established meaning for the term *fair market value* by enunciating seven standards that must be considered in determining fair market value:

1. The buyer and the seller are a willing buyer and a willing seller.
2. Neither the willing buyer nor the willing seller is under a compulsion to buy or sell the item in question.
3. The willing buyer and the willing seller are both hypothetical persons.
4. The hypothetical willing buyer and the hypothetical willing seller are both aware of all facts and circumstances involving the item in question.
5. The item in question is valued at its highest and best use, regardless of its current use.
6. The item in question is valued without regard to events occurring after the valuation date, unless the event was reasonably foreseeable at the valuation date or was relevant to the valuation.[13]
7. The transaction is for cash and will be consummated within a reasonable commercial time frame.

These standards have evolved over many decades.

---

[9]Rev. Rul. 59-60.

[10]*United States v. Cartwright*, 411 U.S. 546 (1973); *Snyder v. Comm'r*, 93 T.C. 529, 539 (1989); *Estate of Hall v. Comm'r*, 92 T.C. 312 (1989); see also *Gillespie v. United States*, 23 F.3d 36 (2d Cir. 1994); *Collins v. Comm'r*, 3 F.3d 625, 633 (2d Cir. 1993), *aff'g.* T.C. Memo 1992-478; Reg. § 20.2031-1(b).

[11]See *Estate of Bright v. United States*, 658 F.2d 999, 1005-1006 (5th Cir. 1981), *aff'g.* 71 T.C. 235 (1978); *Estate of Newhouse v. Comm'r*, 94 T.C. 193 (1990).

[12]See, e.g., *Estate of Scanlan v. Comm'r*, T.C. Memo. 1996-331, *aff'd. without published opinion,* 116 F.3d 1476 (5th Cir. 1997); *Estate of Cloutier v. Comm'r*, T.C. Memo. 1996-49, 71 T.C.M. (CCH) 2001 (1996).

[13]For a full discussion, see Chapter 2.

When estimating the fair market value of a business interest, one must give meaning to each of the words found in the Treasury's definition:

> . . .*the price at which the property would change hands between a willing buyer and a willing seller, neither being under any compulsion to buy or sell and both having reasonable knowledge of relevant facts.*[14]

We parse the definition as follows:

1. *Property.* Any business valuation must identify with particularity the precise property that is the subject of the valuation. In most cases, this is easy to do. If we are valuing some shares of MEL Corporation, we can often value the entire corporation and then assign value based on the number of shares being valued. It is a misconception, however, to believe that we must always value a company this way; sometimes, it is possible to value minority interests by themselves, or by reference to other minority interests, without needing to value the entire corporation.

   The valuation becomes more difficult if the item is a partial interest in a royalty, patent, or other intellectual property, but it is still comprehensible. The important thing to stress is that what is being valued is some property interest. On occasion, the valuation expert may need a legal opinion to ascertain the identity and nature of the property being valued. The precise definition of the word *property* has legal connotations and significance, particularly where the property is intangible. Business appraisers who are not also lawyers may have difficulty if they carelessly assume the definition of the property being valued.

2. *Would change hands.* The definition of value assumes that a hypothetical transaction will occur, whether it be a gift, sale, or exchange. The hypothetical transaction is assumed to be happening in a hypothetical market; identifying the hypothetical market and analyzing it is part of the valuer's task. There need not be an actual market for an item to have a fair market value; the item is valued on the basis of what a willing buyer and willing seller would buy and sell for, based on hypothetical sales of the item.

3. *Between a willing buyer and a willing seller.* The willing buyer and the willing seller are not the real persons involved in the actual transaction, which is the subject of the valuation. Rather, the willing buyer and seller are hypothetical persons. These hypothetical buyers and hypothetical sellers are characteristic of a universe of somewhat sophisticated persons. Imagine such hypothetical persons living in a hypothetical world doing business in a hypothetical market. The market may be described as follows:

   > [A] *"market" itself presupposes enough competition between buyers and sellers to prevent the exigencies of an individual from being exploited. It may well imply that the goods have several possible buyers, so that a necessitous seller shall not be confined to one; and that there are several possible sellers of the same goods or their substantial equivalent, so that a hard-pressed buyer shall not have to accept the first offer.*[15]

   In this universe, there are trades and exchanges of property happening on a routine and somewhat frequent basis. It is not important to the definition of fair market value that in the real world there may not be such trades or that they may not be frequent. Instead, the

---

[14]Reg. § 1.170A-1(c)(2).

[15]*Helvering v. Walbridge*, 70 F.2d 683,684 (2d Cir. 1934), *cert. denied*, 293 U.S. 594 (1934).

hypothetical buyer and seller are among a multitude of buyers and sellers who in the aggregate constitute a hypothetical market based on hypothetically frequent arm's-length transactions for the subject property.

Occasionally, a court may permit the item's subjective value to the taxpayer to enter into the definition of fair market value,[16] but almost all the cases recognize that objective, hypothetical evidence of value should dictate the valuation. Thus, the taxpayer's opinion that her diamond has great sentimental value must be disregarded if that sentiment is not a view that is held by the universe of hypothetical buyers and sellers.

We realize, however, that real transactions take place with real persons in real markets. When real considerations exist, and those real considerations are essential to the valuation,[17] those realities must be taken into consideration.[18] The valuation task, therefore, is to perform the valuation in the context of the real market, with real persons, without individualizing the hypothetical willing seller and willing buyer to such an extent that they lose their hypothetical character. Obviously, there must be some individualizing of the willing buyer and willing seller, or the valuation will lose relevance. For instance, the valuation of a urological medical practice must involve narrowing the consideration of buyers and sellers to physicians.

If this sounds complicated, it is. As a result of this hypothetical model, there is an inevitable tension in trying to describe the hypothetical willing buyer and willing seller without identifying and describing a real buyer and real seller.

In summary, the willing buyer and willing seller are hypothetical persons, but on occasion the individual or subjective characteristics of the buyer and seller are considered, where doing so makes the valuation more accurate.

4. *Neither being under any compulsion to buy or sell.* The hypothetical willing buyer and the hypothetical willing seller are assumed to be performing without any compulsion to buy or to sell, other than the normal concerns that buyers and sellers have. Thus, a forced liquidation is not within the definition of fair market value. Examples of forced transactions that do not meet the definition of fair market value are bankruptcies, sales compelled by creditors, and sales of property subject to an unexercised option.

The primary reason why forced sales should not be determinative of fair market value is this: When people sell under a compulsion, they act in haste and do not allow for the normal time it takes to market property so as to achieve its true value. Indeed, common sense suggests that a buyer may get a better deal by buying from a seller who is in a hurry to unload the property. One could, of course, argue that all sales are probative of market value, and that disregarding forced sales may taint the true market, which does involve sales compelled by financial necessity.

5. *Both having reasonable knowledge of relevant facts.* This aspect of the definition is critical in that it requires both the hypothetical buyer and seller to be not just well informed, but to also have reasonably full knowledge of all relevant facts. Therefore, a sale of an interest in

---

[16]See *Turner v. Comm'r*, 13 T.C.M. 463, 465 (1954).
[17]*True v. United States*, 547 F.Supp. 201, 204 (D. Wyo. 1982).
[18]*Estate of Winkler v. Comm'r*, 57 T.C. Memo 382 (1989).

a business by a seller who did not have reasonable knowledge of relevant facts cannot be the basis for a market comparable under the market comparability approach.

The requirement of full knowledge imposes a burden on the hypothetical buyer and seller to investigate the circumstances relating to the property, the market, and all relevant facts that reasonably are known or could be discovered. In some cases, the hypothetical seller or buyer may be better informed than the actual buyer or seller. Although this might seem illogical, remember that actual buyers or sellers have individual characteristics that are not taken into account when creating the hypothetical buyer and the hypothetical seller.[19]

In another example, suppose that a person owns stock in a closely held corporation. She believes the stock is worth $30 a share based on the assertions of the corporation's chief financial officer and a review of a two-year-old appraisal of the business performed by a reputable, independent business valuer. On that basis, gifts are made and gift tax returns are filed with the Service. Assume that the Service audits the taxpayer and concludes that the gifts are worth $50 a share. Resolution of this controversy will involve, in part, whether the actual taxpayer's "investigation" of the stock's value measures up to the kind of thorough investigation the hypothetical buyer or seller could have performed.

For example, would a hypothetical taxpayer be satisfied with a two-year-old appraisal? Would a hypothetical taxpayer rely on the assertions of the chief financial officer without looking for other comparable transactions to verify the accuracy of the valuation? The answers to these questions turn on all of the facts and circumstances of the transaction. The point is that, regardless of what the actual taxpayer did or failed to do, the hypothetical buyer or seller is presumed to have conducted an investigation to discover all relevant facts. Failure to be informed of all relevant facts means the valuation does not meet the fair market value standard and can be successfully challenged by the Service.

Finally, even though the hypothetical buyer and seller have reasonable knowledge of all relevant facts, they are not presumed to be omniscient of all obscure or minuscule information. As with many areas of the law, reasonableness permeates valuation controversies and grants some relief for the honestly mistaken taxpayer.

Valuation Approaches

Generally, three approaches are used to determine fair market value: the market approach, the income approach, and the asset-based approach.

The market approach values an item by looking at the market price of a comparable item. The income approach computes the present value of the estimated future cash flows of the item by taking the sum of the present value of the available cash flow and the present value of the residual value, or by capitalizing the indicated future level of maintainable cash flows or earnings. The asset-based approach examines the underlying company assets and liabilities to assess a value for the company.[20]

---

[19]*Estate of Trenchard v. Comm'r*, 69 T.C. Memo 2169 (1995) ("The willing buyer and the willing seller are hypothetical persons, rather than specific individuals or entities and the individual characteristics of these hypothetical persons are not necessarily the same as the individual characteristics of the actual seller or the actual buyer.")
[20]See Chapters 14, 15, and 16.

Fair Value

The term *fair value* is used in many state statutes as well as in GAAP. In state statutes, fair value is the valuation definition employed for dissenting stockholders' appraisal rights and sometimes for marital dissolution.

With respect to GAAP, *fair value* is often associated, and used interchangeably, with *fair market value*, and is employed by accountants in the preparation of financial statements.

State Law

The Revised Model Business Corporation Act (RMBCA) defines fair value as:

> the value of the shares immediately before the effectuation of the corporate action to which the dissenter objects, excluding any appreciation or depreciation in anticipation of the corporate action unless exclusion would be inequitable.

As previously observed:

> The statutory definition of fair value in 32 states is similar to the definition provided by the RMBCA. . . . The definition in several other states is similar, but without the "unless exclusion would be inequitable" clause. . . . The definition of fair value in Delaware and Oklahoma is similar to that of the several other states, but includes a clause that states, "In determining such fair value, the court should take into account all relevant factors."[21]

Most state courts have not equated fair value with fair market value when interpreting their own statutes. Accordingly, business valuations that are performed for state controversies adopt a different standard than that which is used for federal tax valuations and controversies.

As noted, each state generally enacts a statute that defines the term *fair value*. We look at Illinois, for example, which defines *fair value* in a manner designed to resemble but not match *fair market value*, as defined by the Treasury.

With regard to a noncash asset, the Illinois Code specifies that:

> (a) [fair value is] the amount at which that asset could be bought or sold in a current transaction between arms-length, willing parties;
> (b) quoted market price for the asset in active markets should be used if available; and
> (c) if quoted market prices are not available, [fair value is] a value determined using the best information available considering values of like assets and other valuation methods.

In ruling on the question of fair value, the Illinois courts have held that the fair value of an item may be the same as its fair market value, but not always.[22] The Illinois courts have also

---

[21]Shannon P. Pratt, *The Lawyer's Business Valuation Handbook* (Chicago: American Bar Association, 2000): 7, quoting from Daniel R. Van Vleet, Chapter 9A: "Fair Value in Dissenting Stockholder Disputes, in *Financial Valuation: Businesses and Business Interests*," U9A-6 (James H. Zukin, ed., 1999). This chapter lists the definitions of fair value in each state.
[22]*Laserage Technology Corp. v. Laserage Laboratories, Inc.*, 972 F.2d 799, 805 (7th Cir. 1992); see also *Institutional Equipment & Interiors, Inc. v. Hughes*, 562 N.E. 2d 662 (Ill. 1990) (holding that the fair market value valuation method did not apply, but fair value did).

noted that the state legislature has given them much flexibility in applying the concept of "fair value."[23] Over time, these courts have created a nonexclusive list of factors that are used in determining the fair value of an asset. These factors include earning capacity, investment value, history and nature of the business, economic outlook, book value, dividend-paying capacity, and market price of stock of similar businesses.[24]

Fair Value and GAAP

As previously noted, accountants use fair value as their standard in the preparation of GAAP financial statements. Financial statements prepared by certified public accountants are used not only by the clients for whom they are prepared but also by lending banks, buyers of businesses, the Securities and Exchange Commission, and countless others.

In one pronouncement, the FASB has defined fair value for financial accounting purposes in this way:

> *Value determined by bona fide bargain between well-informed buyers and sellers, usually over a period of time; the price for which an [asset] can be bought or sold in an arm's-length transaction between unrelated parties; value in a sale between a willing buyer and a willing seller, other than in a forced or liquidation sale; an estimate of such value in the absence of sales or quotations.*[25]

Sometimes, practitioners use *fair value* and *fair market value* interchangeably. Since the GAAP definition of fair value is so important, it is worthwhile to examine whether GAAP fair value is in fact the same as Treasury's fair market value.

Comparison of GAAP Fair Value to Fair Market Value

The *fair market value* standard requires the buyer and seller to be aware of all facts and circumstances that are relevant to the valuation. The fair value standard does not require any such knowledge, nor is it required of both parties. Fair value anticipates that the willing buyer and willing seller will be "well informed." While the terms *well informed* and *reasonably aware of all relevant facts and circumstances* appear similar, they are not. One can be well informed and still be unaware of all the facts and circumstances relevant to the valuation.

Second, fair market value requires that neither the willing buyer nor the willing seller be under any compulsion to buy or sell the property that is the subject of the valuation. Fair value states that the property should not be the subject of a forced sale or liquidation.

Are the two terms the same? No. A liquidation is not the same as being under a compulsion to buy or sell: One can liquidate voluntarily without being under some internal com-

---

[23]*Weigel Broad. Co. v. Smith*, 682 N.E. 2d 745, 749 (Ill. 1996).

[24]Id.; *Stanton v. Republic Bank of S. Chicago*, 581 N.E. 2d 678, 682 (Ill. 1991); *Independence Tube Corp. v. Levine*, 535 N.E. 2d 927, 930 (Ill. 1988) (more extensive list); *Stewart v. Stewart & Co.*, 346 N.E. 2d 475, 481 (Ill. 1976) (referencing Rev. Rul. 59-60).

[25]Statement of Federal Financial Accounting Standards #11: Amendments to Accounting for Property, Plant and Equipment (July 1999). See *Kohler's Dictionary for Accountants*, "Fair Value" (5th ed., 1983).

pulsion. Also, it is possible for one party to be forced into the transaction while the other party is not. Fair market value requires that neither party be under any compulsion.

Thus, GAAP fair value is a broader term than is fair market value for tax purposes. In some respects, fair value encompasses fair market value.

Investment Value

We have observed that fair market value necessarily involves hypothetical buyers, hypothetical sellers, and a hypothetical marketplace. The term *investment value* differs significantly from fair market value in that investment value denotes value to a *particular* buyer, seller, owner, or investor.

Investment value therefore considers and examines value from the perspective of a particular individual, owner, or investor. Unlike the hypothetical buyer and seller, we take into consideration a multitude of individualized factors when considering investment value, including these seven:

1. The respective economic needs and abilities of the parties to the transaction or event
2. Risk aversion or tolerance
3. Motivation of the parties
4. Business strategies and business plans
5. Synergies and relationships
6. Strengths and weaknesses of the target business
7. Form of organization of the target business

Intrinsic Value

Intrinsic value is a concept of value commonly used by an analyst in evaluating publicly held securities. It is distinguished from investment value in that investment value considers the circumstances of a particular investor or owner, while intrinsic value considers value from the perspective of the analyst. For example, if a stock is trading on the New York Stock Exchange at $30 per share, and a security analyst says, "I believe it is worth $40 per share based on my fundamental analysis," the $30 is fair market value, and the $40 is that analyst's estimate of intrinsic value.

PREMISE OF VALUE

In a fair market value analysis, one must make an assumption regarding the transactional facts and circumstances applicable to the subject being valued. This assumption will have a significant influence on the valuation itself and therefore should be considered as part of the business valuation. The various assumptions may be summarized as follows:

1. *Value as a going concern.* Value in continued use, as a mass assemblage of income-producing assets, and as a continuing business enterprise.

2. *Value as an assemblage of assets.* Value in place, as part of a mass assemblage of assets, but not in current use in the production of income, and not as a going-concern business enterprise.

3. *Value as an orderly disposition.* Value in exchange, on a piecemeal basis (not part of a mass assemblage of assets), as part of an orderly disposition. This premise contemplates that all the assets of the business enterprise will be sold individually, and that they will enjoy normal exposure to their appropriate secondary market.

4. *Value as a forced liquidation.* Value in exchange, on a piecemeal basis (not part of a mass assemblage of assets), as part of a forced liquidation. This premise contemplates that the assets of the business enterprise will be sold individually and that they will experience less-than-normal exposure to their appropriate secondary market.[26]

CONCLUSION

The correct standard of valuation for federal tax purposes is fair market value. The definition of fair market value is found in Treasury materials and has been refined over the years by the many courts that have dealt with the issue (see Chapter 22). Proper valuation for federal tax purposes requires an intricate knowledge of this complex concept.

---

[26]Shannon P. Pratt, et al., *Valuing a Business*, 4th ed. (New York: McGraw-Hill, 2000): 33.

Subsequent Events

SUMMARY

Generally, since valuation is determined as of a specific date, events subsequent to the valuation date should not affect the value of property as of the valuation date. This rule is subject to some notable exceptions.

Subsequent events may be relevant to show what knowledge the hypothetical buyer and seller could reasonably be expected to have at the valuation date. Some authorities hold that subsequent events evidence need only meet the standard test of relevancy. Courts may admit such evidence if probative of value.

Some courts use a subsequent sale of the property to establish its presumed fair market value, adjusting that number for intervening events between the date of valuation and the date of sale.

Some authorities use subsequent sales as evidence of value rather than as something that affects value.

KEY QUESTION

Should events occurring subsequent to the valuation date affect the value of the property as of the valuation date? This question, while seemingly capable of a simple answer, has produced a disconcerting array of responses in the many courts that have addressed the issue.

VALUATION DATE

We start with the obvious. To value a business interest, we must pick a point in time in which the valuation is to be performed. Sometimes, this date is simply the client's fiscal year-end or is established by mutual agreement. In an employee stock ownership plan, the valuation date is set forth in the plan and is usually the last day of that plan's fiscal year. In a merger, the valuation date is the date of such merger.

In the case of federal estate and gift taxes, the valuation date is set by Regulations. For example, in gift tax matters the gift is valued as of the date the gift is transferred.[1] With respect to income taxes and charitable contributions of property, the valuation date is the date when the gift is effectively and legally transferred.[2] For estate tax matters, the valuation date is the date of death or, alternatively, six months after death.[3]

The valuation date is important for determining fair market value. Fair market value requires that we value property at the price at which it would change hands between a willing buyer and seller, both having reasonable knowledge of relevant facts. To ascertain what facts the willing buyer/seller would know, we need to establish the valuation date as the focal point for determining the knowledge relevant to our valuation. Events subsequent to the valuation date, in most cases, are not known by the hypothetical buyer/seller and therefore are not relevant to the valuation.

The Court of Federal Claims stated the rule this way:

> [T]he valuation for income tax purposes must be made as of the relevant date without regard to events occurring subsequently.[4]

In some instances, a day, perhaps even an hour can make a difference in valuations. Stock markets can change value rapidly. Even real estate is subject to quick fluctuations depending on economic and political situations. Consider the value of the World Trade Center on September 10, 2001, compared to September 11, 2001, or consider the value of real property in downtown Baghdad a week before the Coalition invasion and again one day after the bombing began. Likewise, consider the value of a home overlooking a scenic river, compared to the same home after a 100-year flood wipes out everything around it and fills the basement with sludge. Finally, consider the value of a lottery ticket on the day of purchase, and then a week later when it is the winning ticket.

To state the obvious, value is highly dependent on reasonable knowledge of relevant facts. The valuation date fixes the time of the valuation and limits the universe of knowledge that can be used to determine value.

The Supreme Court stated this rule for subsequent events in *Ithaca Trust Co. v. United States*,[5] where Justice Holmes considered the value of a charitable remainder subject to a life estate. The question before the court was whether the charitable remainder became more valuable (as a deduction from the gross estate) because the life tenant, who survived the testator, died before reaching her actuarial life expectancy. The court held that the

---

[1]Reg. § 25.2512-1.
[2]Reg. § 1.170A-1(b).
[3]Reg. § 20.2031-1(b); Code §§ 2031(a), 2032(a).
[4]*Grill v. United States*, 303 F.3d 922 (Ct. Cl. 1962).
[5]279 U.S. 151 (1929). See also *First National Bank v. United States*, 763 F.2d 891 (7th Cir. 1985); *Estate of Smith v. Comm'r*, 198 F.3d 515 (5th Cir. 1999) *rev'g.* 108 T.C. 412 (1997); *Estate of McMorris v. Comm'r*, 243 F.3d 1254 (10th Cir. 2001), *rev'g.* 77 T.C.M. (CCH) 1552 (1999); *Propstra v. United States*, 680 F.2d 1248 (9th Cir. 1982); *Estate of McCord v. Comm'r*, 120 T.C.M. (CCH) 13 (2003) (Judge Foley dissenting).

value of the thing to be taxed must be valued as of the time when the act is done. The court stated:

> *The estate so far as may be is settled as of the date of the testator's death. The tax is on the act of the testa-*
> *tor not on the receipt of property by the legatees. . .[T]he value of the thing to be taxed must be estimated as*
> *of the time when the act is done. . .[I]t depends largely on more or less certain prophecies of the future; and*
> *the value is no less real at that time if later the prophecy turns out false than when it becomes true. Tempting*
> *as it is to correct uncertain probabilities by the now certain fact, we are of [the] opinion that it cannot be*
> *done, but that the value of the wife's life interest must be estimated by the mortality tables.*[6]

SUBSEQUENT EVENTS—EXCEPTIONS

This seemingly neat conclusion is undone by the word *relevant*.

Recall that fair market value assumes that the willing seller and buyer have reasonable knowledge of relevant facts on the valuation date. In deciding what is relevant, some courts have enlarged the focal point of the valuation date by deeming subsequent events "relevant" to taxpayers' perceptions at that time.

Reasonable Foreseeable Events

Some courts find certain events, transactions, and circumstances that happen after the valuation date to be relevant to the valuation if they are reasonably foreseeable as of the valuation date.[7]

It is natural to think that the willing hypothetical buyer will consider the future when deciding whether to buy. To the extent that such willing buyer is reasonably able to project into the future, it would seem that one may consider subsequent events that are foreseeable when performing a valuation.

An old but still viable tax case states:

> *Serious objection was urged by [the government] to the admission in evidence of data as to events which oc-*
> *curred after [the valuation period]. It was urged that such facts were necessarily unknown on that date and*
> *hence could not be considered. . . . It is true that value . . . is not to be judged by subsequent events. There*
> *is, however, substantial importance of the reasonable expectations entertained on that date. Subsequent*
> *events may serve to establish that the expectations were entertained and also that such expectations were*
> *reasonable and intelligent. Our consideration of them has been confined to this purpose.*[8]

Thus, the logic of permitting subsequent events to affect valuation is that they may be helpful and therefore relevant in proving that the hypothetical buyer/seller did reasonably foresee such events. In this manner, the later-occurring events are to be given consideration in the valuation. The weight to be given such evidence may, however, be negligible.[9]

---

[6]*Ithaca Trust Co. v. United States*, supra note 5, 279 U.S. 15 (1929).
[7]*Estate of Sprull v. Comm'r*, 88 T.C.M. (CCH) 1197 (1987 (subsequent events "could not have been reasonably foreseen at the time of the decedent's death").
[8]*Couzens v. Comm'r*, 11 B.T.A. 1040 (1928).
[9]*Campbell v. United States*, 661 F.2d 209 (Ct. Cl. 1981).

Estate Claims

A tax is imposed on the transfer of a taxable estate of every decedent who is a citizen or resident of the United States. The taxable estate is the gross estate less those deductions allowable under Code sections 2051 through 2056. Accordingly, the issue arises as to whether post-death facts can be considered in valuing claims against the estate that are allowable in the jurisdiction where the estate is being administered. On this issue, there is a split of authority in the Circuit Courts of Appeal.

The Ninth Circuit, in *Propstra v. United States*, 680 F.2d 1248 (9th Cir. 1982), held that the *Ithaca Trust* date-of-death valuation principle requires that at the instant of death, the net value of property should, as nearly as possible, be ascertained.

In contrast to *Propstra*, the Eighth Circuit in *Estate of Sachs v. Commissioner*[10] held that the date-of-death principle of valuation does not apply to claims against the estate deducted under section 2053(a)(3). In this case, the trial court held that the estate was permitted to deduct the subsequently refunded tax liability because it existed at the decedent's death. The appellate court then stated:

> *We hold that where, prior to the date on which the estate tax return is filed, the total amount of a claim against the estate is clearly established under state law, the estate may obtain under [predecessor to section 2053(a)(3)] no greater deduction than the established sum, irrespective of whether this amount is established through events occurring before or after the decedent's death.*

In essence, the court held that an estate loses its section 2053(a)(3) deduction for any claim against the estate that ceases to exist legally.

In a recent case, the Fifth Circuit was persuaded that the Ninth Circuit decision in *Propstra* correctly applied the *Ithaca Trust* date-of-death valuation principle to enforceable claims against the estate. In *Estate of Smith v. Commissioner*[11] the Court stated:

> *As we interpret* Ithaca Trust, *when the Supreme Court announced the date-of-death valuation principle, it was making a judgment about the nature of the federal estate tax specifically, that it is a tax imposed on the act of transferring property by will or intestacy and, because the act on which the tax is levied occurs at a discrete time, i.e., the instant of death, the net value of the property transferred should be ascertained as nearly as possible as of that time. This analysis supports broad application of the date-of-death valuation rule. We think that the Eighth Circuit's narrow reading of* Ithaca Trust, *a reading that limits its application to charitable bequests, is unwarranted.*
> *. . . [W]hen Congress wants to derogate from the date-of-death valuation principle it knows how to do so. We note in passing that since* Ithaca Trust, *Congress has made countless other modifications to the statute, but has never seen fit to overrule* Ithaca Trust *legislatively.*

Adjustments

Courts sometimes make adjustments to the valuation for events subsequent to the date of valuation.

---

[10]856 F.2d 1158, 1160 (8th Cir. 1988), *rev'g.* 88 T.C. 769 (1987).
[11]198 F.3d 515 (5th Cir. 1999).

In *Estate of Scanlan v. Commissioner*[12] the court used a stock redemption value more than 2 years from the valuation date as a starting point in determining fair market value. In this regard the court stated:

> *We start with the redemption price . . . because we believe that it represents the arm's length value for all . . . stock in August 1993. We adjust this price to account for the passage of time, as well as the change in the setting from the date of Decedent's death to the date of the redemption agreement.*

The court went on to say:

> *Federal law favors the admission of evidence, and the test of relevancy under federal law is designed to reach that end. . . . Tax Court Rules of Practice and Procedure provides broadly that evidence is "relevant: if it has 'any tendency' to make the existence of any fact that is of consequence to the determination of the action more probable or less probable than it would be without the evidence." Rule 401 of the Federal Rules of Evidence favors a finding of relevance, and only minimal logical relevancy is necessary if the disputed act's existence is of consequence to the determination of the action. . . . In fact, the Federal Rules and practice favor admission of evidence rather than exclusion if the proffered evidence has any probative value at all. Doubts must be resolved in favor of admissibility.*

The court then described how it considers post-death factors by stating:

> *This passage of time, as well as the financial data referenced by petitioner and the fact that the offer was for all of [the company's] stock, are facts that we must consider in harmonizing the offering and redemption prices with the value of the subject shares on the Valuation Dates. . . . Of course, appropriate adjustments must be made to take account of differences between the valuation date and the dates of later-occurring events. For example, there may have been changes in general inflation, people's expectations with respect to the industry, performances of the various components of the business, technology, and the provisions of the tax law that might affect fair market values between the valuation date and the subsequent date of sale. "Although any such changes must be accounted for in determining the evidentiary weight to be given to the later-occurring events, those changes ordinarily are not justification for ignoring the later-occurring events (unless other comparable offer significantly better matches to the property being valued)" [citations omitted].*

In *Estate of Jung v. Commissioner*,[13] the court took into consideration whether the events were foreseeable as of the valuation date. It then proceeded to examine sales of assets more than two years after decedent's death and stated the following:

> Of course, appropriate adjustments must be made to take account of differences between the valuation date and the dates of later-occurring events. For example, there may have been changes in general inflation, people's expectations with respect to that industry, performances of the various components of the business, technology, and the provisions of tax law that might affect fair market value.

The court in *Jung* then drew a line between two categories of later-occurring events, distinguishing between later-occurring events that affect fair market value as of the valuation date, and later-occurring events that may be used as evidence of fair market value as of the valuation date. This latter point is important because some courts do not use subsequent

---

[12]T.C. Memo. 1996-331.
[13]101 T.C. 412 (1993).

events to determine fair market value initially, but rather use such later-occurring events to affirm their fair market valuation conclusions, provided that the events were foreseeable and relevant.[14]

The Federal Circuit weighed in on the issue recently, in *Okerlund v. United States*:[15]

> *Valuation must always be made as of the donative date relying primarily on ex ante information; ex post data should be used sparingly. As with all evidentiary submissions, however, the critical question is relevance. The closer the profile of the later-date company to that of the valuation-date company, the more likely ex post data are to be relevant (though even in some cases, they may not be). The greater the significance of exogenous or unforeseen events occurring between the valuation date and the date of the proffered evidence, the less likely ex post evidence is to be relevant—even as a sanity check on the assumptions underlying a valuation model.*[16]

In *Okerlund*, the issue was whether estate plan provisions requiring the purchase of stock upon the decedent's death were properly included as affecting value when the stock was gifted to decedent's children, two years prior to the decedent's untimely (and unexpected) demise. The Court of Federal Claims held that it should not have been included as an item of value when the stock was gifted because there was no reason to believe the decedent would pass away in the near future. The Federal Circuit affirmed. The subsequent event of decedent's demise was held not relevant to determining the correct value at the time of death, although the court did say that such evidence *could* be considered, if relevant.

The question, at least in the Federal Circuit, is thus what subsequent events may be relevant to judging the correctness of a valuation. One Eighth Circuit case is instructive on the issue, if not dispositive. In *Polack v. Commissioner*,[17] the taxpayer wished to introduce subsequent (unaudited) financial statements to support his valuation. The court refused to consider this evidence, holding that the statements were not relevant because an arm's-length buyer could not have relied on them had she purchased the business in the year it was valued.[18]

The following formula may be considered as a starting point when adjusting for subsequent events:

Value at valuation date

- \+   Inflation
- +/–   Industry changes, or changes in expectations regarding industry
- +/–   Changes in business component results if relevant in time and type
- +/–   Societal changes, such as changes in technology, macroeconomics, or tax laws
- +/–   The actual occurrence (or lack thereof) of an event included (excluded) from original valuation, if relevant in time and type
- +/–   The occurrence or nonoccurrence of any other events or facts that an arm's-length buyer could have reasonably foreseen had she purchased the business in the year of valuation
- =   Adjusted valuation

---

[14]See, e.g., *Estate of Fitts v. Comm'r*, 237 F.2d 729, 731 (8th Cir. 1956); *Estate of Myler v. Comm'r*, 28 B.T.A. 633 (1933).

[15]93 365 F.3d 1044 (Fed. Cir. 2004).

[16]Id. at 1053.

[17]T.C. Memo 2002-145.

[18]Id. at 612.

One will note that the key to many of these adjustments is relevance, as dictated by the Eighth Circuit and the Federal Circuit. Rule 401, Federal Rules of Evidence, defines relevant evidence as evidence having any tendency to make the existence of any fact that is of consequence to the determination of the matter more or less probable than it would be without the evidence. Relevance is a legal concept beyond the scope of this book, but there is a plethora of case law on relevance and its limitations.[19]

Two types of relevance have been identified by the courts thus far: relevance in time and relevance in type. Relevance in time means that the event is not so far removed from the valuation date as to have been unforeseeable. Relevance in type means that the subsequent event is similar to something that was foreseeable and predictable as of the valuation date.

Okerlund and *Polack* shed some light on this inquiry, but valuers, if they choose to do so, must carefully consider all relevant factors in determining the impact, if any, of subsequent events. The formula just given is merely offered as a starting point, should the client wish to consider subsequent events. It is by no means exhaustive, and the valuer should be guided in its application by her experience and the facts of the valuation.

Subsequent Sales

Sometimes, courts allow subsequent events such as sales of the actual property or comparable properties to be used in determining fair market value. This is so even if the sales were not foreseeable as of the valuation date. This exception seems to be founded in the belief that the sale of the actual or comparable property is such strong evidence that it is worthy and therefore reliable evidence of fair market value.[20]

CONCLUSION

Events subsequent to the valuation date should not be taken into consideration when valuing business interests, unless at least one of these five conditions is true:

1. The subsequent events were reasonably foreseeable as of the valuation date.
2. The subsequent events are relevant to the valuation, and appropriate adjustments are made to account for the differences between the valuation date and the date of such subsequent events.
3. The subsequent events are not used to arrive at the valuation, but to confirm the valuation already concluded.
4. The subsequent events relate to property that is comparable to the property being valued, and the subsequent events are probative of value.
5. Subsequent events may be evidence of value rather than as something that affects value.

---

[19]*Estate of Gilford v. Comm'r*, 88 T.C. 38 (1987); *Krapf v. United States*, 977 F.2d 1454 (1992); *Krapf v. United States*, 35 Fed. Cl. 286 (1996).

[20]*Estate of Jung*, supra note 13, at 431–432 (as evidence of value rather than as something that affects value—later-occurring events are no more to be ignored than earlier-occurring events).

Business Valuation Experts

SUMMARY

This chapter covers the use of business valuation experts in valuation controversies. To qualify under the Federal Rules of Evidence (FRE) as an "expert" in business valuation, the appraiser must have sufficient training or experience. Preferably, the expert also will be certified by one of the relevant accrediting bodies. See the appendix at the end of this chapter for a detailed discussion of expert certifications. Certification recognizes that the expert, whose job it is to render an opinion on valuation issues, is qualified to do so.

Before trial, the expert will compile all of the information she needs, review it, and render a written opinion as to value. This opinion will then be presented to the trier of fact.

Effective use of experts requires five conditions:

1. *The expert must be qualified to perform the necessary analysis and formulate the needed expert opinions.* Appraisers are specialists, and it is important to select the right one for the job. An accredited appraiser is almost inevitably more qualified than one who is not.

2. *The expert has credibility with the court.* Credibility means that the expert is worthy of belief. One way in which credibility of the witness may be discovered is by researching prior cases where the expert has testified; courts often comment on the qualifications and reliability of the expert, providing a treasure chest of knowledge on the consistency and thoroughness of that expert.

3. *The expert refrain from advocacy.* In theory, the expert is a dispassionate analyst who will guide the trier of fact to truth, even if that truth conflicts with the client's position. In practice, expert opinions are perceived to be purchased by the word, lessening their credibility. Attorneys should thus refrain from making the expert nothing more than a surrogate advocate for the client's position. Because of these concerns, some courts are now avoiding the expert-advocate problem altogether by appointing their own experts under FRE 706.

4. *If the expert is a public accountant, it is recommended that she refrain from providing audit and valuation services at the same time.* The Sarbanes-Oxley Act could be read to prohibit an accountant from serving in both valuation and audit capacities. Good practice suggests that accountants should refrain from valuing a business they are contemporaneously auditing, pending clarification from the Securities and Exchange Commission (SEC).

5. The expert must offer reliable and relevant analysis and opinions.

INTRODUCTION

Taxpayers frequently need to prove business value for a variety of transactions, such as buy-outs, mergers, or gifts. Business valuations are also required as part of many tax-reportable transactions and in a multitude of business transactions that must be valued before the transaction can be consummated.

PROVING BUSINESS VALUE

How do you prove the value of a business?

There are a multitude of factors that enter into the establishment of business value. For instance: earnings, assets, liabilities, cash flow, economic conditions, competition, technological advancements, and local, regional and world events may all affect valuation.[1]

By themselves, or even in combination, however, these factors do not prove value; at best, they are limited indicators of value. Someone is needed to identify and assimilate the correct valuation indicators, to interpret them, and to formulate an opinion as to valuation.

In many tax-related valuations, taxpayers perform their own valuations or utilize the services of anyone who claims some knowledge of valuation. Many tax forms require little, if any, information about who performs the valuation. On other tax forms, taxpayers can perform their

---

[1]Rev. Rul. 59-60 lists the following as factors to be considered when arriving at business value: (a) the nature of the business and the history of the enterprise, (b) economic outlook, (c) book value, (d) earning capacity, (e) dividend-paying capacity, (f) goodwill or intangible value, (g) comparable sales, and (h) comparable companies. See Chapter 22.

own valuations without even having to describe the method used to estimate value. This loose valuation policy contributes to inconsistency and unreliability in business valuation.

In many cases, however, estimating the value of an interest in a closely held business is beyond the competency of anyone who is not a professional (and credentialed) business appraiser. Customarily, the best procedure to prove business value for federal tax purposes requires that a professional person—someone skilled, educated, and experienced in understanding and analyzing the various factors pertaining to valuation—express an opinion of value. That opinion must be based on careful and thorough research of the events and circumstances surrounding the business valuation object or event. We generally refer to the person providing such an opinion as an *appraiser* or *valuer*.

THE EXPERT APPRAISER

Merely being qualified as a business appraiser does not qualify one as an expert in the field. Instead, experts are distinguished by their credentials, skills, experience, and training. To be recognized as an expert, courts often require that the appraiser has distinguished herself among her peers, has exceptional qualifications or training, has spoken at professional meetings on the topic, and/or has published scholarly articles on the relevant subject matter.[2]

Author Nina Crimm states:

> *For centuries, the judiciary has utilized expert witnesses. There are English cases dating back to the fourteenth century in which courts summoned skilled persons for advice. These skilled persons acted as non-partisan advisers to the presiding judge or jury when questions of fact arose about which the judge or jury lacked particular knowledge. For example, the courts in several instances called surgeons to advise them of the freshness or permanency of wounds when central to the questions before the courts. In other cases, the courts obtained advice of grammarians to assist in the interpretation of commercial instruments and other documents. Sometimes the court impaneled a special jury of experts to decide questions requiring a special knowledge. More recently, but as far back as the seventeenth century, parties to controversies summoned skilled persons to testify to their observations and conclusions drawn therefrom. Typical of such cases were those in which the prosecution in a criminal trial called a physician to testify as to his observations during the autopsy of a deceased individual and to draw conclusions on the probable cause of death.*
>
> *The need to summon one or more experts to participate in judicial proceedings, either as impartial consultants to the trier of fact or as to partisan advisers, arises from the reality that the trier of fact cannot be a 'jack of all trades.' Often the trier of fact is asked to intelligently decide issues that depend upon specialized knowledge or experience beyond that of the fact finder. (citations omitted).*[3]

TYPES OF EXPERTS

There are as many different kinds of valuers as there are uses for them. Some valuers concentrate only on real estate or perhaps further subspecialize in certain types of real estate such as

---

[2]For a history of the utilization of experts by the judiciary, see Lloyd L. Rosenthal, "The Development of the Use of Expert Testimony," 2 *Law & Contemporary Probs.* 403 (1935).

[3]"A Role for Expert Arbitrators" in "Resolving Valuation Issues before the United States Tax Court: A Remedy to Plaguing Problems,"26 *Indiana Law Review* 41, 43 (1992). Copyright 1991, The Trustees of Indiana University. Reproduced with permission from the *Indiana Law Review*.

commercial land. Others, business valuers, specialize in closely held businesses, or even single aspects of closely held businesses, such as compensation issues pertaining to executives or owners. Still other valuers may address issues such as transfer pricing, employee stock ownership plans (ESOPs), or limited partnerships.

Before one hires an expert, it is essential first to understand the special experience, training, education, and abilities of the expert. It would be a huge mistake to utilize the wrong expert when attempting to prove value. To state the obvious, an expert in accounting may not be the expert one needs for establishing the value of a patent in a high-tech computer company. Although both may be business valuation experts, one is not qualified to do the other's job.[4]

The following story highlights the importance of hiring the right "expert." Around the end of the twentieth century, there was a factory employing 300 people in the hills of Virginia. One day, the machine that controlled essential functions at the factory broke down. The managers could not find the problem that caused the machine to fail. If the machine was not fixed right away, the factory would be forced to curtail operations and all the employees would be sent home. The manager learned about a very knowledgeable and skilled person who lived fifty miles away in another town. (It seems that all experts come from at least fifty miles away and carry a briefcase.)

The manager sent for him, and before long this expert arrived at the factory with his small black bag and approached the problematic machine. He studied it and then took a hammer out of his black bag. With great precision, he hit the machine at a certain angle and intensity, whereupon the machine started to work. The factory was saved and all the employees went back to their jobs.

Days later, the manager received a bill from the expert for $50,100. This was a huge amount, and particularly so when the expert was only at the plant for less than one hour. The manager asked the expert to explain his bill. "Well," said the expert, "the $100 is for the time it took me to travel to the plant and return, and included the time for striking the machine."

"Yes, but how do you justify the $50,000?" asked the manager.

"Well," said the expert, "that was for knowing where to hit the machine."

VARIOUS ROLES OF EXPERTS

An expert's role in a business valuation event may include the following:

- *Advising counsel or a client on a business valuation independent of, and prior to, a controversy relating to the valuation.* The vast majority of business valuation studies are performed for a client in everyday business transactions that do not become the subject of a tax controversy. One strong reason some transactions do not become controversial is that the valuation event is supported by a credentialed business appraiser who provides a well-reasoned report.

Business executives and owners frequently make fundamental decisions with respect to the assets they sell or purchase based on the opinions of valuation experts. Among the many

---

[4]In *ACM Partnership. v. Comm'r*, 157 F.3d 231 (3d Cir. 1998), *aff'g. in part and rev'g. in part*. T.C. Memo 1997-115, a person, qualified as an expert in economics, was vigorously cross-examined when he offered an opinion on cost accounting, a subject in which he was not experienced as an expert.

and diverse business events or transactions requiring valuations are major asset sales, mergers, acquisitions, spinoffs, corporate liquidations, financial restructuring, incentive stock options, incorporations, and issues relating to corporate compensation.

- *Providing an opinion that will be used before the Service in an audit, or at the Appellate Division in an appeals conference.* For example, experts are often used at the audit stage to explain the valuation estimates for taxable gifts or estates. Most tax controversies are resolved at this level, based on the taxpayer's providing adequate support for the transaction.

- *Assisting counsel out of court in understanding technical issues and preparing for the case.* Frequently, experts educate counsel about the various valuation approaches or methods. In this manner counsel gains a proper understanding of technical issues and knows better how to question the valuation-related witnesses.

- *Testifying in court to an opinion that will be included in a trial record.*

Each of these tasks requires different skills from the expert, and one needs to select an expert based on the purpose for the valuation, as well as the skills and abilities of the expert.

BUSINESS VALUATION LITIGATION WITNESSES

Lay Witnesses

It is important to distinguish lay opinion testimony from *expert* opinion testimony. If a witness is testifying in court but is not qualified as an expert, the witness's opinion testimony is limited to those opinions that are rationally based on the personal knowledge and perception of the witness, are helpful in determining a fact in issue, and are not based on hypothetical facts (which is reserved for experts). This is called lay opinion testimony.

Most courts have permitted the owner or officer of a business to testify to the value or projected profits of the business, without the necessity of qualifying the witness as an accountant, appraiser, or similar expert.[5] Such lay opinion testimony is allowed because of the knowledge that the witness has by virtue of her position in the business—not because of experience, training, or specialized, acquired knowledge, as is the case with an expert.

Expert Testimony

In contrast, the purpose of expert testimony is to help the trier of fact better understand the evidence, or to decide a fact in issue that is based on scientific, technical, or specialized knowledge. Once qualified as an expert, the witness can offer ultimate opinions and conclusions on issues that the trier of fact might not otherwise understand.

---

[5]Some argue that the use of the term *expert* is ill advised because it inadvertently puts too much credence on the witness. See, e.g., Hon. Charles Richey, "Proposals to Eliminate the Prejudicial Effect of the Use of the Word 'Expert' under the Federal Rules of Evidence in Criminal and Civil Jury Trials," 154 F.R.D. 537, 559 (1994).

ADMISSIBILITY OF EVIDENCE UNDERLYING EXPERT OPINIONS

The Federal Rules of Evidence govern the admissibility of evidence in federal court.[6] FRE 702: Testimony by Experts specifically provides:

> *If scientific, technical or other specialized knowledge will assist the trier of fact to understand the evidence or to determine a fact in issue, a witness qualified as an expert by knowledge, skill, training, or education, may testify thereto in the form of an opinion or otherwise, if (1) the testimony is based upon sufficient facts or data, (2) the testimony is the product of reliable principles and methods, and (3) the witness has applied the principles and methods reliably to the facts of the case.*

The Rule is broadly worded. The fields of knowledge for which a witness can qualify as an expert are not just scientific and technical, but include skills such as business appraisal. The expert assembles before trial all of the necessary information, data, and documents upon which to base an opinion. The expert then reviews those records and forms an opinion. Expert testimony need not be in opinion form, however. Although it is very common for valuation experts to testify in the form of an opinion, the Federal Rules of Evidence recognize that an expert may give an explanation of the principles relevant to the case and leave the trier of fact to apply them to the facts. The ultimate opinion of the expert is thus not of primary importance.

The expert will examine carefully all of the data he or she accumulates. Information gathering, and the review of such information, is crucial not only for the expert to formulate an opinion, but also for others to be able to see, at least in part, the information upon which the opinion is based.

Generally, experts reveal their data in a written report. Well-prepared attorneys carefully review such data to test the thoroughness and reliability of the expert's analysis and ultimate opinion. Often, opposing counsel will seek to discover the expert's raw data, or prior drafts of written reports, as part of preparing for the deposition of the expert or for trial purposes.

Generally, the expert is given considerable discretion in selecting the data that will form the basis of the opinion. A good expert is trained to know what resources are available and the reliability of those resources. If the expert utilizes the wrong data, or outdated information, the ultimate opinion will be affected. Thus, anyone examining the opinion of the expert should first review the data and information underlying the expert's opinion. Remember, however, that simply because the expert may rely upon certain data does not mean that such data will be admissible at trial. Accordingly, FRE 703: Bases of Opinion Testimony by Experts provides the following:

> *The facts or data in the particular case upon which an expert bases an opinion or inference may be those perceived by or made known to the expert at or before the hearing. If of a type reasonably relied upon by experts in the particular field in forming opinions or inferences upon the subject, the facts or data need not be admissible in evidence in order for the opinion or inference to be admitted. . . .*

---

[6]See, e.g., Tax Ct. R. Practice & Proc. R. 143(a). Trials before the Court will be conducted in accordance with the rules of evidence in trials without a jury in the United States District Court for the District of Columbia. See I.R.C. § 7453. To the extent applicable to such trials, those rules include the rules of evidence in the Federal Rules of Civil Procedure (FRCP) and any rules of evidence generally applicable in the Federal courts.

Facts or data upon which the expert's opinion is based may be derived from three possible sources. The first is the firsthand observation of the witness. Some appraisers who are asked to perform valuations may indeed be able to observe the event or transaction.

In many cases, however, experts are asked to opine on valuation events that occurred months or years earlier. In such cases, firsthand observation is not possible. Therefore, a second source of data comes from experts attending the trial and gaining information from the testimony of others. Based upon this information, the expert is then asked to give an opinion.

Third, the facts may be presented to the expert outside of court and before the trial. The expert is then asked to review those facts and express an opinion.

LIMITATIONS TO ADMISSIBILITY

Hearsay

Various documents or other evidence are often not admitted because of a party's objections that such material is hearsay. Hearsay evidence is generally not admissible, with some exceptions, due to its presumed unreliability.[7]

Experts, however, may rely on hearsay. FRE 703 specifically allows the expert to rely upon such otherwise nonadmissible evidence. Thus, FRE 703 is, in essence, an exception to the hearsay rule, allowing inadmissible evidence to be incorporated into the record through an expert. This clever backdoor around the hearsay rule must be used carefully, however, because an expert's utilization of such evidence may contribute to the court's skepticism as to the reliability of the expert's opinion.

Scope of Expert Testimony

Experts may testify in the form of an opinion based on underlying facts or data. Experts may also testify in response to hypothetical questions, unlike most fact witnesses who must answer based on personal knowledge or observation. FRE 705: Disclosure of Facts or Data Underlying Expert Opinion provides:

> *The expert may testify in terms of opinion or inference and give reasons therefore without first testifying to the underlying facts or data, unless the court requires otherwise. The expert may in any event be required to disclose the underlying facts or data on cross examination.*

In the U.S. Tax Court, expert testimony is governed by the following:

> *Rule 143(f): A written report of the expert must be submitted to the Court and opposing party no later than 30 days before trial, unless otherwise permitted by the Court. The written report is intended to serve as the direct testimony of the expert and will be received into evidence unless the Court determines that the witness is not qualified as an expert. Additional direct testimony with respect to the report may, in the discretion of*

---

[7]FRE 801(c) describes hearsay as a statement, other than one made by the declarant while testifying at the trial or hearing, offered in evidence to prove the truth of the matter asserted.

the Court, be allowed to clarify or emphasize matters in the report, to cover matters arising after the preparation of the report, or for other reasons.

Rule 143(f) further provides that the expert witness report must include three things:

1. The qualifications of the expert witness
2. The witness's opinion and the facts or data on which that opinion is based
3. Detailed reasons for the conclusion

The expert may be given little or no opportunity at trial to supplement the report, except to discuss matters that arose subsequent to the submission of the report. By having the written report serve as the expert's direct testimony, the expert's testimony at trial generally is limited to clarification of the report.

RELIABILITY OF THE EXPERT

The trial judge must decide whether a particular witness qualifies as an expert. Once that is determined, the judge must rule whether the expert's testimony is admissible into the trial record. In almost half of the reported cases in a recent survey of federal judges, the judges indicated that admissibility of the expert testimony was not disputed.[8]

In *Daubert v. Merrell Dow Pharmaceuticals, Inc.*, the Supreme Court held that FRE 702 requires the federal trial judge to act as a gatekeeper to "ensure that any and all scientific testimony or evidence admitted is not only relevant but reliable."[9] In *Kumho Tire Co., Ltd. v. Carmichael*,[10] the Supreme Court clarified that *Daubert*'s requirements of relevance and reliability apply not only to scientific testimony but to all expert testimony, including that from business valuation experts.

Daubert emphasized that two elements precondition the admissibility of the expert's testimony in court: The testimony must be relevant and it must be reliable. In ruling on the issue of reliability, the court must consider all relevant facts, including the methodology employed by the expert, the facts and data relied upon by the expert in formulating conclusions, and the expert's application of the specific methodology to those facts and data.

In *Daubert*, the Supreme Court discussed four nonexclusive factors that trial judges may consider in ruling on the issue of whether the expert's testimony is reliable:

1. Whether the theory or technique can be and has been tested
2. Whether the theory or technique has been subjected to peer review and publication

---

[8]See Molly Treadway Johnson et al., *Expert Testimony in Federal Civil Trials, A Preliminary Analysis*, Federal Judicial Center (2000).
[9]509 U.S. 579 (1993).
[10]See also *Frymire-Brinati v. KPMG Peat Marwick*, 2 F.3d 183, 186 (7th Cir. 1993) (requiring application of *Daubert* to accountant tendered as an expert witness); *Gross v. Comm'r*, T.C. Memo 1999-254 (concluding that the gatekeeper function of *Daubert* applies in the Tax Court). A court has broad latitude in determining how it will decide whether expert testimony is reliable. The focus of the determination, however, must be on the expert's approach in reaching the conclusions provided in her opinion, rather than on the validity of the conclusions themselves.

3. The method's known or potential rate of error
4. Whether the theory or technique finds general acceptance in the relevant subject matter's community

The court in *Kumho* held that these factors might also be applicable in assessing the reliability of skilled experts, depending on the particular circumstances of the case.

No attempt has been made to codify any specific factors. *Daubert* emphasized that its factors are not exclusive, and they do not apply neatly to business valuation experts. Accordingly, subsequent courts have found four other factors to be relevant in determining whether expert testimony is reliable:

1. Whether the expert is proposing to testify about matters related to research conducted independent of the litigation
2. Whether the expert has unjustifiably extrapolated from an accepted premise to an unsubstantiated conclusion
3. Whether the expert has accounted for alternative explanations
4. Whether the expert employs in the courtroom the same level of intellectual rigor that characterizes the practice of the expert in the expert's workplace

Still other factors may be relevant to the determination of the reliability of the expert. The trial judge is given considerable leeway, and no single factor is necessarily dispositive. Even so, the focus must be on principles and methodology and not on the conclusions they generate.

One court described the parameters for use of expert opinions in *Estate of True et al. v. Commissioner:*[11]

> As is customary in valuation cases, the parties rely primarily on expert opinion evidence to support their contrary valuation positions. We evaluate the opinions of experts in light of their demonstrated qualifications and all other evidence in the record. We have broad discretion to evaluate "the overall cogency of each expert's analysis." [sic] Although expert testimony usually helps the Court determine values, sometimes it does not, particularly when the expert is merely an advocate for the position argued by one of the parties.
>
> We are not bound by the formulas and opinions proffered by an expert witness and will accept or reject expert testimony in the exercise of sound judgment. We have rejected expert opinion based on conclusions that are unexplained or contrary to the evidence.
>
> Where necessary, we may reach a determination of value based on our own examination of the evidence in the record. Where experts offer divergent estimates of fair market value, we decide what weight to give those estimates by examining the factors they used in arriving at their conclusions. We have broad discretion in selecting valuation methods, and in determining the weight to be given the facts in reaching our conclusions, inasmuch as "finding market value is, after all, something for judgment, experience, and reason." While we may accept the opinion of an expert in its entirety, we may be selective in the use of any part of such opinion, or reject the opinion in its entirety. Finally, because valuation necessarily results in an approximation, the figure we arrive at need not be directly attributable to specific testimony if it is within the range of values that may properly be arrived at from consideration of all the evidence (citations omitted).[12]

---

[11]*Estate of True et al. v. Comm'r*, T.C. Memo. 2001-167.
[12]Id. at 205.

MINIMUM THRESHOLDS FOR THE BUSINESS VALUATION EXPERT

There are no absolute mandated standards to qualify an individual to be a valuation expert, with the exception of the rules laid down in Regulation section 1.170A-13c, for Qualified Appraisers, discussed later in this chapter. However, there are certain qualifications for experts upon which there is general agreement.

The minimum thresholds for the business valuation expert are that the expert must have four qualities:

1. *An expert must be qualified by knowledge, skill, experience, training, or education.* Valuing closely held businesses requires a review and analysis of a multitude of factors ranging from financial analysis to economics, from product mix to management, and from statistics to securities. Business valuers are required to understand and assimilate complex and sometimes incomplete and confusing data. Ultimately, they are asked to make sense out of such data and to provide an opinion. These challenges often require a valuer to receive special training and education to prepare for her tasks and to thereby earn the designation *expert*.

   Fortunately, several professional organizations have, in recent years, developed excellent programs for formal training and education of valuation experts. Among the well known are these:

   • American Society of Appraisers (ASA)
   • American Institute of Certified Public Accountants (AICPA)
   • Institute of Business Appraisers (IBA)
   • National Association of Certified Valuation Analysts (NACVA)[13]

   These organizations issue designations and credentials for those who successfully complete their accreditation programs. Judges and others can and should be able to rely on persons possessing such credentials.

2. *An expert must be credible.* Simply stated, the expert must be believable. Credibility is best achieved when individuals conduct themselves over a period of time so as to earn a reputation for sincerity, integrity, and honesty. Judges use their own experience to determine the credibility of witnesses and will disregard the testimony of experts whom they find not credible.

   In the case of fact witnesses, the trier of fact sometimes looks at the eyes of the witnesses or their *body language* to assess believability. This is not necessarily true of experts, whose credibility is determined by their integrity, knowledge, skill, and experience. An expert who admits weakness in an area due to lack of data may gain more credibility with the trier of fact (which can be either a judge or a jury, depending on venue and the choice of the parties) than one who blindly defends a deficient position. Credibility means, at a minimum, that the expert is worthy of belief.

   Those interested in retaining the services of an expert should research the published writings of the expert to see if they contain views contrary to the taxpayer's position. In

---

[13]See appendix to this chapter for a full discussion of these and other organizations that provide training and issue certifications for those who complete the educational programs they offer.

addition, former court cases should be reviewed for comments or case histories relating to the expert. Judges frequently comment on the credibility of experts in their published opinions. Lawyers and others should review those comments carefully to determine the credibility of the expert.[14]

3. *An expert must be unbiased.* It is elementary that experts have a duty to be objective with respect to their valuation opinions. Valuation experts should not be alter egos of the attorneys or clients who hire them. Their opinions should be their best judgment based on data, knowledge, and experience. An expert who advocates the position of one side in a controversy does not help the trier of fact and actually does a disservice to the court and the expert's client.[15]

Experts are sometimes used to settle valuation controversies by meeting with their counterparts and resolving the differences between them. Experts might find it difficult to define the line they should not cross when they are asked by attorneys or clients to settle the case. An expert should not be an advocate for a position, but may defend an opinion through the demonstration of data and underlying facts. There certainly is no problem with experts explaining in a settlement negotiation why they used various assumptions. Advocating the client's position is the attorney's duty, however, not the expert's; the expert will be expected to testify in court in an unbiased manner.

4. *An expert must assist and educate the court in understanding the valuation evidence.* The court generally will not allow the expert to testify if the trier of fact did not need assistance in understanding the valuation evidence. However, most judges are not experts in business valuation and do not claim to be so. It is a rare judge who has in-depth knowledge of economics, generally accepted methods of accounting, and financial ratios.

The most helpful and persuasive experts are those who realize that their job is to explain and educate in comprehensible terms the intricacies of business valuation approaches, the mysteries of capitalization rates, and the importance of restricted stock and pre-IPO studies. Experts should not assume that the trier of fact understands the underlying data or analysis, and should carefully and meticulously support their conclusions. Most importantly, experts must show the trier of fact how their ultimate opinions were arrived at as a product of analysis. No trier of fact will be able to accept the conclusions of the expert if it cannot be shown that the underlying data and facts, together with the analysis of such data, logically lead to the opinions derived therefrom.

SARBANES-OXLEY ACT OF 2002

On July 30, 2002, President Bush signed into law the Sarbanes-Oxley Act of 2002. The Act was passed by Congress in response to various accounting scandals, creating a new federal oversight board for the purpose of monitoring public accounting firms.

---

[14]Trial courts intentionally comment on the credibility of experts in their opinions in order to make a solid record for appeal. Appellate courts require that the lower courts explain the rationale behind their conclusions. See *Leonard Pipeline Contractors, Ltd. v. Comm'r*, T.C. Memo 1996-316, *rev'd.* 72 T.C.M. (CCH) 83, *and remanded* 142 F.3d 1133 (9th Cir. 1998).

[15]*Neonatology Assoc. v. Comm'r*, 115 T.C. 43, 86 (2000), *Laureys v. Comm'r*, 92 T.C. 101, 129 (1989).

Among other things, the Act imposes certain restrictions with respect to nonaudit functions such as valuation services. The Act lists nine activities, called "Prohibited Activities," which a public accounting firm is expressly prohibited from providing contemporaneously with an audit of the client. Among those nine prohibited activities is valuation services.

In another section of the Act there is a provision that states that an accounting firm may engage in any nonaudit service if the activity is approved in advance by the audit committee. Some commentators conclude that tax-related valuation services may be provided to the audit client if the audit committee approves such service in advance.

However, it is unclear whether all valuation services may be provided to an audit client, even with approval by the audit committee. Further clarification is needed, and it is expected that the Securities and Exchange Commission may provide such clarification through regulations. At this time, however, we must assume that valuation services performed by an accounting firm for an audit client may be prohibited when performed contemporaneously with the audit.

ATTORNEY ASSISTANCE TO THE EXPERT

There is little published authority that discusses the proper limits of attorney assistance to the expert in the formulation of her report. Experienced counsel and experts know that in order to preserve the independence and integrity of the expert's opinion, counsel should refrain from assisting the expert in the formulation of the analysis and in the ultimate opinion of the expert.

Counsel's role is appropriately that of an advocate, but this does not extend to expert witnesses. If counsel exceeds the legitimate limits of assistance by influencing the expert's opinion, counsel has tainted the expert's opinion with advocacy and thus rendered the expert unreliable. If an expert is found to be unreliable, the court may disregard her testimony in its entirety, admit only portions of it, draw a negative inference against the expert, or exclude the expert from testifying altogether.

There are several ways in which an expert may appear unreliable to the court as a result of attorney assistance.

The first deals with *spoliation* of evidence, which is a legal term for destruction of evidence. In the context of expert opinions, recent case law suggests that spoliation rules have broad application. To avoid appearing unreliable, experts should retain copies of all their work in a given case so that the court can see the factual background for their analysis and conclusions. Without such background, the court will be unable to determine the basis for the expert's opinion, and can impose any of the sanctions previously outlined.

Federal Rule of Civil Procedure (FRCP) 26(a)(2)(B) prescribes what experts must disclose to opposing counsel prior to trial in a federal district court. In relevant part, it requires that lawyers disclose to opposing counsel the expert's report, as well as the following:

a complete statement of all opinions to be expressed and the basis and reasons therefore; the data or other information considered by the witness in forming the opinions; any exhibits to be used as a summary of or support for the opinions; the qualifications of the witness, including a list of all publications authored by the witness within the preceding ten years; the compensation to be paid for the study and testimony; and a listing of any other cases in which the witness has testified as an expert at trial or by deposition within the preceding four years.

FRCP 26(a)(2)(B) is broadly worded, and some courts have shown a willingness to strictly enforce its provisions. If the expert (or the lawyer) has destroyed any evidence covered by this Rule, the expert's opinion will likely be deemed unreliable. To be safe, the expert should retain such things as the following:

- Drafts of reports and opinions
- Results of studies
- Copies of all treatises, articles, reports, and so forth relied upon by the expert
- Memoranda from subordinates whose research and/or opinions are incorporated into the expert's report at any stage—even if such work is not used in the final draft of the report

Another way in which an expert may appear unreliable is by becoming nothing more than a surrogate advocate for the attorney. When experts do not write their own opinions, but instead sign off on those drafted by the lawyers, they have abandoned their impartial role.

The notes to FRCP 26(a)(2)(B) state that:

> *[The rule] does not preclude counsel from providing assistance to experts in preparing reports, and indeed, with experts such as automobile mechanics, this assistance may be needed. Nevertheless, the report, which is intended to set forth the substance of the direct examination, should be written in a manner that reflects the testimony to be given by the witness and it must be signed by the witness.*

Assistance, however, may exceed the limits acceptable to the court. In *In re Jackson Nat'l. Life Insurance Co.*,[16] the court affirmed a magistrate's refusal to allow plaintiffs' expert to testify at trial. The magistrate had found, in part, that plaintiffs had violated FRCP 26(a)(2)(B) by providing the defendant with a report that was not prepared by their expert. The court stated:

> *The record clearly supports the finding that the language of [the expert's] report, including the formulation of his opinions, was not prepared by him, but was provided to him by plaintiff's counsel. Granted, Rule 26(a)(2) contemplates some assistance of counsel in the preparation of an expert's report. See* Marek v. Moore, *171 F.R.D. 298 (D. Kan. 1997). However, undeniable substantial similarities between [the expert's] report and the report of another expert prepared with assistance from the same counsel in an unrelated case, demonstrate that counsel's participation so exceeded the bounds of legitimate "assistance" as to negate the possibility that [the experts] actually prepared his own report within the meaning of Rule 26(a)(2). Plaintiffs' failure to furnish defendant with a report prepared by [the experts] constitutes a violation of Rule 26(a)(2).*

In a recent district court case, the taxpayer alleged the government's experts had not authored their opinions, but had instead signed off on opinions ghostwritten by others. The court could not find enough evidence to support the taxpayer's contention and held for the government.

In the process, however, the court defined ghostwriting as "the preparation of the substance writing of the report by someone other than the expert purporting to have written it," and held such to be a violation of FRCP 26(a)(2)(B). The court further explained that, al-

---

[16]2000 WL 33654070 (W.D. Mich. 2000), 2000 U.S. Dist. LEXIS 1318.

though the Rule does not preclude some assistance from counsel in the preparation of the report, the report itself must not be prepared by a third party, and it must be "based on the expert's own valid reasoning and methodology."[17]

Experts, rather than counsel, should thus be responsible for drafting both the analysis and the ultimate opinion in the report. Counsel's participation should be minimal and nonessential, and should relate only to assisting the expert in complying with the court rules or the FRCP. Further, good practice suggests that experts should be cautious in blindly relying on the work of others. An expert's report should be drafted by the *expert*: The broad language of FRCP 26(a)(2)(B) could operate to preclude the expert from testifying to a report written in substance by a colleague or the client's attorney.[18]

Another problematic area is where the expert report is authored by more than one person but only one expert is available to testify as to its contents. In some courts (e.g., the Tax Court), the report is the direct testimony of the witness. Thus, if the report of the expert is admitted, it is the equivalent of live, in-court testimony by the expert. When the report is authored by more than one person, but only one expert is available to be cross-examined, the court and the opposing party are unable to examine all of the report's authors. This inability may be sufficient for a court to deny admission of the report. Even in cases where all of the authors can be cross-examined, the report may still be excluded if the authors cannot clearly establish who wrote precisely what. In the final analysis, good practice will ensure that all of the signers of a report are available to testify as to, and can confidently identify, their portion of the work.

The Service has recently opined that the witness must sign expert opinions and must be available for trial testimony. The chief counsel put it this way: "The proponent of the report must establish that the words, analysis and opinions in the report are the expert's own work and a reflection of the expert's own expertise. . . . To avoid the possibility that the tax court will exclude all or a portion of an expert witness report signed by nontestifying experts, Counsel attorneys must produce as witnesses all of the experts who prepared the report."[19]

QUALIFIED APPRAISER

In a few circumstances, the Service *requires* the use of an appraiser to establish value. For example, Regulations describe the qualifications and restrictions applicable to appraisers who perform certain valuations in connection with charitable contributions.

Regulation section 1.170A-13(c) requires a summary appraisal by a qualified appraiser in conjunction with any charitable contribution of a closely held business interest valued at over $10,000. The section defines a qualified appraiser as having these characteristics:

- The appraiser is publicly represented as an appraiser who regularly performs appraisals.
- The appraiser is qualified to appraise property.
- The appraiser is aware of the appraiser penalties associated with the overvaluation of charitable contributions.

---

[17]Id. at 3.
[18]For further analysis, see Stuart M. Hermitz and Richard Carpenter, "Can an Attorney Participate in the Writing of an Expert Witness's Report in the Tax Court?" *Journal of Taxation* (June 2004): 358.
[19]CC- 2004-023.

Certain individuals, however, may not act as qualified appraisers:

- The property's donor (or the taxpayer who claims the deduction)
- The property's donee
- A party to the property transaction (with certain, very specific exceptions)
- Any person employed by, married to, or related to any of the above persons
- An appraiser who regularly appraises for the donor, donee, or party to the transaction and does not perform a majority of his or her appraisals for other persons

Although it is laudable that the Service has taken some steps to establish rules and qualifications for appraisers used for tax purposes, the rules are limited and without substantial vigor. For instance, the regulations state that the appraiser must be qualified. Apparently, anyone is qualified who holds herself out as an appraiser having the requisite skills and knowledge of valuation penalties. The Service does not require evidence of competency, such as a designation earned from a reputable professional appraisal organization.

This is questionable. At the minimum, taxpayers should utilize credentialed, competent appraisal experts who meet the standards set forth previously in the "Minimum Thresholds for the Business Valuation Expert" section of this chapter.

CONCERNS ABOUT EXPERT TESTIMONY

Not surprisingly, experts' opinions are susceptible to abuse, as well as error and misjudgment. The Supreme Court recognized the difficulties and uncertainty of expert opinion when it stated that:

Experience has shown that opposite opinions of persons professing to be experts may be obtained to any amount; and it often occurs that not only many days, but even weeks, are consumed in cross-examinations, to test the skill or knowledge of such witnesses and the correctness of their opinions, wasting the time and wearying the patience of both court and jury, and perplexing, instead of elucidating, the questions involved in the issue.[20]

The literature and case law are replete with discussions concerning the problems associated with expert opinion.[21] Among the noteworthy concerns are these:

- Experts who abandon objectivity and become advocates for the side that hired them
- Excessive expense of party-hired experts

---

[20]*Winans v. N.Y. & Erie R.R. Co.*, 62 U.S. 88, 99 (1958).

[21]Some of these problems are quite old. See Nina Crimm, "A Role for 'Expert Arbitrators' in Resolving Valuation Issues Before the United States Tax Court: A Remedy to Plaguing Problems," 256 *Indiana Law Review* 41,44 (1992). "As early as 1876, an English judge expresses discontentment with the partisan expert witness system: The mode in which expert evidence is obtained is such as not to give the fair result of scientific opinion to the court. A man may go, and does some times, to half-a-dozen experts. . . He takes their honest opinions, he finds three in his favor, and three against him; he says to the three in his favor, "will you be kind enough to give evidence?" and he pays the three against him their fees and leaves them alone; the other side does the same. . . . I am sorry to say the result is that the Court does not get that assistance from the experts which, if they were unbiased and fairly chosen, it would have a right to expect. *Thorn v. Worthing Skating Rink Co.* (M.R. 1876, August 4) (Jessel, M.R.), quoted in *Plimpton v. Spiller*, 6 Ch.D 412 (1877), in Charles T. McCormick, Evidence 35 (1954)." Copyright 1991, The Trustees of Indiana University. Reproduced with permission from the *Indiana Law Review*.

- Expert testimony that appears to be of questionable validity or reliability
- Conflict among experts that defies reasoned assessment
- Disparity in level of competence of experts
- Expert testimony not comprehensible to the trier of fact
- Expert testimony that is comprehensible but does not assist the trier of fact
- Failure of parties to provide discoverable information concerning experts
- Attorneys unable to adequately cross-examine experts
- Experts poorly prepared to testify[22]

Another very important concern is whether the expert is able to support her valuation with empirical, solid data. Is the expert's analysis leading to his or her conclusion as to value apparent and logical? Judges permit experts to testify in business valuation controversies because they find the specialized knowledge of the experts to be helpful in understanding the facts of the case. Where, however, the experts do not adequately connect the data to the analysis, and the analysis to the conclusion, the expert is not helpful to the trier of fact.

Do judges and other triers of fact find the opinions of the experts in business valuation cases to be persuasive? According to one study of valuation cases in the U.S. Tax Court, the judges did not accept the opinions of the experts in more than 65 percent of the valuation cases examined.[23]

Taxpayers and their counsel invest considerable time and expense in selecting and preparing experts to prove their cases, and yet the referenced study suggests that there is a serious disconnect between the experts' conclusions and the findings of the trier of fact.

The problem with expert testimony may be in the nature of the expert witness procedure itself, rather than any deficiency or inadequacy of the experts.

It is not unexpected that some judges are skeptical of expert witnesses. On the one hand, judges are accustomed to fact witnesses who come to court in order to testify about an incident or observation of which the witnesses have personal knowledge. An expert, on the other hand, is governed by different circumstances. Consider the following hypothetical dialogue between the court and the attorney:

COURT: You may call the next witness, but before you do, please describe the witness.

ATTORNEY: Your Honor, the next witness is someone who was never there when the event or circumstance happened. She has no first-hand, personal knowledge. She has created her understanding of the event by recreating it.

COURT: Oh, . . . anything else?

ATTORNEY: Yes, your Honor, you know all of that hearsay evidence that you excluded from the trial record because it was unreliable? Well, . . . this witness has relied almost exclusively on that hearsay evidence.

COURT: Oh, really . . . anything else I should know?

---

[22]Molly Treadway Johnson, Carol Krafka, Joe S. Cecil, "Expert Testimony in federal Civil Trials, A Preliminary Analysis," Federal Judicial Center, 2000. In 1998, the Federal Judicial Center surveyed federal judges about their experiences with expert testimony in civil cases. The judges identified the problems cited.

[23]Crimm, supra.

ATTORNEY: Yes. This witness will be paid to come to court to testify. And, by being paid, I don't mean the customary $40 a day that the fact witnesses get. I mean $25,000, just to testify, your Honor.

COURT: And what will we get from this witness that will be helpful to the disposition of this case?

ATTORNEY: Just her opinion. That's all . . . just her opinion.

Given these unsettling characteristics inherent in expert testimony, it is no wonder that some experts make the trier of fact uncomfortable. Despite this, courts nevertheless need experts and their ultimate opinions.

COURT-APPOINTED EXPERT

The practice of shopping for experts has become a matter of deep concern. Too often, experts are hired for the obvious purpose of advocating, a function more appropriately left to the lawyers.

Moreover, it is not unusual for the court to reject the valuation opinions of both parties' experts.[24] When this happens, the court may then be left in the unenviable position of having to come to a conclusion without the benefit of an expert opinion upon which it may rely. It is not surprising that there is an increasing trend to look to experts appointed by the court to provide the specialized knowledge that the court requires.

Approximately 20 percent of the federal district courts around the country have chosen to appoint their own experts.[25] The Court of Federal Claims and the U.S. Tax Court have also appointed their own experts.[26]

Federal courts appoint experts under FRE 706: Court-Appointed Experts, which provides:

(a) Appointment. The court may on its own motion or on the motion of any party enter an order to show cause why expert witnesses should not be appointed, and may request the parties to submit nominations. The court may appoint any expert witnesses agreed upon by the parties, and may appoint expert witnesses of its own selection. An expert witness shall not be appointed by the court unless the witness consents to act. A

[24]See *Seagate Technology v. Comm'r*, 102 T.C. 149 (1994); *Bausch & Lomb, Inc. v. Comm'r*, 92 T.C. 525 (1989), *aff'd.* 993 F.2d 1084 (2d Cir. 1991).

[25]Joe S. Cecil and Thomas E. Willging, "Court-Appointed Experts: Defining the Role of Experts Appointed under Federal Rule of Evidence 706," Federal Judicial Center 15 (1993).

[26]See *Bank One v. Comm'r*, 120 T.C. 174 (2003), where the court appointed two experts and describes in the opinion the court's procedure with respect to the appointments. Prior to *Bank One*, which is the only case in which the Tax Court has appointed an expert under Federal Rule 706, the parties in *Argro Science Co. v. Comm'r*, T.C. Memo 1989-687, *aff'd.* 934 F.2d 573 (5th Cir. 1991) stipulated to the appointment of a joint expert witness. There was no court order appointing the expert witness. In their Joint Stipulation on the Use of the Witness Roger H. Kennett, PhD, the parties agreed that: (1) the proposed witness was an expert in the area of monoclonal antibody research; (2) they would agree to share the costs specified therein; (3) the expert would have specified documents available to him; (4) the expert would not produce a written report for purposes of trial; (5) the expert would be subject to direct and cross-examination by both petitioner and respondent; and (6) the parties would not communicate *ex parte* with the expert before trial. Also, in *Holland v. Comm'r*, 835 F.2d 675 (6th Cir. 1987), *aff'g.* T.C. Memo 1985-627, the Court of Appeals for the Sixth Circuit affirmed the Tax Court's direction for one party to procure an expert witness at the party's expense.

witness so appointed shall be informed of the witness's duties by the court in writing, a copy of which shall be filed with the clerk, or at conference in which the parties shall have the opportunity to participate. A witness so appointed shall advise the parties of the witness' findings, if any; the witness' deposition may be taken by any party; and the witness may be called to testify by the court or any party. The witness shall be subject to cross-examination by each party, including a party calling the witness.
(b) Compensation. Expert witnesses so appointed are entitled to reasonable compensation in whatever sum the court may allow. . . In other civil actions and proceedings, the compensation shall be paid by the parties in such proportion and at such time as the court directs . . .

***

(d) Parties experts of own selection. Nothing in this rule limits the parties in calling expert witnesses of their own selection.

The primary advantage of the court's using its own expert is that the court-appointed witness may educate the court using neutral, unbiased knowledge. Also, the court-appointed expert may be used by the court to evaluate the opinions of the other experts and thus give the court information by which it can resolve differences of opinion on technical matters that may be confusing to the judge. Another, but less cited, advantage of court-appointed experts is that it may be far less expensive to have one court expert opine on matters than to have two opposing parties hire multiple experts. The cost of a court-appointed expert is allocated, at the discretion of the court, to the parties. Despite the obvious economies of court-appointed experts, parties often prefer to have their own experts, adding to the perception that the parties' experts are in essence substitute advocates.

There are, however, disadvantages to court-appointed experts. Among them is that court-appointed experts sometimes acquire an aura of infallibility to which they may not be entitled.[27] This concern may be legitimate, as a judicial study found that judges often decide cases consistent with the advice and testimony of court-appointed experts.[28] Also, some argue that court-appointed experts are an unwise departure from the usual adversarial process where opposing counsel introduce evidence to the court in the light most favorable to their respective clients.[29]

CONCLUSION

Almost 100 years ago, Judge Learned Hand stated that "[n]o one will deny that the law should in some way effectively use expert knowledge wherever it will aid in settling disputes. The only real question is as to how it can do so best."[30]

The following appendix details the requirements to obtain various professional credentials relating to business valuation. Questions to evaluate the quality of experts' credentials can be found at the beginning of Chapter 24.

---

[27]Cecil & Willging, supra at 52, 56.
[28]Id. at 20–21.
[29]Gross, "Expert Evidence, 1991 *Wisconsin Law Review* 1113, 1220–1221 (1991).
[30]Judge Learned Hand, "Historical and Practical Considerations Regarding Expert Testimony," 15 *Harvard Law Review* 40 (1901).

APPENDIX: EXPERT CREDENTIALS AND QUALIFICATIONS

There are no mandatory criteria for qualifications of business appraisers. This is so because there is resistance in the valuation community to establishing criteria for fear of excluding a few individuals whose testimony has the potential to be helpful in court. But the court can rely only on the evidence presented to it in the specific case at bar, and bad evidence produces bad case law. Therefore, it is the responsibility of the legal profession to select well-qualified experts for their clients' cases. This appendix presents qualification criteria for several business valuation professional designations.

In addition to checking into an expert's professional qualifications, the attorney may want to check professional references. The attorney might also want to search court cases to see what positions the expert has taken in past cases and the court's reaction to the expert.

Professional Organizations Offering Certification in Business Appraisal

There are four major professional associations in the United States and one in Canada that offer certifications in business appraisal. Three of the organizations offer more than one designation.

The requirements to achieve the designations vary greatly from organization to organization and also are subject to change. The attorney retaining an appraiser to perform a business valuation for tax purposes should be aware of the basic requirements for each designation, but should also ask the potential expert about such requirements during the interview prior to the retention.

Exhibits 3.1, 3.2, and 3.3 are summaries of professional accreditation criteria (including the existing requirements to attain various professional designations), business valuation professional designations, and professional association contact information. In addition to those listed in the exhibits, the CFA Institute offers the well-respected designation of chartered financial analyst (CFA). This is primarily oriented to analysis of publicly traded securities and investment portfolio management, but there are some holders of the CFA designation who specialize in valuation of privately held securities.

Exhibit 3.1 Professional Accreditation Criteria

Organization	Certification	Prerequisites	Course/Exam	Reports	Experience/Other
American Institute of Certified Public Accountants (AICPA)	ABV—Accredited in Business Valuation	AICPA certificate or member with current CPA license.	Pass an 8-hour comprehensive multiple-choice exam.		Substantial involvement in at least ten business valuation engagements. Provide evidence of 75 hours of continuing professional education related to the business of valuation body of knowledge.
American Society of Appraisers (ASA)	AM—Accredited Member	Obtain four-year college degree or equivalent.	Complete four courses of three days each, and pass one half-day exam following each course or complete one all-day challenge exam and USPAP exam.	Submit of two actual reports from within the last two years to satisfaction of board examiners.	Two years full time or equivalent (e.g., five years 400 hours business appraisal work per year equals one year full-time equivalent). One full year of requirement is granted to anyone who has a CPA, CFA, or CBI designation with five years of practice held.
	ASA—Accredited Senior Appraiser	Meet AM requirements.			Five years of full-time or equivalent experience including two years for AM.
	FASA—Fellow of American Society of Appraisers	Meet ASA requirements, plus be voted into College of Fellows on the basis of technical leadership and contribution to the profession of the Society.			
Institute of Business Appraisers (IBA)	AIBA—Accredited by IBA	Complete four-year college degree or equivalent; possess business appraisal designation from AICPA, ASA, or NACVA, or complete IBA eight-day Appraisal Workshop.	Complete comprehensive written exam.	Submit one report for peer review.	Provide four references of character and fitness.
	CBA—Certified Business Appraiser	Complete four-year college degree or equivalent. Complete IBA's 16-hour course 1010 (Report Writing).	Pass six-hour exam. Applicants may be exempt from the exam if they hold the ASA, ABV, CVA, or AVA designation	Submit two business-appraisal reports showing professional competence	Successfully complete 90 hours of upper-level business valuation course work (at least 24 hours from IBA) or five years full-time active experience as a business appraiser. Provide four references (two personal, two professional).
	BVAL—Business Valuator Accredited for Litigation	Obtain business appraisal designation from IBA, AICPA, ASA, NACVA, or CVA candidate who has passed the exam.	Five-day Expert Witness Skills Workshop and four-hour exam.		Provide letters of reference from two attorneys or complete 16 hours of education in the area of law in which the appraiser will testify.

(Continued)

Exhibit 3.1 (Continued)

Organization	Certification	Prerequisites	Course/Exam	Reports	Experience/Other
	MCBA—Master Certified Business Appraiser	Obtain four-year college degree and two-year post graduate degree or equivalent; hold CBA designation for at least five years and hold one other designation (ASA, CVA, or ABV)			Ten years full-time practice. Provide three references from MCBAs with personal knowledge of applicant's work.
	FIBA—Fellow of the Institute of Business Appraisers	Meet all CBA requirements, plus be voted into College of Fellows on basis of technical leadership and contribution to the profession and the Institute.			
National Association of Certified Valuation Analysts (NACVA)	AVA—Accredited Valuation Analyst, includes prior GVA designation	Obtain business degree and/or an MBA or higher; member in good standing of NACVA.	Complete five-day course; four-hour exam; additional eight-hour exam for applicants without accounting fundamentals background.	Provide case study for exam.	Two years full-time or equivalent business valuation or related experience, or ten or more business valuations. Provide three personal references, three business references, and a minimum of one letter of recommendation from an employer or another CPA.
	CVA—Certified Valuation Analyst	Have college degree, unrevoked CPA license, and be a member in good standing of NACVA.	Complete five-day course; pass two-part exam: four-hour proctored exam plus take-home exam with case study.	Pass case study for exam.	Two years experience as a CPA. Provide three personal references and three business references.
	CFFA—Certified Financial Forensic Analyst	Possess one of the following designations: CVA, AVA, AM, ASA, CBA, CBV, CFA, CMA, CPA, or CA; hold advanced degree in economics, accounting, or finance, or undergraduate degree and MBA.	Complete two-week course, and 8 days of training at NACVA's Forensic Institute; pass two-part exam: four-hour proctored exam plus take-home exam with case study.	Submit case study report under Fed. Rule 26, or report admitted into evidence within the last three years.	Provide one business and two legal references. Substantial experience in ten litigation matters, including five in which a deposition or testimony was given.

Organization	Designation	Education	Examination	Experience
Canadian Institute of Chartered Business Valuators (CICBV)	CBV—Chartered Business Valuator	Have college degree or equivalent: accounting or finance encouraged.	Successfully complete six courses, including assignments and exams for each course plus the required experience, followed by the writing of the Membership Entrance Exam. Writing of exam can be challenged without successful completion of courses if applicant has at least five years full-time experience in business valuations.	Have two years full-time experience or the equivalent of part-time obtained over a five-year period, attested to by a sponsoring CICBV member.
	CA-CBV	Hold CA (Chartered Accountant) designation; complete CICBV Program of Studies or five years of full-time business valuation experience may allow for exemption.	Obtain at least 60% in the CICBV's Membership Entrance Exam comprising two three-and-one-half-hour examinations.	Submit a letter from a CBV that sponsors and confirms applicant's two full years of full-time business valuation experience and recommends applicant for membership; agree to uphold CICBV's Code of Ethics and Practice Standards.
	FCBV—Fellow of the Canadian Institute of Chartered Business Valuators	Be a member; have rendered outstanding service to the business valuation profession; or have earned distinction and brought honor through achievements in professional life or in the community.		Two years full-time experience or the equivalent of part-time obtained over a five-year period, attested to by a sponsoring CICBV member.

Source: Business Valuation Resources, LLC. All rights reserved. Used with permission.

Exhibit 3.2   Business Valuation Professional Designations Summary

AIBA	Accredited by IBA (Institute of Business Appraisers)
AM	Accredited Member (American Society of Appraisers)
ASA	Accredited Senior Appraiser (American Society of Appraisers)
AVA	Accredited Valuation Analyst (National Association of Certified Valuation Analysts)
BVAL	Business Valuator Accredited for Litigation (Institute of Business Appraisers)
CA-CBV	Chartered Accountant–Chartered Business Valuator (The Canadian Institute of Chartered Business Valuators)
CBA	Certified Business Appraiser (Institute of Business Appraisers)
CBV	Chartered Business Valuator (The Canadian Institute of Chartered Business Valuators)
CFA	Chartered Financial Analyst (CFA institute, formerly Association for Investment Management and Research)
CFFA	Certified Financial Forensic Analyst (National Association of Certified Valuation Analysts)
CPA/ABV	Certified Public Accountant Accredited in Business Valuation (American Institute of Certified Public Accountants)
CVA	Certified Valuation Analyst (National Association of Certified Valuation Analysts)
FASA	Fellow of the American Society of Appraisers
FCBV	Fellow of the Canadian Institute of Chartered Business Valuators
FIBA	Fellow of the Institute of Business Appraisers
MCBA	Master Certified Business Appraiser (Institute of Business Appraisers)

Exhibit 3.3   Professional Association Contact Information

American Institute of Certified Public Accountants (AICPA)
1211 Avenue of the Americas
New York, NY 10036-8775
Phone: (888) 777-7077 or
(212) 596-6200
Fax: (212) 596-6213
Web site: *www.aicpa.org*

American Society of Appraisers (ASA)
555 Herndon Parkway, Suite 125
Herndon, VA 20170
Phone: (800) 272-8258 or
(703) 478-2228
Fax: (703) 742-8471
E-mail: *asainfo@apo.com*
Web site: *www.appraisers.org*
BV Discipline Web site: *www.bvappraisers.org*
Contact: Jerry Larkins, Executive Vice President; (703) 733-2108; *jerry@appraisers.org*

Association for Investment Management and Research (AIMR)
P. O. Box 3668
Charlottesville, VA 22903-0668
Phone: (434) 951-5499
Fax: (434) 951-5262
E-mail: *info@aimr.org*
Web site: *www.aimr.org*

CFA Institute
(Formerly Association for Investment Management and Research [AIMR])
560 Ray C. Hunt Dr.
Charlottesville, VA 22903-2981
Phone: (800) 247-8132 (U.S. and Canada) or (434) 951-5499 (outside the United States and Canada)
Fax: (434) 951-5262
E-mail: *info@cfainstitute.org*
Web site: *www.cfainstitute.org*

Institute of Business Appraisers (IBA)
P.O. Box 17410
Plantation, FL 33318
Phone: (800) 299-4130 or (954) 584-1144
Fax: (954) 584-1184
E-mail: *ibahq@go-iba.org*
Web site: *www.go-iba.org*
Contacts: Michele G. Miles, Executive Director; Raymond Miles, Technical Director; Mary Lou Clemente, Controller

National Association of Certified Valuation Analysts (NACVA)
1111 Brickyard Road, Suite 200
Salt Lake City, UT 84106-5401
Phone: (800) 677-2009 or (801) 486-0600
Fax: (801) 486-7500
E-mail: *nacva@nacva.com*
Web site: *www.nacva.com*

The Canadian Institute of Chartered Business Valuators (CICBV)
277 Wellington Street West, 5th Floor
Toronto, Ontario M5V 3H2
Phone: (416) 204-3396
Fax: (416) 977-8585
E-mail: *admin@cicbv.ca*
Web site: *www.businessvaluators.com*

Sources of Law and Choice of Courts

SUMMARY

The American legal framework consists of dual systems: state and federal. Within each system, cases are resolved by considering constitutions, statutes, regulations, and common law. Taxes are imposed by both the state and federal governments. Each state has its own constitution, statutes, regulations, and common law, but often this is not considered by federal courts in resolving federal tax issues. Federal tax issues are the focus of this book.

Sources of federal tax law and administrative guidance include the Internal Revenue Code, Treasury Regulations, Revenue Rulings, Revenue Procedures, Private Letter Rulings, and court decisions. Tax cases are heard by the United States Supreme Court, Federal Circuit Courts of Appeal, the United States Tax Court, the various federal district courts, the Court of Federal Claims, and, occasionally, United States Bankruptcy Courts.

STRUCTURE OF THE AMERICAN LEGAL SYSTEM

State laws may conflict with federal law. When this happens, federal law trumps, and all courts, state and federal, must follow federal law under the doctrine of Supremacy. State tax issues are resolved in state court, but such issues are beyond the scope of this book.

The Constitution, Statutes, and Regulations

The United States Constitution is the supreme law of the land. If the U.S. Constitution speaks to an issue, it trumps any other law. To the extent any other law conflicts, it is unconstitutional and invalid.

The statutes of the United States, enacted by Congress and contained in the United States Code, are the next level of authority in the federal system. Where a state law conflicts, the federal statute controls. The Code deals with complex issues, and Congress usually does not attempt to write minute administrative details into statutes, instead delegating its decision-making authority to the U.S. Treasury Department.

By empowering the Treasury to make its decisions, Congress avoids dealing with administrative issues and eases the daily functioning of the tax administration. When a statute delegates congressional decision making to the Treasury, the rules created by the Treasury are called Regulations, and are published in the Code of Federal Regulations (CFR).

If no statute or regulation exists, or if the regulation or statute is ambiguous and must be interpreted and applied to the facts of the case, the proper recourse may be to the courts.

The Courts: Statutory Interpretation and Common Law

Within the federal system, the United States is divided into twelve judicial *circuits*, numbered 1 through 11, and the District of Columbia. A thirteenth circuit, the Federal Circuit, has no geographic boundaries; its jurisdiction is defined by its subject matter. The Federal Circuit has exclusive jurisdiction of all patent cases as well as appeals from the Court of Federal Claims. By contrast, the twelve geographical circuits have general jurisdiction of all claims within their geographical boundaries, regardless of subject matter.

Within each federal circuit (an archaic name left over from the days when United States appellate judges still "rode the circuit" on horseback to hear cases), there are district courts. The district courts have jurisdiction of all cases that involve an issue of federal law or that meet certain other requirements. At trials, witnesses are examined and cross-examined, each side's case is argued, and then the judge or jury determines what the facts are and who should win. There are also three federal courts with specialized jurisdiction—the U.S. Tax Court, the U.S. Court of Federal Claims, and the U.S. Court of International Trade. (For a full discussion, see the Tax Litigation section, infra.)

TAX LAW

The Code

Tax law's primary source is, of course, the Internal Revenue Code. Created by Congress, the Code is a product of society's perceived needs, current political philosophy, and complex political compromises. Not surprisingly, this array of sometimes contradictory considerations often produces the most complex legislation to emerge from Congress and not infrequently produces inadvertent aberrations called *loopholes*.

Any research into a tax issue should start in the Code. Despite its daunting complexity, the

Code frequently offers creative ways to solve a tax problem. In drafting the Code, however, Congress often uses a broad brush, choosing to leave to the Treasury Department the chore of interpreting what the Code is intended to accomplish. Thus, the Treasury has broad authority to further define the intent of a section and to issue "all needful rules and regulations" for the enforcement of its provisions. (I.R.C. § 7805(a)). As a result, a large body of tax law has its source in administrative regulations.

Administrative Regulations

In exercising the power delegated to the Treasury by Congress, the Service often issues *interpretive regulations*. These are intended to show how a particular Code section operates and to illustrate what Congress intended the Code section to accomplish. Ambiguities and other drafting issues are frequently addressed by such regulations.

Another form of regulation promulgated by the Service is the *legislative regulation*, done under specific directives from Congress—as, for example, when Congress simply delegates to the Treasury the authority to make law on a particular tax issue. Legislative regulations are not interpretive, since the Treasury is actually making the law under a direct delegation of authority from Congress.

Both forms of Treasury regulations, whether interpretive or legislative, are accorded considerable weight by the courts. Legislative regulations generally may be accorded more weight than interpretive ones.

Treasury regulations are typically issued in a tentative form called a *proposed regulation*, which allows public comment prior to adoption. When the process of public comment on a proposed regulation is completed, the Service may withdraw it or promulgate it as a final regulation in the Code of Federal Regulations.

Occasionally, temporary regulations may be issued without the usual protocol of public comment, and these are flagged by adding the suffix "T" to the citation. In general, Treasury regulations are cited in numerical format, with the number *1* followed by a decimal and the Code section they refer to. For example, a regulation applicable to § 368 of the code would be cited as Treas. Reg. §1.368. (Were this a temporary regulation, the cite would be §1.368T).

Acquiescence

When issues are decided in the court, the Service may publish an acquiescence or nonacquiescence to the result. The latter simply means that the Service does not agree with the outcome and will continue to challenge the issue should others raise it in court.

Revenue Rulings and Revenue Procedures

Often referred to as "Rev. Ruls." ("Rev. Rul." in the singular), Revenue Rulings are published by the Service in the Internal Revenue Bulletin each week, and are later compiled in the *Cumulative Bulletin*. They are cited numerically, using the year of the Rev. Rul. followed by a dash, followed by the number of the ruling—as, for example, 99-25, for the twenty-fifth ruling issued in 1999.

Rev. Ruls. provide a detailed analysis by the Service of certain tax issues. The facts of the issue being addressed will be described, the Service will analyze the law on the subject, and then reach a conclusion as to how the issue should be decided.

Revenue Procedures, known as Rev. Procs., are similar to Rev. Ruls. and deal with ways in which the Service will administer the Code and litigate cases. To the extent that there is a distinction between them, it is this: Rev. Ruls. deal with the substantive law, while Rev. Procs. deal with administrative issues, although both should be consulted, since the Service may put substantive law into Rev. Procs.

Rev. Ruls. and Rev. Procs. can be extremely helpful to a taxpayer when they favor her position, since such a rule is binding on the Service.[1]

Private Letter Rulings

Private Letter Rulings are responses by the Service to a taxpayer's request for an advance ruling on a specific tax issue. The taxpayer specifies the factual elements of the transaction and requests a ruling on its tax effect. Private Letter Rulings are deemed by the Service to apply only to the taxpayer in question. Private tax services publish these and they can be useful in determining what the Service's position is likely to be given similar facts. Often, they are used as the basis for opinion letters by tax attorneys.

One can find Private Letter Rulings by using their numerical citations: the first four numbers represent the year in which the ruling is issued, the next two numbers represent the week, and the last three represent the number of the ruling that week.

TAX LITIGATION

Tax matters can be litigated in a variety of forums. If a federal tax case involving valuation is not settled through the Service's administrative procedures (e.g., audits and appeals), the taxpayer is faced with litigating in federal court. The taxpayer receives a letter from the Service indicating that in the view of the Service, the taxpayer is deficient in the amount of taxes owed the government.

At this point, the taxpayer can simply concede and pay the tax due, together with interest and any applicable penalties. If the taxpayer prefers to litigate, the taxpayer has a choice of venue. The taxpayer may pay the tax and then sue for a refund in the Court of Federal Claims, or may sue for a refund in the taxpayer's U.S. district court. The other choice for the taxpayer is to not pay the tax and instead sue the government in the U.S. Tax Court, asking that the Court redetermine the correct amount of the deficiency. About 95 percent of taxpayers choose to go to the U.S. Tax Court.

---

[1]To see an example of a Rev. Rul. and Rev. Proc., see Chapter 22.

United States Tax Court

The U.S. Tax Court is a court with national jurisdiction over income, estate, gift, and many other federal tax cases. The Tax Court has nineteen judges, each of whom is appointed by the president with the consent of the Senate. The perpetual defendant in the Tax Court is the Commissioner of Internal Revenue Service. Cases begin when the taxpayer petitions the court asking for a redetermination of the deficiency in taxes that the Service has proposed in its Notice of Deficiency. After filing the petition, it takes about a year or less for her case to come before the Tax Court judge.

The Tax Court may hear the case in Washington, D.C., where the court maintains its offices, or in various cities around the country. The court tries to accommodate the preferences of the taxpayer so as to make it as convenient as possible for the taxpayer to litigate her claims. The clerk of the court prepares trial calendars for various cities on the basis of the number of cases eligible for trial in each city. Cases are not placed on calendars until the commissioner has filed an answer to the taxpayer's petition. Generally, each petitioning taxpayer designates the city where the case should be heard, choosing among approximately sixty-five cities where the Tax Court officially sits. The court sits in each of these cities at least once a year and sits in some of the larger cities several times a year. The chief judge circulates among the judges a list of the trial sessions, and the judges make their preferences known. The chief judge then assigns the calendars to the judges on the basis of their seniority and preferences.

Following a trial in the Tax Court, the judge receives the trial briefs of the parties and deliberates on the case. In due course, the judge will write a report. The report, generally speaking, consists of two sections, the first being the findings of fact and the second being the opinion as to those facts. It is in the opinion portion of the report that the judge sets forth her legal analysis. Unlike a judge in the U.S. District Court who is not subject to any peer-level review of that opinion before its release, the Tax Court judge must follow a statutory review process before the opinion is released. After the report is written, it is sent to the chief judge, who reviews it. In this manner, the opinions of the Tax Court are reviewed in part to make sure that the legal analysis is compatible with the views of a majority of the judges on the court. There are nineteen judges, and accordingly, views may differ on a point of law. It is important that the federal tax laws be uniformly applied to all taxpayers. The review process attempts to assure that the various opinions of the court will be consistent and uniform.

During review, the chief judge may take several actions upon reviewing a proposed report. First, the chief judge may approve the report as a *Division Opinion*. Division Opinions are officially published by the Government Printing Office in the Tax Court Reports and are binding precedent among all the judges on the court. Second, the chief judge may approve a report as a *Memorandum Opinion*. Memorandum Opinions are not officially published and generally turn on the facts of the case or on established law. Memorandum Opinions are not considered by some judges on the court as binding precedent. Other judges and some appellate courts view the Memorandum Opinions differently. Valuation opinions are highly fact intensive and, unless there is some novel aspect of law involved, are almost always issued as Memorandum Opinions. In this regard, valuation opinions may not be precedent for future valuation cases. Third, the chief judge may return the proposed report to the authoring judge with comments and suggestions. If the authoring judge does not accept the suggestions, then the chief judge may send the proposed report to the Court Conference for review by all of the regular judges. Each regular judge has one vote on each conference decision.

Generally, the court conferees meet monthly. In preparation for their conference, the conferees receive copies of each proposed report set for review, and each conferee independently researches and analyzes the underlying issues. Typically, one or more conferees will circulate a memorandum before conference, articulating his or her position as to the case.

At the conference, the conferees discuss and vote upon the case. If a majority of the judges participating in the conference vote for the proposed report, the proposed report is adopted and becomes a Division Opinion. An exception to this rule is where the proposed report overrules a previous Tax Court opinion. In that case, the proposed report is adopted only if it receives a vote of the majority of the conferences. If a proposed report is not adopted, the authoring judge may ask that the case be reassigned to another judge. In that case, the presiding judge usually files a side opinion in which he or she dissents to the majority's contrary opinion.

Traditionally, a proposed report is sent to the Court Conference if it: (1) overrules a prior Tax Court opinion, (2) invalidates a Regulation of the Treasury Department, or (3) decides an issue inconsistently with the opinion of a Court of Appeals other than the court to which an appeal of the case lies.

A proposed report may also be sent to the Court Conference for other reasons, such as: (1) the issue is recurring in nature; (2) the issue is a matter of first impression; (3) the chief judge questions the validity of the legal approach that the proposed report has adopted; and (4) the chief judge receives notification from other judges that there is disagreement on a report that is about to be issued. In the latter case, opinions that have been adopted by the court, either with or without court review, are circulated around the court the morning of the day they are to be issued. The judges have until 3:00 P.M. of the day when the opinion is officially released to the parties and to the public to notify the chief judge of any disagreement.

Federal District Court

The U.S. district courts are located throughout the United States. The U.S. district courts are the only courts where the taxpayer can have a federal tax–related valuation case tried before a jury. To have the right to litigate in the U.S. district court, the taxpayer must have the deficiency assessed and then must pay the deficiency. Then the taxpayer must file a claim for refund with the Service within two years of paying the deficiency or three years from the filing of the return, whichever is later. If the refund claim is ignored or rejected, the taxpayer can file suit no earlier than six months after the claim is filed and no later than two years after the Service rejects the claim. Appeals from the U.S. district courts are made to the Court of Appeals for the circuit in which the taxpayer resides.

Court of Federal Claims

The Court of Federal Claims is located in Washington, D.C., and here taxpayers and others may sue the United States for various claims within the jurisdiction of the court. Included among the claims for which one may sue are federal tax refunds. The taxpayer must follow the same refund procedures as she would take in the instance of preparing a case to go to the U.S. district court, as just described. Cases are tried before a single judge and without a right to a jury. Tax cases are a small percentage of the court's caseload. A claim for refund can be filed anytime within two years after paying the tax or three years from the filing of the return. Appeals from the Court of Federal Claims are made to the U.S. Court of Appeals for the Federal Circuit.

United States Bankruptcy Courts

The bankruptcy courts of the United States will occasionally hear tax matters when they arise in the context of a bankruptcy. Usually, this occurs when bankrupt taxpayers seek to have their tax debts discharged pursuant to 11 U.S.C. § 523 (a)(1)(c). This seldom involves valuation issues, and is thus not discussed at length.

Chapter 5

Burden of Proof in Valuation Controversies

SUMMARY

This chapter discusses the burden of proof as it relates to valuation. *Burden of proof* is a concept used to assess facts in trials; it determines which party must do two distinct things. First, the burden of proof determines which party must initially produce evidence so as to avoid having her suit dismissed. This is called the *burden of production.* Second, it determines which party must ultimately persuade the court as to the correctness of its position. This is termed the *burden of persuasion. Note:* The two burdens are totally distinct. Thus, the burden of production is not inevitably assigned to the party that bears the burden of persuasion.

The burden of proof can be outcome determinative in cases where there is little evidence on the issue in controversy. Normally, the burden rests upon the taxpayer, and the position of the Internal Revenue Service Commissioner is presumed to be correct. This is not inevitable, however. The burden may be shifted by the court, in its discretion, or by statute, where the taxpayer establishes four threshold facts:

1. All items required by law to be substantiated are substantiated.
2. The taxpayer has maintained all records required by law to be maintained.
3. The taxpayer cooperates with the Service.
4. The taxpayer does not exceed a certain net worth (not applicable to individuals).

In planning a transaction involving a valuation event, one needs to assess a multitude of factors. Among them is the burden of proof.

Although it is true that only a small percentage of all of the valuation reports produced in the planning process ultimately are involved in litigation, planners need to know what the burden of proof is and which party must carry it in order to prepare proper documentation in the event that the valuation becomes controversial.

Audits and Appeals

Although burden of proof is a concept utilized in court, the importance of who has the burden of proof should be analyzed and considered long before the controversy goes to court.

For example, when the Service audits a taxpayer, the auditing agent may dispute issues with the taxpayer. About 95 percent of these disputes are resolved at the audit stage, but the remaining 5 percent move to the Service's appeals stage for resolution.

There, a representative of the Service's Appellate Division will meet with the taxpayer and/or the taxpayer's representative to resolve issues. It is at this level that the appellate conferee is able to take into consideration a multitude of factors in an effort to settle the case. A very important consideration from the government's perspective is an understanding of what litigation hazards the government will encounter if it declines to settle.

KEY THOUGHT

An appellate conferee is a representative of the Service who meets with the taxpayer at an appellate conference and has settlement authority.

Obviously, if the appellate conferee concludes that the government has a litigation hazard, he or she will factor that in when deciding whether and how to settle the case. A litigation hazard is, among other things, whether the government has the burden of proof should the case go to court. Thus, without ever having set foot in a courtroom, the taxpayer may be able to achieve a better settlement at the administrative level merely by establishing that the government has the burden of proof.[1]

Presumption of Correctness

To explain the nature and importance of the burden of proof, it is helpful to understand some basics relating to federal tax litigation. The Commissioner of the Internal Revenue Service ("the Commissioner") issues a notice of deficiency if the taxpayer and the Service cannot resolve their controversy administratively at the audit or appeals level.[2]

The notice serves to advise the taxpayer that the Commissioner means to assess a deficiency and proceed in court.[3]

---

[1]Some taxpayers prefer to skip proceeding to the Appellate Division and go directly to court to resolve their controversies. However, in order to shift the burden of proof from the taxpayer to the government under a motion pursuant to I.R.C. § 7491, the taxpayer must first cooperate with the Service. Cooperation means, in part, that the taxpayer must first exhaust his or her administrative remedies, which include taking the issues to the appellate conference for resolution. See the legislative history of I.R.C. § 7491(a)(2)(B).

[2]I.R.C. § 6212(a) provides that such notice shall include a notice to the taxpayer of the taxpayer's right to contact a local office of the taxpayer advocate and the location and phone number of the appropriate office.

[3]*Olsen v. Helvering*, 88 F.2d 650, (2d Cir. 1937).

The U.S. Supreme Court has stated that the notice of deficiency has a presumption of correctness. Thus, the government is presumed to be correct when it informs the taxpayer that the taxpayer owes the government taxes. If the taxpayer is to prevail in a dispute with the government, the taxpayer now bears the burden of proving the government's deficiency notice erroneous. In some sense, the presumption of correctness may be nothing more than a way of characterizing who bears the burden of proof. The presumption of correctness is essentially the same hurdle of proof, in loose terms, as is the burden of proof, which we shall discuss in the remainder of this chapter.

If the deficiency notice is found to be *arbitrary and erroneous*, or *arbitrary and excessive*, the presumption of correctness is negated and the burden of proof may shift to the government.[4]

Note, however, that there is a difference between a deficiency notice that is arbitrary and erroneous and one that is merely incorrect. An incorrect notice may still be entitled to a presumption of correctness while an arbitrary and erroneous notice may lose the presumption of correctness.

All that is required to support the presumption of correctness is that the Commissioner's determination have some minimal factual predicate. It is only when the Commissioner's assessment is shown to be "without rational foundation" or "arbitrary and erroneous" that the presumption should not be recognized.

The general rebuttable presumption that the Commissioner is correct is a fundamental element of any federal tax controversy.[5]

Now, let us assume that the taxpayer decides to go to court to dispute the determination set forth in the deficiency notice. By virtue of the presumption of correctness in favor of the government, the taxpayer must begin by offering some evidence or she will lose. The presumption of correctness therefore imposes on the party against whom it is directed the burden of going forward with evidence to rebut the presumption.

BURDEN OF PROOF

Judge Richard A. Posner, in his book, *Economic Analysis of Law*, explains that the burden of proof has two components. He states:

> *Burden of proof has two aspects. The first is important only in an adversarial system, where the tribunal does not participate in the search for evidence. This is the burden of producing (submitting) evidence to the*

---

[4]*Welch v. Helvering*, 290 U.S. 111 (1933). If, however, the deficiency notice is found to be "arbitrary and erroneous," or "arbitrary and excessive," the presumption of correctness is negated and the burden of proof may shift to the government.

[5]Although this presumption is judicially created, rather than legislatively based, there is considerable evidence that the presumption has been repeatedly considered and approved by Congress. The Internal Revenue Code contains a number of civil provisions that explicitly place the burden of proof on the Commissioner in certain circumstances. Presumably, if Congress had wanted to place the general presumption of correctness on the Commissioner, it could have done so but instead chose to do so only in specific cases such as (1) fraud, §§ 7454(a) and 7422(e); (2) transferee liability, § 6902(a); (3) illegal bribes, § 162(c)(1) and (2); and (4) income tax return preparer's penalty, Sec 6703(a). See footnote 17 of Townsend, Burden of Proof in Tax Cases: Valuation and Ranges, Tax Notes, October 1, 2001, wherein he states that "Congress was aware that the BTA (Board of Tax Appeals) imposed the burden of proof on the taxpayer. During hearings leading to the 1926 Tax Act, a member of the BTA testified to the House Ways and Means Committee that if the burden of proof were to be placed on the Commissioner instead of the taxpayer, Congress might as well repeal the income tax law and pass the hat, because you will practically be saying to the taxpayer, 'How much do you want to contribute toward the support of the government?' and in that case they would have to decide for themselves."

tribunal, as distinct from the burden of persuading the tribunal that one ought to win the case. Failing to carry either burden means that the party having the burden loses. The two burdens are intertwined; for one thing the burden of persuasion generally determines who has the burden of production. The plaintiff's burden in an ordinary civil case is to show that his position is more likely than not correct. In other words, if at the end of the trial the jury either thinks the defendant should win or doesn't know which side should win—the evidence seems in equipoise—the plaintiff loses.[6]

Burden of Production Component

The burden of proof is a single concept that consists of two parts: the burden of production and the burden of persuasion. Together, they are commonly called the burden of proof.

The burden of production is the obligation to go forward with evidence or lose the case. Since this burden is normally on the taxpayer, the taxpayer must begin by introducing some evidence of a credible nature that supports the taxpayer's argument. The burden of production serves to ensure that the evidence is of a certain minimum level to satisfy the trier of fact. Customarily, once this minimum has been met, the burden of production will then shift to the opposition.

Burden of Persuasion Component

The second part of the burden of proof is the burden of persuasion. In civil tax cases, one carries the burden of persuasion by producing a preponderance of credible evidence. A preponderance of evidence is not the same standard used in criminal cases. In criminal cases the standard of proof is "beyond a reasonable doubt." Thus, the government must show that the defendant is guilty beyond a reasonable doubt in order to prevail.

However, in civil cases, the standard is lower. As noted, taxpayers can prevail in a non-criminal tax case, in most instances, by convincing the trier of fact that they have provided a preponderance of evidence. To carry the burden of persuasion by a preponderance of evidence means essentially that one has produced and supported the case with more than 50 percent of the credible evidence required to prove the point.[7]

The burden of persuasian is yet another hurdle. After satisfying the procedural burden of producing evidence to rebut the presumption in favor of the Commissioner, the taxpayer must still carry his ultimate burden of proof or persuasion.

WHO BEARS THE BURDEN OF PROOF

It is customary in litigation for each party to inform the court as to who bears the burden of proof. In most cases there is no dispute. In some instances, the issue of who has the burden of proof is contested and the parties will pursue their arguments on this issue as vigorously as

---

[6]Judge Richard A. Posner, *Economic Analysis of Law* (New York: Aspen Publishers, 2002): 617. Reprinted with permission of Aspen Publishers. All rights reserved.
[7]For a good discussion of this, see Townsend, "Burden of Proof in Tax Cases: Valuation and Ranges," *Tax Notes* (October 1, 2001). In civil fraud cases, the evidentiary minimum threshold is what is called "clear and convincing" evidence considered to be higher than more than 50-plus percent. See section 7454(a).

any substantive issue of the case.[8] Who has the burden of proof is determined according to one or more of the following:

- Court Rules of Practice and Procedure[9]
- The Internal Revenue Code[10]
- Relevant case law[11]

In the U.S. Tax Court, where 95 percent of all federal tax litigation is adjudicated,[12] the burden of proof is provided for by Court Rule 142(a), which states, in part:

> *The burden of proof shall be upon the petitioner, [the taxpayer], except as otherwise provided by statute or determined by the Court; and except that, in respect of any new matter, increases in deficiency, and affirmative defenses, pleaded in the answer, it shall be upon the respondent [government].*

Reasons that are often given for placing the burden of proof on the taxpayer are historically founded. In the early years of the income tax, before there was a Tax Court, a common remedy for taxpayers to dispute their taxes was to sue for a refund after first paying the tax. Typically, in a refund suit, the plaintiff has the burden of proof. This historical foundation has generally carried over to modern-day tax litigation.

In addition, taxpayers presumably have, or should have, the dispositive records within their possession. If a taxpayer has the records, it makes sense that the taxpayer should have the burden of presenting those records to prove that the government's determination of tax liability is in error.

Finally, if the government has the burden of proof, one can question whether the government would have to be more intrusive in order to sustain its burden. If the records to prove the correct tax liability are in the possession of the taxpayer, and the government has the burden of proof, the government would be expected to take efforts to obtain that evidence and thus become more intrusive. Generally, it is felt that a more intrusive government is not desirable.

For all of these reasons, in most business valuations that become controversial and go to court, the taxpayer has the burden of proof—at least initially.

BURDEN OF PROOF: EXCEPTIONS TO THE GENERAL RULE

There are certain exceptions to the general rule that the taxpayer has the burden of proof in tax litigation. For instance, in any case involving the issue of fraud with intent to evade tax, the burden is on the government and that burden of proof is required to be carried by clear and convincing evidence.[13] There are other exceptions to the general rule that also put the

---

[8]See *Estate of Paul Mitchell v. Comm'r*, 250 F.3rd (9th Cir. (2001).

[9]For example, see Tax Court Rules of Practice and Procedure, Rule 142(a).

[10]I.R.C. § 7491(a).

[11]For example, see *Welch v. Helvering* (op. cit.) where the Supreme Court stated that the Commissioner's "ruling has the support of a presumption of correctness, and the petitioner has the burden of proving it wrong."

[12]Section 7454(a).

[13]Tax Ct. Rule 142(b). See also I.R.C. § 7454(a).

burden of proof on the government, such as issues relating to the knowing conduct of a foundation manager,[14] transferee liability,[15] alleged bribes, and certain penalties relating to tax return preparers.

Generally, there are two ways by which the burden of proof can be shifted from the taxpayer to the government. First, a court has discretion under certain circumstances to shift the burden to the government and away from the taxpayer. Second, the burden can be shifted to the government if the taxpayer meets certain statutory thresholds, enacted recently by Congress in response to the public's concerns that it is unfair to have the burden of proof on the taxpayer.

Let us examine each possibility.

Shifting the Burden through Judicial Discretion: An Example

Assume the following: A taxpayer makes a gift of her closely held corporate stock to her children. She values the stock at $2 million and reports the transaction in a gift tax return. The Service audits the taxpayer and concludes that the stock is undervalued. The Service believes that the stock is worth $3 million. The parties are unable to resolve their disagreement through administrative means and therefore the Service issues a notice of deficiency, determining that the gift of the stock should be increased by $1 million.

Now, assume that the taxpayer files a timely petition for redetermination of her tax liability with the U.S. Tax Court. Sometime after the litigation has begun, assume that the Service learns by way of discovery that the appropriate value should be $4 million, rather than $3 million. Under the circumstances, it adjusts its pleadings accordingly and seeks a new tax liability for the taxpayer based on the higher valuation.

Under these facts, Tax Court Rule 143(a) places the burden of proving the higher amount, the extra million dollars, on the government. The government increased its deficiency and therefore has assumed the burden of proving the new, higher amount. In this case, the government must go forward with the production of evidence to prove the higher amount, and must carry the burden of persuasion, in order to prevail. So far, no one will argue that this seems unfair or inappropriate.

Change the facts: Assume that instead of increasing the deficiency after the deficiency notice was served, the government learns via the discovery process that the amount should be less than the $3 million it originally asserted. The government therefore appropriately concedes to the lesser amount, which we will assume is $2.5 million.

Now, who has the burden of proof? Remember that the burden of proof has two aspects: The burden of production, that is the burden of going forward with the evidence, and the burden of persuading the trier of fact of the correctness of this position

The view expressed by most courts is that when the government concedes to the lower deficiency amount, only the burden of production shifts to the government.[16] Under this view, if the government does not go forward with its evidence, it loses. If, however, the government

---

[14]Tax Ct. Rule 142(c).
[15]Id. at Rule 142(d).
[16]See, for example, *Cozzi v. Comm'r*, 88 T.C. 435 (1987); *Weimerskirch v. Comm'r*, 596 F.2d 358, 360-61 (9th Cir. 1979), *rev'g* 67 T.C. 672 (1977).

does go forward with its evidence, the taxpayer then still has the burden of going forward with its own evidence, and ultimately still has the burden of persuasion.[17]

However, the Ninth Circuit Court of Appeals took a different path, and has ruled recently to the contrary in certain valuation cases and held that, where the government lowers the value from the amount it first determined in its deficiency notice, it has both the burden of production and the burden of persuasion. In other words, the whole burden of proof shifts to the government where the government, in a valuation case, concedes an issue or lowers the amount it first determined to be correct. This result seems contrary to the ruling of the Supreme Court in *Welch v. Helvering*, which puts the burden of proof squarely on the taxpayer.[18]

Certain questions arise by virtue of the position recently taken in the Ninth Circuit. First, what incentive does the government have in a valuation case to make a concession with respect to the valuation amount, if the government knows that by lowering its first determination it now has the burden of proof? Second, suppose that the government makes a concession on a nonvaluation issue in a case with several issues implicating valuation, such as travel and entertainment deductions. Does this concession also mean that the government bears the burden of proof on the remaining valuation issue? If so, what incentive does the government have to make any concession once a case is in litigation?

Shifting of the Burden of Proof by Statute: Section 7491

Earlier, we stated that there were other circumstances where the burden of proof would shift to the government when the taxpayer met certain thresholds established by Congress. Congress recently changed the rules relating to burden of proof because it felt that individuals and small business taxpayers were at a disadvantage when they litigated against the government in tax matters. Congress felt that shifting the burden of proof to the Commissioner would create a better balance between the Service and such taxpayers, without encouraging tax avoidance.[19]

In 1998, Congress enacted Code section 7491 to provide that the Commissioner shall bear the burden of proof in any court proceeding with respect to a factual issue, if the taxpayer introduces credible evidence on the issue that is relevant to ascertaining the taxpayer's income tax liability.

For the taxpayer to shift the burden to the government, four conditions must be met. The taxpayer must

1. Substantiate any item required by law to be substantiated.[20]
2. Maintain records required by law to be kept.[21]

---

[17]See *Hardy v. Comm'r*, 181 F.3d 1002 (9th Cir. 1999); *Rapp v. Comm'r*, 774 F.2d 932 (9th Cir. 1985). (Once the government has carried its initial burden of introducing some evidence . . . , the burden shifts to the taxpayer to rebut the presumption by establishing a preponderance of the evidence that the deficiency determination is arbitrary or erroneous.)

[18]For an excellent discussion of this subject see Lederman, "Arbitrary Stat Notices in Valuation Cases or Arbitrary Ninth Circuit?" *Tax Notes*, June 29, 2001. Note that in some prior cases, the Ninth Circuit has held that the burden of persuasion remains with the taxpayer. See *Hardy v. Comm'r*, 181 F.3rd 1002,1004 (9th Cir. 1999), *Rapp v. Comm'r*, 774 F.2d 932, 935 (9th Cir. 1985).

[19]See the Committee Reports to the Internal Revenue Service Restructuring and Reform Act of 1998, Sec. 3001.

[20]I.R.C. § 7491(a)(2)(A).

[21]I.R.C. § 7491(a)(2)(B).

3. Cooperate with reasonable requests by the Service for meetings, interviews, witness information, and documents.[22] Cooperation includes the taxpayer's providing reasonable access to, and inspection of, witnesses, information, and documents. Cooperation also includes providing reasonable assistance to the Service in obtaining access to evidence not within the control of the taxpayer, including witnesses, information, and documents. This element of cooperation implies that the taxpayer will also cooperate with respect to any witnesses, information, or documents located in any foreign country. A necessary element of cooperation is that the taxpayer must exhaust other administrative remedies, including any appeal rights provided by the Service.

4. Meet certain net worth limitations,[23] except in the case of an individual. Corporations, partnerships, and trusts whose net worth exceeds $7 million are not eligible for the benefits of shifting the burden of proof.

Finally, the taxpayer bears the burden of proving that each of these conditions is met before it can be established that the burden of proof is on the government.

The burden will shift to the government only if the taxpayer meets these conditions and introduces credible evidence with respect to a factual issue relevant to ascertaining the taxpayer's liability.

In addition, if the case involves the imposition of penalties or additions to tax, the Commissioner bears the burden of production in any court proceeding.[24]

Credible evidence is the quality of evidence that the court would find sufficient to base a decision upon if no contrary evidence were submitted, without regard to the judicial presumption of governmental correctness. A taxpayer has not produced credible evidence if the taxpayer merely makes implausible factual assertions, frivolous claims, or tax-protester arguments. For the evidence to be credible, the court must be convinced that it is worthy of belief. If, after evidence from both sides, the court believes that the evidence is equally balanced, the court likely will find that the taxpayer has not sustained its burden of proof.

---

[22]Id.
[23]I.R.C. § 7491(a)(2)(C).
[24]I.R.C. § 7491(c).

Penalties and Sanctions

SUMMARY

The tax law is designed to provide disincentives, or sanctions, for valuations that are substantially misstated. These sanctions can seriously increase the costs related to the valuation transactions. Accordingly, great care must be taken to ensure that the valuation is realistic and within a reasonable range.

An incorrect valuation can result in one or more penalties or sanctions, which can be grouped into three categories:

1. Valuation penalties
2. General penalties
3. Discretionary sanctions

The valuation penalty (I.R.C. § 6662) may be imposed when there is a substantial valuation misstatement (I.R.C. § 6662(b)(3)), or substantial estate or gift tax valuation understatement (I.R.C. § 6662(b)(5)). General penalties may be imposed where the taxpayer was negligent (I.R.C. § 6662(b)(1)) or fraudulent (I.R.C. § 6663). Discretionary sanctions are imposed by courts, in their discretion, where the taxpayer uses the Court primarily for delay, takes a "frivolous or groundless" position, or unreasonably fails to pursue administrative remedies.

INTRODUCTION

The Big Picture

Some may believe that business valuation is merely an exercise in guessing or estimating, even if based on some abstract financial principles. Courts, albeit unintentionally, contribute to this belief when they merely split the difference between appraisals and do not make the effort to arrive at precise values.

If valuation is nothing more than a good guess, there is nothing to prevent appraisers from providing lawyers or clients whatever appraisal they need to justify their transaction. After all, who can dispute that the guess is not legitimate?

Although it is true that the valuation of a business involves using common sense to make sound judgments, valuation is not merely a guess as to value. Certainly, valuation is a judgment; but it is a studied judgment, and should be withheld by ethical business appraisers until all reasonable and relevant facts are analyzed in the context of established financial and appraisal principles.

To discourage mere valuation guesses, and to deter those who would perform a valuation with the purpose of accommodating a client who needs a certain result, the tax law has a series of penalties, nondeductible from taxes, that apply to valuations done for tax purposes. These penalties are designed to inhibit over- and undervaluations, as well as negligent or fraudulent valuations.

Penalties are important to both the Service and the taxpayer. To the Service, penalties are a meaningful deterrent against abusive valuation misstatement. To taxpayers, penalties are real dollars that they would not pay the government but for a valuation misstatement.

If a taxpayer underpays taxes as a result of a substantial valuation misstatement, the Service can collect three types of monetary remedies: the actual back taxes owed, interest on the amount owed, and penalties. Excluding potential criminal liability, in business terms the first two remedies would be analogous to repaying a loan—the taxpayer repays the principal, plus the interest that she denied the government. Penalties are how the Service financially discourages underpayment of taxes, and they are far from trivial.[1]

For the aggressive taxpayer assessed with a deficiency due to a valuation misstatement, this multitude of penalties can add up to significant amounts of money. The statutory penalty expressly designed for valuation cases is in two subsections within Code section 6662, but other penalties may be applied by the Service in special cases.

WHAT YOU NEED TO KNOW

Five sections in the Internal Revenue Code provide for penalties that may be applied in cases of valuation misstatement.

To avoid confusion, remember that some sections contain multiple penalties. For instance, section 6662 contains both valuation and general penalties. For this reason, it is highly recommended that you read I.R.C. §§ 6662, 6663, 6700(a)(2)(B), 6701, and 6673 before reading the rest of the chapter.

---

[1]Additions to tax under sections 6651(a)(1) (failure to file a tax return) and 6651(a)(2) (failure to pay taxes) are not penalties and are not discussed in this chapter. They are, however, another way in which the Service may penalize certain valuation misstatements. See, e.g., *Estate of Young v. Comm'r*, 110 T.C. 297 (1998) and *Estate of Campbell v. Comm'r*, T.C. Memo 1991-615.

VALUATION PENALTIES

The penalty directly applicable to valuation misstatement is contained in Code sections 6662(b)(3) and (b)(5). Generally, where a taxpayer "substantially" misstates value for income or estate tax purposes, she will be liable for a penalty equal to 20 percent of the resulting underpayment, after the back taxes are paid with interest.

Section 6662: Imposition of Accuracy-Related Penalty provides in relevant part:

(a)   Imposition of Penalty. If this section applies to any portion of an underpayment of tax required to be shown on a return, there shall be added to the tax an amount equal to 20 percent of the portion of the underpayment to which this section applies.

(b)   Portion of Underpayment to Which Section Applies. This section shall apply to the portion of any underpayment which is attributable to one or more of the following:

(1)   Negligence or disregard of rules or regulations.

(2)   Any substantial understatement of income tax.

(3)   Any substantial valuation misstatement under chapter 1.

(4)   Any substantial overstatement of pension liabilities.

(5)   Any substantial estate or gift tax valuation understatement.

. . .

(e)   Substantial valuation misstatement under chapter 1.

(1)   In general. For purposes of this section, there is a substantial valuation misstatement under chapter 1 if—

(A) the value of any property (or the adjusted basis of any property) claimed on any return of tax imposed by chapter 1 is 200 percent or more of the amount determined to be the correct amount of such valuation or adjusted basis (as the case may be), or

(B) (i) the price for any property or services (or for the use of property) claimed on any such return in connection with any transaction between persons described in section 482 is 200 percent or more (or 50 percent or less) of the amount determined under section 482 to be the correct amount of such price, or

(ii) the net section 482 transfer price adjustment for the taxable year exceeds the lesser of $5,000,000 or 10 percent of the taxpayer's gross receipts.

(2) Limitation. No penalty shall be imposed by reason of subsection (b)(3) unless the portion of the underpayment for the taxable year attributable to substantial valuation misstatements under chapter 1 exceeds $5,000 ($10,000 in the case of a corporation other than an S corporation or a personal holding company (as defined in section 542)).

. . .

(g) Substantial estate or gift tax valuation understatement.

(1) In general. For purposes of this section, there is a substantial estate or gift tax valuation understatement if the value of any property claimed on any return of tax imposed by subtitle B is 50 percent or less of the amount determined to be the correct amount of such valuation.

(2) Limitation. No penalty shall be imposed by reason of subsection (b)(5) unless the portion of the underpayment attributable to substantial estate or gift tax valuation understatements for the taxable period (or, in the case of the tax imposed by chapter 11, with respect to the estate of the decedent) exceeds $5,000.

Key aspects of section 6662 include:

- The penalty for any violation of the section is 20 percent of the underpayment—not the misstatement, but the amount by which taxes were underpaid.
- The penalty applies for both income and transfer taxes. In other words, you cannot escape the penalty by moving from the income to the transfer tax regime.
- No penalty will be imposed for overstating property values for income-tax purposes unless the overstatement is 200 percent of the correct value.
- No penalty will be imposed for understating property values for transfer tax purposes unless the understatement is 50 percent of the correct value and the resulting underpayment exceeds $5,000.

Consider a routine court case involving a valuation penalty. In *Estate of Reiner v. Commissioner,*[2] the court had to decide whether the estate is liable for an addition to tax under section 6662(a) for a substantial estate or gift tax valuation understatement.

The Reiner family owned a 7,200-square-foot strip mall in Dubuque, Iowa, selling consumer electronics. At the time of his death, the father owned 22,100 private shares of the company, which the estate reported as worth $33.02 each. After lengthy analysis, the court found the fair market value of those shares to equal $952,000, for a price per share of $43.08. The estate reported the shares as worth $33.02 per share. The Commissioner sought to impose a penalty under section 6662(b)(5).

The court stated:

> *[The Commissioner] also determined that the estate was liable for an addition to tax under section 6662(a), which imposes a 20-percent addition for certain underpayments of tax. The addition is imposed where there is an underpayment of estate tax resulting from a substantial estate tax valuation understatement. See sec. 6662(b)(5). A substantial tax estate valuation understatement occurs if the value of any property claimed on an estate tax return is 50 percent or less of the amount determined to be correct. See sec. 6662(g)(1). In the instant case, the estate reported Reiner's stock on its return as having a value of $33.02 per share. As we have found that the correct value is $43.08 per share, no substantial estate or gift tax valuation understatement has occurred. Given our conclusion, we need not address whether the estate qualifies for the reasonable cause exception contained in section 6664(c)(1).*

As this case reflects, application of valuation penalties is fairly mechanical. The court merely compares the amount of the value claimed by the taxpayer with what it determines is the (correct) fair market value. Within these doctrinal confines, however, is an enormous uncertainty for the taxpayer: What will the court determine fair market value to be? Without being able to predict what measure of value the court will use or how it will apply the measure used, the taxpayer cannot be certain whether he or she will face penalties if the Service assesses a deficiency.

Section 6662 "shall" apply in the case of underpayment due to substantial misstatement of value. Section 6664(c) provides for a reasonable cause and/or good faith exception to section 6662, but this requires the taxpayer to establish that she either had reasonable cause to believe the valuation was reasonable, or that she acted in good faith. Neither of these is easy to estab-

---

[2]T.C. Memo 2000-298, 80 T.C.M. (CCH) 401, T.C.M. (RIA) 54054.

lish, given the uncertain nature of valuation, but having a recognized valuation expert (and preferably several of them) value the property using several different valuation techniques will strengthen the taxpayer's argument.[3]

There is another clause in section 6662(d)(2)(B), which waives the penalty where the underpayment was due to: (a) items supportable with "substantial authority," or (b) items that are "adequately disclosed" on the return. However, neither of these exceptions is available where the underpayment was the result of investment in a tax shelter. Since many valuation cases arise from use of tax shelters, section 6662(d)(2)(B) may be of limited usefulness.

Whether the taxpayer faces the stiff 20 percent penalty will thus hinge largely on what the fair market value of the property is determined to be. As we have repeatedly noted, determining *fair market value* is a factual matter about which there may be a difference of opinion.

GENERAL PENALTIES

General penalties are applicable to all cases, but can be, and often are, applied to valuation cases. There are four relevant general penalties:

1. Negligence—section 6662(b)(1)
2. Fraud—section 6663
3. Promoting abusive shelters by making, or encouraging another to make, a gross valuation overstatement—section 6700(a)(2)(B)
4. Aiding and abetting understatement of tax liability—section 6701

We will discuss only the negligence and fraud penalties, as they are the most likely to be applied in a valuation case.

Negligence

Consider section 6662(c):

> *(c) Negligence. For purposes of this section, the term negligence includes any failure to make a reasonable attempt to comply with the provisions of this title, and the term disregard includes any careless, reckless, or intentional disregard.*

The statute states: "failure to make a reasonable attempt to comply." If one thinks of levels of neglect on a continuum, careless disregard is the least egregious and is typified by just being sloppy. Reckless disregard is the next level of misbehavior and may include things like not observing the tax law at all. Intentional disregard is the highest form of negligence and may occur where one read and understood the law, but did not follow the law.

---

[3]There is, however, no guarantee the court will accept either the taxpayer's or government's experts. See, e.g., *Pulsar Components v. Comm'r*, T.C. Memo 1996-129, 71 T.C.M. (CCH) 2436 (1996) (dismissing the taxpayer's expert as "unconvincing" and having "difficulty" accepting the government's expert, the court concluded, "we are not persuaded by either of the experts," and proceeded to conduct its own valuation.)

Where a taxpayer is justified in relying on a tax advisor and continues to monitor the status of an investment, he or she may not be liable for the negligence penalty. Negligence penalties are not excused where the taxpayer's reliance on another was unjustified.

Fraud

Imposition of Fraud Penalty is rarely applicable to valuation cases. It is applied, as the name would suggest, to cases of willful abuse, and the penalties are stiff.

Section 6663 states:

(a)   IMPOSITION OF PENALTY. If any part of any underpayment of tax required to be shown on the return is due to fraud, there shall be added to the tax an amount equal to 75 percent of the portion of the underpayment which is attributable to fraud.

(b)   DETERMINATION OF PORTION ATTRIBUTABLE TO FRAUD. If the Secretary establishes that any portion of an underpayment is attributable to fraud, the entire underpayment shall be treated as attributable to fraud, except with respect to any portion of the underpayment which the taxpayer establishes (by a preponderance of the evidence) is not attributable to fraud.

DISCRETIONARY SANCTIONS

Discretionary sanctions are those that may be awarded against taxpayers when a court feels they are justified. Under section 6673, discretionary sanctions may be awarded in one of three instances: when the court feels the taxpayer (1) is litigating the case solely for delay, (2) is taking a frivolous position, or (3) unreasonably failed to pursue administrative remedies.

Section 6673 provides:

(a) Tax court proceedings.

(1) Procedures instituted primarily for delay, etc. Whenever it appears to the Tax Court that—

(A) proceedings before it have been instituted or maintained by the taxpayer primarily for delay, (B) the taxpayer's position in such proceeding is frivolous or groundless, or (C) the taxpayer unreasonably failed to pursue available administrative remedies, the Tax Court, in its decision, may require the taxpayer to pay to the United States a penalty not in excess of $ 25,000.

(2) Counsel's liability for excessive costs. Whenever it appears to the Tax Court that any attorney or other person admitted to practice before the Tax Court has multiplied the proceedings in any case unreasonably and vexatiously, the Tax Court may require—

(A) that such attorney or other person pay personally the excess costs, expenses, and attorneys' fees reasonably incurred because of such conduct, or (B) if such attorney is appearing on behalf of the Commissioner of Internal Revenue, that the United States pay such excess costs, expenses, and attorneys' fees in the same manner as such an award by a district court.

(b) Proceedings in other courts.

(1) Claims under section 7433. Whenever it appears to the court that the taxpayer's position in the proceedings before the court instituted or maintained by such taxpayer under section 7433 is frivolous or groundless, the court may require the taxpayer to pay to the United States a penalty not in excess of $ 10,000. (2) Collection of sanctions and costs. In any civil proceeding before any court (other than the Tax Court) which

is brought by or against the United States in connection with the determination, collection, or refund of any tax, interest, or penalty under this title, any monetary sanctions, penalties, or costs awarded by the court to the United States may be assessed by the Secretary and, upon notice and demand, may be collected in the same manner as a tax. (3) Sanctions and costs awarded by a court of appeals. In connection with any appeal from a proceeding in the Tax Court or a civil proceeding described in paragraph (2), an order of a United States Court of Appeals or the Supreme Court awarding monetary sanctions, penalties or court costs to the United States may be registered in a district court upon filing a certified copy of such order and shall be enforceable as other district court judgments. Any such sanctions, penalties, or costs may be assessed by the Secretary and, upon notice and demand, may be collected in the same manner as a tax.

Valuation and Choice of Entity

SUMMARY

This chapter explores five different types of business entities and then examines some of their unique characteristics to see what relationship, if any, these varying characteristics may have with valuation.

The five types of entities considered are:

1. Corporations
2. Limited liability companies
3. Partnerships
4. Limited partnerships
5. Sole proprietorships

Corporations (C or S corporations) are distinguished by their centralized management, difficulty of formation, limited liability for owners, perpetual existence, centralized management, and free transferability of ownership. Their primary disadvantages are cost of formation and, for C corporations, double taxation, with income being taxed when earned by the corporation *and* when distributed to shareholders.

Limited liability companies (LLCs) share many corporate attributes, including limited liability. LLC members may participate in management (if accorded that right) without destroying limited liability. Unlike corporations, however, they are not taxed twice on their earnings; all earnings pass through to the owners.

Partnerships can exist any time two or more people or entities act in a joint activity for profit. They are easily formed and permit each partner full participation in the business. However, they impose unlimited joint and several liability on each partner, allowing creditors to come after the partners' personal assets to satisfy partnership debts. They also have a limited life, terminating, in the case of a two-member partnership, on the death of either partner.

Limited partnerships (LPs) are similar to LLCs in many ways, affording limited liability to limited partners and pass-through tax treatment to all partners. LPs differ in several important ways, however. First, there must be a general partner in an LP who takes unlimited liability for the LPs debts, unlike an LLC. Second, unlike LLC members, limited partners must not participate in management of the LP or they may be treated as a general partner and lose limited liability.

Sole proprietorships exist whenever one person engages in business. They are limited in duration to the life of the proprietor, who has unlimited liability.

Some of these inherent differences among the entities can lead to significant differences in value when exploited by sophisticated tax planners.

INTRODUCTION

We now turn to the role that the choice of business organization may have on valuation.

A brief example will be helpful to our discussion. Assume that Rachel has been in the business of selling computers for the last several years, operating as a sole proprietor. Business has been good and so she decides to expand. She needs additional investment capital and decides to solicit a few investors.

Assume that she has the choice of incorporating her business or organizing as a limited partnership. Will the choice of organization alter value? Would it make any difference to the value of the business if Rachel incorporated and then her corporation elected to be taxed as an S corporation? In essence, does the form of the organization affect its valuation for federal tax purposes?

Among the major organizational choices or forms are:

- Corporations
- Limited liability companies
- Partnerships
- Limited partnerships
- Sole proprietorships

There are approximately 4.6 million corporations, 1.7 million partnerships, and 17 million unincorporated proprietorships in the United States. Although corporations represent only about one-fifth of all business entities, they account for roughly 90 percent of all business income.[1]

---

[1] U.S. Census Bureau, Statistical Abstract of the United States 545 (1999).

A complete analysis of each business organization, examining each organization and comparing one to another in great detail, is beyond the scope of this book. The focus of this chapter is the importance, if any, of the form of business entity to valuation.

We begin with the corporation.

CORPORATIONS

A corporation is an artificial person or legal entity created under the laws of a state; it has six major attributes:

1. *A corporation is created by filing articles of incorporation.* The articles of incorporation contain information about authorized shares and possible restrictions on the shares. The bylaws of the corporation come into existence at about this time and may also address restrictions applicable to the shares. For instance, the corporation may decide to restrict the number of shares to be issued, establish rules for voting control, or define how directors are elected. Restrictive provisions may inhibit transferability of shares and thus negatively impact the value of the shares in the corporation.

2. *The corporation is a separate legal entity.* The corporation does business in its own name and on its own behalf, rather than in the name of its shareholders. The corporation may contract in its own name, similar to a person doing business; it has powers to do all things necessary to conduct business.

3. *A corporation has centralized management that is distinct from the owners of the corporation.* A corporation is run by its board of directors. Each director is elected by the shareholders. The board, in turn, appoints management to conduct the daily affairs of the corporation. This means that investors may remain passive. Valuers pay careful attention to management, as they want to know if management is talented and capable enough to create a successful business. Valuers must also look at management's compensation to ensure that it is structured to reward successful management, and thereby ensure the continued vitality of the business.

4. *A corporation has perpetual life.* The corporation endures by law until merger, dissolution, or some other matter causes it to terminate. It is never destroyed by a person's death. Valuers may consider perpetual life to be an advantage over a form of organization with a finite life, such as ten years or the life of the owner.

5. *Corporate ownership is freely transferable.* Absent restrictions adopted by shareholders or the corporation itself, shareholders are free to sell, gift, or transfer their shares. When, however, the transferability of the shares is restricted, either by law or agreement, the restrictions are likely to reduce the value of the shares. This reduction in value is sometimes desirable. For instance, family members may want to have a buy-sell agreement that defines and restricts the sale of shares to only family members. Such restrictions may inhibit value, but the Service closely scrutinizes such agreements out of concern that values may be artificially reduced.

6. *Limited liability.* Shareholders, management, and board members do not become personally liable for corporate obligations. This alone is a strong attraction of the corporation. Members of limited liability companies, and limited partners in a limited partnership, also

enjoy some aspects of limited liability. However, partners in a general partnership are personally liable for the obligations of the partnership. Valuers must take into consideration exposure to liabilities as an element of value. Since the corporate form limits the liability of the shareholders, the corporate form itself has added value. Quantifying that value depends on the facts and circumstances of the particular business being valued.

The biggest downside of traditional corporations is double-taxation. C corporations, governed by Subchapter C of the Code, which are taxed as legal entities separate from their shareholders. Income, taxed at the corporate level, is taxed again, either as ordinary income when distributed as a dividend, or as capital gains when shareholders sell their shares.

To avoid this, a corporation may elect to become a pass-through entity under Subchapter S of the Code.[2] The virtue of this election is that the taxable income of the corporation is passed through to the shareholders without first being taxed at the corporate level. At the same time, the shareholders continue to enjoy the benefits of limited liability. It can be difficult to qualify as an S corporation, however—the Code specifies several requirements that must be met before a corporation can elect S status. For a further discussion, see Chapter 8.

LIMITED LIABILITY COMPANIES

A limited liability company is a hybrid, unincorporated business organization that shares some aspects of corporations and partnerships. The Service has ruled that the LLC can be taxed as a partnership, if the taxpayers so elect. Gains and losses are not taxed at the entity level, but are passed through to its members. LLC members may actively participate in management.

The LLC nominally offers limited liability to its members similar to that of a corporation. And it is not as hard to qualify as an LLC as it is to qualify for S corporation status. All states have statutes governing LLCs, but the provisions vary from state to state. There is one downside: LLCs are relatively new (the first LLC statute was enacted in 1977), and it is too early to know with certainty how courts will treat them on the issue of limited liability.

GENERAL PARTNERSHIPS

A general partnership is an association of two or more people or entities engaged in an activity for profit. The partnership is not taxed; the gains and losses are passed through to the partners, who are taxed on their share of partnership gains. Each partner is jointly and severally liable for the partnership obligations, for the acts of the other partners, and for acts of the partnership's agents in furtherance of partnership business. Potential liability is unlimited, and partners can be pursued personally for partnership debts.

---

[2]Though it is beyond the scope of the book, readers should be aware that if a corporation was formerly organized as a C corporation, certain types of profits may be subject to double taxation for a period of 10 years.

LIMITED PARTNERSHIPS

The limited partnership (or limited liability company) seems to be the entity of choice for practitioners who desire to maximize discounts for lack of marketability and minority interests. Limited partnerships and limited liability companies lend themselves to valuation discounts.

A limited partnership is a partnership formed pursuant to state statute. A majority of the states have adopted a limited partnership statute permitting limited partnerships. These statutes substantially reflect the provisions of the Revised Uniform Limited Partnership Act (RULPA).

To create a limited partnership, one must file a certificate of limited partnership with the state where the partnership is formed. The certificate identifies key features of the partnership and indicates whom its partners are.

A limited partnership has at least two classes of partners: a general partner, who has unlimited liability and is responsible for making the major partnership business decisions; and limited partners, whose liability exposure is limited to the capital that they have invested. Limited partners have limited liability similar to that of shareholders in a corporation. To achieve this limited liability, however, limited partners must refrain from participating in most business decisions of the partnership. Those decisions, instead, are made by the general partner, who is liable for them.

Since the limited partnership is a partnership for federal tax purposes, the entity pays no federal tax. Income or loss passes through to the partners, who have the responsibility to report it and pay any resulting tax.

An important wrinkle is that, while gains and losses are passed through to the partners, the decision to distribute cash is left to the general partner. Thus, if a general partner withholds cash distributions, a limited partner must pay taxes on money he does not receive. This aspect is particularly important to creditors of limited partners, who cannot access partnership assets to pay the partnerships debts. In this regard, the limited partnership provides some asset protection.

An important remedy for a judgment creditor is to obtain a charging order against the debtor's partnership interest (RULPA § 703). A charging order entitles the creditor to receive any distributions to which the debtor partner would be entitled. However, federal tax law requires the creditor to pay the tax due on the debtor partner's portion of the partnership's income even if the general partner does not make any distributions. This is usually sufficient to deter creditors from seeking a charging order against the debtor partner's interest.

There are three more typical features of limited partnerships:

1. Limited partners usually are not able to assign or pledge their limited partnership interest as collateral. (Notwithstanding prohibitions in the partnership agreement, most lending institutions would not make a loan based on a limited partnership interest, anyhow.)
2. General partners control the decisions of the partnership pertaining to the acquisition of assets and the incurring of partnership liabilities.
3. Limited partners who desire to sell must usually first offer their partnership interests to the partnership or other partners.

Further, a limited partner must not participate in the business decisions of the partnership as a matter of law; limited partnership agreements are drafted to reflect this and prohibit limited partner participation. Thus, decisions regarding cash distributions, payment of salaries to partnership employees, marketing, and so forth are within the sole discretion of the general partner. Limited partners sacrifice many of the rights and privileges normally attendant to business ownership in exchange for the benefits just discussed.

Since limited partners cannot control business decisions, they are automatically subject to the same detriments that may give rise to minority discounts and lack of marketability discounts with certain corporate shares.

The minority discount is established when it can be demonstrated that the business interest in question does not enjoy the same benefits and powers of a controlling interest. In most states, owning 51 percent of the shares in a closely held corporation gives the owner a controlling interest and the ability to name directors, set executive salaries, arrange mergers, and so forth. By the same token, a limited partner cannot participate in management or make any of those decisions, and is therefore likely entitled to some amount of valuation discount.

The lack of marketability discount is established and enhanced when the property being valued is determined to be less marketable than property that is freely traded in a market within three business days. Most limited partner units are not freely tradable on an established market within three business days, so limited partners usually command a lack of marketability discount.

The limited partnership entity is popular because it serves multiple purposes: It is flexible enough to be taxed as a partnership, it protects assets from creditors, it affords pass-through taxation, it provides limited liability, and it usually results in valuation discounts for tax purposes.

Because of this, the limited partnership can be especially valuable for family-owned businesses. Family limited partnerships (FLPs) are favorites of tax planners, and have been challenged repeatedly by the Service on valuation issues. When legitimately used, the FLP allows parents to maintain control as general partners while at the same time giving their children considerable ownership interests as limited partners.

SOLE PROPRIETORSHIPS

A sole proprietorship is an individual carrying on business under her own name or under an assumed name. She is taxed for federal purposes as an individual. She has unlimited tort and contract liability.

Previously, the classification of an entity was uncertain due to characteristics normally associated with one entity's being designed into another, mostly by choice of the planner. Most of this confusion went away after the Treasury adopted regulations whereby taxpayers are allowed to determine their choice of entity and tax status by checking a box on the appropriate election form.

VALUATION CONSIDERATIONS

There is little, if any, empirical evidence that establishes that one form of business organization inherently commands a higher or lower valuation as compared to the alternatives. Some will argue that an S corporation may have a different value than a C corporation. See Chapter 8 for a complete discussion.

When attorneys structure certain elements of any business organization, they can affect its ultimate valuation by the terms and conditions of that business entity.

For instance, restrictions pertaining to free transferability of ownership generally depress value. If an attorney prepares a buy-sell agreement among shareholders or partners, the value of the shares or partnership interest is negatively impacted. Thus, by design, one can deliberately impact value when preparing legal terms and agreements. As long as there are legitimate, arm's-length business purposes for preparing such documents, the Service will respect the documents and value may be affected accordingly.

Also, business agreements that increase the risk to the investor of not receiving cash flow from the business tend to reduce value. All business organizations strive for good cash flow. Organizations that create cash flows and provide for such cash to be returned to the investors unimpeded are more valuable than those that do not. When a partnership agreement has terms that put in question whether cash will be distributed, and the law requires that the partner pay tax on undistributed gains, value is diminished. The role of the valuer is to assimilate all of this information and apply a commonsense judgment as to value in the context of sound financial and valuation principles.

Understandably, this involves many questions, such as the thirteen that follow:

1. How will the business be taxed—at the entity level or as a pass-through to the owner?
2. Are there any limits on the number or kind of owners, as with an S corporation?
3. Can the owners participate in management?
4. Are the ownership interests freely transferable?
5. Is there a fixed term for the life of the entity?
6. Are there specified events for dissolution?
7. Are there provisions for distributions and special allocations?
8. What kinds of fringe benefits are available?
9. What limitations apply to sale or transferability of ownership interests?
10. What are the possibilities of going public with the entity?
11. What is the extent of the liability exposure?
12. What governmental limitations or rules apply to the conduct of this business?
13. What rules or laws apply upon liquidation? How does the investor get his or her money out of the investment?

Exhibit 7.1[3] is helpful in comparing and contrasting some of the differences among the various entities examined.

---

[3]This chart is for illustrative purposes only. A more detailed comparison is necessary when making a legal decision of choice of entity. For a good chart describing the tax considerations among various entities, see Mary McNulty and Michelle M. Kwon, "Tax Considerations in Choice of Entity Decisions," *Business Entities* (November/December, 2002): 1.

Exhibit 7.1 Differences among Various Entities

Feature	C Corp	S Corp	LLC	Limited Partnership	General Partnership
Tax	Double: Corporation and shareholders	Shareholders only, with exceptions	Member only	Partner	Partner
Number of Owners	One or more	1 to 100	One, but at least two if taxed as a partnership	Two or more	Two or more
Types of Owners	Unrestricted	Restrictions apply	Unrestricted	Unrestricted	Unrestricted
Different Classes of Ownership	Permitted	One class	Permitted	Permitted	Permitted
State Law Liability	Entity only is liable.	Entity only is liable.	Entity only is liable.	General partner is liable.	Partners are liable.

CHOICE OF JURISDICTION

Choice of jurisdiction can also affect the valuation of the entity, as each state has different enabling statutes, many provisions of which can alter value. To illustrate the point, we have compiled a brief summary of the laws of six states dealing with LLC issues: transferability of membership interests, rights of assignee upon transfer, rights of assignor on transfer, and rights of creditors.

Restrictions on transferability have an effect on value through the lack of marketability discount. More rights for assignees after transfer will make the membership interests more valuable, as they will be more marketable if the assignee can, for example, become a member easily, or inspect entity records. When assignors continue to have some rights of ownership after transfer, value may be affected. Finally, strong creditor rights may have an impact on value.

Consider what discounts would be available in each state represented in Exhibit 7.2.

CONCLUSION

Valuers must carefully consider the various features of each business organization when performing a business valuation. An organization's characteristics affect valuation because they define and influence such things as cash flow and transferability of the business interest. Federal and state laws determine many parameters of the entity, but counsel can also

Exhibit 7.2   Differences in LLC Form among Various States

Feature	New York	Illinois	California	Nevada	Arkansas	Texas
Assignable?	Freely	No	Only with majority approval by members.	If articles do not prohibit.	Freely	Freely
Can assignee access LLC records and books?	No	No	No	No	No	Yes
How does assignee become member?	Majority vote, excluding assignor.	Member cannot dissociate.	Only with majority approval by members.	Majority vote, excluding assignor.	Only with unanimous vote.	All members consent, or regulations.
Is assignor still member after assignment?	Not if it transfers 100% of interest.	Dissociation not allowed.	Yes, if only economic interest is assigned.	Transfer does not release it from liability.	Transfer does not release it from liability.	Until assignee becomes member.
How is creditor treated?	Assignee	Interest must be sold at auction. Purchaser has rights of assignee.	Interest must be sold at auction. Purchaser has rights of assignee.	Assignee	Assignee	Assignee

contribute to the ultimate valuation of an entity by drafting agreements with terms and conditions that restrict ownership of securities and conduct of the business. By adding a put or call option to a limited partnership interest, by restricting shares with the right of first refusal, or by limiting dividends on corporate shares, one seriously impacts the rights and privileges of those property interests and correspondingly affects their value for tax purposes.

Chapter 8

Valuation of S Corporations and Other Pass-Through Tax Entities: Minority and Controlling Interests

INTRODUCTION

Valuation of Subchapter S corporations and other pass-through entities has been one of the most controversial issues the appraisal profession has faced over the last several years. It has also been one of the most difficult to resolve, as divergent and complex financial theories have surfaced and competed for attention. For the valuation practitioner, the application of reasoned financial theory has proven to be an extremely difficult undertaking, given the multitude of viewpoints and uncertainties of the IRS audit process.

While the issue was brought to a head with a string of Tax Court cases that weighed in the IRS's favor, it is one that had been rising as an emerging issue for several years. The benefits of single taxation had been debated for years. With S corporations increasing nearly fivefold in a fifteen-year period and surpassing the number of C corporations by the mid to late 1990s, the issue finally came to a head in *Walter L. Gross, Jr., et ux, et al. v. Commissioner.*[1] The appraisal

---

[1]T.C. Memo. 1999-254, No. 4460-97 (July 29, 1999), *aff'd.* 272 F.3d 333 (6th Cir. 2001).

community was quick to react, citing the violations of basic valuation principles, common sense, and unfairness to taxpayers. A multitude of theories and viewpoints ensued, with no consensus. Meanwhile, the IRS enjoyed three more victories in Tax Court.

Since the *Gross* decision, four models for valuing interests in S corporations have emerged and taken prominence in the valuation community. They are each presented in this chapter, and were developed by the following individuals:

- Roger J. Grabowski
- Z. Christopher Mercer
- Chris D. Treharne
- Daniel R. Van Vleet

While these experts on S corporation valuation issues have differences, they also share common bases for their theories.

To begin, the experts agree that the appropriate standard of value is fair market value as defined in Rev. Rul. 59-60:

> [T]he price at which the property would change hands between a willing buyer and a willing seller when the former is not under any compulsion to buy and the latter is not under any compulsion to sell, both parties having reasonable knowledge of relevant facts.

Thus, all of the experts presented in this chapter maintain that their valuation strategies consider both the buyer's and seller's perspectives. Additionally, they recognize that the buyer and seller are hypothetical—rather than specific (e.g., family members)—investors. However, in at least one of the theories, the notion of who comprises the hypothetical pool is further refined.

These experts agree that the role of a business valuation analyst is to estimate the present value of an investor's future economic benefits. Finally, all concede that the cash flow generated by company operations is available for distribution to equity holders, may be retained by the company, or it may be partially distributed to investors and partially retained by the company.

Regardless of which model you use, there are three important concepts for the business valuation analyst to be aware of when using these materials:

- The models presented are minority interest valuation models, except where specifically noted.
- Each entity and each ownership interest in an entity will have *unique characteristics that must be examined and considered*. As a result, no valuation model can be applied blindly without consideration of the specific attributes of the subject ownership interest.
- In some cases, ownership interests in S corporations will be worth less than otherwise similar C corporation interests; in some cases, they will be worth the same; and in some cases, they will be worth more than otherwise similar C corporation interests.

This chapter deals with one of the most controversial issues in business valuation today. The opinions, expressed or implied, contained in this chapter do not necessarily represent the views of the authors of this book and are the sole product of the experts whose views are contained within this chapter. The reader is responsible for his/her own use and due diligence in the application of the material presented. The collective experts make no warranty as to fitness for any use and accept no liability for any application of any of the material presented.

CASE LAW BACKGROUND

We are aware of four Tax Court opinions and one Appeals Court opinion that suggest S corporation earnings should not be tax affected for valuation purposes:

1. *Walter L. Gross, Jr., et ux, et al. v. Commissioner*, T.C. Memo. 1999-254, No. 4460-97 (July 29, 1999), *aff'd.* 272 F.3d 333 (6th Cir. 2001)
2. *Estate of John E. Wall v. Commissioner*, T.C. Memo. 2001-75
3. *Estate of William G. Adams, Jr. v. Commissioner*, T.C. Memo. 2002-80
4. *Estate of Heck v. Commissioner*, T.C. Memo. 2002-34, 83 T.C.M. (CCH) 1181.

Note that each opinion is a "T.C. Memo." It is our understanding that such opinions are case-fact specific and do not necessarily reflect the opinion of the Tax Court as a whole on a particular topic.

In *Gross*, the subjects of the valuation were small, minority interests (less than 1 percent of the outstanding stock each) in a name-brand soft drink bottling company, not 100 percent of the underlying business owned by the S corporation. The shareholders had historically received distributions approximately equal to taxable net income. A shareholder agreement limited potential willing buyers of the subject interest to persons who met the legal requirements for the corporation to retain its S corporation status, and none of the shareholders had expressed interest in selling his or her shares.

There was no reason to expect the business would be sold, nor any reason to believe that S corporation status would be in jeopardy if the subject interests were sold. No facts were presented that contradicted the expectation that distributions would continue as they had in the past.

Despite these unique characteristics, the taxpayer's expert applied a traditional valuation approach and fully tax-affected the S corporation's earnings as if it were a C corporation. The Commissioner's expert applied no income tax to the S corporation's earnings because S corporation distributions to its shareholders are not taxed at the entity level.

The court agreed with the Commissioner's approach, noting that the taxpayer's expert introduced a "fictitious tax burden" that reduced earnings by 40 percent. In rejecting this artificial tax affecting, the court noted the necessity of matching the tax characteristics of an entity's cash flow with the discount rate applied. The court stated:

> *If in determining the present value of any future payment, the discount rate is assumed to be an after-shareholder-tax rate of return, then the cash flow should be reduced ("tax affected") to an after-shareholder-tax amount. If, on the other hand, a pre-shareholder-tax discount rate is applied, no adjustment for taxes should be made to the cash flow. . . . We believe that the principal benefit that shareholders expect from an S corporation election is a reduction in the total tax burden imposed on the enterprise. The owners expect to save money, and we see no reason why that savings ought to be ignored as a matter of course in valuing the S corporation.*

Prior to *Gross*, the Service had supported the traditional approaches it opposed in *Gross*.[2]

In the second case, *Heck*, neither expert deducted taxes from their minority cash flows in valuing a minority interest. Both experts also took discounts for the risk the minority interest shareholder takes on due to the S corporation status. The court agreed that a 10 percent discount was appropriate for such additional risks, in addition to a 15 percent marketability discount.

In *Wall*, the taxpayer's expert presented a traditional tax-affected valuation. The court again rejected this approach. In *Wall*, the court stated:

> . . . We believe it is likely to result in an undervaluation of (the subject S corporation) stock. . . . We also note that both experts' income-based analyses probably understated value, because they determined cash flows on a hypothetical after tax basis, and then used market rates of return on taxable investments to determine the present value of those cash flows.

The preceding suggests that at least some judges would agree with Mercer, Van Vleet, Treharne, and Grabowski's analysis of minority interests and conclude that the absence of double taxation in S corporations could make an interest in them more valuable than an interest in an equivalent C corporation. However, the traditional approach of tax-affecting an S corporation's income, and then determining the value of that income by reference to the rates of return on C corporation investments, means that an appraisal of a minority interest done in this manner will give no value to S corporation status, according to the decision in *Wall*.

These three rejections of the traditional valuation approaches have left business valuation analysts searching for an acceptable method.

In *Adams*, the petitioner's expert attempted to match S corporation tax characteristics in discounting by converting his after-entity-level-taxes rate of return to a pre-entity-level-taxes rate of return. The intention was to put the discounted cash flow analysis on an equal pretax basis for all its elements. The court rejected that expert's approach, saying:

> The result here of a zero tax on estimated prospective cash flows and no conversion of the capitalization rate from after corporate tax to before corporate tax is identical to the result in Gross v. Commissioner *of zero corporate tax rate on estimated cash flows and a discount rate with no conversion from after corporate tax to before corporate tax.*

These cases point to a rejection of the traditional valuation practice of automatically income tax–affecting S corporation pretax income when valuing an interest in an S corporation or other pass-through entity.

Grabowski, Mercer, Van Vleet, and Treharne all agree that these cases indicate the need for a wholly fact-driven inquiry when valuing minority interests, taking into consideration the facts and circumstances in each case.

Under this imprecise standard, the choice between methods thus remains with the analyst, who must be guided by the facts of the case and the perceived appropriateness of each model.

---

[2]Citing the *IRS Valuation Guide for Income, Estate, and Gift Taxes* and the *Examination Techniques Handbook*.

S CORPORATION MINORITY INTEREST APPRAISALS

In this section, four theories for valuing S corporation minority interests will be offered. The four experts all agree that these theories and models likely are not appropriate for the valuation of S corporation controlling ownership interests, except as specifically noted. These models are referred to in this chapter as follows:

- Roger J. Grabowski's model
- Z. Christopher Mercer's model
- Chris D. Treharne's model
- Daniel R. Van Vleet's model

Roger J. Grabowski's Model[3]

Roger J. Grabowski holds that interests in S corporations and other pass-throughs may have a greater value than an interest in an otherwise identical C corporation. Grabowski champions a facts-and-circumstances analysis. Grabowski's theory holds that one is not typically valuing an abstract business entity, but rather, one is typically asked to value a specific interest in an entity. That interest comes with characteristics inherent in the entity—legal and tax. Unless one is valuing absolute controlling interests, the hypothetical willing seller is selling an interest subject to those characteristics and the hypothetical willing buyer is buying an interest subject to those characteristics.

Grabowski urges consideration of the following factors on a case-by-case basis.

Comparative Benefits to Pass-Throughs

There are three major benefits of owning a business through a pass-through entity:

1. *Income is subject to only one level of taxation at the individual shareholder level, with no double taxation.* Minority shareholders may perceive a disadvantage in holding an interest in a pass-through entity, since the owners become liable for income taxes, whether or not they receive any cash distributions. Unless an agreement requires distributions at least equal to the imputed income tax owed, an owner may be liable for income taxes in excess of cash distributions received.[4]

   C corporations can accumulate earnings, paying income tax only at the corporate level, without its shareholders being individually taxed. A pass-through entity's accumulation of earnings without distributions (such as for business expansion) could make owners subject to taxes on phantom income. Since a minority shareholder cannot compel a distribution, the potential for phantom income adds considerably to shareholder risk.

---

[3]Roger J. Grabowski, "S Corporation Valuation in the Post-*Gross* World—Updated," *Business Valuation Review* (September 2004).

[4]In the case of REITs the law generally requires distributions of 95% of the taxable income to the REIT interest owners.

2. *Owners of the pass-through entity receive an increase in their basis to the extent that taxable income exceeds distributions to shareholders.* In other words, income retained by the S corporation adds to the tax basis of the shareholders' stock, reducing the shareholder's capital gain upon sale. This requires some analysis of the investment horizon of buyers.[5]

3. *Owners of the pass-through entity may realize more proceeds upon sale if the buyer can realize increased tax savings by pushing the purchase price down to the underlying assets and getting a step-up in basis.* For example, upon selling the entire business, a seasoned S corporation will sell assets to a buyer, thereby increasing buyer's basis.[6]

The buyer of stock in a C corporation generally realizes future depreciation and amortization based on carry-over income tax basis of the underlying assets.

KEY THOUGHT

A step-up in basis *increases the buyer's basis to the amount of the purchase price, thereby reducing the buyer's income taxes in future years, through increased depreciation and/or amortization, or reducing the buyer's future capital gains on the sale of the entity's assets.* A carryover basis *gives the buyer the same basis as the seller in the entity's assets, thereby increasing the buyer's future capital gain on a sale of the entity's assets, assuming the asset has appreciated since seller purchased it.*

All else being equal, the buyer will be willing to pay a greater amount for a business in which assets receive a step-up in basis, because the buyer's effective future income taxes will be reduced.

Further, pass-through entity owners receive proceeds upon sale that are taxed only once. Gains on sale of assets by a C corporation are taxed at the corporate level, and then distributions are taxed again at the shareholder level.[7] Likely exit strategies therefore become an important consideration for valuation.

If one is valuing a *minority* interest in an S corporation, the noncontrolling shareholder can be assured of only two benefits: single taxation and a step-up in basis when taxable income exceeds distributions. The benefit to S corporation shareholders of selling assets can be realized only where the controlling shareholder(s) decides to sell the assets of the S corporation.

However, if the entity structure is considered a partnership for federal income tax purposes (such as an LLC that has so elected), even a minority owner may benefit from a buyer's ability to take assets with a step-up in basis.[8]

---

[5]Note that this represents increase in basis from the perspective of what a hypothetical buyer might determine as realizable upon their ultimate exit from the firm.

[6]The owner of an S corporation can sell stock (subject to capital gains treatment) with an I.R.C. § 338 election being made that treats the sale of stock as if it were the sale of assets, allowing for a "set-up in basis" of the assets.

[7]In the sale of an interest in a partnership, the buyer may also benefit through a *step-up in basis* of his proportionate share of the assets if an I.R.C. § 754 election is made (which may be allowed under the partnership agreement typically by election of the incoming partner or only upon agreement of the general partner), in essence equalizing his *outside basis* (i.e., investment cost) and his proportionate *inside basis*. See Matthew A. Melone, "Partnership Final Regs," *Valuation Strategies* (May/June 2000).

[8]See footnote 17.

Analysts are often asked to value interests in pass-through entities where available public data on discount rates and market multiples can be derived only from public C corporations, whose tax structures differ from that of a pass-through entity.

In *Adams*, the taxpayer's expert simply converted the C corporation after-entity-level-taxes rate of return to a pre-entity-level-taxes equivalent. The court found that he did not match tax characteristics of the cash flows with the tax character of the discount rate; the court's decision did not, however, preclude adjustments to S corporation earnings or applicable discount rates for differences in income tax rates, risks, and probable investment.[9]

Unlike S corporations, shares of a nonpublicly traded or private REIT can be valued directly through observation of rates of return and market multiples for guideline public REITs (applying the market approach). Publicly traded REITs are pass-through entities with the same tax characteristics as the private REIT being valued. Tax characteristics are matched.

Considerations in Valuing Minority Interests

Grabowski's model for valuation of minority interests starts with the value of 100 percent of an equivalent C corporation and 100 percent of the free or available cash flow is distributed.

He then makes five adjustments to reflect the items previously discussed:

1. *Present value of taxes saved as S.* Grabowski takes 100 percent of the tax savings from avoiding double taxation and converts the savings to preowner-level tax equivalent amount (dividing by 1 minus owner-level dividend tax rate). This is added to the equivalent C value.
2. *Less tax savings on S retained earnings* as the shareholder pays income taxes on the net income of the entity whether the cash is distributed or not.
3. *Less higher shareholder-level taxes.* S shareholders pay 40 percent higher personal income tax rates on S income than do C shareholders, who pay only 20 percent on dividends.

Note that up to this point, Grabowski makes the same adjustments as does Treharne (following), albeit with different names. By adding the present value of tax savings, then deducting the lost value from lower taxes on C corporation dividends, Grabowski has adjusted the equivalent C corporation value to reflect the tax benefit associated with distributions in excess of taxes, and the value impact from the differences in tax rates. (See the Treharne Model section in this chapter.) From this point, however, Grabowski goes beyond the Treharne model.

4. *Plus present value of basis buildup.* Grabowski projects the excess of net income over distributions and adds this amount to basis. He then adds value for the additional basis, assuming that it will provide value to the owners through reduced taxes when they sell in the future.
5. *Plus present value of step-up in basis benefit.* Grabowski urges that where the facts support it, analysts include the present value of the tax benefit received from buyers being able to depreciate or amortize the price of assets when they are sold in the future.

---

[9]The court found that the taxpayer's expert did not match the tax characteristics of the cash flow (pre–personal income tax) with the characteristics of the discount rate (pre–corporate income tax).

To calculate either four or five, one must be able to project exit strategy and timing of what may be many years into the future, thus requiring assumptions that buyers will pay today for the ability to build up basis in the future and that assets will be worth some premium in the future that can and will be depreciated and/or amortized in an asset sale that the current buyer will be unable to control.

To counter this impediment, Grabowski's theory holds that willing buyers and sellers must be constructed with some consideration of the makeup of the pool of likely buyers. Thus, for minority interests in S corporations, Grabowski urges that willing buyers would likely be those qualified to buy an S corporation and take advantage of the listed benefits. For example, in a recent case, one court found that the owners of interests in a series of real estate entities had a long and intertwined history of investing together. That court concluded that a willing seller of the subject minority interest would sell to other insiders to maximize his selling price. Insiders, the court concluded, would pay a premium to exclude outsiders. Therefore, the interests were to be valued as if sold to an insider.[10]

Grabowski states that possible tax benefits from a proposed exit strategy may, in some circumstances, be so speculative that they should not be included in the valuation. This highlights the importance of a rigorous facts-and-circumstances analysis in each case—no one formula exists for valuing pass-throughs, and different elements should be included as warranted by the facts. Each valuation of a pass-through must be driven by the facts of the case, and individual elements of value should be included only where there is a justifiable basis for doing so.

As a further area of inquiry, many S corporation shareholder agreements require distributions at least equal to the accrued income taxes due by the shareholders, unless such distributions would result in the corporation's becoming insolvent. The analyst should investigate whether such an agreement exists.

If there is no such contractual income tax protection, the historical practice of the subject S corporation's distributions often serves as the basis for establishing future distribution expectations. If history shows that distributions have always been sufficient for shareholders to pay the income taxes due, then one may assume this will continue. The presumption is particularly strong in cases where the controlling shareholder(s) do not have other sources of cash with which to pay income taxes.

Such historical precedent does not, however, provide the same level of risk reduction as a shareholder agreement. Absent shareholder agreement protection, the theoretical benefit of avoiding double taxation may be offset in whole or in part by an increased discount that results.[11] Controlling shareholders may reduce distributions for any number of reasons, including retaining income for capital investments or squeezing out nonconforming minority shareholders. These specific risks should be weighed against the theoretical advantages of an S corporation.

Finally, Grabowski may apply a minority interest discount since his model starts with 100 percent of free cash flow of the entity that minority shareholders cannot be assured will be distributed.

---

[10]Unpublished decision, Tax Court of New Jersey, *Wilf v. Wilf, Essex County, NJ.*

[11]By either increasing the discount rate or increasing the percentage discount for lack of control and/or lack of ready marketability applied to the indicated value at the end of the valuation process.

Considerations in Valuing a Controlling Interest

Grabowski contends that buyers often give up some (and sometimes a great deal) of synergistic value to sellers so as to outbid other buyers. Although the hypothetical willing buyer is an abstraction and not a single buyer with unique circumstances, Grabowski urges that, for many sellers, *highest and best use* may equate to sale of the subject business to any one of several buyers willing to pay extra for the seller's tax advantages. The Tax Court has stated that the hypothetical buyer and hypothetical seller must be disposed to maximum economic gain.[12]

In valuing a *controlling* interest in an S corporation, one must assess the probability that the pool of likely buyers of a controlling interest will be able to avail themselves of continuing the S corporation status. If the pool of likely buyers is made up of qualified S corporation shareholders, then those buyers of a controlling interest can realize all three of the benefits, according to Grabowski (no double taxation, pass-through-basis adjustment, and increased proceeds upon sale of assets).

Grabowski urges that even a 100 percent interest often has value since it is an *existing* S Corp, especially if it has been an S corp since its incorporation or for the past ten years. First, because the S corp election requires unanimous consent of the shareholders, any buyer of less than 100 percent of the stock cannot unilaterally make an S corp election and thus the current election has value.

Second, unless the S corp is an *old-and-cold* S corp (an S corp since its incorporation or for at least 10 years), the sale of assets of an S corp is subject to a built-in gains tax. This will reduce the desirability to the owners of selling the stock at what may be the optimum time. Although the tax does not reduce the price for which the assets will sell, the presence of the built-in gains tax *reduces the marketability of the stock* compared to the stock of an old-and-cold S corporation, according to Grabowski.

When the *Gross* case was decided, some commentators from the business appraisal community immediately disagreed with the court, urging that there could not be any difference in the value of an S and a C corporation, since any willing buyer could purchase a C corporation and convert it to an S. This criticism, argues Grabowski, fails to recognize what the court was valuing: stock of an S corporation, not 100 percent of the underlying business. Stock comes with certain inherent characteristics, and the courts recognized that the advantages and disadvantages of S corporation election may vary based on specific facts and circumstances in each case.

Grabowski further notes that the studies of C corporation versus S corporation multiples have failed to distinguish new-and-hot S corporations, whose retained earnings are treated like C corporations, from old-and-cold S corporations, whose retained earnings are taxed like a partnership. Thus, he contends they may have failed to capture this element of value of these older S corporations.

---

[12]*BTR Dunlop Holdings, et al. v. Comm'r*, T.C. Memo 1999-377, 78 T.C.M. (CCH) 557.

Exhibit 8.1 Assumptions

Table G-1		
(1)	Growth rate	5.0%
(2)	Pretax margin	12.5%
(2)	Entity-level tax rate (C corp)	40.0%
	Personal income tax rate	41.5%
(3)	Depreciation as a % of sales	4.0%
(4)	Reinvestment rate	150.0%
(5)	Net working capital as a % of sales	10.0%
(6)	Rate of return on equity	15.0%

Example: Grabowski Model

Following is an example that incorporates the elements of Grabowski's model, applying the discounted cash flow method.[13]

We start with a common set of assumptions, found in Exhibit 8.1 (Table G-1), to be used in the examples in Tables G-2, G-3, and G-4. Assume a debt-free corporation with cash flows less than the corporation's income before taxes expected to be distributed to the owners, increasing at a long-term sustainable growth rate of 5 percent per annum.

We begin with a basic S corporation valuation using the traditional method (Table G-2) and the valuation following the method adopted by the Court in *Gross* (Table G-3). We are assuming: C corporation entity-level income tax rate of 40 percent (combined federal and effective state rate); owner-level income tax rate on ordinary income of 41.5 percent (combined federal and effective state rates); and owner-level income tax rate on dividends and capital gains of 20 percent (combined federal and effective state rates).

In *Gross* and *Heck*, the subjects of the valuations were minority interests; in *Adams*, the subject of the valuation was a controlling interest in a small corporation. In all three cases, the courts assumed that the S corporation election would continue indefinitely. Note that the relative values are dependent on the specific facts assumed.

Traditional Method

Exhibit 8.2 presents the valuation of a 5 percent common equity interest in an S corporation using the DCF method. We are converting to present value the distributions expected by minority shareholders after subtraction of assumed entity-level taxes. In other words, we value the stock as if the entity were a C corporation by subtracting a (hypothetical) entity-level tax (for simplicity we assume the entity is and will remain debt free with long-term sustainable growth in cash flows of 5 percent).

The appropriate C corporation equity rate of return (discount rate) used to discount the after-entity-level-tax cash flows may be derived from historical returns on stocks. For example, the total, historical return on publicly traded very small (micro-cap) stocks through year-

---

[13]Grabowski presents four methods to value an interest in a pass-through entity (Modified Traditional, Modified *Gross*, C Corp Equivalent, and Pretax Discount Rate methods) in "S Corp Valuation in the Post-*Gross* World—Updated," *Business Valuation Review* (September 2004). We present one method here for simplicity.

Exhibit 8.2 Traditional Method

Table G-2	Assumption (Table G-1) or Line #	Projected Fiscal Year 1	2	3	4	Stabilized as if C Corp
(7) Revenue		5,000,000	5,250,000	5,512,500	5,788,125	6,077,531
(8) Income before tax	(2) × (7)	625,000	656,250	689,063	723,516	759,691
(9) Entity-level tax rate (C corp)		40.0%	40.0%	40.0%	40.0%	40.0%
(10) Entity-level tax	(8) × (9)	(250,000)	(262,500)	(275,625)	(289,406)	(303,877)
(11) Net income	(8) – (10)	375,000	393,750	413,438	434,109	455,815
(12) Depreciation	(3) × (7)	200,000	210,000	220,500	231,525	243,101
(13) Capital expenditures	(4) × (12)	(300,000)	(315,000)	(330,750)	(347,288)	(364,652)
(14) Net working capital (increase)/ decrease	(5) × D (7)	(23,810)	(25,000)	(26,250)	(27,563)	(28,941)
(15) Free cash flow	Σ (11) to (14)	251,190	263,750	276,938	290,784	305,324
(16) Present value factor	15.0%	0.8696	0.7561	0.6575	0.5718	
(17) Discounted cash flows	(15) × (16)	218,427	199,433	182,091	166,257	
(18) Sum of discounted cash flows	Σ (17)	766,207				
(19) PV terminal value	See Box A	1,745,698				
(20) Pass-through basis adjustment		N/A				
(21) Asset sale amortization benefit		N/A				
(22) Indicated value (marketable, 100%)	Σ (18) to (21)	**2,511,905**				

Box A

Capitalization rate	10%
Terminal value	3,053,236
Present value factor	.5718
PV of terminal value	1,745,698

end 2002 was 15.2 percent.[14] That is, as an alternative to investing in the typical small, closely-held S corporation, one could purchase a portfolio of small public stocks. From historic returns, the investor would expect a 15.2 percent rate of return on such a portfolio (15 percent rounded).

We will use this 15 percent rate as the appropriate C corporation discount rate, after entity-level tax but pre-owner-level tax. Our example assumes that the pool of willing buyers at the valuation date are qualified S corporation shareholders who expect to hold a 5 percent interest for four years (assumed investment holding period) at which point the business is expected to be sold at the terminal value (calculated by capitalizing the normalized cash flow expected in the fifth year).

Table G-1 displays the calculations. The indicated value of $2,511,905 for 100 percent of the equity, multiplied by 5 percent, equals $125,595 (before application of any discount for lack of control and/or reduced marketability).

Gross Method

In Exhibit 8.3 we are valuing the 5 percent interest consistent with *Gross*, *Heck*, and *Adams*, so we replace the 40 percent entity-level income tax with any state/local income taxes that are

---

[14] Ibbotson Associates' *Stocks, Bonds Bills & Inflation (SBBI) Valuation Edition 2003 Yearbook*, Table 2-1, average of Geometric mean returns (12.1%) and Arithmetic return (18.2%) for 1926–2002 = 15.2% (rounded).

Exhibit 8.3 *Gross* Method

Table G-3	Assumption (Table G-1) or Line #	Projected Fiscal Year				Stabilized as if C Corp
		1	2	3	4	
(8) Revenue		5,000,000	5,250,000	5,512,500	5,788,125	6,077,531
(9) Income before tax	(2) × (8)	625,000	656,250	689,063	723,516	759,691
(10) Entity-level tax rate		1.5%	1.5%	1.5%	1.5%	40.0%
(11) Entity-level tax	(9) × (10)	(9,375)	(9,844)	(10,336)	(10,853)	(303,877)
(12) Net income	(9) − (11)	615,625	646,406	678,727	712,663	455,815
(13) Depreciation	(3) × (8)	200,000	210,000	220,500	231,525	243,101
(14) Capital expenditures	(4) × (13)	(300,000)	(315,000)	(330,750)	(347,288)	(364,652)
(15) Net working capital (increase)/ decrease	(5) × D (8)	(23,810)	(25,000)	(26,250)	(27,563)	(28,941)
(16) Free cash flow	Σ (12) to (15)	491,815	516,406	542,227	569,338	305,324
(17) Present value factor	15.0%	0.8696	0.7561	0.6575	0.5718	
(18) Discounted cash flows	(16) × (17)	427,666	390,477	356,523	325,521	
(19) Sum of discounted cash flows	Σ (18)	1,500,187				
(20) PV terminal value as if a C corp (a)		1,745,698				
(21) Asset sale amortization benefit	*See Box A*	161,849				
(22) Indicated value (marketable, 100%)	(19) + (20) + (21)	**3,407,733**				

Box A

Terminal value before benefit	3,053,236
Estimated % of intangible assets	50%
Intangible assets	1,526,618
Step-up factor (15-yr period) (b)	1.1854
Step-up value of intangible assets	1,809,693
Addition to selling price	283,075
PV of addition to selling price (c)	161,849

(a) Calculated as (stabilized cash flow) / (discount rate – growth rate) × year 4 PV factor.
(b) Calculated using a 15% discount rate and a 40% tax rate.
(c) Applies year 4 present value factor.

tax deductions at the entity level (we assume 1.5 percent of taxable income) and use the same discount rate. S corporations may be required to file state tax returns as well as federal returns. Many states have state income taxes, franchise taxes, or personal property taxes that apply to S corporations at the entity level. In Illinois, for example, S corporations are subject to a state personal property replacement income tax of 1.5 percent.

In *Gross*, *Heck*, and *Adams* there was the presumption that the S corporation election would continue indefinitely. That is, these cases assumed that the willing buyer is a noncontrolling shareholder with no expectation that the entity will be sold at the end of his four-year expected investment period. Terminal value was calculated without subtracting an entity-level income tax (consistent with the assumption that the S corporation benefit of eliminating the entity-level tax would continue indefinitely).

There will be no additional purchase price paid due to any pushdown of the purchase price to the underlying assets of the S corporation (and resulting asset step-up in basis) because the succeeding noncontrolling interest buyer will only receive the tax benefits from the carryover tax basis of the entity's assets (there is no Code section 754 election available to an S corporation shareholder).

But assume that the controlling shareholder is elderly with no heirs active in the business.

Both hypothetical willing buyers and sellers of minority interests at the valuation date would expect the business to be sold.[15]

To the extent that there is a likelihood that the controlling shareholders of the S corporation will sell the business, and the pool of likely willing buyers includes C corp (or other non-eligible S corporation shareholders), those buyers will not pay for the benefit of single taxation or the pass-through basis adjustment. That pool of likely willing buyers will pay a premium for tax savings from the step-up in basis. Selling to a nonqualified S corporation shareholder will end the S corporation election, and this buyer will value the entity as a C corporation. The current, qualified buyer will realize upon resale to a nonqualified buyer at the end of the fourth year:

- The C corporation value (assuming carryover income tax basis of the entity's assets)
- Plus the tax savings resulting from any basis adjustment from cash flows in excess of distributions while the stock was held
- Plus the additional price the likely succeeding buyer will pay because the deal can be structured as an asset purchase with a resultant step-up in basis, thereby increasing depreciation and amortization and lowering entity income taxes in future periods

The indicated value is $3,407,733 for 100 percent of the equity multiplied by five percent equals $170,387 (before application of any discount for lack of control and/or reduced marketability). This example addresses the assumed investment holding period and the effect on value if it is assumed that the business will be sold to a C corporation at the end of the investment holding period. But it simply applies the *Gross* method with a change in the terminal value. A more robust model is needed to quantify the differences between an S corporation and a C corporation.

Grabowski Modified Traditional Method

We begin with the results of the traditional method (Table G-2). In Exhibit 8.4 we:

- Add the present value of the entity-level income taxes saved (and assumed to be distributed to the owners) during the four years of the assumed investment holding period during which the S corporation election is effective
- Add the present value of pass-through-basis adjustment
- Subtract the income taxes paid on the excess of taxable income over cash flow
- Subtract the income taxes paid due to the higher ordinary income tax rate on S corporation taxable income (even if the taxable income equaled or was less than the cash flow)
- Add the present value of the proceeds upon sale including the added proceeds from sale of assets due to the step-up in basis realized by the willing buyer.

Again, we are assuming that the entity will be sold at the end of the fourth year and the likely buyer is not a qualified S corporation shareholder.

In the traditional method, the S corporation is assumed to pay (hypothetical) entity-level income taxes as if it were a C corporation. The sum of the present value of the cash flows after

---

[15]The example includes such facts to display how to take them into account. If there is little likelihood of sale of the business, hypothetical willing buyers and sellers will not value any such theoretical value increment.

Exhibit 8.4   Grabowski Modified Traditional Method

Table G-4	Assumption (Table G-1) or Line #	Projected Fiscal Year 1	2	3	4	Stabilized as if C Corp
(7) Revenue		5,000,000	5,250,000	5,512,500	5,788,125	6,077,531
(8) Income before tax	(2) × (7)	625,000	656,250	689,063	723,516	759,691
(9) Entity-level tax rate (C corp)		40.0%	40.0%	40.0%	40.0%	40.0%
(10) Entity-level tax	(8) × (9)	(250,000)	(262,500)	(275,625)	(289,406)	(303,877)
(11) Net income	(8) – (10)	375,000	393,750	413,438	434,109	455,815
(12) Depreciation	(3) × (7)	200,000	210,000	220,500	231,525	243,101
(13) Capital expenditures	(4) × (12)	(300,000)	(315,000)	(330,750)	(347,288)	(364,652)
(14) Net working capital (increase)/ decrease	(5) × D (7)	(23,810)	(25,000)	(26,250)	(27,563)	(28,941)
(15) Free cash flow	Σ (11) to (14)	251,190	263,750	276,938	290,784	305,324
(16) Present value factor	15.0%	0.8696	0.7561	0.6575	0.5718	
(17) Discounted cash flows	(15) × (16)	218,427	199,433	182,091	166,257	
(18) Sum of discounted cash flows	Σ (17)	766,207				
(19) Tax savings of S Corp election	(32)	917,474				
(20) Pass-through-basis adjustment	(40)	76,277				
(21) Tax on income in excess of free cash flow	(45)	(195,909)				
(22) Taxes paid due to tax rate differential	(52)	(586,670)				
(23) PV terminal value as if C corp (a)		1,745,698				
(24) Asset sale amortization benefit	See Box A	161,849				
(25) Indicated value (marketable, 100%)	Σ (18) to (24)	**2,884,925**				

Box A	
Terminal value before benefit	3,053,236
Estimated % of intangible assets	50%
Intangible assets	1,526,618
Step-up factor (15-yr period) (b)	1.1854
Step-up value of intangible assets	1,809,693
Addition to selling price	283,075
PV of addition to selling price (c)	161,849

(a) Calculated as (stabilized cash flow) / (discount rate – growth rate) × year 4 present value factor.

(b) Calculated using a 15% discount rate and a 40% tax rate.

(c) Applies year 4 present value factor.

		Projected Fiscal Year 1	2	3	4
(26) Entity-level taxes for S corp	Table G-3, Line 11	(9,375)	(9,844)	(10,336)	(10,853)
(27) Entity-level taxes for C corp	Table G-2, Line 10	(250,000)	(262,500)	(275,625)	(289,406)
(28) Difference in entity-level taxes	(26) – (27)	240,625	252,656	265,289	278,554
(29) Pretax equivalent (owner-level dividend tax rate)	(28) / (1 – 20%)	300,781	315,820	331,611	348,192
(30) Present value factor	(16)	.8696	.7561	.6525	.5718
(31) Discounted tax savings of S corp election	(29) × (30)	261,549	238,806	218,040	199,080
(32) Tax savings of S corp election	Σ (31)	**917,474**			

Exhibit 8.4 *(Continued)*

		Projected Fiscal Year			
		1	2	3	4
(33) S corp net income	Table G-3, Line 12	615,625	646,406	678,727	712,663
(34) S corp free cash flow	Table G-3, Line 16	491,815	516,406	542,227	569,338
(35) Net income less free cash flow	(33) – (34)	123,810	130,000	136,500	143,325
(36) Sum of cash flow differential	Σ (35)	533,635			
(37) Tax benefit of 20% (capital gains rate)	(36) × 20%	106,727			
(38) Pretax equivalent cash flow	(37) / (1 – 20%)	133,409			
(39) Present value factor	(16)	.5718			
(40) **Pass-through-basis adjustment**	(38) × (39)	**76,277**			

		Projected Fiscal Year			
		1	2	3	4
(41) Tax on income in excess of free cash flow	(35) × 41.5%	51,381	53,950	56,648	59,480
(42) Pretax equivalent (owner-level dividend tax rate)	(41) / (1 – 20%)	64,226	67,438	70,809	74,350
(43) Present value factor	(16)	.8696	.7561	.6575	.5718
(44) Discounted tax adjustment	(42) × (43)	55,849	50,992	46,558	42,510
(45) **Tax on income in excess of free cash flow**	Σ (44)	**195,909**			

		Projected Fiscal Year			
		1	2	3	4
(46) Owner-level taxes if C corp	(15) × 20%	50,238	52,750	55,388	58,157
(47) Owner-level taxes if S corp	(34) × 41.5%	204,103	214,309	225,024	236,275
(48) Income tax differential	(46) – (47)	153,865	161,559	169,637	178,118
(49) Pre-tax equivalent (owner-level dividend tax rate)	(48) / (1 – 20%)	192,332	201,948	212,046	222,648
(50) Present value factor	(16)	.8696	.7561	.6575	.5718
(51) Discounted tax adjustment	(49) × (50)	167,245	152,702	139,423	127,300
(52) **Tax increase due to tax rate differential**	Σ (51)	**586,670**			

paying the hypothetical income tax for the first four years, using a C corporation, pre-owner-level discount rate of 15 percent, equals $766,207.

But the S corporation pays a reduced or no entity-level income tax. The sum of the present value of the tax savings for the first 4 years, using a C corporation, pre-owner-level discount rate of 15 percent, equals $733,980. The sum of these two amounts ($766,207 plus $733,980) is equal to the sum of the first four years' discounted cash flows using the court's

Gross method. Assuming that the entity tax savings increases the cash distributions to the shareholders of the S corporation stock, the entity-level tax savings are converted to their pretax equivalent cash flow using the owner-level dividend tax rate (dividing by 1 minus 20 percent). The present value of the four-year savings in entity-level income taxes, calculated using the C corporation, pre-owner-level discount rate of 15 percent, equals $917,474.

In *Gross*, distributions approximated the taxable income; therefore, the pass-through-basis adjustment was not addressed.

In *Heck*, even though cash flows (distributions) as determined by the court were less than taxable income, neither the pass-through-basis adjustment nor the fact that the taxable income exceeded free cash flows were addressed.

In *Adams*, any difference between taxable income and distributions was not addressed.

The pass-through-basis adjustment results in income tax savings upon sale; the added basis reduces the owner-level capital gains tax upon sale. To be consistent with the C corporation pre-owner-level-tax discount rate of 15 percent, we converted the owner-level capital gains tax savings to a pretax equivalent cash flow (dividing by 1 minus 20 percent) and converted that amount to present value using the same 15 percent discount rate. The present value of the pass-through-basis adjustment equals $76,277.

Because the cash flows in this example are less than the income subject to income taxes to the S corporation shareholders, we need to reduce the indicated value by the present value of the income taxes due on the taxable income in excess of distributions. The added income taxes are converted to their pretax equivalent cash flow using the owner-level dividend tax rate (dividing by 1 minus 20 percent). The present value of the four-year difference, calculated using the C corporation, pre-owner-level discount rate of 15 percent, equals $195,909 (a reduction in value).

We then adjust for the difference in the owner-level income tax rates even if the cash flow equaled the taxable income. If the entity were a C corporation, the owner-level income tax rate on dividends and capital gains would be 20 percent while the owner-level income tax rate on the S corporation income taxable to the S corporation shareholder is an ordinary income tax rate of 41.5 percent, a rate differential of 21.5 percent. The added income taxes due to income tax rate differential on the cash flow are converted to their pretax equivalent cash flow at an owner-level dividend tax rate (dividing by 1 minus 20 percent). The present value of the four-year difference, calculated using the C corporation, pre-owner-level discount rate of 15 percent, equals $586,670 (a reduction in value)

In this example, the S corporation shareholder suffers two negative adjustments: Cash flows distributed are less than the income subject to income taxes, and the income tax rate is the ordinary income tax rate.

In *Gross*, *Heck*, and *Adams* it was assumed that the S corporation election continued in perpetuity. Therefore, the benefits to a succeeding buyer from step-up in basis were not addressed. In this example, the terminal value is calculated with the succeeding buyer valuing the entity as a C corporation and able to obtain the benefits of a step-up in the basis of the underlying assets, thereby increasing depreciation/amortization in future periods. We have assumed that:

- One-half of the cash flow valued in the terminal value calculation results from intangible assets (amortizable to the buyer using 15-year straight-line amortization consistent with I.R.C. § 197).

- In an asset sale the buyer would be willing to pay an additional purchase price equal to the present value of the tax savings from the step-up in basis of the intangible assets.[16]

In Table G-4, we calculate the present value of the terminal value (valued as a C corporation) using the C corporation, pre-owner-level discount rate of 15 percent; that present value equals $1,745,698;[17] the additions to the selling price due to the step-up equals $283,075; that present value equals $161,849.

In summary, Grabowski's method nets the following:

Sum of discounted cash flows for 4 years (as if the entity were a C corporation)	766,207
Plus tax savings of S corporation election at the entity level	917,474
Plus pass-through-basis adjustment	76,277
Minus tax on income in excess of free cash flow	195,909
Minus tax increase due to tax rate differential	586,670
Plus present value of the terminal value assuming carryover asset basis at entity level	1,745,698
Plus present value of added purchase price due to step-up in asset basis at entity level	161,849
Equals indicated value for 100 percent of the equity	$2,884,925
Multiplied by 5 percent equals	$ 144,246

(Before application of any discounts for lack of control and/or reduced marketability to account for the liquidity differences between stocks of publicly traded companies and the private S corporation investment)

Some are skeptical as to whether hypothetical willing buyers can and will project their holding periods and, therefore, assign any value to the pass-through-basis adjustment. Similarly, in the real world they would assign little probability to any increase in value due to a sale of the business. Grabowski assumes that where the facts dictate, these elements need to be measured.

---

[16]For simplicity we have assumed only a step-up in the value of the intangible assets; the willing buyer would also be willing to pay for the step-up in the value of the tangible assets.

[17]The generally accepted formula for calculating the present value of the increase in the fair market value due to the step-up in basis attributable to say I.R.C. § 197 is as follows: Let n = amortization life (in years; in the case of I.R.C. § 197 = 15 years), t = corporate tax rate, k = discount rate for tax savings due to step-up benefit, $\text{PVAF}_{k,n}$ = present value of annuity factor, discounted at k over n years (= $1/k - 1/(k(1+k)^n)$ if one uses an end of year convention without partial periods), VBAB = value before amortization benefits due to step-up, FMV = the fair market value; Then $\$1/n$ = annual amortization charge per $1 purchase price; and $t(1/n) = t/n$ = annual tax savings per $1 purchase price. Finally, $(t/n)\,\text{PVAF}_{k,n}$ = present value of tax shield benefits per $1 purchase price = ratio of the value of amortization benefits to fair market value. Now, the value of the amortization benefit equals FMV times $(t/n)\,\text{PVAF}_{k,n}$. Therefore: FMV = VBAB + FMV$(t/n)\,\text{PVAF}_{k,n}$. Solving for FMV, we get: FMV = VBAB/$(1 - (t/n)\,\text{PVAF}_{k,n})$ = VBAB $(1/(1 - (t/n)\,\text{PVAF}_{k,n}))$.

Mercer's Model[18]

In at least three recent cases, *Gross*, *Heck*, and *Adams*, the Tax Court has essentially opined that S corporations are worth more than otherwise identical C corporations.[19] This chapter provides only a cursory discussion of the cases. However, the Mercer article reaches a different conclusion[20]:

- At the level of the enterprise, an S corporation has the same value as an *otherwise identical* C corporation.
- At the level of the *shareholder*, an S corporation interest may be worth somewhat less than, the same as, or somewhat more than an *otherwise identical* interest in an *otherwise identical* C corporation.

Mercer bases his conclusions on basic financial theory, the nature of S corporations relative to C corporations, and discounted cash flow analysis. In terms of the levels of value, the relative values of S and C corporations and interests in them is depicted in Exhibit 8.5.

Value at the *enterprise level* is the present value of expected cash flows discounted to the present at an appropriate discount rate. Because no differences in enterprise cash flows are created by the S election, there are no differences in enterprise values for C and otherwise identical S corporations.

Value at the *shareholder level* is the present value of the expected cash flows of shareholders, for the duration (or expected holding period) of their investment, discounted to the present at an appropriate discount rate. Mercer utilizes a discounted cash flow model known as the quantitative marketability discount model (QMDM) to determine the present value of shareholder cash flows for both C and S corporations.[21] At the shareholder level, there are obvious tax benefits for distributing S corporations. There are also incremental risks. The (net) interaction of the incremental benefits and risks, for the duration of the expected holding period of minority investments in illiquid securities, determines the relative values of S versus C corporation minority interests in otherwise identical corporations.

Enterprise Level: Value Equivalency

Mercer considers key facts about S and C corporations, including:

- *Enterprise cash flows are unaffected by the choice of form of organization.* The S election has no impact on the revenues of a converted C corporation, and it has no impact on the operating costs of that corporation.

---

[18]Z. Christopher Mercer, "Are S Corporations Worth More than C Corporations?" *Business Valuation Review* (September 2004).

[19]*Gross v. Comm'r*, T.C. Memo. 1999-254, *aff'd.* 272 F.3d 333 (6th Cir. 2001). *Heck v. Comm'r*, T.C. Memo. 2002-34, filed February 5, 2002. *Estate of Adams v. Comm'r*, T.C. Memo. 2002-80, filed March 28, 2002.

[20]Supra note 18.

[21]Z. Christopher Mercer, *Valuing Shareholder Cash Flows: Quantifying Marketability Discounts*, an e-book (Memphis, TN: Peabody Publishing, LP, 2005); Mercer, *Quantifying Marketability Discounts* and its revised reprint (Memphis, TN: Peabody Publishing, LP, 1997, 2001). Available from the publisher at *www.integratedtheory.com*.

Exhibit 8.5 Levels of Value

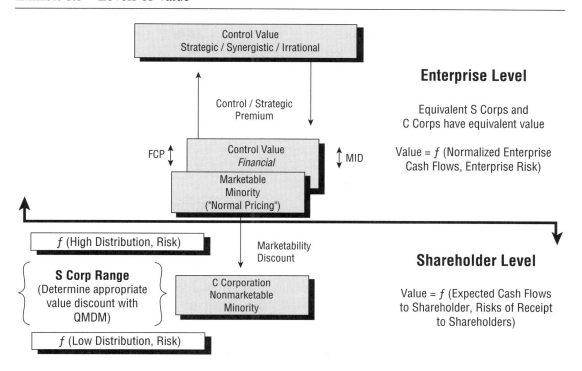

- *The ability to elect S corporation status is a shareholder election.* Electing S corporation status is essentially a costless election for qualifying shareholders.[22] Shareholders make the election, presumably for perceived shareholder benefits, which include:
  - Taxes that otherwise would be paid by a C corporation are passed through to the shareholders, who pay them at their individual income tax rates. The result is that a layer of taxation can be avoided by S corporations and other pass-through entities. Dividends beyond the level necessary to pay the required pass-through taxes are therefore tax free.
  - Retained earnings of an S corporation add to the basis in the stock of its shareholders. As a result, future capital gains upon exit from an investment in an S corporation are sheltered from capital gains taxes.
  - An S corporation has the ability to sell its assets, rather than its stock, and in so doing, achieve capital gains status on the sale. C corporations cannot sell assets without incurring corporate gains taxes at the level of the corporation. Therefore, a mature S corporation may achieve greater proceeds upon sale than a mature C corporation may, because purchasers will consider the embedded capital gains on the assets in their purchase decisions. In addition, purchasers of S corporations may be able to step up

---

[22]Mercer asks the question: Why would rational purchasers of an S corporation pay "extra" for an election they can obtain costlessly following an acquisition? There appears to be no rationale for the existence of two layers of pricing for S and C corporations. If such value exists, every C corporation would have the *option to convert*, and C corporation sellers would not accept lower value because of the existence of the option.

the basis in the assets, thereby allowing a tax shelter benefit on the increased amortization that results.[23]

However, S corporation shareholders also bear certain risks not present for holders of otherwise identical C corporation interests. For example, it could be costly to an S corporation shareholder if the S election were broken, a risk that exists with many, if not most, S corporations. In addition, under current tax law, there are certain disadvantages for significant S corporation shareholders (related to medical benefits and others) that essentially create phantom income, which is taxed at ordinary income rates. This is an ongoing penalty for many S corporation shareholders.

Mercer then makes the following observations:

- C corporations must pay federal and state income taxes on their earnings. This is simply the law.
- S corporations *will* distribute pass-through taxes to their shareholders who, in turn, will pay taxes at ordinary income tax rates. If it were not so, then one or more shareholders of a nondistributing S corporation would likely take steps to break the S election.
- To simplify analysis, Mercer assumes that the corporate federal/state blended income tax rate is identical to that of the personal federal/state blended rate.[24]

Under these realistic facts and assumptions, identical S and C corporations will be in *exactly* the same position following the payment of taxes (C corporation) or the distribution of taxes on pass-through income (S corporation), and will have *exactly* the same potential to make shareholder distributions or dividends and to retain earnings to finance future growth. It should be clear that no value to the *enterprise* is created if a C corporation makes the S election.

Mercer constantly emphasizes two words, *otherwise identical*, when discussing the relative values of S and C corporations. All analysts, he suggests, should agree that *nonidentical* corporations, whether S or C corporations, will likely not have identical values.

Mercer states that, unless reversed, the momentum of *Gross*, as well as *Heck* and *Adams*, will create a situation similar to that which existed for several years regarding the economic treatment of embedded capital gains in C corporations. The Tax Court's position was that consideration of embedded gains was improper unless liquidation of the subject corporation's as-

---

[23]Mercer suggests that, at the time of such sales, the S and C corporations are no longer identical. The fact is that the C corporation has a liability that does not exist for the S corporation. He further argues that the potential difference is not a difference in value, but is rather a difference in proceeds to shareholders. What most writers ignore is that the purchaser of an S corporation's assets avoids acquiring the corporation with its potential "tail" liability, which is retained by the shareholders of the S corporation. Reported transaction prices never quantify the expected magnitude of this tail liability retained by S corporation sellers. The significance of this liability, however, should not be underestimated. It is one compelling reason that purchasers desire to acquire assets, rather than stock, and similarly, a compelling reason that sellers desire to sell stock, rather than assets (whether S or C corporations are involved).

[24]In the current tax environment, personal rates exceed corporate rates, so to the extent that an S corporation makes full distributions for pass-through taxes, it will have less retained earnings than an otherwise equivalent C corporation and, arguably, would be worth less.

sets was imminent. The court maintained this economic position, considered by many a matter of law, until the liability was recognized, at least partially, in *Davis* in 1998.[25] A bit later, the Second Circuit Court of Appeals reversed a 1997 Tax Court decision on the issue in *Eisenberg*.[26] Until then, analysts were forced to choose one of three options:

1. Ignore the Tax Court's noneconomic ruling and treat embedded gains as real liabilities. This was the position taken by Mercer Capital and many other firms.
2. Ignore the liabilities and still attempt to achieve reasonable valuation results.
3. Attempt to get around the court's position by considering the embedded gains liability as part of another discount, such as the marketability discount. This was the position taken by two analysts in *Davis*.

As this area of valuation theory has crystallized in the appraisal profession since the *Gross*, *Wall*, *Heck*, and *Adams* cases, it is hoped the Tax Court will have the opportunity in the future to hear a clearer presentation of the sound economic reasoning for valuing such interests.

Shareholder Level: Value Can Differ

The Tax Court's quandary when considering the value of S versus C corporation minority interests is understandable. The court recognizes the obvious benefits of owning minority interests in S corporations, and rightly insists that analysts recognize the benefits in their appraisals. However, treating the earnings stream of the corporation as if taxes do not exist is not the appropriate economic way to consider the benefit. Every corporation, whether C or S, will pay taxes, either directly to the government or to their shareholders in tax pass-through distributions.

Mercer provides an example of two otherwise identical corporations, both of which pay taxes at blended rates of 40 percent (corporate taxes for the C corporation, and pass-through taxes for the S corporation). He then considers the potential value impact of being an S or a C corporation from the viewpoint of their shareholders under three assumed *economic distribution* policies. He defines economic distributions as dividends or distributions to shareholders *after the payment/distribution of corporate-level taxes*.

The valuation analysis considers the example corporation(s) shown in Exhibit 8.6. Uniform assumptions are made that relate both to a C corporation and an otherwise identical S corporation.

---

[25]*Davis v. Comm'r*, 110 T.C. 530, 35 (1998). Mercer wrote briefly about *Davis* in an early issue of *E-Law* (*E-Law* 1998-02, "The Good News and the Not So Good News about the *Davis* Case" (October 1998). In addition, he published a substantive analysis of the issue of embedded capital gains (Z. Christopher Mercer, "Imbedded Capital Gains in C Corporation Holding Companies," *Valuation Strategies* (November/December 1998): 30–41). Mercer makes the point that one of the primary reasons that the Tax Court maintained the noneconomic position regarding embedded capital gains was the absence of realistic, economic evidence in many of the cases presented to it.

[26]*Eisenberg v. Comm'r*, 155 F.3d 50 (2d Cir. 1998), vacating T.C.M. 1997-483.

Exhibit 8.6   S Corporation (or Otherwise Identical C Corporation)

1. Uniform Operating Assumptions		
a. Year One Sales	$ 5,000.00	
b. Forecast for	4 Years	
c. Enterprise Discount Rate (Reinvestment Rate)	15.0%	
d. Interim Base Earnings Growth Rate	15.0%	
e. Long-Term Growth Rate—Terminal Value	5.0%	
f. Pretax Margin	12.5%	
g. Earnings Retention Rate	100.0%	*All earnings reinvested*
h. Dividend Payout Ratio	0%	*No economic distributions*
2. Uniform Tax Rate Assumptions		
a. C Corp Federal/State Blended Rate	40.0%	
b. Federal/State Blended Rate on Ordinary Income	40.0%	*The pass-through tax*
c. Federal/State Blended Rate on Capital Gains	20.0%	
d. Federal/State Blended Rate on Dividends	15.0%	

Under these assumptions, C corporation and S corporation net earnings (and cash flows) are identical. An underlying premise of this analysis is that all undistributed economic earnings (after the payment of C corporation taxes or pass-through taxes for an S corporation) are reinvested into the businesses at the discount rate. This ensures that, regardless of (economic) distribution policy, the business will always provide a basic return of its enterprise discount rate. The (identical) enterprise valuations are shown in Exhibit 8.7.

The enterprise value for both corporations is $3.75 million. All nondistributed earnings are assumed to be reinvested in the corporations at the enterprise discount rates, which are the same (15 percent) for both C and S corporations.[27] This is an important assumption, since any assumption of suboptimal reinvestment (at less than the discount rate) would create a drain on expected shareholder return that should be considered separately. Further, there is no leakage of enterprise shareholder cash flows to controlling shareholders. All distributions are assumed to occur pro rata to ownership. The subject interests are assumed to be 10 percent minority interests.

Mercer then varies economic distributions assuming no distributions (0 percent dividend payout or 100 percent earnings retention), 50 percent distributions (50 percent earnings retention) and 100 percent distributions (0 percent earnings retention). He uses the QMDM to determine the present value of expected shareholder level cash flows for both the C and the S corporations under each of the three distribution assumptions.

It is important to note that the QMDM assumptions model expected shareholder cash flows *for the duration of the expected holding period*. In this fashion, the tax benefit of the S election is considered appropriately. The tax benefit of the S election is determined by grossing up the (after taxes paid) S corporation economic distributions to their C corporation equiv-

---

[27]Mercer notes that any other assumption regarding the enterprise, such as suboptimal reinvestment and the accumulation by a corporation of excess cash, or the leakage of cash flow through non–pro rata distributions to a controlling shareholder, injects additional elements of *shareholder concerns*, which can cause marketability discounts to be increased further. The controlling shareholder has the option, today, of selling the business under the market assumption of optimal reinvestment. If he or she chooses another strategy, both controlling and noncontrolling shareholders will experience suboptimal performance and lower returns.

Exhibit 8.7 S Corporation (or Otherwise Identical C Corporation) Discounted Cash
Flow Valuation

	0	1	2	3	4	5	
Sales	**$4,545.00**	**$5,000.00**	**$5,750.00**	**$6,612.50**	**$7,604.38**	**$8,745.03**	
Pretax Margin		12.5%	12.5%	12.5%	12.5%	12.5%	
Pretax Earnings	**543.5**	**625.0**	**718.8**	**826.6**	**950.5**	**1093.1**	
State Taxes	2%	($9.38)	($10.78)	($12.40)	($14.26)	($16.40)	
After State Taxes		$615.625	$707.969	$814.164	$936.289	$1,076.732	
Federal Taxes	39.08629%	($240.63)	($276.72)	($318.23)	($365.96)	($420.85)	
Net Income		**$375.000**	**$431.250**	**$495.938**	**$570.328**	**$655.877**	
Reinvestment		($375.0)	($431.3)	($495.9)	($570.3)	$0.0	
Net Cash Flow		**$0.000**	**$0.000**	**$0.000**	**$0.000**	**$655.877**	
Periods to Discount		1.000	2.000	3.000	4.000	4.000	
Present Value Factors	15%	0.86960	0.75610	0.65750	0.57180	0.57180	
Present Value of Interim Cash Flows		**$0.00**	**$0.00**	**$0.00**	**$0.00**	**$6,558.77**	Terminal Value
Present Value of Terminal Value					$3,750.31		
Enterprise Value	**$3,750.3**						
Multiple of Pretax	**6.000**						
Multiple of Net Income	**10.00**						

alency. So S corporation dividend yields are determined by dividing the C corporation yield by 1 minus Personal Tax Rate on Dividends.

The five key assumptions of the QMDM are summarized in Exhibit 8.8 for the 10 percent minority interests in both the C corporation and the S corporation across the assumed range of economic distributions.

A brief discussion of each of the QMDM assumptions follows:

- *The expected growth in value.* From the previously determined marketable minority value of the enterprise of $3.75 million, what value growth for the enterprise is expected *over the assumed holding period*? With no distributions, all earnings are retained and reinvested at the discount rate, so value grows at 15 percent per year. With 50 percent distributions, value grows at 10 percent, and with 100 percent distributions, value growth will be 5 percent. These assumptions are identical for both the S corporation and the C corporation interests.

- *The expected distribution yield.* With no dividends, there is a 0 percent distribution yield for both S and C corporation interests. With 50 percent distributions, the C corporation yield is 5.0 percent, and the S corporation yield is 5.9 percent (5.0 percent / 1 – 15 percent tax rate on dividends). With 100 percent distributions, the C corporation yield is 10 percent and the S corporation yield, calculated as with the 50 percent distributions, is 11.8 percent. This is how the tax benefit of S corporation status should be reflected in the valuation of an S corporation interest.

- *The expected growth in distributions.* With no distributions, growth is not an issue. Since the total return must be 15 percent at the enterprise level, if the distribution yield is 5 percent, the expected growth must be 10 percent. Similarly, if the distribution yield is 10 percent, the expected growth in distributions must be 5 percent.

Exhibit 8.8   Assumptions for a DCF Analysis of Minority Interests

		C Corporation			S Corporation		
Retention %		100%	50%	0%	100%	50%	0%
DPO %		0%	50%	100%	0%	50%	100%
Expected Growth in Value	QMDM #1	**15.0%**	**10.0%**	**5.0%**	**15.0%**	**10.0%**	**5.0%**
Expected Distribution Yield	QMDM #2	**0.0%**	**5.0%**	**10.0%**	**0.0%**	**5.9%**	**11.8%**
Expected Growth in Distributions	QMDM #3	**na**	**10.0%**	**5.0%**	**na**	**10.0%**	**5.0%**
Expected Holding Period (Years)	QMDM #4	**4.0**	**4.0**	**4.0**	**4.0**	**4.0**	**4.0**
Discount Rate for Enterprise		15.0%	15.0%	15.0%	15.0%	15.0%	15.0%
Combined Shareholder Risk Factors		6.0%	5.0%	4.0%	7.0%	6.0%	5.0%
Required Holding Period Return	QMDM #5	**21.0%**	**20.0%**	**19.0%**	**22.0%**	**21.0%**	**20.0%**
Marketable Minority Value	**$375.0**	*(of 10% of the Enterprise)*					

- *The expected holding period.* For purposes of this example, it is assumed that the expected holding period is exactly four years. In actual appraisals, analysts must make reasonable estimates of the holding period. Mercer advises that implicit in the selection of *every* marketability discount is an assumed expected holding period (or range of periods). Analysts (and courts) cannot dodge making this estimate just because of uncertainty—all investment decisions (and appraisals) are made in the face of uncertainties.

- *The required holding period return (shareholder discount rate).* The enterprise discount rate of 15 percent provides the base for developing the shareholder required holding period return. A range of premiums to this discount rate (15 percent) is estimated for the different distribution policies for C corporations. Higher dividends imply more rapid receipt of returns and therefore less risk than lower (or no) dividends. The incremental risk of holding S corporation shares is estimated at 1 percent more than the assumed shareholder risk factors for the C corporation.[28]

With these assumptions, Mercer ran the QMDM Companion, the Excel spreadsheet developed to perform the discounted cash flow assumptions of the QMDM. The model run assuming no distributions for the C corporation is shown in Exhibit 8.9 for illustration. The model was run for each of the assumption sets, and the results are further summarized in the exhibit.

The calculated marketability discount with the assumed required shareholder return of 21 percent and a holding period of exactly four years is 18.4 percent. This is lower than the typical benchmark discount of 35 percent or so. It is lower because of the attractive growth prospects of the investment. Note that if the assumed holding period were 10 years, the calculated marketability discount would have been 39.9 percent, within a range of about 35 percent

---

[28]Mercer notes that the estimation of specific risk factors relating to *shareholder risks* is conceptually no different than estimating specific company risk factors when using the Adjusted Capital Asset Pricing Model (or a build-up method) to estimate enterprise discount rates. Appraisers can test the reasonableness of their derived required holding period returns through comparisons with the implied returns from restricted stock transactions, from venture capital and equity fund returns (involving illiquid investments in enterprises), from returns from investments in illiquid real estate limited partnerships, and other sources.

Exhibit 8.9 Quantitative Marketability Discount Model

S VERSUS C CORPORATION VALUATION—NO ECONOMIC DISTRIBUTIONS ASSUMED

Base Value (Marketable Minority Interest)	$1.00	Reference/Brief Explanation
Basic Assumptions of the Model		
1. Expected Growth Rate of Underlying Value	15.0%	1. Value growth at R = 15% because of reinvestment
2. Expected Dividend Yield	0.0%	2. No distributions assumed
3. Expected Growth Rate of Dividend	0.0%	3. Therefore, no growth in distributions
4. Midpoint Required Return	21.0%	4. Assumed 6% holding period premium to R
5a. Minimum Holding Period	4	5. Four-year expected holding period assumed
5b. Maximum Holding Period	4	

QMDM Modeling Assumptions

Dividends Received End of Year ("E") or Mid-Year ("M")	E
Premium(+) / Discount(–) to Marketable Minority Value at Exit	0.0%

Average Indicated Discounts for Selected Holding Periods (Mid-Point Return +/- 1%)

Average of 2–4-Year HP	14%		Average of 5–10-Year HP	31%
Average of 5–7-Year HP	26%		Average of 10–15-Year HP	46%
Average of 8–10-Year HP	37%		Average of 15–20-Year HP	58%
Average of 10–20-Year HP	52%			

Concluded Marketability Discount   **18.4%**

Implied Marketability Discounts

Required Holding Period Return (%)	Assumed Holding Periods in Years													
	1	2	3	4	5	6	7	8	9	10	15	20	25	30
17.0%	2%	3%	5%	7%	8%	10%	11%	13%	14%	16%	23%	29%	35%	40%
18.0%	3%	5%	7%	10%	12%	14%	16%	19%	21%	23%	32%	40%	47%	54%
19.0%	3%	7%	10%	13%	16%	19%	21%	24%	26%	29%	40%	50%	57%	64%
20.0%	4%	8%	12%	16%	19%	23%	26%	29%	32%	35%	47%	57%	65%	72%
21.0%	5%	10%	14%	18.4%	22%	26%	30%	33%	37%	39.9%	53%	64%	72%	78%
22.0%	6%	11%	16%	21%	26%	30%	34%	38%	41%	45%	59%	69%	77%	83%
23.0%	7%	13%	18%	24%	29%	33%	38%	42%	45%	49%	64%	74%	81%	87%
24.0%	7%	14%	20%	26%	31%	36%	41%	45%	49%	53%	68%	78%	85%	90%
25.0%	8%	15%	22%	28%	34%	39%	44%	49%	53%	57%	71%	81%	88%	92%

PV = 100%   Calculations performed using QMDM Companion (*www.integratedtheory.com*)

© Z. Christopher Mercer 1997, 2001, 2005

103

to 45 percent. This simple illustration should illustrate that one discount (or small range) does not fit all assumptions. The assumptions matter, as is again illustrated in Exhibit 8.10, when the marketability discounts for the C and S corporations are calculated based on the preceding range of QMDM assumptions. The table presents the actual present value math employed by the QMDM, together with the respective conclusions.

The marketability discount for the S corporation with no economic distributions is 21.1 percent, or about 2.6 percent of discount points higher than the 18.4 percent for the C corporation's marketability discount. There were no dividends to offset the higher risk of holding the S corporation interest. The marketability discounts for the C and S corporations assuming 50 percent economic distributions were 14.7 percent and 14.8 percent, respectively, or almost identical. The benefits of tax-free distributions offset the incremental S corporation risk. Finally, the C corporation with 100 percent distributions has a marketability discount of 11.3 percent, versus the S corporation's discount of 8.9 percent. In this case, heavy distributions offset the incremental S corporation risk, yielding a lower marketability discount.

As noted in the conclusion stated at the outset, the value of a minority interest of an S corporation relative to an otherwise identical interest in a C corporation is perhaps a bit less assuming no distributions, about the same assuming 50 percent (or some distributions), and a bit more assuming 100 percent distributions.[29]

In the final analysis, Mercer uses a discounted cash flow method to determine the present value of expected future benefits of either S or C corporations. These expected benefits are discounted to the present at the shareholders' required holding period rate of return over the duration of the expected holding period. Clearly, suggests Mercer, assumptions must be made, but in the context of the facts and circumstances of each valuation situation.

Consideration of Other Potential Benefits

Some analysts take the analysis of expected benefits of the S election a step further. They suggest, rightly, that S corporation shareholders can shelter future capital gains from taxation to the extent of earnings retained. To the extent that an analyst believes that willing buyers and sellers of S corporation interests will negotiate over the incremental value of the expected basis buildup, it is not inappropriate to consider this factor.

However, for fully distributing or heavily distributing S corporations, Mercer notes there will be no or very little basis buildup and, therefore, very little potential capital gains shelter.

---

[29]Mercer notes that some readers may be concerned by the small size of the concluded marketability discounts in this analysis in relationship to a "benchmark range" of 35% to 45% based on restricted stock and pre-IPO studies. However, more attractive investments should have lower discounts (and higher prices) than less attractive investments. By way of comparison, if all other assumptions remain the same except that the expected holding period is increased to 10 years, the marketability discounts for the C corporation are 39.0% (no distributions), 29.1% (50% economic distributions), and 20.4% (100% distributions). The marketability discounts for the S corporation assuming a ten year holding period are 44.6% (no distributions), 28.6% (50% distributions) and 15.0% (100% distributions). So, assuming a ten year holding period, the S corporation with no distributions is worth about 5% less than otherwise identical C corporation (because of incremental risk), about the same for the 50% distribution case (where incremental risk and benefits approximately offset each other), and about 5% more for the 100% distribution case (where the prolonged benefit more than offsets the incremental risk).

Exhibit 8.10 Summary of Results: Marketability Discounts for 10% Interests of Otherwise Identical C and S Corporations

Shareholder Cash Flows	C Corp	1	2	3	4	S Corp	1	2	3	4	Value Diff.	
0% Distributions												
Interim Cash Flows		$0.0	$0.0	$0.0	$0.0		$0.0	$0.0	$0.0	$0.0		
Terminal Value					$655.9					$655.88		
Present Value Factors @	21.0%	0.8264	0.6830	0.5645	0.4665	22.0%	0.8197	0.6719	0.5507	0.4514		
Present Value of Cash Flows	$305.97	$0.0	$0.0	$0.0	$306.0	$296.06	$0.0	$0.0	$0.0	$296.1	−3.2%	in $ value
Implied Marketability Discount	18.4%					21.1%					2.6%	in points of discount
50% Distributions												
Interim Cash Flows		$18.8	$20.6	$22.7	$25.0		$22.1	$24.3	$26.7	$29.4		
Terminal Value					$549.0					$549.0		
Present Value Factors @	20.0%	0.8333	0.6944	0.5787	0.4823	21.0%	0.8264	0.6830	0.5645	0.4665		
Present Value of Cash Flows	$319.89	$15.6	$14.3	$13.1	$276.8	$319.70	$18.2	$16.6	$15.1	$269.8	−0.1%	in $ value
Implied Marketability Discount	14.7%					14.8%					0.1%	in points of discount
100% Distributions												
Interim Cash Flows		$37.5	$39.4	$41.3	$43.4		$44.1	$46.3	$48.6	$51.1		
Terminal Value					$455.8					$455.8		
Present Value Factors @	19.0%	0.8403	0.7062	0.5934	0.4987	20.0%	0.8333	0.6944	0.5787	0.4823		
Present Value of Cash Flows	$332.80	$31.5	$27.8	$24.5	$248.9	$341.53	$36.8	$32.2	$28.1	$244.4	2.6%	in $ value
Implied Marketability Discount	11.3%					8.9%					−2.3%	in points of discount

The maximum benefit would occur with nondistributing or low distributing (on an economic basis) S corporations, of which, in Mercer's experience, there are relatively few.

Finally, it has been suggested that willing buyers and sellers today will negotiate over the form of a *future* liquidity transaction (i.e., at the end of the expected holding period when a sale of the business is contemplated as the exit strategy) for an enterprise when transacting in minority interests. Proponents of this suggestion rely on the fact that buyers know that they may be able to purchase assets from an S corporation, and may factor into their offers the present value of their expected tax savings from writing up the basis of assets purchased.

Such consideration would be extremely facts and circumstances based. It requires that buyers and sellers of minority interests today agree on the *form* of a sale transaction in the future in addition to estimating *when* (expected holding period) and at what future value (based on the expected growth in value) that transaction might occur.

While Mercer agrees that calculations regarding the benefit of a future buyer's potential tax amortization benefit can be calculated based on enough assumptions, he does not believe that willing buyers, either real or hypothetical, would take such calculations into account today and consider them to be overly speculative. For example, a rational, defensive purchaser of a minority S corporation interest is unlikely to pay money today based on the seller's assertion that a future sale will take a particular form and provide benefits if it does. First, it might not. And second, the tax law could change in the interim, eliminating some or all of the potential benefit. At the very least, it would appear that analysts considering the present value of such benefits in an appraisal of a minority interest in an S corporation should use a higher discount rate than applied to interim distributions and the terminal value to bring their future values to the present.

Treharne's Model[30]

The Discount Rate

As background for his model, Chris D. Treharne begins with a discussion of the discount rate. Business analysts generally utilize either the build-up method or the capital asset pricing model (CAPM) to determine a discount rate, often by relying on data derived from public stock transaction data published by Ibbotson Associates ("Ibbotson"). Ibbotson states:

> *The equity cost of capital is equal to the expected rate of return for a firm's equity; this return includes all dividends plus any capital gains or losses.*[31]

Note Ibbotson's reference to two components of value, "dividends" and "capital gains or losses."

Because Ibbotson solely analyzes publicly traded stocks (which are C corporations), Ibbotson's rates of return reflect satisfaction of tax liabilities associated with entity income. Furthermore, it is critical to recognize that C corporation dividends are an after-entity-tax component

---

[30]*Valuation of Pass-Through Entities: Minority and Controlling Interests*, Chris D. Treharne, ASA, MCBA, BVAL, Gibraltar Business Appraisals and Nancy J. Fannon, CPA, ABV, MCBA, submitted by the S Corporation to the Treasury Department.

[31]*Stocks, Bonds, Bills and Inflation Valuation Edition, 2002 Yearbook* (Ibbotson Associates, 2002), 37.

of net cash flow. Clearly, C corporation net cash flow and retained cash flow are diminished when the tax liability associated with entity income is paid. Thus, the payment of C corporation tax liabilities associated with entity income affects the discount rates reported by Ibbotson.

In *Adams*, the court quoted the following from Ibbotson:

> *All of the risk premium statistics included in this publication are derived from market returns by an investor. The investor receives dividends and realizes price appreciation* after the corporation has paid its taxes. *Therefore, it is implicit that the market return data represents returns after corporate taxes but before personal taxes.* [emphasis added] *When performing a discounted cash flow analysis, both the discount rate and the cash flows should be on the same tax basis.*[32]

Ibbotson's position (as quoted in the *Adams* case) is consistent with the conclusions that rates of return derived from its data are after taxes associated with entity income and that cash flow is diminished by the payment of tax liabilities.

More importantly, even though S corporations—at the company (versus investor) level—have no income tax liability (i.e., the income tax liability associated with entity income is passed on to the shareholders), *it is unreasonable to assume that rates of return derived from Ibbotson data can be used with a net cash flow stream that does not reflect the tax liability associated with entity income.* Accordingly, the reader should not casually dismiss the necessary symmetry between the rates of return arrived at by using Ibbotson data and the subject ownership interest's economic income.

Instead, both the income stream and the discount rate—if the latter is derived from public stock data, as is Ibbotson's data—must reflect the satisfaction of income taxes associated with entity income. Who pays the taxes—the C corporation, as an entity, or the S corporation shareholder—is not relevant. Either way, the dollars used to satisfy the liability are not available for reinvestment and do not create wealth for the entity or its owners. As a result, the income stream must be normalized to reflect the satisfaction of taxes associated with entity income if one derives a discount rate using the Ibbotson data.

Ibbotson also states that an inaccurate conclusion will result from the misapplication of rates of return to improper income streams:

> *One important aspect of the income approach model is that the discount rate and the cash flows need to be estimated on the same basis. For instance, if pre-tax cash flows are projected in the model, they must be discounted to present using a pre-tax cost of capital (as opposed to an after-tax cost of capital). . . . Failure to properly match the discount rate with the cash flows will produce an inaccurate value.*[33]

Said in another way: If Ibbotson discount rates are used in a present value calculation, the economic income stream must reflect equivalent C corporation tax liabilities. If not, the "[f]ailure to properly match the discount rate with the cash flows will produce an inaccurate value."[34]

---

[32]Id. at. 87.
[33]Id. at 16.
[34]Id.

Discount rates (arrived at using Ibbotson data) and market multiples (e.g., the P/E ratio) derived from public stocks reflect returns after taxes associated with entity income and before owner-level taxes. However, there are examples in the public securities marketplace when investors will consider the impact of personal taxes. More explicitly, investors will consider this extra analysis when doing so affects the ranking of potential investments.

In particular, investors will accept lower rates of return (i.e., discount rates) on double-tax-exempt municipal bonds because their personal net cash flow is not reduced by personal income taxes related to the investment (i.e., there are no personal income tax liabilities associated with double-tax-exempt municipal bonds). In contrast, proceeds from corporate bonds of quality equal to the municipal bonds are taxable at the personal level, and the marketplace therefore demands higher rates of return so that the investor's net proceeds associated with the investments are identical. Said in another way, to yield the same net cash flow to the investor (i.e., after payment of personal taxes associated with proceeds from the investment), corporate bonds must have a higher interest rate (on an investor's pre–personal tax basis) to yield the same return on a post–personal tax basis as the double-tax-exempt municipal bonds.

A comparative example is shown in Exhibit 8.11. Note that both bonds have the same face value (line 1), the same net cash flow to the investor (line 7), and the same after-tax yield (line 8). Yet, because the investor will incur a personal tax liability with the corporate bond (line 5), it must have a higher interest rate (i.e., discount rate, line 2) to yield the same net cash flow (line 7) after the satisfaction of personal tax liabilities associated with the investment. Only then will the knowledgeable investor be indifferent toward the two investments.

The existence of lower rates of return for double-tax-exempt municipal bonds relative to corporate bonds of similar risk is market evidence that investors focus on net cash flow after personal taxes (line 7) when valuing securities.

As a result, Treharne concludes that investors make investment decisions based on net proceeds after the satisfaction of tax liabilities directly attributable to the investment, whether those tax liabilities are associated with the security or the individual investor.

Furthermore, the preceding analysis demonstrates that premiums for minority interests in S corporations can arise when the net proceeds after the satisfaction of all tax liabilities

Exhibit 8.11   Investor Cash Flow: Corporate versus Municipal Bonds

			Corporate Bond	Municipal Bond
1	Face value		1,000	1,000
2	Interest rate (discount rate)		10.0%	5.9%
3			——	——
4	Interest earned by investor		100	59
5	Income taxes (personal)	41%	(41)	0
6			——	——
7	Net cash flow to investor		59	59
8	Yield to investor (after personal taxes)		5.9%	5.9%

Exhibit 8.12 New Cash Flow and Retained Cash Flow

1	Pretax income
2	Income taxes (C corp)
3	————————————
4	Net income
5	Noncash expenses
6	Changes in working capital
7	Fixed asset acquisitions
8	Debt principal payments
9	————————————
10	Net cash flow
11	C corp dividends paid
12	S corp tax distribution paid
13	S corp "excess distributions" paid
14	————————————
15	Retained cash flow

(personal or entity) directly attributable to the investment are greater for the S corporation shareholder than they are for an equivalent C corporation shareholder.

Treharne begins by defining net cash flow in Exhibit 8.12, lines 1 to 10. Additionally, lines 11 to 15 restate the components of net cash flow and—depending on the form of the entity, C or S corporation—also depict components (i.e., dividends and distributions) of the company's "Retained cash flow."

Before proceeding, it is critical for the reader to recognize that net cash flow (as traditionally defined for valuation purposes) may not be the same as net cash flow to the company (defining the latter as "Retained cash flow," line 15) if the company is distributing cash to investors. In other words, net cash flow and retained cash flow will not be identical if the company pays dividends to C corporation investors or distributions to S corporation investors. As will be demonstrated later, within these two discrepant cash flows lies the potential for value differences between minority interests in C and S corporations.

Treharne offers an example, beginning with discount rate assumptions, as shown in Exhibit 8.13, where the discount rate is assumed to be derived from Ibbotson.

Also, a larger discount rate for the present value calculation associated with the double taxation adjustment in Exhibit 8.14 (lines 34 to 43, the shaded portion of the model) was chosen. As discussed in detail later, the choice of a larger discount rate reflects the greater risk associated with the minority owner's inability to control and receive distributions.

Exhibit 8.13 Equity Discount and Capitalization Rates

	Retained Cash Flow	Double Taxation Adj.
Discount rate	20%	21%
Growth rate	5%	5%
Capitalization rate	15%	16%

Exhibit 8.14 Discount Rate Assumptions

	Tax Rates	C Corporation				S Corporation											
						Scenario A				Scenario B				Scenario C			
		2004	2005	2006	Present Value	2004	2005	2006	Present Value	2004	2005	2006	Present Value	2004	2005	2006	Present Value
Retained Cash Flow:																	
1 Pretax income	40%	1,000	1,200	1,800		1,000	1,200	1,800		1,000	1,200	1,800		1,000	1,200	1,800	
2 Income taxes (C corp)		400	480	720													
3																	
4 Net income		600	720	1,080		1,000	1,200	1,800		1,000	1,200	1,800		1,000	1,200	1,800	
5 Noncash expenses		60	72	108		60	72	108		60	72	108		60	72	108	
6 Changes in working capital		(15)	(18)	(27)		(15)	(18)	(27)		(15)	(18)	(27)		(15)	(18)	(27)	
7 Fixed asset acquisitions		(65)	(78)	(117)		(65)	(78)	(117)		(65)	(78)	(117)		(65)	(78)	(117)	
8 Debt principal payments		(25)	(30)	(45)		(25)	(30)	(45)		(25)	(30)	(45)		(25)	(30)	(45)	
9																	
10 Net cash flow		555	666	999		955	1,146	1,719		955	1,146	1,719		955	1,146	1,719	
11 C corp dividends paid		0	0	0													
12 S corp tax distribution paid	41%					(410)	(492)	(738)		(410)	(492)	(738)		0	0	0	
13 S corp "excess distributions" paid						0	0	0		(590)	(708)	(1,062)		0	0	0	
14																	
15 Retained cash flow		555	666	999		545	654	981		(45)	(54)	(81)		955	1,146	1,719	
16 C corp valuation adjustment		0	0	0		0	0	0		0	0	0		(400)	(480)	(720)	
17																	
18 Retained cash flow (C corp basis)		555	666	999		545	654	981		(45)	(54)	(81)		555	666	999	
19 Terminal value				6,993				6,867				(567)				6,993	
20																	
21 Total		555	666	7,992		545	654	7,848		(45)	(54)	(648)		555	666	7,992	
22 Present value (retained cash flow)		463	463	4,625	5,550	454	454	4,542	5,450	(38)	(38)	(375)	(450)	463	463	4,625	5,550
23 **Net cash flow to investor**																	
24 S corp tax distribution paid		0	0	0		410	492	738		410	492	738		0	0	0	
25 S corp "excess distributions" paid		0	0	0		0	0	0		590	708	1,062		0	0	0	
26 Personal taxes on S corp operations	41%	0	0	0		(410)	(492)	(738)		(410)	(492)	(738)		(410)	(492)	(738)	
27																	
28 Net cash flow to investor		0	0	0		0	0	0		590	708	1,062		(410)	(492)	(738)	
29 Terminal value		0	0	0		0		0				7,434				(5,166)	
30																	
31 Total		0	0	0		0	0	0		590	708	8,496		(410)	(492)	(5,904)	
32 Present value		0	0	0	0	0	0	0	0	492	492	4,917	5,900	(342)	(342)	(3,417)	(4,100)
33																	
34 **Double Taxation Adj.**																	
35 Total S corp distributions		0	0	0		410	492	738		1,000	1,200	1,800		0	0	0	
36 C corp entity-related taxes		0	0	0		(400)	(480)	(720)		(400)	(480)	(720)		(400)	(480)	(720)	
37																	
38 S corp "excess distributions" paid	21%	0	0	0		10	12	18		600	720	1,080		0	0	0	
39 S Corp "excess dist" tax benefit		0	0	0		2	3	4		126	151	227		0	0	0	
40 Terminal value				0				25				1,488				0	
41																	
42 Total		0	0	0		2	3	29		126	151	1,715		0	0	0	
43 Present value (double taxation adj.)		0	0	0	0	2	2	16	20	104	103	968	1,176	0	0	0	0

Exhibit 8.14 *(Continued)*

	Tax Rates	C Corporation				S Corporation Scenario A				Scenario B				Scenario C			
		2004	2005	2006	Present Value	2004	2005	2006	Present Value	2004	2005	2006	Present Value	2004	2005	2006	Present Value
44																	
45 **Tax-Rate Differential Adj.**																	
46 S corp entity-related taxes	41%	0	0	0		(410)	(492)	(738)		(410)	(492)	(738)		(410)	(492)	(738)	
47 C corp entity-related taxes	40%	0	0	0		(400)	(480)	(720)		(400)	(480)	(720)		(400)	(480)	(720)	
48																	
49 S corp benefit (liability)		0	0	0		(10)	(12)	(18)		(10)	(12)	(18)		(10)	(12)	(18)	
50 Terminal value				0				(126)				(126)				(126)	
51																	
52 Total		0	0	0		(10)	(12)	(144)		(10)	(12)	(144)		(10)	(12)	(144)	
53 Present value (tax-rate differential adj.)		0	0	0	0	(8)	(8)	(83)	(100)	(8)	(8)	(83)	(100)	(8)	(8)	(83)	(100)
54																	
55 Present value (cash to investor)					0				(80)				6,976				(4,200)
56																	
57 **PV of retained & investor cash flows**					5,550				5,370				6,526				1,350

As the benchmark against which S corporation minority interest values will be measured, the value of an otherwise similar C corporation minority interest was first determined in Exhibit 8.14.

Moving on to the S corporation examples in Exhibit 8.14, three scenarios are presented. Note that the C corporation and personal tax rates (40 percent and 41 percent, respectively) differ.

- Scenario A shows the valuation strategy for an S corporation distributing only enough of its income to satisfy the minority owner's tax liability associated with entity income.
- Scenario B represents the valuation of an S corporation minority ownership interest in an entity distributing 100 percent of net income to minority owners (facts similar to the *Gross* case).
- Scenario C demonstrates the valuation strategy for an S corporation paying no distributions to the minority owner.

General comments and observations for Exhibit 8.14:

- Retained cash flow (line 15) differs for each of the four scenarios.
- Net cash flows (line 10) for the three S corporation scenarios are identical but greater than the same measure for the C corporation scenario. If net cash flow is the basis for valuing the C corporation minority interest, the knowledgeable investor will always prefer the S corporation investment opportunities. Using the information previously presented in this paper in combination with Exhibit 8.14, the folly of this position will be demonstrated.
- Relative to the C corporation and other S corporations, larger S corporation distributions (lines 12 and 13, as well as 24, 25, and 35) favorably affect the value of the minority investment (line 57). Conversely, smaller S corporation distributions adversely affect the value of a minority investment. If only net cash flow (line 10) is used as a basis in the valuation analysis, the conclusion will be wrong.
- The three S corporation scenario entries on line 53—the present value of the tax-rate differential adjustments—are and always will be identical if the taxable incomes, line 1, are identical.

C Corporation Scenario

Because the C corporation pays no dividends (line 11) to its minority shareholders, its net cash flow (line 10) is the same as its retained cash flow (line 15).

Particularly note that the present value of the cash to the investor is zero (line 55) because the investor receives no dividends. Additionally, because the entity is a C corporation, there are no double-taxation (line 43) or tax-rate differential (line 53) adjustments. Hence, the value of the benchmark C corporation minority interest is the value of its retained cash flow (line 22, which is identical to line 57). Logically, the traditional method of calculating the present value of a C corporation is consistent with determining the present value of net cash flow (line 10) because net cash flow and retained cash flow (line 15) are identical and there are no adjustments (lines 23 to 53) to this value.

S Corporation Scenarios

Scenario A: Distributions equal tax liability associated with entity income. If C corporation and personal tax rates (lines 2 and 12, respectively) are identical, the present value components (lines 22, 32, 43, 53, and 57) of the C corporation and the Scenario A S corporation will be identical and the knowledgeable investor will be indifferent toward the two investments.

However, if tax rates differ (as indicated in Treharne's example), the investor will choose the C corporation minority investment since its Scenario A value (line 57) is slightly greater relative to the otherwise identical S corporation. Logically and all other factors identical, different tax rates (e.g., C corporation versus personal) affect an investor's opinion of value.

Scenario B: Distributions exceed the tax liability associated with entity income. The Scenario B conclusion indicates that this particular S corporation minority interest is worth more than an S corporation minority interest receiving no distributions and is worth more than a C corporation paying no dividends (line 57). Note that the premium for the value of the S corporation minority interest versus the C corporation will vary with the amount of excess distributions and the likelihood of continued receipt (the latter affecting the choice of a discount rate for the excess distribution). Contrary to *Gross*, also note that both premiums are much smaller than would be derived without tax-affecting S corporation income.

Because Treharne's example represents the extreme case of distributing all income (lines 12 and 13), the result is negative retained cash flow (line 15), which infers that the entity will be unable to fully generate or service the operating, investment, and financing activities on lines 1 to 8 and still pay owner distributions at the indicated level. Over the long term, distributions cannot exceed net cash flow (line 10).

However, if the entity in Scenario B is in a mature industry with minimal growth prospects (i.e., has minimal demands for additional working capital, line 6), does not require investment in capital equipment (line 7) greater than its depreciation expense (line 5), and has no debt service requirements (line 8), net income (line 4) and net cash flow (line 10) will be similar. In such circumstances, the S corporation can afford to pay all of its income to its minority owners without jeopardizing the entity's future. The preceding unusual circumstances are similar to the facts of *Gross* and do not represent the facts of a typical S corporation valuation assignment.

Scenario C: Distributions less than the tax liability associated with entity income. Because the C corporation income taxes have been recognized in the C corporation scenario (line 2) and in Scenario A and Scenario B (line 12) cash flows, retained cash flow (line 15) does not need to be further adjusted to reflect the satisfaction of tax liabilities associated with entity income.

However, the C corporation tax liability has not been recognized in Scenario C's retained cash flow (line 15). As a result, for the purposes of a valuation analysis, a C corporation tax liability adjustment must be made on line 16 so that the discount rate and the cash flow streams are symmetric. If the C corporation tax liability is not recognized and Ibbotson discount rates are used, the conclusion will be wrong.

Because S corporation distributions (line 35) do not exceed C corporation taxes (line 36), there is no double-taxation benefit (line 39). In general, when S corporation distributions do not exceed C corporation taxes, no double-taxation benefit will be recognized.

Conclusions

The valuation conclusions are summarized on line 57 of Exhibit 8.14 and in Exhibit 8.15.

Valuation Model Summary

Consistent with the market's expectations for evaluating tax-exempt investment opportunities, Treharne recommends identifying the incremental cash flow differences between C and S corporation minority interests and determining their present values using the following strategy:

1. Determine the present value of retained cash flow (Exhibit 8.14, line 22) by tax-affecting the S corporation's cash flow at C corporation income tax rates (Exhibit 8.14, line 12). C corporation rates must be used to normalize the economic income stream to the same basis as the Ibbotson derived discount rates (i.e., the tax liability associated with entity income has been paid).

2. Value attributed to investor's cash flow (line 28) should be adjusted for the tax benefits associated with the S corporation shareholder's not having to pay a second level of taxes on excess distributions (i.e., S corporation distributions in excess of the equivalent C corporation's tax liability, Exhibit 8.14, line 38). When determining the present value of the S corporation minority shareholder's tax benefit, the discount rate may be increased to reflect greater uncertainty associated with receiving S corporation distributions. More specifically, the risk and discount rate associated with distributions may be greater than the risk and discount rate associated with the company's net cash flow stream because distributions are subordinate to, and dependent upon, net cash flow. Furthermore, distributions are made at the discretion of the controlling owner. When the company's history of distributions has been consistent, the additional premium will be minimal, maybe zero. Alternately, an inconsistent history of distributions may justify a larger discount rate.

3. The present value of the cash flow to the investor (line 28) should be adjusted for the income tax differences between C corporations and individuals (the latter being responsible for the tax liability associated with an S corporation's income).

Exhibit 8.15 Minority Interests' Valuation Summary

(Minority marketable basis)

	C Corporation	S Corporation		
		Scenario A	Scenario B	Scenario C
Net cash flow for 2004	555	955	955	955
Present value (retained cash flow)	5,550	5,450	(450)	5,550
Present value (cash to investor)	0	(80)	6,976	(4,200)
Value to investor	5,550	5,370	6,526	1,350

In addition to the preceding adjustments to a C corporation minority interest valuation analysis, Treharne recognizes that the ability of a buyer to build up S corporation basis (i.e., increase retained earnings) may have a favorable impact on the valuation conclusion. However, its impact is mitigated by one of the implicit, key assumptions of the multi-period discounting model used in Treharne's example (Exhibit 8.14). More specifically, because the implicit holding period in the example is perpetuity, the present value of any benefit associated with S corporation basis increases is negligible.

From a more practical perspective, the analyst may choose to recognize that a holding period of 10 years may approximate perpetuity at a 25 percent equity discount rate and a long-term growth rate of 5 percent. More specifically, the tax benefit attributed to basis buildup is only 0.83 percent at 10 years, assuming a 20 percent capital gain tax rate (federal plus state). In general, the longer the investment holding period, the larger the discount rate, and/or the lower the growth rate, the smaller the impact of basis changes on value. Unless one of these variables is at an opposite extreme to those identified in the preceding sentence, Treharne believes the impact of basis buildup is negligible when valuing a minority S corporation interest.

Because Treharne's model produces a marketable minority interest value, one final adjustment, a discount for lack of marketability (DLOM), also should be considered if the objective is a nonmarketable minority interest value. Many analysts recognize the contribution of C corporation dividends by adjusting the benchmark-DLOM averages (e.g., the pre-IPO or restricted stock studies' averages) downward. Because Treharne's S corporation valuation model quantifies similar adjustments in terms of dollars (instead of a percentage), the analyst needs to be wary of and avoid double counting the favorable impact of an S corporation's excess distributions.

Van Vleet's Model[35]

Introduction

The S corporation economic adjustment model developed by Daniel R. Van Vleet contemplates the following: (1) the economic characteristics of generally accepted business valuation approaches; (2) the disparate income tax attributes of S corporations, C corporations, and their respective shareholders; and (3) the net economic benefits derived by S corporation and C corporation shareholders. This model should be used only when the following conditions are present: (1) the assignment is to value a non-controlling equity interest in an S corporation and (2) empirical market data of publicly traded C corporation equity securities is used to estimate the value of the subject S corporation equity securities.

There are two basic premises that are relevant to a discussion of the Van Vleet model. The first premise is that there are significant differences in the income tax treatment of

---

[35]Daniel R. Van Vleet, ASA, CBA, "The S Corporation Economic Adjustment Model," Chapter 4, *The Handbook of Business Valuation and Intellectual Property Analysis* (New York: McGraw-Hill, 2004).

S corporations, C corporations, and their respective shareholders. These differences are briefly described as follows:

- C corporations are subject to corporate income taxes at the entity level. Conversely, the shareholders of S corporations recognize a pro rata share of the net income[36] of the S corporation on their personal income tax returns.
- Dividends from C corporations are subject to dividend income tax rates at the shareholder level.[37] Conversely, dividends received by shareholders of S corporations are not subject to income taxes.
- The undistributed income of an S corporation increases the income tax basis of its equity securities. Conversely, the undistributed income of a C corporation does not change the income tax basis of its equity securities.

The second premise is that capital markets are efficient, at least over the long term. Consequently, equity investment rates of return, equity security prices, and price/earnings multiples of publicly traded C corporations inherently reflect the income tax treatment of C corporations and their respective shareholders.

Based on these two premises, there is a theoretical mismatch between (1) the economic characteristics of the empirical market data of publicly traded C corporations and (2) the economic attributes of noncontrolling equity interests in S corporations. This mismatch may distort the appraised value of S corporation equity securities when empirical studies of C corporations are used to estimate such value. These potential distortions may occur when publicly traded C corporation data is used to (1) estimate the capitalization rate or present value discount rate used in the income approach, (2) estimate the price/earnings multiples used in the market approach, or (3) estimate the discount for lack of control used in the income approach, market approach, or asset-based approach.

Currently, there is a lack of good empirical data related to transactions involving minority equity interests in S corporations. Consequently, Van Vleet argues the need for a mathematical framework that conceptually addresses the relevant income tax–related differences between S corporations, C corporations, and their respective shareholders. This mathematical framework should permit the adjustment of estimated values of noncontrolling equity interests in S corporations when empirical market data of publicly traded C corporations is used in the valuation analysis. This mathematical framework should be generally applicable to each of the generally accepted approaches and methods to business valuation, not just the income approach.

Business Valuation Approaches

There are three basic approaches to the valuation of an equity interest in a business enterprise: (1) the income approach, (2) the market approach, and (3) the asset-based approach. In order to assess whether the S corporation organization form has an impact on any of these business

---

[36]S corporation net income is defined as net income prior to the payment of federal and state income tax at the shareholder level.

[37]The term *shareholder level* refers to a noncontrolling equity interest in the subject business enterprise.

valuation approaches, it is necessary to understand (1) the general economic nature of corporate transactions and (2) how empirical studies of these transactions are reflected within the various business valuation approaches. In order to simplify the following explanations, the three business valuation approaches are grouped into two categories: (1) income-based approaches and (2) asset-based approaches.

For purposes of this discussion, the income approach and market approach are both classified as *income-based approaches*. The indicated value of equity provided by each of these approaches is based on (1) a measurement of income and (2) the application of a capitalization factor. The capitalization factor is a percentage—or multiple—used to convert a measurement of income into an indication of value. Capitalization factors used in the income approach may take the form of a single-period capitalization rate or a multiperiod present value discount rate. Capitalization factors used in the market approach may take the form of a price/earnings multiple.

Income Approach

The two most commonly used income approach methods are (1) the discounted cash flow method and (2) the single-period direct capitalization method.[38] These methods use either a capitalization rate or present value discount rate—both of which are typically derived from empirical studies of investment rates of return on noncontrolling equity interests in publicly traded C corporations—to estimate the value of the subject S corporation equity securities.

A fundamental business valuation principle is that the economic attributes of income and the capitalization rate or present value discount rate should be conceptually consistent. In order to assess whether this consistency is present in a valuation analysis, it is necessary to understand how investment rates of return on publicly traded C corporation equity securities are calculated.

Public market equity investors expect to receive an investment rate of return that is comprised of some combination of income (i.e., cash dividends) and capital gains or losses. The following formula is the mathematical representation of this relationship:

$$k_1 = \frac{(S_1 - S_0) + d_1}{S_0}$$

where:

k_1 = Investment rate of return during period 1
S_1 = Stock price at end of period 1
S_0 = Stock price at beginning of period 1
d_1 = Dividends paid during period 1

The formula illustrates the principle that investment rates of return on equity securities— and, therefore, the capitalization rates and present value discount rates used in the income

---

[38]Either of these methods can be constructed to provide either a controlling interest or a noncontrolling interest indication of value. However, for purposes of our discussion, the income approach methods discussed in this portion of the chapter are assumed to provide a noncontrolling indication of value.

approach—are derived from a combination of capital appreciation of the security $(S_1 - S_0)$ and dividend payments (d_1).

Theoretically, capital appreciation and dividend payments are derived from the net income of the corporation. In other words, net income is either (1) paid to the shareholders in the form of dividends or (2) retained by the company (resulting in the capital appreciation[39] of equity). Consequently, equity investment rates of return inherently reflect (1) corporate income taxes at the entity level and (2) capital gains taxes and dividend income taxes at the shareholder level. When the income approach uses capitalization rates or present value discount rates derived from publicly traded equity securities, and when the projected net income of the subject S corporation is tax-affected using an appropriate C corporation equivalent income tax rate, the resulting indication of value of equity is a C corporation publicly traded equivalent value.

Market Approach

Within the market approach, there are a variety of valuation methods. The two most commonly used methods are (1) the guideline publicly traded company method and (2) the guideline merger and acquisition method.

The guideline publicly traded company method estimates the value of equity based on the application of price/earnings multiples derived from empirical studies of stock prices and earnings fundamentals of comparative publicly traded companies. Investment theory tells us that these price/earnings multiples are based on the same fundamental principles as the equity investment rates of return used to estimate the capitalization rates and present value discount rates used in the income approach. The indication of value provided by the guideline publicly traded company method is a C corporation publicly traded equivalent value.

The guideline merger and acquisition method estimates the value of the subject company based on the application of market-derived pricing multiples extracted from transaction prices and earnings fundamentals of target companies involved in merger or acquisition transactions. The guideline merger and acquisition method initially provides a controlling interest indication of value. When using this method to value an equity interest that lacks control, a discount for lack of control (DLOC) is typically estimated and applied. The DLOC is typically estimated using empirical studies of acquisition price premiums paid for the equity securities of publicly traded companies in control-event merger or acquisition transactions. The inverse of this premium is generally considered a reasonable proxy for the DLOC. When the DLOC is estimated and applied, the analyst has essentially adjusted the indication of value provided by the guideline merger and acquisition method from a controlling interest value to a C corporation publicly traded equivalent value.

---

[39]There are many economic factors that contribute to the capital appreciation (or depreciation) of an equity security. It is not feasible to mathematically model all of the components that either contribute to or detract from the capital appreciation of an equity security. Consequently, the most reasonable assumption is that, over the long term, capital appreciation is derived from retained earnings. The discussion contained in this portion of the chapter is consistent with this assumption.

Asset-Based Approaches

The asset-based approach is not commonly used to value a noncontrolling equity interest of a profitable going-concern business enterprise. Typically, the asset-based approach provides an indication of equity value on a controlling interest basis. As such, the indication of value is typically adjusted with a DLOC when valuing a noncontrolling equity interest. When this discount is estimated using empirical studies of acquisition price premiums paid for the equity securities of publicly traded companies in control event merger or acquisition transactions, the analyst has effectively adjusted the indication of value to a C corporation publicly traded equivalent value.

Summary

The income approach, market approach, and asset-based approach can be used to estimate the C corporation publicly traded equivalent value of a noncontrolling equity interest in a C corporation or an S corporation. Exhibit 8.16 illustrates this concept.

The C corporation publicly traded equivalent value assumes that the equity interest being valued is (1) a noncontrolling equity interest, (2) readily marketable, and (3) subject to C corporation entity-level income taxation, and (4) subject to dividend and capital gains income tax treatment at the shareholder level. Also, the indication of value assumes that investors are indifferent between dividends and capital gains, since both forms of investment returns are (1) readily liquid and (2) subject to identical federal income tax rates.

Since there are significant differences among the income, dividend, and capital gains income tax treatment of S corporations, C corporations and their respective shareholders, the C corporation publicly traded equivalent indication of value may not be appropriate when valuing a noncontrolling equity interest in an S corporation. Also, the S corporation shareholders may or may not be indifferent between investment returns in the form of distributions (i.e., dividends) or capital gains.

Conceptual Mismatch between S Corporations and C Corporations

There are income tax differences between S corporations, C corporations and their respective shareholders. These income tax differences result in differing economic benefits attributable

Exhibit 8.16 Business Valuation Approaches

to the shareholders of S corporations and C corporations. Exhibit 8.17 illustrates these differences and was created using the following assumptions:

- Distribution (i.e., dividend) payout ratio of 50 percent of net income
- C corporation corporate income tax rate of 35 percent
- Individual ordinary income tax rate of 35 percent
- Dividend income tax rate of 15 percent
- Capital gains income tax rate of 15 percent
- Capital gains tax liability is economically recognized when incurred.
- Capital appreciation of equity is derived from increases in retained earnings on a dollar-for-dollar basis.

As demonstrated in Exhibit 8.17, the total net economic benefit of $65,000 derived by S corporation shareholders is different from the total net economic benefit of $55,250 derived by C corporation shareholders. Historically, business valuation analysts have attempted to correct for these differences by estimating income taxes and subtracting this amount from the net income of the subject S corporation. Unfortunately, this adjustment does not properly resolve the economic mismatch.

Exhibit 8.17   Net Economic Benefits to Shareholders

	C Corp. ($)	S Corp. ($)
Income before Corporate Income Taxes	100,000	100,000
Corporate Income Taxes	(35,000)	NM
Net Income	65,000	100,000
Dividends		
Distributions to S Corporation Shareholders	NM	50,000
Income Tax Due by S Corporation Shareholders	NM	(35,000)
Net Cash Flow Benefit to S Corporation Shareholders	NM	15,000
Dividends to C Corporation Shareholders	32,500	NM
Dividend Tax Due by C Corporation Shareholders	(4,875)	NM
Net Cash Flow Benefit to C Corporation Shareholders	27,625	NM
Capital Appreciation		
Net Income	65,000	100,000
Dividends and Distributions	(32,500)	(50,000)
Retained Earnings (i.e., Net Capital Appreciation)	32,500	50,000
Effect of Increase in Income Tax Basis of Shares	NM	(50,000)
Taxable Capital Appreciation	32,500	0
Capital Gains Tax Liability	(4,875)	0
Net Capital Appreciation Benefit to Shareholders	27,625	50,000
Net Cash Flow Benefit to Shareholders	27,625	15,000
Net Capital Appreciation Benefit to Shareholders	27,625	50,000
Total Net Economic Benefit to Shareholders	**55,250**	**65,000**

The S Corporation Economic Adjustment

Van Vleet developed the S corporation economic adjustment (SEA) as a means to address the differences in net economic benefits between S corporation and C corporation shareholders.

The SEA contemplates the differing income tax treatments of S corporations, C corporations, and their respective shareholders. As such, the SEA is the first step in creating a mathematical framework that may be used to adjust the indicated value of noncontrolling equity interests in S corporations. The SEA is based on equations that model the net economic benefits to (1) C corporation shareholders (NEB_C) and (2) S corporation shareholders (NEB_S).

The NEB_C equation is comprised of two principle components: (1) net cash received by shareholders from dividends after the payment of income taxes at the entity level and income taxes on dividends at the shareholder level and (2) net capital appreciation of the equity security after recognition of capital gains taxes at the shareholder level.

The equation for the first component of the NEB_C equation is:

$$\text{Net Cash from dividends} = I_p \times (1 - t_c) \times D_p \times (1 - t_d)$$

where:

I_p = Income prior to federal and state income tax ($I_p > 0$)
t_c = C corporation effective income tax rate
D_p = Dividend payout ratio
T_d = Income tax rate on dividends

The equation for the second component of the NEB_C equation is:

$$\text{Net capital appreciation} = I_p \times (1 - t_c) \times (1 - D_p) \times (1 - t_{cg})$$

where:

I_p = Reported income prior to federal and state income tax ($I_p > 0$)
t_c = C corporation effective income tax rate
D_p = Dividend payout ratio
t_{cg} = Capital gains tax rate

Adding together the first and second components of the NEB_C equation results in an equation that models the total net economic benefit to the C corporation shareholder. The NEB_C equation follows in its entirety:

$$NEB_C = [I_p \times (1 - t_c) \times D_p \times (1 - t_d)] + [I_p \times (1 - t_c) \times (1 - D_p) \times (1 - t_{cg})]$$

The NEB_S equation is less complex. The NEB_S equation simply multiplies S corporation net income by one minus the individual ordinary income tax rate $(1 - t_i)$. This is the only adjustment necessary due to the fact that the income tax paid at the shareholder level represents the only income tax–related economic drain to the net income of the S corporation. The remaining S corporation net income (i.e., after payment of income tax at the shareholder level) provides either tax-free dividends or tax-free capital appreciation[40] of the equity security. The NEB_S equation is:

$$NEB_S = I_p \times (1 - t_i)$$

Obviously, there is a mathematical inequality between the NEB_C and NEB_S equations. This inequality represents the difference between the net economic benefit derived by S corporation shareholders and the net economic benefit derived by C corporation shareholders. This inequality is referred to as the SEA.

$$NEB_C = NEB_S - SEA$$

An algebraic manipulation of the preceding formula produces the SEA equation:

$$SEA = NEB_S - NEB_C$$

A detailed version of the SEA equation is:

$$SEA = [I_p \times (1 - t_i)] - \{[I_p \times (1 - t_c) \times D_p \times (1 - t_d)] + [I_p \times (1 - t_c) \times (1 - D_p) \times (1 - t_{cg})]\}$$

The algebraically simplified version of the SEA equation is:

$$SEA = I_p \times (t_c + t_{cg} - t_i - t_c t_{cg} + D_p t_d - D_p t_{cg} - D_p t_c t_d + D_p t_c t_{cg})$$

The SEA equation quantifies the incremental net economic benefit of being an S corporation shareholder vis-à-vis a C corporation shareholder. As such, the SEA equation is useful in creating a factor that may be used to adjust the appraised value of a noncontrolling equity interest in an S corporation. A description of the development of this factor is provided in the following section of this chapter.

S Corporation Equity Adjustment Multiple (SEAM)

The SEA can be used to estimate the percentage economic benefit of being an S corporation shareholder vis-à-vis a C corporation shareholder by dividing the SEA by the NEB_C. This percentage is added to 1.0 to calculate a multiple that may then be used to adjust the indicated equity value of an S corporation when empirical studies/analyses of C corporations are used to estimate such value. This multiple is referred to as the S corporation equity adjustment multiple (SEAM).

The basic SEAM equation is:

$$SEAM = 1 + \frac{SEA}{NEB_C}$$

---

[40]The capital appreciation of equity is derived from the undistributed earnings of the S corporation. Since undistributed earnings increase the income tax basis of the S corporation shares, the capital appreciation is thereby tax free.

A detailed version of the SEAM equation is:

$$\text{SEAM} = 1 + \frac{[I_p \times (1 - t_i)] - \{[I_p \times (1 - t_c) \times D_p \times (1 - t_d)] + [I_p \times (1 - t_c) \times (1 - D_p) \times (1 - t_{cg})]\}}{[I_p \times (1 - t_c) \times D_p \times (1 - t_d)] + [I_p \times (1 - t_c) \times (1 - D_p) \times (1 - t_{cg})]}$$

The algebraically simplified version of the SEAM equation is:

$$\text{SEAM} = 1 + \frac{(t_c + t_{cg} - t_i - t_c t_{cg} + D_p t_d - D_p t_{cg} - D_p t_c t_d + D_p t_c t_{cg})}{(1 - t_c - t_{cg} + t_c t_{cg} - D_p t_d + D_p t_{cg} + D_p t_c t_d - D_p t_c t_{cg})}$$

Application of the SEAM

Once the SEAM has been calculated, the application in business valuation analysis is relatively simple. The analyst (1) estimates the C corporation publicly traded equivalent value of the subject S corporation equity and (2) multiplies this concluded value by the SEAM.

When estimating the C corporation publicly traded equivalent value of the equity of the S corporation, the following guidelines generally apply:

- When using the income approach, the analyst should estimate corporate-level income taxes and deduct this amount from the projected net income of the S corporation.
- When using the market approach, the price/earnings multiples of the guideline C corporations should be applied to the same earnings fundamentals of the subject S corporation as those used in the calculation of the price/earnings multiples.
- When using any valuation approach that results in a controlling interest indication of value, a DLOC should be considered. If used, the DLOC should be estimated using empirical studies of acquisition price premiums paid for the equity securities of publicly traded companies in control-event merger or acquisition transactions.

When the analyst multiplies the C corporation publicly traded equivalent value by the SEAM, the resulting indication of value is an S corporation publicly traded equivalent value. In other words, the SEAM-adjusted indication of equity value is the hypothetical value of the subject S corporation equity as though an efficient capital market existed for S corporation equity securities. An illustration of this concept is provided in Exhibit 8.18.

The selection of the numerical components of the SEAM equation is properly left to the discretion of the analyst. However, the following is provided for consideration:

- C Corporation Effective Income Tax Rate (t_c): The effective income tax rate of the publicly traded C corporations selected as comparative to the subject S corporation.

Exhibit 8.18 Application of the SEAM

| C Corporation Publicly Traded Equivalent Value | X | S Corporation Equity Adjustment Multiple (SEAM) | = | S Corporation Publicly Traded Equivalent Value |

- Capital Gains Tax Rate (t_{cg}): A composite of combined federal and state long-term capital gains tax rates
- Individual Ordinary Income Tax Rate (t_i): A composite of combined federal and state individual income tax rates
- Income Tax Rate on Dividends (t_d): A composite of combined federal and state individual income tax rate on dividends
- Dividend Payout Ratio (D_p): The dividend payout ratio of publicly traded C corporations selected as comparative to the subject S corporation

The application of the SEAM is merely a step in the process of estimating the value of a noncontrolling equity interest in an S corporation. Other factors—most notably the DLOM—should be considered when estimating the value of a noncontrolling equity interest in an S corporation. A discussion of the SEAM-specific factors to consider when estimating the appropriate DLOM is provided in the following section of this chapter.

Discount for Lack of Marketability (DLOM)

The DLOM is typically one of the more important and economically significant adjustments that a business valuation analyst makes in the course of valuing a noncontrolling equity interest in a closely held company. The DLOM is intended to adjust the indicated value of the subject equity security from a publicly traded equivalent value (i.e., noncontrolling, marketable value) to an indication of value that represents the illiquid nature of the closely security (i.e., noncontrolling, nonmarketable value). This valuation adjustment is relevant when valuing a noncontrolling equity interest in a closely held C corporation, as well as an S corporation. When valuing an equity interest in a closely held C corporation, the analyst adjusts the C corporation publicly traded equivalent value with a DLOM. The same holds true when the analyst has used the SEAM to estimate the S corporation publicly traded equivalent value. Exhibit 8.19 illustrates this procedure.

When using the SEAM in the valuation analysis, there are certain inherent assumptions that should be considered to properly estimate the DLOM. Also, it is important to consider the conceptual and theoretical characteristics of the empirical studies and/or quantitative methods

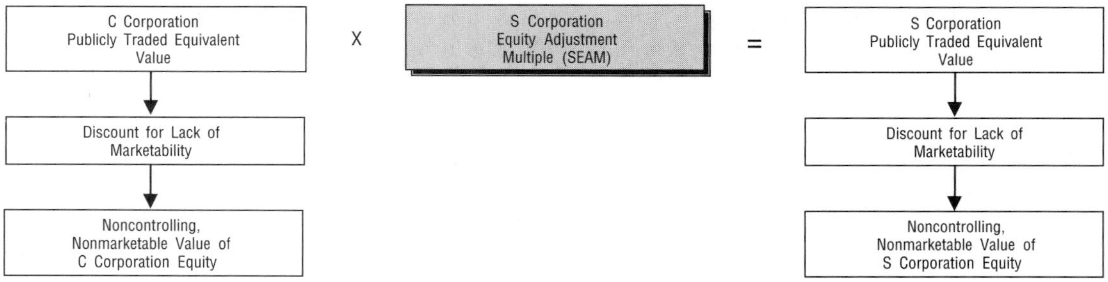

Exhibit 8.19   Application of the Discount for Lack of Marketability

used to estimate the DLOM. Following is a discussion of the principal assumptions of the SEAM that may affect the selection of the DLOM.

Principal Assumptions of the SEAM and the DLOM

The SEAM is based on the following principal assumptions:

- The subject company will continue as an S corporation in perpetuity.
- Investors are indifferent between distributions and capital gains.
- There is a pool of qualified S corporation equity security buyers.
- Current law related to the income tax treatment of S corporations vis-à-vis C corporations will continue in perpetuity.
- The subject S corporation will continue to be a profitable enterprise in perpetuity.

A brief discussion of each these principal assumptions—and potential analytical adjustments to the DLOM—follows.

S Corporation Perpetuity Assumption

Investors would not be willing to pay a price premium for an S corporation equity security if the S election would be revoked upon purchase. If the revocation of the S election of the subject company is a foreseeable near-term possibility, the SEAM should either not be used or adjusted to reflect the foreseeable revocation. Even if the S election is expected to continue in perpetuity, the SEAM does not specifically contemplate the risk of revocation. This is a unique risk to S corporations that is not contemplated by the DLOM used for C corporation equity security valuations. Consequently, when applying the SEAM, analysts should consider (1) whether the terms and conditions of shareholder agreements discourage shareholder behavior that may endanger the S election and (2) whether the subject S corporation is in danger of revocation of the S election. The presence of either of these conditions may require an adjustment to the DLOM or, in the case of an imminent S election revocation, the elimination of the SEAM from the analysis.

Distributions and Capital Gains

The SEAM adjusts the C corporation publicly traded equivalent value to an S corporation publicly traded equivalent value. As such, the SEAM inherently assumes that S corporation equity investors are indifferent between investment returns in the form of either cash distributions or capital appreciation. Given the closely held nature of S corporations, this is typically not the case.

The S corporation publicly traded equivalent value (as estimated by the SEAM) assumes that S corporation equity investors are indifferent between distributions and capital gains. This is because both elements of investment return are assumed to be equally liquid in an efficient capital market. Since S corporations are privately held, the capital gains investment return is rarely considered to be a liquid investment return. Consequently, the SEAM equation inherently assumes that the subject S corporation will distribute 100 percent of its net income, as this is the only way the total S corporation investment return could be considered liquid. To the extent that the subject S corporation is expected to distribute less than 100 percent of its net income, the analyst should consider whether to make an adjustment to the DLOM. This type of analysis should be considered for both closely held S corporations and C corporations.

Under current U.S. tax law, capital gains taxes are not assessed until the asset is sold. However, both investment components of publicly traded equity securities (i.e., dividends and capital gains) are equally liquid and the investor can obtain the capital gains return by simply selling the security. Consequently, investors in publicly traded equity securities are assumed to recognize—and their investment behavior is influenced by—the capital gains tax liability when incurred rather than when realized. Since the SEAM quantifies an S corporation publicly traded equivalent value, the inherent assumption is that S corporation equity investors recognize the economic impact of the capital gains tax treatment of S corporation equity securities when incurred rather than when realized. As discussed earlier, the SEAM assumes (1) capital gains are derived from retained earnings and (2) retained earnings increase the income tax basis of the S corporation equity securities. Consequently, the capital gains investment returns to the S corporation equity security are assumed to be tax free.

To the extent that the subject S corporation is retaining its income to fund future growth, the capital gains income tax benefit attributable to S corporation retained earnings may not be realized for some period of time. Consequently, the present value of this income tax benefit may be less than assumed in the SEAM-adjusted indication of value. This factor should be considered in conjunction with the expected future distributions of the subject S corporation when estimating the DLOM.

When conducting a fair market value analysis, the business valuation analyst should be cautious when adjusting the DLOM for the assumed future capital gains tax benefit of S corporation equity securities. The fair market value standard inherently assumes the existence of (1) a willing buyer and a willing seller and (2) a liquidity event. Given these assumptions, the fair market value standard assumes the seller could liquidate his ownership interest at the price estimated by the business valuation analyst. Consequently, the investor could theoretically obtain the S corporation capital gains tax benefit associated with retained earnings at any time. This fact diminishes the argument that the S corporation capital gains tax benefit associated with retained earnings has minimal economic relevance.

Tax Status of Buyers and Sellers

The SEAM inherently assumes there is a pool of qualified S corporation equity security buyers that are willing to pay a price premium—over the C corporation publicly traded equivalent value—for the income tax attributes of an S corporation equity security. To the extent that there are no qualified S corporation buyers, the business valuation analyst may wish to adjust the DLOM or consider whether it is appropriate to use the SEAM in the analysis.

Current Income Tax Law

The SEAM inherently assumes that current law related to the income tax treatment of S corporations vis-à-vis C corporations will continue in perpetuity. Given the uncertainty of future income tax law for both S corporations and C corporations, this is the most reasonable assumption. To the extent that disparate changes in income tax law for S corporations or C corporations are foreseeable, the analyst should assess the probability of this change and either adjust the DLOM or the model components of the SEAM. The business valuation analyst should be aware that most of the risk of change in income tax law is contemplated in the security prices of publicly traded equity securities.

Profitability Assumption

To the extent that the subject S corporation is not expected to be profitable for some or all of the foreseeable future, the analyst should consider the fact that the income tax attributes of an S corporation—as well as a C corporation—are dependent upon the ability of the subject corporation to generate a pretax profit. If the subject S corporation is not expected to be profitable, the analyst should consider whether the use of the SEAM is appropriate.

Summary and Conclusion

The SEAM may be used to adjust the value of a noncontrolling equity interest in an S corporation from a C corporation publicly traded equivalent value to an S corporation publicly traded equivalent value. The SEAM contemplates the differences in net economic benefit attributable to shareholders resulting from the disparate income tax treatments of S corporations, C corporations, and their respective shareholders. When using the SEAM to value a noncontrolling equity interest in an S corporation, it is necessary to (1) conduct a careful and reasoned approach to the initial C corporation publicly traded equivalent value, (2) carefully consider the components and theoretical aspects of the SEAM, and (3) conduct a thorough analysis of the DLOM in order to conclude meaningful and appropriately supported indications of value.

COMPARISON OF MINORITY INTEREST THEORIES— A SUMMARY OF THE ISSUES

The reader has been presented with four sound, yet diverse approaches to valuing interests in S corporations. In this section, we will examine the ways in which these models differ from each other. These differences highlight the issues the practitioner needs to consider in approaching the valuation of an interest in an S corporation; selection of the appropriate model for a particular valuation may depend on the extent to which the facts and circumstances fit with a particular model.

The differences in the minority valuation models, and the issues that give rise to valuation differences between S corporations and C corporations, include the following:

- The starting point for the valuation
- The extent to which current cash distributions affect value
- The impact on value of retained cash flow (basis)
- The extent that shareholder benefits (i.e., personal taxes saved) impact the value determination

- The amount, extent, and manner that discounts are taken against the value determined by the model
- The impact on today's value of the asset sale amortization benefit resulting from future transactions

We will review how each model handles these issues.

The Starting Point for the Minority Interest Valuation

One of the reasons for the differences in the models is the point from which they start; if the analyst is not starting from the same base, the same adjustments to it would not be expected.

- Grabowski's model begins with the value of an equivalent C corporation after reinvestment needs are met, assuming 100 percent of remaining *free cash flow* is distributed—but for minority, he advises the analyst to adjust for either expected cash flows or to take a discount against the value determination.
- Mercer's model begins with the value of an identical C corporation at the marketable minority level, and calculates the S premium or discount by reference to C corporation equivalent yields on distribution: (S corporation Distribution Yield / (1 − Dividend Tax)) and employs the QMDM to determine the values.
- Treharne's model begins with the value of an equivalent C corporation after reinvestment of all necessary cash flows, making additions or subtractions to the C corporation value depending on the extent of distributions to the minority owner, and any tax rate differentials.
- Van Vleet's SEAM model begins with a C corporation publicly traded equivalent value—as estimated by the income approach, market approach, and/or asset-based approach—and adjusts this value to an S corporation publicly traded equivalent value based on the disparate income tax treatment of S corporations, C corporations, and their respective shareholders. This indication of value is then adjusted with a DLOM based on the theoretical assumptions of the SEAM model.

Distributions and Their Impact on Value

Each model, one way or another, distinguishes for the level of distribution:

- Grabowski says to adjust to expected cash flow for noncontrolling interests, or treat income as being 100 percent distributed and take discounts for lack of control or illiquidity as appropriate.
- Mercer says that enterprise (marketable minority) value of *otherwise identical C and S corporations* are the same regardless of the level of distributions; however, the risks associated with receiving varying distributions at the shareholder level are considered by use of the QMDM, resulting in potential value differentials *from equivalent Cs making the same distribution*.
- Treharne makes value distinctions for each level of distribution.

- Van Vleet recognizes that the distributions for the subject company can impact value, and recognizes it through the extent of the lack of marketability discount.

Retained Net Income (Basis)

The analyst should consider the facts and circumstances of the particular situation, including consideration of the prospects for realizing the benefit of the retained net income. The facts of the particular interest would then dictate whether or not such inclusion was appropriate.

- Grabowski discounts the expected tax savings due to retained net income from a selected date in the future.
- Mercer estimates differing relative values to retained earnings shelter depending on expected distribution policies.
- Treharne has said that you need to consider the facts and circumstances and the likelihood of realizing the benefit of basis in the future.
- Van Vleet's SEAM model assumes that shareholders are indifferent between distributions and capital gains, which would be true for a publicly traded company. Therefore, the SEAM assumes that the subject S corporation is paying 100 percent of its earnings in distributions. To the extent that the subject S corporation is paying less than 100 percent of earnings, Van Vleet argues that the lack of marketability discount should be adjusted.

Recognizing Asset Amortization Benefit Currently

Grabowski alone says the asset amortization benefit should be considered where the facts indicate the entity may be sold at a reasonably foreseeable time in the future.

Discounts for Lack of Control and Lack of Marketability

Regardless of the model used, the business valuation analyst should consider what has already been taken into consideration by the application of the model itself.

- If the model begins with marketable minority cash flows, then there would be no apparent need to take a further discount for lack of control (unless there were other issues of control to be considered). However, a DLOM likely will be required.
- If the model starts with a controlling interest valuation, then the analyst should consider a DLOC, in addition to the lack of marketability.
- If there is an adjustment made for basis buildup, the analyst should consider the likelihood of its ever being realized.
- If the analyst makes an adjustment for step-up in basis (asset amortization benefit), the analyst should consider the possibly more remote likelihood of its ever being realized. Note that this can also be considered in the discount rate applied to the amortization benefit.

Questions to Ask When Valuing Noncontrolling Interest

An examination of the components of the models, and the points on which their applications differ, gives rise to the following questions for the analyst to consider:

- From what base am I going to start? Total C corporation? Identical minority C corporation interest making identical distributions?
- What tax advantage does the interest have over a comparable C corporation or interest in a C corporation?
- What is the distribution versus retention policy, and how does that impact value? Does the past policy reflect future expectations?
- What is the likely exit strategy of the hypothetical buyer, including:
  - What is the expected holding period?
  - Is there a reasonable chance that retained net income will be realized and that the buyer will pay for the ability to use and make use of the increased basis; if so, at what point in the future?
  - Is there a reasonable belief that an opportunity for step-up in the basis of assets exists for the hypothetical buyer, and if so, how do you measure that, and at what point in the future?

Each of these issues should be carefully considered and the valuation driven by the particular facts and circumstances of the interest being valued.

S CORPORATION CONTROLLING INTEREST APPRAISALS

Mercer and Treharne believe that the value differences between controlling interests in C and S corporations are minimal, if existent at all. Grabowski and Van Vleet believe that differences may exist, if an examination of the facts leads one to that conclusion.

The issues affecting controlling interest valuation include:

- Some empirical studies of C and S corporation transactions in the marketplace do not support the notion that S corporations are worth more than C corporations; in fact, they point to the opposite conclusion. However, given the complexity of corporate transaction structuring, not everyone agrees that this evidence is conclusive.
- A 100 percent ownership interest in an S corporation does not necessarily come with a bundle of rights and obligations attached to it any more than does a 100 percent ownership interest in a C corporation. This is distinctly different than a minority interest in an S corporation or a C corporation.
- The controlling shareholder can mimic the favorable tax characteristics of an S corporation (i.e., avoid the double-taxation disadvantage of C corporation dividends by paying additional salary). However, there are income tax regulations related to excess executive compensation that limit the ability of C corporation owners to pursue this strategy.
- Buyers will not pay for an election that they can make themselves for free, unless it has some value to them. Grabowski points out that in some instances it can, and says that buy-

ers will pay a premium for the possible benefits that come with an old-and-cold S corporation. Further, no buyer of less than absolute controlling interest in a C corporation can make an S corporation election unilaterally; any such election requires unanimous election of all shareholders.

- S corporations logically make distributions of funds necessary to support taxes on corporate earnings. This is no different from a C corporation; in either case, the money is gone and no longer available for corporate investment and growth.

The analyst must make an informed, thoughtful conclusion, taking into consideration the facts and circumstances of the company and the ownership interest being valued. If the analyst determines that a premium for S corporation status exists, he or she should be clear regarding its reasoning and derivation.

SUMMARY

This chapter has presented four reasoned theories for the valuation of S corporations and minority interests in them. They are each based on sound valuation theory, sound economic theory, and market evidence.

To value an S corporation ownership interest, the analyst first should determine if the subject is a controlling or minority interest.

- If the subject interest is a *minority interest*, the analyst should consider the minority interest valuation models presented and determine which one(s) best address(es) the specific facts and circumstances of the valuation assignment.
- If valuing a *controlling interest*, the experts generally agree that there may be no difference in value between S corporations and C corporations. Logically, the experts' consensus is that C corporation valuation methods may be used for valuing controlling ownership interests in S corporations.

Finally, the experts presented in this chapter agree that the change in tax basis attributable to retained earnings of an S corporation can affect the value of the S corporation equity security, yet they disagree as to where in the valuation process this characteristic should be considered. As a result, the analyst should evaluate the facts and circumstances surrounding the valuation assignment and be knowledgeable of the theoretical aspects of the various models presented in this chapter.

S CORPORATION VALUATION ISSUES—PARTIAL BIBLIOGRAPHY

We appreciate the efforts of Mercer Capital in providing the following comprehensive bibliography of articles that have appeared on the issue of S corporation valuation. This bibliography is presented in publication date sequence, through November 2004 (with the most recent articles appearing first).

Articles

Mercer, Z. Christopher, "Are S Corporations Worth More Than C Corporations?" *Business Valuation Review*, September 2004.

Grabowski, Roger J., "S Corporation Valuations in a Post-*Gross* World," *Business Valuation Review*, September 2004.

Treharne, Chris D., "Valuation of Minority Interests in Subchapter S Corporations," *Business Valuation Review*, September 2004.

Van Vleet, Daniel, "The S Corp Economic Adjustment Model," *Business Valuation Review*, September 2004.

Reto, James J. "A Simplified Method to Value an S Corp Minority Interest," *Shannon Pratt's Business Valuation Update*, July 2004.

Elam, Thomas E., "Quantifying the S Value Premium," *Business Appraisal Practice*, Summer 2004, pp. 26–34.

Phillips, John R., "S Corp. or C Corp.? M&A Deal Prices Look Alike," *Business Valuation Resources*, *Shannon Pratt's Business Valuation Update*, March 2004.

Treharne, Chris D., and Nancy J. Fannon, "Valuation of Pass-Through Tax Entities: Minority and Controlling Interests," S-Corp. Association, *www.S-Corp.org*, February 2004.

Van Vleet, Daniel, "The S Corporation Economic Adjustment Model Revisited," *Willamette's Insight*, Winter 2004.

Crow, Matthew R., and Brent A. McDade, "The Hypothetical Willing Seller: Maybe C Corporations Are Worth More Than S Corporations," *Mercer Capital's Value Matters*, November 26, 2003.

Vinso, Joseph, "Distributions and Entity Form: Do They Make a Difference in Value?" *Valuation Strategies*, September/October 2003.

Van Vleet, Daniel, "The Valuation of S Corporation Stock: The Equity Adjustment Multiple," *Pennsylvania Family Lawyer*, May–June 2003.

Pratt, Shannon, "Editor Attempts to Make Sense of S versus C Debate," *Business Valuation Resources*, *Shannon Pratt's Business Valuation Update*, March 2003.

Van Vleet, Daniel, "A New Way to Value S Corporation Securities," *Trusts & Estates*, March 2003.

Van Vleet, Daniel, "The Valuation of S Corporation Stock: The Equity Adjustment Multiple," *Willamette's Insight*, Winter 2003.

Erickson, Merle, and Shiing-wu Wang, "Response to the 'Erickson-Wang Myth,' " *Shannon Pratt's Business Valuation Update*, February 2003, pp. 1–5.

Alerding, R. James, Travis Chamberlain, and Yassir Karam, "S Corporation Premiums Revisited: The Erickson-Wang Myth," *Shannon Pratt's Business Valuation Update*, January 2003.

Finnerty, John D., "Adjusting the Comparable-Company Method for Tax Differences When Valuing Privately Held 'S' Corporations and LLCs," *Journal of Applied Finance*, Fall/Winter 2002, pp. 15–30.

Mattson, Michael, Donald Shannon, and Upton, David, "Part 2: Empirical Research Concludes S Corporation Values Same as C Corporations," *Shannon Pratt's Business Valuation Update*, December 2002.

Mattson, Michael, and Donald Shannon, "Part 1: Empirical Research Concludes S Corporation Values Same as C Corporations," *Shannon Pratt's Business Valuation Update*, November 2002.

Grabowski, Roger J., "S Corporation Valuations in the Post-*Gross* World," *Business Valuation Review*, September 2002, pp. 128–141.

Treharne, Chris D., "Comparing Three Payout Assumptions' Impact on Values of S versus C Corps," *Shannon Pratt's Business Valuation Update*, September 2002.

Mercer, Z. Christopher, and Travis W. Harms, "S Corporation Valuation in Perspective: A Response to the Article 'S Corporation Discount Rate Adjustment,' " *AICPA ABV E-Valuation Alert*, Volume 4, Issue 7, July 2, 2002.

Barad, Michael W., "S Corporation Discount Rate Adjustment," *AICPA ABV E-Valuation Alert*, Volume 4, Issue 6, June 3, 2002.

Mercer, Z. Christopher, "S Corporation Versus C Corporation Values," *Shannon Pratt's Business Valuation Update*, June 2002.

Jalbert, Terrance, "Pass-Through Taxation and the Value of the Firm," *American Business Review*, June 2002.

Reilly, Robert F., "S Corporation Commercial Bank Valuation Methods and Issues," *Valuation Strategies*, May/June 2002, pp. 28–33, 48.

Massey, Susan G., "How Do Unrealized Capital Gains Affect Valuation of S Corporation Stock?" *The Valuation Examiner*, May/June 2002, pp. 26–29.

Erickson, Merle, "Tax Benefits in Acquisitions of Privately Held Corporations: The Way Companies Are Organized for Tax Purposes Affects Their Selling Price in an Acquisition," *Capital Ideas*, Vol. 3, No. 3, Winter 2002, Chicago GSB.

Hawkins, George B., and Michael A. Paschall, "A Gross Result in the Gross Case: All Your Prior S Corporation Valuations Are Invalid," *Business Valuation Review*, March 2002, pp. 10–15.

Johnson, Owen T., "Letter to the Editor," *Business Valuation Review*, March 2002, pp. 44–45.

Burke, Brian H., "Letter to the Editor," *Business Valuation Review*, March 2002, p. 44.

Luttrell, Mark S., and Jeff W. Freeman, "Taxes and the Undervaluation of 'S' Corporations," *American Journal of Family Law*, Winter 2001, pp. 301–306.

Johnson, Owen T., "Letter to the Editor," *Business Valuation Review*, December 2001, p. 56.

Finkel, Sidney R., "Is There an S Corporation Premium?" *Valuation Strategies*, July/August 2001, pp. 14–27.

Burke, Brian H., "The Impact of S Corporation Status on Fair Market Value," *Business Valuation Review*, June 2001, pp. 15–24.

Barber, Gregory A., "Valuation of Pass-Through Entities," *Valuation Strategies*, March/April 2001, pp. 4–11, 44–45.

Erickson, Merle, "To Elect or Not to Elect, That Is the Tax Question," Capital Ideas, Volume 2, No. 4, Winter 2001.

Buckley, Allen, Crouse, Lynda M., and Kniesel, Greg, "S Corporation ESOPs in Dispositive Sales and Reorganization Transactions," *Valuation Strategies*, January/February 2001, pp. 20–29, 46–48.

Bowles, Tyler J., and W. Cris Lewis, "Tax Considerations in Valuing Nontaxable Entities," *Business Valuation Review*, December 2000, pp. 175–185.

Giardina, Edward, "The Gross Decision Revisited," *Business Valuation Review*, December 2000, pp. 213–218.

Sonneman, Donald, "Business Valuation Controversies and Choices: Understanding Them and Their Impact (Controversy No. 7)," *Business Valuation Review*, June 2000, p. 85.

Wiggins, C. Donald, S. Mark Hand, and Laura L. Coogan, "The Economic Impact of Taxes on S Corporation Valuations," *Business Valuation Review*, June 2000, pp. 88–94.

Reto, James J., "Are S Corporations Entitled to Valuation Discounts for Embedded Capital Gains?" *Valuation Strategies*, January/February 2000, pp. 6–9, 48.

Light, David C., and Richard C. May, "Stock Valuation Issues for S Corporation ESOPS," *Shannon Pratt's Business Valuation Update*, August 1999.

Miller, Scott D., "New Opportunities for ESOP's—Subchapter S Corporations," *Valuation Examiner*, February/March 1999.

Sliwoski, Leonard, "Reflections on Valuing S Corporations," *Business Valuation Review*, December 1998, pp. 141–146.

Avener, Leslie, "An Appraiser Looks at *Davis v. Commissioner*," *Business Valuation Review*, September 1998, pp. 72–78.

Gasiorowski, John R., "Tax Basis Does Matter in the Valuation of Asset Holding Companies," *Business Valuation Review*, September 1998, pp. 79–84.

Serro, James A, "Valuing C-Corporations versus S-Corporations," *Valuation Examiner*, June/July 1998.

Julius, J. Michael, "Converting Distributions from S Corporations and Partnerships to C Corporation Dividend Equivalent Basis," *Business Valuation Review*, June 1997, pp. 65–67.

Graber, Adrian, "Business Valuations for S Corporation Elections," *Business Valuation Review*, December 1996, pp. 174–175.

Dufendach, David C., "Valuation of Closely Held Corporations: 'C' vs. 'S' Differentials," *Business Valuation Review*, December 1996, pp. 176–179.

Johnson, Bruce A., "Tax Treatment When Valuing S-Corporations Using the Income Approach," *Business Valuation Review*, June 1995, pp. 83–85.

Kramer, Yale, "Letter to the Editor," *Business Valuation Review*, December 1994, p. 177.

Sliwoski, Leonard J., "Capitalization Rates Developed Using the Ibbotson Associates Data: Should They Be Applied to Pre-tax or Aftertax Earnings?" *Business Valuation Review*, March 1994, pp. 8–10.

Cassiere, George G., "The Value of S-Corp Election—The C-Corp Equivalency Model," *Business Valuation Review*, June 1994, pp. 84–95.

Duffy, Robert E., and George L. Johnson, "Valuation of 'S' Corporations Revisited: The Impact of the Life of an 'S' Election Under Varying Growth and Discount Rates," *Business Valuation Review*, December 1993, pp. 155–167.

Condren, Gary, "S Corporations and Corporate Taxes," *Business Valuation Review*, December 1993, pp. 168–171.

Fowler, Bradley A., "How Do You Handle It?," *Business Valuation Review*, March 1992, p. 39.

Leung, T.S. Tony, "Letter to the Editor," *Business Valuation Review*, March 1991, p. 41–42.

Kato, Kelly, "Valuation of 'S' Corporations Discounted Cash Flow Method," *Business Valuation Review*, December 1990, pp. 117–122.

Gilbert, Gregory, "Letter to the Editor," *Business Valuation Review*, June 1989, pp. 92–93.

Hempstead, John E., "Letter to the Editor," *Business Valuation Review*, March 1989, p. 42.

Shackelford, Aaron L., "Valuation of 'S' Corporations," *Business Valuation Review*, December 1988, pp. 159–162.

Leung, T.S. Tony, "Tax Reform Act of 1986: Considerations for Business Valuators," *Business Valuation Review*, June 1987, pp. 60–61.

Books

Mercer, Z. Christopher, *Valuing Enterprise and Shareholder Cash Flows: The Integrated Theory of Business Valuation* (Memphis, TN: Peabody Publishing, LP, 2004).

Van Vleet, Daniel, Chapter 4: "The S Corporation Economic Adjustment," *The Handbook of Business Valuation and Intellectual Property Analysis* (New York: Reilly/Schweihs, McGraw-Hill, 2004).

Grabowski, Roger J., and William McFadden, Chapter 5: "Applying the Income Approach to S Corporation and Other Pass-Through Entity Valuations" *The Handbook of Business Valuation and Intellectual Property Analysis* (New York: Reilly/Schweihs, McGraw-Hill, 2004).

Hitchner, James R., *Financial Valuation: Application and Models* (New York: John Wiley & Sons, 2003).

Pratt, Shannon P., Robert F. Reilly, and Robert P. Schweihs, *Valuing a Business*, 4th ed. (New York: McGraw-Hill, 2000), pp. 568–569.

Trugman, Gary R., *Understanding Business Valuation* (New York: AICPA, 1998), pp. 197–199.

Reilly, Robert F., and Robert P. Schweihs, Chapter 6: "S Corporations—Premium or Discount," *The Handbook of Advanced Business Valuation* (New York: Reilly/Schweihs, McGraw-Hill, 1999), pp. 119–138.

Mercer, Z. Christopher, *Quantifying Marketability Discounts* (Memphis, TN: Peabody Publishing, LP, 1997), pp. 233–239.

Pratt, Shannon P., Reilly, Robert F., and Schweihs, Robert P., *Valuing a Business*, 3rd ed. (New York: Irwin, 1996), pp. 518–520.

Walker, Donna J., Chapter 24: "S Corporations," *Valuing Small Businesses and Professional Practices*, 2nd ed. (Pratt/Reilly/Schweihs, Business One Irwin, New York, 1993), pp. 345–356.

Presentations

Mercer, Z. Christopher, Daniel Van Vleet, Chris D. Treharne, and Nancy J. Fannon, "Valuation of Pass-Through Entities," Presented to the American Institute of Certified Public Accountants, November, 2004.

Treharne, Chris D., James Hitchner, and Nancy J. Fannon, "Valuation of Pass-Through Entities," Presented to the American Society of Appraisers' Advanced Business Valuation Conference, October 8, 2004.

Crow, Matthew R., and Daniel Van Vleet, "S Corporation Valuation Issues," Presented to the Business Valuation Association of Chicago, September 22, 2004.

Van Vleet, Daniel, Chris D. Treharne, and James Hitchner, "S Corporation Valuation Issues," Shannon Pratt's Business Valuation Update Audio Conference, June 29, 2004.

Treharne, Chris D., James Hitchner, and Nancy J. Fannon, "Valuation of Pass-Through Entities, Presented to the Institute of Business Appraisers Conference, Las Vegas, NV, June 10, 2004.

Van Vleet, Daniel, "The S Corporation Economic Adjustment Model," Presented to the Institute of Business Appraisers Conference, Las Vegas, NV, June 10, 2004.

Treharne, Chris, James Hitchner, and Nancy J. Fannon, "Valuation of Pass-Through Entities: What's All the Fuss?" Presented to the American Institute of Certified Public Accountants, November 2003.

Grabowski, Roger, Z. Christopher Mercer, and Daniel Van Vleet, "S Corporation Valuation Issues," Presented to the American Society of Appraisers' Advanced Business Valuation Conference, October 17, 2003.

Mercer, Z. Christopher, "S Corporation Valuation Issues," Presented to the American Bar Association S Corporation Committee Mid-Year Meeting, January 24, 2003.

Mercer, Z. Christopher, "S Corporation Valuation," Presented to the Business Valuation Association of Chicago, September 19, 2002.

Bajaj, Mukesh, Z. Christopher Mercer, and George Hawkins, "Tax-Affecting S Corporation Earnings for the Purpose of Valuing Stock," Business Valuation Resources Audio Conference, August 13, 2002.

Mercer, Z. Christopher, and Joseph D. Vinso, "S Corporation Valuation," Presented to the American Society of Appraisers' 2002 International Appraisal Conference, August 27, 2002.

Griswald, Terrence, Z. Christopher Mercer, and Richard Schleuter, "Are S Corporations Worth More Than C Corporations," Presented to the New York City Chapter of the ASA's Current Topics in Business Valuations—2002 Conference, New York, NY, May 9, 2002.

Johnson, Bruce A., "S Corporation Tax Treatment," Presented to the 2001 International Appraisal Conference of the American Society of Appraisers, Pittsburgh, PA, July 25, 2001.

Walker, Donna J., "S Corporation Valuation for ESOPS," Presented to the 2001 International Appraisal Conference of the American Society of Appraisers, Pittsburgh, PA, July 24, 2001.

Crow, Matthew R., "Are S Corporations Worth More?," Presented to the New York City Chapter of the ASA's Current Topics in Business Valuations—2000 Conference, New York, NY, May 5, 2000.

Smith, Philip M., "The Continuing Subchapter S Controversy," Presented to the 1998 International Appraisal Conference of the American Society of Appraisers, Maui, HI, June 24, 1998.

Wilusz, Edward A., "Does the S Corporation Election Create Value?" Presented to the 15th Annual Advanced Business Valuation Conference of the American Society of Appraisers, Memphis, TN, October 10, 1996.

Danyluk, Anne, "Valuing S Corporations: A Look at Adjustments," Presented to the 1991 International Appraisal Conference of the American Society of Appraisers, Philadelphia, PA, June 18, 1991.

Chapter 9

Valuation of International Transactions[1]

SUMMARY

International transactions present valuation issues principally in two contexts: when the convoluted transfer pricing rules of Code section 482 are implicated, and when businesses attempt to import goods into the United States and must value them for customs duties.

Section 482 is designed to prevent related entities from artificially shifting income, expenses, or deductions between themselves, and thereby avoiding federal income tax. Section 482 allows the Service to reapportion income between related entities to reflect the amount of tax that would have been paid had the entities been unrelated. To do so, the Service asserts the entities were subject to common control, and as a result the value of the transaction was different from the value of an uncontrolled, arm's-length transaction.

Section 482 applies to transactions involving the international transfer of tangible property, intangible property, loans, advances, and services. While we will focus on section 482's effect on valuation of intellectual property rights that are transferred internationally,

---

[1]This chapter was contributed by L. Richard Walton, Esq., of Chain, Younger, Cohn & Stiles.

the principles relating to valuation of intellectual property also apply to other types of section 482 property, since the basic arm's-length standard remains the same.

In determining the appropriate price for an arm's-length, uncontrolled transaction, one of four methods may be used:

1. Comparable uncontrolled transaction
2. Comparable profits
3. Profit split
4. An *unspecified method*, a catchall provision permitting use of any reasonable method

No one method is preferred, although the first is usually thought to give the best results. A result under any of the methods may be subject to collateral and periodic adjustments. Valuers may also be asked to apportion value between the owner and any other controlled entities that assisted the owner in developing the intellectual property.

Customs valuation is standardized among countries pursuant to treaty, with each country applying one of six valuation methods to determine the value of imported goods for the purpose of imposing duties. These valuation methods, in descending order of preference, follow:

6. Transaction value of the imported goods, with adjustments
5. Transaction value of identical merchandise, with adjustments
4. Transaction value of similar merchandise, with adjustments
3. Resale price after importation (deductive value), with adjustments
2. Computed value, using production costs, profit, and overhead, with adjustments
1. Derived value

INTRODUCTION

International transactions raise complex valuation issues, requiring the valuer to understand relevant tax laws and revenue goals, as well as valuation methods. Valuation issues in international transactions revolve around the twin concepts of equality and reciprocity. We will consider valuation of intellectual property under Code section 482, and valuation of imported goods under the *Agreement on Implementation of Article VII of the General Agreement on Tariffs and Trade* (the "Customs Valuation Agreement").

Under section 482, the United States seeks to promote equality in taxation by preventing domestic corporations from shifting income offshore to foreign corporations, and thereby avoiding payment of federal income tax. Under the Customs Valuation Agreement (a treaty), signatory countries guarantee reciprocity in valuation methods so that every country values goods in the same way when determining the amount of import duties.[2]

---

[2]I.R.C. § 1059A states that a determination of value for section 482 purposes also fixes the value for Customs. This reasonable and clear policy is modified by several Service pronouncements that arguably allow different valuations under section 482 and the Customs Valuation Agreement, so long as they are not unreasonably different.

TRANSFER PRICING

The purpose of section 482 is to prevent taxpayers from shifting income between entities that they control, thereby reducing their federal income tax. In the context of international taxes, section 482 applies when U.S. businesses attempt to shift their income to controlled foreign entities.

To understand how this could happen, assume you are the best-selling author of 13 books. You assign all of your copyrights to your Delaware corporation, thereby shifting royalty income to the corporation. At dinner one evening with your friend, an Irish author, you discover that Ireland has a 12 percent income tax rate, as opposed to the 35 percent you are paying in the United States.

You form a second corporation in Ireland, selling all of your past copyrights to the Irish corporation in exchange for a note, but maintaining your Delaware corporation so you can copyright your new work in the United States. Absent section 482, this clever bit of planning could save you 23 percent a year in income tax.

Section 482 seeks to avoid this result and, under the principle of equality, effectively taxes such a transaction as if you left your copyrights in Delaware. Under section 482, the Service will reapportion income between corporations with the same owner so as to accurately reflect income. When two corporations transfer intellectual property between themselves, thereby shifting income and avoiding federal income tax, valuers will be called upon to determine a reasonable price for the intellectual property under section 482. The transferor must recognize income in that amount.

The problem becomes more complex when there are multiple transfers between parent and subsidiary, involving both intellectual property and tangible goods. Where the parent buys a finished product from its foreign subsidiary, and the foreign subsidiary licenses intellectual property rights from the parent that are used in the creation of the finished product, the valuer must separate the tangible goods purchase by the parent from the intellectual property license by the subsidiary. Each has independent significance and must be separately analyzed to determine if both parent and subsidiary reflect the proper amount of income.[3] In other words, you cannot net Irish sub's royalty payments against parent's transfer payment for the finished product—you must separately determine that each is fair and reasonably priced.

Section 482 is designed to equate controlled transactions with noncontrolled transactions. Thus, it applies only when two or more business entities:

1. Are under common control, *and*
2. Reallocation of income or deduction is necessary to reflect each entity's proper income, or to prevent an evasion of federal income tax.[4]

First, the Service must show that the two entities are subject to common control. This is a practical inquiry, concerned with whether the common controller exercised practical, rather than theoretical, control when the transaction in question was negotiated. Thus, *common*

---

[3]*Bausch & Lomb, Inc. v. Comm'r*, 933 F.2d 1084, 1093 (2d Cir. 1991).
[4]*Local Finance Corp. v. Comm'r*, 407 F.2d 629 (7th Cir. 1969).

control is determined on a transactional basis, and the valuer must determine what control was actually used in the transaction.[5]

The presence of a third party in negotiations is not dispositive on the common control issue. In one case, the subsidiary was granted an option to purchase the parent's trademark as part of an acquisition of the subsidiary by a third party. Although the third-party purchaser was present during the negotiations between parent and subsidiary regarding the option price, the court found that it had no interest in the transaction and was thus not a reliable check to ensure that the price for the trademark was equivalent to what would be paid in an arm's-length transaction. In fact, the court hypothesized, the purchaser's goal could be to have the subsidiary pay as little as possible for the trademark, an interest congruent with the parent's interest in minimizing federal income tax by artificially lowering the option's strike price.[6]

The inquiry is whether corporations were subject to common control such that the price paid was less than that which would have been paid had the transaction been at arm's length. There is no formula for determining this, but common sense is applied to a range of factors:

- Common management
- *Percentage of holdings in each company.* Such percentages need not be a simple majority of shares, so long as the owner exercises practical control of business decisions, such that the transaction was not arm's length.
- *Relationship between owners.* Familial relationship is not necessarily sufficient to establish common control, so long as there is no plan to shift income, and family members do not cross-own interests in each other's businesses. However, where businesses are intertwined and mutually dependent, relationship between owners is sufficient.
- *Retention of interests.* Owners must be heavily involved in the business after it is sold or changes form; otherwise, retention of ownership is not sufficient to subject the owners to section 482.
- Parent/subsidiary relationship

If the Service establishes common control *during the transaction in question* by showing one or more of these factors, it must then assert that such common control resulted in a deal different from that which would have resulted from an uncontrolled transaction between an arm's-length buyer and seller. The question is whether the transaction—in both price and terms—was substantially similar to a transaction where there was not common control of the buyer and seller. If the Service determines that the transaction was *not* substantially similar, the taxpayer bears the burden of showing that the Service's determination was arbitrary or capricious—a difficult but not insurmountable task.

An example would be HAC, the financing subsidiary of automaker HM. When HM obtains a loan from HAC, section 482 asks whether the contract is identical in terms and interest rate to what HM could obtain from an unrelated financing company. If the answer is no, the two-part test of section 482 has been met: There is common control, which has influenced the deal, and some of HAC's profit is transferred to HM via favorable loan terms. Since HM pays

---

[5]*DHL Corp. v. Comm'r*, 285 F.3d 1210 (9th Cir. 2002).
[6]Id at 1210, 1219.

less for the loan than it otherwise would have, its profits are artificially inflated, and the Commissioner may reallocate some of HM's profits to HAC.[7]

In the context of international transfers of intellectual property between related parties, the second prong of section 482's two-part test raises the following issues:

- What valuation methods may be used?
- Which is the best method in a given circumstance?
- What adjustments should be made to the valuation?
- How does one apportion value between joint holders of intellectual property?[8]

Methods

Arm's-length value of intellectual property must be commensurate with the income attributable to the intellectual property.[9] Where the payment is made in a lump sum, the sum must be equal to the present value of the stream of royalties anticipated over the life of the intellectual property.[10] There are four methods that may be used to determine this amount: comparable uncontrolled transaction, comparable profits, profit split, and unspecified methods.

Comparable Uncontrolled Transaction

Valuers will find this market-comparables method the easiest one to employ, as it requires a comparable, but not identical, transaction between an uncontrolled buyer and seller, with adjustments for differences.

Consider the previous example of HM. Assume HM licensed its MetroHopper trademark to an unrelated company in China 10 years ago as part of a pre-WTO transfer of intellectual property. In exchange, HM receives 3 percent of all Chinese gross sales. This year, HM licenses the same MetroHopper trademark to a related subsidiary in Poland. As long as the license fee was 3 percent of gross Polish sales, HM could argue that its valuation of the Polish license was reasonable under the market comparables method.

Reliability of this method increases as the uncontrolled transaction becomes more similar to the controlled transaction. For instance, if the two transactions had different contractual terms or occurred under different economic conditions, adjustments would have to be made to the uncontrolled value, and reliability of the method is decreased.

At least ten factors influence comparability:

1. Whether the intellectual properties were used in connection with similar products or processes

---

[7]We assume for purposes of the illustration that the interest rate charged by HAC is below the Applicable Federal Rate. There is a safe harbor for such loans, and the Service will not challenge transactions where the interest rate is equal to or greater than a specified percentage of the Applicable Federal Rate. If the interest rate is below this number, however, the arm's-length test applies.

[8]The following rules apply to taxable years after 1993. While pre-1993 Regulations are of historic interest, they are unlikely to be relevant to current valuations and thus are not discussed in this chapter.

[9]Reg. § 1.482-4(a).

[10]Reg. § 1.482-4(f)(5)(i).

2. Whether the intellectual properties have similar profit potential

3. Whether the terms of transfer are the same

4. What stage of development each property is in

5. Whether there are similar rights to receive updates

6. The uniqueness of the properties, and the comparative periods for which the properties will remain unique

7. The duration of the grant of use

8. Comparative economic and product-liability risks assumed by the purchaser

9. The existence and extent of any collateral transactions or business relationship between the buyer and seller

10. The functions to be performed by the transferor and transferee[11]

A prior transfer of the same intellectual property to an uncontrolled party may serve as the comparable transaction. However, an alleged arm's-length transaction may not be used as a comparable if it was not made in the ordinary course of business or if one of its principal purposes was to establish an arm's-length result for purposes of section 482.[12]

Thus, the valuer will ideally find an identical arm's-length transaction that can be used to directly value the controlled transaction. Failing this, the valuer should locate a similar transaction and make adjustments to it as necessary to reflect differences in the factors just listed.

Comparable Profits

This method requires the valuer to apply an objective measure of profitability, derived from uncontrolled taxpayers with similar businesses, to the controlled transaction. Applying an uncontrolled profit margin to "the most narrowly identifiable business activity" for which data are available will theoretically determine the uncontrolled value of the transaction.[13] Although this standard may, at first blush, seem difficult to apply to a transfer, recall that section 482 equates sales price with the income attributable to the intellectual property. Thus, by projecting the profit derived from the intellectual property and discounting it to present value, the valuer can determine uncontrolled value.

In reality, the comparable profits method can only be used in hindsight, and thus is almost inevitably used solely for litigation purposes.

Using the previous HM example, the comparable profits method could only be applied *after* the Polish license had generated revenue. HM could not use it to prospectively value the transaction, since profits data simply is not available. The Service and HM can, however, use the method in fighting over the value of the deal years later when the transaction is challenged and profits figures are available. Thus, if HM's license in China had a net operating profit of 5 to 6 percent of sales, and its Polish license net operating profits were roughly comparable, HM would have a good argument that the deal was fair.

---

[11]Reg. § 1.482-4(c)(2)(iii).
[12]Reg. § 1.482-1(d)(4)(iii).
[13]Reg. § 1.482-5(b)(1).

Two profit-level indicators may be used:

1. Rate of return on capital employed. Here, the valuer would determine the rate of return (or cost savings) as against the book value of the intellectual property.
2. Various financial ratios, including operating profit/sales, gross profit/operating expenses, and other ratios that accurately reflect the uncontrolled income and which do not rely solely on internal data.

Use of any profit-level indicator requires a close analysis of comparability between the uncontrolled taxpayer and the controlled taxpayer to determine that the same relationships hold true for both. To the extent that the uncontrolled taxpayer differs from the controlled taxpayer, adjustments must be made. However, as similarity decreases, all factors considered, the reliability of the analysis will rapidly decline—perhaps indicating that another method is more appropriate. All relevant differences between the two entities must be considered, including differing accounting methods, management efficiency, cost structures, and risks, to name a few.[14]

Profit Split Method

Where more than one controlled taxpayer contributes to the overall profitability of the intellectual property, the profit split method is appropriate. Where intellectual property is partially transferred, but the seller continues to contribute to, or benefit from, its profitability (by, for instance, manufacturing the product or exploiting the trademark), the profit split method determines what each controlled taxpayer contributes to the combined operating profit or cost savings, and whether the apportionment of profit is comparable to an arm's-length apportionment.

To find the comparability of profit apportionment between controlled and uncontrolled taxpayers, the valuer must establish the value of each controlled taxpayer's contribution to the intellectual property. Such a determination must reflect the functions each performs, the risks each assumes, and the resources each employs.

If the arm's-length apportionment of profits does not equate with the actual apportionment, the Service may seek to reallocate income from the intellectual property, and therefore revalue the transfer price. As already discussed, section 482 equates the price of the option with the present value of its projected stream of earnings. Thus, an apportionment of profit dissimilar to the uncontrolled apportionment will result in a different value for the intellectual property.

One of two methods is available under profit splitting, but only one is likely to be employed in allocating profit when intellectual property is involved.

Comparable profit split determines what percentage of the combined operating profit or cost savings each uncontrolled taxpayer receives from using the same, or substantially the same, intellectual property. Like the previous methods, profit split relies on external industry benchmarks, and the reliability of the analysis decreases as the comparability between the external transaction and the controlled transaction decreases. All of the comparability factors listed for the previous methods should be considered, especially the contractual relationship between the uncontrolled taxpayers.

Residual profit split will probably never be applicable to intellectual property valuation,

---

[14]Reg. § 1.482-5.

as it applies to profit-splitting situations where the controlled taxpayers are contributing intellectual property as part of a larger shifting of income. It thus uses a two-step process. First, income is allocated to routine contributions by the controlled parties so as to provide them with a market return on their routine contributions. (*Routine contributions* are those contributions similar to ones made by uncontrolled taxpayers. The valuer performs a functional analysis to determine what each party contributes to create revenue. Market returns are then applied to each of these categories of contribution.) Second, residual profit is allocated based on the fair market value, or capitalized cost of development, of the intangible property contributed.[15]

Reliability and comparability will be determined using the factors discussed in the Comparable Uncontrolled Transactions section, earlier in this chapter.

Unspecified Methods

This is the catchall valuation provision, permitting the use of any reasonable method not specified in the Regulations. The basic guideline for determining when a method is reasonable is whether the method provides information on the prices and profits of realistic alternatives to the controlled transaction. This is based on the premise that taxpayers choose to enter into transactions after considering realistic alternatives. If the taxpayer's valuation is outside the arm's-length range, discussed *infra*, the Service may reallocate income. To the extent that the method relies on internal data, its reliability is reduced.[16]

Arm's-Length Range

Given the uncertainties associated with valuation, the Regulations recognize that application of a single method may produce more than one result. An example of this would be the existence of several similar transactions when using the comparable uncontrolled transactions method. If each of the comparables has a different value, the valuation result will be a range of possible values.

If the price paid falls within this range, there will be no section 482 reallocation. If each of the valuation results is not sufficiently reliable, statistical methods can be applied to adjust the range and increase reliability to the 75th percentile. If the price is outside the arm's-length range, the Service can adjust the price to any value within the range.[17]

Choice of Method: The Best-Method Rule

There is no priority of methods: Any method may be used so long as it is reliable. The court will apply whichever method is deemed the most reliable for the transaction in question. When more than one of the methods could be applied, or there is more than one way to apply a single method, a transaction between unrelated parties is the benchmark of reliability.

In determining the best method, the two factors that must be considered are the degree of comparability between the controlled transaction and any uncontrolled comparables, and the

---

[15]Reg. § 1.482-6.
[16]Reg. § 1.482-4(d).
[17]Reg. § 1.482-1(e)(2).

quality of data used and its analysis. When relevant, the valuer will also want to consider whether the results under one method are consistent with the results under another.

As the controlled and uncontrolled transactions become less comparable, the normal presumption that the uncontrolled transaction method is the most reliable will be weakened, making it more likely that another method will apply. Other factors to consider are the completeness and accuracy of the underlying data, the reliability of the assumptions used, and the sensitivity of the result to possible deficiencies in data or assumptions. Deficiencies can be corrected to some extent with adjustments, but the court's inquiry is a broad one, encompassing both comparability of the transactions and reliability of the method as applied to the transaction.[18]

Given these imponderables, savvy valuers will use more than one method to ensure that, should the court not find their method of choice the most reliable, the valuation will still be accepted.

Adjustments

There are two types of adjustments that can be made to a section 482 valuation: collateral adjustments and periodic adjustments.

Collateral Adjustments

Collateral adjustments are made once the difference between the controlled and uncontrolled transactions is calculated. There are three types of collateral adjustments: correlative allocations, conforming adjustments, and setoffs.

Correlative allocations are balancing adjustments where the Service reallocates income from one corporation to another. In the preceding example, if the Service reallocates income to HM, then there must be a correlative allocation reducing the income of HAC.[19]

Conforming accounts to reflect section 482 allocations determines the nature of income that is reallocated. If HM's income is increased by $5 million, the Service must classify the nature of the increase—capital gains, ordinary income, and so on. In this case, HM could petition under Rev. Proc. 65-17 for the increase to be treated as an account receivable, due on the last day of the year of the transaction, with interest accruing.[20]

Setoffs occur when there are other non-arm's-length transactions between the controlled taxpayers. Such transactions are netted for purposes of computing the total tax owed.[21]

Periodic Adjustments

Where intellectual property is transferred under an agreement extending beyond one year, the consideration charged for it in each taxable year may be adjusted to equate the compensation recognized with the income realized. All relevant factors are considered in determining whether to adjust the original amount of compensation in subsequent years, and periodic

---

[18]Reg. § 1.482-1(c).
[19]Reg. § 1.482-1(g)(2).
[20]Reg. § 1.482-1(g)(3).
[21]Reg. § 1.482-1(g)(4).

adjustments may be made even where the transaction was considered equivalent to an arm's-length transaction in years past.[22]

Periodic adjustments may not be used under these conditions:[23]

- Basis for uncontrolled transaction method was transfer of same property with similar terms to an uncontrolled taxpayer.
- Basis for uncontrolled transaction method was comparable property transferred under comparable circumstances, where there was a written agreement setting forth an arm's-length amount of consideration in the first year and limiting use of the intellectual property to a specified purpose, there were no substantial changes in the functions performed by the controlled transferee, the aggregate profits were not less than 80 percent and not more than 120 percent of foreseeable profits, and the controlled agreement was substantially the same as the uncontrolled agreement.
- Under any method other than the uncontrolled transaction method, there was a written agreement setting forth an arm's-length amount of consideration in the first year, with no substantial changes in the functions performed by the controlled transferee, and the aggregate profits were not less than 80 percent and not more than 120 percent of foreseeable profits.
- Extraordinary events beyond the control of the taxpayers make the actual profits less than 80 percent, or greater than 120 percent, of the reasonably expected profit, and all of the other requirements of the second and third conditions are met.
- Lapse of a five-year period during which all of the requirements of the second and third conditions are met.

Any one of these exceptions will bar periodic adjustments, but valuers must be wary of future income altering the value of a controlled international transfer of intellectual property.

Apportioning Value among Joint Holders

Lastly, we address the issue of how one apportions value between joint owners of intellectual property. Given its ease of assignment, it is not uncommon for several people to claim ownership of intellectual property. No allocation of value is made until transfer, at which time the valuer must determine how to divide the total value of the intellectual property among its various owners.

Specifically, the Regulation provides:

> *If another controlled taxpayer provides assistance to the owner in connection with the development or enhancement of an intangible, such person may be entitled to receive consideration with respect to such assistance.*[24]

The problem is, of course, identifying the owner. Where intellectual property is legally protected, the legal owner is deemed to be the owner for tax purposes. The Service may im-

---

[22]Reg. § 1.482-4(f)(2).
[23]Reg. § 1.482-4(f)(2)(ii).
[24]Reg. § 1.482-4(f)(3).

pute an agreement to transfer ownership where the conduct of the parties suggests that such was their intent. Where intellectual property is not legally protected, its developer will be considered the owner. If two people jointly develop intellectual property, there can be only one owner for purposes of the statute. The owner will be whichever developer bore the largest portion of the direct and indirect costs of development, absent an agreement to the contrary that was entered into before the success of the project became known.

Once the owner is determined, valuers know who will bear the primary burden of reallocation. However, people who assisted in developing the intellectual property will also be subject to reallocation, receiving an amount sufficient to repay the arm's-length value of their contributions, except for routine expense items that would have been incurred regardless of the development. The value of such contributions must be determined using one of the four methods previously described.[25]

CUSTOMS VALUATION

The purpose of the Customs Valuation Agreement, a treaty among signatory countries that prescribes five possible valuation methods for taxes on imported goods, is to provide reciprocity between nations when they impose import duties. By using the same valuation methods in every signatory country, countries avoid having valuation become a tool for trade wars. Further, corporations can predict their cost of doing business in another country, as the import duties they will have to pay will be easily predicted: Using the same valuation methods, each country then applies its own *ad valorem* import duty to the product. This takes much of the uncertainty out of predicting the cost of exporting products, thereby encouraging trade.

There are six possible valuation methods:

1. *Transaction value of the imported goods*, with adjustments for certain costs. This is the primary method. When it is inapplicable, one of the following will be employed, in descending order of preference.
2. *Transaction value of identical merchandise*, with adjustments so as to approximate the primary method
3. *Transaction value of similar merchandise*, with adjustments so as to approximate the primary method
4. *Resale price after importation* ("deductive value"), with adjustments so as to approximate the primary method
5. *Computed value*, using production costs, profit, and overhead, with adjustments so as to approximate the primary method
6. *Derived value*, which is a formula derived from an otherwise unacceptable method, using reasonable adjustments[26]

We consider each in turn.

---

[25]Reg. § 1.482-4(f)(3).
[26]19 U.S.C. § 1401a.

Transaction Value

Under the primary standard, goods should be priced at the actual quantity and level of trade, not at usual wholesale quantities. There are five permissible additions to price:[27]

1. Packing costs incurred by the buyer
2. Selling commission incurred by the buyer
3. Apportioned value of any assists (see discussion *infra*)
4. Any royalty or license fee the buyer must pay (see discussion *infra*)
5. Proceeds from any subsequent sale, which are payable to the seller

In addition, three items must be deducted from the market price of goods:[28]

1. Any reasonable costs incurred for construction, assemblage, maintenance, and so on, of the good after importation
2. Any reasonable cost for transportation following importation
3. Any U.S. Customs duties or other import taxes, or any federal excise taxes

Transaction value is the preferred valuation method. There are times, however, when this method may *not* be used:[29]

- There are no restrictions on the buyer regarding the disposition or use of the imported goods, except restrictions that are imposed by law on the geographical area of resale or that do not substantially affect value.
- The price of the goods is subject to any condition or consideration for which a value cannot be determined when the goods are imported. For instance, where the goods are part of an overall package deal that artificially lowers the price of the goods in question, the transaction value method may not be used.
- The proceeds from disposal or use by the buyer are in any way payable to the seller.
- The parties are related, unless the relationship between the parties did not influence the price, or the actual price derived from this method closely approximates the value derived from other methods. Thus, where it can be shown that the parties dealt at arm's length, the primary method may be used. In this situation, section 482, discussed *supra*, also comes into play. Unfortunately for the taxpayer, the interests of the Service and of Customs are diametrically opposed. The Service is concerned with inflated values that reduce income by increasing cost of goods sold. Customs is worried about values being understated so as to avoid import duties. The loser is, predictably, the taxpayer, although the two agencies have indicated a willingness to work together to achieve a common valuation.[30]

---

[27]19 U.S.C. § 1401a(b).
[28]19 U.S.C. § 1401a(b)(3).
[29]19 U.S.C. § 1401a(b)(2)(A).
[30]Customs Hq. Ruling 546879 (August 30, 2000).

Transaction Value of Identical Merchandise

Under this method, valuers may consider the price of any identical merchandise produced in the same country, by the same or a different manufacturer. Additions and deductions are identical to those used for the primary method. In addition, an adjustment must be made for any differences in commercial and quantity levels between the identical merchandise and the merchandise being imported. If there are several different values for identical merchandise, the lowest value should be used.[31]

Transaction Value of Similar Merchandise

This method is identical to the transaction value of identical merchandise method discussed *supra*, with the only difference being the use of *similar merchandise*. Similar merchandise is merchandise produced in the same country by the same or a different person, similar in nature to, and commercially interchangeable with, the goods being imported. Factors that must be considered in determining whether the merchandise is similar are: the quality of the merchandise, its reputation, and whether it is trademarked.[32]

Resale Price after Importation

Deductive value is the price at which the imported goods, identical goods, or similar goods (in that order of preference) will be resold in the United States, with adjustments, and factoring in the condition of the goods on resale and the time of resale. This is determined by looking at the unit price for which the goods are sold in the greatest quantity. To illustrate, assume the following facts:

Quantity	Unit Price
2,000	$10
2,500	$15
1,200	$17
3,300	$20
3,900	$15
5,700	$ 9

Here, the deductive value unit price would be $15, as the highest quantity of goods sold is at $15 (2,500 + 3,900 = 6,400).

Four items must be deducted from this amount:

1. Commissions, importer's profits, and/or general expenses included in the unit price (taken from the importer's figures, unless such figures are not congruent with industry standards)

---

[31]19 U.S.C. § 1401a(c) & (h).
[32]Id.

2. Transportation and insurance costs related to shipping the goods from a foreign country to their destination point in the United States

3. Customs duties and other federal taxes incurred as part of importation

4. Cost of additional processing in the United States[33]

Computed Value

Computed value is a mathematical equation, usually used to define value in the context of related-party transactions. The formula is as follows:

$$CV = C + M + P + O + A + S$$

where:

$$
\begin{aligned}
CV &= \text{Computed value} \\
C &= \text{Cost or value of materials} \\
M &= \text{Manufacturing costs} \\
P &= \text{Profit} \\
O &= \text{Overhead (general expenses) normally allocated to such products} \\
A &= \text{Any assist (see discussion later in this chapter)} \\
S &= \text{Packing costs}
\end{aligned}
$$

The cost of materials and overhead will be derived from the producer, unless such figures are inconsistent with industry standards. Profit and overhead are netted so that even if the individual figures differ from the industry, they will be used so long as their sum is consistent with industry standards.

As between deductive and computed value, Customs must use deductive value unless all of the required elements are not present or the importer elects treatment under the computed value method.[34]

Derived Value

Derived value allows use of any formula that is derived from one of the unacceptable methods, where necessary to accurately reflect value, with appropriate adjustments to approximate the results derived from one or more acceptable methods. The following seven methods may not, however, be used:

1. Selling price of goods manufactured in the United States

2. Any method allowing for appraisement of good at the higher of two values

3. Price of merchandise in the exporting country

4. Any cost of production, other than that for identical or similar merchandise under the computed value method

---

[33] 19 U.S.C. § 1401a(d).
[34] 19 U.S.C. § 1401a(e).

5. Price of merchandise exported to countries other than the United States
6. Minimum values for appraisement
7. Arbitrary or fictitious values[35]

Assists

An *assist* is a production or selling input that is provided to the foreign producer at a reduced or zero cost. It is assumed that such an assist proportionally reduces the price charged by the foreign manufacturer; the valuer must determine what constitutes an assist and place a value on it.

Most items directly related to production of the good will be deemed an assist. Examples include tools, raw materials, and engineering. Engineering services are an assist only if performed outside the United States, and even some engineering work done overseas is not considered an assist so long as the engineering was primarily undertaken in the United States. Indirect services, such as legal work or management input, are not assists.

Where an assist is received from an unrelated party, value is defined as the item's acquisition cost. Where, however, the assist was received from a related party, the value is normally the cost of production. Apportionment of the value of the assist is at the discretion of the valuer, so long as the valuer follows GAAP. Valuers may apportion the assist over all shipments to the United States, entirely to the first shipment, or to the number of units produced and sent in the first shipment.[36]

Royalties

Whether royalties and license fees are added to the cost of the product depends on the type of intellectual property involved. Where the buyer pays a patent royalty connected with importing and using the product, such payment is added to the cost of the good. However, where the buyer pays a license fee to market the good in the United States, such payment will not be added to the cost of the good. Valuers should consider to whom the buyer is paying royalty fees and under what circumstances.

Customs has laid out a three-part test to determine whether royalties will be added to the cost of the imported good: Was the good manufactured under a patent, is the royalty involved in the good's production or sale, and could the buyer acquire the good without paying the fee? If the answer is no to the first two questions, and yes to the third, the royalty is likely not includable in the cost of the good.[37]

Currency Conversion

All valuations are to be made in U.S. dollars. Where prices are stated in foreign currency, the valuer must convert the price to U.S. dollars, using a quarterly rate promulgated by the

---

[35]19 U.S.C. § 1401a(f).
[36]19 U.S.C. § 1401a(h).
[37]19 U.S.C. § 1401a(b).

secretary of the Treasury, where available. If the quarterly rate is unavailable, or if the daily exchange rate fluctuates more than 5 percent from the quarterly rate, the daily rate must be used.[38]

CONCLUSION

International valuation issues involving non-arm's-length transactions, while complex, are eminently manageable, requiring the valuer to apply well-known standards of market-comparable valuation in the context of international deals. Mastery of section 482 and the Customs Valuation Agreement alone is not enough, however. The two provisions often interact, requiring the valuer to understand not only the methods of valuation, but also the competing revenue goals of the Service and Customs and the way such competing goals can negatively impact valuation results for the client.

---

[38] 19 C.F.R. § 159.35.

Adjustments to Financial Statements

SUMMARY

Almost all business valuations use information from financial statements. This chapter discusses adjusting the financial statements to provide a relevant basis for fair market value opinions. Chapter 11 discusses analyzing the statements to provide insights to be used in the valuation.

In most valuation cases, certain adjustments to the subject company's historical financial statements should be made. This chapter discusses, in broad terms, the categories of such adjustments and why each is appropriate. If no adjustments were made to the subject company's statements, the report should contain a statement that the analyst has reviewed the company's statements and that no adjustments were considered appropriate.

If a publicly traded guideline company method is used, the same categories of adjustments should be made to the guideline companies as to the subject company.[1] If the analyst has made no adjustments to the guideline companies, the report should contain a statement to the effect that the analyst has reviewed the guideline company statements and no adjustments were necessary.

There are six categories of financial statement adjustments:

1. Separating nonoperating items from operating items
2. Adjusting for excess assets or asset deficiencies
3. Adjusting for contingent assets and/or liabilities
4. Adjusting the cash-basis financial statements to accrual-basis statements (if the company accounts are on a cash basis)

---

[1]See Chapter 15.

5. Normalizing adjustments
6. Controlling adjustments

The financial statement adjustments section of the report should be reviewed with these questions in mind:

- Were all the adjustments that should have been made actually made (including parallel adjustments to the financial statements of the guideline companies)?

  Note: The authors have seen reports where extensive adjustments were made to the subject company's financial statements, with no mention of comparable adjustments to the guideline company's financial statements. This can sometimes lead to an invalid conclusion of value in the market approach.

- Were any adjustments made that were inappropriate?
- Is there convincing rationale for the magnitude of the adjustments?

SEPARATING NONOPERATING ITEMS FROM OPERATING ITEMS

Generally speaking, when valuing an operating company, nonoperating assets on the balance sheet should be removed and treated separately from the value of the company as an operating company. When nonoperating assets are removed from the balance sheet, any income or expense associated with them should also be removed from the income statement.

For example, some companies own portfolios of marketable securities. These should be removed from the balance sheet, and any related income should be removed from the income statement. The fair market value of the marketable securities should be added to the value of the company as an operating company (i.e., aggregated with the going-concern value of the business operation to arrive at the value of the company and its issued shares).

An exception would be when the securities are required to be held to meet certain contingent liabilities of the operating company.

Another example of a nonoperating item would be real estate not involved in the company's operation.

There can be legitimate controversy over whether certain items are operating or nonoperating. Most nonoperating assets are worth more on a liquidation basis than they are based on the value of the income they contribute to the operation. Therefore, those who want a high value usually argue to classify questionable items as nonoperating, while those who want a low value argue to classify the items as operating assets. A case in point would be defunct drive-in theaters owned by a theater chain, used for swap meets at the valuation date. (They were classified for tax purposes as nonoperating assets.)

In any case, where an asset approach is being used in a tax context, any write-ups of assets should be offset by the capital gains liability on the write-ups.[2]

Some argue for not reclassifying nonoperating items when valuing minority interests. The

---

[2]*Estate of Dunn v. Comm'r*, T.C. Memo 2000-12, *rev'd. and remanded*, 301 F.3d 339 (5th Cir. 2002).

minority stockholder does not have the power to liquidate the assets; therefore, reclassifying nonoperating items and adding back their value would usually result in overvaluation for a minority stockholder. An alternative for minority interest valuations would be to find the fair market value of nonoperating assets, net of a minority interest discount, and add it to the value of the operating company.

ADDRESSING EXCESS ASSETS AND ASSET DEFICIENCIES

Excess assets or asset deficiencies should be treated similarly to nonoperating assets. That is, to the extent that there are excess assets or asset deficiencies, their value should be added to or subtracted from the value of the operating company.

If valuing a minority interest, a minority interest discount may be applied to the value of the nonoperating assets. This is because the minority interest holder has no power to liquidate the excess assets, and the market usually does not give full credit to excess assets in the stock price.

The most common category of controversy regarding excess or deficient assets involves working capital. The most common measurement of the adequacy of working capital is the amount of working capital as a percentage of the company's sales. Benchmarks can be industry averages or working capital-to-sales percentages of guideline companies. Either of these benchmarks usually produces a range. If working capital is within a reasonable range relative to the benchmarks, no adjustment is ordinarily required.

The following example is typical of the treatment of excess assets, in this case for the valuation of stock in a bank:

> The bank held cash and marketable securities—primarily intermediate term Treasury notes, equal to 22 percent of assets, compared to 9 percent or less for peer groups. [The Service expert] separated out cash and securities representing 13 percent of the total assets and calculated an adjusted operating book value. He separated out the earnings from the excess assets and calculated adjusted operating earnings. He then estimated the company's value on an operating basis and added the value of the excess assets, the latter net of a 10 percent minority interest discount.[3]

The same calculation can be performed in reverse in case of a working capital deficiency.

HANDLING CONTINGENT ASSETS AND LIABILITIES

Many companies have contingent liabilities, and some have contingent assets. The contingent liabilities often arise from environmental issues. They can also arise from product liability lawsuits and from other actual or potential lawsuits. Contingent assets sometimes arise from unknown collections or lawsuits where the subject company is a plaintiff.

Contingent assets or liabilities are often handled as percentage adjustments at the end of the valuation process (see Chapter 17). However, they are sometimes handled as specific financial statement adjustments.

---

[3]*Shannon Pratt's Business Valuation Update* (Business Valuation Resources, LLC, October 1999): 5, commenting on *Estate of Hendrickson v. Comm'r*, T.C. Memo 1999-278, 78 T.C.M. (CCH) 322.

ADJUSTING CASH-BASIS STATEMENTS
TO ACCRUAL-BASIS STATEMENTS

Some companies, usually small businesses and professional practices, use cash-basis accounting. This means that both revenues and expenses are recorded when they are received or paid, rather than when they are incurred.

Accrual-basis accounting, by contrast, records revenues and expenses when they are earned, measurable, and collectible, based on the accounting principle of matching costs with related revenues. Most valuations use accrual-basis accounting. Therefore, for any given period, figures should be adjusted to reflect revenues earned and expenses incurred during the period. Accounts receivable and accounts payable should also be adjusted.

NORMALIZING ADJUSTMENTS[4]

The general idea of normalizing adjustments is to present data in conformance with GAAP and any industry accounting principles and to eliminate nonrecurring items. The goal is to present information on a basis comparable to that of other companies and to provide a foundation for developing future expectations about the subject company. Another objective is to present financial data on a consistent basis over time.

The following are some examples of normalizing adjustments:

- Adequacy of allowance and reserve accounts:
  - Allowance for doubtful accounts (correct to reasonable amount, in light of historical results and/or management interviews)
  - Pension liabilities
- Inventory accounting methods:
  - First in, first out (FIFO); last in, first out (LIFO); and other methods (adjust to methods usually used in the industry)
  - Write-down and write-off policies (adjust to normal industry practices)
- Depreciation methods and schedules
- Depletion methods and schedules (adjustments to industry reporting norms often appropriate)
- Treatment of intangible assets:
  - Leasehold interest (adjust to market value)
  - Other intangible assets
- Policies regarding capitalization or expensing of various costs (adjust to industry norms)
- Timing of recognition of revenues and expenses:
  - Contract work (including work in progress; e.g., percentage of completion or completed contract)
  - Installment sales

---

[4]Shannon Pratt, *Business Valuation Body of Knowledge*, 2nd ed. (New York: John Wiley & Sons, Inc., 2003): 205–207.

- Sales involving actual or contingent liabilities (e.g., guarantees, warranties)
- Prior period adjustments (e.g., for changes in accounting policy or items overlooked)
- Expenses booked in one year applying to other years
- Net operating losses carried forward
- Treatment of interests in affiliates
- Adequacy or deficiency of assets:
  - Excess or deficient net working capital (adjust to industry average percent of sales)
  - Deferred maintenance (based on plant visit and management interviews)
- Adequacy or deficiency of liabilities:
  - Pension termination liabilities
  - Deferred income taxes
  - Unrecorded payables
- Unusual gains or losses on sale of assets
  Note: It does not have to be extraordinary in a GAAP sense to be nonrecurring in a financial analysis sense. This factor is a matter for the analyst's judgment (e.g., rental income).
- Nonrecurring gains or losses:
  - Fire, flood, or other casualty, both physical damage and business interruption to extent not covered by insurance
  - Strikes (unless common in the industry and considered probable to recur)
  - Litigation costs, payments, or recoveries
  - Gain or loss on sale of business assets
  - Discontinued operations

A valuer should consider all of these adjustments, whether they have been made, and, if not, why not.

CONTROLLING ADJUSTMENTS[5]

A control owner or potential owner might make control adjustments, but a minority owner, generally, could not force the same changes. Therefore, control adjustments normally would be made only in the case of a controlling interest valuation, unless there was reason to believe that the changes were imminent and probable. These include:

- Excess or deficient compensation and perquisites
- Gains, losses, or cash realization from sale of excess assets
- Elimination of operations involving company insiders (e.g., employment, non-market-rate leases)
- Changes in capital structure

---

[5]Id. at 207.

The most common control adjustment is for reasonable compensation. The following is a typical illustration of a court's treatment of an excess compensation issue:

> *The Court rejected [the estate's witness's] opinion that [taxpayer] paid $15,000 per year in excess compensation, for a total excess compensation figure of $86,663. The Court found that [the estate's witness'] opinion was "unsupported by any objective criteria." Some of his data and assertions were "no more than a conclusory guess."*

> *The Court accepted [the Service's] basic methodology, which was based upon a determination of the market replacement cost of the various positions fulfilled by family-member employees. However, he erred with respect to the number of hours that would be required to fulfill the duties of those employees. Therefore, the Court used the market wage and benefit figures that [the Service's witness] presented, but recalculated the reasonable compensation based upon the number of hours the Court determined, based upon testimony in the record, the employees were required to work to fulfill their duties.*[6]

When experts present objective evidence to support their opinion, the objective evidence will almost always be scrutinized by opposing experts and will be subject to criticism. The more sources that are available, the greater is the onus on the expert to defend his source.[7]

Note: There is a minority (but legitimate) school of thought that considers what we have just classified as control adjustments to be normalizing adjustments, even in a minority interest valuation where the minority holder cannot force the company policy to change. The reason for this is to put the subject company on a basis comparable to the guideline companies. The minority interest factor is then handled as a separate discount at the end of the valuation.

CONCLUSION

In this chapter we have classified financial statement adjustments into six categories:

1. Separating nonoperating items from operating items
2. Addressing excess assets and asset deficiencies
3. Handling contingent assets and liabilities
4. Adjusting cash-basis statements to accrual-basis statements
5. Normalizing adjustments
6. Controlling adjustments

There is nothing wrong with an analyst's using a different categorization of financial statement adjustments; this categorization is merely presented for the convenience of the reader. However, if any of the items in this chapter are relevant, adjustments to the financial statements should be made, however categorized. If no adjustments are warranted, the analyst should include a statement in the report that the financial statements were analyzed and no adjustments were warranted.

Once the financial statements have been adjusted to provide a relevant basis for arriving at fair market value, the next step is to analyze them so as to recognize trends, strengths, and weaknesses.

---

[6]*Shannon Pratt's Business Valuation Update* (Business Valuation Resources, LLC, November 2000): 6, commenting on *Estate of Renier v. Comm'r*, T.C. Memo. 2000-298, 80 T.C.M. (CCH) 401 (September 25, 2000).

[7]There are many sources of reasonable compensation data. Many of these sources are listed in the *Business Valuation Data, Publications, and Internet Directory* (Portland, OR: Business Valuation Resources, LLC, published annually).

Chapter 11

Comparative Financial Statement Analysis

SUMMARY

Once the financial statements have been adjusted to provide a sound basis for arriving at an opinion as to fair market value, the next step is to analyze the statements to reveal trends, strengths, and weaknesses.

Objective of Financial Statement Analysis

The objective of financial statement analysis is to provide analytical data to guide the valuation. The reliability of a valuation report may be evaluated partially on whether the financial analysis is adequate, and on the relevance of that analysis to the valuation conclusion.

    Since "valuation . . . is, in essence, a prophecy [sic] as to the future,"[1] the relevance of historical financial statements is merely as a guide for what to expect in the future. For most companies, a pure extrapolation of past results would provide a misleading prophecy as to the company's future.

---

[1]Rev. Rul. 59-60.

Assessment of Risk

Risk can be defined as the degree of certainty (or lack thereof) of achieving future expectations at the times and in the amounts expected.

One of the most important products of financial statement analysis is to provide an objective basis for assessment of risk relative to industry average risk and/or risk of specific guideline companies. Risk analysis is of critical importance because, *other things being equal, the higher the risk, the lower the fair market value of the company.*

In the income approach, the higher the risk, the higher the market's required rate of expected return on investment. The market's required rate of return on investment is called the *discount rate*, the rate at which projected cash flows are discounted back to a present fair market value. The discount rate represents the *total* expected rate of return on the value of the investment, including both cash distributions and capital appreciation, whether realized or unrealized. The higher the risk, the higher the discount rate, and thus the lower the value of the company or interest in the company (see Chapter 14).

In the market approach, risk is reflected in valuation multiples. The higher the risk, the lower the valuation multiples, and thus the lower the fair market value of the company or interest in the company (see Chapter 15).

Risk also affects the discount for lack of marketability. Other things being equal, the higher the risk, the higher the discount for lack of marketability (see Chapter 18).

Assessment of Growth Prospects

Another purpose of financial statement analysis is to provide a basis for assessing the prospects for growth. The higher the company's prospective growth in net cash flows (or earnings, or some other measure of benefit to shareholders), all else being equal, the higher the present fair market value of the company.

In the discounted cash flow method within the income approach, growth is reflected directly in the projections. Financial statement analysis can provide a basis for evaluating the reasonableness of the projections. The discounted cash flow method, discussed in Chapter 14, requires that all projected future benefits to the owners be discounted back to a present value at a discount rate that reflects the risk of realizing the benefits projected.

In the capitalization method within the income approach, growth is reflected by subtracting the rate of expected long-term growth from the discount rate to arrive at the capitalization rate (see Chapter 14). Financial statement analysis can help to evaluate the reasonableness of the estimate of the long-term growth rate. The capitalization method discussed in Chapter 14 consists of dividing some measure of benefit by a capitalization rate, which is either the discount rate minus the expected long-term growth rate or a rate observed from comparative companies.

In the market approach, expected growth is reflected in the valuation multiples. Financial statement analysis can be helpful in evaluating the reasonableness of the multiples applied to the subject company's fundamentals.

COMPARABLE RATIO ANALYSIS

For convenient analytical purposes, ratios can be arbitrarily classified into half a dozen categories:

1. Activity ratios
2. Performance ratios
3. Return-on-investment ratios
4. Leverage ratios
5. Liquidity ratios
6. Other risk-analysis ratios

   The following list of financial statement ratios is not all-inclusive, but presents those most commonly used.

Activity Ratios (sometimes also called Asset Utilization Ratios)

Activity ratios relate an income statement variable to a balance sheet variable. Ideally, the balance sheet variable would represent the average of the line item for the year, or at least the average of the beginning and ending values for the line item. However, many sources of comparative industry ratios are based only on year-end data. *For the ratios to have comparative meaning, it is imperative that they be computed from the subject company on the same basis as the average or individual company ratios with which they are being compared.* It also should be noted that many ratios can be distorted significantly by seasonality, so it may be important to match comparative time periods.

Accounts receivable turnover:

$$\frac{\text{Sales}}{\text{Accounts receivable}}$$

The higher the accounts receivable turnover, the better the company is doing in collecting its receivables.

Inventory turnover:

$$\frac{\text{Cost of goods sold}}{\text{Inventory}}$$

The higher the inventory turnover, the more efficiently the company is using its inventory. *Note:* Some people use sales instead of cost of goods sold in this ratio. This method inflates the ratio, since it does not really reflect the physical turnover of the goods.

Sales to net working capital:

$$\frac{\text{Sales}}{\text{Net working capital (Current assets} - \text{Current liabilities)}}$$

The higher the sales to net working capital, the more efficiently the company is using its net working capital. However, too high a sales-to-working-capital ratio could indicate the risk of inadequate working capital.

Sales to net fixed assets:

$$\frac{\text{Sales}}{\text{Net fixed assets (Cost} - \text{Accumulated depreciation)}}$$

Sales to total assets:

$$\frac{\text{Sales}}{\text{Total assets}}$$

Generally speaking, activity ratios are a measure of how efficiently a company is utilizing various balance sheet components.

Performance Ratios (Income Statement)

The four most common measures of operating performance are:

Gross profit as a percentage of sales:

$$\frac{\text{Gross profit}}{\text{Sales}}$$

Operating profit (earnings before interest and taxes [EBIT]) as a percentage of sales:

$$\frac{\text{EBIT}}{\text{Sales}}$$

Pretax income as a percentage of sales:

$$\frac{\text{Pretax income}}{\text{Sales}}$$

Net profit as a percentage of sales:

$$\frac{\text{Net profit}}{\text{Sales}}$$

All four measures can be read directly from the common size income statements, which are discussed in the following section. A higher performance ratio means that a higher price-to-sales multiple can be justified.

Return-on-Investment Ratios

Like activity ratios, return-on-investment ratios relate an income statement variable to a balance sheet variable. Ideally, the balance sheet variable would represent the average of the line item for the year, or at least the average of the beginning and ending values for the line item. Unlike activity ratios, return-on-investment ratios sometimes are computed on the basis of the balance sheet line item at the *beginning* of the year. However, many sources of comparative ratios are based only on year-end data. For the ratios to have comparative meaning, it is imperative that they be computed for the subject company on the same basis as the average or individual company ratios with which they are being compared.

Return on equity:

$$\frac{\text{Net income}}{\text{Equity}}$$

Note: The preceding ratio normally is computed based on book value of equity. It also may be enlightening to compute it based on market value of equity.

Return on investment:

$$\frac{\text{Net income} + [(\text{Interest})(1 - \text{Tax rate})]}{\text{Equity} + \text{Long-term debt}}$$

Return on total assets:

$$\frac{\text{Net income} + [(\text{Interest})(1 - \text{Tax rate})]}{\text{Total assets}}$$

Note: These ratios are normally computed based on book values.

Each measure of investment returns provides a different perspective on financial performance. In valuation, return on equity influences the price-to-book-value multiple, and return on investment influences the market-value-of-invested-capital (MVIC)-to-EBIT multiple. A higher return on various balance sheet components justifies a higher value multiple relative to those components.

Leverage Ratios

The general purpose of balance sheet leverage ratios (capital structure ratios) is to aid in quantifiable assessment of the long-term solvency of the business and its ability to deal with financial problems and opportunities as they arise. Balance sheet leverage ratios are important in assessing the risk of the individual components of the capital structure. Above-average levels of debt may increase both the cost of debt and the company-specific equity risk factor in a build-up model for estimating a discount or capitalization rate. Alternatively, above-average debt may increase the levered beta in the capital asset pricing model (CAPM). The CAPM, discussed in Chapter 14, is a procedure for developing a discount rate applicable to equity.

Total debt to total assets:

$$\frac{\text{Total liabilities}}{\text{Total assets}}$$

Equity to total assets:

$$\frac{\text{Total equity}}{\text{Total assets}}$$

Long-term debt to total capital:

$$\frac{\text{Long-term debt}}{\text{Long-term debt} + \text{Equity}}$$

Equity to total capital:

$$\frac{\text{Total equity}}{\text{Long-term debt} + \text{Equity}}$$

Fixed assets to equity:

$$\frac{\text{Net fixed assets}}{\text{Total equity}}$$

Debt to intangible equity:

$$\frac{\text{Total liabilities}}{\text{Total equity}}$$

Note: The preceding ratio sometimes is computed using total equity minus intangible assets in the denominator.

Leverage ratios are a measure of the overall financial risk of the business.

Liquidity Ratios

Liquidity ratios are indications of the company's ability to meet its obligations as they come due—in this sense, they are factors that may be considered in assessing the company-specific risk.

Current ratio:

$$\frac{\text{Current assets}}{\text{Current liabilities}}$$

Quick (acid test) ratio:

$$\frac{\text{Cash } + \text{ Cash equivalents } + \text{ Short-term investments } + \text{ Receivables}}{\text{Current liabilities}}$$

times interest earned:

a. $$\frac{\text{EBIT}}{\text{Interest expense}}$$

or

b. $$\frac{\text{EBDIT}}{\text{Interest expense}}$$

Note: Depreciation in the preceding formula is usually construed to include amortization and other noncash charges, sometimes expressed by the acronym EBITDA (earnings before interest, taxes, depreciation, and amortization).

Coverage of fixed charges:

$$\frac{\text{Earnings before interest, taxes, and lease payments}}{\text{Interest } + \text{ Current portion of long-term debt } + \text{ Lease payments}}$$

Other Risk-Analysis Ratios

Business risk (variability of return over time):

$$\frac{\text{Standard deviation of net income}}{\text{Mean of net income}}$$

Business risk measures volatility of operating results over time. The higher the historical business risk, the less predictable future results are likely to be. Variability of past results is a better predictor of variability of future results (risk) than a past upward or downward trend is of a future upward or downward trend.

Note: This measure is called the *coefficient of variation.* It can be applied to any measure of income, including sales, EBITDA, EBIT, gross profit, pretax profit, or net cash flow.

Degree of operating leverage:

$$\frac{\text{Percentage change in operating earnings}}{\text{Percentage change in sales}}$$

Note: This is really another measure of business risk. The numerator could be any of the measures of income listed earlier.

Financial risk (degree of financial leverage):

$$\frac{\text{Percentage change in income to common equity}}{\text{Percentage change in EBIT}}$$

COMMON SIZE STATEMENTS

A *common size statement* is a balance sheet that expresses each line item as a percentage of total assets or an income statement that expresses each line item as a percentage of revenue.

When several years of financial statements are available for a company, common size statements can be used to compare the company against itself over time. This is called *trend analysis.*

The Chapter 15 appendix section contains two examples, one being five years of common size balance sheets, and the other, five years of common size income statements for Optimum Devices. Note that five years of statements produce only four years of year-to-year changes and thus a four-year compound rate of growth, or decline, in each line item.

When a number of years' worth of common size statements are used, the volatility of each line item can be measured using the standard deviation of the year-to-year changes.

When a comparable number of years of common size statements are available for industry averages or specific guideline companies, the relative volatility of each line item can be compared. Higher volatility is indicative of higher risk.

A single year's common size statements can be used to compare subject company to industry averages or to specific guideline companies. Exhibit 15.10 is an example of a subject company's common size statements relative to industry averages; Exhibit 15.13 is an example of a subject company's common size statements compared with specific guideline companies. (See Chapter 15.)

TYING THE FINANCIAL STATEMENT ANALYSIS TO THE VALUE CONCLUSION

The implications of the financial statement analysis for the conclusion of value should be identified in the financial statement analysis section, the valuation section, or both. Some reports have an extensive financial analysis section with no mention of implications for value either in the analysis or valuation section. To be convincing, the report should be *cohesive*; the report should hang together, with each section lending support for the value conclusion. The connection should be explained, not leaving the reader to guess. Many readers will not be financial experts, and a connection that might be apparent to a financial analyst might not be obvious to a less sophisticated reader.

CONCLUSION

The primary objectives of financial statement analysis are to identify trends and to identify the strengths and weaknesses of the subject company relative to its peers. Perhaps the most important outgrowth of financial statement analysis is objective evidence of the subject company's risk relative to its peers. This relative riskiness plays a part in the discount and capitalization rates in the income approach, and in the valuation multiples in the market approach.

Economic and Industry Analysis

SUMMARY

Almost every company is affected to some extent by economic conditions and by conditions in the industry in which it operates. No discussion of business valuation would be complete without at least a brief discussion of external factors. Various economic and industry factors affect each company differently, and the key to effective economic and industry analysis is to show how each factor impacts the subject company.

Some companies are affected by certain aspects of the national economy. Others are affected primarily by regional and local economic factors. Some are affected more heavily than others by conditions in the industry in which they operate. Economic and industry analysis identifies those factors that affect the subject company.

OBJECTIVE OF ECONOMIC AND INDUSTRY ANALYSIS

The objective of economic and industry analysis is to provide relevant data on the context within which the company is operating.

The key word here is *relevant*.

No company operates in a vacuum. All companies are impacted to a greater or lesser extent by external conditions. These could be national, regional, or local economic conditions and/or conditions in the industry in which the company operates.

The extent to which various economic and industry conditions affect differing companies varies widely from company to company.

It is the appraiser's job to identify what aspects of economic and/or industry conditions tend to affect the subject company, to identify how those conditions are expected to change in the future, and to assess the impact of those changes on the subject company. "It is essential for the appraiser to relate economic indicators and outlook to the specific circumstances of the subject company and valuation engagement."[1]

A great deal of economic and industry data are available online. The most comprehensive source of economic and industry data available online is *Best Websites for Financial Professionals, Business Appraisers, and Accountants*, 2nd ed.[2] (referred to in subsequent sections of this chapter as *Best Websites*).

NATIONAL ECONOMIC ANALYSIS

Companies in some industries are heavily impacted by certain aspects of the U.S. economy. In some cases those aspects of the national economy have little or no relevance.

Major components of national economic analysis include the following:

- General economic conditions:
  - Gross domestic product (GDP)
  - Consumer spending
  - Government spending
  - Business investments
  - Inventories (increases or decreases)
  - Trade deficit
- Consumer prices and inflation rates
- Interest rates
- Unemployment
- Consumer confidence
- Stock markets
- Construction
- Manufacturing

The analyst should identify which of these economic variables affects the subject company, and should concentrate the economic analysis on those variables. Long-term outlooks

---

[1] Shannon Pratt in *Economic Outlook Update* 4Q 2002 (Portland, OR: Business Valuation Resources, LLC, published quarterly).

[2] Eva M. Lang and Jan Davis Tudor, *Best Websites for Financial Professionals, Business Appraisers, and Accountants*, 2nd ed. (Hoboken, N.J.: John Wiley & Sons, Inc., 2003).

for certain national economic variables can be very important to some companies, especially the long-term growth forecast. Projections of long-term growth in excess of the sum of forecasted growth in real gross domestic product (GDP), plus inflation, should generally be viewed with suspicion and require strong justification. For example, some valuating practitioners use the expected growth in a company or industry for the coming five years with the assumption that this is going to continue for the long term. This is usually wrong, and can lead to an inflated estimate of value.

Some sources of national economic data are listed in the bibliography at the end of this chapter and others are described in the *Business Valuation Data, Publication, and Internet Directory*.[3] Web sites for collecting economic research are available in *Best Websites*.[4]

REGIONAL AND LOCAL ECONOMIC ANALYSIS

Regional and/or local economic analysis is relevant to those companies whose fortunes are affected primarily by regional and/or local economic conditions. These would include such companies as regional or local financial institutions, retailers, building contractors, and various types of service companies.

Sources of regional and local economic analysis include banks, public utilities, state departments of economic development, and chambers of commerce.

INDUSTRY ANALYSIS

Industry analysis can be categorized into three components:

1. General industry conditions and outlook
2. Comparative industry financial statistics
3. Management compensation information[5]

Web sites for industry analysis are available in *Best Websites*.[6]

General Industry Conditions and Outlook

Almost all industries have one or more trade associations. Many also have other independent publications devoted to industry conditions. Also, most national stock brokerage companies publish outlook information for the industries in which they specialize. There are several directories of these sources included in the bibliography at the end of this chapter.

---

[3]*Business Valuation Data, Publications, and Internet Directory* (Portland, OR: Business Valuation Resources, LLC, published annually).

[4]See note 2, Chapter 3, pp. 37–56.

[5]Shannon P. Pratt, Robert F. Reilly, Robert P. Schweihs, *Valuing a Business: The Analysis and Appraisal of Closely Held Companies*, 4th ed. (New York: McGraw-Hill, 2000).

[6]See note 2, Chapter 4, pp. 57–73.

Comparative Industry Financial Statistics

Industry average financial statistics can be useful to compare the subject company's financial performance with industry norms. The comparisons can take either or both of two forms:

1. *Ratio analysis.* Comparing a company's financial ratios to industry norms
2. *Common size statements.* Income statements and balance sheets where each line item is expressed as a percentage of total revenue or total assets

Each of these types of analysis is discussed in Chapter 11.

Several general sources of comparative industry financial statistics are included in the bibliography at the end of this chapter. Sources for specific industry financial statistics can be found in the directories of trade associations and industry information (also in the bibliography at the end of this chapter), and in the *Business Valuation Data, Publications, and Internet Directory.*[7]

Each source of industry information has its own source of data. The valuation analyst should be aware of the sources for each industry information compilation and the potential distortions or biases that might result from the source. For example, compilations based on the Department of Commerce's *Sources of Income* are compiled from federal tax returns, with data about three to four years old. For industries in which statistics remain relatively stable over time, this is a good source, because it has the advantage of more company-size breakdowns than any other. However, in industries for which statistics are volatile over time, a comparison to four-year-old data may not be valid.

Also, each source has its own definitions. When using comparative industry data, the analyst must be certain that the definitions used for the subject company are the same as those used in the industry source. Otherwise, the comparisons will not be valid. For example, Risk Management Association's (RMA's) *Annual Statement Studies* use only year-end data. Therefore, when comparing inventory turnover with data published by RMA, an accurate comparison requires use of year-end inventory, even though average inventory is more valid for financial analysis.

Management Compensation Information

The most frequent (and controversial) adjustment to the subject company's income statement is to management compensation. There are whole income tax cases where the sole issue is reasonable compensation.

There are many sources of average industry compensation, some more specific as to job description than others, but all having some weaknesses. For example, RMA does not publish how many people are included in its line item "Officers, Directors, Owners Compensation/Sales."

Also, even in the case where specific compensation by position is available for an industry, adjustments may need to be made for the specific individual's contribution to the company versus the average industry executive's contribution.

Some general sources of compensation are included in the bibliography at the end of this

---

[7]See note 3.

chapter. More specific sources by industry are found in the directories of trade associations and industry information (also in the bibliography at the end of this chapter) and in the *Business Valuation Data, Publication, and Internet Directory*.[8] Web sites for salary and executive compensation surveys are available in *Best Websites*.[9]

CONCLUSION

Economic and industry information is such a broad subject that we could only address it briefly in this chapter. Some companies are affected by various national or regional economic factors. Others are affected largely by local conditions. The importance of industry conditions varies greatly from one industry to another. As with financial statement analysis, the analyst should point out the connection between the economic and industry factors and the valuation of the subject company.

PARTIAL BIBLIOGRAPHY OF SOURCES FOR ECONOMIC AND INDUSTRY ANALYSIS

National Economic Information

Economic Outlook Update. Portland, OR: Business Valuation Resources, quarterly. Each *Economic Outlook Update* quarterly report presents the general economic climate that existed at the end of the respective quarter. Topics addressed include general economic conditions, consumer prices and inflation rates, interest rates, unemployment, consumer spending, the stock markets, construction, manufacturing, and economic outlook. The economic outlook section contains short- and long-term forecasts for major economic indicators such as gross domestic product, inflation, interest rates, and major stock market indexes. The reports are available quarterly and are delivered via e-mail to subscribers as a PDF file, Word document, or Excel document. (*www.bvlibrary.com*)

Economic Report of the President. Washington, D.C.: Government Printing Office, annual.

Federal Reserve Bank Periodicals (a sampling):

Federal Reserve Bank of Atlanta. *Economic Review.*

Federal Reserve Bank of Atlanta. *Econ South.*

Federal Reserve Bank of Boston. *Regional Review.*

Federal Reserve Bank of Boston. *New England Economic Indicators.*

Federal Reserve Bank of Boston. *New England Economic Review.*

Federal Reserve Bank of Chicago. *Ag Letter.*

Federal Reserve Bank of Chicago. *Economic Perspectives.*

Federal Reserve Bank of Cleveland. *Economic Commentary.*

Federal Reserve Bank of Cleveland. *Economic Review.*

Federal Reserve Bank of Cleveland. *Economic Trends.*

Federal Reserve Bank of Dallas. *Economic & Financial Review.*

---

[8]Id.

[9]See note 2, Chapter 8, pp. 111–128.

Federal Reserve Bank of Dallas. *Southwest Economy.*

Federal Reserve Bank of Kansas City. *Economic Review.*

Federal Reserve Bank of Minneapolis. *Fedgazette.*

Federal Reserve Bank of Minneapolis. *Quarterly Review.*

Federal Reserve Bank of New York. *Economic Policy Review.*

Federal Reserve Bank of Philadelphia. *Business Review.*

Federal Reserve Bank of Richmond. *Economic Quarterly.*

Federal Reserve Bank of Richmond. *Region Focus.*

Federal Reserve Bank of St. Louis. *International Economic Conditions.*

Federal Reserve Bank of St. Louis. *The Regional Economist.*

Federal Reserve Bank of St. Louis. *Review.*

Federal Reserve Bank of St. Louis. *U.S. Financial Data.*

Federal Reserve Bank of San Francisco. *Economic Review.*

Federal Reserve Bank of San Francisco. *Fed in Print* (index).

Federal Reserve Bank of San Francisco. *Economic Letter.*

Federal Reserve Bulletin. Washington, D.C.: Board of Governors of the Federal Reserve System, monthly. (*www.federalreserve.gov/publications.htm*)

FRASER (Federal Reserve Archival System for Economic Research). St. Louis: Federal Reserve Bank of St. Louis. On the FRASER Web site (*http://fraser.stlouisfed.org/*) you can find scanned information that was previously available only in print. The item includes historical economic statistical publications, releases, and documents, which provide valuable economic information and statistics.

FRED II (Federal Reserve Economic Data). St. Louis: Federal Reserve Bank of St. Louis. *FRED II* is a database with more than 2,900 economic time series; the data are downloadable in Microsoft Excel or text formats. (*http://research.stlouisfed.org/fred2/*)

Monthly Labor Review. U.S. Bureau of Labor Statistics, Department of Labor. Washington, D.C.: Government Printing Office, monthly (*www.bls.gov/opub/mlr/mlrhome.htm*). A compilation of economic and social statistics. Most are given as monthly figures for the current year and one prior year. Features articles on the labor force, wages, prices, productivity, economic growth, and occupational injuries and illnesses. Regular features include a review of developments in industrial relations, book review, and current labor statistics.

Statistical Abstract of the United States. Washington, D.C.: Government Printing Office, annual. (*www.census.gov/statab*)

Survey of Current Business. Washington, D.C.: Government Printing Office, monthly. (*www.bea.doc.gov/bea/pubs.htm*)

Regional Economic Information

City and County Databook and the State Metropolitan Area Databook. U.S. Bureau of the Census, Deportment of Commerce. Washington, D.C.: Government Printing Office. (*www.census.gov/statab/www/ccdb.html*)

Consensus Forecasts USA. London, UK: Consensus Economics, monthly. Detailed forecasts for 20 economic and financial variables for the United States. (*www.consensuseconomics.com*)

Economic Census. U.S. Bureau of the Census, Department of Commerce. Washington, DC: Government Printing Office (*www.census.gov*). *The Economic Census* is grouped into report by NAICS code. It profiles the U.S. economy every five years from the national to local levels. Contains statistics on housing, population, construction activity, and many other economic indicators.

Survey of Buying Power. San Diego: Claritas, Inc., annual. This survey, published annually by *Sales & Marketing Management* magazine, breaks down demographic and income data by state, metropolitan area, and county or parish. Retail sales data are presented for store groups and merchandise lines. Also included are population and retail sales forecasts for local areas. (*www.salesandmarketing.com*)

The Complete Economic and Demographic Data Source. Washington, D.C.: Woods and Poole Economics, Inc., annual. (*www.woodsandpoole.com/main*)

U.S. Bureau of Economic Analysis. Department of Commerce. Washington, D.C. This organization has a regional economics program that provides estimates analyses, and projections by region, state metropolitan statistical area, and county or parish, Regional reports are released approximately six times a year with summary estimates of state personal income. (*www.bea.doc.gov*)

WEBEC, Finland: Lauri Saarinen. This is an extensive online library that provides links to free economic data. Categories include economic data, regional economics, financial economics, labor and demographics, a list of economic journals, and business economics. (*http://netec.wustl.edu/WebEc/WebEc.html*)

Industry Information

Almanac of Business and Industrial Financial Ratios. Leo Troy, Ph.D., ed. Englewood, Cliffs, N.J.: Prentice Hall, annual. Includes ratios for more than 175 industries. Statistics are based on corporate activity during the latest year for which figures from IRS tax returns are published.

B&E Datalinks. Web site. Provides links to economic and financial data. Categories include macroeconomics, finance, labor and general microeconometrics, and business datasets. Each category lists of hundreds of Web sites with a brief description, date modified, and rating. (*www.econ-datalinks.org*)

ECONDATA.NET. Web site. A guide to finding economic data on the Web. Includes more than 1,000 links. Searchable by provider, including Census, federal, and private, and by subject, including income, employment, demographics, and industry sector. Also includes the ten best sites. (*www.econdata.net*)

Economic Forecasts Reports and Industry Forecasts. West Chester, Penn.: Economy.com, Inc. *Economic Forecast Reports* available by country, state, or metropolitan area. Includes five-year forecasts, written analysis, and key statistics on income, migration, top employers, business/living costs, and more. Subscriptions include current report and two updates. Samples are available for each report. *Industry Forecast Reports* include five-year forecasts for up to 50 financial variables, current and forecasted trends, risk factors, and so on. Each report also includes data on macroeconomic conditions, trends, and outlooks. Reports are four pages and updated three times yearly. Subscriptions include current report and two updates. Samples are available for each report. (*www.economy.com/research*)

Encyclopedia of American Industries (2 volumes), 3rd ed., Kevin Hillstrom, ed. Farmington Hills, MI: Thomson Gale, 2000. Provides information on many industries, broken down by SIC code. Information includes an industry "snapshot," organization and structure of the industry, current conditions, a discussion of industry leaders, information on the workforce, foreign competition and trade information, and additional sources of information. (*www.gale.com*)

Encyclopedia of Associations. Farmington Hills, Mich.: Thomson Gale, annual. Available in print, electronic, and Web-based formats. This is the largest compilation of nonprofit associations and organizations available anywhere. Contains descriptions of professional associations, trade and business associations, labor unions, chambers of commerce, and groups of all types in virtually every field.

FED STATS. Washington D.C. Provides access to statistical data from the federal government. Data are searchable by subject, agency, and geographical location. Topics of interest include economic and population trends, health care costs, foreign trade, employment statistics, and more. (*www.fedstats.gov*)

First Call Database. New York: Thomson Financial. Research covering more than 34,000 companies in more than 130 countries. Current and historical data, public filings, and forecasted data available. Forecasts include: P/E ratios, growth rates, return on assets, earnings, cash flow, sales, and more. Thomson Financial has completed the full integration of I/B/E/S onto the First Call Web site. (*www.firstcall.com*)

Industry Norms and Key Business Ratios. New York: Dun & Bradstreet, Inc., annual. Balance sheet and profit-and-loss ratios based on a computerized financial statements file. The 14 key ratios are broken down into median figures, with upper and lower quartiles. Covers over 800 lines of business, broken down into three size ranges by net worth for each SIC. (*www.dnb.ca/products/indnorm.html*)

Industry Valuation Update. Portland, Ore.: Business Valuation Resources, LLC. *The Industry Valuation Update* is a six-volume series on industry valuation topics. Each volume includes seven general business valuation chapters, two industry-specific chapters including articles by valuation experts, and insights on the best valuation approaches for each industry. Each volume also includes rules of thumb, SIC and NAICS codes, industry analysis, court cases, and Pratt's Stats analysis. (*www.bvstore.com*)

Industry Profiles: First Research. More than 140 industry profiles available. Information includes recent developments, industry challenges and overview, important questions, and new links. Financial data include ratios, profitability trends, economic statistics, and benchmark statistics. Most reports provide a free summary before initial purchase. (*www.bvmarketdata.com or http://firstresearch.com/profiles*)

Industry Reports: The Center for Economic and Industry Research. Industry studies that provide information for a particular area and length of time. Studies range anywhere from 15 to 20 pages. (*www.c-e-i-r.com*)

Manufacturing & Distribution USA, 2nd ed. Farmington Hills, Mich.: Thomson Gale, 2000. Presents statistics on more than 500 SIC and NIACS classifications in the manufacturing, wholesaling, and retail industries. Information is compiled from the most recent government publications and includes projections, maps, and graphics. Classification of leading public and private corporations in each industry is also included. (*www.gale.com*)

Market Research Reports. Cleveland, Ohio: The Freedonia Group, Inc., ten new titles published monthly. Provides industry analysis, including product and market forecasts, industry trends, and competitive strategies. Studies can be searched by title, table of content, or full text. Individual reports or parts of reports are available. (*www.freedoniagroup.com*)

Market Share Reporter. Farmington Hills, Mich.: Thomson Gale, annual. Presents comparative business statistics in a clear, straightforward manner. Arranged by four-digit SIC code; contains data from more than 2,000 entries. Each entry includes a descriptive title, data and market description, a list of producers/products along with their assigned market share, and more. (*www.gale.com*)

Mergent's Industry Review. Charlotte, N.C.: Mergent. *Mergent's Industry Review* contains comparative rankings by industry for items like revenues, net income, profit margins, assets, return on investment, return on equity, and cash position. In addition to the comparative rankings, this publication offers comparative statistics like key business ratios and special industry specific ratios. (*www.mergent.com*)

National Economic Review. Memphis, Tenn.: Mercer Capital, quarterly. *National Economic Review* is an overview of the major factors affecting the economy and includes discussions of the current and expected performance of the national economy, interest rates, employment, inflation, the stock and bond markets, construction, housing, and real estate. It consists of four to eight pages of text and two pages of exhibits (annual/quarterly economic indicators and investment trends). (*www.mercercapital.com or www.bizval.com*)

National Trade and Professional Associations of the United States. Washington, D.C.: Columbia Books, annual. Excellent source book for trade and industry sources of industry information. Restricted to trade and professional associations and labor unions with national memberships.

Online Industry and Benchmark Reports. Kennesaw, Ga.: Integra. The type of reports available from Integra: *Five Year Reports, Industry Growth Outlook Reports, Industry Narrative Reports, Industry QuickTrends Reports, Integra's Comparative Profiler, Three Year Industry Reports.* (*www.integrainfo.com*)

Plunkett's Industry Almanacs. Houston, Tex.: Plunkett Research, Ltd. Includes profiles of approximately 500 companies, financial trends, salary information, market and industry analysis, and more. Choose from a variety of industries, including energy, computers and Internet, entertainment and media, and retail. (*www.plunkettresearch.com*)

Predicasts PROMT. Foster City, Calif.: Information Access Company. This multi-industry resource provides broad, international coverage of companies, products, markets, and applied technologies for all industries. Available through online services, *PTS PROMT* is comprised of abstracts and full-text records from more than 1,000 of the world's important business publications, including trade journals, local newspapers and regional business publications, national and international business newspapers, trade and business newsletters, research studies, S1 SEC registration statements, investment analysts' reports, corporate news releases, and corporate annual reports.

RMA Annual Statement Studies. Philadelphia: Risk Management Association, annual. Standard & Poor's Analyst's Handbook. New York: Standard & Poor's Corporation, Inc., annual. (*www.standardandpoors.com*)

Standard & Poor's Industry Surveys. New York: Standard & Poor's Corporation, Inc., biannual. (*www.standardandpoors.com*)

University of Michigan Documents Center: Ann Arbor, Mich. This Web site from the University of Michigan Documents Center is one of the most comprehensive resources for statistical data. Categories of interest include agriculture, business and industry, government finances, labor, finance and currency, foreign economics, and demographics. (*www.lib.umich.edu/govdocs/stats.html*)

Management Compensation Sources

Executive Compensation Assessor. Redmond, Wash.: Economic Research Institute, quarterly. ERI's *Executive Compensation Assessor* reports salaries and bonuses for 371 top management positions within multiple industries. Data may be adjusted for geographic area, organization size, and compensation valuation date. This source provides analysis of data compiled from virtually all publicly available executive compensation surveys, along with direct analysis of SEC EDGAR proxy data. Other compensation products are also available. (*www.erieri.com*)

National Executive Compensation Survey Results. Illinois: The Management Association of Illinois, annual. This survey reports annual salaries for 10,451 executives in 33 positions at 1,544 participating organizations throughout the country. (*www.ercnet.org*)

Source Book Statistics of Income. Washington, D.C.: Internal Revenue Service, annual. *Standard & Poor's Execucomp.* New York: Standard & Poor's, quarterly. Available online or on CD-ROM, *Execucomp* is a comprehensive database that covers S&P 500, S&P mid-cap 400, and S&P small cap companies. The study includes more than 80 different compensation, executive, director, and company items, including breakdowns of salary, bonuses, options, and director compensation information.

Watson Wyatt Data Services Compensation Survey Reports. Rochelle Park, N.J.: Watson Wyatt Data Services, annual. Watson Wyatt publishes several different compensation surveys annually—some are industry specific (e.g., Survey of Hospital & Health Care Management Compensation) and some are position specific (e.g., Survey of Top Management Compensation). The companies surveyed range from emerging growth businesses to *Fortune* 1000 companies. The surveys together encompass more than one million employees.

Site Visits and Interviews

SUMMARY

When an appraiser does site visits and management interviews, the appraiser usually gains an improved understanding of the subject company. For this reason, although site visits are not required, more credibility is accorded to an expert who has performed site visits and management interviews than to one who has not.

The primary objectives of site visits and interviews are twofold:

1. To gain an understanding of the subject company's operations and *the economic reason for its existence*, and
2. Since "valuation . . . is, in essence, a prophecy [sic] as to the future,"[1] *to identify those factors that will cause the company's future results to be different from an extrapolation of its recent past results.*

SITE VISITS

A site visit can enhance the understanding of such factors as the subject company's operations, the efficiency of its plant, the condition of its equipment, the advantages and disadvantages of its location, the quality of its management, and its general and specific strengths and weaknesses.

MANAGEMENT INTERVIEWS

Management interviews can be helpful in understanding the history of the business, compensation policy, dividend policy, markets and marketing policies and plans, labor relations, regu-

---

[1]Rev. Rul. 59-60.

latory relations, supplier relations, inventory policies, insurance coverage, reasons for financial analysis to reveal deviations from industry or guideline company norms, and off-balance-sheet assets or liabilities.

Inquiries should be made as to whether there were any past transactions in the company's ownership and, if so, whether they were arm's length. Another related inquiry should be whether there were any bona fide offers to buy the company and, if so, the details of such offer(s).

Areas of investigation for the management interview could include, for example:

- Management's perspective on the company's position in its industry
- Any internal or external facts that could cause future results to differ materially from past results
- Prospects, if any, for a liquidity event (e.g., sale of the company, public offering of stock)
- Why the capital structure is organized as it is, and any plans to change it
- Identification of prospective guideline companies, either publicly traded companies or private companies that have changed ownership

The management interview can also be a good occasion on which to identify sources of industry information. The following questions are a good place to start:

- What trade associations do you belong to?
- Are there any other trade associations in your industry?
- What do you read for industry information?

Most appraisers have checklists of areas of inquiry for site visits and management interviews.[2] At the end of each interview, many experienced appraisers ask a catch-all question such as, "Is there any information that we haven't covered which might bear on the value?" This can accomplish two objectives:

1. Protect the appraiser against material omissions
2. Place the burden on management to not withhold relevant information

INTERVIEWS WITH PERSONS OUTSIDE THE COMPANY

Sometimes it is also helpful to interview persons outside the company, such as the outside accountant, the company's attorney, the company's banker, industry experts, customers, suppliers, and even competitors.

---

[2]An excellent checklist for site visits and management interviews can be found in Jay Fishman et al., *Guide to Business Valuations*, 15th ed. (Ft. Worth, TX.: Practitioners Publishing Company, 2005).

The company's outside accountant has two key functions:

1. Explain or interpret appraiser's questions about items on the financial statements.
2. Provide audit working papers for additional details regarding the financial statements.

The company's attorney may be helpful in interpreting the legal implications of various documents or in assessing the potential impact of contingent assets or liabilities, especially unsettled law suits.

The company's banker may provide a perspective on the company's risk, as well as on the availability of bank financing. Documents submitted by the company to its bankers for borrowing purposes may also provide certain insight.

Industry experts may be helpful in a variety of ways, such as:

• Assessing industry trends and their potential impact on the company
• Assessing the impact of imminent changes in the industry or its regulations
• Assessing the potential impact of various contingent liabilities, such as environmental concerns or liability from, for example, asbestos lawsuits

Customers, former customers, suppliers, and competitors may be helpful in assessing such things as the company's position in the industry and the market's perceived quality of the company's products and services.

CONCLUSION

Site visits and interviews with management and possibly others can provide the analyst with insights available from no other source. These insights strengthen the appraiser's understanding of the company, its business risks, and its growth prospects.

Armed with this background information, we can now proceed to the valuation methodology. We deal first with the three basic approaches to value (income, market, and asset-based), then to discounts and/or premiums, and finally to the weight to be accorded to each so as to reach a final opinion of value.

Chapter 14

The Income Approach

SUMMARY OF APPROACHES, METHODS, AND PROCEDURES

In the hierarchy of widely used business valuation terminology, there are approaches, methods, and procedures. In business valuation, as in real estate appraisal, there are three generally recognized approaches: *income*, *market* (sales comparison), and *asset-based* (cost).

Within these approaches, there are methods. Within the income approach, the methods are *discounting* and *capitalizing*. Within the market approach, the primary methods are *guideline publicly traded companies* and the *guideline transaction* (mergers and acquisitions) method (sales of entire companies). Also conventionally classified under the market approach are *prior transactions*, *offers to buy*, *buy/sell agreements*, and *rules of thumb*. Within the asset approach, the methods are the adjusted net asset method and the excess earnings method.

Procedures are techniques used within these methods, such as the direct equity procedure versus the invested capital procedure. For example, in any of the three approaches, the procedure could be to value the common equity directly or to value all of the invested capital and then subtract the value of all the senior securities to arrive at the value of the common equity.

Although not every business appraiser follows these conventional classifications, this book will proceed with a chapter on each of the recognized approaches, within which we discuss the methods in the order just outlined.

INTRODUCTION TO THE INCOME APPROACH

Theoretically, the income approach is the most valid way to measure the value of a business or business interest. Most corporate finance texts say that the value of a company (or an interest in a company) is the value of all of its future benefits to its owners (usually measured in net cash flows) discounted back to a present value at a discount rate (cost of capital) that reflects the time value of money and the degree of risk of realizing the projected benefits.

The income approach is widely used by corporate acquirers, investment bankers, and institutional investors who take positions in private companies. The Chancery Court of Delaware has declared it the preferred approach in valuing stock for dissenting stockholder suits, stating, for example, that the discounted cash flow method is "increasingly the model of choice for valuations in this Court."[1]

As noted in the summary, within the income approach are two basic methods:

1. *Discounting.* All expected future benefits are projected and discounted back to a present value.
2. *Capitalizing.* A single benefit is divided by a capitalization rate to get a present value.

As will be explained, the latter method is simply a derivation of the former method.

The income approach requires two categories of estimates:

1. Forecasts of future results, such as net cash flow or earnings
2. Estimation of an appropriate discount rate (cost of capital or cost of equity)

Reasonable business appraisers may disagree widely on each of these inputs. As with the market approach, the income approach can be used to value common equity directly or to value all invested capital (common and preferred stock and long-term debt). As with the market approach, if it is invested capital that was valued, the value of the debt and preferred stock included in the valuation must be subtracted to arrive at the value of the common equity. Some business valuation practitioners also subtract all the cash and cash equivalents from the subject company and omit the returns applicable to the cash equivalents, and then add the value of the cash to the indicated value of the operating company.

NET CASH FLOW: THE PREFERRED MEASURE OF ECONOMIC BENEFIT IN THE INCOME APPROACH

The income approach can be applied to any level of economic benefits, such as earnings, dividends, or various measures of returns. However, the measure of economic benefits preferred

---

[1]*Grimes v. Vitalink Comm. Corp.*, 1997 Del. Ch. LEXIS 124 (Del. Ch. 1997). (*Shannon Pratt's Business Valuation Update*, Oct. 1997).

Exhibit 14.1   Definition of Net Cash Flow to Equity

In valuing *equity* by discounting or capitalizing expected cash flows (keeping in mind the important difference between discounting and capitalizing, as discussed elsewhere), *net cash flow to equity* is defined as

Net income to common stock (after tax)

+	Noncash charges
−	Capital expenditures*
±	Additions to net working capital*
−	Dividends on preferred stock
±	Changes in long-term debt (add cash from borrowing, subtract repayments)*
=	Net cash flow to equity

*Only amounts necessary to support projected operations

Source: Shannon P. Pratt, *Cost of Capital: Estimation and Applications*, 2nd ed. (New York: John Wiley & Sons, Inc., 2002): 16. All rights reserved. Used with permission.

by most professional valuation practitioners for use in the income approach is net cash flow. Net cash flow to equity is defined in Exhibit 14.1; net cash flow to invested capital is defined in Exhibit 14.2.

There are three reasons for the general preference to use net cash flow as the economic benefit to be capitalized or discounted in the income approach:

1. Net cash flow represents the amounts of cash that owners can withdraw or reinvest at their discretion without disrupting ongoing operations of the business.
2. More data are readily available to develop an empirically defensible discount rate for net cash flow than any other economic benefit measure.
3. Net cash flow is one variable not normally used in the market approach. Therefore, use of net cash flow in the income approach makes the income and market approaches more independent from each other and thus more reliable checks on each other.

For these reasons, the authors will use net cash flow in the text and examples throughout this chapter. Any other economic income variable may be discounted or capitalized,

Exhibit 14.2   Definition of Net Cash Flow to Invested Capital

In valuing the entire *invested capital* of a company or project by discounting or capitalizing expected cash flows, *net cash flow to invested capital* is defined as

Net income to common stock (after tax)

+	Noncash charges (e.g., depreciation, amortization, deferred revenue, deferred taxes)
−	Capital expenditures*
+	Additions to net working capital*
+	Dividends on preferred stock
+	Interest expense (net of the tax deduction resulting from interest as a tax-deductible expense)
=	Net cash flow to invested capital

*Only amounts necessary to support projection operations

Source: Shannon P. Pratt, *Cost of Capital: Estimation and Applications*, 2nd ed. (New York: John Wiley & Sons, Inc., 2002): 16. All rights reserved. Used with permission.

but the discount or capitalization rate must be modified to match the definition of the economic income variable being discounted or capitalized. Development of discount or capitalization rates to be used with income variables other than net cash flow is beyond the scope of this book.

DISCOUNTING VERSUS CAPITALIZING

The income approach is applied using one of two methods:

1. Discounted future economic benefits
2. Capitalization of economic benefits

It would be redundant to use both methods in the same valuation because capitalization is simply a shortcut form of discounting.

RELATIONSHIP BETWEEN DISCOUNT RATE AND CAPITALIZATION RATE

When the applicable standard of value is fair market value, the market drives the discount rate. It represents the market's required expected total rate of return to attract funds to an investment (in the case of stock, dividends plus capital appreciation). It is comprised of a "safe" rate of return plus a premium for risk. Development of discount rates is the subject of a later section of this chapter.

The capitalization rate in the income approach is based on the discount rate. The capitalization rate is calculated by subtracting the long-term expected growth rate in the variable being capitalized from the discount rate.

Many people confuse discount rates with capitalization rates. The only case in which the discount rate equals the capitalization rate is where the amount of the variable being discounted or capitalized remains constant (i.e., there is a zero growth rate), theoretically in perpetuity.

Capitalization

The *International Glossary of Business Valuation Terms* defines *capitalization* as "the conversion of a single period of economic benefits into value." It also has the following definitions:

- *Capitalization factor.* Any multiple or divisor used to convert anticipated economic benefits of a single period into value
- *Capitalization-of-earnings method.* A method within the income approach whereby economic benefits for a representative single period are converted to value through division by a capitalization rate
- *Capitalization rate.* Any divisor (usually expressed as a percentage) used to convert anticipated economic benefits of a single period into value

One important assumption is implicit in the capitalization method: that the income variable being capitalized will either remain constant or will grow or decline at a reasonably constant and predictable rate over a long period of time. The "long period of time" theoretically is in perpetuity, but, as a practical matter, changes after 10 years have very little impact on present value.

Constant Level Assumption

The simplest use of the capitalization method involves an assumption that the variable being capitalized remains constant (i.e., a no-growth scenario). In this case, we merely divide the variable being capitalized by the discount rate:

$$\frac{\text{Expected net cash flow per year}}{\text{Discount rate (rate of return) or (cost of capital)}}$$

For example, if expected net cash flow is $20 per year and the capitalization rate is 10 percent, the value of $20 per year capitalized at 10 percent is $200:

$$\$20 \div .10 = \$200$$

In this unique (and unrealistic) case, the discount rate equals the capitalization rate because there is no growth to subtract from the discount rate.

Constant Growth or Decline Assumption (The "Gordon Growth Model")

If one assumes a constant rate of growth in net cash flow, one can simply multiply the latest 12 months' normalized net cash flow by one plus the growth rate and then divide that amount by the discount rate minus the growth rate. This is called the Gordon Growth Model.

$$\frac{\text{Net cash flow } (1 + \text{Growth rate})}{(\text{Discount rate } - \text{Growth rate})}$$

To illustrate the model, assume that the latest 12 months' normalized net cash flow was $10 and the assumed growth rate is 5 percent. The amount to be capitalized would be:

$$\$10.00 \times 1.05 = \$10.50$$

If one assumes that the discount rate is 15 percent, the capitalization rate would be:

$$15\% - 5\% = 10\%$$

One would then divide the amount of next year's anticipated cash flow by the capitalization rate to arrive at the value:

$$\$10.50 \div .10 = \$105$$

In this example, the company's fair market value is $105, the amount a willing buyer would expect to pay and a willing seller would expect to receive (before any transaction costs or valuation discounts or premiums).

The investor in this example thus earns a *total* rate of return of 15 percent, comprised of 10 percent current return (the capitalization rate), plus 5 percent annually compounded growth in the value of the investment.

This is shown in formula form in Exhibit 14.3.

The Discounting Method

The following material is by far the most quantitative section in this book, but is the very core of valuation theory.

Even though the discounting method is complex, we encourage readers to review it until they have a basic understanding of how it works. Whether or not the discounting method is used, the results from any valuation method should be compatible with results from the discounting method.

Description of the Discounting Method

In arithmetic terms, discounting is the opposite of compounding. We understand compounding because we make deposits in savings accounts at compound interest and calculate how

---

Exhibit 14.3   Gordon Growth Model

The assumption is that cash flows will grow evenly in perpetuity from the period immediately preceding the valuation date. This scenario is stated in a formula known as the Gordon Growth Model:

$$PV = \frac{NCF_0(1+g)}{k-g}$$

where:

PV = Present value
NCF_0 = Net cash flow in period 0, the period immediately preceding the valuation date
k = Discount rate (cost of capital)
g = Expected long-term sustainable growth rate in net cash flow to investor

Note that for this model to make economic sense, NCF_0 must represent a normalized amount of cash flow from the investment for the previous year, from which a steady rate of growth is expected to proceed. Therefore, NCF_0 need not be the actual cash flow for period zero but may be the result of certain normalization adjustments, such as elimination of the effect of one or more nonrecurring factors (see Chapter 10 for a discussion of normalization adjustments).

In fact, if NCF_0 is the actual net cash flow for period 0, the valuation analyst must take reasonable steps to be satisfied that NCF_0 is indeed the most reasonable base from which to start the expected growth embedded in the growth rate. Furthermore, the valuation report should state the steps taken and the assumptions made in concluding that last year's actual results are the most realistic base for expected growth. Mechanistic acceptance of recent results as representative of future expectations is one of the most common errors in implementing the capitalization method of valuation.

Source: Shannon P. Pratt, *Cost of Capital: Estimation and Applications,* 2nd ed. (New York: John Wiley & Sons, Inc., 2002): 25–26. All rights reserved. Used with permission.

much the deposit will be worth some years in the future at a given rate of interest. In discounting, we do the opposite. We are calculating what a given amount of dollars, to be received at some time in the future, will be worth in today's dollars, assuming the market requires a particular expected rate of return to attract funds to the investment.

This relationship is shown graphically in Exhibit 14.4.

In theory, the discounting method projects the expected returns over the life of the business. These expected returns are then discounted back to present value at a discount rate that reflects the time value of money and the market's required rate of return for investments of similar risk characteristics.

In other words, we are trying to determine what the investment's future cash flows are worth to an investor in today's dollars. Thus, if our projected cash flow and rate of return are accurate, the present value of the business, if invested today, will ultimately yield the expected cash flows to an investor.

The Terminal Value in the Discounting Method

For some types of investments, such as proposed utility-plant investments based on feasibility studies, analysts actually do make forecasts for the entire expected life of the business. More commonly, however, analysts make projections for a finite number of years—often five to ten years. At the end of the specific projection period, analysts estimate what is referred to as a *terminal value*, or the investment's expected present value as of the end of the specific projection period. Terminal value is then discounted back to today's dollars at an appropriate discount rate. The present value of the terminal value is then added to the present value of the projected cash flows from the specified projection period to arrive at the total estimated present value of the investment.

Exhibit 14.4   Discounted Present Value of an Annuity

	Amount to Be Received at End of Each Year		
Today's Value (Present Value)	Year 1 $1,000	Year 2 $1,000	Year 3 $1,000
$ 925.93 ◄——— 1 year @ 8%			
$ 857.34 ◄————————— 2 years @ 8%			
$ 793.83 ◄——————————————— 3 years @ 8%			
$2,577.10			
	Total present value of 3-year annuity of $1,000 per year with a compound rate of return of 8% per year		

Note how this is the opposite of compounding: If you invested $925.93 for a year at 8 percent, it would be worth $1,000 at the end of the year. If you invested $857.34 for 2 years at 8 percent compounded annually, it would be worth $1,000 at the end of 2 years, and so forth.

$$\$925.93 \times 1.08 = \$1,000$$
$$\$857.34 \times 1.08 \times 1.08 = \$1,000$$
$$\$793.83 \times 1.08 \times 1.08 \times 1.08 = \$1,000$$

Source: Shannon P. Pratt, The Lawyer's Business Valuation Handbook (Chicago: American Bar Association, 2000): 108. All rights reserved. Used with permission.

The terminal value may be estimated either by the Gordon Growth Model or by market valuation multiples. Generally, most professional business valuation analysts prefer estimating the terminal value by the Gordon Growth Model because this preserves the independence of the income approach from the market approach. However, most investment bankers prefer to estimate the terminal value with valuation multiples, on the basis that this best represents the manner in which the business might be sold at the end of the projected period.

Each year's expected cash flows, and the terminal value, are divided by one plus the discount rate, raised to the power of the number of years into the future that the cash flows are expected. The terminal value is discounted by the number of years in the specific forecast period, because the terminal value represents the value of the company as of the end of the specific forecast period. Each year's cash flows are discounted using the year in which they occur as the exponent.

An Example of the Discounting Method

Assume: Discount rate (market's requirement as to expected compound annual return to attract funds to an investment of this level of risk) = 20%

Expected Net Cash Flows	
Year 1	$1,200
Year 2	$1,500
Year 3	$1,700

Expected long-term growth rate following year 3 = 5%

Using the Gordon Growth Model to estimate the terminal value, these assumptions would result in the following calculations:

$$PV = \frac{\$1,200}{(1+.20)} + \frac{\$1,500}{(1+.20)^2} + \frac{\$1,700}{(1+.20)^3} + \frac{\dfrac{\$1,700 \times (1+.05)}{.20-.05}}{(1+.20)^3}$$

$$= \frac{\$1,200}{1.20} + \frac{\$1,500}{1.44} + \frac{\$1,700}{1.728} + \frac{\dfrac{\$1,785}{.15}}{(1+.20)^3}$$

$$= \frac{\$1,200}{1.20} + \frac{\$1,500}{1.44} + \frac{\$1,700}{1.728} + \frac{\$11,900}{1.728}$$

$$= \$1,000 + \$1,041.67 + 983.96 + \$6886.57$$

$$= \$9,912.20$$

This is the amount that a willing buyer would expect to pay and a willing seller would expect to receive for this investment (before considering any transaction costs).

Note how much of the present value is accounted for by the terminal value. This is so because, in this example, we kept the specific projection period unusually short; it is not, however, unusual for the terminal value to account for half or more of the present value. Thus, it is extremely important to assess the reasonableness of the terminal value in determining the reasonableness of an estimated present value.

Exhibit 14.5 Formula for Discounted Cash Flow Calculation Using Gordon Growth Model for Terminal Value

$$PV = \frac{NCF_1}{(1+k)} + \frac{NCF_2}{(1+k)^2} + \ldots + \frac{NCF_n}{(1+k)^n} \quad \frac{\dfrac{NCF_n(1+g)}{k-g}}{(1+k)^n}$$

where:

$NCF_1 \ldots NCF_n$	=	Net cash flow expected in each of the periods 1 through n, n being the last period of the discrete cash flow projections.
k	=	Discount rate (cost of capital)
g	=	Expected long-term sustainable growth rate in net cash flow, starting with the last period of the discrete projections as the base year.

Source: Shannon P. Pratt, *Cost of Capital: Estimation and Applications*, 2nd ed. (New York: John Wiley & Sons, Inc., 2002): 27–28. All rights reserved. Used with permission.

The discounting method is shown in formula form in Exhibit 14.5.

Note how this works in reverse. If we deposited the present value of each of the cash flows and their values grew over the discount period at the discount rate, we would have the following:

Year	PV of Cash Flow	Discount Rate Compounded for n year	Future Value
1	$1,000.00	× 1.20 =	$ 1,200
2	$1,041.67	× 1.20 × 1.20 =	$ 1,500
3	$ 983.96	× 1.20 × 1.20 × 1.20 ≅	$ 1,700
Terminal value	$6,886.57	× 1.20 × 1.20 × 1.20 ≅	$11,900

The present value calculation is sometimes presented in tabular form using capitalization factors for each year's cash flows and for the terminal value. These *capitalization factors* are the reciprocals of the divisors just presented:

$$1/1.20 = 0.833333$$
$$1/(1.20)^2 = 0.694444$$
$$1/(1.20)^3 = 0.578704$$

When using such a table, the presentation looks like this:

Year	Cash Flow	Capitalization Factor	Present Value
1	$ 1,200.00	× 0.833333 =	$1,000.00
2	$ 1,500.00	× 0.694444 =	$1,041.67
3	$ 1,700.00	× 0.578704 =	$ 983.80
Terminal value	$11,900.00	× 0.578704 =	$6,886.57
Present value of investment			$9,912.04

The slight difference between this presentation and the previous presentation is due to rounding off the capitalization factors to six digits. If the capitalization factors were carried out to a few more digits, the values would be exactly the same.

PROJECTED AMOUNTS OF EXPECTED RETURNS

Sometimes the valuation analyst will undertake the task of developing projections for expected returns independently, but usually the projections are provided by management.

Some companies routinely make projections of net cash flows for budgeting and other purposes. There is a presumption that projections prepared in the normal course of business are free of any bias that may creep into projections prepared for litigation.

If management routinely prepares projections, the analyst may request prior projections and compare them with actual results to evaluate the reliability of management's projections.

In any case, all assumptions underlying the projections should be clearly explained in the valuation report. The analyst should understand any underlying assumptions and evaluate them for reasonableness.

If the analyst believes that the projections supplied by management are either too high or too low, she has several possible courses of action, including:

- Reject the income approach as unreliable.
- Adjust the projections in light of more reasonable assumptions.
- Adjust the discount rate for company-specific risk. (Estimating the appropriate discount rate is the subject of a subsequent section.)
- Accept the projections on their face, and disclaim any responsibility for independent verification.

Some analysts regularly use *sensitivity analysis*. That is, they change one or more of the assumptions and rerun the calculations to see how the change in assumptions affects the results. The degree of sensitivity to reasonable changes in assumptions can impact the reliability of the results. For example, when very low discount rates are used, a few points' change in the discount rate can have a major impact on the indicated value.

Projections are usually denominated in *nominal* dollars, which include the effects of inflation. This is because discount rates are usually estimated in nominal terms. In the unusual cases where projections are made in real dollars (not reflecting inflation), then the estimated rate of inflation must be removed from the discount rate to make the calculations consistent.

DEVELOPING DISCOUNT AND CAPITALIZATION RATES
FOR EQUITY RETURNS

Arguably, even more challenging than projecting future results is estimating an appropriate discount rate by which to discount the expected cash flows back to a present value.

Discount rates applicable to debt are readily observable in the market. Unlike stocks, bonds have a fixed amount of promised future payments of interest and principal.

Yield to maturity (an approximation of the discount rate) data are published daily in the financial press for bonds of all risk grades (AAA, AA, A, BBB, etc.). The requirements for each risk grade are published by rating services, so the analyst can easily value a company's debt by estimating the risk category into which it falls and looking up the yields to maturity for that risk category.[2]

Since there are no such published expected rates of return for stocks, the analyst must estimate the rate of return the market would require to invest in the subject stock. This market-driven required rate of return is called the *discount rate*.

There are many models for developing discount rates for equity. Two are most widely used:

1. The build-up model
2. The capital asset pricing model (CAPM)

The Build-Up Model

The *build-up model* incorporates some or all of the following elements:

- A risk-free rate
- A general "equity risk premium" (a premium over the risk-free rate for the added risk of investing in any kind of stocks over the risk-free rate)
- A size premium
- An industry risk adjustment
- A company-specific risk adjustment

The Risk-Free Rate

The *risk-free rate* is the yield to maturity on U.S. government obligations. The most-used rate is the yield to maturity on 20-year Treasury bonds as of the valuation date.

This incorporates a *real* rate of return, which is compensation for giving up the use of money until the maturity of the bond. It also incorporates the market's expectation of the amount of inflation expected over the term of the bond. This means that the rate is a *nominal* rate, which includes expected inflation.

It is called a *risk-free rate* because it is presumably free of risk of default. However, it also incorporates *horizon risk* or *maturity risk*, the risk that the market value of the principal may fluctuate with changes in the general level of interest rates.

The Equity Risk Premium

The *equity risk premium* is the amount of return over and above the risk-free rate for investing in a portfolio of large common stocks, such as the Standard & Poor's 500 stock index.

Much research and controversy are devoted to estimating the level of the equity risk premium at any given time. Estimates range from 2 percent to more than 7.5 percent. To the extent

---

[2]For a discussion of valuing debt investments, see Shannon P. Pratt, Robert F. Reilly, and Robert P. Schweihs, *Valuing a Business: The Analysis and Appraisal of Closely Held Companies*, 4th ed. (New York: McGraw-Hill, 2000), Chapter 23, pp. 515–530.

there is a consensus as of this writing, it is probably between 5 and 6 percent. In any case, the analyst's report should disclose the source of the estimated equity risk premium.

The Size Premium

In general, small companies are more risky than large ones, all other things being equal. Size can be measured in many dimensions, such as market value of equity, revenues, or assets, to name a few. Research suggests that the risk premium for small size relative to average size of the companies making up the S&P 500 is about the same regardless of which measure of size is used in the analysis.

Since most companies are much smaller than the average size of the companies included in the S&P 500, a size premium is usually incorporated into the estimation of the discount rate. Estimates of the size premium usually fall in the range of 3 to 9 percent, although it is possible to be outside that range.

In any case, the analyst's report should indicate how any applicable size premium was derived.

The Industry Adjustment

In 2001, Ibbotson Associates, in its annual *Stocks, Bonds, Bills and Inflation*,[3] started publishing suggested adjustments to the discount rate based on industry groups for use with the build-up model. Beginning in 2003, the list of companies from which the data were compiled for each industry group was made available on Ibbotson's Web site, *www.Ibbotson.com.*

The industry groups are quite broadly defined. If the subject company conforms well to one of Ibbotson's broadly defined industries, their adjustments may be useful.

The industry adjustment is applied to the combined equity risk premium and size premium based on Ibbotson data, and can be either positive or negative.

The Company-Specific Risk Adjustment

This company-specific element of the discount rate captures any aspects of risk factors unique to the subject company, as opposed to the risk factors incorporated in the companies from which the discount rate was otherwise derived. It is usually positive, but could be negative. If an industry adjustment is not used, the company-specific risk adjustment may incorporate industry risk factors not generally characteristic of other companies in the size range.

The company-specific adjustment is usually in the range of a negative 2 percent to a positive 5 percent, but sometimes falls outside that range, and is occasionally as high as positive 10 percent. A 10 percent adjustment could be warranted in extreme circumstances such as a start-up company or a financially distressed company. It could even be much higher for a true start-up in a venture-capital situation. This adjustment is based entirely on the appraiser's analysis and judgment, so it should be well supported in the narrative discussion of risk factors.

The Capital Asset Pricing Model (CAPM)

The CAPM differs from the build-up model in that it incorporates a factor called beta as a modifier to the general equity risk premium. *Beta* is a measure of systematic risk, that is, the

---

[3]Ibbotson Associates. *Stocks, Bonds, Bills and Inflation* (Chicago: Ibbotson Associates, annual).

Exhibit 14.6 Developing Equity Discount Rates Using the Build-Up Model with and without an Industry Adjustment and Using the Capital Asset Pricing Model

	Build-Up Model w/Industry Adjustment	Build-Up Model w/o Industry Adjustment	Capital Asset Pricing Model
Risk-free rate[a]	5.4%	5.4%	5.4%
Equity risk premium[b]	7.0%	7.0%	
× Beta of .8[c]			
(7.0 × .8 = 5.6)			5.6%
Size premium[d]	3.5%	3.5%	3.5%
Industry adjustment[e]	–3.6%	—	—
Estimated Equity Discount Rate	12.3%	15.9%	14.5%

[a]20-year U.S. Treasury bond yield to maturity as of the valuation date, July 31, 2003.

[b]1926–2002 arithmetic average of excess return on S&P 500 stocks over 20-year U.S. Treasury bonds per Ibbotson Associates, *Stocks, Bonds, Bill and Inflation*, 2003 Valuation Edition, p. 248.

[c]Average beta for selected guideline companies in SIC 422, Public Warehousing and Transportation.

[d]Size premium in excess of CAPM for micro-cap stocks (smallest quintile on NYSE) according to *SBBI*, 2003 Valuation Edition, p. 127.

[e]Industry risk adjustment for SIC 422, Public Warehousing and Transportation, per *SBBI*, 2003 Valuation Edition, p. 46.

Source: Ibbotson data used with permission. All rights reserved. *www.ibbotson.com.*

correlation of fluctuations in the *excess* returns on the specific stock with the *excess* returns on the market as a whole as measured by some index, usually the S&P 500. *Excess returns* are those returns over and above the risk-free rate of return.

The average beta for the market is, by definition, 1.0. Thus, for a company with a beta of 1.2, the company's excess returns can be expected to fluctuate by 120 percent above the market; a company with a beta of 0.8 can be expected to fluctuate by 80 percent of the market as a whole.

Because private companies do not have public market prices, when valuing a private company using the CAPM, average betas of companies in the same industry are usually used as a proxy for the beta of the subject private company.

In the CAPM, the equity risk premium is modified by multiplying it by the assumed beta. Because the beta reflects the risk of the industry, the industry risk adjustment is not used in the CAPM.

The size premium factor is used for companies smaller than those in the S&P 500. The company-specific risk adjustment is used where appropriate.

Exhibit 14.6 is a comparative sample illustration of the development of the equity discount rate using three models:

1. The build-up model with an industry adjustment
2. The build-up model without an industry adjustment. The industry adjustment is an attempt to replace beta. It works reasonably well in the cases where the companies used to calculate the industry adjustment are adequately homogeneous with the subject company.
3. The CAPM

Estimating Capitalization Rates

Capitalization rates are used in the income approach for the capitalization method, and for the discounting method in cases where the Gordon Growth Model is used to develop the terminal value.

In the context of the income approach, the capitalization rate is derived by subtracting the estimated long-term growth rate from the discount rate. Since the capitalization rate is such a crucial factor in the income approach, it is important that both the discount rate and the long-term growth rate be estimated very carefully in order to obtain a reliable value estimate.

WEIGHTED AVERAGE COST OF CAPITAL (WACC)

When valuing a company's invested capital by the income approach, the projected cash flows include those available to all the invested capital. Therefore, the market rate of return at which they should be discounted is the weighted average of the components of the capital structure (common equity, preferred equity, and long-term debt), known as the weighted average cost of capital (WACC).

The components of the WACC are weighted at their respective market values, NOT their book values. Since market values (at least for the equity component) are unknown, calculating the WACC often requires an *iterative process,* that is, repeating the calculations at various weightings of the components until they balance. Fortunately, modern computer programs can perform the necessary iterations in seconds.

Since interest paid on debt is tax deductible, the actual cost of debt to the company is the after-tax cost. Thus, the company's tax rate should be deducted from the pretax cost of debt when calculating the debt component of the weighted average cost of capital.

The following is an example of the weighted average cost of capital.

Assume:

	Cost	Weight
Common equity	20%	70%
Long-term debt	10%	30%
Tax rate	40%	

Then:

Component	Cost	Weight	Weighted Cost
Equity	0.20	$\times 0.70 =$	14.0%
Long-term debt	$0.10 \times (1 - 0.40) = 0.60$	$\times 0.30 =$	1.8%
Weighted average cost of capital			15.8%

This would be used as a discount rate when valuing invested capital. (In appraisals for property tax purposes, the weighted average cost of capital is often referred to as the *band of investment* theory.)

One question that arises in estimating the WACC is whether to use the company's actual capital structure or a hypothetical capital structure. In general, when valuing a minority interest, the company's actual capital structure should be used because the minority owner has no power to change the capital structure. However, when valuing a controlling interest, the control holder has the power to change the capital structure, so in some cases analysts use an industry average capital structure.

THE MIDYEAR CONVENTION

The capitalization and discounting procedures previously discussed implicitly reflect the assumption that the cash flows will be received at the end of each projected year. This is a reasonable assumption for many companies because management may wait until the end of the year to determine the capital expenditure and working capital requirements for the following year before deciding on distributions, if any.

However, some companies receive cash flows more or less evenly throughout the year. To reflect this situation, some business valuation practitioners employ a modification to the capitalization and discounting calculations called the midyear convention.

The midyear convention, in effect, assumes that investors receive cash flows in the middle of each year. This assumption approximates the value that would be calculated from receiving cash flows evenly throughout the year.

The Midyear Convention in the Capitalization Method

In the Gordon Growth Model, the modification to reflect the midyear convention is to raise the growth factor to the exponential level of 0.5. In the previous example ($10 last year's cash flow and 5 percent growth rate), the calculation for the amount to be capitalized would be $10.50 \times (1.05)^{.5} = \$10.76$. This would be divided by the capitalization rate, which was .10, to arrive at the value:

$$\$10.76 \div .10 = \$107.60$$

Note that this compares to a value of $105 with the year-end convention. The midyear convention will always produce a higher value than the year-end convention so long as the cash flows are positive, because investors are assumed to have received each projected cash flow six months earlier.

The formula for the Gordon Growth Model using the midyear convention is shown in Exhibit 14.7.

Exhibit 14.7   Formula for the Gordon Growth Model Incorporating the Midyear Convention

$$PV = \frac{NCF_1(1+k)^{0.5}}{k-g}$$

where:

PV = Present value
NCF_1 = Net cash flow expected in period 1, the period immediately following the valuation date
k = Discount rate (cost of capital, total required rate of return)
g = Long-term growth rate

Exhibit 14.8 Formula for the Discounting Method Incorporating the Midyear Convention

$$PV = \frac{NCF_1}{(1+k)^{0.5}} + \frac{NCF_2}{(1+k)^{1.5}} + \ldots + \frac{NCF_n}{(1+k)^{n-.05}} + \frac{\dfrac{NCF_n(1+g)}{k-g}}{(1+k)^{n-.05}}$$

where:

PV	=	Present value
$NCF_1 \ldots NCF_n$	=	Net cash flows expected in periods 1 through n
k	=	Discount rate (cost of capital, total required rate of return)
g	=	Long-term growth rate

Alternatively, the modified Gordon Growth Model formula may be used for the terminal value, in which case the terminal value would be discounted for n periods instead of $n - 0.5$ periods.

The Midyear Convention in the Discounting Model

The midyear modification to the discounting model is accomplished by raising each component of the divisors to an exponent of 0.5 less than would be the case in the year-end procedure.

In the previous example, the computations would be revised as follows:

$$
\begin{aligned}
PV &= \frac{\$1,200}{(1+.20)^5} + \frac{\$1,500}{(1+.20)^{1.5}} + \frac{\$1,700}{(1+.20)^{2.5}} + \frac{\dfrac{\$1,700 \times (1+.05)}{(.20-.05)}}{(1+.20)^{2.5}} \\
&= \frac{\$1,200}{1.095445} + \frac{\$1,500}{1.314534} + \frac{\$1,700}{1.577441} + \frac{\$11,900}{1.577441} \\
&= \$1,095.45 + \$1,141.09 + \$1,077.69 + \$7,543.86 \\
&= \$10,858.09
\end{aligned}
$$

This compares with $9,912.20 by the year-end convention; the assumption that investors receive their cash earlier can make a significant difference in the indicated value.

The formula for the discounting method incorporating the midyear convention is shown as Exhibit 14.8.

THE INCOME APPROACH IN THE COURTS

Following are excerpts from a few instructive court cases that explain why the income approach was or was not accepted.

In *Estate of Furman*,[4] both experts used the CAPM to estimate a discount rate, and the court rejected both—but for different reasons, basing its conclusion on the market approach.

---

[4]*Estate of Furman v. Comm'r*, T.C. Memo 1998-157, 75 T.C.M. (CCH) 2206.

The court criticized the taxpayer expert's conversion of the discount rate to a capitalization rate for failing to reflect any real growth in the assumed growth rate:

> *Our major criticism of [taxpayer's expert's] application of the income method was their construction of the capitalization rate. In deducting a long-term growth factor from the expected rate of return, [taxpayer's expert] deducted 8 percent for the 1980 capitalization rate and 7 percent for the 1981 rate. Since these figures are identical to the inflation estimates of the Value Line Investment Survey that were cited by [taxpayer's expert] in its report, the growth factors used represented only the expectation of nominal earnings growth: the growth in earnings caused by price inflation. FIC was a growing business; real sales and earnings growth could be expected, both from increased volume at existing restaurants and from the construction of new stores in the Exclusive Territory, which was an area of rapid population growth.*

The court criticized the Service's expert for calculating WACC based on book values rather than market values, and for arbitrary selection of beta:

> *After determining a cost of equity using CAPM, [the Service's expert] purported to compute the WACC of FIC in order to arrive at a capitalization rate. Without providing any explanation, [the Service's expert] computed WACC in a manner that did not conform to the accepted method. See Brealey & Myers, Principles of Corporate Finance 465-469 (4th ed. 1991); Pratt et al., Valuing a Business 180, 184, 189-190 (3d ed. 1996). First, [the Service's expert] modified the WACC formula by weighting FIC's debt and equity based on book value, rather than market value, to arrive at a WACC of 11.0 percent. Considering that the parties have stipulated risk-free rates of 11.86 percent and 14.4 percent in 1980 and 1981, respectively, it is obvious that [the Service's expert's] result is incorrect.*

In *Estate of Klauss*,[5] the court accepted the taxpayer's use of the build-up method for estimating the discount rate and rejected the Service's use of CAPM for estimating the discount rate.

The Service relied on an article by Bajaj & Hakala[6] for the proposition that there is no small-stock premium. The court stated that "[the taxpayer's expert] reasonably based the small-stock premium he used in his report on data from Ibbotson Associates" and commented further on the use of the small-stock premium by stating, "We find [the taxpayer's reports'] analysis to be more persuasive."

The court also criticized the Service's selection of beta:

> *In applying the CAPM method, [the Service's expert] chose a beta of .7 to estimate Green Light's systematic risk. . . . We disagree with [the Service's expert's] use of a .7 beta because Green Light was a small, regional company, had customer concentrations, faced litigation and environmental claims, had inadequate insurance, was not publicly traded, and had never paid a dividend. . . . [The Service's expert] stated that he selected the beta based on a review of comparable companies. However, he did not identify these comparable companies or otherwise give any reason for this use of a .7 beta. We believe [the Service's expert's] use of a .7 beta improperly increased his estimate of the value of the Green Light stock.*

---

[5]*Estate of Klauss v. Comm'r*, T.C. Memo 2000-191, 79 T.C.M. (CCH) 2177 (June 27, 2000).
[6]Mukesh Bajaj and Scott D. Hakala, "Valuation for Smaller Capitalization Companies," *Financial Valuation: Businesses and Business Interests*, James H. Zukin, ed. (New York: WG&L/RIA Group, 1998): U12A-1–U12A-39.

The court also criticized the Service's expert's inconsistency in the use of source data in developing the discount rate he used in his CAPM:

> *[The Service's expert] testified that it is appropriate to use the Ibbotson Associates data from the 1978–92 period rather than from the 1926–92 period because small stocks did not consistently outperform large stocks during the 1980's and 1990's. We give little weight to [the Service's expert's] analysis. [The Service's expert] appeared to selectively use data that favored his conclusion. He did not consistently use Ibbotson Associates data from the 1978–92 period; he relied on data from 1978–92 to support his theory that there is no small-stock premium but used an equity risk premium of 7.3 percent from the 1926–92 data (rather than the equity risk premium of 10.9 percent from the 1978–92 period). If he had used data consistently, he would have derived a small-stock premium of 5.2 percent and an equity risk premium of 7.3 percent using the 1926–92 data, rather than a small-stock premium of 2.8 percent and an equity risk premium of 10.9 percent using the 1978–92 data.*

In *Estate of Hendrickson*,[7] the court ultimately relied on the market approach and gave the Service's discounted cash flow (DCF) method no weight, but the court's lengthy discussion of the Service's DCF methodology is instructive. The Service's expert used CAPM. His discount rate essentially consisted of the following:

Risk-free rate		7.0%
Equity risk premium	7.3%	
× Beta	1.0	
		7.3%
Total discount rate		14.3%

The court criticized the Service's use of CAPM on three bases:

1. *CAPM inadequate because it fails to capture unsystematic risk.* This shortcoming might be overcome by a specific company risk factor, but the Service's expert did not address the issue.

> *[B]ecause CAPM assumes that an investor holding a diversified portfolio will encounter only systematic risk, the only type of risk for which an investor can be compensated is systematic or market risk, which represents the sensitivity of the future returns from a given asset to the movements of the market as a whole* (citing Brealey & Myers, Principles of Corporate Finance *137–138, 143–144 (4th ed. 1991)*; Pratt et al., Valuing a Business *166 (3d ed. 1996))*. . . .
>
> *[The Service's expert] followed the principles of CAPM and did not make any provision for Peoples' unsystematic risk, based on the assumption that such risk was diversifiable. . . . [[R]espondent and SERVICE'S expert] have overlooked the difficulties in diversifying an investment in a block of stock they argued is worth approximately $8.94 million. Construction of a diversified portfolio that will eliminate most unsystematic risk requires from 10 to 20 securities of similar value. See Brealey & Myers, supra at 137–139. Thus, proper diversification of an investment in the Peoples shares owned by petitioner, as valued by respondent, would require a total capital investment of at least $89 million. We do not think the hypothetical buyer should be*

---

[7]*Estate of Hendrickson v. Comm'r*, T.C. Memo 1999-278, 78 T.C.M. (CCH) 322.

limited only to a person or entity that has the means to invest $ 89 million in Peoples and a portfolio of nine other securities. . . .

2. *Beta of 1.0 too low.* [The Service's expert] derived his beta estimate from banks in Value Line, which are much larger, and the court noted that smaller companies have higher average betas.

Beta, a measure of systematic risk, is a function of the relationship between the return on an individual security and the return on the market as a whole. See Pratt et al., supra at 166. . . . However, because the betas for small corporations tend to be larger than the betas for larger corporations, it may be difficult to find suitable comparables when valuing a small, closely held corporation . . . there are substantial differences in size and operations between Peoples and the banks on the VL bank list; we do not believe that their betas are representative of the greater business risks faced by Peoples. . . .

We do not believe that an investment in Peoples, a small, single-location bank, whose earnings were susceptible to impending interest rate mismatches and sluggish local economic conditions, presents the same systematic risk as an investment in an index fund holding shares in 500 of the largest corporations in the United States.

3. *Failed to add small-stock premium.*

Although [the Service's expert] cited Ibbotson as his source for equity risk premium, in his initial report he ignored a crucial aspect of the Ibbotson approach to constructing a cost of capital-the small-stock premium. In his rebuttal report, [the Service's expert] unsuccessfully tried to persuade us that the small-stock premium is not supported by financial theory, characterizing the risk associated with a firm's size as unsystematic risk, for which the market does not compensate. The relationship between firm size and return is well known. Size is not an unsystematic risk factor and cannot be eliminated through diversification. "On average small companies have higher returns than large ones." Ibbotson at 125 (citing Banz, The Relationship Between Returns and Market Value of Common Stock, 9 J. Fin. Econ., 3–18 (1981)). We have already alluded to the likelihood that small stocks will have higher betas than larger stocks, because of greater risk. See Ibbotson at 126. However, it has been found that the greater risk of small stocks is not fully reflected in CAPM, in that actual returns may exceed those expected based on beta. Consequently, when calculating a cost of capital under CAPM on a small stock, it is appropriate to add a small stock premium to the equity risk premium, to reflect the greater risk associated with an investment in a small stock in comparison to the large stocks from which the equity-risk premium is calculated. Based on Peoples' size, a microcapitalization equity size premium of 3.6 percent should have been added See Ibbotson at 161. Consequently, even if we accepted [the Service's] beta of 1, which we do not, Peoples' cost of capital should have been at least 18 percent.

In *Polack v. Commissioner*[8] (a gift tax case), the difference between the experts' values using the income approach came down to the question of which expert's projection was more reliable. The court found that the taxpayer's witness's projection was not based on any evidence or personal knowledge, and was therefore not probative, but that the Service's witness's projection was based on objective and reliable evidence.

The opinion stated that the evidence introduced "though sparse, was not equally compelling. . . . [W]e have based our conclusion on the preponderance of evidence. . . ." Two primary differences between the appraisals were (1) the amount of "Value Added Refund

---

[8]*Polack v. Comm'r*, T.C. Memo 2002-145, 2002 Tax Ct. Memo LEXIS 149.

Income" the company would retain (as opposed to passing it along to customers), and (2) the amounts of capital expenditures the company would incur.

The Service's expert visited the facility and interviewed the persons primarily responsible for daily operations. His projections were based on statements in the interview (and also were consistent with the company's past history), while "petitioner's bald projection . . . does not appear to be based on any evidence or knowledge personal to the petitioner."

The foregoing excerpts from court case opinions illustrate well-grounded analyses of the application of the income approach. Although, as noted in the introduction to this chapter, the income approach is the most theoretically valid way to value a business or business interest, its validity is destroyed if it is not applied properly. The analyst must use well-accepted procedures and well-documented evidence to support discount rates, capitalization rates, and projected returns.

A sample valuation using the income approach is the subject of this chapter's appendix.

CONCLUSION

We presented the income approach first because it represents the theory around which business valuation revolves. However, as noted in the introduction to this chapter, the inputs necessary for the income approach can be subject to substantial differences, even among reasonable experts. We turn to the market approach in Chapter 15.

APPENDIX: AN ILLUSTRATION OF THE INCOME APPROACH TO VALUATION

Introduction

Optimum Software is a hypothetical corporation used to illustrate the application of the two methods of the income approach to valuation—the discounted cash flow method and the capitalized economic income method. The valuation techniques presented in this appendix are only examples of what the analyst may choose to include in his or her valuation. Also, in an actual valuation report, the analyst would be expected to explain his or her assumptions, methodology, and conclusions in much greater detail than presented here. An illustration of the application of the market approach to valuation can be found in Chapter 15, Appendix.

Valuation Assignment

At their 20X5 annual board meeting, the directors of Optimum Software Corporation decided to sell the company in the upcoming year. They were interested in obtaining an estimate of the value of the company as of December 31, 20X4. At the request of the board shareholders, a limited appraisal of the company was conducted with the objective of estimating the value of a 100 percent controlling interest in Optimum Software Corporation as of December 31, 20X4. The purpose of the appraisal was to assist the board in their initial negotiations with possible buyers. The standard of value used is fair market value and the premise of value is that the business will continue to function as a going concern in the foreseeable future.

Summary Description of the Company

Optimum Software Corporation is a closely held C corporation specializing in the design, development, and production of prepackaged computer software. For the software products it develops, Optimum Software also provides services such as preparation of installation documentation, and training the user in the use of the software. The two main lines of products currently developed by Optimum Software are online commerce software solutions and computer games. As of December 31, 20X4, Optimum Software reported operating income of $4.9 million, with net income of $2.9 million on sales of $17 million and assets of $6.2 million. The company was founded in 1998 and it has a workforce of roughly 100 employees, of whom 40 percent are professionals involved in the production process and 60 percent are in sales and support. The company has no preferred stock.

Financial Statements and Forecasts

Audited and unaudited financial statements were provided by the management of Optimum Software and were accepted and used without third-party independent verification. The management was also the source of the financial forecasts used in the income approach to valuation. These forecasts were checked for reasonableness against the historical performance of the company as well as the broader industry outlook and economic environment, and were found to be reasonable. This valuation is limited to information available as of the date of valuation, and the opinion of value expressed in this limited valuation is applicable only to the purpose stated above. Selected financial information for Optimum Software is presented in Exhibits 14.9 and 14.10.

Valuation of Optimum Software

In a series of exhibits, we present the basic procedures for two different methods under the income approach to valuation. Both the discounted cash flow method and the capitalized economic income method are applied to value 100 percent of equity in Optimum Software as of December 31, 20X4. Basic information such as 20X4 and five years of forecasted information for balance sheets, income statements, statements of stockholders' equity and the net cash flow to invested capital are presented in Exhibits 14.11, 14.12, 14.13, and 14.14.

Valuation Methods Applied

The analysis presented here is a very brief one. This analysis is typically presented in the valuation report, not in the footnotes to the exhibits. As noted earlier, *explaining the assumptions, methodology, and the valuation conclusion is an essential part of the valuation and should be allotted much more detail and space than we have available here.* This analysis led to its opinion of value by the application of a set of assumptions, procedures, and subjective judgment calls. A different set of assumptions, procedures, and subjective judgments may be applied, possibly resulting in a different opinion of value. For instance, here we used the net cash flow to invested capital, and we discounted or capitalized it to arrive at the market value of the invested capital in Optimum Software. Then, we subtracted the market value of the long-term debt to arrive at the value of the equity. Alternatively, the net cash flow to equity could be computed and then discounted or capitalized to arrive directly at the value of equity.

Estimating a Discount Rate

Exhibits 14.15 and 14.16 illustrate the computation of the cost of equity and the weighted average cost of capital (WACC), respectively. The cost of equity was estimated using two methods—the build-up method, and the capital asset pricing model (CAPM). The data sources are presented as footnotes to the exhibits. Since we are valuing a controlling interest in Optimum Software, we used an industry average capital structure for the market value weights in the computation of the WACC. If we were valuing a minority interest, we would most likely have used the company's own capital structure. Since we are discounting net cash flow to all invested capital, the WACC will be used as a discount rate in the discounted cash flow model and also as the base rate to arrive at the capitalization rate for the capitalized economic income method.

Exhibit 14.9 Optimum Software Adjusted Balance Sheets

Fiscal Year Ended	December 31 ($000)					December 31 (Common Size)				
	20X4	20X3	20X2	20X1	20X0	20X4	20X3	20X2	20X1	20X0
Cash and equivalents	$1,833	$1,715	$1,628	$1,925	$1,963	29%	26%	31%	30%	27%
Receivables	$3,059	$3,297	$2,813	$3,083	$3,031	49%	50%	54%	49%	42%
Inventories	$ 731	$ 645	$ 630	$ 754	$ 954	12%	10%	12%	12%	13%
Current assets	$5,623	$5,657	$5,070	$5,761	$5,948	90%	86%	97%	91%	83%
Fixed assets (net)	$ 600	$ 619	$ 83	$ 474	$1,157	10%	9%	2%	7%	16%
Intangibles (net)	$ 12	$ 269	$ 98	$ 95	$ 58	0%	4%	2%	1%	1%
Total assets	$6,234	$6,544	$5,250	$6,330	$7,163	100%	100%	100%	100%	100%
Notes payable	$ 895	$ 778	$ 758	$ 596	$1,199	14%	12%	14%	9%	17%
Current portion of long-term debt	$ 232	$ 322	$ 135	$ 78	$ 433	4%	5%	3%	1%	6%
Trade payables	$ 520	$ 483	$ 450	$ 690	$ 564	8%	7%	9%	11%	8%
Taxes payable	$ 77	$ 161	$ 68	$ 78	$ 87	1%	2%	1%	1%	1%
Current liabilities	$1,725	$1,744	$1,410	$1,442	$2,282	28%	27%	27%	23%	32%
Long-term debt	$ 565	$ 537	$ 465	$ 346	$ 636	9%	8%	9%	5%	9%
Total liabilities	$2,290	$2,281	$1,875	$1,789	$2,918	37%	35%	36%	28%	41%
Common stock, $0.1 par	$ 28	$ 28	$ 28	$ 28	$ 28	0%	0%	1%	0%	0%
Additional paid-in capital	$ 353	$ 293	$ 343	$ 408	$ 352	6%	4%	7%	6%	5%
Retained earnings	$3,563	$3,943	$3,004	$4,105	$3,865	57%	60%	57%	65%	54%
Total equity	$3,945	$4,263	$3,375	$4,541	$4,245	63%	65%	64%	72%	59%
Total liabilities and equity	$6,234	$6,544	$5,250	$6,330	$7,163	100%	100%	100%	100%	100%
Working Capital	$3,898	$3,913	$3,660	$4,319	$3,666					

Exhibit 14.10 Optimum Software Adjusted Income Statements

Fiscal Year Ended	December 31 ($000)					December 31 (Common Size)				
	20X4	20X3	20X2	20X1	20X0	20X4	20X3	20X2	20X1	20X0
Sales	$17,045	$15,246	$13,790	$16,030	$18,620	100%	100%	100%	100.00%	100%
Cost of goods sold	$ 8,550	$ 7,788	$ 7,200	$ 8,400	$ 9,576	50%	51%	52%	52%	51%
Gross margin	$ 8,495	$ 7,458	$ 6,590	$ 7,630	$ 9,044	50%	49%	48%	48%	49%
SG&A	$ 2,220	$ 2,112	$ 2,160	$ 2,340	$ 2,520	13%	14%	16%	15%	14%
Research and development	$ 1,020	$ 1,056	$ 1,080	$ 1,320	$ 1,008	6%	7%	8%	8%	5%
Depreciation and amortization	$ 330	$ 264	$ 120	$ 210	$ 504	2%	2%	1%	1%	3%
Total operating expenses	$ 3,570	$ 3,432	$ 3,360	$ 3,870	$ 4,032	21%	23%	24%	24%	22%
Income (loss) from operations	$ 4,925	$ 4,026	$ 3,230	$ 3,760	$ 5,012	29%	26%	23%	23%	27%
Interest expense	$ 62	$ 70	$ 75	$ 86	$ 112	0%	0%	1%	1%	1%
Income (loss) before taxes	$ 4,863	$ 3,956	$ 3,155	$ 3,674	$ 4,900	29%	26%	23%	23%	26%
Provision for income taxes	$ 1,945	$ 1,582	$ 1,262	$ 1,470	$ 1,960	11%	10%	9%	9%	11%
Net income	$ 2,918	$ 2,374	$ 1,893	$ 2,204	$ 2,940	17%	16%	14%	14%	16%
EBITDA	$ 5,255	$ 4,290	$ 3,350	$ 3,970	$ 5,516					

Exhibit 14.11 Optimum Software Forecast of Balance Sheets

Balance Sheets ($000) End of Year	Actual 20X4	Projected 20X5	20X6	20X7	20X8	20X9
Current assets	$5,623	$6,185	$6,803	$7,484	$8,232	$9,055
Fixed assets (net)	600	660	726	799	878	966
Intangibles (net)	12	13	14	16	17	19
Total assets	**6,234**	**6,858**	**7,544**	**8,298**	**9,128**	**10,041**
Current liabilities	1,725	1,898	2,087	2,296	2,526	2,778
Long-term debt	565	621	683	752	827	910
Total equity	3,945	4,339	4,773	5,250	5,775	6,353
Total liabilities and equity	**6,234**	**6,858**	**7,544**	**8,298**	**9,128**	**10,041**
Working capital	$3,898	$4,287	$4,716	$5,188	$5,707	$6,277
Change in working capital		$390	$429	$472	$519	$571

Notes:

Expected growth rate for the high-growth period is 10% for the first 5 years.

Market value of debt = Book value of debt

Exhibit 14.12 Optimum Software Forecast of Income Statements

Income Statements ($000)	Actual 20X4	Projected 20X5	20X6	20X7	20X8	20X9
Sales	$17,045	$18,750	$20,624	$22,687	$24,956	$27,451
Cost of goods sold	8,550	9,405	10,346	11,380	12,518	13,770
Gross margin	8,495	9,345	10,279	11,307	12,438	13,681
SG&A	2,220	2,442	2,686	2,955	3,250	3,575
Research and development	1,020	1,122	1,234	1,358	1,493	1,643
Depreciation and amortization	330	363	399	439	483	531
Total operating expenses	3,570	3,927	4,320	4,752	5,227	5,750
Income (loss) from operations	4,925	5,418	5,959	6,555	7,211	7,932
Interest expense	62	68	75	83	91	100
Income (loss) before taxes	4,863	5,349	5,884	6,473	7,120	7,832
Provision for income taxes	1,945	2,140	2,354	2,589	2,848	3,133
Net Income	2,918	**3,210**	**3,531**	**3,884**	**4,272**	**4,699**

Note:

Expected growth rate for the high-growth period is 10% for the first 5 years.

Exhibit 14.13 Optimum Software Forecast of Stockholders' Equity

Statements of Stockholders' Equity ($000)	Projected 20X5	20X6	20X7	20X8	20X9
Balance at beginning of year	$3,945	$4,339	$4,773	$5,250	$5,775
Plus net income	3,210	3,531	3,884	4,272	4,699
Minus dividends paid	2,815	3,097	3,406	3,747	4,122
Equals balance at end of year	**4,339**	**4,773**	**5,250**	**5,775**	**6,353**

Exhibit 14.14   Calculation of Net Cash Flow to Invested Capital ($000)

	Projected				
	20X5	20X6	20X7	20X8	20X9
Net income	$3,210	$3,531	$3,884	$4,272	$4,699
Plus depreciation	363	399	439	483	531
Minus capital expenditures	500	550	605	666	732
Minus increase in working capital	390	429	472	519	571
Plus interest expense net of tax effect	41	45	50	54	60
Equals net cash flow to invested capital	2,724	2,996	3,296	3,625	3,988

Note:

Capital expenditures in year 20X5: $500 million

Exhibit 14.15   Optimum Software Cost of Equity
Computation as of December 31, 20X4

Build-up Model

Risk-free rate (1)		4.80%
Plus equity risk premium (2)		5.75%
Plus firm size premium (3)		3.53%
Plus industry premium (4)		5.35%
Cost-of-Equity Build-up Model		**19.43%**

Capital Asset Pricing Model (CAPM)

Risk-free rate (1)		4.80%
Plus equity risk premium (2)	5.75%	
Times beta (5)	1.82	10.47%
Plus firm size premium (3)		3.53%
Cost of Equity CAPM		**18.80%**

Average Value Cost of Equity

Build-up Model	19.43%	50%
Capital Asset Pricing Model	18.80%	50%
Total		**19.11%**

Notes:

(1) Long-term (20-year) U.S. Treasury coupon bond yield.

(2) Long-horizon expected equity risk premium. S&P 500 market benchmark. Adjusted downward by 1.25%.

(3) Size premium (Return in excess of CAPM) for micro-caps. *SBBI Valuation Edition 2003 Yearbook*, p. 125.

(4) Industry premium for SIC Code group 737. "Computer Programming, Data processing and Other Computer Services," *SBBI Valuation Edition 2003 Yearbook*, p. 48.

(5) Adjusted levered beta for SIC Composite SIC Code 7372. *Cost of Capital 2003 Yearbook* (Ibbotson Associates, *www.ibbotson.com*): 7–16.

Exhibit 14.16 Optimum Software Weighted Average Cost of Capital Computation as of December 31, 20X4

Capital Component	Capital Structure (1)	Cost of Capital Component	Tax Effect	Weighted Average Cost
Market value of debt	50.00%	10.98%	0.60	3.29%
Market value of equity	50.00%	19.11%	1.00	9.56%
Weighted average cost of capital				12.85%

Note:

(1) Capital Structure Ratios for the SIC Composite SIC Code 7372. *Cost of Capital 2003 Yearbook* (Ibbotson Associates, *www.ibbotson.com*): 7–16.

Discounting Net Cash Flow to Invested Capital

Exhibit 14.17 illustrates discounting the net cash flow to invested capital using the projected net cash flows developed in Exhibit 14.14 and the weighted average cost of capital developed in Exhibit 14.16. This is a two-stage discounted cash flow model using a five-year period of high growth at 10 percent followed by 5 percent growth in perpetuity, in the computation of the terminal value. When discounting the net cash flow to invested capital, the resulting value is the market value of all invested capital. The market value of debt, as of the valuation date, is subtracted from

Exhibit 14.17 Optimum Software Estimation of Value as of December 31, 20X4 (Discounted Cash Flow Method)

	Projected					
	20X5 1	20X6 2	20X7 3	20X8 4	20X9 5	Terminal Value 5
Net cash flow to invested capital	$ 2,723,734	$2,996,108	$3,295,719	$3,625,290	$3,987,819	$53,345,724
Present value factor	0.886	0.785	0.696	0.617	0.546	0.546
Discounted net cash flow to invested capital	$ 2,413,605	$2,352,667	$2,293,267	$2,235,367	$2,178,929	$29,147,900
Market value of invested capital	$40,621,737					
Less: Market value of interest-bearing debt (20X4)	$ 564,844					
Indicated value of equity	**$40,056,893**					

Notes:

Discounted cash flows and terminal value computed using weighted average cost of capital of: 12.85%

Terminal value computed using the Gordon Growth Model assuming a growth rate in perpetuity of: 5.00%

Market value of debt = Book value of debt

Exhibit 14.18   Optimum Software Estimation of Equity
Value as of December 31, 20X4
(Capitalized Income Method)

	Year 1
Net cash flow to invested capital	$ 2,723,734
WACC minus expected growth rate in perpetuity (1)	6.60%
Indicated value of business entity	$41,268,703
Less: Market value of interest bearing debt (20X4)	$ 564,844
Indicated value of equity	**$40,703,859**

Notes:
(1) WACC less the growth rate = 12.85% – 6.25%. The 6.25% is a
blend of the short-term growth rate of 10% for 20X5–20X9 and the
long-term rate of 5% after year 20X9.

Market value of debt = Book value of debt

the market value of invested capital to arrive at the value of equity. If cash was deducted before
the forecasted cash flows were computed, it would be added back at this point.

Capitalizing Net Cash Flow to Invested Capital

Exhibit 14.18 illustrates capitalizing the net cash flow to invested capital. This model assumes
a 6.25 percent growth in perpetuity (a blending of the 10 percent growth for five years followed
by a 5 percent growth thereafter, using a readily available computer program), and it subtracts
this rate from the WACC to arrive at a capitalization rate of 6.60 percent in our case. Just as in
the discounting method, when capitalizing net cash flow to invested capital, the resulting value
is the market value of all invested capital. The market value of debt, as of the valuation date, is
subtracted from the market value of invested capital to arrive at the value of equity.

Opinion of Value

The application of the two methods of the income approach (the discounted net cash flow
method and the capitalized economic income method) indicates values for the equity of Optimum Software of $40.1 million and $40.7 million, respectively, as shown in Exhibit 14.19.
*The analyst normally would not employ both the discounting and capitalization methods, be-
cause the capitalization method is just a shortcut version of the discounting method, and theoretically both should produce the same answer.* The difference in this case is due to rounding
in estimating the capitalization rate.

Exhibit 14.19   Indications of Equity Value
Derived from the Application of
the Income Approach to Valuation

Method	Indicated Equity Value
Discounted cash flow method	$40,056,893
Capitalized income method	$40,703,859

The Market Approach

SUMMARY

Although the income approach as addressed in the previous chapter is *theoretically* the best approach to business valuation, it requires estimates (the projections and the discount rate) that are subject to potential disagreement. The market approach is quite different in that it relies on more observable data, although there can be (and often are) disagreements as to the comparability of the guideline companies used and the appropriate adjustments to the observed multiples to reach a selected multiple to apply to the subject company's fundamental data.

THE MARKET APPROACH

The *market approach* to business valuation is a pragmatic way to value businesses, essentially by comparison to the prices at which other similar businesses or business interests changed hands in arm's-length transactions. It is widely used by buyers, sellers, investment bankers, brokers, and business appraisers.

The market approach to business valuation has its roots in real estate appraisal, where it is known as the *comparable sales method*. The fundamental idea is to identify the prices at which other similar properties changed hands in order to provide guidance in valuing the property that is the subject of the appraisal.

Of course, business appraisal is much more complicated than real estate appraisal because there are many more variables to deal with. Also, each business is unique, so it is more challenging to locate companies with characteristics similar to those of the subject business, and more analysis must be performed to assess comparability and to make appropriate adjustments for differences between the guideline businesses and the subject being valued.

Different variables are relatively more important in appraising businesses in some industries than in others, and the analyst must know which variables tend to drive the values in the different industries. These variables are found on (or developed from) the financial statements of the companies, mostly on the income statements and balance sheets. There are also qualitative variables to assess, such as quality of management.

REVENUE RULING 59-60 EMPHASIZES MARKET APPROACH

Rev. Rul. 59-60 suggests the market approach in several places. For example:

> As a generalization, the prices of stocks which are traded in volume in a free and active market by informed persons best reflect the consensus of the investing public as to what the future holds for the corporations and industries represented. When a stock is closely held, is traded infrequently, or is traded in an erratic market, some other measure of value must be used. In many instances, the next best measure may be found in the prices at which the stocks of companies engaged in the same or a similar line of business are selling in a free and open market.

> Section 2031(b) of the Code states, in effect, that in valuing unlisted securities the value of stock or securities of corporations engaged in the same or similar line of businesses which are listed on an exchange should be taken into consideration along with all other factors. An important consideration is that the corporations to be used for comparisons have capital stocks which are actively traded by the public. . . . The essential factor is that whether the stocks are sold on an exchange or over-the-counter there is evidence of an active, free public market for the stock as of the valuation date. In selecting corporations for comparative purposes, care should be taken to use only comparable companies. Although the only restrictive requirements as to comparable corporations specified in the statute is that their lines of business be the same or similar, yet it is obvious that consideration must be given to other relevant factors in order that the most valid comparison possible will be obtained.[1]

---

[1]Rev. Rul. 59-60.

THE GUIDELINE PUBLICLY TRADED COMPANY AND THE GUIDELINE TRANSACTION (MERGER AND ACQUISITION) METHOD

When Rev. Rul. 59-60 was written (more than 40 years ago), there were no databases of transaction information on acquisitions of entire companies. Today, while listings of publicly traded companies have been declining (to less than 7,500 as shown in Exhibit 15.1), one online source presents details on more than 18,000 merged or acquired companies (as shown in Exhibit 15.2). Other databases of merged and acquired companies are also available, as listed in Appendix C.

Thus, the professional business appraisal community now breaks the market approach down into two methods:

1. The guideline publicly traded company method
2. The guideline transaction (merger and acquisition) method

The guideline publicly traded company method consists of prices relative to underlying financial data in day-to-day trades of minority interests in active publicly traded companies, either on stock exchanges or the over-the-counter market.

The guideline transaction (merger and acquisition) method consists of prices relative to underlying fundamental data in transfers of controlling interests in companies that may have been either private or public before the transfer of control. The transactions in the databases usually were done through intermediaries (business brokers, M&A specialists, or investment bankers), so they are virtually all on an arm's-length basis.

Both methods are implemented by computing multiples of price of the guideline company transactions to financial variables (earnings, sales, etc.) of the guideline companies, and then applying the multiples observed from the guideline company transactions to the same financial variables in the subject company.

Also generally subsumed under the market approach are the following:

- Past transactions in the subject company
- Bona fide offers to buy
- Rules of thumb
- Buy–sell agreements

There is no compiled source of transactions in minority interests in private companies. The vast majority of brokers do not accept listings for minority interests in private companies because there is no market for them. The fact that brokers will not even accept listings for minority interests in privately held companies is evidence of the wide gulf in degree of marketability between minority interests in private companies and restricted stocks of public companies.

In any method under the market approach, the *price* can be either the price of the common equity (equity procedure) or the price of all the invested capital (market value of invested capital, or MVIC). When the invested capital procedure is used, the result is the value of all the invested capital (usually common equity and long-term debt), so the long-term debt must be subtracted in order to reach the indicated value of the common equity. If cash was eliminated for the purpose of the comparison, it should be added back.

Exhibit 15.1 Number of Listed Companies:
Yearly Comparison of
NASDAQ, NYSE, and AMEX

Year	NASDAQ	NYSE	AMEX	Total
1975	2,467	1,557	1,215	5,239
1976	2,456	1,576	1,161	5,193
1977	2,456	1,575	1,098	5,129
1978	2,475	1,581	1,004	5,060
1979	2,543	1,565	931	5,039
1980	2,894	1,570	892	5,356
1981	3,353	1,565	867	5,785
1982	3,264	1,526	834	5,624
1983	3,901	1,550	822	6,273
1984	4,097	1,543	792	6,432
1985	4,136	1,541	783	6,460
1986	4,417	1,575	796	6,788
1987	4,706	1,647	869	7,222
1988	4,451	1,681	896	7,028
1989	4,293	1,720	859	6,872
1990	4,132	1,774	859	6,765
1991	4,094	1,885	860	6,839
1992	4,113	2,089	814	7,016
1993	4,611	2,361	869	7,841
1994	4,902	2,570	824	8,296
1995	5,122	2,675	791	8,588
1996	5,556	2,907	751	9,214
1997	5,487	3,047	771	9,305
1998	5,068	3,114	770	8,952
1999	4,829	3,025	769	8,623
2000	4,734	2,862	765	8,361
2001	4,109	2,798	691	7,598
2002	3,663	2,783	698	7,144
2003	3,335	2,755	700	6,790
30 June 04	3,293	2,742	711	6,746
2003 versus Peak	**60.0**	**88.5**	**57.6**	**73.0**

*Source: www.nasdaq.marketdata.com/asp/Sec1Com
Comp.asp.* Copyright 2004, The NASDAQ Stock Market,
Inc. Reprinted with permission. All of 1999 data was
missing in original document but was provided by Tim
McCormick (Academic Liaison) of NASDAQ. Source
document was corrected with NYSE data from:
*http://www.nysedata.com/factbook/viewer_edition.asp?
mode=table&key=76&category=4.*

Exhibit 15.2 Business Valuation Guideline Merged and Acquired Company Databases Available at *BVMarketData.com*, Sorted by Sale Price

	Pratt's Stats™ Private	Public Stats™	BIZCOMPS®	Mergerstat®/Shannon Pratt's Control Premium Study™
Type of data	Private	Public	Private	Public
Data fields per transaction	80	62	21	51
Birth year of database	1996	2000	1990	1998
Earliest transaction year	1990	1995	1992	1998
Sale Price				
Under $250,001	1,720	2	5,324	1
$250,001 to 500,000	640	1	1,225	3
$500,001 to $1 million	471	5	552	6
$1,000,001 to $2 million	447	9	214	33
$2,000,001 to $5 million	652	44	102	124
$5,000,001 to $10 million	585	62	21	194
$10,000,001 to $20 million	609	120	8	291
$20,000,001 to $50 million	708	258	3	627
$50,000,001 to $100 million	366	243	0	629
$100,000,001 to $500 million	146	447	0	1,206
Over $500 million	9	119	0	987
Total	**6,353**	**1,310**	**7,449**	**4,101**

Notes:

All data are as of 11/4/04.

BIZCOMPS sale price = Actual sale price + Transferred inventory

Pratt's Stats sale price = Equity price + Liabilities assumed = MVIC (market value of invested capital)

Mergerstat/Shannon Pratt's Control Premium Study Sale price = The aggregate purchase price given to shareholders of the target company's common stock by the acquiring company

Sources:

BIZCOMPS (San Diego: BIZCOMPS) at *www.BVMarketData.com*

Pratt's Stats (Portland, OR: Business Valuation Resources, LLC) at *www.BVMarketData.com*

Mergerstat/Shannon Pratt's Control Premium Study (Los Angeles: Mergerstat LP) at *www.BVMarketData.com*

See Exhibit 15.3 for a list of the market value multiples generally employed in the equity procedure. See Exhibit 15.4 for a list of market value multiples generally employed in the invested capital procedure. Neither of these lists is all-inclusive, but they include the multiples most commonly found in business valuation reports. It usually is not appropriate to use all the multiples in a single business valuation. The appraiser should select one or a few that are most relevant to the subject company.

HOW MANY GUIDELINE COMPANIES?

For a market approach valuation by the publicly traded guideline company method or the transaction (merger and acquisition) method, the analyst usually will select about three to seven guideline companies, although there may be more. The more data there are available for

Exhibit 15.3   Market Value Multiples Generally Employed in the Equity Procedure

In the publicly traded guideline company method, market value multiples are conventionally computed on a per-share basis, while in the merged and acquired company methods they are conventionally computed on a total company basis. Both conventions result in the same values for any given multiple.

Price/Earnings

Assuming that there are taxes, the term *earnings*, although used ambiguously in many cases, is generally considered to mean earnings *after* corporate-level taxes, or, in accounting terminology, net income.

Price/Gross Cash Flow

Gross cash flow is defined here as net income plus all noncash charges (e.g., depreciation, amortization, depletion, deferred revenue).

The multiple is computed as

$$\frac{\text{Price per share}}{\text{Gross cash flow per share}} = \frac{\$10.00}{\$1.96} = 5.1$$

Price/Cash Earnings

Cash earnings equals net income plus amortization, but not other traditional noncash charges, such as depreciation. This is a measure developed by investment bankers in recent years for pricing mergers and acquisitions as an attempt to even out the effects of very disparate accounting for intangibles.

The multiple is computed as

$$\frac{\text{Price per share}}{\text{Cash earnings per share}} = \frac{\$10.00}{\$1.40} = 7.1$$

Price/Pretax Earnings

The multiple is computed as

$$\frac{\text{Price per share}}{\text{Pretax income per share}} = \frac{\$10.00}{\$1.67} = 6.0$$

Price/Book Value (or Price/Adjusted Net Asset Value)

Book value includes the amount of par or stated value for shares outstanding, plus retained earnings.

The multiple is computed as

$$\frac{\text{Price per share}}{\text{Book value per share}} = \frac{\$10.00}{\$1.72} = 5.8$$

Price/Adjusted Net Asset Value

Sometimes it is possible to estimate adjusted net asset values for the guideline and subject companies, reflecting adjustments to current values for all or some of the assets and, in some cases, liabilities. In the limited situations where such data are available, a price to adjusted net asset value generally is a more meaningful indication of value than price/book value. Examples could include real estate holding companies where real estate values are available, or forest products companies for which estimates of timber values are available. This procedure can be particularly useful for family limited partnerships.

Tangible versus Total Book Value or Adjusted Net Asset Value

If the guideline and/or subject companies have intangible assets on their balance sheets, analysts generally prefer to subtract them out and use only price/tangible book value or price/tangible net asset value as the valuation multiple.

This is to avoid the valuation distortions that could be caused because of accounting rules. On one hand, if a company purchases intangible assets, the item becomes part of the assets on the balance sheet. If, on the other hand, a company creates the same intangible asset internally, it usually is expensed and never appears on the balance sheet. Because of this difference, tangible book value or tangible net asset value may present a more meaningful direct comparison among companies that may have some purchased and some internally created assets.

Exhibit 15.3 *(Continued)*

Price/Dividends (or Partnership Withdrawal)

If the company being valued pays dividends or partnership withdrawals, the multiple of such amounts can be an important valuation parameter. This variable can be especially important when valuing minority interests, since the minority owner normally has no control over payout policy, no matter how great the company's capacity to pay dividends or withdrawals.

The market multiple is computed as follows:

$$\frac{\text{Price per share}}{\text{Dividend per share}} \quad \frac{\$10.00}{\$0.50} = 20$$

This is one market multiple that is more often quoted as the reciprocal of the multiple; that is, the capitalization rate (also called the yield). The yield is computed as

$$\frac{\text{Dividend per share}}{\text{Price per share}} \quad \frac{\$0.50}{\$10.00} = 5.0\% \text{ yield}$$

Price/Sales

This multiple is more often used as an invested capital multiple, because all of the invested capital, not just the equity, is utilized to support the sales. If the subject and guideline companies have different capital structures, the equity price/sales can be very misleading. However, if none of the companies has long-term debt, then the equity is equal to the total invested capital, and the multiple is meaningful on an equity basis.

This multiple is computed as

$$\frac{\text{Price per share}}{\text{Sales per share}} \quad \frac{\$10.00}{\$13.89} = 0.72$$

Price/Discretionary Earnings

The International Business Brokers Association defines *discretionary earnings* as pretax income plus interest plus all noncash charges plus all compensation and benefits to one owner/operator. Because the multiple of discretionary earnings is normally used only for small businesses where no debt is assumed, it is usually computed on a total company basis.

The multiple is computed as

$$\frac{\text{MVIC (or price)}}{\text{Discretionary earnings}} \quad \frac{\$10,200,000}{\$2,450,000} = 4.2$$

The multiple of discretionary earnings is used primarily for smaller businesses and professional practices where the involvement of the key owner/operator is an important component of the business or practice. For such businesses or practices, meaningful multiples generally fall between 1.5 and 3.5, although some fall outside that range.

Source: Adapted from Shannon P. Pratt, *The Market Approach to Valuing Businesses* (New York: John Wiley & Sons, Inc., 2001), pp. 10–17. All rights reserved. Used with permission.

Exhibit 15.4   Market Value Multiples Generally Employed in the Invested
Capital Procedure

MVIC stands for market value of invested capital, the market value of all the common and preferred equity and long-term debt. Some analysts also include all interest-bearing debt.

MVIC/EBITDA (Earnings before Interest, Taxes, Depreciation, and Amortization)
The multiple is computed as

$$\frac{\text{MVIC}}{\text{EBITDA}} \quad \frac{\$10,200,000}{\$\ 1,950,000} = 5.2$$

EBITDA multiples are particularly favored to eliminate differences in depreciation policies.

MVIC/EBIT (Earnings before Interest and Taxes)
The multiple is computed as

$$\frac{\text{MVIC}}{\text{EBIT}} \quad \frac{\$10,200,000}{\$\ 1,500,000} = 6.8$$

EBIT multiples are good where differences in accounting for noncash charges are not significant.

MVIC/TBVIC (Tangible Book Value of Invested Capital)
The multiple is computed as

$$\frac{\text{MVIC}}{\text{TBVIC}} \quad \frac{\$10,200,000}{\$\ 3,100,000} = 3.3$$

This MVIC multiple can be used on TBVIC and also with adjusted net asset value instead of book value if data are available.

MVIC/Sales
The multiple is computed as

$$\frac{\text{MVIC}}{\text{Sales}} \quad \frac{\$10,200,000}{\$10,000,000} = 1.02$$

MVIC/Physical Activity or Capacity
The denominator in a market value multiple may be some measure of a company's units of sales or capacity to produce. Analysts generally prefer that the numerator in such a multiple be MVIC rather than equity for the same reasons as the sales multiple—that is, the units sold or units of capacity are attributable to the resources provided by all components of the capital structure, not just the equity.

Source: Adapted from Shannon P. Pratt, *The Market Approach to Valuing Businesses* (New York: John Wiley & Sons, Inc., 2001): 17–20. All rights reserved. Used with permission.

each company and the greater the similarity between the guideline companies and the subject company, the fewer guideline companies are needed.

The court summed up this notion in *Estate of Heck*,[2] which involved valuing shares of F. Korbel and Bros., Inc., a producer of champagne, brandy, and table wine. The opinion explained the court's rejection of the market approach as follows:

> *As similarity to the company to be valued decreases, the number of required comparables increases in order to minimize the risk that the results will be distorted to attributes unique to each of the guideline companies.*

---

[2]*Estate of Heck v. Comm'r*, T.C. Memo 2002-34, 83 T.C.M. (CCH) 1181.

In this case, we find that Mondavi and Canandaigua were not sufficiently similar to Korbel to permit the use of a market approach based upon those two companies alone.

In *Estate of Hall*,[3] there was one very good comparable to Hallmark Cards; it was American Greetings. One appraiser relied entirely on American Greetings; the other appraiser used it and about 10 other consumable-product manufacturers with dominant market shares, such as Parker Pens. While acknowledging that American Greetings was an excellent comparable, the court based its conclusion on the broader list, noting that a single comparable is not necessarily representative of a market. The court noted:

"[a]ny one company may have unique individual characteristics that may distort the comparison." . . . A sample of one tells us little about what is normal for the population in question.

In *Estate of Gallo*,[4] there were no other wineries available with dominant market share. Both appraisers selected distillers, brewers, soft-drink manufacturers, and other food manufacturers with dominant market shares. The court based its conclusion entirely on the market approach, using the 10 guideline companies that both appraisers agreed were comparable.

SELECTION OF GUIDELINE COMPANIES

A major area of controversy in the market approach in some cases is the selection of guideline companies. There are cases where the court gave no weight whatsoever to the market approach, even though both sides used it, because the court felt that the guideline companies selected were not adequately comparable. There are other cases where the court accepted one side's market approach over the other's because of inadequate comparability of companies on the side that was rejected. There are cases, such as *Gallo*, where the court accepted a subset of the guideline companies proffered and did its own valuation based on the subset.

Rev. Rul. 59-60 uses the expression *comparable companies*. In recognition of the fact that no two companies are exactly alike, the business valuation professional community has adopted the expression *guideline companies*.

There are two indexes in use today for selecting companies by line of business:

1. SIC (Standard Industrial Classification) codes

2. NAICS (North American Industrial Classification System) codes

See Exhibit 15.5 for an explanation of these two classification systems.

In addition, many databases (including all that are available online at *BVMarketData*) can be searched by a verbal description of the industry or industries of interest.

Rev. Rul. 59-60 contains the language "the same or a similar line of business." The primary criteria for similar line of business are the economic factors that impact the company's rev-

---

[3]*Estate of Hall v. Comm'r*, 92 T.C. 312 (1989).
[4]*Estate of Gallo v. Comm'r*, T.C. Memo 1985-363, 50 T.C.M. (CCH) 470.

Exhibit 15.5   Standard Industrial Classifications and the North American Industry
Classification System

Late in 1998, the new industrial classification system called the North American Industry Classification System (NAICS) was introduced. As the name implies, it is a joint effort of Mexico, the United States, and Canada. Eventually, this will replace the SIC system.

The biggest advantage of the NAICS system is its breadth of coverage, especially in new service sectors of the economy. There are 1,100 industry classifications, of which 387 are new since the last edition of the SIC directory (1987).

The latest update of NAICS was in 2002.

Pratt's Stats™, BIZCOMPS®, and Mergerstat/Shannon Pratt Control Premium Study™ all now cross-classify for both SIC and NAICS codes. Lists of industry descriptions and their SIC and NAICS codes are online at the site of the databases, *www.BVMarketData.com.*

enues and profits, such as markets, sources of supply, and products. For example, for a company manufacturing electronic controls for the forest products industry it would make much more sense to select companies manufacturing a variety of capital equipment for the forest products industry than to select companies manufacturing electronic controls for unrelated industries. This is so because the companies manufacturing capital equipment for the forest products industry would be subject to the same economic conditions as the subject company.

An excellent discussion of why a court relied on one expert's selection of guideline companies over those of the opposing expert is found in *Estate of Hendrickson*.[5] The valuation involved an ownership interest in a thrift institution (Peoples), and the conclusion of value was based entirely on the market approach. Both experts valued the interest using guideline companies. The court made this comment:

> *Because value under the guideline method is developed from the market data of similar companies, the selection of appropriate comparable companies is of paramount importance.*

In selecting the guideline companies for his analysis, the estate expert's primary criterion was geography. All of the companies he chose were significantly larger than Peoples, offered more services than Peoples, and were multibranch operations.

In contrast, the Service's selection of guideline companies was "significantly more exacting than [the estate expert's]," and the Court relied on its data because "criteria for the selection of comparable companies produced a group of companies that more closely resembled the size and operating characteristics of Peoples than [the estate expert's] guideline companies."

The Service's first selection criterion was that the guideline companies had to be thrifts comparable in size to Peoples. Further, he divided his guideline companies into two groups, one that reflected minority interests and the other that reflected controlling interests.

The court stated:

> *To examine thrift pricing on a control basis, [the Service's expert] selected six thrifts (the control group) meeting the following criteria: (1) Thrifts that sold in the Midwest, (2) return on average assets greater*

---

[5]*Estate of Hendrickson v. Comm'r*, T.C. Memo 1999-278, 78 T.C.M. (CCH) 322.

than 1 percent, (3) total assets less than $100 million, and (4) transactions that were pending or completed between January 1 and December 31, 1992. In order to examine thrift pricing on a minority basis, [the Service's expert] selected 10 thrifts (the minority group) meeting the following criteria: (1) Thrift organizations in the United States, (2) total assets less than $150 million, (3) not subject to announced or rumored acquisition, and (4) publicly traded securities as evidenced by listing on a major exchange [or trading market].

DOCUMENTING THE SEARCH FOR GUIDELINE COMPANIES

The guideline company search criteria should be clearly spelled out in the report so that another analyst could replicate the same criteria and expect to produce the same source list. The search criteria should include, for example, these six factors:

1. The line or lines of businesses searched (e.g., SIC and/or NAICS code or codes)
2. Size range (e.g., $ revenue, $ assets)
3. Geographical location, if applicable (location may be of great importance in certain industries, such as retailing, yet of no importance in other industries such as software)
4. Range of profitability (e.g., net income, EBITDA)
5. If using the guideline merger and acquisition method, range of transaction dates
6. The database(s) searched

If any companies that meet the stated search criteria are eliminated, the analyst should list the companies and the reason they were eliminated (e.g., ratio analysis far from subject company). The analyst should then give a brief description of each company selected. This procedure should be sufficient to assure the court that there is no bias in the selection of guideline companies.

CHOOSING MULTIPLES BASED ON OBJECTIVE EMPIRICAL EVIDENCE

In *Estate of Renier*,[6] in addition to using an income approach, the estate's witness used a market approach procedure that he (correctly) called the *business broker method*. The court described the business broker method as follows:

[T]he business broker method postulates that the purchase price of a business equals the market value of the inventory and fixed assets plus a multiple of the seller's discretionary cash-flow, defined as the total cash-flow available to the owner of the business.

The court rejected the estate's application of this method because its expert failed to justify the multiple he applied to the company's discretionary cash flow. He used "his own judg-

---

[6]*Estate of Renier v. Comm'r*, T.C. Memo 2000-298, 80 T.C.M. (CCH) 401.

ment" rather than providing adequate supporting data. Accordingly, the court found that "on this record the reliability of the business broker method has not been established."

WHAT PRICES TO USE IN THE NUMERATORS OF THE MARKET VALUATION MULTIPLES

First of all, the prices must be *market values*, *NOT book values*. For invested capital multiples, book value of debt is usually assumed to equal market value, but it may require adjustment from book value to market value if market conditions have changed significantly since the issuance of the debt.

In the guideline publicly traded company method the price is almost always the closing price of the companies' stock on the valuation date. However, on occasion, such as in an extremely volatile market, it might be an average of some period of time (usually 20 trading days) either immediately preceding, or preceding and following, the valuation date.

In the guideline merger and acquisition method, the price is as of the guideline company transaction closing date. That price may require adjustment if industry conditions (e.g., typical valuation multiples for the industry) have changed significantly between the guideline company transaction date and the subject company valuation date.

CHOOSING THE LEVEL OF THE VALUATION MULTIPLE

Valuation pricing multiples calculated from guideline publicly traded companies can vary widely. For example, price/earnings multiples for the guideline companies may range between 8 and 20 times the trailing 12 months' earnings. A great deal of analyst's judgment goes into the choice of where the valuation multiple to be applied to the subject company should fall relative to the multiples observed in the guideline companies. However, this judgment should be backed up by quantitative and qualitative analysis to the greatest extent possible. This requires a thorough analysis of the financial statement, as discussed in Chapter 10. At a minimum, every step in the analysis should be described so a reader can recreate it.

The preferred measure of central tendency in most arrays is the median (the middle observation in the array, or, in the case of an even number of observations, the number halfway in between the numbers immediately above and immediately below the middle of the array). The median is generally preferred over the average (the mean) because the average may be distorted by one or a few very high numbers.

In general, there are two main determinants of the multiple that should be applied to the subject company relative to the guideline companies:

1. Relative degree of risk (uncertainty as to achievement of expected results)
2. Relative growth prospects

In addition, other financial analysis variables, such as return on sales and return on book value, may impact the selection of specific market multiples.

Relative Degree of Risk

Risk is the degree of uncertainty regarding the achievement of expected future results, especially future cash flows. In the market approach, risk is factored into value through market multiples, while risk in the income approach is factored in through the discount rate.

High risk for the subject company relative to the guideline companies should have a downward impact on the multiples chosen for the subject company relative to the guideline company multiples, and vice versa.

Leverage (debt-to-equity ratio) is one measure of relative risk. The relative degree of stability or volatility in past operating results is another measure of relative risk.

Although objective financial analysis should be utilized in assessing risk, the analyst must also use subjective judgment based on management interviews, site visits, economic and industry conditions, past experience, and other sources that may impact the assessment of risk. Both objective and subjective adjustments must be thoroughly explained.

Relative Growth Prospects

In the market approach, growth prospects are factored into the valuation through market multiples, while growth prospects in the income approach are factored in through projected operating results. High growth prospects for the subject company relative to the guideline companies should have an upward impact on the multiples chosen for the subject company relative to the guideline company multiples, and vice versa. The key phrase here is *relative to the guideline companies*.

Relative growth between the subject and guideline companies should be considered, if available, but there is no assurance that relative past trends will continue in the future. The analyst should assess growth prospects carefully in light of the management interviews, the site visit (for example, is there evidence of future costs for deferred maintenance?), and analysis of how economic and industry conditions will impact the subject company relative to the guideline companies.

Return on Sales

If the subject company has a higher return on sales than the guideline companies, it would deserve a higher price/sales multiple than the guideline companies, all other things being equal, assuming that the higher relative return on sales is expected to continue in the future.

Return on Book Value

To the extent that the subject company's return on book value of equity or invested capital is higher than the guideline companies' returns on book value of equity or invested capital, it would deserve a higher price/book value multiple than those of the guideline companies, all other things being equal and assuming that the higher relative return on book value is expected to continue in the future.

Mechanics of Choosing Levels of Market Multiples

In light of these factors, the analyst should select the level of each market multiple to apply to the subject company. There are several acceptable procedures for doing this.

Medians of multiples from the guideline companies provide a good starting point. However, analysis of relative risk, growth prospects, return on sales, and return on book value will usually lead the analyst to select one or even all of the multiples at levels above or below the medians of the guideline companies. If median multiples are chosen, the analyst should demonstrate that the subject and guideline companies are relatively homogeneous.

There are many techniques for choosing multiples other than the median. One is to select a subset of the guideline companies whose characteristics most resemble the characteristics of the subject and to use the averages or medians of their multiples. Another is to choose a percentage above or below the mean. Still another is to choose a point in the array of multiples such as the upper or lower quartile, quintile, or decile.

Regression analysis may be used to select the price/sales and price/book value multiples.

It is not necessary that all multiples chosen bear the same relationship to the median multiple. For example, if return on book value for the subject company is above that of the guideline companies, the selected price or MVIC-to-book-value multiple may be higher than that of the guideline companies, while if return on sales for the subject company is lower than that of the guideline companies, the selected price or MVIC-to-sales multiple may be lower than that of the guideline companies.

Occasionally, in extreme circumstances, the multiple selected to apply to the subject company may even be outside of the range observed for the guideline companies. For example, if return on book value is outside the range of observed returns on book value, the selected price or MVIC to book value may be outside the range of observed price or MVIC-to-book-value multiples.

SELECTING WHICH VALUATION MULTIPLES TO USE

From the array of valuation multiples in Exhibits 15.3 and 15.4 (or other possible multiples), the analyst must select which one or ones to use. The analyst should explain in the report why he or she chose the particular multiples used.

Generally speaking, invested capital multiples (which reflect the value of all equity and long-term debt) are preferable for controlling interests. This is because a control owner is not bound by the existing capital structure. A control owner has the right to increase or decrease leverage; the minority owner does not have this right.

Sometimes, however, invested-capital multiples are used when valuing minority interests. Invested-capital multiples are especially relevant where the degree of leverage (ratio of debt to equity) varies significantly between the subject and guideline companies.

Some appraisers use invested-capital multiples in *all* their valuations. Others use both invested-capital and equity-valuation multiples, depending on the circumstances.

Three criteria have the most impact on the choice of valuation multiples:

1. The relevance of the particular multiple to the subject company
2. The quantity of guideline company data available for the multiple
3. The relative tightness or dispersion of the data points within the multiple

Relevance of Various Valuation Multiples to the Subject Company

The degree of relevance of any valuation multiple for a subject company depends on both the industry and the company's financial data. Exhibit 15.6 gives some suggestions as to when certain valuation multiples are appropriate to be used.

For example, property and casualty insurance agencies are usually valued on a price/sales basis because they are service businesses, they are asset light, and they have relatively homogeneous cost structures.

By contrast, many manufacturing companies are valued largely or entirely on the basis of MVIC/EBITDA multiples to even out potentially significant differences in depreciation schedules.

Availability of Guideline Company Data

Data used to compute certain valuation multiples might not be available for all selected guideline companies. If too few guideline companies' data are available for a certain valuation multiple, this may be reason to eliminate that multiple from consideration.

Exhibit 15.6   When to Use a Valuation Multiple

Price/Net Earnings
- Relatively high income compared with depreciation and amortization
- When depreciation represents actual physical wear and tear
- Relatively *normal* tax rates

Price/Pretax Earnings
- Same as above except company has relatively temporary abnormal tax rate
- "S" corporations may be valued using pretax income or may be taxed hypothetically at "C" corporation rates or personal tax rates

Price/Cash Flow (often defined as net income plus depreciation and amortization)
- Relatively low income compared with depreciation and amortization
- Depreciation represents low physical, functional, or economic obsolescence

Price/Sales
- When the subject company is "homogeneous" to the guideline companies in terms of operating expenses
- Service companies and asset-light companies are best suited for this ratio

Price/Dividends or Dividend-Paying Capacity
- Best when the subject company actually pays dividends
- When the company has the ability to pay representative dividends and still have adequate ability to finance operations and growth
- In minority interest valuation, actual dividends are more important

Price/Book Value
- When there is a good relationship between price/book value and return on equity
- Asset-heavy companies

Source: American Society of Appraisers, *BV-201, Introduction to Business Valuation, Part I*, from Principles of Valuation course series, 2002. Used with permission. All rights reserved.

Relative Tightness or Dispersion of the Valuation Multiples

Generally speaking, multiples that have tightly clustered values are the most relevant, because the tight clustering usually indicates that the particular multiple is one that the market relies on. Widely dispersed valuation multiples provide less reliable valuation guidance.

One way to judge the tightness or relative dispersion of the data is just to look at it. A mathematical tool for measuring the relative tightness or dispersion of the data is called the *coefficient of variation* (the standard deviation divided by the mean). Valuation multiples with lower coefficients of variation are usually more reliable than multiples with higher coefficients of variation.

ASSIGNING WEIGHTS TO VARIOUS MARKET MULTIPLES

In unusual cases, one valuation multiple may dominate the concluded indication of value. In most cases, however, two or more market value multiples will have a bearing on value, and the analyst must deal with how much weight to accord to each.

The same factors considered in choosing the relevant multiples should also be considered in deciding the weight to be accorded to each. For example, where assets are important to a company's value—such as holding companies, financial institutions, and distribution companies—weight should be given to price/book-value multiples. Where earnings are of paramount importance—such as service and manufacturing companies—weight should be given to operating multiples, such as price/sales, price/earnings, price (MVIC)/EBITDA, and so on.

The analyst may either use subjective weighting or assign mathematical weights. Although there is no formula for assigning mathematical weights, doing so may be helpful in understanding the analyst's thinking. If assigning weights, the analyst should include a disclaimer to the effect that there is no empirical basis for the weights and that they are shown only as guides to the analyst's thinking.

SAMPLE MARKET VALUATION APPROACH TABLES

This chapter's appendix includes a sample of typical tables that may be included in a report using the guideline public company method. Both methods may be used, depending on the facts of the valuation.

Of course, considerable explanatory text should accompany the tables.

OTHER METHODS CLASSIFIED UNDER THE MARKET APPROACH[7]

Four other methods are conventionally classified under the market approach:

1. Past transactions in the subject company
2. Offers to buy

---

[7]Much of this section was adapted from Shannon P. Pratt, *The Market Approach to Valuing Businesses* (New York: John Wiley & Sons, 2001). All rights reserved. Used with permission.

3. Rules of thumb
4. Buy–sell agreements

Past Transactions in the Subject Company

The analyst should inquire as to whether there have been any past transactions in the company's equity, either on a control or a minority basis. The analyst should also inquire as to whether the company has made any acquisitions. If past transactions occurred, the next question is whether they were on an arm's-length basis.

If past arm's-length transactions did take place, they should be analyzed like any other guideline company transactions. The past transactions method may be one of the most useful market methods, yet it is often overlooked.

Several court cases address the issue of defining what "arm's length" is. For example, in *Morrisey v. Commissioner,*[8] two sales of blocks of 3.25 percent and 4.67 percent of the outstanding stock, respectively, occurred two months after the valuation date. In essence, the Ninth Circuit found that the actual sales were arm's-length transactions that were the best evidence of fair market value. The court noted that the sellers were under no compulsion to sell, that they reasonably relied on a Merrill Lynch valuation presented by the buyer, and that the evidence of a distant family relationship between the parties did not indicate a lack of arm's-length negotiations.

In transactions between related or affiliated parties, the arm's-length character of the pricing may be established by use of an independent expert. For example, The Limited Inc. established four separate companies to hold the trademarks applicable to each of its four subsidiaries: Victoria's Secret, Lane Bryant, Express Inc., and The Limited Stores.[9] The New York State Division of Taxation alleged that the companies were *shell organizations* that should have filed combined returns, and that failure to do so resulted in approximately $4.5 million underpayments of tax under New York state franchise tax law.

If the trademark companies could be proven to be viable business entities operating on an arm's-length basis, the Division of Taxation could not require each retailer to file combined franchise tax reports with its respective trademark protection company. Of particular interest are the criteria by which the court judged whether the transactions with affiliates were or were not on an arm's-length basis.

Key factors were engagement of independent experts in initially establishing royalty rates and testimony of experts at trial backed by empirical evidence. When The Limited Inc. first set up royalty fees, it retained an independent business and intangible valuation firm "to determine an appropriate Fair Market Royalty Rate."[10]

The court concluded that one of the expert's reports "clearly established that the petitioners respective rates of return after payment of royalties exceeded the rates of return experienced by most U.S. retailers during the period at issue."[11]

---

[8]*Estate of Morrisey et al. v. Comm'r* 243 F.3d 1145, (9th Cir. Cal. 2001) *rev'd* T.C. Memo 1999-199, 77 T.C.M. (CCH) 1779.
[9]*Matter of Express Inc.*, Nos. 812330, 812331, 812332 (N.Y. Division of Tax Appeals).
[10]Id.
[11]Id.

Another issue was whether the interest paid by the trademark companies qualified as arm's length based on compliance with the federal "safe harbor" rates, which were "not less than 100 percent or greater than 130 percent of the applicable federal rate." The court concluded that the taxpayer's expert "establishes that the interest rates on the loans made by the trademark companies to the retailers fell within the safe haven range. . . . The report thus indicates that the loans were made at arms-length rates."[12]

Past Acquisitions by the Subject Company

Past acquisitions by the subject company are often a fertile field for very valid guideline market transaction data, and are a source often overlooked. We would suggest, "Have you made any acquisitions?" as a standard question in management interviews. Appropriate adjustments must be made, as just discussed.

Offers to Buy

For offers to buy to be probative evidence of value, they must be: (1) firm, (2) at arm's length, (3) with sufficient detail of terms to be able to estimate the cash equivalent value, and (4) from a source with the financial ability to consummate the offer (i.e., a bona fide offer). It is rare that all of these requirements are met.

If the requirements are met, the offer to buy can be handled in the same way as a past transaction to arrive at one indication of value as of the valuation date. Since the offer did not conclude in a consummated transaction, however, the weight accorded its indication of value may be limited.

Rules of Thumb

Many industries, especially those characterized by very small businesses, have valuation rules of thumb, some more valid than others. If they exist, they should be considered if they have a wide industry following. However, they should never be relied on as the only valuation method.

Nature of Rules of Thumb

Rules of thumb come in many varieties, but the most common are:

- Multiple of sales
- Multiple of some physical nature of activity
- Multiples of discretionary earnings
- Assets plus any of the above

---

[12]Id.

Proper Use of Rules of Thumb

Rules of thumb are best used as a check on the reasonableness of the conclusions reached by other valuation methods, such as capitalization of earnings or a market multiple method. A good source for guidance on when to use rules of thumb is in the American Society of Appraisers Business Valuation Standards:

> *Rules of thumb may provide insight on the value of a business, business ownership interest, or security. However, value indications derived from the use of rules of thumb should not be given substantial weight unless supported by other valuation methods and it can be established that knowledgeable buyers and sellers place substantial reliance on them.*[13]

Problems with Rules of Thumb

One problem with rules of thumb is the lack of knowledge about the derivation of the rules. Several other problems are:

- *Not knowing what was transacted.* Most, but not all, rules of thumb presume that the valuation rule applies to an asset sale. Few of them, however, specify what assets are assumed to be transferred. The asset composition may vary substantially from one transaction to another.

   It is also important to remember that the rules of thumb almost never specify whether they assume a noncompete agreement or an employment agreement, even though such types of agreements are very common for the kinds of businesses for which rules of thumb exist.

- *Not knowing assumed terms of the transactions.* Most transactions for which there are rules of thumb are not all-cash transactions, but involve some degree of seller financing. The financing terms vary greatly from one transaction to another, and affect both the face value and the fair market value (which, by definition, assumes a cash or cash equivalent value).

- *Not knowing the assumed level of profitability.* The level of profitability impacts almost all real-world valuations. However, for rules of thumb that are based on either gross revenue or some measure of physical volume, there is no indication of the average level of profitability that the rule of thumb implies.

- *Uniqueness of each entity.* Every business is, to some extent, different from every other business. Rules of thumb give no guidance for taking the unique characteristics of any particular business into account.

- *Multiples change over time.* Rules of thumb rarely change, but in the real world market valuation multiples do change over time. Some industries are more susceptible than others to changes in economic and industry conditions. Changes occur in the supply/demand relationship for valuing various kinds of businesses and professional practices because of many factors, sometimes including legal/regulatory changes. When using market transaction multiples, adjustments can be made for changes in conditions from the time of the guideline transaction to the subject valuation date, but there is no base date for rules of thumb.

---

[13]American Society of Appraisers, Business Valuation Standards, BVS-V. Used with permission. All rights reserved.

Sources for Rules of Thumb

Two popular sources for rules of thumb are Glenn Desmond's *Handbook of Small Business Valuation Formulas and Rules of Thumb*[14] and Tom West's annual *Business Reference Guide.*[15] The rules of thumb section in West's reference guide has expanded every year in recent years.

For some industries, articles or trade publications may provide some industry rules of thumb.

Buy-Sell Agreements

Buy–sell agreements are included here as a market approach category on the assumption that they represent parties' agreements on pricing transactions that are expected to occur in the future. The pricing mechanism set forth in the buy–sell agreement may be determinative of value in certain circumstances, such as where it is legally binding for the purposes of the valuation. In other cases, the buy–sell agreement price might be one method of estimating value, but not determinative. In still other instances, the buy–sell agreement might be ignored because it does not represent a bona fide arm's-length sale agreement.

For estate tax purposes, for example, a buy–sell agreement price is binding for estate tax determination only if it meets all of the following conditions:

- The agreement is binding during life as well as at death.
- The agreement creates a determinable value as of a specifically determinable date.
- The agreement has at least some bona fide business purpose (this could include the promotion of orderly family ownership and management succession, so this is an easy test to meet).
- The agreement results in a fair market value for the subject business interest, *when executed.* Often, buy–sell agreement values will generate future date of death or gift date values substantially above or below what the fair market value otherwise would have been for the subject interest—even though the value was reasonable when the agreement was made.
- Its terms are comparable to similar arrangements entered into by persons in arm's-length transactions.[16]

If a buy–sell agreement does not meet these conditions, it is entirely possible to have a buy–sell value that is legally binding on an estate for transaction purposes, but not for estate tax purposes, and that may not even provide enough money for estate taxes.

---

[14]Glenn Desmond, *Handbook of Small Business Valuation Formulas and Rules of Thumb*, 3rd ed. (Camden, Me.: Valuation Press, 1993).

[15]Tom West, *The Business Reference Guide* (Concord, Mass.: Business Brokerage Press), published annually.

[16]This requirement was added as part of section 2703 of Internal Revenue Code Chapter 14 and is only mandatory for buy–sell agreements entered into or amended after October 8, 1990. For an extensive discussion of buy–sell agreements, see "Buy–Sell Agreements" in Shannon P. Pratt, Robert F. Reilly, and Robert P. Schweihs, *Valuing a Business*, 4th ed. (New York: McGraw Hill, 2000), Chapter 29.

A buy–sell agreement may not be binding for gift tax purposes even though it would be considered binding for estate tax purposes. Following is the complete text of section 8 of Rev. Rul. 59-60, which addresses the effect of stockholder agreements on gift and estate tax values:

> *Frequently in the valuation of a closely held stock for estate and gift tax purposes, it will be found that the stock is subject to an agreement restricting its sale or transfer. Where shares of stock were acquired by a decedent subject to an option reserved by the issuing corporation to repurchase at a certain price, the option price is usually accepted as the fair market value for estate tax purposes. See Rev. Rul. 54-76, C.B. 1954-1, 194. However, in such case the option price is not determinative of fair market value for gift tax purposes. Where the option, or buy and sell agreement, is the result of voluntary action by the stockholders and is binding during the life as well as at the death of the stockholders, such agreement may or may not, depending upon the circumstances of each case, fix the value for estate tax purposes. However, such agreement is a factor to be considered, with other relevant factors, in determining fair market value. Where the stockholder is free to dispose of his shares during life and the option is to be-come effective only upon his death, the fair market value is not limited to the option price. It is always necessary to consider the relationship of the parties, the relative number of shares held by the decedent, and other material facts, to determine whether the agreement represents a bona fide business arrange-ment or is a device to pass the decedent's shares to the natural objects of his bounty for less than an ad-equate and full consideration in money or money's worth. In this connection, see Rev. Rul. 157 C.B. 1953-2, 255, and Rev. Rul. 189, C.B. 1953-2, 29.*[17]

CONCLUSION

Sample tables typically used in the market approach are contained in the appendix to this chapter.

The two primary methods within the market approach are the guideline publicly traded company method and the guideline transaction (merger and acquisition) method. Other meth-ods often classified under the market approach are past transactions, offers to buy, rules of thumb, and buy–sell agreements.

The income and market approaches are the main approaches used for operating compa-nies when the premise of value is a going-concern basis. For holding companies and operating companies for which the appropriate premise of value is a liquidation basis, an asset approach is typically employed. The asset approach is the subject of Chapter 16.

---

[17]Rev. Rul. 59-60, section 8. For a full discussion, please see Chapter 22.

APPENDIX: AN ILLUSTRATION OF THE MARKET APPROACH TO VALUATION

Introduction

Optimum Software is a hypothetical corporation used to illustrate the application of the two methods of the market approach to valuation—the guideline publicly traded company method and the guideline transaction (merged and acquired company) method. The valuation techniques presented in this appendix are only examples of what an analyst may choose to include in his or her valuation. Also, in a real valuation report, the analyst would be expected to explain his or her assumptions, methodology, and conclusions in much greater detail than presented here. An illustration of the income approach to valuation can be found in Chapter 14, Appendix.

Valuation Assignment

At its 20X5 annual board meeting, the directors of Optimum Software Corporation decided to sell the company in the upcoming year. They were interested in obtaining an estimate of the value of the company as of December 31, 20X4. At the request of the board shareholders, a limited appraisal of the company was conducted with the objective of estimating the value of a 100 percent controlling interest in Optimum Software Corporation as of December 31, 20X4. The purpose of the appraisal was to assist the board in their initial negotiations with possible buyers. The standard of value used is fair market value and the premise of value is that the business will continue to function as a going concern in the foreseeable future.

Summary Description

Optimum Software Corporation is a closely held C corporation specializing in the design, development, and production of prepackaged computer software. For the software products it develops, Optimum Software also provides services such as preparation of installation documentation and training the user in the use of the software. The two main lines of products currently developed by Optimum Software are online commerce software solutions and computer games. As of December 31, 20X4, Optimum Software reported operating income of $4.9 million, with net income of $2.9 million on sales of $17 million and assets of $6.2 million. The company was founded in 1998 and it has a workforce of roughly 100 employees, of whom 40 percent are professionals involved in the production process and 60 percent are in sales and support. The company has no preferred stock.

Financial Statements and Forecasts

Audited and unaudited financial statements were provided by the management of Optimum Software and were accepted and used without third-party independent verification. This valuation is limited to information available as of the date of valuation, and the opinion of value expressed in this limited valuation is applicable only to the purpose just stated. Selected financial information for Optimum Software is presented in Exhibits 15.7, 15.8, and 15.9.

Gathering of Market Data

To value Optimum Software, both major market valuation methods were applied—the guideline publicly traded company method and the guideline transaction (merged and acquired company) method. For each method, a group of comparable companies were selected and their market prices were used to develop pricing multiples for Optimum Software.

To ensure that the search for market data yielded companies similar to the subject, the following search criteria were applied uniformly to both guideline publicly traded companies and guideline merged and acquired companies:

- Primary SIC Code 7372—Prepackaged Software (NAICS Code 511210—Software Publishers)
- Similar business description
- Positive operating earnings and positive cash flow for the last reported fiscal period
- Revenues between $2 million and $200 million
- Transactions taking place as close as possible to the valuation date for the merged and acquired company method (within the last three years in our example)
- Stock sales for the guideline merged and acquired company method (as opposed to asset sales)
- Actively traded stocks and companies with at least five years of historic financial data for the guideline publicly traded company method

The search for public companies' data was conducted online by querying EDGAR, an Internet search engine that allows access to filings made by public companies with the Securities and Exchange Commission (*http://www.sec.gov/edgar.shtml*). The guideline public companies that met the search criteria are as follows:

- Catapult Communications, Corp.
- Group 1 Software, Inc.
- Ansys, Inc.
- Manhattan Associates, Inc.
- Serena Software, Inc.

More information about the guideline public companies can be found in Exhibits 15.12, 15.13, 15.14, and 15.15.

The search for guideline merged and acquired company data was conducted by querying the following online databases of transactions of both public and private companies:

- Pratt's Stats™
- Mergerstat®/Shannon Pratt's Control Premium Study™
- Public Stats™

These databases can be accessed online at *www.BvmarketData.com*.

The five companies that met our search criteria are closely held companies:

- CygnaCom Solutions, Inc.
- Symitar
- Bonson Information Technology
- Dome Imaging Systems, Inc.
- Data Control Systems, Inc.

More information about the guideline merged and acquired companies can be found in Exhibits 15.23, 15.24, and 15.25.

Financial Statements Analysis

Optimum Software's audited financial statements for the years ended December 31, 20X0 through 20X4, were used. To analyze the operations and position of Optimum at the end of each year and over time, common size balance sheets and income statements were examined, from which financial and operating ratios were computed. These are presented in Exhibits 15.7, 15.8, and 15.9.

In addition, the company's performance was compared to that of other companies in SIC Code 7372—Prepackaged Software (NAICS Code 511210—Software Publishers). Optimum Software was compared to three different samples of companies in the same industry, as follows:

- *Comparison with broad industry statistics:* Optimum Software was compared to companies in the same SIC Code as reported by Integra Information in their *5-Year Industry Report* for SIC Code 7372 (*http://www.integrainfo.com/*). As of the date of the report, financial information from more than 6,000 companies was included in the analysis. Common size balance sheets and income statements, as well as financial and operating ratios for Optimum Software, were compared to those reported by Integra for the industry as a whole. The analysis is presented in Exhibits 15.10 and 15.11.
- *Comparison with selected guideline publicly traded companies:* Common size balance sheets and income statements, as well as financial and operating ratios for Optimum Software, were compared to those of the selected guideline public companies. The analysis is presented in Exhibits 15.12, 15.13, and 15.14.
- *Comparison with the selected guideline merged and acquired companies:* Common size balance sheets and income statements, as well as financial and operating ratios for Optimum Software, were compared to those of the selected guideline merged and acquired companies. The analysis is presented in Exhibits 15.23, 15.24, and 15.25.

Identification and Application of Valuation Multiples

The comparative financial and operating analysis of Optimum Software, relative to the selected guideline publicly traded companies and guideline transactions, revealed that Optimum Software's degree of leverage was considerably different from the comparable companies. Thus, we have elected to value Optimum Software using market multiples based on the market value of invested capital (MVIC). Benefit streams to all stakeholders were used in the denominators of the MVIC market multiples. As a result, the final opinion of the equity value in Optimum Software was determined by subtracting the market value of long-term debt from the resulting MVIC figure.

The following MVIC-based multiples were computed as part of the guideline public company method:

- MVIC/Sales
- MVIC/EBITDA
- MVIC/5-year average EBITDA
- MVIC/EBIT
- MVIC/5-year average EBIT
- MVIC/BVIC

The computation of the valuation multiples for the guideline public companies is presented in Exhibits 15.15 through 15.19. Exhibit 15.20 is a summary of the valuation multiples for the selected guideline publicly traded companies; it computes the mean, median, standard deviation, and coefficient of variation for each multiple. (The multiples computed are shown for illustration, not necessarily because they are applicable to a software company.)

The following MVIC-based multiples were computed as part of the guideline merged and acquired company method:

- MVIC/Sales
- MVIC/EBITDA
- MVIC/EBIT
- MVIC/BVIC

Exhibit 15.26 is a summary of the valuation multiples for the selected guideline merged and acquired companies, and it computes the mean, median, standard deviation, and coefficient of variation for each multiple.

Valuation of Optimum Software

Exhibits 15.21, 15.22, 15.27, 15.28, and 15.29 present the adjustment of the selected valuation multiples, the application of the adjusted multiples to the fundamentals of Optimum Software, the weighting of the values resulting from the application of each multiple, the indications of value resulting from the application of each method, and, finally, the weighting of these two values to reach a final opinion of value. These exhibits include footnotes that explain the processes of adjusting and weighting the multiples, of applying the adjusted multiples, and of arriving at an opinion of value.

The analysis presented here is a very brief one. This analysis is typically presented in the valuation report, not in the footnotes to the exhibits. As noted earlier, *explaining the assumptions, methodology, and the valuation conclusion is an essential part of the valuation and should be allotted much more detail and space than we have available here.* This analysis led to its opinion of value by the application of a set of assumptions, procedures, and subjective judgment calls. A different set of assumptions, procedures, and subjective judgments may be applied, resulting in a different opinion of value. For instance, here we used MVIC multiples, but multiples based on equity could also be computed; other multiples which could provide stronger support to the final opinion of value could be computed as well. In the same way, the weights assigned were based on financial statement analysis, subjective judgment, and the experience of the appraiser. Another appraiser could logically reach different results.

The application of the two market methods indicated similar values of $42 million and $43 million, respectively, as shown in Exhibit 15.29. We chose to assign equal weights to both methods, with a resulting value of $42.5 million for the equity of Optimum Software as of December 31, 20X4.

Exhibit 15.7 Optimum Software Adjusted Balance Sheets

Fiscal Year Ended	December 31 ($000)					December 31 (Common Size)				
	20X4	20X3	20X2	20X1	20X0	20X4	20X3	20X2	20X1	20X0
Cash and equivalents	$1,833	$1,715	$1,628	$1,925	$1,963	29%	26%	31%	30%	27%
Receivables	$3,059	$3,297	$2,813	$3,083	$3,031	49%	50%	54%	49%	42%
Inventories	$ 731	$ 645	$ 630	$ 754	$ 954	12%	10%	12%	12%	13%
Current assets	$5,623	$5,657	$5,070	$5,761	$5,948	90%	86%	97%	91%	83%
Fixed assets (net)	$ 600	$ 619	$ 83	$ 474	$1,157	10%	9%	2%	7%	16%
Intangibles (net)	$ 12	$ 269	$ 98	$ 95	$ 58	0%	4%	2%	1%	1%
Total assets	$6,234	$6,544	$5,250	$6,330	$7,163	100%	100%	100%	100%	100%
Notes payable	$ 895	$ 778	$ 758	$ 596	$1,199	14%	12%	14%	9%	17%
Current portion of long-term debt	$ 232	$ 322	$ 135	$ 78	$ 433	4%	5%	3%	1%	6%
Trade payables	$ 520	$ 483	$ 450	$ 690	$ 564	8%	7%	9%	11%	8%
Taxes payable	$ 77	$ 161	$ 68	$ 78	$ 87	1%	2%	1%	1%	1%
Current liabilities	$1,725	$1,744	$1,410	$1,442	$2,282	28%	27%	27%	23%	32%
Long-term debt	$ 565	$ 537	$ 465	$ 346	$ 636	9%	8%	9%	5%	9%
Total liabilities	$2,290	$2,281	$1,875	$1,789	$2,918	37%	35%	36%	28%	41%
Common stock, $0.1 par	$ 28	$ 28	$ 28	$ 28	$ 28	0%	0%	1%	0%	0%
Additional paid-in capital	$ 353	$ 293	$ 343	$ 408	$ 352	6%	4%	7%	6%	5%
Retained earnings	$3,563	$3,943	$3,004	$4,105	$3,865	57%	60%	57%	65%	54%
Total equity	$3,945	$4,263	$3,375	$4,541	$4,245	63%	65%	64%	72%	59%
Total liabilities and equity	$6,234	$6,544	$5,250	$6,330	$7,163	100%	100%	100%	100%	100%
Working Capital	*$3,898*	*$3,913*	*$3,660*	*$4,319*	*$3,666*					

Exhibit 15.8 Optimum Software Adjusted Income Statements

Fiscal Year Ended	December 31 ($000)					December 31 (Common Size)				
	20X4	20X3	20X2	20X1	20X0	20X4	20X3	20X2	20X1	20X0
Sales	$17,045	$15,246	$13,790	$16,030	$18,620	100%	100%	100%	100.00%	100%
Cost of goods sold	$ 8,550	$ 7,788	$ 7,200	$ 8,400	$ 9,576	50%	51%	52%	52%	51%
Gross margin	$ 8,495	$ 7,458	$ 6,590	$ 7,630	$ 9,044	50%	49%	48%	48%	49%
SG&A	$ 2,220	$ 2,112	$ 2,160	$ 2,340	$ 2,520	13%	14%	16%	15%	14%
Research and development	$ 1,020	$ 1,056	$ 1,080	$ 1,320	$ 1,008	6%	7%	8%	8%	5%
Depreciation and amortization	$ 330	$ 264	$ 120	$ 210	$ 504	2%	2%	1%	1%	3%
Total operating expenses	$ 3,570	$ 3,432	$ 3,360	$ 3,870	$ 4,032	21%	23%	24%	24%	22%
Income (loss) from operations	$ 4,925	$ 4,026	$ 3,230	$ 3,760	$ 5,012	29%	26%	23%	23%	27%
Interest expense	$ 62	$ 70	$ 75	$ 86	$ 112	0%	0%	1%	1%	1%
Income (loss) before taxes	$ 4,863	$ 3,956	$ 3,155	$ 3,674	$ 4,900	29%	26%	23%	23%	26%
Provision for income taxes	$ 1,945	$ 1,582	$ 1,262	$ 1,470	$ 1,960	11%	10%	9%	9%	11%
Net income	$ 2,918	$ 2,374	$ 1,893	$ 2,204	$ 2,940	17%	16%	14%	14%	16%
EBITDA	$ 5,255	$ 4,290	$ 3,350	$ 3,970	$ 5,516					

Exhibit 15.9 Optimum Software Financial and Operating Ratio Analysis (Based on Adjusted Financial Statements)

	December 31				
Fiscal Year Ended	20X4	20X3	20X2	20X1	20X0
Liquidity/Solvency Ratios					
Quick ratio	2.8	2.9	3.1	3.5	2.2
Current ratio	3.3	3.2	3.6	4.0	2.6
Accounts receivables to sales	17.9%	21.6%	20.4%	19.2%	16.3%
Accounts payable to sales	3.1%	3.2%	3.3%	4.3%	3.0%
Current liabilities to net worth	43.7%	40.9%	41.8%	31.8%	53.8%
Turnover					
Sales to average receivables	5.4	5.0	4.7	5.2	na
Sales to average working capital	4.4	4.0	3.5	4.0	na
Sales to average fixed assets	28.0	43.5	49.6	19.7	na
Sales to total assets	2.7	2.3	2.6	2.5	2.6
Debt/Risk					
EBIT to interest expense	79.4	57.5	43.1	43.7	44.8
Current assets to current liabilities	3.3	3.2	3.6	4.0	2.6
Current liabilities to total debt	75.3%	76.5%	75.2%	80.6%	78.2%
Long-term debt to total assets	9.1%	8.2%	8.9%	5.5%	8.9%
Total debt to total assets	36.7%	34.9%	35.7%	28.3%	40.7%
Total debt to net worth	58.1%	53.5%	55.6%	39.4%	68.7%
Fixed assets to net worth	15.2%	14.5%	2.4%	10.4%	27.3%
Profitability					
Gross margin	49.8%	48.9%	47.8%	47.6%	48.6%
EBITDA to sales	30.8%	28.1%	24.3%	24.8%	29.6%
Operating margin	28.9%	26.4%	23.4%	23.5%	26.9%
Pretax retun on assets	78.0%	60.5%	60.1%	58.0%	68.4%
After-tax return on assets	46.8%	36.3%	36.1%	34.8%	41.0%
Pretax retun on net worth	123.3%	92.8%	93.5%	80.9%	115.4%
After-tax return on net worth	74.0%	55.7%	56.1%	48.5%	69.3%
Pretax return on sales	28.5%	25.9%	22.9%	22.9%	26.3%
After-tax return on sales	17.1%	15.6%	13.7%	13.8%	15.8%
Working Capital					
Working capital to sales	22.9%	25.7%	26.5%	26.9%	19.7%
Net income to working capital	74.9%	60.7%	51.7%	51.0%	80.2%
Inventory to working capital	18.8%	16.5%	17.2%	17.5%	26.0%
Current liabilities to working capital	44.3%	44.6%	38.5%	33.4%	62.3%
Long-term debt to working capital	14.5%	13.7%	12.7%	8.0%	17.4%
Operating Efficiency					
Operating expenses to gross margin	42.0%	46.0%	51.0%	50.7%	44.6%
Operating expenses to sales	20.9%	22.5%	24.4%	24.1%	21.7%
Depreciation to sales	1.9%	1.7%	0.9%	1.3%	2.7%
Total assets to sales	36.6%	42.9%	38.1%	39.5%	38.5%
Sales to net worth	4.3	3.6	4.1	3.5	4.4
Sales to fixed assets	28.4	24.6	167.2	33.8	16.1

Notes:

na = not available because turnover ratios are based on average asset data

Data from Integra Information for years 1998 through 2002 was used with permission in this example.

Exhibit 15.10 Optimum Software and Integra Information Common Size Financial Statements

SIC Code 7372—Prepackaged Software

	20X4		20X3		20X2		20X1		20X0	
	Subject	Integra	Subject	Integra	Subject	Integra	Subject	Integra	Subject	Integra
Year-to-Year Growth										
Revenue	11.80%	5.50%	10.56%	3.00%	-13.97%	8.80%	-13.91%	12.30%	na	na
EBITDA	22.49%	5.40%	28.06%	2.20%	-15.62%	9.60%	-28.03%	7.30%	na	na
Pretax income	22.93%	5.50%	25.39%	0.50%	-14.13%	9.30%	-25.02%	-2.60%	na	na
Common Size Balance Sheets										
Cash and equivalents	29.40%	18.80%	26.21%	18.80%	31.00%	18.80%	30.40%	17.20%	27.40%	17.10%
Receivables	49.06%	22.10%	50.38%	22.10%	53.57%	22.10%	48.70%	20.20%	42.31%	20.10%
Inventories	11.73%	2.90%	9.85%	2.90%	12.00%	2.90%	11.91%	2.70%	13.32%	2.70%
Current assets	90.19%	52.70%	86.44%	52.60%	96.57%	52.60%	91.01%	48.10%	83.04%	48.20%
Fixed assets (net)	9.62%	29.00%	9.45%	29.00%	1.57%	28.90%	7.49%	26.60%	16.15%	26.10%
Intangibles (net)	0.19%	0.00%	4.10%	0.00%	1.86%	2.00%	1.50%	8.40%	0.81%	8.40%
Total assets	100.00%	100.00%	100.00%	100.00%	100.00%	100.00%	100.00%	100.00%	100.00%	100.00%
Notes payable	14.36%	7.80%	11.89%	7.70%	14.43%	7.80%	9.41%	7.60%	16.73%	6.90%
Trade payables	8.35%	7.60%	7.38%	7.60%	8.57%	7.50%	10.91%	7.40%	7.87%	7.00%
Current liabilities	27.67%	29.20%	26.64%	29.00%	26.86%	29.00%	22.79%	28.40%	31.86%	26.30%
Long-term debt	9.06%	25.50%	8.21%	25.30%	8.86%	25.40%	5.47%	24.80%	8.88%	23.30%
Total liabilities	36.73%	54.70%	34.85%	54.30%	35.71%	54.40%	28.26%	53.20%	40.74%	49.60%
Total equity	63.27%	45.30%	65.15%	45.70%	64.29%	45.60%	71.74%	46.80%	59.26%	50.40%
Total liabilities and equity	100.00%	100.00%	100.00%	100.00%	100.00%	100.00%	100.00%	100.00%	100.00%	100.00%

Common Size Income Statements

Sales	100.00%	100.00%	100.00%	100.00%	100.00%	100.00%	100.00%	100.00%	100.00%	100.00%
Cost of goods sold	50.16%	0.00%	51.08%	0.00%	52.21%	0.00%	52.40%	0.00%	51.43%	0.00%
Gross margin	49.84%	100.00%	48.92%	100.00%	47.79%	100.00%	47.60%	100.00%	48.57%	100.00%
Total operating expenses	20.94%	97.60%	22.51%	97.70%	24.37%	97.60%	24.14%	97.70%	21.65%	97.30%
Income (loss) from operations	28.89%	2.40%	26.41%	2.30%	23.42%	2.40%	23.46%	2.30%	26.92%	2.70%
Interest expense	0.36%	1.30%	0.46%	1.30%	0.54%	1.40%	0.54%	1.30%	0.60%	1.30%
Income (loss) before taxes	28.53%	2.00%	25.95%	2.00%	22.88%	2.10%	22.92%	2.10%	26.32%	2.40%
Provision for income taxes	11.41%	0.80%	10.38%	0.80%	9.15%	0.80%	9.17%	0.80%	10.53%	0.90%
Net income	17.12%	1.30%	15.57%	1.30%	13.73%	1.30%	13.75%	1.30%	15.79%	1.50%

Notes:

Data from Integra Information used with permission.

Balance Sheet and Income statement line items for which comparison data were not available from Integra were not included in this exhibit.

Data from Integra Information for years 1998 through 2002 were used in this example.

na = not available

Exhibit 15.11 Optimum Software and Integra Information Financial and Operating Ratio Analysis

SIC Code 7372 - Prepackaged Software

	20X4		20X3		20X2		20X1		20X0	
	Subject	Integra	Subject	Integra	Subject	Integra	Subject	Integra	Subject	Integra
Liquidity/Solvency Ratios										
Quick ratio	2.84	1.41	2.87	1.42	3.15	1.42	3.47	1.33	2.19	1.43
Current ratio	3.26	1.81	3.24	1.82	3.60	1.81	3.99	1.70	2.61	1.83
Accounts receivables to sales	17.94%	18.00%	21.62%	18.00%	20.40%	17.00%	19.23%	16.00%	16.28%	na
Accounts payable to sales	3.05%	6.00%	3.17%	6.00%	3.26%	6.00%	4.31%	6.00%	3.03%	na
Current liabilities to net worth	43.73%	64.40%	40.90%	63.50%	41.78%	63.60%	31.76%	60.60%	53.76%	52.20%
Turnover										
Sales to receivables	5.36	5.86	4.99	5.78	4.68	6.15	5.24	6.46	na	na
Sales to working capital	4.36	5.50	4.03	5.40	3.46	5.98	4.02	6.26	na	na
Sales to fixed assets	27.98	4.47	43.49	4.40	49.56	4.67	19.66	4.93	na	na
Sales to total assets	2.73	1.30	2.33	1.28	2.63	1.30	2.53	1.30	2.60	na
Debt/Risk										
EBIT to Interest expense	79.44	1.75	57.51	1.75	43.07	1.78	43.72	1.77	44.75	2.00
Current assets to current liabilities	3.26	6.75	3.24	6.80	3.60	6.79	3.99	6.36	2.61	6.96
Current liabilities to total debt	75.33%	14.30%	76.45%	14.20%	75.20%	14.20%	80.64%	14.20%	78.20%	14.00%
Long-term debt to total assets	9.06%	19.20%	8.21%	19.00%	8.86%	19.10%	5.47%	18.60%	8.88%	17.30%
Total debt to total assets	36.73%	54.70%	34.85%	54.30%	35.71%	54.40%	28.26%	53.20%	40.74%	49.60%
Total debt to net worth	0.58	1.21	0.53	1.19	0.56	1.19	0.39	1.14	0.69	0.98
Fixed assets to net worth	0.15	0.64	0.15	0.64	0.02	0.63	0.10	0.57	0.27	0.52
Profitability										
Gross margin	49.84%	100.00%	48.92%	100.00%	47.79%	100.00%	47.60%	100.00%	48.57%	100.00%
EBITDA to sales	30.83%	6.20%	28.14%	6.20%	24.29%	6.20%	24.77%	6.20%	29.62%	6.50%
Operating margin	28.89%	2.40%	26.41%	2.30%	23.42%	2.40%	23.46%	2.30%	26.92%	2.70%
Pretax retun on assets	78.00%	2.60%	60.45%	2.60%	60.10%	2.60%	58.04%	2.60%	68.41%	3.00%
After-tax return on assets	46.80%	1.60%	36.27%	1.60%	36.06%	1.60%	34.82%	1.60%	41.05%	1.80%
Pretax retun on net worth	123.28%	5.70%	92.79%	5.60%	93.48%	5.80%	80.90%	5.50%	115.44%	5.90%
After-tax return on net worth	73.97%	3.60%	55.68%	3.50%	56.09%	3.60%	48.54%	3.40%	69.26%	3.60%
Pretax return on sales	28.53%	2.00%	25.95%	2.00%	22.88%	2.10%	22.92%	2.10%	26.32%	2.40%
After-tax return on sales	17.12%	1.30%	15.57%	1.30%	13.73%	1.30%	13.75%	1.30%	15.79%	1.50%

Working Capital

Working capital to sales	22.87%	18.20%	25.67%	18.50%	26.54%	16.70%	26.94%	16.00%	19.69%	17.90%
Net income to working capital	74.86%	6.90%	60.66%	6.70%	51.72%	6.90%	51.04%	8.10%	80.20%	8.40%
Inventory to working capital	18.76%	12.40%	16.47%	12.30%	17.21%	12.30%	17.46%	13.50%	26.03%	12.20%
Current liabilities to working capital	44.26%	33.20%	44.56%	32.70%	38.52%	32.80%	33.40%	38.30%	62.25%	31.60%
Long-term debt to working capital	14.49%	81.60%	13.72%	80.50%	12.70%	80.80%	8.02%	94.10%	17.35%	79.10%

Operating Efficiency

Operating expenses to gross margin	42.02%	97.60%	46.02%	97.70%	50.99%	97.60%	50.72%	97.70%	44.58%	97.30%
Operating expenses to sales	20.94%	97.60%	22.51%	97.70%	24.37%	97.60%	24.14%	97.70%	21.65%	97.30%
Depreciation to sales	1.94%	3.80%	1.73%	3.80%	0.87%	3.80%	1.31%	3.80%	2.71%	3.80%
Total assets to sales	36.58%	78.90%	42.92%	79.70%	38.07%	79.30%	39.49%	81.00%	38.47%	81.60%
Sales to net worth	4.32	2.80	3.58	2.75	4.09	2.76	3.53	2.64	4.39	2.43
Sales to fixed assets	28.41	4.37	24.65	4.33	167.15	4.36	33.82	4.63	16.10	4.69

Notes:

Data from Integra Information used with permission.

Data from Integra Information for years 1998 through 2002 were used in this example.

na = not available

Exhibit 15.12 Optimum Software and Selected Guideline Public Companies Balance Sheet and Income Statement Data

Fiscal Year Ended	Catapult 9/30/20X4	Group 1 3/31/20X4	Ansys 12/31/20X4	Manhattan 12/31/20X4	Serena 1/31/20X4	Median	Subject 12/31/20X4
Balance Sheets							
Cash and equivalents	$ 12,575,000	$ 22,936,000	$ 46,198,000	$ 64,664,000	$ 85,954,000	$ 46,198,000	$1,832,813
Receivables	$ 11,009,000	$ 17,551,000	$ 15,875,000	$ 32,384,000	$ 14,111,000	$ 15,875,000	$3,058,594
Inventories	$ 3,869,000	$ 0	$ 0	$ 0	$ 0	$ 0	$ 731,250
Current assets	$ 55,656,000	$ 70,093,000	$ 92,491,000	$159,208,000	$153,377,000	$ 92,491,000	$5,622,656
Fixed assets (net)	$ 3,874,000	$ 5,797,000	$ 4,302,000	$ 12,352,000	$ 3,036,000	$ 4,302,000	$ 600,000
Intangibles (net)	$ 57,148,000	$ 12,686,000	$ 23,713,000	$ 33,644,000	$ 50,135,000	$ 33,644,000	$ 11,719
Total assets	$117,850,000	$111,879,000	$127,001,000	$220,196,000	$231,070,000	$127,001,000	$6,234,375
Accounts payable	$ 2,594,000	$ 1,198,000	$ 627,000	$ 6,754,000	$ 710,000	$ 1,198,000	$ 895,313
Current portion of notes payable	$ 0	$ 3,496,000	$ 0	$ 0	$ 0	$ 0	$ 232,031
Accrued liabilities	$ 18,829,000	$ 5,857,000	$ 5,645,000	$ 11,171,000	$ 11,762,000	$ 11,171,000	$ 520,313
Other current liabilities	$ 5,381,000	$ 32,565,000	$ 29,336,000	$ 16,604,000	$ 23,527,000	$ 23,527,000	$ 77,344
Current liabilities	$ 26,804,000	$ 43,116,000	$ 35,608,000	$ 34,529,000	$ 35,999,000	$ 35,608,000	$1,725,000
Long-term debt	$ 18,081,000	$ 3,630,000	$ 0	$ 381,000	$ 0	$ 381,000	$ 564,844
Total liabilities	$ 44,885,000	$ 51,477,000	$ 35,608,000	$ 34,910,000	$ 46,294,000	$ 44,885,000	$2,289,844
Common equity	$ 13,000	$ 6,918,000	$ 166,000	$ 290,000	$ 40,000	$ 166,000	$ 28,125
Additional paid-in capital	$ 0	$ 0	$ 0	$ 0	$ 0	$ 0	$ 352,969
Retained earnings	$ 50,556,000	$ 28,903,000	$ 79,388,000	$ 61,808,000	$ 71,571,000	$ 61,808,000	$3,563,438
Shareholders' equity	$ 72,965,000	$ 60,402,000	$ 91,393,000	$185,286,000	$184,776,000	$ 91,393,000	$3,944,531
Total liabilities and equity	$117,850,000	$111,879,000	$127,001,000	$220,196,000	$231,070,000	$127,001,000	$6,234,375
Working Capital	$ 28,852,000	$ 26,977,000	$ 56,883,000	$124,679,000	$117,378,000	$127,001,000	$3,897,656

Income Statements

Sales	$40,039,000	$89,428,000	$91,011,000	$175,721,000	$98,641,000	$91,011,000	$17,045,000
Cost of goods sold	$ 3,872,000	$32,853,000	$11,760,000	$ 67,565,000	$12,955,000	$12,955,000	$ 8,550,000
Gross margin	$36,167,000	$56,575,000	$79,251,000	$108,156,000	$85,686,000	$79,251,000	$ 8,495,000
SG&A	$15,670,000	$40,100,000	$30,283,000	$ 47,356,000	$38,639,000	$38,639,000	$ 2,220,000
Research and development	$ 8,920,000	$10,345,000	$19,605,000	$ 22,250,000	$13,308,000	$13,308,000	$ 1,020,000
Depreciation and amortization	$ 0	$ 0	$ 2,289,000	$ 1,772,000	$ 8,336,000	$ 1,772,000	$ 330,000
Total operating expenses	$24,590,000	$50,445,000	$52,177,000	$ 71,378,000	$60,283,000	$52,177,000	$ 3,570,000
Income (loss) from operations	$11,577,000	$ 6,130,000	$27,074,000	$ 36,778,000	$25,403,000	$25,403,000	$ 4,925,000
Interest expense	$ 0	$ 372,000	$ 0	$ 147,000	$ 0	$ 0	$ 62,000
Income (loss) before taxes	$12,785,000	$ 7,278,000	$27,385,000	$ 39,579,000	$31,371,000	$27,385,000	$ 4,863,000
Provision for income taxes	$ 3,636,000	$ 2,852,000	$ 8,426,000	$ 14,383,000	$12,862,000	$ 8,426,000	$ 1,945,200
Net Income	$ 9,149,000	$ 4,426,000	$18,959,000	$ 25,196,000	$18,509,000	$18,509,000	$ 2,917,800
EBITDA	*$11,577,000*	*$ 6,130,000*	*$29,363,000*	*$ 38,550,000*	*$33,739,000*		*$ 5,255,000*

Exhibit 15.13 Optimum Software and Selected Guideline Public Companies Common Size Comparison

Fiscal Year Ended	Catapult 9/30/20X4	Group 1 3/31/20X4	Ansys 12/31/20X4	Manhattan 12/31/20X4	Serena 1/31/20X4	Median	Subject 12/31/20X4	Comment
Balance Sheets								
Cash and equivalents	11%	21%	36%	29%	37%	29%	29%	At median
Receivables	9%	16%	12%	15%	6%	12%	49%	Above median
Inventories	3%	0%	0%	0%	0%	0%	12%	Above median
Current assets	47%	63%	73%	72%	66%	66%	90%	Above median
Fixed assets (net)	3%	5%	3%	6%	1%	3%	10%	Above median
Intangibles (net)	48%	11%	19%	15%	22%	19%	0%	Below median
Total assets	100%	100%	100%	100%	100%	100%	100%	
Accounts payable	2%	1%	0%	3%	0%	1%	14%	Above median
Current portion of notes payable	0%	3%	0%	0%	0%	0%	4%	Above median
Accrued liabilities	16%	5%	4%	5%	5%	5%	8%	Above median
Other current liabilities	5%	29%	23%	8%	10%	10%	1%	Below median
Current liabilities	23%	39%	28%	16%	16%	23%	28%	Above median
Long-term debt	15%	3%	0%	0%	0%	0%	9%	Above median
Total liabilities	38%	46%	28%	16%	20%	28%	37%	Above median
Common equity	0%	6%	0%	0%	0%	0%	0%	At median
Additional paid-in capital	0%	0%	0%	0%	0%	0%	6%	Above median
Retained earnings	43%	26%	63%	28%	31%	31%	57%	Above median
Shareholders' equity	62%	54%	72%	84%	80%	72%	63%	Below median
Total liabilities and equity	100%	100%	100%	100%	100%	100%	100%	

244

Income Statements

Sales	100%	100%	100%	100%	100%	100%	100%	Above median
Cost of goods sold	10%	37%	13%	38%	13%	13%	50%	Below median
Gross margin	90%	63%	87%	62%	87%	87%	50%	Below median
SG&A	39%	45%	33%	27%	39%	39%	13%	Below median
Research and development	22%	12%	22%	13%	13%	13%	6%	Above median
Depreciation and amortization	0%	0%	3%	1%	8%	1%	2%	Below median
Total operating expenses	61%	56%	57%	41%	61%	57%	21%	Above median
Income (loss) from operations	29%	7%	30%	21%	26%	26%	29%	At median
Interest expense	0%	0%	0%	0%	0%	0%	0%	Slightly below median
Income (loss) before taxes	32%	8%	30%	23%	32%	30%	29%	
Provision for income taxes	9%	3%	9%	8%	13%	9%	11%	Above median
Net Income	23%	5%	21%	14%	19%	19%	17%	Slightly below median

Notes:

When compared to the sample of guideline public companies, Optimum Software has:

- Higher than median current assets and fixed asset and lower intangible assets
- Higher than median current liabilities and long-term debt and lower equity
- Lower gross margin and higher EBIT because of higher COGS and lower operating expenses
- The income before taxes and net income is slightly below median but in the higher part of the range

245

Exhibit 15.14 Optimum Software and Selected Guideline Public Companies Financial and Operating Ratio Analysis

Fiscal Year Ended	Catapult 9/30/20X4	Group 1 3/31/20X4	Ansys 12/31/20X4	Manhattan 12/31/20X4	Serena 1/31/20X4	Median	Subject 12/31/20X4	Comment
Liquidity/Solvency Ratios								
Quick ratio	0.9	0.9	1.7	2.8	2.8	1.7	2.8	Above median
Current ratio	2.1	1.6	2.6	4.6	4.3	2.6	3.3	Above median
Accounts receivable to sales	27.5%	19.6%	17.4%	18.4%	14.3%	18.4%	17.9%	Below median
Accounts payable to sales	6.5%	1.3%	0.7%	3.8%	0.7%	1.3%	5.3%	Above median
Current liabilities to net worth	36.7%	71.4%	39.0%	18.6%	19.5%	36.7%	43.7%	Above median
Turnover								
Sales to receivables	3.6	5.1	5.7	5.4	7.0	5.4	5.6	Slightly above median
Sales to working capital	1.4	3.3	1.6	1.4	0.8	1.4	4.4	Above median
Sales to fixed assets	10.3	15.4	21.2	14.2	32.5	15.4	28.4	Above median
Sales to total assets	0.3	0.8	0.7	0.8	0.4	0.7	2.7	Above median
Debt/Risk								
EBIT interest expense	na	0.0	na	250.2	na	125.1	79.4	Below median
Current liabilities to total debt	59.7%	83.8%	100.0%	98.9%	77.8%	83.8%	75.3%	Below median
Long-term debt to total assets	15.3%	3.2%	0.0%	0.2%	0.0%	0.2%	9.1%	Above median
Total debt to total assets	38.1%	46.0%	28.0%	15.9%	20.0%	28.0%	36.7%	Above median
Total debt to net worth	61.5%	85.2%	39.0%	18.8%	25.1%	39.0%	58.1%	Above median
Fixed to net worth	5.3%	9.6%	4.7%	6.7%	1.6%	5.3%	15.2%	Above median
Profitability								
Gross margin	90.3%	63.3%	87.1%	61.5%	86.9%	86.9%	49.8%	Below median
EBITDA to sales	28.9%	6.9%	32.3%	21.9%	34.2%	28.9%	30.8%	Slightly above median
Operating margin	28.9%	6.9%	29.7%	20.9%	25.8%	25.8%	28.9%	Above median
Pretax return on assets	10.8%	6.5%	21.6%	18.0%	13.6%	13.6%	78.0%	Above median
After-tax return on assets	7.8%	4.0%	14.9%	11.4%	8.0%	8.0%	46.8%	Above median
Pretax return on net worth	17.5%	12.0%	30.0%	21.4%	17.0%	17.5%	123.3%	Above median
After-tax return on net worth	12.5%	7.3%	20.7%	13.6%	10.0%	12.5%	74.0%	Above median
Pretax return on sales	31.9%	8.1%	30.1%	22.5%	31.8%	30.1%	28.5%	Slightly below median
After-tax return on sales	22.9%	4.9%	20.8%	14.3%	18.8%	18.8%	17.1%	Slightly below median

Working Capital

Working capital to sales	72.1%	30.2%	62.5%	71.0%	119.0%	71.0%	22.9%	Below median
Net income to working capital	31.7%	16.4%	33.3%	20.2%	15.8%	20.2%	74.9%	Above median
Inventory to working capital	13.4%	0.0%	0.0%	0.0%	0.0%	0.0%	18.8%	Above median
Current liabilities to working capital	92.9%	159.8%	62.6%	27.7%	30.7%	62.6%	44.3%	Below median
Long-term debt to working capital	62.7%	13.5%	0.0%	0.3%	0.0%	0.3%	14.5%	Above median

Operating efficiency

Operating expenses to gross margin	68.0%	89.2%	65.8%	66.0%	70.4%	68.0%	42.0%	Below median
Operating expenses to sales	61.4%	56.4%	57.3%	40.6%	61.1%	57.3%	20.9%	Below median
Depreciation to sales	0.0%	0.0%	2.5%	1.0%	8.5%	1.0%	1.9%	Above median
Total assets to sales	294.3%	125.1%	139.5%	125.3%	234.3%	139.5%	36.6%	Below median
Sales to net worth	0.5	1.5	1.0	0.9	0.5	0.9	4.3	Above median
Sales to fixed assets	10.3	15.4	21.2	14.2	32.5	15.4	28.4	Above median

Notes:

When compared to the sample of guideline public companies, Optimum Software has:

• Higher than the median liquidity and lower than median solvency
• Higher than the median turnover ratios indicating better use of assets
• Debt and risk ratios above the median for the group indicating higher risk
• Profitability slightly below median or above median except for the gross margin
• Better than median operating efficiency and use of fixed and total assets

247

Exhibit 15.15 Guideline Public Company Market Value of Invested Capital

Company	Symbol	Market	Market Value per Share	Number of Shares	Long-Term Debt	Market Value of Equity	Preferred Stock	Market Value of Invested Capital
Catapult	CATT	NASDAQ	$12	13,039,000	$18,081,000	$155,816,050	$ 0	$173,897,050
Group 1	GSOF	NASDAQ	$12	6,237,000	$ 3,630,000	$ 74,532,150	$916,000	$ 79,078,150
Ansys	ANSS	NASDAQ	$20	14,598,000	$ 0	$294,879,600	$ 0	$294,879,600
Manhattan	MANH	NASDAQ	$24	28,653,000	$ 381,000	$677,929,980	$ 0	$678,310,980
Serena	SRNA	NASDAQ	$16	38,522,000	$ 0	$608,262,380	$ 0	$608,262,380

Note:
Information was obtained from SEC filings for the public companies selected.

Exhibit 15.16 Guideline Public Company MVIC/Sales

Company	20X4	20X3	20X2	20X1	20X0	Compound Growth (%)	MVIC	MVIC/ Sales (1)
Catapult	$ 40,039,000	$ 39,886,000	$ 27,046,000	$28,955,000	$18,206,000	21.78	$173,897,050	4.34
Group 1	$ 89,428,000	$ 94,235,000	$ 82,529,000	$65,291,000	$61,004,000	10.03	$ 79,078,150	0.88
Ansys	$ 91,011,000	$ 84,836,000	$ 74,467,000	$63,139,000	$56,553,000	12.6	$294,879,600	3.24
Manhattan	$175,721,000	$156,378,000	$138,619,000	$81,292,000	$62,065,000	29.72	$678,310,980	3.86
Serena	$ 98,641,000	$103,609,000	$ 75,406,460	$48,316,458	$32,147,036	32.35	$608,262,380	6.17
Mean								3.70
Median								3.86
Standard deviation								1.91
Coefficient of variation								0.52
Subject company	$ 17,045,000	$ 15,246,000	$ 13,790,000	$16,030,000	$18,620,000	-2.19		

Note:
(1) The sales figure in the denominator is for year 20X4.

Exhibit 15.17   Guideline Public Company MVIC/EBITDA

Company	20X4	20X3	20X2	20X1	20X0	Compound Growth (%)	MVIC	MVIC/ EBITDA (1)	MVIC/ Av. EBITDA (2)
Catapult	$11,577,000	$14,521,000	$ 7,699,000	$14,424,000	$ 7,590,000	11.13	$173,897,050	15.02	15.58
Group 1	$ 6,130,000	$12,101,000	$ 9,807,000	$ 4,924,000	$ 2,800,000	21.64	$ 79,078,150	12.90	11.06
Ansys	$29,363,000	$23,819,000	$21,813,000	$18,098,000	$16,090,000	16.23	$294,879,600	10.04	13.50
Manhattan	$38,550,000	$28,890,000	$24,455,000	$ 437,000	$ 9,261,000	42.84	$678,310,980	17.60	33.38
Serena	$33,739,000	$40,500,000	$24,139,645	$13,294,495	$ 7,693,567	44.71	$608,262,380	18.03	25.48
Mean								14.72	19.80
Median								15.02	15.58
Standard deviation								3.34	9.36
Coefficent of variation								0.23	0.47
Subject company	$ 5,255,000	$ 4,290,000	$ 3,350,000	$ 3,970,000	$ 5,516,000	−1.20			

Notes:

(1) The EBITDA figure in the denominator is for year 20X4.

(2) The EBITDA figure in the denominator is the five-year average for 20X0–20X4.

Exhibit 15.18 Guideline Public Company MVIC/EBIT

Company	20X4	20X3	20X2	20X1	20X0	Compound Growth (%)	MVIC	MVIC/ EBIT (1)	MVIC/ Av. EBIT (2)
Catapult	$11,577,000	$14,521,000	$ 7,699,000	$14,424,000	$ 7,590,000	11.13	$173,897,050	15.02	15.58
Group 1	$ 6,130,000	$12,101,000	$ 9,807,000	$ 4,924,000	$ 2,800,000	21.64	$ 79,078,150	12.90	11.06
Ansys	$27,074,000	$18,548,000	$19,579,000	$17,214,000	$15,235,000	15.46	$294,879,600	10.89	15.10
Manhattan	$36,778,000	$23,650,000	$23,290,000	$ 437,000	$ 9,261,000	41.17	$678,310,980	18.44	36.31
Serena	$25,403,000	$35,354,000	$21,913,294	$12,555,825	$ 7,693,567	34.80	$608,262,380	23.94	29.55
Mean								16.24	21.52
Median								15.02	15.58
Standard deviation								5.13	10.83
Coefficient of variation								0.32	0.50
Subject company	$ 4,925,000	$ 4,026,000	$ 3,230,000	$ 3,760,000	$ 5,012,000	−0.44			

Notes:

(1) The EBIT figure in the denominator is for year 20X4.

(2) The EBIT figure in the denominator is the five-year average for 20X0–20X4.

Exhibit 15.19 Guideline Public Company MVIC/BVIC

Company	20X4	20X3	20X2	20X1	20X0	Compound Growth (%)	MVIC	MVIC/ BVIC (1)
Catapult	$ 91,046,000	$ 63,490,000	$ 50,887,000	$43,589,000	$10,150,000	73.06	$173,897,050	1.91
Group 1	$ 67,528,000	$ 54,539,000	$ 45,085,000	$35,728,000	$27,646,000	25.02	$ 79,078,150	1.17
Ansys	$ 91,393,000	$ 74,393,000	$ 69,364,000	$65,631,000	$52,367,000	14.94	$294,879,600	3.23
Manhattan	$185,667,000	$143,389,500	$115,867,000	$59,405,000	$56,475,000	34.65	$678,310,980	3.65
Serena	$184,776,000	$157,145,000	$114,524,307	$38,105,050	$ 6,984,754	126.79	$608,262,380	3.29
Mean								2.65
Median								3.23
Standard deviation								1.06
Coefficent of variation								0.40
Subject company	$ 4,509,375	$ 4,800,188	$ 3,840,000	$4,887,600	$ 4,880,625	−1.96		

Note:

(1) The BVIC figure used in the denominator is for year 20X4.

251

Exhibit 15.20 Selected Guideline Public Company Method Pricing Multiples

Company	MVIC/Sales (1)	MVIC/EBITDA (1)	MVIC/Av. EBITDA (2)	MVIC/EBIT (1)	MVIC/Av. EBIT (2)	MVIC/BVIC (1)
Catapult	4.34	15.02	15.58	15.02	15.58	1.91
Group 1	0.88	12.90	11.06	12.90	11.06	1.17
Ansys	3.24	10.04	13.50	10.89	15.10	3.23
Manhattan	3.86	17.60	33.38	18.44	36.31	3.65
Serena	6.17	18.03	25.48	23.94	29.55	3.29
Mean	3.70	14.72	19.80	16.24	21.52	2.65
Median	3.86	15.02	15.58	15.02	15.58	3.23
Standard deviation	1.91	3.34	9.36	5.13	10.83	1.06
Coefficient of variation (3)	0.52	0.23	0.47	0.32	0.50	0.40

Notes:

(1) The figures for Sales, EBITDA, EBIT, and BVIC in the denominators of these multiples are for year 20X4.

(2) The figures for Av. EBITDA, and Av. EBIT in the denominator of these multiples are five-year averages for 20X0–20X4.

(3) The coefficient of variation is computed as the standard deviation divided by the mean.

Exhibit 15.21   Guideline Public Company Method MVIC Multiple Adjustments

Selected Pricing Multiple	Median Pricing Multiple	Adjustment Factor	Adjusted Pricing Multiple	Multiple Weight
MVIC/Sales (1)	3.86	−30.0%	2.70	20.0%
MVIC/EBITDA (2)	15.02	−20.0%	12.02	35.0%
MVIC/Av. EBITDA (2)	15.58	−20.0%	12.46	20.0%
MVIC/BVIC (3)	3.23	−10.0%	2.90	25.0%

Notes:

(1) Due to lower returns to sales compared to the guideline public companies, negative compound growth of revenue stream and higher risk, this multiple was adjusted downward by 30 percent. See Exhibits 15.12, 15.13, 15.14, and 15.16 for details. Due to the relatively higher coefficient of variation, a weight of 20 percent was allotted to this multiple.

(2) The subject company exhibited higher operating margins and superior asset turnover ratios compared to the guideline sample. On the other hand, even if in 20X3 and 20X4 the EBITDA started increasing, it posted negative growth in the last five years. See Exhibits 15.12, 15.13, 15.14, 15.17, and 15.18 for details. Thus, these multiples were adjusted downward 20 percent. A higher weight was assigned to the MVIC/EBITDA compared to MVIC/Av. EBITDA because of its lower coefficient of variation.

(3) The subject company posted higher return on assets and return on equity compared to the guideline sample. Also, the subject company exhibited superior asset turnover ratios. One the other hand, even if in 20X3 and 20X4 the BVIC started increasing, it posted negative growth in the last five years. See Exhibits 15.12, 15.13, 15.14, and 15.19 for details. This multiple was adjusted downward 10 percent and a weight of 25 percent was assigned because of its relatively lower coefficient of variation.

Exhibit 15.22   Guideline Public Company Method Weighting and MVIC Calculation

Selected Pricing Multiple	Adjusted Pricing Multiple	Optimum Software Fundamental	Indicated Value	Multiple Weight	Weighted Method Value
Guideline public company data					
MVIC/Sales	2.70	$17,045,000	$46,057,486	20.0%	$ 9,211,497
MVIC/EBITDA (20X4)	12.02	$ 5,255,000	$63,147,897	35.0%	$22,101,764
MVIC/EBITDA (5-year average)	12.46	$ 4,476,200	$55,788,140	20.0%	$11,157,628
MVIC/BVIC	2.90	$ 4,509,375	$13,094,552	25.0%	$ 3,273,638
Guideline public company MVIC					$42,470,889
Less: Market value of interest-bearing debt (20X4)					$ 564,844
Equals: Indicated value of common equity					$41,906,045

Note:

See footnotes to Exhibit 15.21 for explanations of the adjusted pricing multiple and the multiple weights.

Exhibit 15.23 Optimum Software and Selected Merged and Acquired Companies Balance Sheet and Income Statement Data

Fiscal Year Ended	CygnaCom 12/31/20X2	Symitar 12/31/20X1	Bonson 12/31/20X3	DOME 12/31/20X1	Data 11/30/20X2	Median	Subject 12/31/20X4
Balance Sheets							
Cash and equivalents	$ 746,848	$5,026,927	$ 5,298,000	$ 4,977,719	$ 512,863	$4,977,719	$1,832,813
Receivables	$1,394,943	$2,417,906	$14,931,000	$ 3,661,206	$2,841,738	$2,841,738	$3,058,594
Inventories	$ 0	$ 346,425	$ 932,000	$ 4,451,740	$ 764,081	$ 764,081	$ 731,250
Current assets	$2,164,047	$7,931,035	$23,619,000	$13,891,597	$4,147,261	$7,931,035	$5,622,656
Fixed assets (net)	$ 21,922	$1,460,215	$ 893,000	$ 1,024,313	$ 34,426	$ 893,000	$ 600,000
Total assets	$2,212,677	$9,465,439	$24,515,000	$15,080,827	$4,431,507	$9,465,439	$6,234,375
Current liabilities	$ 216,817	$5,823,144	$14,151,000	$ 6,698,386	$2,808,810	$5,809,782	$1,725,000
Long-term debt	$ 62,142	$ 0	$ 0	$ 2,030,734	$ 13,362	$ 13,362	$ 564,844
Total liabilities	$ 278,959	$5,823,144	$14,151,000	$ 8,729,120	$2,822,172	$5,823,144	$2,289,844
Shareholders' equity	$1,933,718	$3,642,295	$10,364,000	$ 6,351,707	$1,609,335	$3,642,295	$3,944,531
Total liabilities and equity	$2,212,677	$9,465,439	$24,515,000	$15,080,827	$4,431,507	$9,465,439	$6,234,375
Working Capital	*$1,947,230*	*$2,107,891*	*$9,468,000*	*$7,193,211*	*$1,338,451*	*$2,107,891*	*$3,897,656*
Book Value of Invested Capital	*$1,995,860*	*$3,642,295*	*$10,364,000*	*$8,382,441*	*$1,622,697*	*$3,642,295*	*$4,509,375*
Income Statements							
Sales	$6,196,099	$32,804,805	$27,065,000	$28,470,310	$8,865,193	$27,065,000	$17,045,000
Cost of goods sold	$3,998,684	$14,503,468	$19,159,000	$10,977,558	$5,858,895	$9,449,856	$ 8,550,000
Gross margin	$2,197,415	$18,301,337	$ 7,906,000	$19,020,454	$3,006,298	$7,906,000	$ 8,495,000
SG&A							$ 2,220,000
Research and development							$ 1,020,000
Depreciation and amortization	$ 26,613	$ 479,163	$ 532,000	$ 498,551	$ 19,354	$ 479,163	$ 330,000
Total operating expenses	$ 524,064	$13,279,035	$ 5,705,000	$10,977,558	$2,156,792	$ 5,705,000	$ 3,570,000
Income (loss) from operations	$1,673,351	$ 5,022,302	$ 2,201,000	$ 8,042,896	$ 849,506	$ 2,201,000	$ 4,925,000
Interest expense	$ 0	$ 0	$ 258,000	$ 0	$ 0	$ 0	$ 62,000
Income (loss) before taxes	$1,721,659	$ 5,345,117	$ 2,043,000	$ 8,096,402	$ 881,568	$ 2,043,000	$ 4,863,000
Provision for income taxes	$ 0	$ 82,826	$ 31,000	$ 2,603,200	$ 147,141	$ 82,826	$ 1,945,200
Net income	$1,721,659	$ 5,262,291	$ 2,012,000	$ 5,493,202	$ 734,427	$ 2,012,000	$ 2,917,800
EBITDA	*$1,699,964*	*$ 5,501,465*	*$ 2,733,000*	*$ 8,541,447*	*$ 868,860*	*$ 2,733,000*	*$ 5,255,000*

Exhibit 15.24 Optimum Software and Selected Merged and Acquired Companies Common Size Comparison

Fiscal Year Ended	CygnaCom 12/31/20X2	Symitar 12/31/20X1	Bonson 12/31/20X3	DOME 12/31/20X1	Data 11/30/20X2	Median	Subject 12/31/20X4	Comment
Balance Sheets								
Cash and equivalents	34%	53%	22%	33%	12%	33%	29%	Below median
Receivables	63%	26%	61%	24%	64%	61%	49%	Below median
Inventories	0%	4%	4%	30%	17%	4%	12%	Above median
Current assets	98%	84%	96%	92%	94%	94%	90%	Below median
Fixed assets (net)	1%	15%	4%	7%	1%	4%	10%	Above median
Total assets	100%	100%	100%	100%	100%	100%	100%	
Current liabilities	10%	62%	58%	44%	63%	58%	28%	Below median
Long-term debt	3%	0%	0%	13%	0%	0%	9%	Above median
Total liabilities	13%	62%	58%	58%	64%	58%	37%	Below median
Shareholders' equity	87%	38%	42%	42%	36%	42%	63%	Above median
Total liabilities and equity	100%	100%	100%	100%	100%	100%	100%	
Income Statements								
Sales	100%	100%	100%	100%	100%	100%	100%	
Cost of goods sold	65%	44%	71%	33%	66%	65%	50%	Below median
Gross margin	35%	56%	29%	67%	34%	35%	50%	Above median
Depreciation and amortization	0%	1%	2%	2%	0%	1%	2%	Above median
Total operating expenses	8%	40%	21%	39%	24%	24%	21%	Slightly below median
Income (loss) from operations	27%	15%	8%	28%	10%	15%	29%	Above median
Interest expense	0%	0%	1%	0%	0%	0%	0%	At median
Income (loss) before taxes	28%	16%	8%	28%	10%	16%	29%	Above median
Provision for income taxes	0%	0%	0%	9%	2%	0%	11%	Above median
Net income	28%	16%	7%	19%	8%	16%	17%	Slightly above median

Notes:

When compared to the sample of guideline merged and acquired companies, Optimum Software has:

- Higher than median fixed asset and lower current assets
- Higher than median long-term debt and equity and lower current and total liabilities
- Higher gross margin and EBIT because of lower COGS and operating expenses
- The income before taxes is above median and the net income is slightly above the median

255

Exhibit 15.25 Optimum Software and Selected Merged and Acquired Companies Financial and Operating Ratio Comparison

Fiscal Year Ended	CygnaCom 12/31/20X2	Symitar 12/31/20X1	Bonson 12/31/20X3	DOME 12/31/20X1	Data 11/30/20X2	Median	Subject 12/31/20X4	Comment
Liquidity/Solvency Ratios								
Quick ratio	9.9	1.3	1.4	1.3	1.2	1.3	2.8	Above median
Current ratio	10.0	1.4	1.7	2.1	1.5	1.7	3.3	Above median
Accounts receivable to sales	22.5%	7.4%	55.2%	12.9%	32.1%	22.5%	17.9%	Below median
Current liabilities to net worth	11.2%	159.9%	136.5%	105.5%	174.5%	136.5%	43.7%	Below median
Turnover								
Sales to receivables	4.4	13.6	1.8	7.8	3.1	4.4	5.6	Above median
Sales to working capital	3.2	15.6	2.9	4.0	6.6	4.0	4.4	Above median
Sales to fixed assets	282.6	22.5	30.3	27.8	257.5	30.3	28.4	Below median
Sales to total assets	2.8	3.5	1.1	1.9	2.0	2.0	2.7	Above median
Debt/Risk								
EBIT/interest expense	na	0.0	na	na	na	na	79.4	NM
Current liabilities to total debt	77.7%	100.0%	100.0%	76.7%	99.5%	99.5%	75.3%	Below median
Long-term debt to total assets	2.8%	0.0%	0.0%	13.5%	0.3%	0.3%	9.1%	Above median
Total debt to total assets	12.6%	61.5%	57.7%	57.9%	63.7%	57.9%	36.7%	Below median
Total debt to net worth	14.4%	159.9%	136.5%	137.4%	175.4%	137.4%	58.1%	Below median
Fixed to net worth	1.1%	40.1%	8.6%	16.1%	2.1%	8.6%	15.2%	Above median
Profitability								
Gross margin	35.5%	55.8%	29.2%	66.8%	33.9%	35.5%	49.8%	Above median
EBITDA to sales	27.4%	16.8%	10.1%	30.0%	9.8%	16.8%	30.8%	Above median
Operating margin	27.0%	15.3%	8.1%	28.3%	9.6%	15.3%	28.9%	Above median
Pretax return on assets	77.8%	56.5%	8.3%	53.7%	19.9%	53.7%	78.0%	Above median
After-tax return on assets	77.8%	55.6%	8.2%	36.4%	16.6%	36.4%	46.8%	Above median
Pretax return on net worth	89.0%	146.8%	19.7%	127.5%	54.8%	89.0%	123.3%	Above median
After-tax return on net worth	89.0%	144.5%	19.4%	86.5%	45.6%	86.5%	74.0%	Below median
Pretax return on sales	27.8%	16.3%	7.5%	28.4%	9.9%	16.3%	28.5%	Above median
After-tax return on sales	27.8%	16.0%	7.4%	19.3%	8.3%	16.0%	17.1%	Above median

Working Capital

Working capital to sales	31.4%	6.4%	35.0%	25.3%	15.1%	25.3%	22.9%	Below median
Net income to working capital	88.4%	249.6%	21.3%	76.4%	54.9%	76.4%	74.9%	Below median
Inventory to working capital	0.0%	16.4%	9.8%	61.9%	57.1%	16.4%	18.8%	Above median
Current liabilities to working capital	11.1%	276.3%	149.5%	93.1%	209.9%	149.5%	44.3%	Below median
Long-term debt to working capital	3.2%	0.0%	0.0%	28.2%	1.0%	1.0%	14.5%	Above median

Operating efficiency

Operating expenses to gross margin	23.8%	72.6%	72.2%	57.7%	71.7%	71.7%	42.0%	Below median
Operating expenses to sales	8.5%	40.5%	21.1%	38.6%	24.3%	24.3%	20.9%	Below median
Depreciation to sales	0.4%	1.5%	2.0%	1.8%	0.2%	1.5%	1.9%	Above median
Total assets to sales	35.7%	28.9%	90.6%	53.0%	50.0%	50.0%	36.6%	Below median
Sales to net worth	3.2	9.0	2.6	4.5	5.5	4.5	4.3	Below median
Sales to fixed assets	282.6	22.5	30.3	27.8	257.5	30.3	28.4	Below median

Notes:

When compared to the sample of guideline merged and acquired companies, Optimum Software has:

• Higher than the median liquidity and solvency ratios as well as turnover ratios except for slightly lower than median fixed asset turnover

• Debt and risk ratios below the median for the group indicating lower risk

• Profitability above median with the exception of the after-tax return on net worth

• Better than median operating efficiency and lower than median use of fixed and total assets

Exhibit 15.26   Selected Merged and Acquired Company Method Pricing Multiples

Company	MVIC/Sales	MVIC/EBITDA	MVIC/EBIT	MVIC/BVIC
CygnaCom	2.58	9.41	9.29	8.02
Symitar	1.34	8.00	8.23	12.08
Bonson	1.75	17.30	23.14	4.56
DOME	2.14	7.14	7.53	7.28
Data	1.61	16.40	16.16	8.78
Mean	1.88	11.65	12.87	8.14
Median	1.75	9.41	9.29	8.02
Standard deviation	0.49	4.83	6.69	2.72
Coefficient of variation (1)	0.26	0.41	0.52	0.33

Notes:

The sales, EBITDA, EBIT, and BVIC figures in the denominators of the multiples are for latest full year.

(1) The coefficient of variation is computed as the standard deviation divided by the mean.

Exhibit 15.27   Guideline Merged and Acquired Company Method MVIC
Multiple Adjustments

Selected Pricing Multiple	Median Pricing Multiple	Adjustment Factor	Adjusted Pricing Multiple	Multiple Weight
MVIC/Sales (1)	1.75	20.0%	2.10	45.0%
MVIC/EBITDA (2)	9.41	15.0%	10.82	20.0%
MVIC/EBIT (2)	9.29	15.0%	10.69	15.0%
MVIC/BVIC (3)	8.02	10.0%	8.82	20.0%

Notes:

(1) Due to higher returns to sales compared to the guideline merged and acquired companies and lower risk, this multiple was adjusted upward by 20 percent. See Exhibits 15.23, 15.24, and 15.25 for details. Due to the relatively lower coefficient of variation, a weight of 45 percent was allotted to this multiple.

(2) The subject company exhibited higher operating margins and superior asset turnover ratios compared to the guideline sample of merged and acquired companies. See Exhibits 15.23, 15.24, and 15.25 for details. Thus, these multiples were adjusted upward by 15 percent. A higher weight was assigned to the MVIC/EBITDA compared to MVIC/EBIT because of its lower coefficient of variation.

(3) The subject company posted higher returns on assets. Also, the subject company exhibited superior asset turnover ratios. See Exhibits 15.23, 15.24, and 15.25 for details. This multiple was adjusted upward 10 percent and a weight of 20 percent was assigned because of its relatively lower coefficient of variation.

Exhibit 15.28 Guideline Merged and Acquired Company Method Weighting and MVIC Calculation

Selected Pricing Multiple	Adjusted Pricing Multiple	Subject Company Fundamental	Indicated Value	Multiple Weight	Weighted Method Value
Guideline merged and acquired company data					
MVIC/Sales	2.10	$17,045,000	$35,725,161	45.0%	$16,076,323
MVIC/EBITDA	10.82	$5,255,000	$56,878,852	20.0%	$11,375,770
MVIC/EBIT	10.69	$4,925,000	$52,635,278	15.0%	$7,895,292
MVIC/BVIC	8.82	$4,509,375	$39,764,813	20.0%	$7,952,963
Guideline merged and acquired company method MVIC					$43,300,347
Less: Market value of interest-bearing debt (20X4)					$564,844
Equals: Indicated value of common equity					$42,735,503

Note:
See footnotes to Exhibit 15.27 for explanations of the adjusted pricing multiple and the multiple weights.

Exhibit 15.29 Opinion of Value Derived from the Application of the Market Approach to Valuation

Method	Indicated Value	Method Weight	Weighted Value
Guideline public company MVIC method	$41,906,045	0.5	$20,953,023
Guideline merged and acquired company MVIC method	$42,735,503	0.5	$21,367,752
Total			$42,320,774

Note:
Equal weight was assigned to each method in this case, but other weights may be appropriate.

The Asset-Based Approach

Summary

SUMMARY

The asset-based approach is relevant for holding companies and for operating companies that are contemplating liquidation or are unprofitable for the foreseeable future. It should also be given some weight for asset-heavy operating companies, such as financial institutions, distribution companies, and natural resources companies such as forest products companies with large timber holdings.

There are two main methods within the asset approach:

1. The adjusted net asset value method
2. The excess earnings method

Either of these methods produces a *controlling interest value*. If valuing a controlling interest, a discount for lack of marketability may be applicable (see Chapter 18). If valuing a minority interest, discounts for both lack of control and lack of marketability would be appropriate in most cases.

ADJUSTED NET ASSET VALUE METHOD

The adjusted net asset value method involves adjusting all assets and liabilities to current values. The difference between the value of assets and the value of liabilities is the value of the company. The adjusted net asset method produces a controlling interest value.

The adjusted net asset value encompasses valuation of all the company's assets, tangible and intangible, whether or not they are presently recorded on the balance sheet. For most companies, the assets are valued on a going-concern premise of value, but in some cases they may be valued on a forced or orderly liquidation premise of value.

The adjusted net asset method should also reflect the potential capital gains tax liability for appreciated assets. (This is discussed in Chapter 17.) In *Dunn*,[1] the Fifth Circuit Court of Appeals opined that the full dollar amount of the tax on the gains can be deducted "as a matter of law" from indications of value using the asset approach. As a result, this can be done as an adjustment to the balance sheet rather than a separate adjustment at the end.

Exhibit 16.1 is a sample of the application of the adjusted net asset value method. In a real valuation, the footnotes should be explained in far greater detail in the text of the report. Intangible assets are usually valued by the income approach.

EXCESS EARNINGS METHOD (THE FORMULA APPROACH)

The excess earnings method is classified under the asset approach because it involves valuing all the tangible assets at current fair market values and valuing all the intangible assets in a big pot loosely labeled *goodwill*. It is also sometimes classified as a *hybrid method*.

The excess earnings method originated in the 1920s as a result of Prohibition. The U.S. government decided that the owners of breweries and distilleries that were put out of business because of Prohibition should be compensated not only for the tangible assets that they lost, but also for the value of their potential goodwill.

Thus, the concept of the excess earnings method is to value goodwill by capitalizing any earnings the company was enjoying over and above a fair rate of return on their tangible assets. Thus the descriptive label, *excess earnings method*.

The result of the excess earnings method is value on a control basis. The latest IRS pronouncement on the excess earnings method is Rev. Rul. 68-609.[2] Specifically, the Ruling states, "The 'formula' approach may be used for determining the fair market value of intangible assets of a business only if there is no better basis therefore available."

Steps in Applying the Excess Earnings Method

1. Estimate net tangible asset value (usually at market values).
2. Estimate a normalized level income.
3. Estimate a required rate of return to support the net tangible assets.
4. Multiply the required rate of return to support the tangible assets (from step 3) by the net tangible asset value (from step 1).
5. Subtract the required amount of return on tangibles (from step 3) from the normalized amount of returns (from step 2); this is the amount of excess earnings. (If the results are negative, there is no intangible value and this method is no longer an appropriate indicator of value. Such a result indicates that the company would be worth more on a liquidation basis than on a going-concern basis.)
6. Estimate an appropriate capitalization rate to apply to the excess economic earnings. (This rate normally would be higher than the rate for tangible assets and higher than the overall capitalization rate; persistence of the customer base usually is a major factor to consider in estimating this rate.)

---

[1]*Estate of Dunn v. Comm'r*, T.C. Memo 2000-12, 79 T.C.M. (CCH) 1337; *rev'd* 301 F.3d 339 (5th Cir. 2002).
[2]See Chapter 22 for a full discussion.

Exhibit 16.1   Adjusted Net Asset Value for XYZ Company

	6/30/94 $	Adjusted $	As Adjusted $
Assets:			
Current Assets:			
Cash Equivalents	740,000		740,000
Accounts Receivable	2,155,409		2,155,409
Inventory	1,029,866	200,300[a]	1,230,166
Prepaid Expenses	2,500		2,500
Total Current Assets	3,927,775	200,300	4,128,075
Fixed Assets:			
Land & Buildings	302,865	(49,760)[b]	253,105
Furniture & Fixtures	155,347	(113,120)[b]	42,227
Automotive Equipment	478,912	(391,981)[b]	86,931
Machinery & Equipment	759,888	(343,622)[b]	416,266
Total Fixed Assets, Cost	1,697,012	(898,483)	798,529
Accumulated Depreciation	(1,298,325)	1,298,325 [c]	0
Total Fixed Assets, Net	398,687	399,842	798,529
Real Estate—Nonoperating	90,879	43,121 [d]	134,000
Other Assets:			
Goodwill, Net	95,383	(95,383)[e]	0
Organization Costs, Net	257	(257)[e]	0
Investments	150,000	20,000 [d]	170,000
Patents	0	100,000 [e]	100,000
Total Other Assets	245,640	24,360	270,000
Total Assets	4,662,981	667,623	5,330,604
Liabilities and Equity:			
Current Liabilities:			
Accounts Payable	1,935,230		1,935,230
Bank Note, Current	50,000		50,000
Accrued Expenses	107,872		107,872
Additional Tax Liability	0	267,049 [f]	267,049
Total Current Liabilities	2,093,103	267,049	2,360,151
Long-Term Debt	350,000		350,000
Total Liabilities	2,443,102	267,049	2,710,151
Equity:			
Common Stock	2,500		2,500
Paid-in Capital	500,000		500,000
Retained Earnings	1,717,379	400,574 [g]	2,117,953
Total Equity	2,219,879	400,574	2,620,453
Total Liabilities and Equity	4,662,981	667,623	5,330,604

Notes:

[a]Add back LIFO reserve.

[b]Deduct economic depreciation.

[c]Remove accounting depreciation.

[d]Add appreciation of value, per real estate appraisal.

[e]Remove historical goodwill. Value identifiable intangibles and put on books.

[f]Add tax liability of total adjustment at 40% tax rate.

[g]Summation of adjustments.

Source: American Society of Appraisers, *BV-201, Introduction to Business Valuation, Part I* from Principles of Valuation course series, 2002. Used with permission. All rights reserved.

7. Divide the amount of excess earnings (from step 5) by a capitalization rate applicable to excess earnings (from step 6); this is the estimated value of the intangibles.

8. Add the value of the intangibles (from step 7) to the net tangible asset value (from step 1); this is the estimated value of the company.

9. Reasonableness check: Does the blended capitalization rate approximate a capitalization rate derived by weighted average cost of capital (WACC)?

10. Determine an appropriate value for any excess or nonoperating assets that were adjusted for in step 1. If applicable, add the value of those assets to the value determined in step 8. If asset shortages were identified in step 1, determine whether the value estimate should be reduced to reflect the value of such shortages. If the normalized income statement was adjusted for identified asset shortages, it is not necessary to further reduce the value estimate.

Example of the Excess Earnings Method

Assumptions:

Net tangible asset value	$100,000
Normalized annual economic income	$ 30,000
Required return to support tangible assets	10%
Capitalization rate for excess earnings	25%

Calculations:

Net tangible asset value		$100,000
Required return on tangible assets	$0.10 \times \$100,000 =$ $10,000	
Excess earnings	$30,000 – $10,000 = $20,000	
Value of excess earnings	$20,000/0.25 =	$ 80,000
Indicated value of company		$180,000

Reasonableness Check for the Excess Earnings Method

$$\frac{\text{Normalized income } \$30{,}000}{\text{Indicated value of company}} = 0.167 \text{ or } 16.7\%$$

If 16.7 percent is a realistic WACC for this company, then the indicated value of the invested capital meets this reasonableness test. If not, then the values should be reconciled. More often than not, the problem lies with the value indicated by the excess earnings method rather than with the WACC.

Problems with the Excess Earnings Method

Tangible Assets Not Well Defined

- Rev. Rul. 68-609 does not specify the appropriate standard of value for tangible assets (e.g., fair market value [FMV] on a going-concern basis or replacement cost); although some type of FMV seems to be implied, some analysts simply use book value due to lack of existing asset appraisals.
- It is not clear whether clearly identifiable intangible assets (e.g., leasehold interests) should be valued separately or simply left to be included with all intangible assets under the heading of *goodwill*.
- Rev. Rul. 68-609 does not address when or whether asset write-ups should be tax affected. Most appraisers will include built-in capital gains, however, if assets are adjusted upward to reflect their fair market value.

Definition of Income Not Specified

Rev. Rul. 68-609[3] says the following:

> *The percentage of return on the average annual value of the tangible assets used should be the percentage prevailing in the industry involved at the date of valuation, or (when the industry percentage is not available) a percentage of 8 to 10 percent may be used.*
>
> *The 8 percent of return and the 15 percent rate of capitalization are applied to tangibles and intangibles, respectively, of businesses with a small risk factor and stable and regular earnings; the 10 percent rate of return and 20 percent rate of capitalization are applied to businesses in which the hazards of business are relatively high.*
>
> *The above rates are used as examples and are not appropriate in all cases. In applying the "formula" approach, the average earnings period and the capitalization rates are dependent upon the facts pertinent thereto in each case.[4]*

- Practice is mixed. Some use net cash flow, but many use net income, pretax income, or some other measure.
- Since some debt usually is contemplated in estimating required return on tangible assets, returns should be amounts available to all invested capital.
- If no debt is contemplated, then returns should be those available to equity.
- The implication of the preceding two bullet points is that the method can be conducted on either an invested capital basis or a 100 percent equity basis.

Capitalization Rates Not Well Defined

- Rev. Rul. 68-609 recommends using rates prevalent in the industry at the time of valuation.

---

[3]For a reference to the valuation of intangible assets see Robert F. Reilly, and Robert P. Schweihs, *Valuing Intangible Assets* (New York: McGraw-Hill, 1998).
[4]Rev. Rul. 68-609. For a full discussion, please see Chapter 22.

- Required return on tangibles is controversial, but usually a blend of the following:
  - Borrowing rate times percentage of tangible assets that can be financed by debt
  - Company's cost of equity capital
- No empirical basis has been developed for estimating a required capitalization rate for excess earnings.

The result of these ambiguities is highly inconsistent implementation of the excess earnings method.

CONCLUSION

Within the asset approach, the two primary methods are the adjusted net asset value method and the excess earnings method. Under the adjusted net asset value method, all assets, tangible and intangible, are identified and valued individually. Under the excess earnings method, only tangible assets are individually valued; all the intangibles are valued together by the capitalization of earnings over and above a fair return on the tangible assets.

Once indications of value have been developed by the income, market, and/or asset approaches, the next consideration is whether to adjust these values by applicable premiums and/or discounts. In valuations for tax purposes, the premiums and/or discounts often are a bigger and more contentious money issue than the underlying value to which they are applied. Premiums and discounts are the subject of Chapters 17, 18 , and 19.

Entity-Level Discounts

SUMMARY

Entity-level discounts are those that apply to the company as a whole. That is, they apply to the values of the stock held by all the shareholders alike, regardless of their respective circumstances. As such, they should be deducted from value indicated by the basic approach or approaches used. Since they apply to the company as a whole, regardless of individual shareholder circumstances, the entity-level discounts should be deducted *before* considering shareholder-level discounts or premiums.

There are four primary categories of entity-level discounts:

1. Trapped-in capital gains discount
2. Key person discount

3. Portfolio (nonhomogeneous assets) discount
4. Contingent liabilities discount

TRAPPED-IN CAPITAL GAINS DISCOUNT

The concept of the trapped-in capital gains tax discount is that a company holding an appreciated asset would have to pay capital gains tax on the sale of the asset. If ownership in the company were to change, the cost basis in the appreciated asset(s) would not change. Thus, the built-in liability for the tax on the sale of the asset would not disappear, but would remain with the corporation under the new ownership.

Logic Underlying Trapped-In Capital Gains Tax Discount

Under the standard of fair market value, the premise for this discount seems very simple. Suppose that a privately held corporation owns a single asset (e.g., a piece of land) with a fair market value of $1 million and a cost basis of $100,000. Would the hypothetical willing buyer pay $1 million for the stock of the corporation, knowing that the underlying asset will be subject to corporate tax on the $900,000 gain, when the asset (or a comparable asset) could be bought directly for $1 million with no underlying embedded taxes? Of course not.

And would the hypothetical, willing seller of the private corporation reduce the asking price of his or her stock below $1 million in order to receive cash not subject to the corporate capital gains tax? Of course.

The most common reason cited in court decisions for denying a discount for trapped-in capital gains is lack of intent to sell. If the reason for rejecting the discount for trapped-in capital gains tax is that liquidation is not contemplated, this same logic could also lead to the conclusion that the asset approach is irrelevant and that the interest should be valued using the income approach or, possibly, the market approach.

General Utilities Doctrine

Prior to 1986, the *General Utilities* Doctrine (named after the U.S. Supreme Court decision in *General Utilities & Operating Co. v. Commissioner*)[1] allowed corporations to elect to liquidate, sell all their assets, and distribute the proceeds to shareholders without paying corporate capital gains taxes. The Tax Reform Act of 1986 eliminated this option, thus leaving no reasonable method of avoiding the corporate capital gains tax liability on the sale of appreciated assets.

With no way to eliminate the capital gains tax on the sale of an asset, it is unreasonable to believe that an asset subject to the tax (e.g., the stock of a company owning a highly appreciated piece of real estate) could be worth as much as an asset not subject to the tax (e.g., a direct investment in the same piece of real estate). Even with no intent to sell the entity or the

---

[1]*General Utilities & Operating Co. v. Comm'r*, 296 U.S. 200 (1935).

appreciated asset in the foreseeable future, it seems that any rational buyer or seller would contemplate a difference in value.

Court Recognition of Trapped-In Capital Gains

In *Eisenberg v. Commissioner*,[2] the Tax Court denied the trapped-in gains discount, relying on Tax Court decisions prior to the 1986 repeal of the *General Utilities* Doctrine. The taxpayer appealed to the Second Circuit Court of Appeals. The Second Circuit opined that, because of the change in the law, pre–*General Utilities* decisions were no longer controlling. The Second Circuit, commenting favorably on the Tax Court's decision in *Estate of Davis v. Commissioner*[3] (which recognized a discount for trapped-in capital gains) vacated the Tax Court decision denying the discount:

> *Fair market value is based on a hypothetical transaction between a wiling buyer and a willing seller, and in applying this willing buyer/willing seller rule, "the potential transaction is to be analyzed from the viewpoint of a hypothetical buyer whose only goal is to maximize his advantage. . . ." our concern in this case is not whether or when the donees will sell, distribute or liquidate the property at issue, but what a hypothetical buyer would take into account in computing [the] fair market value of the stock. We believe it is common business practice and not mere speculation to conclude a hypothetical willing buyer, having reasonable knowledge of the relevant facts, would take some account of the tax consequences of contingent built-in capital gains. . . . The issue is not what a hypothetical willing buyer plans to do with the property, but what considerations affect the fair market value. . . . We believe that an adjustment for potential capital gains tax liabilities should be taken into account in valuing the stock at issue in the closely held C corporation though no liquidation or sale of the Corporation or its asset was planned. . . .*

The Second Circuit remanded the case for a revaluation, which recognized trapped-in capital gains.

In *Estate of Simplot v. Commissioner*, the company being valued owned a large block of highly appreciated stock in a publicly traded company, Micron Technology.[4] Experts for both the taxpayer and the Service deducted 100 percent of the trapped-in capital gains tax in valuing this nonoperating asset held by the operating company, and the Tax Court accepted this conclusion. The decision was appealed and reversed on other grounds, but the holding regarding trapped-in capital gains tax was not challenged.[5]

Internal Revenue Service Acquiesces to Trapped-in Capital Gains Discount

The Service finally posted a notice acquiescing that there is no legal prohibition against a discount for trapped-in capital gains.

Referring to the *Eisenberg* case, the notice states:

> *The Second Circuit reversed the Tax Court and held that, in valuing closely held stock, a discount for the built-in capital gains tax liabilities could apply depending on the facts presented. The court noted that the Tax Court itself had recently reached a similar conclusion in* Estate of Davis v. Commissioner *110 T.C. 530 (1998).*

---

[2]*Eisenberg v. Comm'r*, 155 F.3d 50 (2d Cir. 1998).
[3]*Estate of Davis v. Comm'r*, 110 T.C. 530 (2d Cir. 1998).
[4]*Estate of Simplot v. Comm'r*, 112 T.C. 130 (1999), *rev'd.* 2001 U.S. App. LEXIS 9220 (9th Cir. 2001).
[5]*Simplot v. Comm'r*, 249 F.3d 1191, 2001, U.S. App. LEXIS 9220.

We acquiesce in this opinion to the extent that it holds that there is no legal prohibition against such a discount. The applicability of such a discount, as well as its amount, will hereafter be treated as factual matters to be determined by competent expert testimony based upon the circumstances of each case and generally applicable valuation principles. Recommendation: Acquiescence.

Subsequent Cases Regularly Recognize Trapped-in Capital Gains Tax Discount

Through the time of this writing, there have been several additional cases involving discounts for trapped-in capital gains, and all, except a partnership case, have recognized the discount, with the amounts varying considerably.

In *Estate of Welch v. Commissioner*, the Tax Court denied the capital gains tax deduction because the appreciated property was real estate subject to condemnation, which made the company eligible for a Code section 1033 election to roll over the sale proceeds and defer the capital gains tax, an option it exercised.[6] On appeal the Sixth Circuit reversed this decision.

The Sixth Circuit specifically addressed the issue of the corporation's potential Code section 1033 election, stating that the availability of the election does not automatically foreclose the application of a capital gains discount, which may be considered as a factor in determining fair market value (FMV).[7]

The point to be gleaned from this case is that while a section 1033 election may be available, the value of that election, and its effect on the value of the stock, still depends on all of the circumstances a hypothetical buyer of the stock would consider. In *Estate of Welch*, the corporation's exercise of the section 1033 election after the valuation date was therefore irrelevant.

In *Estate of Borgatello v. Commissioner*, the estate held an 82.76 percent interest in a real estate holding company.[8] Both experts applied a discount for trapped-in capital gains, but used very different methods.

The expert for the taxpayer assumed immediate sale. On that basis, the combined federal and California state tax warranted a 32.3 percent discount.

The expert for the Service assumed a 10-year holding period and a 2 percent growth rate in asset value. On the basis of these assumptions, he calculated the amount of the combined federal and California tax and discounted that amount back to a present value at a discount rate of 8.3 percent. On that basis, the discount worked out to be 20.5 percent.

The court held that the taxpayer expert's methodology was unrealistic because it did not account for any holding period by a potential purchaser. The court also found that the Service's 10-year holding period was too long. Therefore, the court looked at the range of discounts used by the experts and tried to find a middle ground between the immediate sale and the 10-year holding period. The court concluded that a 24 percent discount for the trapped-in capital gains was reasonable.

---

[6]*Estate of Welch v. Comm'r*, T.C. Memo 1998-167, 75 T.C.M. (CCH) 2252.
[7]Id.
[8]*Estate of Borgatello v. Comm'r*, T.C. Memo 2000-264, 80 T.C.M. (CCH) 260 (2000) 172, 175, 242.

Fifth Circuit Concludes Reduction of 100 Percent of Capital Gains Tax "as a Matter of Law" Is Appropriate

Estate of Dunn was appealed from the Tax Court to the Fifth Circuit. The case involved a 62.96 percent interest in Dunn Equipment, Inc., which owned and rented out heavy equipment, primarily in the petroleum refinery and petrochemical industries.

> *In deciding to apply only a 5% capital gains discount, the Tax Court had reasoned that there was little likelihood of liquidation or sale of the assets. The court of appeals rejected this reasoning because the underlying assumption of an asset-based valuation is the premise of liquidation. The court of appeals stated:*

> *We hold as a matter of law that the built-in gains tax liability of this particular business's assets must be considered as a dollar-for-dollar reduction when calculating the asset-based value of the Corporation, just as, conversely, built-in gains tax liability would have no place in the calculation of the Corporation's earnings-based value.*[9]

Capital Gains Discount Denied in Partnership Case

The only case since *Davis* in which the capital gains tax discount was denied was *Estate of Jones v. Commissioner*, where the estate owned an 83.08 percent partnership interest.[10] In denying the discount, the Court elaborated at length to distinguish the circumstances from *Davis*:

> *The parties and the experts agree that tax on the built-in gains could be avoided by a section 754 election in effect at the time of sale of partnership assets. If such an election is in effect, and the property is sold, the basis of the partnership's assets (the inside basis) is raised to match the cost basis of the transferee in the transferred partnership interest (the outside basis) for the benefit of the transferee. See sec. 743(b). Otherwise, a hypothetical buyer who forces a liquidation could be subject to capital gains tax on the buyer's pro rata share of the amount realized on the sale of the underlying assets of the partnership over the buyer's pro rate share of the partnership's adjusted basis in the underlying assets. See sec. 1001. Because the [limited partnership] agreement does not give the limited partners the ability to effect a section 754 election, in this case the election would have to be made by the general partner.*

> *[Taxpayer's expert] opined that a hypothetical buyer would demand a discount for built-in gains. He acknowledged in his report a 75- to 80-percent chance that an election would be made and that the election would not create any adverse consequences or burdens on the partnership. His opinion that the election was not certain to be made was based solely on the position of [decedent's son], asserted in his trial testimony, that, as general partner, he might refuse to cooperate with an unrelated buyer of the 83.08-percent limited partnership interest (i.e., the interest he received as a gift from his father). We view [decedent's son's] testimony as an attempt to bootstrap the facts to justify a discount that is not reasonable under the circumstances.*

> *[The Service's expert,] on the other hand, opined, and respondent contends, that a hypothetical willing seller of the 83.08-percent interest would not accept a price based on a reduction for built-in capital gains. The owner of that interest has effective control, as discussed above, and would influence the general partner to make a section 754 election, eliminating any gains for the purchaser and getting the highest price for the seller. Such an election would have no material or adverse impact on the preexisting partners. We agree with [the Service's expert]. . . .*

---

[9]*Dunn v. Comm'r*, 2002 U.S. App. LEXIS 15453 (5th Cir. 2002).
[10]*Estate of Jones v. Comm'r*, 116 T.C. 11, 67, 199, 242, 243, 290 (2001).

In the cases in which the discount was allowed, there was no readily available means by which the tax on built-in gains would be avoided. By contrast, disregarding the bootstrapping testimony of [decedent's son] in this case, the only situation identified in the record where a section 754 election would not be made by a partnership is an example by [taxpayer's expert] of a publicly syndicated partnership with "lots of partners . . . and a lot of assets" where the administrative burden would be great if an election were made. We do not believe that this scenario has application to the facts regarding the partnerships in issue in this case. We are persuaded that, in this case, the buyer and seller of the partnership interest would negotiate with the understanding that an election would be made and the price agreed upon would not reflect a discount for built-in gains.

KEY PERSON DISCOUNT

Sometimes the impact or potential impact of the loss of the entity's key person may be reflected in an adjustment to a discount rate or capitalization rate in the income approach or to valuation multiples in the market approach. Alternatively, the key person discount may be quantified as a separate discount, sometimes as a dollar amount, but more often as a percentage. It is generally considered to be an enterprise-level discount (taken before shareholder-level adjustments), because it impacts the entire company. All else being equal, a company with a *realized* key person loss is worth less than a company with a *potential* key person loss.

Internal Revenue Service Recognizes Key Person Discount

The Service recognizes the key person discount factor in Rev. Rul. 59-60, section 4.02:

. . . The loss of the manager of a so-called "one-man" business may have a depressing effect upon the value of the stock of such business, particularly if there is a lack of trained personnel capable of succeeding to the management of the enterprise. In valuing the stock of this type of business, therefore, the effect of the loss of the manager on the future expectancy of the business, and the absence of management-succession potentialities are pertinent factors to be taken into consideration. On the other hand, there may be factors which offset, in whole or in part, the loss of the manager's services. For instance, the nature of the business and of its assets may be such that they will not be impaired by the loss of the manager. Furthermore, the loss may be adequately covered by life insurance, or competent management might be employed on the basis of the consideration paid for the former manager's services. These, or other offsetting factors, if found to exist, should be carefully weighed against the loss of the manager's services in valuing the stock of the enterprise.

Moreover, the Service discusses the key person discount in its *IRS Valuation Training for Appeals Officers Coursebook*:

A key person is an individual whose contribution to a business is so significant that there is certainty that future earning levels will be adversely affected by the loss of the individual. . . .

Rev. Rul. 59-60 recognizes the fact that in many types of businesses, the loss of a key person may have a depressing effect upon value. . . .

Some courts have accounted for this depressing effect on value by applying a key person discount. In determining whether to apply a key person discount certain factors should be considered:

1. Whether the claimed individual was actually responsible for the company's profit levels.

2. If there is a key person, whether the individual can be adequately replaced.

Though an individual may be the founder and controlling officer of a corporation, it does not necessarily follow that he or she is a key person. Earnings may be attributable to intangibles such as patents and copyrights or long-term contracts. Evidence of special expertise and current significant management decisions should be presented. Finally, subsequent years' financial statements should be reviewed to see if earnings actually declined. In many situations, the loss of a so-called key person may actually result in increased profits.

The size of the company, in terms of number of employees, is also significant. The greater the number of employees, the greater the burden of showing that the contributions of one person were responsible for the firm's earnings history.

Even where there is a key person, the possibility exists that the individual can be adequately replaced. Consideration should be given to whether other long-term employees can assume management positions. On occasion, a company may own key-person life insurance. The proceeds from this type of policy may enable the company to survive a period of decreased earnings and to attract competent replacements.

There is no set percentage or format for reflecting a key person discount. It is essentially based on the facts and circumstances of each case.[11]

Factors to Consider in Analyzing the Key Person Discount

Some of the attributes that may be lost upon the death or retirement of the key person include:

- Relationships with suppliers
- Relationships with customers
- Employee loyalty to key person
- Unique marketing vision, insight, and ability
- Unique technological or product innovation capability
- Extraordinary management and leadership skill
- Financial strength (ability to obtain debt or equity capital, personal guarantees)

Some of the other factors to consider in estimating the magnitude of a key person discount, in addition to special characteristics of the person just listed, include:

- Services rendered by the key person and degree of dependence on that person
- Likelihood of loss of the key person (if still active)
- Depth and quality of other company management
- Availability and adequacy of potential replacement
- Compensation paid to key person and probable compensation for replacement
- Lag period before new person can be hired and trained
- Value of irreplaceable factors lost, such as vital customer and supplier relationships, insight and recognition, and personal management styles to ensure companywide harmony among employees

---

[11]Internal Revenue Service, *IRS Valuation Training for Appeals Officers Coursebook* (Chicago: Commerce Clearing House Incorporated, 1998): 9-11–9-13. Published and copyrighted by CCH Incorporated, 1998, 2700 Lake Cook Road, Riverwoods, IL 60015. Reprinted with permission of CCH Incorporated.

- Risks associated with disruption and operation under new management
- Lost debt capacity

There are three potential offsets to the loss of a key person:

1. Life or disability insurance proceeds payable to the company and not earmarked for other purposes, such as repurchase of a decedent's stock
2. Compensation saved (after any continuing obligations), if the compensation to the key person was greater than the cost of replacement
3. Employment and/or noncompete agreements

Quantifying the Magnitude of the Key Person Discount

Ideally, the magnitude of the key person discount should be the estimated difference in the present value of the net cash flows with and without involvement of the key person. If the key person is still involved, the projected cash flows for each year should be multiplied by the mean of the probability distribution of that person's remaining alive and active during the year. Notwithstanding, the fact is that most practitioners and courts express their estimate of the key person discount as a percentage of the otherwise undiscounted enterprise value.

In any case, the analyst should investigate the key person's actual duties and areas of active involvement. A key person may contribute value to a company both in day-to-day management duties and in strategic judgment responsibilities based on long-standing contacts and reputation within an industry.[12] The more detail presented about the impact of the key person, the better.

Court Cases Involving Decedent's Estate

In *Estate of Mitchell v. Commissioner*, the court commented that the moment-of-death concept of valuation for estate tax purposes is important, because it requires focus on the *property transferred*.[13] This meant that, at the moment of death, the company was without the services of Paul Mitchell. Because (1) the court considered him a very key person, (2) alleged earlier offers to acquire the entire company were contingent upon his continuing services, and (3) there was a marked lack of depth of management, the court determined a 10 percent discount from the company's enterprise stock value.

The court's discussion of the key person factor is instructive:

> *We next consider the impact of Mr. Mitchell's death on [John Paul Mitchell Systems]. Mr. Mitchell embodied JPMS to distributors, hair stylists, and salon owners. He was vitally important to its product development, marketing, and training. Moreover, he possessed a unique vision that enabled him to foresee fashion trends in the hair styling industry. It is clear that the loss of Mr. Mitchell, along with the structural inadequacies of JPMS, created uncertainties as to the future of JPMS at the moment of death.*

---

[12]Shannon Pratt, Robert Reilly, and Robert Schweihs, "Loss of Key Person," *Valuing a Business*, 4th ed. (New York: McGraw-Hill, 2000), pp. 601–602.

[13]*Estate of Mitchell v. Comm'r*, 250 F.3d 696, 2001 U.S. App. LEXIS 7990 (9th Cir. 2001).

Accordingly, after determining an enterprise value of $150 million for John Paul Mitchell Systems stock, the court deducted $15 million to arrive at $135 million, before calculation of the estate's proportionate value or applying discounts for minority interest, lack of marketability, and litigation risk.

In *Estate of Feldmar v. Commissioner*, the court gave a lengthy explanation before ultimately arriving at a 25 percent key person discount:[14]

> Management *[United Equitable Corporation] was founded by decedent in 1972. . . . Throughout the company's history, decedent had been heavily involved in the daily operation of UEC. Decedent was the creative driving force behind both UEC's innovative marketing techniques, and UEC's creation of, or acquisition and exploitation of, new products and services. . . .*
>
> *We further recognize, however, that where a corporation is substantially dependent upon the services of one person, and where that person is no longer able to perform services for the corporation by reason of death or incapacitation, an investor would expect some form of discount below fair market value when purchasing stock in the corporation to compensate for the loss of that key employee (key employee discount). See* Estate of Huntsman v. Commissioner, *66 T.C. 861 (1976):* Edwards v. Commissioner, *a Memorandum Opinion of this Court dated January 23, 1945. We find that Milton Feldmar was an innovative driving force upon which UEC was substantially dependent for the implementation of new marketing strategies and acquisition policies. Therefore, we find that a key employee discount is appropriate.*
>
> *Respondent asserts that no key man discount should be applied because, respondent argues, any detriment UEC suffered from the loss of decedent's services is more than compensated for by the life insurance policy upon decedent's life. We do not find merit in such a position. The life insurance proceeds UEC was to receive upon decedent's death are more appropriately considered as a non-operating asset of UEC. See* Estate of Huntsman v. Commissioner, *supra. We did this when we determined a value of UEC's stock by using the market-to-book valuation method.*
>
> *Respondent also argues that the key employee discount should not be applied because, respondent asserts, UEC could rely upon the services of the management structure already controlling UEC, or UEC could obtain the services of a new manager, comparable to the decedent, by using the salary decedent had received at the time of his demise. With respect to the existing management, [taxpayer's expert] conducted interviews of such managers and found them to be inexperienced and incapable of filling the void created by decedent's absence. By contrast, neither of respondent's experts offered an opinion on such management's ability to replace decedent. From the evidence represented, we conclude the UEC could not compensate for the loss of decedent by drawing upon its management reserves as such existed on the valuation date. . . .*

In *Estate of Rodriguez v. Commissioner*, the company subject to valuation was Los Amigos Tortilla Manufacturing, a corn and flour tortilla manufacturing business providing tortillas and shells used by Mexican restaurants for tacos, burritos, and so forth.[15]

Respective experts for the Service and the taxpayer presented diverging testimony on the key person issue. The taxpayer's expert adjusted pretax income to account for the loss of the decedent. The expert for the Service said that he normally would adjust the capitalization rate to account for the loss of a key person, but did not in this case because of the $250,000 corporate-owned life insurance policy on the decedent. He also testified that decedent's salary would pay for a replacement.

---

[14]*Estate of Feldmar v. Comm'r*, T.C. Memo 1988-429, 56 T.C.M. (CCH) 118.
[15]*Estate of Rodriguez v. Comm'r*, T.C. Memo 1989-13, 56 T.C.M. (CCH) 1033.

The court decided the issue in favor of the taxpayer:

[W]e do not agree with [Service's] expert that no adjustment for the loss of a key man is necessary in this case. [Service] argues that an adjustment is inappropriate because Los Amigos maintained $250,000 of insurance on decedent's life. Also, [Service's] expert witness testified that he did not make any allowance for the value of decedent as a key man because his replacement cost was equal to his salary. These arguments understate the importance of decedent to Los Amigos and the adverse effect his death had on business. We agree with [taxpayers] that an adjustment is necessary to account for the loss of decedent.

The evidence shows that decedent was the dominant force behind Los Amigos. He worked long hours supervising every aspect of the business. At the time of his death, Los Amigos' customers and suppliers were genuinely and understandably concerned about the future of the business without decedent. In fact, Los Amigos soon lost one of its largest accounts due to an inability to maintain quality. The failure was due to decedent's absence from operations. Profits fell dramatically without decedent to run the business. No one was trained to take decedent's place.

Capitalizing earnings is a sound valuation method requiring no adjustment only in a case where the earning power of the business can reasonably be projected to continue as in the past. Where, as in this case, a traumatic event shakes the business so that its earning power is demonstrably diminished, earnings should properly be adjusted. See Central Trust Co. v. United States, *305 F.2d at 403. An adjustment to earnings before capitalizing them to determine the company's value rather than a discount at the end of the computation is appropriate to reflect the diminished earnings capacity of the business. We adopt petitioners' expert's adjustment to earnings for the loss of the key man.*

In *Estate of Yeager v. Commissioner*, decedent was the controlling stockholder of a complicated holding company with several subsidiaries.[16] The court decided on a 10 percent discount for the loss of the key person. In its opinion, the court commented:

Until his death, the decedent was president, chief executive officer, and a director of Cascade Olympic, Capital Cascade, and Capitol Center. He was the only officer and director of these corporations who was involved in their day-to-day affairs. The decedent was critical to the operation of both Cascade Olympic and the affiliated corporations.

Court Case in which Key Person Is Still Active

In *Estate of Furman v. Commissioner*, the issue was the valuation of minority interests in a 27-unit Burger King chain.[17] The court rejected in total the Service's valuation. Besides rejecting his methodology, the court noted that he had represented he possessed certain qualifications and credentials to perform business valuations, which he did not, in fact, have.

The taxpayer's appraisal used a multiple of earnings before interest, taxes, depreciation, and amortization (EBITDA) and applied discounts of 30 percent for minority interest, 35 percent for lack of marketability, and a 10 percent key person discount, for a total discount of 59.05 percent. The court adjusted the EBITDA multiple upward, decided on a combined 40 percent minority and marketability discount, and agreed with the application of a 10 percent key person discount, for a total discount of 46 percent.

---

[16]*Estate of Yeager v. Comm'r*, T.C. Memo 1986-48, 52 T.C.M. (CCH) 524.
[17]*Furman v. Comm'r*, T.C. Memo 1998-157, 75 T.C.M. (CCH) 2206.

It is instructive to read the court's discussion supporting the key person discount:

Robert Furman a Key Person

At the time of the 1980 Gifts and the Recapitalization, Robert actively managed [Furman's, Inc.], and no succession plan was in effect. FIC employed no individual who was qualified to succeed Robert in the management of FIC. Robert's active participation, experience, business contacts, and reputation as a Burger King franchisee contributed to value of FIC. Specifically, it was Robert whose contacts had made possible the 1976 Purchase, and whose expertise in selecting sites for new restaurants and supervising their construction and startup were of critical importance in enabling FIC to avail itself of the expansion opportunities created by the Territorial Agreement. The possibility of Robert's untimely death, disability, or resignation contributed to uncertainty in the value of FIC's operations and future cash-flows. Although a professional manager could have been hired to replace Robert, the following risks would still have been present: (i) Lack of management until a replacement was hired; (ii) the risk that a professional manager would require higher compensation than Robert had received; and (iii) the risk that a professional manager would not perform as well as Robert.

Robert was a key person in the management of FIC. His potential absence or inability were risks that had a negative impact on the fair market value of FIC. On February 12, 1980, the fair market value of decedent's gratuitous transfer of 6 shares of FIC's common stock was subject to a key-person discount of 10 percent. On August 24, 1981, the fair market value of the 24 shares of FIC's common stock transferred by each decedent in the Recapitalization was subject to a key-person discount of 10 percent.

PORTFOLIO (NONHOMOGENEOUS ASSETS) DISCOUNT

A *portfolio discount* is applied, usually at the entity level, to a company or interest in a company that holds disparate or nonhomogeneous operations and/or assets. This section explains the principle and discusses empirical evidence of its existence and magnitude. Finally, we note that it has been accepted by some courts.

Investors generally prefer to buy *pure plays* rather than packages of dissimilar operations and/or assets. Therefore, companies, or interests in companies, that hold a nonhomogeneous group of operations and/or assets frequently sell at a discount from the aggregate amount those operations and/or assets would sell for individually. The latter is often referred to as the *breakup value*. This disinclination to buy a miscellaneous assortment of operations and/or assets, and the resulting discount from breakup value, is often called the *portfolio effect*.

It is quite common for family-owned companies, especially multigenerational ones, to accumulate an unusual (and often unrelated) group of operations and/or assets over the years. This often happens when different decision makers acquire holdings that particularly interest them at different points in time. For example, a large privately owned company might own a life insurance company, a cable television operation, and a hospitality division.

The following have been suggested as some of the reasons for the portfolio discount:

- The diversity of investments held within the corporate umbrella
- The difficulty of managing the diverse set of investments
- The expected time needed to sell undesired assets

- Extra costs expected to be incurred upon sale of the various investments
- The risk associated with disposal of undesired investments[18]

The portfolio discount effect is especially important when valuing noncontrolling interests, because minority stockholders have no ability to redeploy underperforming or nonperforming assets, nor can they cause a liquidation of the asset portfolio and/or a dissolution of the company. Minority stockholders place little or no weight on nonearning or low-earning assets in pricing stocks in a well-informed public market. Thus, the portfolio discount might be greater for a minority position because the minority stockholder has no power to implement changes that might improve the value of the operations and/or assets, even if the stockholder desires to.

Empirical Evidence Supports Portfolio Discounts

Three categories of empirical market evidence strongly support the prevalence of portfolio discounts in the market:

1. Prices of stocks of conglomerate companies
2. Breakups of conglomerate companies
3. Concentrated versus diversified real estate holding companies

The empirical evidence shows portfolio discounts from 13 percent up to as high as 65 percent. The courts have allowed portfolio discounts of 15 percent and 17 percent on two occasions. The discount for conglomerates is supported by prospective breakup valuations and historical breakup values.

Stocks of Conglomerate Companies

Stocks of conglomerate companies usually sell at a discount to their estimated breakup value.

Several financial services provide lists of conglomerate companies, most of which are widely followed by securities analysts. The analyst reports usually provide an estimate as to the aggregate prices at which the parts of the company would sell if spun off. This breakup value is consistently more than the current price of the conglomerate stock.

Actual Breakups of Conglomerate Companies

Occasionally, a conglomerate company actually does break up.[19] The resulting aggregate market value of the parts usually exceeds the previous market value of the whole.

---

[18]Wayne Jankowske, "Second-Stage Adjustments to Value," presented at American Society of Appraisers International Appraisal Conference, Toronto, June 16–19, 1996. Available online at *www.BVLibrary.com* with the author's permission.
[19]For example, in 1995 both AT&T and ITT broke up into companies that had different lines of business.

Evidence from Real Estate Holding Companies

An article on real estate holding companies made the point that the negative effect of a disparate portfolio also applies to real estate holding companies, such as real estate investment trusts (REITs): "REITs that enjoy geographic concentrations of their properties and specialize in specific types of properties, e.g., outlet malls, commercial office buildings, apartment complexes, shopping centers, golf courses . . . etc., are the most favored by investors. This is similar to investor preferences for the focused 'pure play' company in other industries."[20]

Portfolio Discounts in the Courts

The courts have recognized the concept of a portfolio discount. Like any discount, however, the portfolio discount must be supported by convincing expert testimony.

Portfolio Discount Accepted

In *Estate of Maxcy v. Commissioner*, the company in question owned citrus groves, cattle and horses, a ranch, mortgages, acreage and undeveloped lots, and more than 6,000 acres of pastureland.[21] The expert for the taxpayer opined that it would require a 15 percent discount from underlying asset value to induce a single purchaser to buy this assortment of assets. The expert for the Service opposed this discount, saying that a control owner could liquidate the corporation and sell the assets at fair market value.

The court agreed with the taxpayer's expert:

> *Without deciding the validity of respondent's contention, we fail to see how this power to liquidate inherent in a majority interest requires a higher value than [taxpayer expert's] testimony indicates. Whether or not a purchaser of a controlling interest in Maxcy Securities could liquidate the corporation and sell its assets is immaterial, as there must still be found a purchaser of the stock who would be willing to undertake such a procedure. [Taxpayer expert's] opinion was that this type purchaser is relatively scarce and not easily found at a sales price more than 85 percent of the assets' fair market value.*

> *Section 20.2031-1(b), Estate Tax Reg., provides that: "The fair market value [of property] is the price at which the property would change hands between a willing buyer and a willing seller, neither being under any compulsion to buy or sell and both having reasonable knowledge of relevant facts." In the instant case, we are attempting to determine the price a willing seller of Maxcy Securities shares could get from a willing buyer, not what the buyer may eventually realize.*

> *[Taxpayer expert's] testimony impresses us as a rational analysis of the value of the stock in issue, and in the absence of contrary evidence, we find and hold on the facts here present that a majority interest in such stock as worth 85 percent of the underlying assets' fair market value on the respective valuation dates.*

Since *Maxcy*, the only other case applying the portfolio discount is *Estate of Piper v. Commissioner*.[22] At issue was the valuation of a gift of stock in two investment companies,

---

[20]Phillip S. Scherrer, "Why REITs Face a Merger-Driven Consolidation Wave," *Mergers & Acquisition, The Dealmaker's Journal* (July/August 1995): 42.
[21]*Estate of Maxcy v. Comm'r*, T.C. Memo 1969-158, 28 T.C.M. (CCH) 783.
[22]*Estate of Piper v. Comm'r*, 72 T.C. 1062 (1979).

Piper Investment and Castanea Realty. The companies each owned various real estate holdings, as well as stock in Piper Aircraft, which manufactured light aircraft.

The Service argued that the discount should be 10 percent, a value in between the values proposed by its two expert witnesses. The estate contended that the discount should exceed 17 percent, the higher of the two values suggested by the Service's experts. Curiously, neither the estate nor its expert witnesses suggested a specific amount for the portfolio discount.

The court discussed each of the expert's methods in turn:

While we consider [the Service's first expert's] approach somewhat superior to that of [the Service's second expert] because [the first] limited his analysis to nondiversified investment companies, we believe that he erred in selecting the average discount of the nondiversified investment companies he considered. The weight of the evidence indicates that the portfolios of Piper Investment and Castanea were less attractive than that of the average nondiversified investment company. We reject [the Service's] attempt to bolster [the first expert's] position by reference to the premiums above net asset value at which certain investment companies, either diversified or specialized in industries other than light aircraft, were selling. Those companies simply are not comparable to Piper Investment and Castanea, nondiversified investment companies owning only realty and [Piper Aircraft] stock.

The court rejected the estate's contention that the discount should exceed 17 percent and chose 17 percent as the appropriate discount:

[The estate] has also failed to introduce specific data to support its assertion that Piper Investment and Castanea were substantially inferior to the worst of the companies considered by [the Service's second expert]. [The estate] made no attempt to elicit evidence as to the portfolios of the companies considered by [the second expert], and its expert witness commented only on [the first expert's], and not on [the second expert's], report. . . .On the basis of the record before us, we conclude that the discount selected by [the first expert] was too low, but that there is insufficient evidence to support [the estate's] position that the discount should be higher than that proposed by [the second expert]. Therefore, we find that 17 percent is an appropriate discount from the net asset value to reflect the relatively unattractive nature of the investment portfolios of Piper Investment and Castanea.

Portfolio Discount Denied

In *Knight v. Commissioner*,[23] the entity in question was a family limited partnership (FLP) that held real estate and marketable securities. Citing the section in *Valuing a Business* on discounts for conglomerates, the expert for the taxpayer claimed a 10 percent portfolio discount. In denying the discount, the court said, "the Knight family partnership is not a conglomerate public company. . . .[Taxpayer's expert] gave no convincing reason why the partnership's mix of assets would be unattractive to a buyer. We apply no portfolio discount. . . ."

DISCOUNT FOR CONTINGENT LIABILITIES

Contingent assets and liabilities are among the most difficult to value simply because of their nature. The challenge lies in estimating just how much may be collected or will have to be paid out, and thus in quantifying any valuation adjustments.

---

[23]*Knight v. Comm'r*, 115 T.C. 506 (2000).

Concept of the Contingent Liability Discount

In real-world purchases and sales of businesses and business interests, such items often are handled through a contingency account. For example, suppose a company with an environmental problem were being sold, and estimates had placed the cost to cure the environmental problem at $10 million to $20 million. The seller might be required to place $20 million in an escrow account to pay for the cleanup, and once the problem was cured, any money remaining would be released back to the seller.

In gift, estate, and certain other situations, however, a point estimate of value is required as of the valuation date, without the luxury of waiting for the actual outcome of a contingent event. In such cases, some estimate of the cost of recovery must be made. It can be added or deducted as a percentage of value, or as a dollar-denominated amount.

Financial Accounting Standard No. 5 May Provide Guidance in Quantifying Contingent Liabilities

Financial Accounting Standard (FAS) No. 5 deals with contingent liabilities for purposes of financial statement reporting. In valuing a company with financial statements that have been compiled, reviewed, or audited by an accountant, valuers might find the accountant's classifications and valuation of contingent liabilities instructive. FAS No. 5 requires consideration of any contingent liabilities, supported by legal letters. (Lawyers are required to respond to accountants' inquiries regarding the probability of contingent liabilities and their potential impact.) This information could be of significant value to the appraiser in determining a discount or reduction in value related to contingent liabilities.

Treatment of Contingencies in the Courts

Discounts for contingent liabilities are recognized where appropriate.

In *Estate of Klauss v. Commissioner*,[24] both the taxpayer's and the Service's experts applied substantial discounts for product liability and environmental claims. The taxpayer's expert enumerated specific items and applied a discount of $921,000. The Service's expert applied a 10 percent discount, which amounted to $1,130,000. The court agreed with the taxpayer's method because "[i]t more accurately accounted for the effect."

In *Payne v. Commissioner*,[25] the Service contended that the value of the stock, $500,000 received and claimed by Payne on his tax returns, was significantly understated. Payne argued that there should be a discount on the stock's value due to pending litigation over the company's business license. The Service's expert valued the stock at $1,140,000 as a going concern and at $230,000 if the company did not receive the business license. The court allowed a 50 percent discount on the going concern value due to the pending litigation and found the stock to be worth $570,000.

The treatment of the contingent liability in *Estate of Desmond v. Commissioner* is quite interesting.[26] Before giving equal weight to the income and guideline public company meth-

---

[24]*Estate of Klauss v. Comm'r*, T.C. Memo 2000-191, 79 T.C.M. (CCH) 2177.
[25]*Payne v. Comm'r*, T.C. Memo 1998-227, 75 T.C.M. (CCH) 2548.
[26]*Estate of Desmond v. Comm'r*, T.C. Memo 1999-76, 77 T.C.M. (CCH) 1529.

ods in valuing a paint manufacturing company's stock, the court applied a 20 percent discount for marketability to the result of the market approach and a 30 percent discount for marketability to the result of the income approach. The extra 10 percent reflected the environmental liability associated with the paint operation.

The reason for not applying the extra contingent liability discount to the market approach was the assumption that the public market multiples of the two guideline paint manufacturing companies already reflected similar contingent liabilities. The Service's expert argued that the companies had higher-than-average betas, and thus the volatility reflected in the income approach betas were due to contingencies. The court said that no evidence was presented to support this argument and rejected it, incorporating a contingent-liability discount only to the result from the market approach.

CONCLUSION

From the indication(s) of value from the basic valuation approach test, entity-level discounts (those that affect *all* the shareholders), if any, should be applied. These entity-level discounts can be categorized largely as follows:

1. Trapped-in capital gains
2. Key person
3. Portfolio (nonhomogeneous assets)
4. Contingent liabilities

Once the entity-level discounts have been considered and applied, we turn to shareholder-level discounts. The most important of these, in most cases, is the discount for lack of marketability, which is the subject of Chapter 18. Other shareholder-level discounts are the subject of Chapter 19.

Discounts for Lack of Marketability

SUMMARY: GENERAL INTRODUCTION TO SHAREHOLDER-LEVEL DISCOUNTS AND PREMIUMS

Valuation discounts and/or premiums are meaningless unless the base to which they are applied is defined. It is therefore necessary to define what level of value is indicated by the results of the income, market, and/or asset approach(es).

The approaches discussed in Chapters 15, 16, and 17 generally produce one of the following levels of value:

1. Control
2. Marketable minority

The income approach can produce either a control or a minority value. The key to which value is indicated is whether the numerators (cash flows, earnings, etc.) represent results that a control owner could be expected to produce by results from business as usual. If a minority value is indicated, it would be considered marketable because the discount rates and capitalization rates used in the income approach are based on publicly traded stock data.

In the guideline publicly traded stock method, the guideline companies are, by definition, minority interests. Therefore, if valuing a minority interest, a minority interest discount normally would not be appropriate, but a discount for lack of marketability would be, because the publicly traded stock can be sold immediately and the proceeds received in three business days, while the privately held stock enjoys no such liquid market. However, as discussed in Chapter 19, minority shares of publicly traded companies may sell at their control value. If the analyst can demonstrate that this is the case, a minority discount might be considered. If valuing a controlling interest, a control premium normally would be appropriate, subject to the caveat in the previous sentence.

The transaction method, being based on acquisitions of entire companies, produces a control value. Therefore, if valuing a minority interest, both minority and marketability discounts would be appropriate. If valuing a controlling interest, it might be appropriate to consider some discount for lack of marketability, as discussed later in this chapter.

If past transactions or buy-sell agreements are used, they should be studied to determine their implications. Rules of thumb normally indicate a control interest value.

Asset-based approaches (both adjusted net asset value and excess earnings) normally result in a control-interest value.

All adjustments to indicated values for any approach should be based on differences between the characteristics of the subject interest and the characteristics implicit in the approach from which the adjustment is made.

DEFINITION OF MARKETABILITY

The discount for lack of marketability is the largest single issue in most disputes regarding the valuation of businesses and business interests, especially in tax matters. This is true both in the number of cases in which the issue arises and the magnitude of the differential dollars involved in the disputes. That is why this is one of the longest chapters in the book and one that the authors consider of significant importance.

Marketability is defined by the *International Glossary of Business Valuation Terms* (see Appendix B) as *the ability to quickly convert property to cash at minimal cost*. The benchmark for marketability for business valuation is the market for active, publicly traded stocks. The holder can have the stock sold in less than a minute at or near the price of the last trade, and have cash in hand in three business days.

Discount for lack of marketability is defined by the *International Glossary of Business Valuation Terms* as an amount or percentage deducted from the value of an ownership interest to reflect the relative absence of marketability. The term *relative* in this definition usually refers to the value of the interest as if it were publicly traded, sometimes referred to as the *publicly traded equivalent value* or the *value if marketable*.

BENCHMARK FOR MARKETABILITY IS CASH IN THREE DAYS

For a discount to have a precise meaning, there must be a precise definition of the benchmark to which it is applied. As one author articulates the benchmark for marketability:

> It is generally accepted within the appraisal profession that the standard for marketability (or liquidity) of minority interests in closely held businesses is "cash in three days." In other words, sellers of publicly traded securities with active markets can achieve liquidity on the third business day, at or very near the market price prevailing at the time of the sale. This is true because current regulations require public market securities transactions to be settled or cleared by the third business day following execution of a transaction. [Footnote omitted.]
>
> If a business interest lacks an active market, it is, by definition, illiquid. Any holder of that interest will experience uncertainty with respect to the ability to "liquefy" the investment, unless that uncertainty is mitigated by contract (e.g., through a buy-sell agreement that specifies the pricing, terms and timing of "liquidity" events), or through other means acceptable to the holder.[1]

The market for securities in the United States is the most liquid market for any kind of property anywhere in the world. This is one of the major reasons companies are able to raise investment capital from both institutional and individual investors—the ability to liquidate the investment immediately, at little cost, and with virtual certainty as to realization of the widely publicized market price.

By contrast, the universe of realistically potential buyers for most closely held minority ownership securities is an infinitesimally small fraction of the universe of potential buyers for publicly traded securities. In the United States securities may not be offered for sale without prior registration and approval by the Securities and Exchange Commission (SEC) or State Securities Commission, absent a few narrow exceptions. Furthermore, *a minority stockholder cannot register stock for public trading*; only the company can register its stock for public trading.[2]

[1]Z. Christopher Mercer, *Quantifying Marketability Discounts* (Memphis, TN: Peabody Publishing, LP, 2001): 6. Used with permission of Peabody Publishing. All rights reserved.
[2]Shannon P. Pratt, *The Lawyer's Business Valuation Handbook* (Chicago: American Bar Association, 2000): 207–208. © 2000 American Bar Association. All rights reserved. Reprinted by permission.

INVESTORS CHERISH LIQUIDITY, ABHOR ILLIQUIDITY

Investors cherish liquidity. The public market allows investors to sell their interest and get cash immediately for any reason: when they believe that the value may go down, when they believe that the company should be managed differently, or when they just desire to have cash with which to do something else. The public market also provides liquidity in that it creates the ability to hypothecate the interest—that is, use it as collateral for a loan.

Consequently, all other things being equal, a stock that can be readily sold in the public market is worth much more than one which cannot be readily sold. When a company first completes an initial public offering (IPO), the price usually will be more than twice the price of the last transaction in the stock when it was private.

Conversely, investors abhor illiquidity. They may be forced to hold a stock and watch it decline in value or even become worthless. They may be forced to hold a stock when they object vehemently to management policies. Whatever their alternative needs or desires, they are generally "locked in" to the stock and are unable to get their money out of it. Banks will rarely accept stock of private companies, even controlling interests, as collateral for loans because of the lack of a market in case of default.

Consequently, all other things being equal, investors demand a large discount from an otherwise comparable public stock to induce them to invest in a private company. For example, there are 1,300 private-equity firms in the United States (firms that are in the business of investing in the equity of private companies). They seek expected returns of 20 percent to 30 percent as compared with average returns of 10 percent to 15 percent for the public stock market. Much of the reason for this higher expected return is to compensate the investor for the lack of marketability of the private-company investment.

DEGREES OF MARKETABILITY OR LACK THEREOF

Marketability is not a black-and-white issue. A stock is considered *marketable* if it is publicly traded, and nonmarketable if it is not. But along the way there are degrees of marketability or lack of marketability. Without attempting to address every conceivable situation, the following gives a general idea of the spectrum of marketability or lack thereof:

- Registered with the SEC and with an active trading market (the benchmark from which some lack of marketability discount usually is indicated)
- Registered with the SEC and fully reporting, but with a somewhat thin trading market
- A stock with contractual *put* rights (right of the owner to sell, usually to the issuing company, under specified circumstances and terms). (The most common example is employee stock ownership plan (ESOP) stock, where the plan includes a put option to sell the stock at the employee's retirement or at certain other times.)
- Registered with the SEC, but not required to file 10K and other reports [citation omitted] (a *nonreporting company*)
- Private company with an imminent (or likely) public offering
- Private company with frequent private transactions
- Private company with few or no transactions

- Private company with interests subject to restrictive transfer provisions
- Private company with ownership interests absolutely prohibited from transfer (for example, tied up in a trust for some period of time)[3]

EMPIRICAL EVIDENCE TO QUANTIFY DISCOUNTS FOR LACK OF MARKETABILITY: RESTRICTED STOCK STUDIES

A *restricted stock* is stock of a publicly traded company that is restricted from public trading for a limited period of time due to restrictions imposed by the SEC. Other than the restrictions imposed by the SEC, it is identical in all respects to its freely tradable counterparts (dividends, voting rights, liquidation rights, etc.).

Although SEC regulations prohibit the sale of restricted stocks in the public market, they might be sold to qualified investors in private transactions, most of which are institutions.

SEC Institutional Investor Study

In 1966, as part of its Institutional Investor Study, the SEC explored extensively the impact of trading restrictions on market value.[4] It compared the prices of transactions of restricted stocks to the prices of the same stock on the public market on the same day. The study encompassed 398 transactions in restricted stocks that took place from January 1, 1966, to June 30, 1969.

The SEC found that the overall average discount for the 398 transactions was about 26 percent. However, the SEC also broke the results down by the market in which the stock was publicly traded. For nonreporting companies trading in the over-the-counter (OTC) market, the average discount was about 33 percent.

A *nonreporting company* is one that is registered with the SEC for public trading but is not required to file annual, quarterly, or special events reports with the SEC. A publicly traded company currently qualifies as a nonreporting company if it has fewer than 500 stockholders, or assets with a book value of less than $10 million. Arguably, these would be the public companies with characteristics most in common with private companies.

The SEC Institutional Investor Study also broke down the companies by size, as measured by earnings and sales. It found that the smaller the company, as measured by either earnings or sales, the larger the discount.

---

[3]Id., pp. 205–206. Copyright 2000 American Bar Association. All rights reserved. Reprinted by permission.
[4]*Institutional Investor Study Report of the Securities and Exchange Commission*, H.R. Doc. No. 64, Part 5, 92nd Congress, 1st Session, 1971.

IRS Recognition of Discounts for Lack of Marketability: Revenue Ruling 77-287

In 1977, the Service officially recognized the factors in the SEC Institutional Investors Study as being relevant in quantifying discounts for lack of marketability. One of the concluding paragraphs of Rev. Rul. 77-287 contains the following language:

> *The market experience of freely tradable securities of the same class as the restricted securities is also significant in determining the amount of discount. Whether the shares are privately held or publicly traded affects the worth of the shares to the holder. Securities traded on a public market generally are worth more to investors than those that are not traded on a public market. Moreover, the type of public market in which the unrestricted securities are traded is to be given consideration.*[5]

It also explicitly recognizes that earnings and sales are factors that impact the amount of the discount.[6] Also, the Ruling states that "the longer the buyer of the shares must wait to liquidate the shares, the greater the discount." It further notes that the expense of liquidating the shares is a factor.[7]

Changes in SEC Rules Affect Restricted Stock Discounts

Since the SEC's Institutional Investor Study, there have been two changes in SEC rules regarding restricted stocks. Each of these changes has constituted a loosening of restrictions, which, in turn, has had the (expected) effect of reducing the discounts for restricted stock transactions.

1990: Elimination of Registration Requirement for Restricted Stock Trades

In 1990, the SEC eliminated the requirement that all restricted stock transactions be registered with it. It issued Rule 144A, which allows qualified institutional investors to trade unregistered securities among themselves without filing registration statements. This created a somewhat more liquid market for unregistered securities, thereby starting a significant trend of reducing the average discounts observed in restricted stock transactions.

1997: Reduction of Minimum Required Holding Period from Two Years to One Year

In February 1997, the SEC announced that, effective April 29, 1997, the required holding period for securities restricted pursuant to Rule 144 would be reduced from two years to one year. This significantly increased the liquidity of restricted securities, and thereby significantly reduced the average discount that the market requires for holding restricted securities.[8]

---

[5]Rev. Rul. 77-287, section 6.04.
[6]Id., section 4.02 (a) and (b).
[7]Id., section 6.02.
[8]Shannon P. Pratt, *Business Valuation Discounts and Premiums* (New York: John Wiley & Sons, Inc., 2001): 82.

Restricted Stock Studies Subsequent to the SEC Institutional Investor Study

There have been a number of studies done since the SEC study, all following the same research pattern. The various studies have broken down the relative impact of different factors, as will be discussed in a subsequent section.

The studies reflect the impact of the changes in the SEC restrictions. They provide an illustration of the effect of higher marketability, higher liquidity, and shorter holding periods on the relative magnitudes of discounts for lack of marketability.

Restricted Stock Studies Prior to 1990

The restricted stock studies prior to 1990 are summarized in Exhibit 18.1. They consistently show discounts from about 31 percent to 36 percent. The Standard Research Consultants study had the fewest transactions and was dominated by oil and gas stocks at a time when the industry was out of favor in the market, which probably accounts for the higher average discounts.

Exhibit 18.1   Summary of Restricted Stock Studies Prior to 1990

Empirical Study	Years Covered in Study	Number of Transactions	Average Price Discount (%)
SEC overall average[a]	1966–1969	398	25.8
SEC nonreporting OTC companies[a]	1966–1969	89	32.6
Gelman[b]	1968–1970	89	33.0
Trout[c]	1968–1972	60	33.5
Moroney[d]	1968–1972	148	35.6
Maher[e]	1969–1973	33	35.4
Standard Research Consultants[f]	1978–1982	28	45.0[i]
Willamette Management Associates[g]	1981–1984	33	31.2[i]
Silber[h]	1981–1988	69	33.8

Notes:

[a]"Discounts Involved in Purchase of Common Stock (1966-1969)," *Institutional Investor Study Report of the Securities and Exchange Commission*, H.R. Doc. No. 64, Part 5, 92nd Congress, 1st Session, 1971, pp. 2444–2456.

[b]Milton Gelman, "An Economist-Financial Analyst's Approach to Valuing Stock in a Closely Held Company," *Journal of Taxation* (June 1972), p. 353.

[c]Robert R. Trout, "Estimation of the Discount Associated with the Transfer of Restricted Securities," *Taxes* (June 1977), pp. 381–385.

[d]Robert E. Moroney, "Most Courts Overvalue Closely Held Stocks," *Taxes* (March 1973), pp. 144–155.

[e]J. Michael Maher, "Discounts for Lack of Marketability for Closely Held Business Interests," *Taxes* (September 1976), pp. 562–571.

[d]William F. Pittock and Charles H. Stryker, "Revenue Ruling 77-276 Revisited," *SRC Quarterly Reports* (Spring 1983), pp. 1–3.

[g]Willamette Management Associates study (unpublished).

[h]William L. Silber, "Discounts on Restricted Stock: The Impact of Illiquidity on Stock Prices," *Financial Analysts Journal* (July–August 1991), pp. 60–64.

[i]Median.

Source: Adapted from Shannon P. Pratt, Robert F. Reilly, and Robert P. Schweihs, *Valuing a Business*, 4th ed. (New York: McGraw-Hill, 2000): 404. Used with permission.

Exhibit 18.2   Summary of Restricted Stock Studies Including Years from 1990 to April 1997

Empirical Study	Years Covered in Study	Number of Transactions	Average Price Discount (%)
FMV Opinions, Inc.[a]	1979–April 1992	>100	23.0
Management Planning, Inc.[b]	1980–1996	53	27.1
Bruce Johnson[c]	1991–1995	72	20.0
Columbia Financial Advisors[d]	1996–April 1997	23	21.0

Notes:

[a]Lance S. Hall and Timothy C. Polacek, "Strategies for Obtaining the Largest Valuation Discounts," *Estate Planning* (January/February 1994), pp. 38–44.

[b]Robert P. Oliver and Roy H. Meyers, "Discounts Seen in Private Placements of Restricted Stock: The Management Planning, Inc., Long-Term Study (1980–1996)" (Chapter 5) in Robert F. Reilly and Robert P. Schweihs, eds., *The Handbook of Advanced Business Valuation* (New York: McGraw-Hill, 2000).

[c]Bruce Johnson, "Restricted Stock Discounts, 1991–1995," *Shannon Pratt's Business Valuation Update* (March 1999): 1–3; "Quantitative Support for Discounts for Lack of Marketability," *Business Valuation Review* (December 1999): 152–155.

[d]Kathryn F. Aschwald, "Restricted Stock Discounts Decline as Result of 1-Year Holding Period," *Shannon Pratt's Business Valuation Update* (May 2000): 1–5.

Restricted Stock Studies from 1990 to April of 1997

The restricted stock studies that included years after 1990 and prior to April 1997 are summarized in Exhibit 18.2. Although Exhibit 18.2 includes some transactions prior to 1990, most of the transactions were in the 1990s because the 1990 SEC Rule change led to more transactions and lower discounts. The transactions during this period show average discounts in the range of 20 percent to 27 percent.

Post-1997 Restricted Stock Studies

The post-1997 restricted stock studies are summarized in Exhibit 18.3. The transactions after 1997 show average discounts ranging from 13 percent to 22 percent.

Exhibit 18.3   Summary of Restricted Stock Studies after April 1997

Empirical Study	Years Covered in Study	Number of Transactions	Average Price Discount (%)
Columbia Financial Advisors[a]	May 1997–1998	15	13.0
FMV Opinions[b]	1997–2003	187	22.5

Notes:

[a]Kathryn F. Aschwald, "Restricted Stock Discounts Decline as Result of 1-Year Holding Period," *Shannon Pratt's Business Valuation Update* (May 2000): 1–5.

[b]Unpublished study of FMV Opinions.

Source: Compiled by Business Valuation Resources, LLC.

Increases in Liquidity in the Public Markets

While the SEC loosened restrictions on trading in restricted stocks, a number of factors also increased liquidity in the public markets:

- The settlement period (length of time between sale and cash in your pocket) has been reduced from five business days to three business days.
- Sales commissions have been drastically reduced with the introduction of the discount broker (e.g., Charles Schwab, Fidelity, Waterhouse, etc.).
- Spreads between bid and ask prices have been reduced considerably with the change from fraction-of-a-dollar prices to decimal prices.
- Derivative securities (puts, calls, and much more sophisticated derivatives) have been developed, allowing hedging on public securities and further enhancing the liquidity of the public markets. (For a thorough discussion on valuing derivatives, please see Chapter 21.) In some cases, even restricted stocks of public companies can be hedged.
- Trading volume for the average public stock has increased several-fold in recent years.

Minority interests in private companies have not benefited from any of this increased liquidity in the public markets. The result is that the differential value between minority interests in private companies and their publicly traded counterparts, other factors being equal, has widened.

Implications for Use of Restricted Stock Studies
for Private-Company Discounts for Lack of Marketability

The results of the several restricted stock studies led Kathryn Aschwald, architect of the Columbia Financial Advisors study, to opine that, to the extent that restricted stock studies are used for guidance in assessing discounts for lack of marketability of private-company interests, the pre-1990 studies are most relevant:

Appraisers have often quoted well-known studies of restricted stock prior to the Rule 144A amendment in 1990 in determining the appropriate discount for lack of marketability for privately held securities. These studies are still applicable for this purpose today.

Many "rumblings" in the appraisal community have centered around the fact that discounts for restricted stock have been declining, and many appear to be concerned about what this might mean in valuing privately held securities. It makes perfect sense that the discounts for restricted securities have generally declined since 1990 as the market (and liquidity) for these securities has increased due to Rule 144A and the shortening of restricted stock holding periods beginning April 29, 1997. Thus, while the newer studies are specifically relevant for determining the appropriate discounts for restricted securities, the studies conducted after 1990 are not relevant for purposes of determining discounts for lack of marketability for privately held stock, because they reflect the increased liquidity in the market for restricted securities. Such increased liquidity is not present in privately held securities.[9]

---

[9]Kathryn F. Aschwald, op cit.

Because of the SEC's *dribble-out* rule,[10] blocks of restricted stock larger than that allowed under the "dribble-out" rule sell at higher discounts. This phenomenon prompted Lance Hall, president of FMV Opinions, to state:

> *The illiquidity of large-percent blocks of restricted stock are more similar to the illiquidity of any-percent-size stock of private company stock than small-percent stocks of restricted stock.*[11]

This is discussed further in a subsequent section on factors that impact levels of discounts for lack of marketability. Although the pre-1990 restricted stock studies may be more relevant for assessing *average* levels of discounts for lack of marketability for private companies, studies since 1990 continue to provide insight into *factors* that impact discounts for lack of marketability.

EMPIRICAL EVIDENCE TO QUANTIFY DISCOUNTS FOR LACK OF MARKETABILITY: PRE-IPO STUDIES

Restricted stocks, by definition, are stocks of companies that already have established public markets. When the restrictions are lifted, an active public market will be available to the owners of the shares. Private companies enjoy no such market, or imminently prospective market. Therefore, it is reasonable to expect that the discount for lack of marketability for minority shares of private companies that have no established market, and which may never have an established market, would be greater than that for restricted stocks.

In an attempt to measure how much greater the discount for lack of marketability might be for a private company stock over the restricted stock of a public company, the first pre-IPO study was introduced into court in 1983 in connection with *Estate of Gallo*. (This was *after* the Service issued Rev. Rul. 77-287 in 1977, which discusses restricted stock studies but not pre-IPO studies.)

When a company undertakes an initial public offering, it is required by the SEC to disclose in its prospectus all transactions in its stock in the three years immediately preceding the offering. These documents are the source of data for private-company transactions.

The pre-IPO studies compare the price at which a private-company stock changed hands with the price of the stock of the same company on the day of the initial public offering (IPO). These are the only studies that capture actual minority interest transactions in stocks of closely held companies.

There are three series of such studies, encompassing more than 3,000 transactions in all. Although each study is independent and has its unique design, all tend to show *average* or *median* discounts for lack of marketability of about 45 to 50 percent.

---

[10]After the minimum holding period, holders of restricted stock may sell per quarter the higher of 1 percent of the outstanding stock or the average weekly volume over a 4-week period prior to the sale.

[11]Lance S. Hall, "The Value of Restricted Stock," ASA Annual International Conference, August 26–28, 2002, San Diego, CA.

The Willamette Management Associates Studies

The Willamette studies include transactions at any time during the full three years prior to the IPO. They exclude options and attempt to exclude any transactions with insiders, leaving only arm's-length transactions.

The discounts are adjusted for changes in the company's earnings and changes in industry price/earnings (P/E) multiples between the private stock transaction and the IPO.

The results of the Willamette studies are available only from 1975 through 1997. They are summarized in Exhibit 18.4. Willamette does not publish the actual transactions underlying its data.

The Emory Studies

The Emory Studies were started by John Emory when he was with Baird & Co., an investment bank. The Emory Studies include transactions within five months prior to the IPO. They include option transactions, and there is no attempt to eliminate insider transactions. If there is more than one private transaction prior to the IPO, the earliest one is selected for the study.

The transaction price is compared to the IPO price, with no adjustments for changes in either earnings or industry price indexes which may have occurred within the months prior to the IPO.

Exhibit 18.4   Summary of Discounts for Private Transaction P/E Multiples Compared to Public Offering P/E Multiples Adjusted for Changes in Industry P/E Multiples

Time Period	Number of Companies Analyzed	Number of Transactions Analyzed	Standard Mean Discount	Trimmed Mean Discount*	Median Discount	Standard Deviation
1975–1978	17	31	34.0%	43.4%	52.5%	58.6%
1979	9	17	55.6%	56.8%	62.7%	30.2%
1980–1982	58	113	48.0%	51.9%	56.5%	29.8%
1983	85	214	50.1%	55.2%	60.7%	34.7%
1984	20	33	43.2%	52.9%	73.1%	63.9%
1985	18	25	41.3%	47.3%	42.6%	43.5%
1986	47	74	38.5%	44.7%	47.4%	44.2%
1987	25	40	36.9%	44.9%	43.8%	49.9%
1988	13	19	41.5%	42.5%	51.8%	29.5%
1989	9	19	47.3%	46.9%	50.3%	18.6%
1990	17	23	30.5%	33.0%	48.5%	42.7%
1991	27	34	24.2%	28.9%	31.8%	37.7%
1992	36	75	41.9%	47.0%	51.7%	42.6%
1993	51	110	46.9%	49.9%	53.3%	33.9%
1994	31	48	31.9%	38.4%	42.0%	49.6%
1995	42	66	32.2%	47.4%	58.7%	76.4%
1996	17	22	31.5%	34.5%	44.3%	45.4%
1997	34	44	28.4%	30.5%	35.2%	46.7%

*Excludes the highest and lowest deciles of indicated discounts.

Source: Willamette Management Associates, *www.willamette.com.* Used with permission.

The studies currently are updated periodically by Emory Business Advisors. The details and data of each study are available online at *BVLibrary.com*, and every transaction in the studies is available free of charge at the Emory Web site, *www.emorybizval.com*. The results of the Emory studies are summarized in Exhibit 18.5.

The Valuation Advisors' Study

The Valuation Advisors' Lack of Marketability Discount Study™ includes transactions within two years prior to every included IPO (excluded are IPOs related to REITs (real estate investment trusts); IPOs without transactions in their stock, convertible-preferred stock, or options prior to the IPO; foreign companies (or U.S. companies with operations that are primarily in foreign countries); master limited partnerships (MLPs); limited partnerships (LPs); closed-end funds; mutual conversions; or American Depository Receipts.). These are transactions in common stock, convertible preferred stock, and options. The database includes data on more than 2,600 transactions, with 15 data points for each transaction, including company sales and operating profit.

No adjustments for changes in earnings or industry price indexes are included in the database. However, the analyst can access the SEC filings and make such adjustments if so desired. Also, both SIC and NAICS codes are included, so the analyst can adjust for changes in industry price indexes.

Studies published using the Valuation Advisors' database break down the number of transactions by length of time that the private transaction occurred prior to the IPO: 1 to 90 days prior, 91 to 180 days prior, 181 to 270 days prior, 271 to 365 days prior, and 1 to 2 years prior. Results for 1999, 2000, 2001, 2002, and 2003 are shown in Exhibit 18.6. The search criteria were the transaction date (1/1/1999 to 12/31/1999, for example), pre-IPO transaction time frame (1 to 90 days) and all transaction types (stock, options, and convertible preferred stocks).

Exhibit 18.5 Emory Studies (after 2002 Revision)

Study	# of IPO Prospectuses Reviewed	# of Qualifying Transactions	Mean Discount	Median Discount
1997–2000*	1,847	266	50%	52%
1995–1997	732	84	43	41
1994–1995	318	45	45	47
1992–1993	443	49	45	43
1990–1992	266	30	34	33
1989–1990	157	17	46	40
1987–1989	98	21	38	43
1985–1986	130	19	43	43
1980–1981	97	12	59	68
Total	4,088	543	46%	47%

*1997–2000 expanded study.

Source: Emory Business Advisors, LLC. Presentation at Institute of Business Appraisers Annual National Conference, Orlando, Florida, June 3, 2003. Used with permission.

Exhibit 18.6 Valuation Advisors' Lack of Marketability Discount Study™, Transaction Summary Results by Year from 1999 to 2003

	Time of Transaction before IPO				
	1–90 Days	91–180 Days	181–270 Days	271–365 Days	1–2 Years
1999 Transaction Results					
Number of transactions	166	223	124	92	104
Median discount	33.4%	53.8%	64.2%	69.2%	74.8%
2000 Transaction Results					
Number of transactions	96	91	45	16	51
Median discount	23.5%	33.3%	43.2%	52.6%	55.0%
2001 Transaction Results					
Number of transactions	13	15	9	16	26
Median discount	14.7%	29.9%	54.8%	54.6%	50.9%
2002 Transaction Results					
Number of transactions	8	10	14	20	65
Median discount	6.6%	17.1%	35.3%	39.6%	53.4%
2003 Transaction Results					
Number of transactions	15	42	51	43	44
Median discount	29.5%	22.3%	37.3%	53.8%	59.3%
1999–2003 Transaction Results					
Number of transactions	298	381	243	187	290
Median discount	28.4%	42.9%	53.8%	61.8%	64.8%

Source: Compiled by Doug Twitchell, Business Valuation Resources, LLC. Used with permission.

The dramatic differences between the 1999 to 2000 results and those of 2001 to 2002 are attributable to the market's reluctance to accept IPOs in 2001 and 2002. This situation resulted in an abnormally low number of IPOs during those two years. Those IPOs that were successful in 2001 to 2002 had much larger average sales and profitability than those in 1999 to 2000, factors that other studies have shown to impact discounts for lack of marketability. Also, 2001 to 2002 IPOs were priced more conservatively, many below investors' expectations of the IPO price at the time of the private transaction, thereby further contributing to lower average discounts between the private transaction price and the price at which the stock was sold to the public.

The Valuation Advisors' database supports the hypothesis that the holding period is an important factor in determining the magnitude of the discount for lack of marketability.

CRITICISMS OF THE PRE-IPO STUDIES

Criticisms of the pre-IPO studies have come from a few widely published sources, particularly the Service.

The most influential of these sources is a paper by Martin Hanan, with input from Dr.

Mukesh Bajaj, presented at a national Service seminar in 1997.[12] Although unpublished, the paper has been widely circulated and relied on in Service circles.

Selection of Transactions

By definition, the pre-IPO databases include only transactions in private companies that eventually had a successful IPO. This has led to a criticism of *selection bias* because it does not include companies that filed for IPOs but were unsuccessful. No study has yet been published on what happened to companies that filed for IPOs but were unsuccessful. This factor could cut either way.

There have been no published criticisms of the Valuation Advisors studies. The Valuation Advisors database includes transaction in the two years preceding *every* IPO.

IPO Prices Inflated by Hype

Some allege that IPO prices are inflated by *hype*. In fact, SEC regulations are designed to do just the opposite. Further, underwriters consciously attempt to price offerings conservatively so that investors can make money on IPOs and will continue to patronize them. In fact, empirical studies show that IPOs are subject to a substantial amount of underpricing.[13]

FACTORS AFFECTING THE MAGNITUDE OF DISCOUNTS FOR LACK OF MARKETABILITY

Several studies have identified factors that impact the size of the discount for lack of marketability. These can largely be categorized under three headings:

1. Amount of dividends or partnership distributions, if any
2. Expected duration of holding period (length of time anticipated before a liquidity event, such as IPO, sale of company, or sale of interest in company)
3. Measures that bear on risk, such as size, level and/or stability of earnings, and so on

Interestingly, the industry in which the company operates normally does not matter much. Exceptions are financial institutions, which tend to have lower discounts than other industries, and certain industries during time periods characterized by extremely unusual industry conditions.

---

[12]Martin D. Hanan, "Current Approaches and Issues to the Valuation of Business and Investment Interests," presented at Continuing Legal Education Seminar for the Estate and Gift Tax Program of the Internal Revenue Service, August 19, 1997.

[13]Roger Ibbotson, and Jay R. Ritter, "Initial Public Offerings," Chapter 30, R.A. Jarrow, V. Maksimovic, W.T. Ziemba, eds., *North-Holland Handbooks of Operations Research and Management Science*, Vol. 9 (Amsterdam: Elsevier, 1995): 993–1016.

Exhibit 18.7   Discount versus Block Size

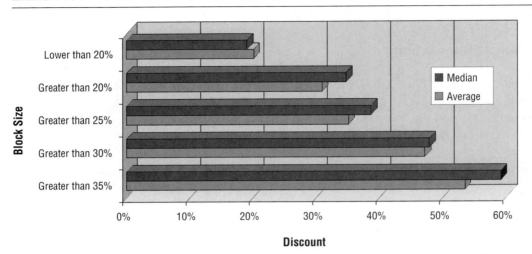

Source: Compiled from *FMV Opinions Restricted Stock Study*, distributed by Business Valuation Resources, LLC, *www.BVMarketData.com*. Used with permission of FMV Opinions, Inc. All rights reserved.

Impact of Distributions on Discounts for Lack of Marketability

Companies that make distributions (either dividends or partnership withdrawals) tend to have lower discounts for lack of marketability than those that do not. The greater the distributions, the lower the discount for lack of marketability.

This is logical, because the greater the distributions, the less dependent the owner is on the ability to liquidate the position to realize some return on the investment. For those stocks or partnership interests that pay no dividends or withdrawals at all, the owner of the interest is *totally* dependent on the sale of the interest in order to realize any return whatsoever on the investment.

Impact of Length of Perceived Holding Period (Prospects for Liquidity) on Discounts for Lack of Marketability

Empirical studies strongly validate the statement in Rev. Rul. 77-287 that "the longer the buyer of the shares must wait to liquidate the shares, the greater the discount."[14]

The FMV Restricted Stock Study

As reported earlier, analysis of the FMV database of restricted stock sales shows that larger blocks as a percentage of shares outstanding have a larger discount for lack of marketability. This is because the shares will take longer to liquidate under the SEC's *dribble-out rule*.

This relationship is depicted graphically in Exhibit 18.7.

---

[14]Rev. Rul. 77-287, section 6.02.

Exhibit 18.8 Emory Studies 1980 to 2000
(after 2002 Revision)

Discounts versus Time between Transactions and IPO

Days	Mean	Median	Count
0–30	30%	25%	18
31–60	40%	38%	72
61–90	42%	43%	162
91–120	49%	50%	161
121–153	55%	54%	130
Total			543

Source: John Emory, Emory Business Advisors, LLC.
Presentation at Institute of Business Appraisers Annual
National Conference, Orlando, Florida, June 3, 2003. Used
with permission of Emory Business Advisors, LLC. All
rights reserved.

The Emory Studies

An analysis of the data in the Emory studies, even though covering only five months prior to the IPO, shows a similar relationship between the size of the discount as the time of the private-company transaction becomes further from the time of the IPO. The results of this relationship are presented in Exhibit 18.8.

Silber Study

The Silber Study, which studied 69 private placements from 1981 through 1989, states, "Discounts are larger when the block of restricted stock is large relative to the shares outstanding."[15]

Standard Research Consultants Study

The Standard Research Consultants Study found that higher trading volume of the unrestricted stock was associated with lower discounts. It concluded that the greater the company's trading volume, the greater the likelihood that, upon expiration of the resale restrictions, the stock could be sold publicly without disrupting the market for the issuer's stock—that is, without having a depressing effect on the stock price.[16]

---

[15]William L. Silber, "Discounts on Restricted Stock: The Impact of Illiquidity on Stock Prices," *Financial Analysts Journal* (July–August 1991): 60–64. Other studies observing this include the SEC Study, the Standard Research Consultants Study, and the Management Planning Study. These findings are summarized in Shannon P. Pratt, *Business Valuation Discounts and Premiums* (New York: John Wiley & Sons, Inc., 2001): 158–159.

[16]William F. Pittock and Charles H. Stryker, "Revenue Ruling 77-276 Revisited," *SRC Quarterly Reports* (Spring 1983): 1–3.

Exhibit 18.9   Standard Research
                    Consultants Study

Profitable Years of Latest Five	Median Discount
5	34%
2 to 4	39%
0 to 1	46%

Source: William F. Pittock and Charles H. Stryker, "Revenue Ruling 77–276 Revisited," *SRC Quarterly Reports* (Spring 1983): 1–3. Used with permission from American Appraisal Associates, Inc. All rights reserved.

SEC Study

Similarly, the SEC study found that companies having the lowest dollar amount of sales during the test period accounted for most of the transactions with higher discounts, while they accounted for only a small portion of the transactions involving lower discounts.[17]

Measures that Bear on Risk

Empirical studies confirm what one would expect, in that higher levels of risk are associated with higher discounts for lack of marketability. This makes sense, since the potential negative impact of risk factors is exacerbated by the holder's inability to readily sell the investment. Risk is embedded in the discount rate in the income approach and in the valuation multiples in the market approach, when estimating the base value to which the discount for lack of marketability is applied. But high risk also makes it more difficult to sell the interest. Therefore, it is not double dipping to count the risk again as a factor exacerbating the discount for lack of marketability.[18]

Level and Volatility of Issuer's Earnings

The SEC study showed that companies with the lowest dollar amount of earnings accounted for most of the transactions having higher discounts, while they accounted for only a small portion of the transactions having lower discounts.

The Standard Research Consultants Study found that the pattern of earnings of the issuer seemed to matter. On average, companies that were profitable in each of the five years prior to the date of placement appeared to sell restricted stock at substantially smaller discounts than did those with two, three, or four unprofitable years during the five-year period. This correlation is shown in Exhibit 18.9.

---

[17]*Institutional Investor Study Report of the Securities and Exchange Commission*, H.R. Doc. No. 64, Part 5, 92nd Congress, 1st Session, 1971.

[18]Shannon P. Pratt, *Business Valuation Discounts and Premiums* (New York: John Wiley & Sons, Inc., 2001): 160. Used with permission. All rights reserved.

The Johnson Study, which studied 72 private placements from 1991 through 1995, showed a differential of seven percentage points for the companies that had positive net income in the current year versus companies that had negative net income in the current year, and the same relationship between companies that had positive and negative net income in the previous year.[19]

Size of Issuer

Many studies document the fact that smaller size increases risk. The empirical data—including the SEC Study, the Standard Research Consultants Study, the FMV Study, the Johnson Study, and the Management Planning Study—all bear out the conclusion that higher risk associated with smaller size of revenue is associated with higher discounts. The Management Planning Study noted, however, that several of the largest companies in terms of revenues had discounts well in excess of the discounts of several of the smaller companies.

USE OF THE DATABASES FOR QUANTIFYING DISCOUNTS FOR LACK OF MARKETABILITY

There is wide dispersion among the individual transaction discounts in both the restricted stock databases and the pre-IPO databases. Most experts in the past have used the restricted stock and pre-IPO studies as *benchmarks*, that is, presenting the average or median discounts from one or more studies and applying either a higher or lower discount to the subject.

However, the most probative evidence is transactions in companies with characteristics as similar to the subject company as possible. Accordingly, a more convincing use of the discount for lack of marketability databases would be to select transactions in companies having characteristics as close as possible to the subject company.

For example, size of the company has been demonstrated to be a factor in discounts for lack of marketability. That is, the larger the company, the lower the discount for lack of marketability. Therefore, company size might be a criterion in the selection of transactions.

(Studies have shown, however, that, except for financial institutions, which have lower discounts for lack of marketability on average than other industries, the line of business is not an important factor with respect to discounts for lack of marketability.)

Starting with Restricted Stock Data

The restricted stock studies can be directly useful for quantifying discounts for restricted stocks of public companies. However, restricted stocks are, by definition, stocks of public companies. When the restrictions expire, the shareholder will have an established public market in which to sell the stock. Absent a plan to sell the company, go public, or create some type of liquidity event, private-company stockholders have no such market to look forward to.

---

[19]Bruce Johnson, "Restricted Stock Discounts 1991–1995," *Shannon Pratt's Business Valuation Update*, Business Valuation Resources, LLC (March 1999): 1–3.

As noted earlier, restricted stocks have become increasingly liquid since 1990. There has been no comparable increase in liquidity for minority interests in private companies. If relying on pre-1990 restricted stock studies or transactions, it is important to point out in the report the loosening of SEC restrictions since 1990, because some are not aware of these changes and otherwise would conclude that more recent studies are more relevant. Exhibit 18.10 is a transaction report from the FMV Restricted Stock database. This database has more than 400 restricted stock transactions with over 50 data fields for each transaction.

Consequently, if starting with restricted stock data to estimate the discount for lack of marketability for a closely held company, a two-step process might be in order:

1. Select companies having financial characteristics in common with the subject company.

2. Add an incremental amount to the discount for lack of marketability to reflect the lack of prospects for liquidity for a closely held as company compared with restricted stocks of public companies.

An example of this two-step process is shown in Exhibit 18.11. Although this example uses only sales and assets for Step 1, the data shown in Exhibit 18.10 provide an infinite variety of opportunities to match the restricted stock transaction to the subject company.

Exhibit 18.10   FMV Restricted Stock Study Transaction Report

Company			
SIC	5812 Eating and Drinking Places		
NAICS	--No description--		
Name	Steakhouse Partners, Inc.		
Company Description			
City			
State			
Country			
Ticker	SIZLQ		
Exchange	NDQ		

Transaction Data		**Financial Data ($000's)**	
Transaction Month	7/1999	Market Value	20,068.71
Registration Rights	M	Book Value	1,552.00
Holding Period(yrs.)	1	MTB Ratio(absolute value)	12.93
Discount (Prior Month)	–0.90%	Intangible Assets	484.00
Discount (Transaction Month)	14.87%	Current Assets	12,219.00
Discount (Subsequent Month)	9.94%	Current Liabilities	51,342.00
Offering Price	$6.81	Total Assets	67,447.00
Prior Month High	$7.50	Debt	36,720.00
Prior Month Low	$6.00	Retained Earnings	–4,982.00
Prior Month High-Low Average	$6.75	Total Revenues	6,519.00
Prior Month Volume	611,100	Depreciation Expense	148.00
Transaction Month High	$10.00	Interest Expense	885.00
Transaction Month Low	$6.00	Pretax Income	–2,678.00
Transaction Month High-Low Average	$8.00	Net Income	–2,962.00
Transaction Month Close	$7.25	Prior Year Dividend ($)	0.00
Transaction Month Volume	1,162,100	EBITDA	0.00
Subsequent Month High	$8.75	Operating Profit Margin(%)	–27.5%
Subsequent Month Low	$6.38	Net Profit Margin(%)	–45.4%
Subsequent Month High-Low Average	$7.56	Volatility(%)	101.40%
Subsequent Month Volume	604,300	Z-Score(absolute value)	–0.46
Shares placed to Volume Ratio	0.29		
Shares Outstanding	2,973,143		
Shares Placed	341,379		
Placement Amount	2,325,000		
Shares Placed/Shares After(%)	10.3%		
% of Prior Month Volume to Total Shares Outstanding(%)	10.3%		

Source: Copyright 2003 Business Valuation Resources, LLC; *www.BVResources.com*, (888) BUS-VALU, (503) 291-7963. All rights reserved.

Exhibit 18.11   FMV Restricted Stock Study Analysis Discount for Lack of
Marketability Evidence

Step 1—Restricted Stock Equivalent Basis

	Revenues ($000)			Median Discount
	Minimum	Maximum	Median	
Quintile 1	—	1,719	417	24.8%
Quintile 2	1,808	9,360	4,518	27.3%
Quintile 3	9,377	21,185	12,436	18.4%
Quintile 4	22,009	57,372	33,422	14.8%
Quintile 5	58,630	1,791,446	156,680	18.3%

	Assets ($000)			Median Discount
	Minimum	Maximum	Median	
Quintile 1	1,002	4,940	2,727	33.4%
Quintile 2	5,064	11,045	8,369	24.7%
Quintile 3	11,045	23,732	16,225	23.4%
Quintile 4	23,899	67,904	44,387	14.2%
Quintile 5	71,061	12,471,366	242,365	12.5%

Valuation Parameters	Value	Quintile	Median Discount
Revenues ($000)	12,209	3	18.4%
Assets ($000)	7,546	2	24.7%

Discount Indication before Adjustment—Restricted Stock Equivalent Basis[a] 21.5%

Step 2—Private Company Adjustment

Percent Shares Placed	Median	Additive	Multiplicative
Small-Block Sample[b]	27.2%	NA	NA
More than 25%	35.3%	8.1%	1.3
More than 30%	47.7%	20.5%	1.8
More than 35%	59.0%	31.8%	2.2

Subject interest block 35.0%

Implied additional additive private-company discount 31.8%

Implied additional multiplicative private-company discount 25.8%

Selected additional private company adjustment[a] 28.8%

Summary – Selected Discount

Step One – Indicated Discount before Adjustment	21.5%
PLUS: Step Two – Indicated Additional Private-Company Adjustment	28.8%
EQUALS: Indicated Discount for Lack of Marketability	50.3%

Notes:

[a]Equals the average of the two indicated discounts.

[b]Includes transactions with block sizes less than 8.7 percent and market values less than $50 million.

Sources: FMV Transaction Database (available from *www.BVMarketData.com*) and Willamette
Management Associates calculations.

Exhibit 18.12   Valuation Advisors Lack of Marketability Discount Study
                     Transaction Report

Company	
Company	Aramark Corporation
Product, Service or Business	Outsourced food services
5812 Eating and Drinking Places	
NAICS	7223 Special Food Services

Transaction Data		Financial Data	
Pre-IPO Timeframe	0 mth(s)	Net Sales	$7,788,690,000
Transaction Date	12/1/2001	Marketability Discount	37.391%
Transaction Price Per Share	$14.40	Total Assets	$3,216,394,000
CPS, S or O	S	Operating Income	$439,507,000
IPO Date	12/10/2001	Operating Profit Margin	5.643%
IPO Price Per Share	$23.00		

Source: Copyright Business Valuation Resources, LLC; *www.BVResources.com*, (888) BUS-VALU, (503) 291-7963. All rights reserved. Used with permission of Brian Pearson, author/creator. All rights reserved.

Starting with Pre-IPO Data

Exhibit 18.12 is a transaction report from the Valuation Advisors pre-IPO database. This, too, provides data from which to select transactions that match the characteristics of the subject company.

If transactions furthest away from the IPO are selected, an adjustment might be needed for earnings as of the private transaction date compared to earnings as of the IPO date. Since these transactions are all from SEC filings, the data to make such adjustments are readily available.

DISCOUNTS FOR LACK OF MARKETABILITY IN THE COURTS[20]

Discounts for lack of marketability have been analyzed primarily on the quality of evidence presented.

Discounts for Lack of Marketability for Minority Interests

In *Estate of Gallo*,[21] the discount for lack of marketability was a major issue, with the Service claiming 10 percent and the estate claiming 36 percent. The Service's witness based his 10 percent discount on the following:

- The popularity and opportunity associated with the wine industry during this period (as reflected by the multitude of acquisitions that took place)
- Gallo's dominant position within the industry

---

[20]Abstracts of the treatment of the discount for lack of marketability in almost every federal and state reported opinion where the issue is adjudicated are found in *Discounts for Lack of Marketability in the Courts* (Portland, OR: Business Valuation Resources, LLC), updated periodically.

[21]*Gallo*, op. cit.

- Ernest and Julio Gallo's unique value to the company's operations, which could enhance the possibility of a merger, acquisition, or public offering, and their respective ages

The opinion also states:

Respondent further argues that a published empirical study, considered by both [Service's] and petitioner's experts, supports the 10 percent discount determined by Service's expert]. The study relied upon by respondent concerned discounts applicable to restricted stock of publicly traded companies. Although such shares were typically issued in private placements and were not immediately tradeable, a purchaser of the shares could reasonably expect them to be publicly traded in the future. The purchaser of Dry Creek shares, by contrast, could foresee no reasonable prospect of his shares becoming freely traded.

One expert for the taxpayer introduced a study of restricted stock transactions prepared internally by Lehman Brothers, indicating a 30 percent average discount for the restricted stocks. He then increased the amount of the discount by 20 percent (six percentage points for a total discount of 36 percent) to account for the fact that the company was private.

Another expert for the estate introduced a pre-IPO study prepared by Willamette Management Associates covering every arm's-length private transaction prior to an IPO in the five years preceding the valuation date.

The court rejected the 10 percent figure offered by the Service's expert as too low and concluded, "considering the entire record, [we] conclude that the 36 percent figure determined by [the estate's expert] . . . was a reasonable discount to reflect the illiquidity . . ."

Howard v. Shay [22] was a shareholder dispute over the value of stock in a terminated employee stock ownership plan (ESOP). Among the major issues was the size of the discount for lack of marketability, which the original valuation report commissioned by the trustees had set at 50 percent.

In support of the 50 percent discount in the original report, the defendants presented evidence from the Willamette Management Associates pre-IPO database. The size of the block of stock in question was approximately 38 percent of the outstanding shares, so the evidence presented was all of the pre-IPO transactions in the Willamette database, which constituted between 25 percent and 49.9 percent of the outstanding shares, for the five years preceding the valuation date. The results indicated an average discount of 49 percent, so the district court affirmed the 50 percent discount in the original report.

The decision was appealed to the 9th Circuit, which found that the trustees had not adequately reviewed and understood the valuation report. The 9th Circuit remanded the case to the district court for further proceedings. On remand, the district court affirmed the valuation and held the trustees liable for attorneys' fees.

Okerlund v. United States [23] was a Court of Federal Claims case in which the expert for the taxpayer selected specific transactions from both the FMV Restricted Stock database and also

[22]*Howard v. Shay*, 1993 U.S. Dist. LEXIS 20153 (C.D. Cal. 1993), *rev'd. and remanded*, 100 F.3d 1484 (9th Cir. 1996), *cert. denied*, 520 U.S. 1237 (1997).
[23]*Okerlund v. United States*, 53 Fed. Cl. 341 (Fed. Ct. 2002), *motion for new trial denied*, 2003 U.S. Claims LEXIS 42 (Fed. Cl. 2003), affirmed by Court of Appeals for the Federal Circuit, *Okerlund v. United States*, 93 AFTR 2d 2004-1715 (Fed. Cir. 2004).

from the Valuation Advisors Pre-IPO database. The case involved the valuation of gifts of stock on two different dates.

Since the prospects for liquidity were remote, the taxpayer's expert selected only the largest-block-size transactions in relation to shares outstanding from the FMV Restricted Stock database. (The relevance of block size to perceived holding period was explained in a previous section.) Since the subject company was very large, and studies show a lower discount for lack of marketability for larger companies than for smaller ones, only transactions in stocks of companies with more than $100 million in sales were selected from the Valuation Advisors Pre-IPO Transaction database. Since the company paid no dividends and was not likely to for the foreseeable future, only non-dividend-paying stocks were selected from both databases.

The expert for the Service testified to 30 percent on both dates, and the expert for the taxpayer testified to 45 percent on both dates. The court concluded that the appropriate discount was 40 percent on one date and 45 percent on the other date, in addition to a 5 percent discount for nonvoting stock (which the experts agreed to), resulting in total discounts of 45 percent on one date and 50 percent on the other date. Excerpts from the court's opinion indicate the importance of strong empirical evidence and analysis:

> *Both experts relied on two sources of empirical data for aid in quantifying the discount for lack of marketability: (1) discounts on sales of restricted shares of publicly traded companies; and (2) discounts on private transactions prior to initial public offerings (IPOs). Based on these studies, and an examination of the perceived risks facing a potential investor in SSE stock, [the estate's expert] concluded that a 45 percent discount for lack of marketability was appropriate, and [the Service's expert] concluded that a 30 percent discount was justified.*

> *[The estate expert's] reports contain a far more detailed analysis of the empirical studies of trading prices of restricted shares and pre-initial public offering transactions than the [Service expert's] Report. The eight independent studies of restricted stock transactions reviewed in the [estate expert's] Report reported average discounts ranging from 25 to 45 percent. According to [the estate's expert], the two most important factors in determining the size of the discount were the amount of dividends paid (more dividends are associated with a lower discount for lack of marketability) and the perceived holding period (the longer the holding period the greater the discount for lack of marketability). The second major line of studies, involving pre-IPO transactions, observed discounts averaging approximately 45 to 47 percent. Unlike the [Service expert's] Report, the [estate expert's] Report considered the pre-IPO studies more relevant for the purpose of determining the appropriate discount for lack of marketability. According to [the estate's expert], the discounts observed in restricted stock studies reflect the existence of a public market for the stock once the temporary restrictions lapse. For a variety of reasons, . . . purchasers of restricted stock "generally expect to be able to resell the stock in the public market in the foreseeable future." Pre-IPO discounts, on the other hand, are based on purely private transactions before a company enters the public market, a situation more comparable to closely held companies such as SSE. . . .*

> *[T]he Court finds [the estate expert's] analysis of the relevant empirical studies and shareholder risks more persuasive than the [Service expert's] report's rather truncated analysis.*

One of the most widely quoted cases is *Mandelbaum et al., v. Commissioner*,[24] where the parties stipulated to freely traded minority interest values, so the only issue was the discount for lack of marketability.

---

[24]*Mandelbaum et al., v. Comm'r*, T.C. Memo 1995-255. Appealed and affirmed, 91 F.3d 124, 1996 U.S. App. LEXIS 17962, 96-2 U.S. Tax Cas. (CCH) P60,240, 78 A.F.T.R.2d (RIA) 5159.

The expert for the Service used three restricted stock studies, including the SEC Institutional Investor Study, from which he testified that the median discount for OTC nonreporting companies was between 30.1 and 40.0 percent. Taxpayer's expert analyzed seven restricted stock studies and three studies on initial public offerings (IPOs).

The court criticized the taxpayer's expert for focusing only on the hypothetical willing buyer. The court observed, "[T]he test of fair market value rests on the concept of the hypothetical willing buyer and the hypothetical willing seller. Ignoring the views of the willing seller is contrary to this well-established test."

The court stated:

Because the restricted stock studies analyzed only "restricted stock", the holding period of the securities studied was approximately 2 years. [The Service's expert] has not supported such a short holding period for Big M stock, and we find no persuasive evidence in the record to otherwise support it. In addition, the restricted stock studies analyzed only the restricted stock of publicly traded corporations. Big M is not a publicly traded corporation. . . .

The length of time that an investor must hold his or her investment is a factor to consider in determining the worth of a corporation's stock. An interest is less marketable if an investor must hold it for an extended period of time in order to reap a sufficient profit. Market risk tends to increase (and marketability tends to decrease) as the holding period gets longer. . . .

We find that the 10 studies analyzed by [the taxpayer's expert] are more encompassing than the three studies analyzed by [the Service's expert]. Because [the taxpayer's] studies found that the average marketability discount for a public corporation's transfer of restricted stock is 35 percent, and that the average discount for IPO's is 45 percent, we use these figures as benchmarks of the marketability discount for the shares at hand.

The court then listed nine factors:

1. Financial statement analysis
2. Dividend policy
3. Nature of the company, its history, its position in the industry, and its economic outlook
4. Management
5. Amount of control in the transferred shares
6. Restrictions on transferability
7. Holding period for the stock
8. Company's redemption policy
9. Costs associated with a public offering.

The court discussed each of these factors in detail. These factors have since become known as the *Mandelbaum factors*. Some commentators have criticized the opinion for possible double counting in that some of the factors would have been reflected in the freely traded value to which the parties stipulated. However, as seen in the prior section Factors Affecting the Magnitude of Discounts for Lack of Marketability, some factors usually considered in fundamental analysis also have a further impact on the marketability discount.

The court concluded:

Based on the record as a whole, and on our evaluation of the above-mentioned factors, we conclude that the marketability discount for the subject shares on each of the valuation dates is no greater than the 30 percent allowed by the respondent.

The *Mandelbaum* case is discussed in numerous subsequent court cases, and the entire text of the decision is produced in the Internal Revenue Service *Valuation Training for Appeals Officers Coursebook.*[25]

In *Estate of Davis*,[26] the issue was the value of stock in a family holding company whose primary asset was more than one million shares of Winn-Dixie stock. The witness for the Service testified to a 23 percent discount for lack of marketability based on certain restricted stock studies. Experts for the taxpayer considered a broader list of restricted stock studies as well as pre-IPO studies, and testified to a 35 percent discount. In concluding a value which reflected approximately a 32 percent discount, the court stated:

> *[W]e found [the taxpayer's experts'] reports and the additional testimony at trial of [one of taxpayer's experts] to be quite helpful in ascertaining the lack-of-marketability discount that we shall apply in this case. . . . [Service's expert] should have considered the pre-valuation date price data reflected in those IPO studies because they, together with the restricted stock studies, would have provided a more accurate base range and starting point for determining the appropriate lack-of-marketability discount. . . .*

In *Gow*,[27] the Service's expert testified to a 10 percent discount for lack of marketability and the taxpayer's expert testified to 30 percent. The court concluded 30 percent was appropriate, noting that the taxpayer's expert used (unnamed) empirical studies that the court believed appropriate, whereas the Service's expert did not. To reiterate a point worth making, this demonstrates the fact that courts like relevant empirical evidence.

In *Barnes*,[28] there were two companies in which stock was gifted. The Service's expert testified to a 25 percent discount for lack of marketability for both, and the taxpayer's expert testified to a 40 percent discount on one and a 45 percent discount on the other. Interestingly, both experts cited mostly the same studies. The court agreed with the taxpayer's expert, and concluded the appropriate discounts were 40 percent and 45 percent. The Service's expert cited eight studies in which the average marketability discount fell in the range of 50 to 60 percent. He admitted that the typical discount for restricted stock was 35 percent and that unregistered stock in a closely held corporation is subject to a larger discount. Thus, the court found the expert's use of a 25 percent discount unconvincing.

In *In re Colonial Reality Co.*,[29] a bankruptcy court case, the court accepted a 35 percent discount for lack of marketability.

Discounts for Lack of Marketability for Controlling Interests

Discount for lack of marketability for controlling interests are usually modest when compared with discounts for lack of marketability for minority interests.

---

[25]Internal Revenue Service, *IRS Valuation Training for Appeals Officers Coursebook* (Chicago: CCH Incorporated, 1998), p. 9-6 and Exhibit 9-3.
[26]*Estate of Davis v. Comm'r*, 110 T.C. 530 (June 30, 1998).
[27]*Gow v. Comm'r*, 19 Fed. Appx. 90; 2001 U.S. App. LEXIS 20882 (2001).
[28]*Estate of Barnes v. Comm'r*, T.C. Memo 1998-413, 76 T.C.M. (CCH) 881, November 17, 1998.
[29]*In re Colonial Realty Co.*, *United States Bankruptcy Court for the District of Connecticut*, 226 B.R. 513 (1998).

The opinion in a 1982 case contained, for example, the following statement:

Even controlling shares in a nonpublic corporation suffer from lack of marketability because of the absence of a ready given private placement market and the fact that flotation costs would have to be incurred if the corporation were to publicly offer its stock.[30]

But the criteria for quantifying discounts for lack of marketability for controlling interests are quite different from those for minority interests. The restricted stock and pre-IPO databases are all minority interest transactions and are, therefore, not relevant empirical evidence to quantify discounts for controlling interests.

Five factors must be analyzed in estimating discounts for lack of marketability for controlling interests:

1. Flotation costs (the costs of implementing an initial public offering [IPO])
2. Professional and administrative costs, such as accounting, legal, appraisals, and management time necessary to prepare the company for a sale or IPO
3. Risk of achieving estimated value
4. Lack of ability to hypothecate (most banks will not consider loans based on private-company stock as collateral, even controlling interests)
5. Transaction costs (payments to an intermediary or internal costs incurred in finding and negotiating with a buyer).

Cases Accepting Discount for Lack of Marketability for Controlling Interests

In *Estate of Hendrickson*,[31] the interest at issue was 49.97 percent, but the court deemed it a controlling interest because the balance of the stock was divided among 29 shareholders. The court allowed a 35 percent discount for the 49.97 percent controlling interest.

Other cases allowing a discount for lack of marketability for a controlling interest include, for example:

- *Estate of Dunn*[32] (15%)
- *Estate of Jameson*[33] (3%)
- *Estate of Dougherty*[34] (25%)
- *Estate of Maggos*[35] (25%)

---

[30]*Estate of Andrews v. Comm'r*, 79 T.C. 938 (1982).

[31]*Estate of Hendrickson v. Comm'r*, T.C. Memo 1999-278, 78 T.C.M. (CCH) 322 (1999).

[32]*Estate of Dunn v. Comm'r*, T.C. Memo 2000-12, 79 T.C.M. (CCH) 1337 (2000).

[33]*Estate of Jameson v. Comm'r*, T.C. Memo 1999-43, 77 T.C.M. (CCH) 1383 (1999).

[34]*Estate of Dougherty v. Comm'r*, T.C. Memo 1990-274, 59 T.C.M. (CCH) 772 (1990).

[35]*Estate of Maggos v. Comm'r*, T.C. Memo 2000-129, 79 T.C.M. (CCH) 1861 (2000). See also *Estate of Desmond*, T.C. Memo 1999-76, 77 T.C.M. (CCH) 1529 (1999) in testimony on marketability discounts combined with other discounts.

Case Denying Discount for Lack of Marketability for Controlling Interest

In *Estate of Cloutier*,[36] the interest at issue was 100 percent of the stock in a company that operated a television station. The taxpayer's expert opined to a 25 percent discount based largely on restricted stock and pre-IPO studies. The court rejected the discount in its entirety because it was based on discounts related to minority interests.

Marketability Discounts Combined with Other Discounts

Although it is preferable to have experts quantify marketability discounts separately from other discounts or premiums, there are some cases where discounts for different factors have been combined.

Estate of Desmond[37] involved an 82 percent interest in a paint and coating manufacturer. The expert for the Service opined to a 0 to 5 percent marketability discount. The expert for the taxpayer opined to a 25 to 45 percent discount, which took into consideration potential environmental liabilities. The court distinguished between the expert's income approach and that expert's market approach in applying that portion of the marketability discount that reflected environmental liabilities on the basis that the market valuation multiples would already reflect the environmental liabilities for the industry:

> [A] 30-percent lack of marketability discount is appropriate. . . . Of this 30-percent discount, 10 percent is attributable to Deft's potential environmental liabilities. We shall apply the 30-percent lack of marketability discount to the unadjusted value we determined under the income method. We however shall apply only a 20-percent lack of marketability discount to the unadjusted value we determined under the market method because as discussed supra, the environmental liabilities have already been included in the unadjusted value under that method.[38]

In *Janda*,[39] the taxpayer's expert testified to a 65.77 percent discount for lack of marketability based on Z. Christopher Mercer's Quantitative Marketability Discount Model (QMDM), essentially a discounted cash flow model which takes as its inputs estimates of (1) the as-if-freely traded "base value," (2) the probable holding period, (3) the growth rate of the base value over the holding period, (4) the interim cash flows over the holding period, and (5) the required holding period rate of return (discount rate).[40] The Service's expert relied on various restricted stock studies and prior Tax Court decisions. The court criticized these studies as being too general. Because information was not presented regarding marketability discounts for companies with the same characteristics as the subject, the court concluded that the Service's analysis was too subjective. The court noted that business appraisers usually rely on "generalized" studies (e.g., restricted stock studies and pre-IPO studies) in determining the appropriate marketability discount, and that the court would prefer to have more specific data

---

[36]*Estate of Cloutier v. Comm'r*, T.C. Memo 1996-49, 71 T.C.M. (CCH) 2001 (1996).

[37]*Estate of Desmond*, op. cit.

[38]*Marketability Discounts in the Courts, 1991–1Q2002* (Portland, Ore.: Business Valuation Resources, LLC, 2002): 30.

[39]*Janda v. Comm'r*, T.C. Memo 2001-24; 2001 Tax Ct. Memo LEXIS 34 (2001).

[40]Z. Christopher Mercer, *Quantifying Marketability Discounts* (Memphis, Tenn.: Peabody Publishing, 2001).

for each appraisal engagement. The court (without any explanation) concluded that a 40 percent combined discount for lack of control and lack of marketability was appropriate.

In *Furman*,[41] the Service's expert testified to a 17 percent discount for lack of marketability, citing the Gelman, Moroney, and Maher studies. The court criticized reliance on the restricted stock studies as follows:

> *We find [the taxpayer's] reliance on the restricted stock studies to be misplaced, since those studies analyzed only restricted stock that had a holding period of 2 years. Inasmuch as we expect the investment time horizon of an investor in the stock of a closely held corporation like FIC to be long term, we do not believe that marketability concerns rise to the same level as a security with a short-term holding period like restricted stock. [footnote omitted.] In light of the foregoing, we find no persuasive evidence in the record to support our reliance on the restricted stock studies in determining an appropriate marketability discount.*

Stating that the determination of a marketability discount was a factual matter, the court looked at the following facts and circumstances regarding the FIC stock:

> *The factors limiting the marketability of stock in FIC in February 1980 and August 1981 included the following: (1) FIC had never paid dividends on its common stock; (2) the corporation was managed and controlled by one individual; (3) the blocks of stock to be transferred were minority interests; (4) a long holding period was required to realize a return; (5) FIC had no custom or policy of redeeming common stock; (6) because FIC's annual sales were only in the $7 million range, it was not likely to go public; and (7) there was no secondary market for FIC stock. While FIC had significant potential for controlled growth, a healthy balance sheet, and robust earnings growth, we find the factors limiting marketability to be significant.*

With no discussion as to how it reached this figure, the court then held that a 40 percent combined minority and marketability discount was most appropriate. Although this may not be the definitive authority on combining the two discounts, the case may be instructive on the evidence and factors considered.

CONCLUSION

The discount for lack of marketability often is the biggest and most controversial issue in a business valuation done for gift and estate tax purposes. There are two distinct categories of empirical databases (and studies based on them):

1. Restricted stock studies (transactions in publicly traded stocks that are temporarily restricted from public funding)
2. Pre-IPO studies (trading in private companies' stocks prior to an initial public offering)

This empirical evidence is based on transactions in minority interests, and is not relevant to controlling interests. Controlling interests may be subject to some marketability discount, but the analyst should explain the factors on which the discounts are based, as discussed in this chapter.

Chapter 19 discusses other shareholder-level discounts and premiums.

---

[41] *Furman v. Comm'r*, T.C. Memo 1998-157, 75 T.C.M. (CCH) 2206 (April 30, 1998).

PARTIAL BIBLIOGRAPHY OF SOURCES FOR DISCOUNTS FOR LACK OF MARKETABILITY

Bajaj, Mukesh, Denis J. David, et al. "Firm Value and Marketability Discounts." *The Journal of Corporation Law* (Fall 2001): 89–115.

_____. "Dr. Bajaj Responds to Dr. Pratt's February 2002 Editorial: Bajaj Attacks Restricted Stock and Pre-IPO Discount Studies; Pratt Replies, Defending Studies, Notes that Debate May Be Semantic." *Shannon Pratt's Business Valuation Update* (March 2002, Vol. 8, No. 3): 12–14.

Bogdanski, John A. "Closely Held Businesses and Valuation: Dissecting the Discount for Lack of Marketability." *Estate Planning* (February 1996, Vol. 23, No. 2): 91–95.

"Discounts for Lack of Marketability: Uses & Misuses of Databases." Business Valuation Resources, LLC. Telephone Conference, May 13, 2003.

Emory Sr., John D. and John D. Emory Jr. Emory Business Valuation, LLC. "Emory Studies: 2002 Revision." Presented to the IBA 25th Annual National Conference, Orlando, Florida (June 3, 2003).

John Emory Sr., F.R. Dengel III, and John Emory Jr. "Emory Responds to Dr. Bajaj: Miniscule Adjustments Warranted." *Shannon Pratt's Business Valuation Update* (May 2002, Vol. 8, No. 5): 1,3.

Grabowski, Roger J. Standard & Poor's Corporate Value Consulting. "The Bubbling Pot in Marketability Discounts." Presented to the Foundation for Accounting Education, New York, NY (June 17, 2002).

Hall, Lance. "The Discount for Lack of Marketability: An Examination of Dr. Bajaj's Approach." *Shannon Pratt's Business Valuation Update* (February 2004, Vol. 10, No. 2): 1–4.

Hertzel, Michael, and Richard L. Smith. "Market Discounts and Shareholder Gains for Placing Equity Privately." *The Journal of Finance* (June 1993, Vol. XLVIII, No. 2): 459–485.

Ibbotson, Roger, and Jay R. Ritter. "Initial Public Offerings," Chapter 30, R. A. Jarrow, V. Maksimovic, W. T. Ziemba, eds., *North-Holland Handbooks of Operations Research and Management Science* 9 (Amsterdam: Elsevier, 1995): 993–1016.

Lerch, Mary Ann. "Yet Another Discount for Lack of Marketability. *Business Valuation Review* (June 1997): 70–106.

Patton, Kenneth W. "The Marketability Discount: Academic Research in Perspective—The Hertzel/Smith Study." *E-Law Business Valuation Perspective* (June 5, 2003, Vol. 2003-02): 1–8.

Pearson, Brian K. "Y2K Marketability Discounts as Reflected in IPOs." *CPA Expert* (Summer 2001): 1–5.

_____. "1999 Marketability Discounts as Reflected in Initial Public Offerings." *CPA Expert* (Spring 2000): 1–6.

Pratt, Shannon P. "Lack of Marketability Discounts Suffer more Controversial Attacks." *Shannon Pratt's Business Valuation Update* (February 2002, Vol. 8, No. 2): 1–3.

Trout, Robert R. "Minimum Marketability Discounts." *Business Valuation Review* (September 2003): 124–126.

See also in Appendix C, other print sources and under "Lack of Marketability Transaction Databases."

Other Shareholder-Level Discounts

SUMMARY

A *shareholder-level* discount or premium is one that affects only a defined group of shareholders rather than the whole company. As with discounts for lack of marketability, other shareholder-level discounts should be applied to the net amount after entity-level discount, if any. Besides the discount for lack of marketability, other shareholder-level discounts and premiums largely fall into three categories:

1. Minority discounts/control premiums
2. Voting versus nonvoting interests
3. Blockage

In addition, there can be discounts for fractional interests in property such as real estate.

MINORITY DISCOUNTS/CONTROL PREMIUMS

Minority discounts are often (and more properly) referred to as *lack of control* discounts because it is possible to have a majority interest and still not have control, and, conversely, a minority interest may have control, perhaps because of voting trusts and other arrangements. For example, on one hand, no limited partner has control, regardless of the percentage interest. On the other hand, in *Estate of Hendrickson v. Commissioner*,[1] a 49.99 percent interest was deemed by the court to constitute control because the balance of the stock was divided among 29 small stockholders.

After marketability, minority/control is the next most frequent issue in disputed valuations. Virtually everyone recognizes that, in most cases, control shares are worth more than minority shares. However, there is little consensus on how to measure the difference. As with lack of marketability, lack of control is not a black-and-white issue, but covers a spectrum:

- 100 percent control
- Less than 100 percent interest
- Less than supermajority where state statutes or articles of incorporation require supermajority for certain actions
- 50/50 interest
- Minority, but enough for *blocking control* (in states or under articles of incorporation that require supermajority for certain actions)
- Minority, but enough to elect one or more directors under cumulative voting
- Minority, but participates in control block by placing shares in voting trust
- Nonvoting stock (covered in following section)
- Minority, with no ability to elect even one director

The value of control lies in the following (partial) list of actions that shareholders with some degree of control can take, and that others cannot:[2]

- Appoint or change operational management.
- Appoint or change members of the board of directors.
- Determine management compensation and perquisites.
- Set operational and strategic policy and change the course of the business.
- Acquire, lease, or liquidate business assets, including plant, property, and equipment.
- Select suppliers, vendors, and subcontractors with whom to do business and award contracts.
- Negotiate and consummate mergers and acquisitions.
- Liquidate, dissolve, sell out, or recapitalize the company.
- Sell or acquire treasury shares.
- Register the company's equity securities for an initial or secondary public offering.
- Register the company's debt securities for an initial or secondary public offering.
- Declare and pay cash and/or stock dividends.
- Change the articles of incorporation or bylaws.
- Set one's own compensation (and perquisites) and the compensation (and perquisites) of related-party employees.

---

[1] *Estate of Hendrickson v. Comm'r*, T.C. Memo 1999-278, 78 T.C.M. (CCH) 322.
[2] Shannon P. Pratt, Robert F. Reilly, and Robert P. Schweihs, *Valuing a Business*, 4th ed. (New York: McGraw-Hill, 2000): 365–366.

- Select joint venturers and enter into joint venture and partnership agreements.
- Decide what products and/or services to offer and how to price those products/services.
- Decide what markets and locations to serve, to enter into, and to discontinue serving.
- Decide which customer categories to market to and which not to market to.
- Enter into inbound and outbound license or sharing agreements regarding intellectual properties.
- Block any or all of the above actions.

The traditional "Levels of Value" chart is shown as Exhibit 19.1. This schematic chart breaks the control premium into two elements:

1. The premium associated with the powers of control
2. The premiums that reflect the value of synergies with the buyer

Exhibit 19.1   Levels of Value in Terms of Characteristics of Ownership

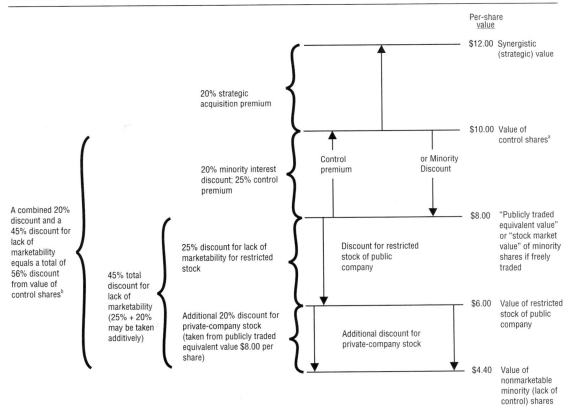

Notes:

a. Control shares in a privately held company may also be subject to some discount for lack of marketability, but usually not nearly as much as minority shares.

b. Minority and marketability discounts normally are multiplicative rather than additive. That is, they are taken in sequence:

$10.00	Control value
− 2.00	Less: Minority interest discount (.20 × $10.00)
$ 8.00	Marketable minority value
− 3.60	Less lack of marketability discount (.45 × $8.00)
$ 4.40	Per-share value of nonmarketable minority shares

Source: Shannon Pratt, " 'Levels of Value' Chart to Reflect Difference in Restricted Stock versus Private Stock," *Shannon Pratt's Business Valuation Update,* Editor's column (Business Valuation Resources, LLC, October 2004): 1.

One question is whether the synergistic portion of the control premium is part of fair market value. Under the hypothetical willing-buyer presumption, the synergies with any *particular* buyer would not be included. But in certain instances where there are enough synergistic buyers to create a market, a case can be made for including the value of synergies in fair market value. An example would be an industry undergoing consolidation through *rollups*, that is, acquisitions of many companies in an industry in order to achieve a target size for some objective, such as an initial public offering.

Measuring the Control Premium/Minority Discount

The minority discount is the same dollar amount as the control premium. Control premiums are usually quoted as a percentage, determined by the dollar amount of the premium divided by of the minority value. Minority discounts are usually quoted as a percentage, determined by the dollar amount of the premium divided by the control value. Where the control premium is $33\frac{1}{3}$ percent, the minority discount would be 25 percent. For example, if a share of stock was worth $30 on a minority basis and $40 on a control basis, the control premium would be $33\frac{1}{3}$ percent ($10 control premium divided by $30 minority value) and the minority discount would be 25 percent ($10 control premium divided by $40 control value). If these figures were based on actual transactions, the control premiums would reflect any synergies between buyer and seller, as well as the value of control.

Measuring Control Premiums/Minority Discounts for Operating Companies

Conceptually, the most accurate analytical method to estimate the magnitude of the control premium/minority discount would be to estimate the value of the shares on a control basis versus their value on a minority basis. In other words, how much value could a control shareholder add, or to what extent is the minority shareholder disadvantaged compared with the control shareholder?

One of the most common examples would be to measure the amount of excess compensation, if any, that the control shareholders are enjoying that otherwise could be shared with the minority shareholders on a pro rata basis. Another example would be to estimate what value could be derived for minority shareholders from liquidating excess assets, and either distributing the proceeds to minority shareholders or redeploying the proceeds so as to generate incremental cash flow to the company.

If a company is being managed in an optimal manner and all shareholders are being treated equally, there might be very little room for a control premium or a minority discount.

Many analysts use the *Mergerstat®/Shannon Pratt's Control Premium Study*™ as an empirical basis to estimate the percentage control premium or implied minority discount. This study records all the takeovers of majority interests in public companies.[3] Misuse of this database often leads to inaccurate results, most often the overstatement of a control premium/minority discount.

---

[3]The database is available online at *BVMarketData.com* for control transactions that have occurred since January 1, 1998.

First, few analysts or valuers realize that more than 15 percent of all takeovers of public companies are at *discounts* from their previous public trading price. The published averages of control premiums in the annual *Mergerstat Review*[4] exclude these transactions at discounts (negative premiums). A more comprehensive measure of average premiums would include those transactions that occurred at discounts.

Second, the averages are distorted by a very few very high takeover premiums (the average—the *mean*—is the sum of the observations divided by the number of observations). A more appropriate measure of central tendency in most cases would be the *median* (the middle number in the array).

Therefore, an appropriate use of the control premium database would be for the analyst to select the relevant transactions (by industry and by time period) and compute the median, *including* the negative premiums. In any case, when control premiums or minority discounts are presented, the reviewers of the appraisal should ask whatever questions are necessary to understand exactly how the relevant premium or discount was estimated.

Also, where synergies are not to be considered as part of fair market value, the transactions used should be examined to estimate what proportion of the control premium reflected synergies. As there is no empirical basis for dividing the premium paid between synergistic and pure premium for control, such a calculation is dependent on the analyst's judgment.

Measuring Minority Discounts for Holding Companies

For holding companies, the base from which minority discounts are applied is usually net asset value. The most common method for estimating the discount is to identify a group of publicly traded companies (e.g., closed-end mutual funds or real estate investment trusts [REITs]) that hold assets similar to the subject company, and to calculate the average discount at which their securities trade in the market relative to their net asset value. If the subject company has two or more classes of assets (e.g., marketable securities and real estate), two or more groups of publicly traded entities may be used for comparison, and the discount for the subject entity assigned in proportion to the net asset value for each class.

Some analysts also use the secondary market for public limited partnerships as a basis for comparison. Data on this market are published annually in the May/June edition of *Partnership Spectrum*,[5] which compares estimates of underlying asset values to the current market prices of the partnership units.

This information can be useful in quantifying minority discounts for some holding companies, especially those that hold real estate as their primary asset. (There are more real estate limited partnerships that trade in the secondary market than all those that hold other types of assets, e.g., oil and gas interests, put together.)

However, the information does have at least three limitations:

1. The secondary market for limited partnerships is not a very active market, so some element of lack of marketability is reflected in the discounts. The analyst must use judgment in deciding how much additional discount for lack of marketability is warranted.

---

[4]*Mergerstat Review* (Santa Monica, CA: FactSet Mergerstat, LLC), published annually.
[5]*Partnership Spectrum* (Dallas, TX: Partnership Profiles, Inc.).

2. The population of limited partnerships that trade in the secondary market has diminished in recent years due to liquidations. This has reduced the number of public limited partnerships with characteristics comparable to any given subject company.

3. Due to the imminence of liquidations, discounts have declined substantially in recent years. Therefore, the analyst should investigate the extent to which imminent liquidation affects any given limited partnership, and eliminate those whose liquidation is imminent.

Control Premiums and Minority Discounts in the Courts

The principle is that whatever is being transferred in a given transaction is what should be valued. Therefore, in the estate tax situation, whatever block is transferred from the decedent to the decedent's estate is what is valued, regardless of how it may ultimately be divided among the estate's beneficiaries. On the other hand, in the gift tax situation, whatever block or blocks are transferred to each donee is what is valued, regardless of the size of the block from which it was transferred. Therefore, if one divided a 100 percent controlling interest and gifted it to each of three children, each gift would be valued as a 33⅓ percent minority interest, even if the gifts were given concurrently.

In *Rushton v. Commissioner*,[6] the donor of gifts made on the same day to each of several donees claimed that the gifts should be aggregated for blockage discount purposes. The Fifth Circuit Court of Appeals affirmed the trial court's decision that several gifts made on the same day to several donees should be valued as individual gifts, rather than in the aggregate.

Rev. Rul. 93-12 allows the consideration of a minority interest discount in valuing each gift as an independent transfer—without regard to the identity of the donor or donee or the aggregation of any separate gifts.

In *Estate of Bosca*,[8] the father recapitalized his company by exchanging his 50 percent share of voting stock for nonvoting stock, thus leaving to his two sons, who each owned 25 percent of the stock, with 50 percent voting control each. The court rejected the argument that no value was transferred. The issue then became whether the stock that was held by the company should be valued as a single block of 50 percent or as two blocks of 25 percent each.

The taxpayer argued that the stock exchanged should be treated as a single block and valued accordingly. The court disagreed, noting that such an approach violates the principle that separate gifts should be valued separately. The indirect gift of the voting rights was held to constitute two gifts: one to each of his sons.

According to stipulation by the parties, had the stocks been valued as a single block, a 25.62 percent premium would have been added to the value of the nonvoting common stock, for an aggregate tax liability of $970,830. Instead, the stocks were treated as two separate blocks of 25 percent each, and a premium of 2.72 percent was applied to the value of nonvoting common stock, for a tax liability of $103,040.

In *Adams v. United States*,[9] the court adopted a 20 percent lack-of-control discount opined by the estate's expert on a 25 percent interest in the estate partnership, because he "provided

---

[6]*Rushton v. Comm'r*, 498 F.2d 88 (5th Cir. 1974).

[7]Rev. Rul. 93-12, 1993-1, C.B. 202.

[8]*Estate of Bosca v. Comm'r*, T.C. Memo 1998-251, 76 T.C.M (CCH) 62.

[9]*Adams v. Comm'r*, No. 3:96-CV-3181-D, 2001 U.S. Dist. LEXIS 13092 (N.D. Tex., August 27, 2001).

the lone specific analysis of the issues, and his reasoning is consistent with numerous cases that plaintiffs cite." (This was in addition to a 10 percent *portfolio discount* and a 35 percent lack of marketability discount.)

In *Estate of Dunn v. Commissioner*,[10] the court used a 7.5 percent lack-of-control discount for a 62.96 percent block, which fell short of the 66 percent needed to compel liquidation. The case was appealed and the appellate court affirmed the lack of control discount.[11]

In *Estate of Godley*,[12] the Fourth Circuit affirmed no premium or discount for a 50 percent interest in a HUD partnership. The court rejected the estate's assertion that it was a question of law whether a 50 percent interest represented lack of control:

> *The question of whether a taxpayer is entitled to a discount is intertwined in the larger question of valuation and valuation determinations are clearly questions of fact.*

The court of appeals held that, absent some explanation of why control has economic value, no premium or discount is warranted. The partnerships were long-term, steady income-producers, the partnership agreements called for annual distribution of all net cash flows, and, although neither decedent nor his sons could alone compel liquidation, the ability to sell was "of little practical import" given the passive nature of the business and "the almost certain prospects of steady profits."

In *Estate of Wright*,[13] the court rejected a control premium put forth by the Service's expert based on a hypothetical scenario in which other investors might purchase decedent's block of stock.

VOTING VERSUS NONVOTING SHARES

In most instances, where there are large numbers of voting and nonvoting shares, the difference in value is quite small because the minority interests in the voting shares can have little impact on the control of the company. Empirical studies of voting versus nonvoting shares in the public markets in the United States have shown differences of 2 percent to 7 percent between the voting and nonvoting classes.[14] A study of the Toronto Stock Exchange showed similar results.[15]

By contrast, where a small number of shares are voting versus a very large number that are nonvoting, a block of voting shares that has the power to control the company is worth

---

[10]*Estate of Dunn v. Comm'r*, T.C. Memo 2000-12, 79 T.C.M. (CCH) 1337 *rec'd* 301 F.3d 339 (5th Cir. 2002).

[11]*Estate of Dunn v. Comm'r*, 301 F.3d 339, 2002 U.S. App. LEXIS 15453.

[12]*Estate of Godley v. Comm'r*, 286 F.3d 210 (4th Cir. 2002).

[13]*Estate of Wright v. Comm'r*, T.C. Memo 1997-53, 73 T.C.M. (CCH) 1863 (1997) 67,257.

[14]See Ronald C. Lease, John J. McConnell, and Wayne H. Mikkelson, "The Market Value of Control in Publicly-Traded Corporations," *Journal of Financial Economics* (1983): 439–471, at 469; Kevin C. O'Shea and Robert M. Siwicki, "Stock Price Premiums for Voting Rights Attributable to Minority Interests," *Business Valuation Review* (December 1991): 165–171; and Paul J. Much and Timothy J. Fagan, "The Value of Voting Rights," *Financial Valuation: Business and Business Interests*, 1996 Update, James H. Zukin, ed. (New York: Warren Gorham & Lamont, 1996).

[15]Chris Robinson, John Rumsey, and Alan White, "The Value of a Vote in the Market for Corporate Control," paper published by York University Faculty of Administrative Studies, February 1996.

considerably more than the nonvoting shares. Studies have shown that the value of a single block of voting stock that controls the company can be worth 10 percent or more of the entire value of the company.[16]

In *Estate of Simplot*, the decedent owned a minority interest in a small control block of stock. Expert witnesses for both the estate and the Service agreed that the company was being run optimally, and that members of the control block were not taking excess compensation or other benefits at the expense of the minority shareholders.

The expert for the Service put a premium of 3 percent of the estimated value of the company as a whole on the entire control block, and then took a 35 percent minority discount from the decedent's pro rata minority interest in the control block. This resulted in a multimillion-dollar control premium on the minority interest in the control block. The taxpayer's position was that the company was being well managed and that a control owner could have nothing more to gain, and therefore there should be zero premium. The trial court accepted the Service's position, and the estate appealed.

The Ninth Circuit reversed the trial court, saying that a buyer of the block could never recover the multimillion-dollar premium. Therefore, with no evidence of any more modest premium presented, the court accepted the taxpayer's position of zero premium.[17]

BLOCKAGE[18]

Blockage refers to an amount of a security such that, when offered for sale all at once, it would have a depressing effect on the market. The term is usually used in connection with publicly traded stock.

It is akin to the concept of *absorption* in real estate. That is, when one property is put on the market, it would sell for X dollars, but when many like properties are put on the market at once, they would sell for X dollars minus an absorption discount.

Section 20.2031-2(e) of the Estate Tax Regulations recognizes blockage discounts as follows:

> *In certain exceptional cases, the size of the block of stock to be valued in relation to the number of shares changing hands in sales may be relevant in determining whether selling prices reflect the fair market value of the block of stock to be valued. If the executor can show that the block of stock to be valued is so large in relation to the actual sales on the existing market that it could not be liquidated in a reasonable time without depressing the market, the prices at which the block could be sold as such outside the usual market, as through an underwriter, may be a more accurate indication of value than market quotations. Complete data in support of any allowance claimed due to the size of the block of stock shall be submitted with the return (Form 706 Estate Tax Return or Form 709 Gift Tax Return). On the other hand, if the block of stock to be*

---

[16]Gil Matthews made an exhaustive study of transactions involving small blocks of shares that controlled companies. His results are tabularized on pages 211–219 in Shannon Pratt *Business Valuation Discounts & Premiums* (New York: John Wiley & Sons, Inc., 2001).

[17]*Estate of Simplot v. Comm'r*, 112 T.C. 130 (1999), *rev'd* 2001 U.S. App. LEXIS 9220 (9th Cir. 2001).

[18]An excellent chapter on blockage by Joseph S. Estabrook can be found in Robert F. Reilly and Robert P. Schweihs, *The Handbook for Advanced Business Valuation* (New York: McGraw Hill, 2000): 139–153.

valued represents a controlling interest, either actual or effective, in a going business, the price at which other lots change hands may have little relation to its true value.[19]

The blockage discount can be thought of as a subset of discounts for lack of marketability. However, the concept of blockage relates to laws of supply and demand, and the depressing effect on the market rather than lack of a market or restrictions on sale. In fact, in *Adams v. Commissioner*,[20] the court allowed both a restricted stock marketability discount and an additional blockage discount on the same block of stock.

There are several ways to dispose of large blocks of stock, and court case decisions have demonstrated that each of these should be considered. The most frequently encountered alternatives are:

- Selling the stock on the open market on a piecemeal basis over a period of time. This involves comparing the size of the block to the average trading volume of the stock.
- Making a private placement through an intermediary.

Exhibit 19.2 presents a summary of blockage discounts adopted in various courts.

Estate of Auker v. Commissioner[21] involved blockage discounts for real estate held in trust. The real estate consisted of three large apartment complexes, accounting for more than 20 percent of the apartment units in the city in which they were located, and a variety of other real estate or interests in real estate.

The estate claimed a 15 percent blockage discount on all the real estate and real estate interests. The Commissioner said no blockage discount should be allowed. Both the estate and the Commissioner presented expert testimony on the blockage issue.

The following is an excerpt from the opinion:

Relevant evidence of value may include consideration of a market absorption discount. Such a discount emanates from the law of blockage, under which courts and the Commissioner have long recognized that the sale of a large block of publicly traded stock over a reasonable period of time usually depresses the price for shares of that stock as quoted on the market. n10 See, e.g., Maytag v. Commissioner, *supra at 965;* Commissioner v. Estate of Stewart, *153 F.2d 17, 18-19 (3d Cir. 1946), affg. a Memorandum Opinion of this Court;* Gross v. Munford, *150 F.2d 825 827-828 (2d Cir. 1945);* Phipps v. Commissioner, *127 F.2d 214,216-217 (10th Cir. 1942), affg. 43 B.T.A. 1010 (1941);* Helvering v. Maytag, *125 F.2d 55, 63 (8th Cir.1942), affg. a Memorandum Opinion of this Court;* Page v. Howell, *116 F.2d 158 (5th Cir. 1940);* Gamble v. Commissioner, *101 F.2d 565 (6th Cir. 1939), affg. 33 B.T.A. 94 (1935);* Helvering v. Kimberly, *97 F.2d 433, 434 (45h Cir. 1938), affg. per curiam a Memorandum Opinion of the Court;* Helvering v. Safe Deposit & Trust Co., *95 F.2d 806, 81-812 (4th Cir. 1938), affg. 35 B.T.A. 259 (1937);* Commissioner v. Shattuck, *97 F.2d 790, 792 (7th Cir. 1938);* Estate of Amon v. Commissioner, *49 T.C. 108, 117 (1967);* Standish v. Commissioner, *8 T.C. 1204, 1210-1212 (1947);* Avery v. Commissioner, *3 T.C. 963, 970-971 (1944);* Estate of McKitterick v. Commissioner, *42 B.T.A. 130, 136-137 91940); sec. 20.2031-2(e), Estate Tax Regs.; n11 sec 25-2512-2(e), Gift Tax Regs. (language similar to that in sec. 20-2031-2(e), Estate Tax Regs.). In other words, the quoted price for shares of a certain type of stock generally reflects the selling price of a relatively small number of those shares, and the presence on the market of a sufficiently large number of those shares tends to depress the quoted price. the market can handle only a certain number of shares of a given stock at*

---

[19]Reg. § 20-2031-2(e).
[20]*Adams*, op. cit.
[21]*Estate of Auker v. Comm'r*, T.C. Memo 1998-185, 75 T.C.M. (CCH) 2321.

Exhibit 19.2　Summary of Selected Tax Cases Involving Blockage Discounts

Year	Case Citation	Blockage Discount	Comments
2000	*Estate of Brocato v. Commissioner*, T.C. Memo 1999-424	11% (on 7 of 8 real properties)	Petitioner asserted a 12.5% blockage discount for all eight real properties, while the IRS argued that a discount of 1.92% should be applied to only seven properties.
1999	*Estate of Millinger v. Commissioner*, 112 T.C. 26	25%	Both parties presented expert testimony for a blockage discount ranging from 15% to 35%; the court made adjustments to petitioner's methods.
1999	*Estate of Foote v. Commissioner*, T.C. Memo 1999-37	3.3%	Court accepted IRS expert opinion of a 3.3% blockage discount based on 16 factors; rejected taxpayer's expert's reliance on past cases and a 22.5% blockage discount.
1998	*Estate of Davis v. Commissioner*, 110 T.C. 530	Zero	Court disallowed a blockage discount because estate failed to carry burden of establishing that a blockage or SEC Rule 144 discount should apply.
1998	*Estate of McClatchy v. Commissioner*, 147 F.3d 1089 (9th Cir.)	15%	IRS conceded a 15% blockage discount opined by petitioner. Issue on appeal related to federal securities law restrictions.
1997	*Estate of Wright v. Commissioner*, T.C. Memo 1997-53	10%	Starting with the over-the-counter price of $50 per share, taxpayer's experts applied a 24% discount for blockage and other factors; IRS expert applied a control premium but no blockage discount.
1987	*Adair v. Commissioner*, T.C. Memo 1987-494	5%	For valuation of petitioner Adair's stock, a blockage discount was inappropriate. For valuation of petitioner Borgeson's stock, IRS expert opined to no blockage discount and petitioner's expert opined to a 15% blockage discount.
1985	*Robinson v. Commissioner*, T.C. Memo 1985-275	18%	Respondent opined to a 6% blockage discount; petitioner Robinson opined to a 40% combined discount for federal securities restrictions and blockage; petitioner Centronics opined to no blockage discount.
1983	*Steinberg v. Commissioner*, T.C. Memo 1983-534	27.5%	Petitioner argued for a 30% blockage discount; IRS argued for a 12.5% blockage discount.
1974	*Rushton v. Commissioner*, 498 F.2d 88 (5th Cir.)	Zero	Commissioner disallowed a blockage discount for sale of four blocks of stock.

Source: Shannon P. Pratt, *Business Valuation Discounts and Premiums* (New York: John Wiley & Sons, Inc., 2001): 257. Reprinted with permission. All rights reserved.

a quoted price, and, when a seller attempts to sell more shares than the market can handle, the large block of shares tends to flood the market, forcing the seller to accept a price of all shares that is less than the price set by the market for some of those shares.

From the four witnesses provided by the two sides, the court had an abundance of data with which to work. Based on prior sales of apartment units, the court estimated that it would require 42 months for the market to absorb all the apartment units at the appraised prices.

The court did not accept the testimony of any of the experts. It did not allow any blockage discount on the several dissimilar properties, but turned its attention to the three large apartment complexes. The court noted that the real estate appraisers assumed an 18-month time on market. The parties had stipulated to the appraised values as a starting point.

In reaching its decision, the court assumed that one of the apartment buildings could be sold within the 18 months, a second could be sold in 30 months (12 months after the assumed sales in the appraisals), and the third one in 42 months (24 months after the assumed sale dates).

To arrive at a discount rate to discount the extended period to the 18-month expectation, the court took the weighted average of capitalization rates used in the appraisals of the three apartment buildings (weighted by the appraised value of each). Using a midyear convention (discussed in Chapter 14), the discount rate was 4.813 percent for the one that would require 12 extra months and 13.754 percent for the one that would require 24 extra months.

The resulting discount was 6.189 percent ((4.813% + 13.754%) ÷ 3). Thus, the court applied a 6.189 percent discount to the appraised value of each of the three apartment complexes to account for blockage. From an aggregate value of a little more than $22 million, this amounted to an aggregate discount for blockage of a little more than $1.3 million.

DISCOUNTS FOR UNDIVIDED FRACTIONAL INTERESTS IN PROPERTY[22]

Discounts for undivided fractional interests in property such as real estate are usually less than those for partnership or corporate interests with comparable underlying assets. This is because of the right to partition, which is not enjoyed by owners of partnership or stock interests.

A partition is the division of the property, whether held by joint tenants or tenants in common, into distinct portions so that the tenants may hold ownership of those portions individually. The right to partition provides the co-tenant with a potential liquidation option. However, the partition action may be costly and require significant time before liquidation occurs. Thus, the time and expense required for a partition action may substantially reduce the desirability of an undivided joint interest to a potential investor.

A court-ordered partition could result in division of the property or, if the property is indivisible, sale of the property. A judicial partition action usually takes from two to six years.

---

[22]A more thorough discussion of discounts for undivided interests can be found in Dan Van Vleet, "Premium and Discount Issues as Undivided Interest Valuations," Chapter 19 in Shannon Pratt, *Business Valuation Discounts and Premiums* (New York: John Wiley & Sons, Inc., 2001): 292–315.

Estimating the Appropriate Discount for an Undivided Interest

In most states, co-tenancy rights require unanimous consent of the undivided-interest owners to manage or liquidate the property. An undivided joint interest thus suffers a significant lack of control when compared to a fee-simple interest. Also, the market for undivided joint interests is very limited compared with the market for fee-simple interests. Therefore, undivided joint interests suffer from both lack of control and lack of marketability. Most of the approaches to quantifying discounts for undivided joint interests encompass both of these disadvantages within a single discount.

There are two main approaches to quantifying the amount of the discount for undivided fractional interests:

1. Comparable sales of undivided interests
2. Partition analysis

Comparable Sales of Undivided Interests

An ideal approach to quantifying discounts for undivided joint interests would be to observe sales of comparable undivided joint interests and to compare these prices to prices of otherwise comparable fee interests. Although this is sometimes feasible, there are so few sales of undivided interests in most markets that little or no comparable sales data are actually available.

Partition Analysis

The analysis most often seen in court cases to quantify the discounts for undivided fractional interests is partition analysis. This essentially involves the discounted cash flow (DCF) method described in Chapter 14.

The partition analysis involves estimates of the following:

- The value at the end of the partition period, either the value of the separate properties if divided, or the net proceeds if the property is sold (the terminal value in the DCF method)
- The length of time before the partition is completed
- The net cash inflows (income from the property) and net cash outflows (attorney expenses and other costs) during the partition period (these correspond to the interim cash flows in the DCF method)
- A present value discount rate that reflects the risks (uncertainties) of the accuracy of the projected cash inflows and outflows, and the value of the proceeds, at the times and in the amounts projected.

Undivided-Interest Discounts in the Courts

Estate of Williams[23] was one case in which the court did consider the minority and marketability issues separately. The decedent owned an undivided 50 percent interest in Florida Timber-

---

[23]*Estate of Williams v. Comm'r*, T.C. Memo 1998-59, 75 T.C.M. (CCH) 1276.

land. The estate's expert applied a 30 percent lack-of-control discount and a 20 percent lack-of-marketability discount in turn for a total discount of 44 percent (100% – 30% = 70%; 70% – (20% of 70%) = 14% = 44% total discount). The court rejected the Service's position that any discount should be limited to the cost of the partition.

In *Estate of Baird v. Commissioner*,[24] experts for the estate presented evidence of fractional sales of timberland in Louisiana and Texas. On the basis of this evidence, the court upheld the 60 percent discount for fractional interests that two estates claimed on their amended estate tax returns.

In *Estate of Busch v. Commissioner*,[25] the decedent owned a 50 percent undivided interest in 90.74 acres of real property. The court used a modified partition analysis. It assumed that the value of the property at termination of the partition period would be the same as the appraised value at date of death, and discounted that value back to present value at a 9 percent discount rate. It then deducted the estimated costs to partition. The result was a 38.4 percent discount.

The court in *Estate of Barge v. Commissioner*[26] applied a full partition analysis, as just described, to an undivided interest in timberland, reflecting positive interim cash flows from timber income and also partition costs. The result was a 26 percent discount from the appraised fee-simple interest value.

CONCLUSION

Shareholder-level discounts (or premiums) should be applied *after* entity-level discounts. As noted in Chapter 18, the most frequent and generally most controversial shareholder-level discount is for lack of marketability. This chapter has presented the three next most often encountered shareholder-level discounts (or premiums):

1. Minority discount/control premiums
2. Voting versus nonvoting shares
3. Blockage (which can apply to both securities and property such as real estate, art, etc.)

This chapter has also discussed discounts for fractional interests in real estate.

If more than one valuation approach has been used, now that any appropriate adjustments have been made, the analyst must decide the relative weight to be accorded to each approach. That is the subject of Chapter 20.

---

[24]*Estate of Baird v. Comm'r*, T.C. Memo 2001-258, 82 T.C.M. (CCH) 666.
[25]*Estate of Busch v. Comm'r*, T.C. Memo 2000-3, 79 T.C.M. (CCH) 1276.
[26]*Estate of Barge v. Comm'r*, T.C. Memo 1997-188, 73 T.C.M. (CCH) 2615.

Weighting of Approaches

SUMMARY

Normally, holding companies are valued by the asset approach and operating companies are valued by the income or market approach. However, some companies may have characteristics of both a holding company and an operating company. In such cases, some weight may be given to the asset approach and some to the income or market approach.

If a company's assets can be divided between operating assets and nonoperating assets, the company's operating assets can be valued by the income and/or market approach, and the nonoperating assets by the asset approach. (See Chapter 10.)

When more than one approach is to be accorded some weight, there is a difference of opinion as to whether the weighting should be mathematical (assigning a percentage to each approach to be accorded some weight) or subjective.

THEORY AND PRACTICE

In theory, the discounted cash flow method within the income approach is the most correct method. There is virtually unanimous agreement that a company is worth the future benefits it will produce for its owners (benefits preferably measured by net cash flows or some other measure of earnings), discounted back to a present value by a discount rate that reflects the risk of achieving the benefits in the amounts and at the times expected. A typical statement of this theory is as follows:

> *[T]he value of an asset is the present value of its expected returns. Specifically, you expect an asset to provide a stream of returns during the period of time you own it. To convert this estimated stream of returns to a value for the security, you must discount this stream at your required rate of return. This process of valuation requires estimates of (1) the stream of expected returns, and (2) the required rate of return on the investment.*[1]

---

[1]Frank K. Reilly and Keith C. Brown, *Investment Analysis and Portfolio Management*, 7th ed. (Mason, OH: South-Western, 2003), p. 374.

Another leading text states it simply:

[W]e calculate NPV [net present value] by discounting future cash flows at the opportunity cost of capital.[2]

In dissenting stockholder litigation, the Chancery Court of Delaware has declared that the discounted cash flow method is its preferred method.

However, the Service leans toward favoring the market approach over the income approach. There are several references to guideline public companies in Rev. Rul. 59-60. (In 1959, when Rev. Rul. 59-60 was written, there were no databases on mergers and acquisitions of either public or private companies.)

If good guideline companies can be found, the market approach provides the most objective and unbiased indication of value. Some in the Service make the point that the income approach can be subject to bias in the projections presented and/or in the discount or capitalization rates chosen. Also, the income approach can produce widely divergent results based on small variations in assumptions such as the growth rate or discount rate.

Often, the quality of the data presented in support of various approaches determines which approach or approaches should be utilized, or how much weight should be accorded to each. Frequently, zero weight is accorded to an approach on the basis that the underlying data is inadequate to support the conclusion reached. (Those instances where zero weight is accorded to an approach are addressed in the chapters on the respective approaches; only examples of partial weight to more than one approach are presented in this chapter.)

MATHEMATICAL VERSUS SUBJECTIVE WEIGHTING

Rev. Rul. 59-60 rejects a mathematical weighting of approaches with the following language:

SEC. 7. AVERAGE OF FACTORS.

Because valuations cannot be made on the basis of a prescribed formula, there is no means whereby the various applicable factors in a particular case can be assigned mathematical weights in deriving the fair market value. For this reason, no useful purpose is served by taking an average of several factors (for example, book value, capitalized earnings and capitalized dividends) and basing the valuation on the result. Such a process excludes active consideration of other pertinent factors and the end result cannot be supported by a realistic application of the significant facts in the case except by means of chance.[3]

But when analysts use subjective weighting, both clients and the courts usually want to know *how much* weight was accorded to the various approaches. So the analysts usually apply mathematical weights when giving weight to two or more approaches, with a disclaimer that there is no empirical basis for assigning mathematical weights, and that the weights are presented only to help clarify the thought process of the analyst. A good report will also go on to demonstrate that all relevant factors were considered.

---

[2]Richard A. Brealey and Stewart C. Myers, *Principles of Corporate Finance*, 7th ed. (New York: McGraw-Hill/Irwin, 2003), p. 995.
[3]Rev. Rul. 59-60.

When courts accord weight to two or more approaches, they often present their conclusion as to weights in percentage terms.

EXAMPLES OF WEIGHTING OF APPROACHES

The *Estate of H. Freeman v. Commissioner*[4] involved valuing a minority interest in a manufacturing company.

The expert for the Service recommended 70 percent weight be given to his value by the market approach and 30 percent weight to his value by the income approach, and the court accepted those weightings. In his market approach, he narrowed down a list of guideline public companies to three that most closely resembled the subject company in such characteristics as line of business and earnings growth. For his income approach, he projected five years of cash flow available for distributions, estimated a terminal value, and discounted the components to a present value.

The court gave zero weight to the taxpayer's value. In his market approach, the taxpayer's expert did not identify any specific guideline companies, instead basing his market multiples on the Dow Jones Industrial Average. In his income approach, he made no projection but merely capitalized the net income from the last full fiscal year.

Estate of Dunn v. Commissioner involved a 62.96 percent interest in a company that owned and rented out heavy equipment. The company's bylaws required a two-thirds supermajority vote for major corporate actions such as liquidation.

On appeal to the Fifth Circuit, the appellate court assigned an 85 percent weight to the value based on the income approach and 15 percent to the value based on the asset approach. It reasoned that if the company was not likely to be liquidated, which the trial court said it was not, then the valuation approach based on liquidation should not be given the greater weight.[5]

Estate of Smith v. Commissioner[6] involved a 33 percent interest in the common stock of Jones Farm, Inc. (JFI). The taxpayer's expert gave 70 percent weight to the value by the asset approach and 30 percent to the value by the income approach. The expert for the Service gave all the weight to the asset approach. The judge accepted the 70/30 weighting used by the taxpayer's expert.

The judge agreed that in addressing the central issue of the case—the valuation of a high-asset-value, low-earning company—asset-based methods are applicable to corporations that hold assets, and earnings-based methods are applicable to going concerns. JFI had characteristics of both. The judge found that assets contributed to the value of JFI, but that JFI's status as an operating business must be taken into account by considering income-based value indicators. Quoting from *Estate of Andrews*,[7] the court noted, "The value of the underlying real estate will retain most of its inherent value even if the corporation is not efficient in securing a stream of income."[8]

---

[4]*Estate of Freeman v. Comm'r*, T.C. Memo 1996-372, 72 T.C.M. (CCH) 373.

[5]*Estate of Dunn v. Comm'r*, T.C. Memo 2000-12, 79 T.C.M. (CCH) 1337; *rev'd* 301 F.3d 339 (5th Cir. 2002).

[6]*Estate of Smith v. Comm'r*, T.C. Memo 1999-368, 78 T.C.M. (CCH) 745.

[7]*Estate of Andrews v. Comm'r*, 79 T.C. 938 (1982).

[8]Id., quote from an abstract of case in *Shannon Pratt's Business Valuation Update*, Business Valuation Resources, LLC (December 1999): 10.

CONCLUSION

For operating companies, most or all of the weight is usually accorded to indications of value from either the income or the market approach. For holding companies, most or all of the weight is normally accorded to value from the asset approach. For operating companies that are operating-asset intensive (e.g., forest products companies with large timber stands), the weight may be divided between the asset approach and the market approach. For operating companies with significant nonoperating assets, the company might be valued by the income or market approaches, plus the value of the nonoperating assets, with some discount in case of a minority interest.

Chapter 21 is on a different but related topic, valuation of stock options.

Valuation of Options[1]

SUMMARY

Options are a prediction of the future worth of an underlying asset. They have no intrinsic value, instead deriving their value from the asset they represent. Thus, valuers might find it necessary to *predict* future value of the underlying asset to ascertain the option's present value.

This task ranges from challenging to difficult, because the Service uses complex valuation methods. Generally speaking, option valuation issues may be thought of in four categories: *when*, *how*, *what*, and *if*.

When determines when options are valued. Tax law limits valuation dates to two possibilities: when the option is received and when it is exercised. The Regulations encourage use of whichever valuation date maximizes tax revenue.

How prescribes valuation methods. There are at least three formulae that are used.

1. *Mean between high and low market prices.* This formula is used only for publicly traded options.
2. *FMV = Value of the Underlying Property – Strike Price + Option Privilege +/– Other Factors.* This is the most prevalent formula, with some variation used for most option valuations.
3. *Black-Scholes variation.* This open-ended method considers all relevant factors in determining value.

---

[1]This chapter was contributed by L. Richard Walton, Esq., of Chain, Younger, Cohn & Stiles.

What considers other factors that might be included in the analysis, such as administrative costs and credit risks.

If asks whether fair market value is *readily ascertainable*. If it is, one valuation date and formula will be used. If not, a different valuation date and formula will be employed.

These broad principles are illustrated by applying them to options received as compensation, as dividends, and as gifts.

INTRODUCTION AND BACKGROUND

Options are a form of derivative investment. Derivatives have no intrinsic value of their own but are valuable because they represent the right to possess an asset that *is* valuable. They *derive* their value from the commodity they represent.

Options are a contract for the purchase or sale of a commodity at some time in the future. In technical terms, an option is the binding right to purchase (a *call*) or sell (a *put*) an underlying commodity at a fixed price (the *strike price*) at some date in the future (the *settlement date*). Some options require no up-front cash outlay by the holder (such as employee stock options), although others cost several hundred thousand dollars (such as an option to purchase a feature film script).

Assume you have just completed a screenplay, *Gone with the Rain*. You pitch your script to Sophie Entertainment, and Sophie is interested. It does not know, however, what movie stars it can package with the movie (a commitment by the star to act in the movie if funding becomes available), or whether a studio will be interested in funding it. Without knowing whether it can sell the script, Sophie is unwilling to pay your asking price of $250,000. They are optimistic, however, and do not want to lose your script to a rival production company.

They offer to pay you $50,000 for a two-year option on the script. If you agree, for the next two years you cannot sell the script to anyone else, and Sophie has the absolute right to buy your script for $250,000 if it chooses to do so. If it does not buy the script within two years, you keep the $50,000.

This is a classic option contract. To put it in the vernacular, Sophie has acquired, for $50,000, a call option with a strike price of $250,000 and a discretionary settlement date within the next two years.

Notice that the only thing that makes the option valuable is the underlying script—there is nothing inherently valuable in the option, which derives its value from the script.

Note also that options are a gamble and someone always loses. Sophie is gambling that it can get a studio to fund the script, at which time it will exercise the option. If it cannot get funding, you keep (and it loses) the $50,000. Consider an option to buy stock: If the strike price for 1,000 shares of IBM is $40 per share in three months, and the current market quote is $35 per share, then the holder of a call option is gambling that the price will exceed $40 in three months. If it does not, the holder must choose between purchasing shares for more than they are worth, or forfeiting the money paid for the option. Conversely, the holder of a put is gambling that stock prices will be lower in three months, thereby allowing him or her to sell shares for more than they are worth.

Options allow savvy investors to hedge against known risks, such as fluctuations in the price of a vital raw material. If a cornmeal manufacturer wishes to hedge against the risk that the price of corn will increase, it can buy a call option with a strike price close to the current cost of corn. If the price of corn goes up, the manufacturer offsets the higher market cost of corn with its gain from the option, thereby keeping its cost of production roughly the same. If, however, the price of corn unexpectedly drops, the manufacturer's loss on the option is offset by the lower cost of corn.

Options can also offer impressive returns to a clever speculator, but remember that every time a person makes money on a derivative, someone always loses.

Options may be encountered in almost any business transaction, from transfers of control in family businesses to executive compensation plans. They are rarely easy to value.

Options present a tricky problem for valuers as they are usually not publicly traded, and vary greatly in their terms and features. The variety of options one will encounter is limited only by the imagination of the people who create them, and each option presents unique features that can alter value. Despite unfavorable tax treatment, options have expanded beyond Hollywood to become one of the most popular forms of derivative investment on the market.

Stating the basic rule for valuing options is easy, while applying it in practice is anything but. We will consider some general rules of valuation and apply them in three specific situations: when options are received as compensation, distributed to owners of a corporation, or received as a gift.

GENERAL PRINCIPLES OF OPTION VALUATION

Fair market value of options is determined using the same basic rules as other property. Property should be valued at the price at which it would change hands between a willing buyer and willing seller, neither being under any compulsion to buy or sell, both having reasonable knowledge of relevant facts.[2] This includes a consideration of all relevant factors.[3]

There are generally three acceptable approaches for determining fair market value:

1. The market approach
2. The income approach
3. The asset-based approach

Note that the same problems discussed in Chapter 1 are present here: There are substantive differences between the Treasury's definition of *fair market value* and the AICPA's definition of *fair value*. These differences are even more complex to resolve following the sweeping changes incorporated in Statements of Financial Accounting Standards 123 and 133, which require firms to recognize, in the year incurred, gains or losses on nonhedge derivatives' *fair value*. The inherently uncertain nature of derivatives, coupled with the yearly valuation requirement, will inevitably create valuation tension between AICPA book value and reportable income or loss for taxes.

---

[2] Reg. § 20.2031-1(b).
[3] *Bank One v. Comm'r*, 120 T.C. 174 (2003); Rev. Rul. 59-60.

In the rare case of an option that is either purchased through, or is traded on, one of the derivative exchanges (Chicago Board of Trade, Chicago Board Options Exchange), valuation is easy: The market itself values the option, and the Service accepts this value.[4]

The problem comes when one encounters the horde of non–publicly traded options, used for everything from executive compensation to transfer of control in a family-owned business. Valuers must determine the value of something that, by itself, has no value. This necessarily involves reference to the value of the underlying asset—and sometimes a prediction of what that asset will be worth at some time in the future. Having determined (using the term loosely) what the asset could be worth in, say, three months, the valuer must then consider other factors that affect an option's value, including, perhaps, such esoteric adjustments as credit risk of the parties and administrative costs.[5]

The Treasury's mandate that all relevant factors be considered in reaching a determination of fair market value thus requires that the valuer have almost omniscient knowledge of a host of unknowns.[6] Fundamentally, options are an attempt to predict and value the future.

Valuing options is difficult as the range of possible scenarios covers a host of variables related not only to the option but also to the underlying asset. Option valuation thus forces the valuer away from the comfortable world of verifiable factors and market comparables into the murky waters of metaphysical projection. Nor does the Service leave much room for error in the valuation, since taxpayers often use options to defer payment of tax. See discussion, *infra*.

To understand the Service's approach to option valuation, one should grasp that, whatever the context, the Service is seeking to impose tax on the full amount of gain, at the highest appropriate marginal tax rate. The Regulations structure valuation issues regarding options so as to leave four questions which the valuer must consider: *when* the option is to be valued, *how* the value should be calculated, *what* should be included in the valuation, and *if* fair market value is *readily ascertainable*.

When: Valuation Date

In theory, options could be valued at any time between receipt and exercise. Recognizing that some options cannot be valued when received due to uncertainty, the Service allows one of

---

[4]See, for example, Reg. § 1.83-7(a).

[5]Paul Carmen & Melanie Gnazzo, "FMV, Mark-to-Market, and Clear Reflection of Income: The Tax Court Takes a Middle Road in Bank One," *Journal of Taxation* (August 2003): 98.

[6]There is a limited safe harbor for so-called "golden parachute" options. For purposes of Code sections 280G and 4999 *only*, use of the Black-Scholes model provides a valuation safe harbor, if it considers the following factors: (1) Volatility of the underlying stock, (2) option exercise price, (3) the spot price, and (4) the option term as of the valuation date. Reg. § 1-280G-1; Rev. Proc. 2003-68; 68 FR 45745. This narrowly limited safe harbor can be relied on only where the option was issued as compensation to a disqualified individual if: (1) issuance is contingent on a change in ownership of corporate stock, assets, or control; and (2) the aggregate projected present value of all payments is at least three times base salary; *or* the payment violates any securities laws. If that list was not confusing enough, imagine trying to determine the present value of options income at some point in the future. It is small wonder the Service granted a safe harbor, lest the task become impossible. Note, however, that this safe harbor will seldom if ever be useful to the practitioner.

two valuation dates, limiting the potential universe of valuation dates to the date of receipt and the date of exercise.

Which of these dates the Service prefers depends on the situation: If options are used as executive compensation, the Service prefers to value on the date of exercise, thereby preventing the taxpayer from locking in the value of the property at receipt of the option and then paying tax on any gain much later at (much lower) capital gain rates. If, however, options are given by a corporation as a dividend-in-kind, the Service prefers to value on the date of receipt, taxing the fair market value of the option as a dividend, thereby preventing the shareholder from avoiding tax altogether by deferring gain until exercise and then arguing that the strike price and property value (measured at receipt) are the same.[7]

These rules are discussed fully *infra*. For the moment, remember that options must be valued on one of two dates: when received or when exercised. A valuer's task is much easier if the valuation is done at exercise, as many of the unknowns are resolved by that time.

How: Valuation Formula

There are at least three formulae used by the Service to value options.

Formula One: If the option is actively traded on an exchange, its value is the mean between the highest and lowest quoted prices—or, if unavailable, bid and asked prices—on the date of the valuation, or as close to that date as possible. Other factors may be included in the valuation if it can be established that the option was not trading for its true fair market value.[8] Thus, if the option, or an option very similar to it, traded on the CBOT for a high of $40 and a low of $30 on the valuation date, the fair market value would be $35. Unfortunately for valuers, such easy answers are rarely available. Where Formula One applies, and the option is part of an employee's compensation, the fair value of the option is recognized as income in the year it is received. Under the game of Now or Later, the taxpayer loses, since she must pay taxes Now and lose the use of her money until Later.

Formula Two: If the option is not actively traded, fair market value may still be "readily ascertainable," discussed *infra*, by applying some variation of this formula:

$$\text{FMV} = \text{Value of the underlying property} - \text{Strike price} + \text{Option privilege} +/- \text{Other factors}$$

Breaking the formula down, if the underlying stock were valued at $30, and the strike price was $25, the value of the option would be $5. The problem, of course, is determining the value of the underlying property. If the value of the property cannot be adequately determined at receipt, then valuation will be deferred until exercise, when the option can be precisely valued because the unknowns are resolved by the consummation of the transaction.

Where the option is being valued at receipt, the valuer must include some value for the potential exercise of the option prior to the settlement date. In simple terms, if one holds a $35 per share option for IBM stock, with a holder-determinable settlement date up to three months

---

[7]See, for example, *Baumer v. United States*, 580 F.2d 863 (5th Cir. 1978) (taxpayer argued that strike price and property value were the same, and therefore, under value – strike price formula, he owed no tax. The court rejected this reading, holding the options to be a dividend, taxable when received for the fair market value of the option).
[8]Reg. § 1.83-7; § 20.2031-2(b).

in the future, and IBM reaches $150 per share one month after the option is purchased, the holder will likely exercise the option and immediately resell IBM for a $115 profit.

The Service terms this the *option privilege* and expects the valuer to calculate the likelihood of its occurrence and include some value for it. In determining the value of an option privilege, the valuer must consider the value of the underlying property (if it can be ascertained), the probability the underlying property will increase or decrease in value, and the option's duration. We consider other factors that might affect value *infra*.

Formula Three: Where the option is a gift, the Service applies a straight fair market value standard that incorporates many of the factors used in the Black-Scholes model.[9] Here, the taxable value of the option is determined by reference to the following formula:

$$\text{Option value} = \text{Fair market value of option} - \text{Price paid for option}$$

Determining the option's fair market value includes consideration of the fair market value of the underlying asset at the date of receipt, the option price, any potential for appreciation or depreciation during the option period, and the time period of the option.[10] This loose standard allows valuers considerable leeway within the Black-Scholes framework.

Which formula one uses depends on whether the option's fair market value is "readily ascertainable" when the option is received by the taxpayer.

What: Additional Factors Affecting Value

Regardless of which formula is used, there may be additional factors that can affect value. These factors may include administrative costs of the parties and the credit risks inherent in the transaction.[11] Valuers should be aware that there may be a host of factors to consider in valuing derivatives.

If: Is FMV "Readily Ascertainable"?

Determining which valuation date and formula to use often hinges on whether the option has a "readily ascertainable" fair market value at the time of receipt. If it does, the option will be valued when received. Otherwise, the Service makes the valuer's task immensely easier by waiting until the date of exercise to value the option.

When options are issued as compensation, the Regulations attempt to force the taxpayer into recognizing income when the options are exercised, rather than when they are received, and *readily ascertainable* is thus very narrowly defined. It is frequently impossible to meet this standard, as discussed *infra*. In other situations, such as gifts of options, valuation may be deferred until exercise for the simple reason that it is not always possible to value options at the time of receipt.

---

[9]A detailed analysis of the Black-Scholes model is beyond the scope of this book, but for an excellent discussion of this revolutionary model, see, generally, Jerry Marlow, *Option Pricing* (New York: John Wiley & Sons, Inc., 2001).
[10]Rev. Rul. 80-186.
[11]For a further discussion, see Paul Carmen & Melanie Gnazzo, op. cit.

Consider a closely held business that has not been appraised. Father gives son an option to purchase 50 percent of father's company for $100,000; at the same time, father gives another person an option to purchase 35 percent of the company for $250,000. Obviously, the son's option is worth considerably more, but it is impossible to determine *how much* more without some idea of what the business is worth.

For this reason, valuation of the option may be deferred until its exercise under the so-called "open transactions doctrine," which defers valuation until the property in question can be valued. Under this standard, the taxpayer does not have as high a burden of proof as she does under the stringent Regulations dealing with compensation, and will find it easier to value options at receipt.

Only rarely will a court find an option to be so hard to value at any time during its life that it holds the option to be worthless. In one old but apparently still viable case, the taxpayer owned options to purchase shares of a bankrupt corporation that had never shown a profit, had no marketable assets, and whose business plan was predicated on an unproven idea. The court held the options, and the assets underlying them, to be so speculative in value as to be worthless—despite the later commercial success of the enterprise.[12]

Although the applicability of this case today is highly in doubt, it is worth noting that at least in times past, a court has found that some options represent assets so inherently speculative in nature that they cannot be valued and are not subject to tax. The case also raises the interesting possibility of claiming a discount for restricted options on restricted property, thereby increasing the amount of valuation discount one can take.

SPECIFIC RULES FOR VALUING OPTIONS

The general principles of option valuation just outlined are applied with considerable nuance, depending on the circumstances surrounding the valuation. This variation in application is the product of two factors: options represent a popular tax-planning technique for deferring and reducing federal income tax, and they vary greatly in both design and purpose. Thus, the Service applies different presumptions and different formulae, depending on context.

We have selected three of the most common uses for options to illustrate how the valuation rules are applied in practice. As you read the following material, remember that the single unifying theme is this: Options can allow taxpayers to reduce tax, and the Service tries to ensure that options cannot be used to circumvent the Code.

Compensation

Where options are used for executive compensation, the Service has promulgated detailed Regulations prescribing their tax treatment. Understanding these complex rules will be simplified if one understands that we are playing the tax game called *Now or Later*. Now or Later is a continuing struggle between the Service and taxpayers to determine when federal income taxes are paid. Taxpayers love to defer federal income taxes because they have the use of their

---

[12]*W.W. Waterson Ass'n. v. Comm'r*, 14 B.T.A. 370, 373 (1928).

money until they must pay it to the government. Thus, Now or Later usually involves the taxpayer's trying to defer recognition of revenue into the indefinite future.

Not so with options. The government cares greatly about overall revenue. When dealing with options, Now or Later is often reversed, with taxpayers seeking to recognize their income at receipt, and the Commissioner seeking to defer recognition until exercise.

To understand why this is so, consider a typical compensatory option: Rather than receiving cash this year, executive Faith receives options entitling her to purchase 1,000 shares of corporate stock for $20 per share. The stock is currently trading at $30 per share, and Faith sincerely hopes the stock will be worth $50 when she exercises her options in two years.

Regulations section 1.83-7 provides for one of two valuation dates: Faith can, if she meets a multitude of tests, recognize the options as ordinary income when received, paying tax on the difference between $20 and $30, or $10 per share. (Using Formula One, *supra*). Her basis in the shares will be $30. She will pay no tax when she exercises the option and receives shares worth $50. That tax is deferred until Later; Faith will pay capital gains tax—at a much lower marginal rate—when she sells the stock at some point in the far distant future.

Alternatively, she will recognize no income when the options are received, instead deferring recognition until she exercises the shares, at which point she will pay tax under Formula One on $30, the difference between the value of the shares ($50) and the strike price ($20), at ordinary income tax rates. Her basis will be $50, and she will still have to pay capital gains tax if she later sells her shares for any amount greater than $50.

Note that if she pays tax on receipt of the options, the executive's compensation income tax is paid in full, and she will pay no more tax until the stock itself is sold. If, however, she does not recognize income until she exercises the options, her taxable compensation is the difference between the fair market value of the thing received (stock) and the price she must pay to acquire it (the strike price). Assuming the stock has increased in value, Faith will pay far more tax if she recognizes income at exercise.

Recognizing income when options are received thus results in huge tax savings for executives, so long as the underlying stock price continues to rise.[13] The Regulations attempt to avoid this result through a unique two-tier test, engineered for the sole purpose of forcing taxpayers to recognize income when options are exercised.[14]

To recognize income when she receives her options, Faith must establish that the options have a "readily ascertainable" fair market value. If the options are actively traded (a highly unlikely scenario), the Service concedes they have a readily ascertainable fair market value.[15] If, however, they are not actively traded, Faith must initially meet a four-part test and show that:

1. The option is transferable by the optionee.
2. The option is exercisable immediately in full by the optionee.

---

[13]The executive takes a risk in recognizing income immediately, however. If the stock price drops and the options become worthless, the executive will have paid tax on income never realized.

[14]Employers also prefer to defer recognition of compensation until exercise of the option, as they receive a larger compensation deduction when the option is exercised.

[15]Reg. § 1.83-7(b)(1). Unfortunately, close probably does not count: If Faith's option is close, but not identical, to traded options, the Service would likely deny it was "actively traded."

3. The option or the property subject to the option is not subject to any restriction or condition (other than a lien or other condition to secure the payment of the purchase price) that has a significant effect on fair market value of the option.
4. The fair market value of the option privilege is readily ascertainable.

Consider how unlikely it is that Faith can meet all four of these tests. First, the option must be freely transferable. Most are not, for the simple reason that companies do not want nonemployees having the right to purchase stock at bargain prices. Second and third, the option must be exercisable in full, immediately, with no significant restrictions. Again, this is highly unlikely. The goal of stock options is to motivate managers to continued excellence, and thus the options, the underlying stock, or both are almost inevitably subject to some forfeiture provisions contingent on remaining with the company, and/or continued corporate earnings growth. It is unlikely that companies will defer this important compensation goal solely for tax-planning reasons—especially if one considers that corporations will receive a larger deduction for wage expense if the tax is deferred until exercise of the option.

Fourth, the fair market value of the option privilege must be readily ascertainable. Enter the second tier of the Service's analysis, of direct interest to valuers. Assuming that Faith can meet the above three tests, she still must prove that the *option privilege* value is readily ascertainable. As just discussed, option privilege attempts to place a value on the fact that Faith will be able to purchase the underlying stock for a fixed price for some time to come, regardless of how much it appreciates in value. This requires valuers to make some prediction of what the underlying asset will be worth in the future, an intentionally impossible task.

Three factors that should be considered in determining whether the value of the option privilege is readily ascertainable, and its value, are:

- Whether the value of the underlying property can be ascertained
- The probability of any ascertainable value of such property increasing or decreasing
- The length of time during which the option can be exercised

Compounding the difficulty of making this determination is the Service's hard-line position on valuation shortcuts, such as the barter-equation method. In one case, the taxpayer sought to equate the value of an option received in a corporate reorganization with the value of the property delivered, following the general rule that when two properties are exchanged, their value is presumed to be equal. The court held for the Service, denying use of the barter-exchange method.[16]

The challenge for valuers is, as discussed, determining a value for property at some date in the future with enough certainty to satisfy these three criteria. Such a task may be possible for a publicly traded company with a strong history of earnings, price/earnings (P/E) ratios, and market prices; it is impossible in the context of closely held business with no significant sales to third parties at the time of grant, and no comparable publicly traded companies.[17]

Where her stock is not publicly traded, Faith must establish all seven elements of the two-tier test outlined above in order to use Formula Two. If enough data exists to make use of For-

---

[16]*Mitchell v. Comm'r*, 590 F.2d 312 (9th Cir. 1979).
[17]*Frank v. Comm'r*, 447 F.2d 552 (7th Cir. 1971).

mula Two, the stock's value is "readily ascertainable." Assume that Faith's options meet the first three standards and are transferrable, exercisable, and not subject to any substantial restriction. Assume further that the option value is reasonably ascertainable. Strike price for the shares is still $20, and the underlying property is valued at $35 per share. To this is added the option privilege that is worth $2 per share. No other adjustments are necessary. Faith will now be taxed on $17 ($35 − $20 + $2) under Formula Two when she receives the shares. If one of these factors cannot be satisfied, however, the stock must be valued at exercise.

Through the simple device of a valuation method impossible to apply in the vast majority of cases, the Service has been very successful in forcing taxpayers to recognize gains at the time most favorable to the Service.

Corporate Distributions

Options are increasingly being used as a vehicle for corporate distributions, granting shareholders the right to purchase shares at less than fair market value. Dividends in kind of stock in the issuing corporation, or options to purchase such stock, are not taxable when received.[18]

However, where a corporation distributes options to purchase stock in another corporation—even a related parent or subsidiary—the Service asserts that a taxable event has occurred. *When* and *How* thus become relevant where Corporation A distributes options to purchase stock in Corporation B, and the tax treatment of such dividends has not yet been authoritatively settled.

In *Palmer v. Commissioner*, the Supreme Court held the following:

> *The mere issue of rights to subscribe and their receipt by stockholders, is not a dividend. No distribution of corporate assets or diminution of the net worth of the corporation results in any practical sense. Even though the rights have a market or exchange value, they are not dividends within the statutory definition.*[19]

Under *Palmer*, no income is recognized when the dividend in kind is received, with tax deferred until sale or exercise of the option, at which time any gain (determined using Formula Two, FMV − Strike Price) is taxed as a dividend. The wrinkle with *Palmer* is that the fair market value of the underlying property is determined on the date of *receipt*. Shareholder receives an option dividend with a strike price equal to current fair market value, and the stock thereafter appreciates in value. Under *Palmer*, shareholder owes no tax when she exercises the option, regardless of current fair market value of the stock.

Such is the Service's concern; if the option's strike price equals fair market value when the option is received, income tax is avoided under Formula Two. The Service has two options to deal with the problem: It can force valuation at exercise, or it can change the valuation method. The Service chose to do the latter in Rev. Rul. 70-251, asserting that such options should be taxed as a dividend when received.

Rev. Rul. 70-251 relies on the fact that *Palmer* was decided before section 317(a) was enacted. The Fifth and Seventh Circuits bought the Service's argument and distinguished

---

[18]I.R.C. § 317(a) specifically excludes stock in the issuing corporation, or options to purchase such, from its definition of *property*, which is taxed as a dividend in kind.

[19]*Palmer v. Comm'r*, 302 U.S. 63, 71 (1937).

Palmer on the statutory issue, holding that options should be valued when received, using Formula Three to determine fair market value of the option, rather than the spread between stock price and strike price.[20] By altering the valuation method to consider the fair market value of the option, the Service defeated taxpayers.

The ultimate outcome is still in doubt, however. *Palmer* is an antiquated holding, but the Supreme Court has never explicitly overruled it. Thus, there may still be a viable argument that *Palmer* is the correct method for valuing such options.

Gifts

We finally turn to gifts[21] of stock options, most commonly encountered in the context of family-owned businesses. Parents, wishing to transfer control of the business to their children, grant them options to purchase stock in the business at some considerable discount, in exchange for a nominal amount of consideration such as $20.

Three questions arise if options are part of a gift to a family member: When is the gift capable of valuation, when should the gift be valued, and what standard should be used?

First, a gifted option is capable of valuation when it is transferred to the donee, and is binding and enforceable under state law. In most states, only options supported by consideration bind the donor. Thus, an option supported by consideration may not be withdrawn prior to exercise, whereas a gratuitous option may be withdrawn (merely a nonbinding promise, and not a true option). To be binding and enforceable, the option must be supported by some nominal consideration. The consideration need not be adequate to be enforceable.

Second, if the above requirements are met, the Service insists that gifted options be valued when received.

Third, the Service encourages an open-ended inquiry into option value, using Formula Three. This loose standard mentions the following factors for valuers to consider, but leaves open the possibility of using other, nonlisted factors[22]:

- Fair market value of underlying property when the option is received
- Option price
- Any potential for appreciation or depreciation in the underlying asset during the option period
- The time period of the option

The standard for gifted options is the easiest of the three to apply, allowing flexibility in both *when* and *how*, leaving it up to planners to determine when the option will be valued, and up to valuers to determine exactly how.

---

[20]*Baumer v. United States*, 580 F.2d 863 (5th Cir. 1978); *Redding v. Comm'r*, 630 F.2d 1169 (7th Cir. 1980).

[21]We use the term *gifts* to connote options for which the recipient paid little or no value.

[22]Rev. Rul. 80-186.

CONCLUSION

Option valuation is a difficult process, made more so because the Service uses unique and at times intricate valuation standards to achieve its revenue goals. Given the increasing popularity of derivative investments, however, it is an issue that valuers will face, and until the Service sees fit to modify its position, business valuers must be at least somewhat comfortable with applying its standards.

IRS Positions

SUMMARY

This chapter explores the Service's positions on valuation as expressed in Tax Advice Memorandums (TAMs), Revenue Rulings (Rev. Rul.), and Revenue Procedures (Rev. Proc.). The chapter covers the following material:

- Rev. Rul. 59-60 is the foundation of modern valuation. It holds that all factors must be considered in valuation and adopts no particular method, although it does list several that can be considered. Originally, it applied only to estate and gift tax issues.
- Rev. Rul. 65-192 expanded Rev. Rul. 59-60 to include income tax and other tax issues, while reserving earlier "formula" approaches for intangible assets. It was replaced by Rev. Rul. 68-609.
- Rev. Rul. 65-193 modified Rev. Rul. 59-60 by deleting any rule for valuation of intangible assets.
- Rev. Proc. 66-49 extended the principles of Rev. Rul. 59-60, with appropriate modifications, to valuation of contributed property.
- Rev. Rul. 68-609 replaced Rev. Rul. 65-192 and clearly stated that the formula approach could be used for intangible assets only when no other method was available.

- Rev. Proc. 77-12 used the principles of Rev. Rul. 59-60 in allocating value among assets for basis purposes where the company was purchased for a lump sum or was a subsidiary merged into its parent.
- Rev. Rul. 77-287 dealt with valuation of stock that is restricted from resale under the federal securities laws. It listed several factors to be considered and the weight each was to be given.
- Rev. Rul. 83-120 outlined how to value preferred and common stock where a closely held business is recapitalized.
- Rev. Rul. 85-75 held that the valuation misstatement penalties now contained in section 6662 of the Code could be applied to beneficiaries who merely use for their basis an (incorrect) valuation adopted by the estate.
- Rev. Rul. 93-12 declined to attribute ownership among family members where each owns an interest in a closely held corporation. As a result, minority discounts are still available to family owners.
- TAM 1994-36-005 was an attempt by the Service to identify some factors that might increase the value of stock, thus minimizing the effects of valuation discounts.
- Rev. Proc. 2003-51 provided guidance for fair market valuation of inventory when acquired as part of an asset purchase or stock purchase for which a section 338(h)(10) election has been made.

INTRODUCTION

This chapter reproduces and analyzes the Service positions on valuation currently in force.

Regulations are drafted by the Treasury and the Service and have the force of law when finalized. They are given deference by the courts, and are overruled only where they are not based on a permissible construction of the statute they interpret. Thus, so long as Regulations are consistent with one potential reading of a statute—not necessarily the best one—they will not be overruled by the courts.

Revenue Rulings are issued by the Service to state its position on various tax issues. Courts of Appeal give varying degrees of deference to Revenue Rulings.[1] The Supreme Court, in *Chevron*[2] and more recently in *Mead Data*[3] implied that Agency rulings are entitled to some degree of deference, albeit small.[4]

Revenue Procedures set forth how the Service will apply certain laws, when it will issue rulings, and so forth. They are seldom used to state the Service's position on substantive issues. Revenue Rulings and Revenue Procedures may be used by the taxpayers as precedent to support their positions.

Historically, Revenue Rulings and Revenue Procedures were not binding on the Service,

---

[1] *Telecom USA v. United States*, 192 F.3d 1068 (D.C. Cir. 1999).
[2] 467 U.S. 837 (1984).
[3] 121 S.Ct. 2164 (2001).
[4] See also *Skidmore v. Swift*, 323 U.S. 134 (1944).

however, and the Service was routinely criticized for litigating against its own guidelines. Recently, the chief counsel of the Internal Revenue Service indicated that the Service will no longer challenge its own rulings in court—an idea that makes eminently good sense. The Service has finally acquiesced, and will follow its own guidelines.

Private Letter Rulings (PLRs) and Tax Advice Memorandums (TAMs), however, have no precedential value and may be relied upon only by the taxpayers who requested them. PLRs are issued where a taxpayer believes a specific transaction is legal under the Tax Code, but wants to know what the Service's position will be in litigation if the transaction is challenged. A taxpayer will thus write the Service and describe the transaction, asking for its opinion. PLRs are the Service's response to these inquiries and cannot be relied upon by anyone other than the taxpayer who asked the question. They are followed closely by practitioners, however, as they are indicative of what the Service is thinking about certain tax plans and tax-planning issues. TAMs are the opinion of the Service, as are PLRs, but TAMs usually are requested by the Service auditing agents in the process of an audit.

We will discuss the materials in chronological order, thereby tracing the evolution of the Treasury's valuation positions. The following material constitutes the entirety of the Service's positions on valuation. Each of the 12 pronouncements reviewed will be preceded by a few short paragraphs summarizing the contents.

REV. RUL. 59-60

Summary

Rev. Rul. 59-60 is considered to be the finest and most comprehensive piece of scholarship on valuation.[5] Rev. Rul. 59-60 underlies everything we have discussed in this book.

Rev. Rul. 59-60 laid the cornerstone of all modern valuation by discarding any use of mechanical formulae in valuing closely held businesses for estate and gift tax purposes. Instead, it urges a case-by-case analysis of all available factors, outlining various general factors that are broadly applicable to all valuation questions. This *ad hoc* analysis leaves enormous discretion to the courts in determining the *fair market value* of a business. Such discretion breeds ambiguity for both taxpayers and the Commissioner, as neither can predict with any certainty what the court will do.[6]

Several things should be noted in reading the Revenue Ruling. First, it applies only to companies that cannot be valued by the market, such as closely held corporations, or corporations whose stock is not traded on any organized exchange. Second, it applies only to the estate and gift tax laws (although Rev. Rul. 65-192 subsequently broadened it to apply to income taxes and all federal tax issues). Third, it rejects any mechanistic formula in valuing such businesses. Fourth, it lists general factors for each valuation situation. Although this list of factors is not exhaustive, it is an excellent starting point for thinking through valuation issues.

---

[5]For a full analysis, see Gary R. Trugman, *Understanding Business Valuation*, 291–308.
[6]See, e.g., *Pulsar Components v. Comm'r*, T.C. Memo 1996-129, 71 T.C.M. (CCH) 2436 (dismissing the taxpayer's expert as "unconvincing" and having "difficulty" accepting the government's expert, the court concluded "we are not persuaded by either of the experts" and proceeded to conduct its own valuation.)

Text

Section 2031: Definition of Gross Estate

26 CFR 20.2031-2: Valuation of stocks and bonds.

(Also Section 2512.)

(Also Part II, Sections 811 (k), 1005, Regulations 105, Section 81.10.)

1959-1 C.B. 237; 1959 IRB LEXIS 303; REV. RUL. 59-60

January 1959. In valuing the stock of closely held corporations, or the stock of corporations where market quotations are not available, all other available financial data, as well as all relevant factors affecting the fair market value must be considered for estate tax and gift tax purposes. No general formula may be given that is applicable to the many different valuation situations arising in the valuation of such stock. However, the general approach, methods, and factors which must be considered in valuing such securities are outlined. Revenue Ruling 54-77, C.B. 1954-1, 187, superseded.

Section 1: Purpose

The purpose of this Revenue Ruling is to outline and review in general the approach, methods, and factors to be considered in valuing shares of the capital stock of closely held corporations for estate tax and gift tax purposes. The methods discussed herein will apply likewise to the valuation of corporate stocks on which market quotations are either unavailable or are of such scarcity that they do not reflect the fair market value.

Section 2: Background and Definitions

.01 All valuations must be made in accordance with the applicable provisions of the Internal Revenue Code of 1954 and the Federal Estate Tax and Gift Tax Regulations. Sections 2031(a), 2032 and 2512(a) of the 1954 Code (sections 811 and 1005 of the 1939 Code) require that the property to be included in the gross estate, or made the subject of a gift, shall be taxed on the basis of the value of the property at the time of death of the decedent, the alternate date if so elected, or the date of gift.

.02 Section 20.2031-1(b) of the Estate Tax Regulations (section 81.10 of the Estate Tax Regulations 105) and section 25.2512-1 of the Gift Tax Regulations (section 86.19 of Gift Tax Regulations 108) define fair market value, in effect, as the price at which the property would change hands between a willing buyer and a willing seller when the former is not under any compulsion to buy and the latter is not under any compulsion to sell, both parties having reasonable knowledge of relevant facts. Court decisions frequently state in addition that the hypothetical buyer and seller are assumed to be able, as well as willing, to trade and to be well informed about the property and concerning the market for such property.

.03 Closely held corporations are those corporations the shares of which are owned by a relatively limited number of stockholders. Often the entire stock issue is held by one family. The result of this situation is that little, if any, trading in the shares takes place. There is,

therefore, no established market for the stock and such sales as occur at irregular intervals seldom reflect all of the elements of a representative transaction as defined by the term "fair market value."

Section 3: Approach to Valuation

.01   A determination of fair market value, being a question of fact, will depend upon the circumstances in each case. No formula can be devised that will be generally applicable to the multitude of different valuation issues arising in estate and gift tax cases. Often, an appraiser will find wide differences of opinion as to the fair market value of a particular stock. In resolving such differences, he should maintain a reasonable attitude in recognition of the fact that valuation is not an exact science. A sound valuation will be based upon all the relevant facts, but the elements of common sense, informed judgment, and reasonableness must enter into the process of weighing those facts and determining their aggregate significance.

.02   The fair market value of specific shares of stock will vary as general economic conditions change from "normal" to "boom" or "depression," that is, according to the degree of optimism or pessimism with which the investing public regards the future at the required date of appraisal. Uncertainty as to the stability or continuity of the future income from a property decreases its value by increasing the risk of loss of earnings and value in the future. The value of shares of stock of a company with very uncertain future prospects is highly speculative. The appraiser must exercise his judgment as to the degree of risk attaching to the business of the corporation which issued the stock, but that judgment must be related to all of the other factors affecting value.

.03   Valuation of securities is, in essence, a prophesy as to the future and must be based on facts available at the required date of appraisal. As a generalization, the prices of stocks which are traded in volume in a free and active market by informed persons best reflect the consensus of the investing public as to what the future holds for the corporations and industries represented. When a stock is closely held, is traded infrequently, or is traded in an erratic market, some other measure of value must be used. In many instances, the next best measure may be found in the prices at which the stocks of companies engaged in the same or a similar line of business are selling in a free and open market.

Section 4: Factors to Consider

.01   It is advisable to emphasize that in the valuation of the stock of closely held corporations or the stock of corporations where market quotations are either lacking or too scarce to be recognized, all available financial data, as well as all relevant factors affecting the fair market value, should be considered. The following factors, although not all-inclusive, are fundamental and require careful analysis in each case:

- The nature of the business and the history of the enterprise from its inception
- The economic outlook in general and the condition and outlook of the specific industry in particular
- The book value of the stock and the financial condition of the business
- The earning capacity of the company

- The dividend-paying capacity
- Whether or not the enterprise has goodwill or other intangible value
- Sales of the stock and the size of the block of stock to be valued
- The market price of stocks of corporations engaged in the same or a similar line of business having their stocks actively traded in a free and open market, either on an exchange or over-the-counter

.02   The following is a brief discussion of each of the foregoing factors:

- The history of a corporate enterprise will show its past stability or instability, its growth or lack of growth, the diversity or lack of diversity of its operations, and other facts needed to form an opinion of the degree of risk involved in the business. For an enterprise which changed its form of organization but carried on the same or closely similar operations of its predecessor, the history of the former enterprise should be considered. The detail to be considered should increase with approach to the required date of appraisal, since recent events are of greatest help in predicting the future; but a study of gross and net income, and of dividends covering a long prior period, is highly desirable. The history to be studied should include, but need not be limited to, the nature of the business, its products or services, its operating and investment assets, capital structure, plant facilities, sales records and management, all of which should be considered as of the date of the appraisal, with due regard for recent significant changes. Events of the past that are unlikely to recur in the future should be discounted, since value has a close relation to future expectancy.
- A sound appraisal of a closely held stock must consider current and prospective economic conditions as of the date of appraisal, both in the national economy and in the industry or industries with which the corporation is allied. It is important to know that the company is more or less successful than its competitors in the same industry, or that it is maintaining a stable position with respect to competitors. Equal or even greater significance may attach to the ability of the industry with which the company is allied to compete with other industries. Prospective competition which has not been a factor in prior years should be given careful attention. For example, high profits due to the novelty of its product and the lack of competition often lead to increasing competition. The public's appraisal of the future prospects of competitive industries or of competitors within an industry may be indicated by price trends in the markets for commodities and for securities. The loss of the manager of a so-called "one-man" business may have a depressing effect upon the value of the stock of such business, particularly if there is a lack of trained personnel capable of succeeding to the management of the enterprise. In valuing the stock of this type of business, therefore, the effect of the loss of the manager on the future expectancy of the business, and the absence of management-succession potentialities are pertinent factors to be taken into consideration. On the other hand, there may be factors which offset, in whole or in part, the loss of the manager's services. For instance, the nature of the business and of its assets may be such that they will not be impaired by the loss of the manager. Furthermore, the loss may be adequately covered by life insurance, or competent management might be employed on the basis of the consideration paid for the former manager's services. These, or other offsetting factors, if found to exist, should be carefully weighed against the loss of the manager's services in valuing the stock of the enterprise.

- Balance sheets should be obtained, preferably in the form of comparative annual statements for two or more years immediately preceding the date of appraisal, together with a balance sheet at the end of the month preceding that date, if corporate accounting will permit. Any balance sheet descriptions that are not self-explanatory, and balance sheet items comprehending diverse assets or liabilities, should be clarified in essential detail by supporting supplemental schedules. These statements usually will disclose to the appraiser (1) liquid position (ratio of current assets to current liabilities); (2) gross and net book value of principal classes of fixed assets; (3) working capital; (4) long-term indebtedness; (5) capital structure; and (6) net worth. Consideration also should be given to any assets not essential to the operation of the business, such as investments in securities, real estate, etc. In general, such nonoperating assets will command a lower rate of return than do the operating assets, although in exceptional cases the reverse may be true. In computing the book value per share of stock, assets of the investment type should be revalued on the basis of their market price and the book value adjusted accordingly. Comparison of the company's balance sheets over several years may reveal, among other facts, such developments as the acquisition of additional production facilities or subsidiary companies, improvement in financial position, and details as to recapitalizations and other changes in the capital structure of the corporation. If the corporation has more than one class of stock outstanding, the charter or certificate of incorporation should be examined to ascertain the explicit rights and privileges of the various stock issues including: (1) voting powers, (2) preference as to dividends, and (3)preference as to assets in the event of liquidation.

- Detailed profit-and-loss statements should be obtained and considered for a representative period immediately prior to the required date of appraisal, preferably five or more years. Such statements should show (1) gross income by principal items; (2) principal deductions from gross income including major prior items of operating expenses, interest and other expense on each item of long-term debt, depreciation and depletion if such deductions are made, officers' salaries, in total if they appear to be reasonable or in detail if they seem to be excessive, contributions (whether or not deductible for tax purposes) that the nature of its business and its community position require the corporation to make, and taxes by principal items, including income and excess profits taxes; (3) net income available for dividends; (4) rates and amounts of dividends paid on each class of stock; (5) remaining amount carried to surplus; and (6) adjustments to, and reconciliation with, surplus as stated on the balance sheet. With profit and loss statements of this character available, the appraiser should be able to separate recurrent from nonrecurrent items of income and expense, to distinguish between operating income and investment income, and to ascertain whether or not any line of business in which the company is engaged is operated consistently at a loss and might be abandoned with benefit to the company. The percentage of earnings retained for business expansion should be noted when dividend-paying capacity is considered. Potential future income is a major factor in many valuations of closely held stocks, and all information concerning past income which will be helpful in predicting the future should be secured. Prior earnings records usually are the most reliable guide as to the future expectancy, but resorting to arbitrary five- or ten-year averages without regard to current trends or future prospects will not produce a realistic valuation. If, for instance, a record of progressively increasing or decreasing net income is found, then greater weight may be accorded the most recent years' profits in estimating earning power. It will be helpful, in judging risk and the extent to which a business is a marginal operator, to consider deductions from income and net income in terms of percentage of sales. Major categories of cost and expense to be so analyzed include the consumption of raw materials and supplies in the case of manufacturers, processors, and fabricators; the cost of purchased merchandise in the case of merchants; utility services; insurance; taxes; depletion or depreciation; and interest.

- Primary consideration should be given to the dividend-paying capacity of the company rather than to dividends actually paid in the past. Recognition must be given to the necessity of retaining a reasonable portion of profits in a company to meet competition. Dividend-paying capacity is a factor that must be considered in an appraisal, but dividends actually paid in the past may not have any relation to dividend-paying capacity. Specifically, the dividends paid by a closely held family company may be measured by the income needs of the stockholders or by their desire to avoid taxes on dividend receipts, instead of by the ability of the company to pay dividends. Where an actual or effective controlling interest in a corporation is to be valued, the dividend factor is not a material element, since the payment of such dividends is discretionary with the controlling stockholders. The individual or group in control can substitute salaries and bonuses for dividends, thus reducing net income and understating the dividend-paying capacity of the company. It follows, therefore, that dividends are less reliable criteria of fair market value than other applicable factors.

- In the final analysis, goodwill is based upon earning capacity. The presence of goodwill and its value, therefore, rests upon the excess of net earnings over and above a fair return on the net tangible assets. While the element of goodwill may be based primarily on earnings, such factors as the prestige and renown of the business, the ownership of a trade or brand name, and a record of successful operation over a prolonged period in a particular locality, also may furnish support for the inclusion of intangible value. In some instances it may not be possible to make a separate appraisal of the tangible and intangible assets of the business. The enterprise has a value as an entity. Whatever intangible value there is, which is supportable by the facts, may be measured by the amount by which the appraised value of the tangible assets exceeds the net book value of such assets.

- Sales of stock of a closely held corporation should be carefully investigated to determine whether they represent transactions at arm's length. Forced or distress sales do not ordinarily reflect fair market value nor do isolated sales in small amounts necessarily control as the measure of value. This is especially true in the valuation of a controlling interest in a corporation. Since, in the case of closely held stocks, no prevailing market prices are available, there is no basis for making an adjustment for blockage. It follows, therefore, that such stocks should be valued upon a consideration of all the evidence affecting the fair market value. The size of the block of stock itself is a relevant factor to be considered. Although it is true that a minority interest in an unlisted corporation's stock is more difficult to sell than a similar block of listed stock, it is equally true that control of a corporation, either actual or in effect, representing as it does an added element of value, may justify a higher value for a specific block of stock.

- Section 2031(b) of the Code states, in effect, that in valuing unlisted securities, the value of stock or securities of corporations engaged in the same or a similar line of business which are listed on an exchange should be taken into consideration along with all other factors. An important consideration is that the corporations to be used for comparisons have capital stocks that are actively traded by the public. In accordance with section 2031(b) of the Code, stocks listed on an exchange are to be considered first. However, if sufficient comparable companies whose stocks are listed on an exchange cannot be found, other comparable companies that have stocks actively traded on the over-the-counter market also may be used. The essential factor is that whether the stocks are sold on an exchange or over-the-counter there is evidence of an active, free public market for the stock as of the valuation date. In selecting corporations for comparative purposes, care should be taken to use only comparable companies. Although the only restrictive requirement as to comparable corporations specified in the statute is that their lines of business be the same or similar, yet it is obvious that consideration must be given to other relevant factors in order that the most valid comparison possible will be obtained. For illustration, a corporation having one or more issues of preferred stock, bonds or debentures in addition to its common stock should not be considered to be directly comparable to one having only common stock outstanding. In like manner, a company with a declining business and decreasing markets is not comparable to one with a record of current progress and market expansion.

Section 5: Weight to Be Accorded Various Factors

The valuation of closely held corporate stock entails the consideration of all relevant factors as stated in section 4. Depending on the circumstances in each case, certain factors may carry more weight than others because of the nature of the company's business. To illustrate:

- Earnings may be the most important criterion of value in some cases, whereas asset value will receive primary consideration in others. In general, the appraiser will accord primary consideration to earnings when valuing stocks of companies which sell products or services to the public; conversely, in the investment or holding type of company, the appraiser may accord the greatest weight to the assets underlying the security to be valued.
- The value of the stock of a closely held investment or real estate holding company, whether or not family owned, is closely related to the value of the assets underlying the stock. For companies of this type the appraiser should determine the fair market values of the assets of the company. Operating expenses of such a company and the cost of liquidating it, if any, merit consideration when appraising the relative values of the stock and the underlying assets. The market values of the underlying assets give due weight to potential earnings and dividends of the particular items of property underlying the stock, capitalized at rates deemed proper by the investing public at the date of appraisal. A current appraisal by the investing public should be superior to the retrospective opinion of an individual. For these reasons, adjusted net worth should be accorded greater weight in valuing the stock of a closely held investment or real estate holding company, whether or not family owned, than any of the other customary yardsticks of appraisal, such as earnings and dividend-paying capacity.

Section 6: Capitalization Rates

In the application of certain fundamental valuation factors, such as earnings and dividends, it is necessary to capitalize the average or current results at some appropriate rate. A determination of the proper capitalization rate presents one of the most difficult problems in valuation. That there is no ready or simple solution will become apparent by a cursory check of the rates of return and dividend yields in terms of the selling prices of corporate shares listed on the major exchanges of the country. Wide variations will be found even for companies in the same industry. Moreover, the ratio will fluctuate from year to year depending upon economic conditions. Thus, no standard tables of capitalization rates applicable to closely held corporations can be formulated. Among the more important factors to be taken into consideration in deciding upon a capitalization rate in a particular case are: (1) the nature of the business; (2) the risk involved; and (3) the stability or irregularity of earnings.

Section 7: Average of Factors

Because valuations cannot be made on the basis of a prescribed formula, there is no means whereby the various applicable factors in a particular case can be assigned mathematical weights in deriving the fair market value. For this reason, no useful purpose is served by taking an average of several factors (for example, book value, capitalized earnings and capitalized dividends) and basing the valuation on the result. Such a process excludes active consideration of other pertinent factors, and the end result cannot be supported by a realistic application of the significant facts in the case except by mere chance.

Section 8: Restrictive Agreements

Frequently, in the valuation of closely held stock for estate and gift tax purposes, it will be found that the stock is subject to an agreement restricting its sale or transfer. Where shares of stock were acquired by a decedent subject to an option reserved by the issuing corporation to repurchase at a certain price, the option price is usually accepted as the fair market value for estate tax purposes. See Rev. Rul. 54-76, C.B. 1954-1, 194. However, in such case the option price is not determinative of fair market value for gift tax purposes. Where the option, or buy and sell agreement, is the result of voluntary action by the stockholders and is binding during the life as well as at the death of the stockholders, such agreement may or may not, depending upon the circumstances of each case, fix the value for estate tax purposes. However, such agreement is a factor to be considered, with other relevant factors, in determining fair market value. Where the stockholder is free to dispose of his shares during life and the option is to become effective only upon his death, the fair market value is not limited to the option price. It is always necessary to consider the relationship of the parties, the relative number of shares held by the decedent, and other material facts, to determine whether the agreement represents a bona fide business arrangement or is a device to pass the decedent's shares to the natural objects of his bounty for less than an adequate and full consideration in money or money's worth. In this connection see Rev. Rul. 157 C.B. 1953-2, 255, and Rev. Rul. 189, C.B. 1953-2,294.

Section 9: Effect on Other Documents

Revenue Ruling 54-77, C.B. 1954-1, 187, is hereby superseded.

REV. RUL. 65-192

Summary

Shortly after Rev. Rul. 59-60 was issued in 1959, the Service began issuing follow-on Revenue Rulings and Private Rulings that expanded its applicability and explained its limits. Revenue Ruling 65-192 extends Rev. Rul. 59-60 to cover income and other tax valuation issues, thereby making Rev. Rul. 59-60 controlling for all tax purposes.

Two earlier rulings, A.R.M. 34 and A.R.M. 68, both issued in 1920, were severely limited. These earlier rulings had adopted a formulaic approach towards valuation for income tax purposes. Rev. Rul. 59-60 rejected this for estate and gift tax purposes, and Rev. Rul. 65-192 limited its application to valuation of intangible assets.

Text

Section 1001. Determination of Amount of and Recognition of Gain or Loss

26 CFR 1.1001-1: Computation of gain or loss.

1965-2 C.B. 259; 1965 IRB LEXIS 80; REV. RUL. 65-192

July 1965. The general approach, methods, and factors outlined in Revenue Ruling 59-60, C.B. 1959-1, 237, for use in valuing closely held corporate stocks for estate and gift tax purposes are equally applicable to valuations thereof for income and other tax purposes and also in determinations of the fair market values of business interests of any type and of intangible assets for all tax purposes.

The formula approach set forth in A.R.M. 34, C.B. 2, 31 (1920), and A.R.M. 68, C.B. 3, 43 (1920), has no valid application in determinations of the fair market values of corporate stocks or of business interests, unless it is necessary to value the intangible assets of the corporation or the intangible assets included in the business interest. The formula approach may be used in determining the fair market values of intangible assets only if there is no better basis therefore available. In applying the formula, the average earnings period and the capitalization rates are dependent upon the facts and circumstances pertinent thereto in such case.

Section 1: Purpose

The purpose of this Revenue Ruling is to furnish information and guidance as to the usage to be made of suggested methods for determining the value as of March 1, 1913, or of any other date, of intangible assets and to identify those areas where a valuation formula set forth in A.R.M. 34, C.B. 2, 31 (1920), as modified by A.R.M. 68, C.B. 3, 43 (1920), both quoted in full below, should and should not be applied. Since it appears that such formula has been applied to many valuation issues for which it was never intended, the Internal Revenue Service reindicates its limited application.

Section 2: Background

A.R.M. 34 was issued in 1920 for the purpose of providing suggested formulas for determining the amount of March 1, 1913, intangible asset value lost by breweries and other businesses connected with the distilling industry, as a result of the passage of the 18th Amendment to the Constitution of the United States. A.R.M. 68 was issued later in the same year and contained a minor revision of the original ruling so that its third formula would be applied in accordance with its purpose and intent.

Section 3: Statement of Position

.01 Although the formulas and approach contained in A.R.M. 34, were specifically aimed at the valuation of intangible assets of distilling and related companies as of March 1, 1913, the last two paragraphs of the ruling seemingly broaden it to make its third formula applicable to almost any kind of enterprise. The final sentences, however, limit the purpose of such formula by stating that "In * * * all of the cases the effort should be to determine what net earnings a purchaser of a business on March 1, 1913, might reasonably have expected to receive from it, * * *," and by providing certain checks and alternatives. Also, both A.R.M. 34 and A.R.M. 68 expressly stated that such formula was merely a rule for guidance and not controlling in the presence of "better evidence" in determining the value of intangible assets. Furthermore, T.B.R. 57, C.B. 1, 40 (1919), relating to the meaning of "fair market value" of property received in exchange for other property, which was published before A.R.M. 34 and A.R.M. 68 and has not been revoked, set forth general principles of valuation that are consistent with Revenue Ruling 59-60, C.B. 1959-1, 237. Moreover, in S.M. 1609, C.B. III-1, 48 (1924) it was stated that "The method suggested in A.R.M. 34 for determining the value of intangibles is * * * controlling only in the absence of better evidence." As said in *North American Service Co., Inc. v. Commissioner*, 33 T.C. 677, 694 (1960), acquiescence, C.B. 1960-2, 6, "an A.R.M. 34 computation would not be conclusive of the existence and value of good will if better evidence were available * * *."

.02 Revenue Ruling 59-60 sets forth the proper approach to use in the valuation of closely held corporate stocks for estate and gift tax purposes. That ruling contains the statement that no formula can be devised that will be generally applicable to the multitude of different valuation issues. It also contains a discussion of intangible value in closely held corporations and some of the elements which may support such value in a given business.

Section 4: Delineation of Areas in Which Suggested Methods Will Be Effective

.01 The general approach, methods, and factors outlined in Revenue Ruling 59-60 are equally applicable to valuations of corporate stocks for income and other tax purposes as well as for estate and gift tax purposes. They apply also to problems involving the determination of the fair market value of business interests of any type, including partnerships, proprietorships, etc., and of intangible assets for all tax purposes.

.02 Valuation, especially where earning power is an important factor, is in essence a process requiring the exercise of informed judgment and common sense. Thus, the suggested formula approach set forth in A.R.M. 34, has no valid application in determinations

of the fair market value of corporate stocks or of business interests unless it is necessary to value the intangible assets of the corporation or the intangible assets included in the business interest. The formula approach may be used in determining the fair market values of intangible assets only if there is no better basis therefor available. In applying the formula, the average earnings period and the capitalization rates are dependent upon the facts and circumstances pertinent thereto in each case. See *John Q. Shunk et al. v. Commissioner*, 10 T.C. 293, 304-5 (1948), acquiescence, C.B. 1948-1, 3, affirmed 173 Fed. (2d) 747 (1949); *Ushco Manufacturing Co., Inc. v. Commissioner*, Tax Court Memorandum Opinion entered March 10, 1945, affirmed 175 Fed. (2d) 821 (1945); and *White & Wells Co. v. Commissioner*, 19 B.T.A. 416, nonacquiescence C.B. IX-2, 87 (1930), reversed and remanded 50 Fed. (2d) 120 (1931).

Section 5: Quotation of A.R.M. 34

For convenience, A.R.M. 34 reads as follows:

The Committee has considered the question of providing some practical formula for determining value as of March 1, 1913, or of any other date, which might be considered as applying to intangible assets, but finds itself unable to lay down any specific rule of guidance for determining the value of intangibles which would be applicable in all cases and under all circumstances. Where there is no established market to serve as a guide the question of value, even of tangible assets, is one largely of judgment and opinion, and the same thing is even more true of intangible assets such as good will, trade-marks, trade brands, etc. However, there are several methods of reaching a conclusion as to the value of intangibles which the Committee suggests may be utilized broadly in passing upon questions of valuation, not to be regarded as controlling, however, if better evidence is presented in any specific case.

Where deduction is claimed for obsolescence or loss of good will or trademarks, the burden of proof is primarily upon the taxpayer to show the value of such good will or trademarks on March 1, 1913. Of course, if good will or trade-marks have been acquired for cash or other valuable considerations subsequent to March 1, 1913, the measure of loss will be determined by the amount of cash or value of other considerations paid therefor, and no deduction will be allowed for the value of good will or trade-marks built up by the taxpayer since March 1, 1913. The following suggestions are made, therefore, merely as suggestions for checks upon the soundness and validity of the taxpayers' claims. No obsolescence or loss with respect to good will should be allowed except in cases of actual disposition of the asset or abandonment of the business.

In the first place, it is recognized that in numerous instances it has been the practice of distillers and wholesale liquor dealers to put out under well-known and popular brands only so much goods as could be marketed without affecting the established market price therefor and to sell other goods of the same identical manufacture, age, and character under other brands, or under no brand at all, at figures very much below those which the well-known brands commanded. In such cases the difference between the price at which whisky was sold under a given brand name and also under another brand name, or under no brand, multiplied by the number of units sold during a given year gives an accurate determination of the amount of profit attributable to that brand during that year, and where this practice is continued for a long enough period to show that this amount was fairly constant and regular and might be expected to yield annually that average profit, by capitalizing this earning at the rate, say, of 20 per cent, the value of the brand is fairly well established.

Another method is to compare the volume of business done under the trade-mark or brand under consideration and profits made, or by the business whose goodwill is under consideration, with the similar volume of business and profit made in other cases where good will or trade-marks have been actually sold for cash, recognizing as the value of the first the same proportion of the selling price of the second, as the profits of the first attributable to brands or good will, is of the similar profits of the second.

The third method and possibly the one which will most frequently have to be applied as a check in the absence of data necessary for the application of the preceding ones, is to allow out of average earnings over a period of years prior to March 1, 1913, preferably not less than five years, a return of 10 per cent upon the average tangible assets for the period. The surplus earnings will then be the average amount available for return upon the value of the intangible assets, and it is the opinion of the Committee that this return should be capitalized upon the basis of not more than five years' purchase -that is to say, five times the amount available as return from intangibles should be the value of the intangibles.

In view of the hazards of the business, the changes in popular tastes, and the difficulties in preventing imitation or counterfeiting of popular brands affecting the sales of the genuine goods, the Committee is of the opinion that the figure given of 20 per cent return on intangibles is not unreasonable, and it recommends that no higher figure than that be attached in any case to intangibles without a very clear and adequate showing that the value of the intangibles was in fact greater than would be reached by applying this formula.

The foregoing is intended to apply particularly to businesses put out of existence by the prohibition law, but will be equally applicable so far as the third formula is concerned, to other businesses of a more or less hazardous nature. In the case, however, of valuation of good will of a business which consists of the manufacture or sale of standard articles of every-day necessity not subject to violent fluctuations and where the hazard is not so great, the Committee is of the opinion that the figure for determination of the return on tangible assets might be reduced from 10 to 8 or 9 per cent, and that the percentage for capitalization of the return upon intangibles might be reduced from 20 to 15 per cent.

In any or all of the cases the effort should be to determine what net earnings a purchaser of a business on March 1, 1943, might reasonably have expected to receive from it, and therefore a representative period should be used for averaging actual earnings, eliminating any year in which there were extraordinary factors affecting earnings either way. Also, in the case of the sale of good will of a going business the percentage rate of capitalization of earnings applicable to good will shown by the amount actually paid for the business should be used as a check against the determination of goodwill value as of March 1, 1913, and if the good will is sold upon the basis of capitalization of earnings less than the figures above indicated as the ones ordinarily to be adopted, the same percentage should be used in figuring value as of March 1, 1913.

Section 6: Quotation of A.R.M. 68

Also for convenience, A.R.M. 68 reads as follows:

The Committee is in receipt of a request for advice as to whether under A.R.M. 34 the 10 per cent upon tangible assets is to be applied only to the net tangible assets or to all tangible assets on the books of the corporation, regardless of any outstanding obligations.

The Committee, in the memorandum in question, undertook to lay down a rule for guidance in the absence of better evidence in determining the value as of March 1, 1913, of good will, and held that in determining such value, income over an average period in excess of an amount sufficient to return 10 per cent upon tangible assets should be capitalized at 20 per cent. Manifestly, since the effort is to determine the value of the good will, and therefore the true net worth of the taxpayer as of March 1, 1913, the 10 per cent should be applied only to the tangible assets entering into net worth, including accounts and bills receivable in excess of accounts and bills payable.

In other words, the purpose and intent are to provide for a return to the taxpayer of 10 per cent upon so much of his investment as is represented by tangible assets and to capitalize the excess of earnings over the amount necessary to provide such return, at 20 per cent.

Section 7: Effect on Other Documents

Although the limited application of A.R.M. 34 and A.R.M. 68 is reindicated in this Revenue Ruling, the principles enunciated in those rulings are not thereby affected.

REV. RUL. 65-193

Summary

Revenue Ruling 65-193 repaired a minor gaffe in Rev. Rul. 59-60. In Rev. Rul. 59-60 the Service had attempted to devise a categorical rule for valuation of the intangible assets of a business, adopting the accounting rule for measuring goodwill: The value of goodwill is equal to the fair market value of the business assets less the net book value of business assets. This rule proved so difficult to apply in practice that, in Rev. Rul. 65-193, the Service withdrew it and declined to use any one standard for intangible valuation.

Text

Section 2031. Definition of Gross Estate

26 CFR 20.2031-2: Valuation of stocks and bonds. (Also Sections 1001, 2512; 1.1001-1, 25.2512-2.)

1965-2 C.B. 370; 1965 IRB LEXIS 89; REV. RUL. 65-193

July 1965. Revenue Ruling 59-60, C.B. 1959-1, 237, is hereby modified to delete the statements, contained therein at section 4.02(f), that "In some instances it may not be possible to make a separate appraisal of the tangible and intangible assets of the business. The enterprise has a value as an entity. Whatever intangible value there is, which is supportable by the facts, may be measured by the amount by which the appraised value of the tangible assets exceeds the net book value of such assets."

The instances where it is not possible to make a separate appraisal of the tangible and intangible assets of a business are rare and each case varies from the other. No rule can be devised which will be generally applicable to such cases.

Other than this modification, Revenue Ruling 59-60 continues in full force and effect. See Rev. Rul. 65-192, page 259, this Bulletin.

REV. PROC. 66-49

Summary

Revenue Procedure 66-49 applies the standard of Rev. Rul. 59-60 in the context of donated property, where the donor seeks to deduct the value of the property donated from his or her taxes. This presents the Service with a problem converse to that addressed by Rev. Rul. 59-60, where the main concern is that the taxpayer will minimize the value of the item so as to minimize taxes. In the context of donated property, the taxpayer seeks to do the opposite and inflate the value of the property, thereby maximizing the deduction.

Despite the opposing goals represented by these two valuation contexts, Rev. Rul. 66-49 legitimated the principles of Rev. Rul. 59-60 while applying it in the context of donated property.

Text

26 CFR 601.602: Forms and instructions. (Also Part I, Section 170; 26 CFR 1.170-1.)

1966-2 C.B. 1257; 1966 IRB LEXIS 213; REV. PROC. 66-49

July 1966. A procedure to be used as a guideline by all persons making appraisals of donated property for federal income tax purposes.

Section 1: Purpose

The purpose of this procedure is to provide information and guidelines for taxpayers, individual appraisers, and valuation groups relative to appraisals of contributed property for federal income tax purposes. The procedures outlined are applicable to all types of noncash property for which an appraisal is required such as real property, tangible or intangible personal property, and securities. These procedures are also appropriate for unique properties such as art objects, literary manuscripts, antiques, etc., with respect to which the determination of value often is more difficult.

Section 2: Law and Regulations

.01   Numerous sections of the Internal Revenue Code of 1954, as amended, give rise to a determination of value for federal tax purposes; however, the significant section for purposes of this Revenue Procedure is section 170, Charitable, Etc., Contributions and Gifts.

.02   Value is defined in section 1.170-1(c) of the Income Tax Regulations as follows:

> * * *. *The fair market value is the price at which the property would change hands between a willing buyer and a willing seller, neither being under any compulsion to buy or sell and both having reasonable knowledge of relevant facts.* * * *

.03   This section further provides that:

> * * *. *If the contribution is made in property of a type which the taxpayer sells in the course of his business, the fair market value is the price which the taxpayer would have received if he had sold the contributed property in the lowest usual market in which he customarily sells, at the time and place of contribution (and in the case of a contribution of goods in quantity, in the quantity contributed).* * * *

.04   As to the measure of proof in determining the fair market value, all factors bearing on value are relevant including, where pertinent, the cost, or selling price of the item, sales of comparable properties, cost of reproduction, opinion evidence and appraisals. Fair market value depends upon value in the market and not on intrinsic worth.

.05   The cost or actual selling price of an item within a reasonable time before or after the valuation date may be the best evidence of its fair market value. Before such information is taken into account, it must be ascertained that the transaction was at arm's length and that the parties were fully informed as to all relevant facts. Absent such evidence, even the sales price of the item in question will not be persuasive.

.06 Sales of similar properties are often given probative weight by the courts in establishing fair market value. The weight to be given such evidence will be affected by the degree of similarity to the property under appraisal and the proximity of the date of sale to the valuation date.

.07 With respect to reproductive cost as a measure of fair market value, it must be shown that there is a probative correlation between the cost of reproduction and fair market value. Frequently, reproductive cost will be in excess of the fair market value.

.08 Generally, the weight to be given to opinion evidence depends on its origin and the thoroughness with which it is supported by experience and facts. It is only where expert opinion is supported by facts having strong probative value, that the opinion testimony will in itself be given appropriate weight. The underlying facts must corroborate the opinion; otherwise such opinion will be discounted or disregarded.

.09 The weight to be accorded any appraisal made either at or after the valuation date will depend largely upon the competence and knowledge of the appraiser with respect to the property and the market for such property.

Section 3: Appraisal Format

.01 When it becomes necessary to secure an appraisal in order to determine the values of items for federal income tax purposes, such appraisals should be obtained from qualified and reputable sources, and the appraisal report should accompany the return when it is filed. The more complete the information filed with a tax return the more unlikely it will be that the Internal Revenue Service will find it necessary to question items on it. Thus, when reporting a deduction for charitable contributions on an income tax return, it will facilitate the review and the acceptance of the returned values if any appraisals which have been secured are furnished. The above-mentioned regulations prescribe that support of values claimed should be submitted and a properly prepared appraisal by a person qualified to make such an appraisal may well constitute the necessary substantiation. In this respect, it is not intended that all value determinations be supported by formal written appraisals as outlined in detail below. This is particularly applicable to minor items of property or where the value of the property is easily ascertainable by methods other than appraisal.

.02 In general, an appraisal report should contain at least the following:

- A summary of the appraiser's qualifications
- A statement of the value and the appraiser's definition of the value he has obtained
- The bases upon which the appraisal was made, including any restrictions, understandings, or covenants limiting the use or disposition of the property
- The date as of which the property was valued
- The signature of the appraiser and the date the appraisal was made

.03 An example of the kind of data that should be contained in a typical appraisal is included below. This relates to the valuation of art objects, but a similar detailed breakdown

can be outlined for any type of property. Appraisals of art objects, paintings in particular, should include:

- A complete description of the object, indicating the size, the subject matter, the medium, the name of the artist, approximate date created, the interest transferred, etc.
- The cost, date, and manner of acquisition
- A history of the item including proof of authenticity such as a certificate of authentication if such exists
- A photograph of a size and quality fully identifying the subject matter, preferably a 10″ × 12″ or larger print
- A statement of the factors upon which the appraisal was based, such as:
  - Sales of other works by the same artist particularly on or around the valuation date
  - Quoted prices in dealers' catalogs of the artist's works or of other artists of comparable stature
  - The economic state of the art market at or around the time of valuation, particularly with respect to the specific property
  - A record of any exhibitions at which the particular art object had been displayed
  - A statement as to the standing of the artist in his profession and in the particular school or time period

.04   Although an appraisal report meets these requirements, the Internal Revenue Service is not relieved of the responsibility of reviewing appraisals to the extent deemed necessary.

Section 4: Review of Valuation Appraisals

.01   While the Service is responsible for reviewing appraisals, it is not responsible for making appraisals; the burden of supporting the fair market value listed on a return is the taxpayer's. The Internal Revenue Service cannot accord recognition to any appraiser or group of appraisers from the standpoint of unquestioned acceptance of their appraisals. Furthermore, the Service cannot approve valuations or appraisals prior to the actual filing of the tax return to which the appraisal pertains and cannot issue advance rulings approving or disapproving such appraisals.

.02   In determining the acceptability of the claimed value of the donated property, the Service may either accept the value claimed based on information or appraisals submitted with the return or make its own determination as to the fair market value. In either instance, the Service may find it necessary to:

- Contact the taxpayer and ask for additional information
- Refer the valuation problem to a Service appraiser or valuation specialist
- Recommend that an independent appraiser be employed by the Service to appraise the asset in question (This latter course is frequently used by the Service when objects requiring appraisers of highly specialized experience and knowledge are involved.)

REV. RUL. 68-609

Summary

In 1968, the Service returned to the issue of applying Rev. Rul. 59-60 to income and other tax issues, specifically those involving intangible assets. Of particular concern was the odd position of Rev. Rul. 65-192, which adopted Rev. Rul. 59-60 for income tax purposes while leaving in effect old precedent using the formula approach rejected in Rev. Rul. 59-60.

In this Revenue Ruling, the Service returned to the topic and definitively outlined when the old formula approach should be applied to intangible asset valuation—almost never—and how Rev. Rul. 59-60 could be harmonized with A.R.M.'s 34 and 68. Rev. Rul. 68-609 supersedes A.R.M.'s 34 and 68, as well as Rev. Rul. 65-192.

Text

Prepared pursuant to Rev. Proc. 67-6, C.B. 1967-1, 576.

Section 1001. Determination of Amount of and Recognition of Gain or Loss

26 CFR 1.1001-1: Computation of gain or loss. (Also Section 167; 1.167(a)-3.) 1968-2 C.B. 327; 1968 IRB LEXIS 239; REV. RUL. 68-609

July 1968. The *formula* approach may be used in determining the fair market value of intangible assets of a business only if there is no better basis available for making the determination; A.R.M. 34, A.R.M. 68, O.D. 937, and Revenue Ruling 65-192 superseded.

The purpose of this Revenue Ruling is to update and restate, under the current statute and regulations, the currently outstanding portions of A.R.M. 34, C.B. 2, 31 (1920), A.R.M. 68, C.B. 3, 43 (1920), and O.D. 937, C.B. 4, 43(1921).

The question presented is whether the formula approach, the capitalization of earnings in excess of a fair rate of return on net tangible assets, may be used to determine the fair market value of the intangible assets of a business.

The formula approach may be stated as follows:

A percentage return on the average annual value of the tangible assets used in a business is determined, using a period of years (preferably not less than five) immediately prior to the valuation date. The amount of the percentage return on tangible assets, thus determined, is deducted from the average earnings of the business for such period and the remainder, if any, is considered to be the amount of the average annual earnings from the intangible assets of the business for the period. This amount (considered as the average annual earnings from intangibles), capitalized at a percentage of, say, 15 to 20 percent, is the value of the intangible assets of the business determined under the "formula" approach.

The percentage of return on the average annual value of the tangible assets used should be the percentage prevailing in the industry involved at the date of valuation, or (when the industry percentage is not available) a percentage of 8 to 10 percent may be used.

The 8 percent rate of return and the 15 percent rate of capitalization are applied to tangibles and intangibles, respectively, of businesses with a small risk factor and stable and regular earnings; the 10 percent rate of return and 20 percent rate of capitalization are applied to businesses in which the hazards of business are relatively high.

These rates are used as examples and are not appropriate in all cases. In applying the formula approach, the average earnings period and the capitalization rates are dependent upon the facts pertinent thereto in each case.

The past earnings to which the formula is applied should fairly reflect the probable future earnings. Ordinarily, the period should not be less than five years, and abnormal years, whether above or below the average, should be eliminated. If the business is a sole proprietorship or partnership, there should be deducted from the earnings of the business a reasonable amount for services performed by the owner or partners engaged in the business. See *Lloyd B. Sanderson Estate v. Commissioner*, 42 F.2d 160 (1930). Further, only the tangible assets entering into net worth, including accounts and bills receivable in excess of accounts and bills payable, are used for determining earnings on the tangible assets. Factors that influence the capitalization rate include (1) the nature of the business, (2) the risk involved, and (3) the stability or irregularity of earnings.

The formula approach should not be used if there is better evidence available from which the value of intangibles can be determined. If the assets of a going business are sold upon the basis of a rate of capitalization that can be substantiated as being realistic, though it is not within the range of figures indicated here as the ones ordinarily to be adopted, the same rate of capitalization should be used in determining the value of intangibles.

Accordingly, the formula approach may be used for determining the fair market value of intangible assets of a business only if there is no better basis therefore available.

See also Revenue Ruling 59-60, C.B. 1959-1, 237, as modified by Revenue Ruling 65-193, C.B. 1965-2, 370, which sets forth the proper approach to use in the valuation of closely-held corporate stocks for estate and gift tax purposes. The general approach, methods, and factors, outlined in Revenue Ruling 59-60, as modified, are equally applicable to valuations of corporate stocks for income and other tax purposes as well as for estate and gift tax purposes. They apply also to problems involving the determination of the fair market value of business interests of any type, including partnerships and proprietorships, and of intangible assets for all tax purposes.

A.R.M. 34, A.R.M. 68, and O.D. 937 are superseded, since the positions set forth therein are restated to the extent applicable under current law in this Revenue Ruling. Revenue Ruling 65-192, C.B. 1965-2, 259, which contained restatements of A.R.M. 34 and A.R.M. 68, is also superseded.

REV. PROC. 77-12

Summary

Revenue Procedure 77-12 reiterates Rev. Rul. 59-60's basic premise in the context of valuing assets acquired through an asset purchase or subsidiary merger. Unlike the usual situations involving Rev. Rul. 59-60, Rev. Proc. 77-12 contemplates the problem of assigning value to specific assets in a business that might be publicly traded.

Where assets are purchased for a lump sum, or a subsidiary is merged into its parent, the total value of the company must be allocated among its assets for basis purposes.[7] In making

---

[7]Basis is the amount at which an asset is carried on the books. This is important for tax purposes, as basis will determine the amount of tax that must be paid on transfer of the asset (tax rate × fair market value − basis).

this determination, Rev. Proc. 77-12 rejects any categorical formula but does suggest three acceptable methods for valuation: cost of reproduction, comparative sales, and income. They are only a guideline, however, in conformity with Rev. Rul. 59-60.

Text

26 CFR 601.105: Examination of returns and claims for refund, credit or abatement; determination of correct tax liability. (Also Part I, Section 334; 1.334-1.)

1977-1 C.B. 569; 1977 IRB LEXIS 712; REV. PROC. 77-12 January, 1977

Section 1: Purpose

The purpose of this Revenue Procedure is to set forth guidelines for use by taxpayers and Service personnel in making fair market value determinations in situations where a corporation purchases the assets of a business containing inventory items for a lump sum or where a corporation acquires assets including inventory items by the liquidation of a subsidiary pursuant to the provisions of section 332 of the Internal Revenue Code of 1954 and the basis of the inventory received in liquidation is determined under section 334(b)(2). These guidelines are designed to assist taxpayers and Service personnel in assigning a fair market value to such assets.

Section 2: Background

If the assets of a business are purchased for a lump sum, or if the stock of a corporation is purchased and that corporation is liquidated under section 332 of the Code and the basis is determined under section 334(b)(2), the purchase price must be allocated among the assets acquired to determine the basis of each of such assets. In making such determinations, it is necessary to determine the fair market value of any inventory items involved. This Revenue Procedure describes methods that may be used to determine the fair market value of inventory items.

In determining the fair market value of inventory under the situations set forth in this Revenue Procedure, the amount of inventory generally would be different from the amounts usually purchased. In addition, the goods in process and finished goods on hand must be considered in light of what a willing purchaser would pay and a willing seller would accept for the inventory at the various stages of completion, when the former is not under any compulsion to buy and the latter is not under any compulsion to sell, both parties having reasonable knowledge of relevant facts.

Section 3: Procedures for Determination of Fair Market Value

Three basic methods an appraiser may use to determine the fair market value of inventory are the cost of reproduction method, the comparative sales method, and the income method. All methods of valuation are based on one or a combination of these three methods.

.01 The cost of reproduction method generally provides a good indication of fair market value if inventory is readily replaceable in a wholesale or retail business, but generally should

not be used in establishing the fair market value of the finished goods of a manufacturing concern. In valuing a particular inventory under this method, however, other factors may be relevant. For example, a well balanced inventory available to fill customers' orders in the ordinary course of business may have a fair market value in excess of its cost of reproduction because it provides a continuity of business, whereas an inventory containing obsolete merchandise unsuitable for customers might have a fair market value of less than the cost of reproduction.

.02   The comparative sales method utilizes the actual or expected selling prices of finished goods to customers as a basis of determining fair market values of those finished goods. When the expected selling price is used as a basis for valuing finished goods inventory, consideration should be given to the time that would be required to dispose of this inventory, the expenses that would be expected to be incurred in such disposition, for example, all costs of disposition, applicable discounts (including those for quantity), sales commissions, and freight and shipping charges, and a profit commensurate with the amount of investment and degree of risk. It should also be recognized that the inventory to be valued may represent a larger quantity than the normal trading volume and the expected selling price can be a valid starting point only if customers' orders are filled in the ordinary course of business.

.03   The income method, when applied to fair market value determinations for finished goods, recognizes that finished goods must generally be valued in a profit motivated business. Since the amount of inventory may be large in relation to normal trading volume the highest and best use of the inventory will be to provide for a continuity of the marketing operation of the going business. Additionally, the finished goods inventory will usually provide the only source of revenue of an acquired business during the period it is being used to fill customers' orders. The historical financial data of an acquired company can be used to determine the amount that could be attributed to finished goods in order to pay all costs of disposition and provide a return on the investment during the period of disposition.

.04   The fair market value of work in process should be based on the same factors used to determine the fair market value of finished goods reduced by the expected costs of completion, including a reasonable profit allowance for the completion and selling effort of the acquiring corporation. In determining the fair market value of raw materials, the current costs of replacing the inventory in the quantities to be valued generally provides the most reliable standard.

Section 4: Conclusion

Because valuing inventory is an inherently factual determination, no rigid formulas can be applied. Consequently, the methods outlined above can only serve as guidelines for determining the fair market value of inventories.

REV. RUL. 77-287

Summary

In applying Rev. Rul. 59-60, the Service found it necessary to provide further guidance on the Ruling's use in the context of securities restricted from immediate resale under federal securities laws. If stock was restricted as to resale because it was, for example, part of a private offering exempt from regulation, taxpayers were unclear as to how the stock should be valued under Rev. Rul. 59-60. The problem was thorny, as other shares issued by the company were often tradable and had a fair market value. The issue was thus how to arrive at an appropriate value for the restricted stock. Revenue Ruling 77-287 was meant to clarify this.

Text

Section 2031. Definition of Gross Estate

26 CFR 20.2031-2: Valuation of stocks and bonds.

(Also Sections 170, 2032, 2512; 1.170A-1, 20.2032-1, 25.2512-2.)

1977-2 C.B. 319; 1977 IRB LEXIS 258; REV. RUL. 77-287

July 1977. Valuation of securities restricted from immediate resale. Guidelines are set forth for the valuation, for federal tax purposes, of securities that cannot be immediately resold because they are restricted from resale pursuant to federal securities laws; Rev. Rul. 59-60 amplified.

Section 1: Purpose

The purpose of this Revenue Ruling is to amplify Rev. Rul. 59-60, 1959-1 C.B.237, as modified by Rev. Rul. 65-193, 1965-2 C.B. 370, and to provide information and guidance to taxpayers, Internal Revenue Service personnel, and others concerned with the valuation, for federal tax purposes, of securities that cannot be immediately resold because they are restricted from resale pursuant to federal securities laws. This guidance is applicable only in cases where it is not inconsistent with valuation requirements of the Internal Revenue Code of 1954 or the regulations thereunder. Further, this ruling does not establish the time at which property shall be valued.

Section 2: Nature of the Problem

It frequently becomes necessary to establish the fair market value of stock that has not been registered for public trading when the issuing company has stock of the same class that is actively traded in one or more securities markets. The problem is to determine the difference in fair market value between the registered shares that are actively traded and the unregistered shares. This problem is often encountered in estate and gift tax cases. However, it is sometimes encountered when unregistered shares are issued in exchange for assets or the stock of an acquired company.

Section 3: Background and Definitions

.01   The Service outlined and reviewed in general the approach, methods, and factors to be considered in valuing shares of closely held corporate stock for estate and gift tax purposes in Rev. Rul. 59-60, as modified by Rev. Rul. 65-193. The provisions of Rev. Rul. 59-60, as mod-

ified, were extended to the valuation of corporate securities for income and other tax purposes by Rev. Rul.68-609, 1968-2 C.B. 327.

.02 There are several terms currently in use in the securities industry that denote restrictions imposed on the resale and transfer of certain securities. The term frequently used to describe these securities is "restricted securities," but they are sometimes referred to as "unregistered securities," "investment letter stock," "control stock," or "private placement stock." Frequently these terms are used interchangeably. They all indicate that these particular securities cannot lawfully be distributed to the general public until a registration statement relating to the corporation underlying the securities has been filed, and has also become effective under the rules promulgated and enforced by the United States Securities & Exchange Commission (Section) pursuant to the Federal securities laws. The following represents a more refined definition of each of the following terms along with two other terms: "exempted securities" and "exempted transactions."

- *Restricted securities* is defined in Rule 144 adopted by the Section as "securities acquired directly or indirectly from the issuer thereof, or from an affiliate of such issuer, in a transaction or chain of transactions not involving any public offering."

- *Unregistered securities* refers to those securities with respect to which a registration statement, providing full disclosure by the issuing corporation, has not been filed with the Section pursuant to the Securities Act of 1933. The registration statement is a condition precedent to a public distribution of securities in interstate commerce and is aimed at providing the prospective investor with a factual basis for sound judgment in making investment decisions.

- *Investment letter stock* and *letter stock* denote shares of stock that have been issued by a corporation without the benefit of filing a registration statement with the Section. Such stock is subject to resale and transfer restrictions set forth in a letter agreement requested by the issuer and signed by the buyer of the stock when the stock is delivered. Such stock may be found in the hands of either individual investors or institutional investors.

- *Control stock* indicates that the shares of stock have been held or are being held by an officer, director, or other person close to the management of the corporation. These persons are subject to certain requirements pursuant to Section rules upon resale of shares they own in such corporations.

- *Private placement stock* indicates that the stock has been placed with an institution or other investor who will presumably hold it for a long period and ultimately arrange to have the stock registered if it is to be offered to the general public. Such stock may or may not be subject to a letter agreement. Private placements of stock are exempted from the registration and prospectus provisions of the Securities Act of 1933.

- *Exempted securities* refers to those classes of securities that are expressly excluded from the registration provisions of the Securities Act of1933 and the distribution provisions of the Securities Exchange Act of 1934.

- *Exempted transactions* refers to certain sales or distributions of securities that do not involve a public offering and are excluded from the registration and prospectus provisions of the Securities Act of 1933 and distribution provisions of the Securities Exchange Act of 1934. The exempted status makes it unnecessary for issuers of securities to go through the registration process.

Section 4: Securities Industry Practice in Valuing Restricted Securities

.01   Investment Company Valuation Practices. The Investment Company Act of 1940 requires open-end investment companies to publish the valuation of their portfolio securities daily. Some of these companies have portfolios containing restricted securities, but also have unrestricted securities of the same class traded on a securities exchange. In recent years the number of restricted securities in such portfolios has increased. The following methods have been used by investment companies in the valuation of such restricted securities:

- Current market price of the unrestricted stock less a constant percentage discount based on purchase discount
- Current market price of unrestricted stock less a constant percentage discount different from purchase discount
- Current market price of the unrestricted stock less a discount amortized over a fixed period
- Current market price of the unrestricted stock
- Cost of the restricted stock until it is registered

The Section ruled in its Investment Company Act Release No. 5847, dated October 21, 1969, that there can be no automatic formula by which an investment company can value the restricted securities in its portfolios. Rather, the Section has determined that it is the responsibility of the board of directors of the particular investment company to determine the "fair value" of each issue of restricted securities in good faith.

.02   Institutional Investors Study. Pursuant to Congressional direction, the Section undertook an analysis of the purchases, sales, and holding of securities by financial institutions, in order to determine the effect of institutional activity upon the securities market. The study report was published in eight volumes in March 1971. The fifth volume provides an analysis of restricted securities and deals with such items as the characteristics of the restricted securities purchasers and issuers, the size of transactions (dollars and shares), the marketability discounts on different trading markets, and the resale provisions. This research project provides some guidance for measuring the discount in that it contains information, based on the actual experience of the marketplace, showing that, during the period surveyed (January 1, 1966, through June 30, 1969), the amount of discount allowed for restricted securities from the trading price of the unrestricted securities was generally related to the following four factors.

1. *Earnings.* Earnings and sales consistently have a significant influence on the size of restricted securities discounts according to the study. Earnings played the major part in establishing the ultimate discounts at which these stocks were sold from the current market price. Apparently earnings patterns, rather than sales patterns, determine the degree of risk of an investment.

2. *Sales.* The dollar amount of sales of issuers' securities also has a major influence on the amount of discount at which restricted securities sell from the current market price. The results of the study generally indicate that the companies with the lowest dollar amount of sales during the test period accounted for most of the transactions involving the highest discount rates, while they accounted for only a small portion of all transactions involving the lowest discount rates.

3. *Trading market.* The market in which publicly held securities are traded also reflects variances in the amount of discount that is applied to restricted securities purchases. According to the study, discount rates were greatest on restricted stocks with unrestricted counterparts traded over-the-counter, followed by those with unrestricted counterparts listed on the American Stock Exchange, while the discount rates for those stocks with unrestricted counterparts listed on the New York Stock Exchange were the smallest.

4. *Resale agreement provisions.* Resale agreement provisions often affect the size of the discount. The discount from the market price provides the main incentive for a potential buyer to acquire restricted securities. In judging the opportunity cost of freezing funds, the purchaser is analyzing two separate factors. The first factor is the risk that underlying value of the stock will change in a way that, absent the restrictive provisions, would have prompted a decision to sell. The second factor is the risk that the contemplated means of legally disposing of the stock may not materialize. From the seller's point of view, a discount is justified where the seller is relieved of the expenses of registration and public distribution, as well as of the risk that the market will adversely change before the offering is completed. The ultimate agreement between buyer and seller is a reflection of these and other considerations. Relative bargaining strengths of the parties to the agreement are major considerations that influence the resale terms and consequently the size of discounts in restricted securities transactions. Certain provisions are often found in agreements between buyers and sellers that affect the size of discounts at which restricted stocks are sold. Several such provisions follow, all of which, other than the third, would tend to reduce the size of the discount:

- A provision giving the buyer an option to "piggyback," that is, to register restricted stock with the next registration statement, if any, filed by the issuer with the Section;
- A provision giving the buyer an option to require registration at the seller's expense;
- A provision giving the buyer an option to require registration, but only at the buyer's own expense;
- A provision giving the buyer a right to receive continuous disclosure of information about the issuer from the seller;
- A provision giving the buyer a right to select one or more directors of the issuer;
- A provision giving the buyer an option to purchase additional shares of the issuer's stock; and
- A provision giving the buyer the right to have a greater voice in operations of the issuer if the issuer does not meet previously agreed upon operating standards. Institutional buyers can and often do obtain many of these rights and options from the sellers of restricted securities, and naturally, the more rights the buyer can acquire, the lower the buyer's risk is going to be, thereby reducing the buyer's discount as well. Smaller buyers may not be able to negotiate the large discounts or the rights and options that volume buyers are able to negotiate.

.03 Summary. A variety of methods have been used by the securities industry to value restricted securities. The Section rejects all automatic or mechanical solutions to the valuation of restricted securities, and prefers, in the case of the valuation of investment company portfolio stocks, to rely upon good faith valuations by the board of directors of each company. The study made by the Section found that restricted securities generally are issued at a discount from the market value of freely tradable securities.

Section 5: Facts and Circumstances Material to Valuation of Restricted Securities

.01   Frequently, a company has a class of stock that cannot be traded publicly. The reason such stock cannot be traded may arise from the securities statutes, as in the case of an "investment letter" restriction; it may arise from a corporate charter restriction, or perhaps from a trust agreement restriction. In such cases, certain documents and facts should be obtained for analysis.

.02   The following documents and facts, when used in conjunction with those discussed in Section 4 of Rev. Rul. 59-60, will be useful in the valuation of restricted securities:

- A copy of any declaration of trust, trust agreement, and any other agreements relating to the shares of restricted stock
- A copy of any document showing any offers to buy or sell or indications of interest in buying or selling the restricted shares
- The latest prospectus of the company
- Annual reports of the company for 3 to 5 years preceding the valuation date
- The trading prices and trading volume of the related class of traded securities 1 month preceding the valuation date, if they are traded on a stock exchange (if traded over-the-counter, prices may be obtained from the National Quotations Bureau, the National Association of Securities Dealers Automated Quotations [NASDAQ], or sometimes from broker-dealers making markets in the shares)
- The relationship of the parties to the agreements concerning the restricted stock, such as whether they are members of the immediate family or perhaps whether they are officers or directors of the company
- Whether the interest being valued represents a majority or minority ownership

Section 6: Weighing Facts and Circumstances Material to Restricted Stock Valuation

All relevant facts and circumstances that bear upon the worth of restricted stock, including those set forth above in the preceding Sections 4 and 5, and those set forth in Section 4 of Rev. Rul. 59-60, must be taken into account in arriving at the fair market value of such securities. Depending on the circumstances of each case, certain factors may carry more weight than others. To illustrate:

.01   Earnings, net assets, and net sales must be given primary consideration in arriving at an appropriate discount for restricted securities from the freely traded shares. These are the elements of value that are always used by investors in making investment decisions. In some cases, one element may be more important than in other cases. In the case of manufacturing, producing, or distributing companies, primary weight must be accorded earnings and net sales; but in the case of investment or holding companies, primary weight must be given to the net assets of the company underlying the stock. In the former type of companies, value is more closely linked to past, present, and future earnings while in the latter type of companies, value is more closely linked to the existing net assets of the company. See the discussion in Section 5 of Rev. Rul. 59-60.

.02   Resale provisions found in the restriction agreements must be scrutinized and weighed to determine the amount of discount to apply to the preliminary fair market value of the company. The two elements of time and expense bear upon this discount; the longer the buyer of the shares must wait to liquidate the shares, the greater the discount. Moreover, if the provisions make it necessary for the buyer to bear the expense of registration, the greater the discount. However, if the provisions of the restricted stock agreement make it possible for the buyer to "piggyback" shares at the next offering, the discount would be smaller.

.03   The relative negotiation strengths of the buyer and seller of restricted stock may have a profound effect on the amount of discount. For example, a tight money situation may cause the buyer to have the greater balance of negotiation strength in a transaction. However, in some cases the relative strengths may tend to cancel each other out.

.04   The market experience of freely tradable securities of the same class as the restricted securities is also significant in determining the amount of discount. Whether the shares are privately held or publicly traded affects the worth of the shares to the holder. Securities traded on a public market generally are worth more to investors than those that are not traded on a public market. Moreover, the type of public market in which the unrestricted securities are traded is to be given consideration.

Section 7: Effect on Other Documents

Rev. Rul. 59-60, as modified by Rev. Rul. 65-193, is amplified.

REV. RUL. 83-120

Summary

Revenue Ruling 83-120 expands Rev. Rul. 59-60 by providing additional factors to consider in the context of closely held corporate recapitalizations. These transactions became popular with taxpayers who entered into them as part of a comprehensive estate plan designed to transfer appreciated assets at a minimal unified estate and gift tax. In an attempt to close some of the most glaring loopholes exploited by taxpayers, the Service issued this Ruling.

Text

Section 2512: Valuation of Gifts

26 CFR 25.2512-2: Stocks and bonds.

(Also Sections 305, 351, 354, 368, 2031; 1.305-5, 1.351-1, 1.354-1, 1.368-1,20.2031-2.) 1983-2 C.B. 170; 1983 IRB LEXIS 147; REV. RUL. 83-120

July 1983. Valuation; stock; closely held business. The significant factors in deriving the fair market value of preferred and common stock received in certain corporate reorganizations are discussed. Rev. Rul. 59-60 amplified.

Section 1: Purpose

The purpose of this Revenue Ruling is to amplify Rev. Rul. 59-60, 1959-1 C.B.237, by specifying additional factors to be considered in valuing common and preferred stock of a closely held corporation for gift tax and other purposes in a recapitalization of closely held businesses. This type of valuation problem frequently arises with respect to estate planning transactions wherein an individual receives preferred stock with a stated par value equal to all or a large portion of the fair market value of the individual's former stock interest in a corporation. The individual also receives common stock which is then transferred, usually as a gift, to a relative.

Section 2: Background

.01   One of the frequent objectives of the type of transaction mentioned above is the transfer of the potential appreciation of an individual's stock interest in a corporation to relatives at a nominal or small gift tax cost. Achievement of this objective requires preferred stock having a fair market value equal to a large part of the fair market value of the individual's former stock interest and common stock having a nominal or small fair market value. The approach and factors described in this Revenue Ruling are directed toward ascertaining the true fair market value of the common and preferred stock and will usually result in the determination of a substantial fair market value for the common stock and a fair market value for the preferred stock which is substantially less than its par value.

.02   The type of transaction referred to above can arise in many different contexts. Some examples are:

- A owns 100 percent of the common stock (the only outstanding stock) of Z Corporation, which has a fair market value of 10,500x. In a recapitalization described in section 368(a)(1)(E), A receives preferred stock with a par value of 10,000x and new common stock, which A then transfers to A's son B.

- A owns some of the common stock of Z Corporation (or the stock of several corporations) the fair market value of which stock is 10,500x. A transfers this stock to a new corporation X in exchange for preferred stock of X corporation with a par value of 10,000x and common stock of corporation, which A then transfers to A's son B.

- A owns 80 shares and his son B owns 20 shares of the common stock (the only stock outstanding) of Z Corporation. In a recapitalization described in section 368(a)(1)(E), A exchanges his 80 shares of common stock for 80 shares of new preferred stock of Z Corporation with a par value of 10,000x. A's common stock had a fair market value of 10,000x.

Section 3: General Approach to Valuation

Under section 25.2512-2(f)(2) of the Gift Tax Regulations, the fair market value of stock in a closely held corporation depends on numerous factors, including the corporation's net worth, its prospective earning power, and its capacity to pay dividends. In addition, other relevant factors must be taken into account. See Rev. Rul. 59-60. The weight to be accorded any evidentiary factor depends on the circumstances of each case. See section 25.2512-2(f) of the Gift Tax Regulations.

Section 4: Approach to Valuation—Preferred Stock

.01   In general, the most important factors to be considered in determining the value of preferred stock are its yield, dividend coverage and protection of its liquidation preference.

.02   Whether the yield of the preferred stock supports a valuation of the stock at par value depends in part on the adequacy of the dividend rate. The adequacy of the dividend rate should be determined by comparing its dividend rate with the dividend rate of high-grade publicly traded preferred stock. A lower yield than that of high-grade preferred stock indicates a preferred stock value of less than par. If the rate of interest charged by independent creditors to the corporation on loans is higher than the rate such independent creditors charge their most credit worthy borrowers, then the yield on the preferred stock should be correspondingly higher than the yield on high quality preferred stock. A yield which is not correspondingly higher reduces the value of the preferred stock. In addition, whether the preferred stock has a fixed dividend rate and is nonparticipating influences the value of the preferred stock. A publicly traded preferred stock for a company having a similar business and similar assets with similar liquidation preferences, voting rights and other similar terms would be the ideal comparable for determining yield required in arms length transactions for closely held stock. Such ideal comparables will frequently not exist. In such circumstances, the most comparable publicly traded issues should be selected for comparison and appropriate adjustments made for differing factors.

.03   The actual dividend rate on a preferred stock can be assumed to be its stated rate if the issuing corporation will be able to pay its stated dividends in a timely manner and will, in fact, pay such dividends. The risk that the corporation may be unable to timely pay the stated dividends on the preferred stock can be measured by the coverage of such stated dividends by the corporation's earnings. Coverage of the dividend is measured by the ratio of the sum of pretax and pre-interest earnings to the sum of the total interest to be paid and the pre-tax earnings needed to pay the after-tax dividends. Standard & Poor's Ratings Guide, 58 (1979). Inadequate coverage exists where a decline in corporate profits would be likely to jeopardize the corporation's ability to pay dividends on the preferred stock. The ratio for the preferred stock in question should be compared with the ratios for high quality preferred stock to determine whether the preferred stock has adequate coverage. Prior earnings history is important in this determination. Inadequate coverage indicates that the value of preferred stock is lower than its par value. Moreover, the absence of a provision that preferred dividends are cumulative raises substantial questions concerning whether the stated dividend rate will, in fact, be paid. Accordingly, preferred stock with noncumulative dividend features will normally have a value substantially lower than a cumulative preferred stock with the same yield, liquidation preference and dividend coverage.

.04   Whether the issuing corporation will be able to pay the full liquidation preference at liquidation must be taken into account in determining fair market value. This risk can be measured by the protection afforded by the corporation's net assets. Such protection can be measured by the ratio of the excess of the current market value of the corporation's assets over its liabilities to the aggregate liquidation preference. The protection ratio should be compared with the ratios for high quality preferred stock to determine adequacy of coverage. Inadequate asset protection exists where any unforeseen business reverses would be likely to jeopardize the corporation's ability to pay the full liquidation preference to the holders of the preferred stock.

.05   Another factor to be considered in valuing the preferred stock is whether it has voting rights and, if so, whether the preferred stock has voting control. See, however, Section 5.02 below.

.06   Peculiar covenants or provisions of the preferred stock of a type not ordinarily found in publicly traded preferred stock should be carefully evaluated to determine the effects of such covenants on the value of the preferred stock. In general, if covenants would inhibit the marketability of the stock or the power of the holder to enforce dividend or liquidation rights, such provisions will reduce the value of the preferred stock by comparison to the value of preferred stock not containing such covenants or provisions.

.07   Whether the preferred stock contains a redemption privilege is another factor to be considered in determining the value of the preferred stock. The value of a redemption privilege triggered by death of the preferred shareholder will not exceed the present value of the redemption premium payable at the preferred shareholder's death (i.e., the present value of the excess of the redemption price over the fair market value of the preferred stock upon its issuance). The value of the redemption privilege should be reduced to reflect any risk that the corporation may not possess sufficient assets to redeem its preferred stock at the stated redemption price. See .03.

Section 5: Approach to Valuation—Common Stock

.01   If the preferred stock has a fixed rate of dividend and is nonparticipating, the common stock has the exclusive right to the benefits of future appreciation of the value of the corporation. This right is valuable and usually warrants a determination that the common stock has substantial value. The actual value of this right depends upon the corporation's past growth experience, the economic condition of the industry in which the corporation operates, and general economic conditions. The factor to be used in capitalizing the corporation's prospective earnings must be determined after an analysis of numerous factors concerning the corporation and the economy as a whole. See Rev. Rul. 59-60, at page 243. In addition, after-tax earnings of the corporation at the time the preferred stock is issued in excess of the stated dividends on the preferred stock will increase the value of the common stock. Furthermore, a corporate policy of reinvesting earnings will also increase the value of the common stock.

.02   A factor to be considered in determining the value of the common stock is whether the preferred stock also has voting rights. Voting rights of the preferred stock, especially if the preferred stock has voting control, could under certain circumstances increase the value of the preferred stock and reduce the value of the common stock. This factor may be reduced in significance where the rights of common stockholders as a class are protected under state law from actions by another class of shareholders, see *Singer v. Magnavox Co.*, 380 A.2d 969 (Del. 1977), particularly where the common shareholders, as a class, are given the power to disapprove a proposal to allow preferred stock to be converted into common stock. See ABA-ALI Model Bus. Corp. Act, Section 60 (1969).

Section 6: Effect on Other Revenue Rulings

Rev. Rul. 59-60, as modified by Rev. Rul. 65-193, 1965-2 C.B. 370 and as amplified by Rev. Rul. 77-287, 1977-2 C.B. 319, and Rev. Rul. 80-213, 1980-2C.B. 101, is further amplified.

REV. RUL. 85-75

Summary

As the Service sought to combat valuation abuses, it started invoking more substantial penalty provisions. One is the valuation overstatement penalty, once contained in section 6659 and now found in section 6662. Revenue Ruling 85-75 involved the interesting situation of a beneficiary's adopting the excessive value used on the decedent's estate tax return as the basis for the property devised. Although the overstatement by the estate clearly invoked section 6659, it was unclear whether the beneficiary could be subject to the same penalty for merely using this excessive valuation figure from the estate.

In Rev. Rul. 85-75, the Service asserted that the beneficiary was, in fact, liable for section 6659 penalties in this situation.

Text

Section 6659. Addition to Tax in the Case of Valuation Overstatements for Purposes of the Income Tax

1985-1 C.B. 376; 1985 IRB LEXIS 240; 1985-23 I.R.B. 19; REV. RUL.

85-75

June 10, 1985

Penalties; valuation overstatement; basis of property acquired from a decedent. The penalty for overvaluation under section 6659 of the Code may apply when a beneficiary of an estate adopts an overstated amount shown on an estate tax return as the beneficiary's adjusted basis under section 1014.

Issue

May the addition to tax under section 6659 of the Internal Revenue Code apply to an income tax return if a beneficiary of an estate adopts an overstated amount shown on an estate tax return as the beneficiary's adjusted basis under section 1014?

Facts

H and W were married at the time of W's death on December 31, 1982. W's will left all property to H. Included in the property was a building with a fair market value of 2,000x dollars. The executor filed Form 706, United States Estate Tax Return, valuing the property at 3,500x dollars. Because the entire estate qualified for the marital deduction under section 2056 of the Code, no estate tax was due.

H filed an income tax return for 1983 claiming an Accelerated Cost Recovery System deduction under section 168 of the Code for the building in question, using a basis under section 1014 of 3,500x dollars. The Internal Revenue Service examined H's 1983 income tax return and determined that the value of the building at the time of W's death was 2,000x dollars. This resulted in an underpayment of $1,000.

Law and Analysis

Section 6659(a) of the Code imposes an addition to tax if an individual or closely held corporation or a personal service corporation has an underpayment of income tax attributable to a valuation overstatement.

Section 6659(c) of the Code provides that there is a valuation overstatement if the value of any property, or the adjusted basis of any property, claimed on any return is 150 percent or more of the amount determined to be the correct amount of such valuation or adjusted basis.

Under section 6659(d) of the Code, the addition to tax is limited to situations in which there is an underpayment attributable to valuation overstatements of at least $1,000.

Section 6659(e) of the Code provides that the Service may waive all or part of the addition to tax on a showing by the taxpayer that there was a reasonable basis for the valuation or adjusted basis claimed on the return and that the claim was made in good faith.

Section 1014 of the Code generally provides that the basis of property in the hands of a person to whom the property passed from a decedent shall be its fair market value at the date of the decedent's death.

The underpayment of H's income tax for 1983 was attributable to a valuation overstatement of 150 percent or more and was at least $1,000. Accordingly, the addition to tax applies, if not waived by the Service. The fact that the adjusted basis of the building on H's income tax return is the same as the value on W's estate tax return does not of itself show the H had a reasonable basis to claim the valuation.

Holding

The addition to tax under section 6659 of the Code applies to an income tax return, absent a waiver by the Service, if a taxpayer adopts an overstated amount shown on an estate tax return as the taxpayer's adjusted basis under section 1014.

REV. RUL. 93-12[8]

Summary

Revenue Ruling 93-12 is one of the most significant valuation rulings issued. In it, the Service declined to attribute voting power based on family relationship. Often, the Service will attribute shares owned by B to A for measuring things like corporate control and ownership percentage, where A and B have a family relationship.

The Service declined to do so for valuation purposes in the context of a closely held corporation. Thus, minority discounts are still available where a parent wishes to gift shares of a private company to family members. Because there is no attribution, the donor can take a minority discount for each gift to a family donee, even though the family together owns the corporation in its entirety.[9]

---

[8]Rev. Rul. 81-253, superseded by Rev. Rul. 93-12, is not included in this chapter.

[9]In the one case, *J.C. Shepard v. Comm'r*, 115 T.C. 30 (2000), where the Service sought to argue that a father's imputed gift to his two sons of 50 percent of his corporate stock should be treated as one gift of 50 percent, the court disagreed, holding the father had in fact made two separate gifts of 25 percent to each of his two sons.

Text

Section 2512. Valuation of Gifts

26 CFR 25.2512-1: Valuation of property; in general.

1993 C.B. 202; 1993 IRB LEXIS 84; 1993-7 I.R.B. 13; REV. RUL. 93-12

February 16, 1993.Valuation; stock; intrafamily transfers; minority discounts. In determining the value of a gift of a minority block of stock in a closely held corporation, the block should be valued for gift tax purposes without regard to the family relationship of the donee to other shareholders. Rev. Rul. 81-253 revoked.

Issue

If a donor transfers shares in a corporation to each of the donor's children, is the factor of corporate control in the family to be considered in valuing each transferred interest, for purposes of section 2512 of the Internal Revenue Code?

Facts

P owned all of the single outstanding class of stock of X corporation. P transferred all of P's shares by making simultaneous gifts of 20 percent of the shares to each of P's five children, A, B, C, D, and E.

Law and Analysis

Section 2512(a) of the Code provides that the value of the property at the date of the gift shall be considered the amount of the gift.

Section 25.2512-1 of the Gift Tax Regulations provides that, if a gift is made in property, its value at the date of the gift shall be considered the amount of the gift. The value of the property is the price at which the property would change hands between a willing buyer and a willing seller, neither being under any compulsion to buy or to sell, and both having reasonable knowledge of relevant facts.

Section 25.2512-2(a) of the regulations provides that the value of stocks and bonds is the fair market value per share or bond on the date of the gift. Section 25.2512-2(f) provides that the degree of control of the business represented by the block of stock to be valued is among the factors to be considered in valuing stock where there are no sales prices or bona fide bid or asked prices.

Rev. Rul. 81-253, 1981-1 C.B. 187, holds that, ordinarily, no minority shareholder discount is allowed with respect to transfers of shares of stock between family members if, based upon a composite of the family members' interests at the time of the transfer, control (either majority voting control or de facto control through family relationships) of the corporation exists in the family unit. The ruling also states that the Service will not follow the decision of the *Fifth Circuit in Estate of Bright v. United States*, 658 F.2d 999 (5th Cir. 1981).

In *Bright*, the decedent's undivided community property interest in shares of stock, together with the corresponding undivided community property interest of the decedent's surviving spouse, constituted a control block of 55 percent of the shares of a corporation. The court held that, because the community-held shares were subject to a right of partition, the decedent's own interest was equivalent to 27.5 percent of the outstanding shares and, therefore, should be valued as a minority interest, even though the shares were to be held by the decedent's surviving spouse as trustee of a testamentary trust. See also, *Propstra v. United States*, 680 F.2d 1248 (9th Cir. 1982). In addition, *Estate of Andrews v. Commissioner*, 79 T.C. 938 (1982), and *Estate of Lee v. Commissioner*, 69 T.C. 860 (1978), nonacq., 1980-2 C.B. 2, held that the corporation shares owned by other family members cannot be attributed to an individual family member for determining whether the individual family member's shares should be valued as the controlling interest of the corporation.

After further consideration of the position taken in Rev. Rul. 81-253, and in light of the cases noted above, the Service has concluded that, in the case of a corporation with a single class of stock, notwithstanding the family relationship of the donor, the donee, and other shareholders, the shares of other family members will not be aggregated with the transferred shares to determine whether the transferred shares should be valued as part of a controlling interest. In the present case, the minority interests transferred to A, B, C, D, and E should be valued for gift tax purposes without regard to the family relationship of the parties.

Holding

If a donor transfers shares in a corporation to each of the donor's children, the factor of corporate control in the family is not considered in valuing each transferred interest for purposes of section 2512 of the Code. For estate and gift tax valuation purposes, the Service will follow *Bright*, *Propstra*, *Andrews*, and *Lee* in not assuming that all voting power held by family members may be aggregated for purposes of determining whether the transferred shares should be valued as part of a controlling interest. Consequently, a minority discount will not be disallowed solely because a transferred interest, when aggregated with interests held by family members, would be a part of a controlling interest. This would be the case whether the donor held 100 percent or some lesser percentage of the stock immediately before the gift.

Effect on Other Documents

Rev. Rul. 81-253 is revoked. Acquiescence is substituted for the non-acquiescence in issue one of Lee, 1980-2 C.B. 2.DRAFTING INFORMATION The principal author of this revenue ruling is Deborah Ryan of the Office of Assistant Chief Counsel (Passthroughs and Special Industries). For further information regarding this revenue ruling, contact Ms. Ryan on (202) 622-3090 (not a toll-free call).

TAX ADVICE MEMORANDUM 1994-36-005

Summary

As Rev. Rul. 59-60 was applied in practice, the pivotal issue became discounts. By taking advantage of certain features of the stock, taxpayers could argue that their stock was less valuable under the comprehensive valuation standard of Rev. Rul. 59-60 and thereby significantly reduce their tax bill. In this TAM, the Service seeks to counter such discounts by pointing out one stock attribute that it argues will increase value: a swing-vote potential for some of the shares, allowing their holder to cast the decisive vote in case of deadlock.

Text

Internal Revenue Service National Office Technical Advice Memorandum

DATE: May 26, 1994

Issue

Should the fact that each of three 30 percent blocks of stock transferred has swing vote attributes be taken into account as a factor in determining the fair market value of the stock?

Facts

The donor owned all of outstanding common stock of Corporation, totaling 28,975 shares. On December 18, 1989, the donor transferred 8,592 shares (approximately 30 percent of the outstanding common stock in Corporation) to each of three children. The donor also transferred 1,509 shares (approximately 5 percent of the stock) to his spouse. The donor retained 1,510 shares or approximately 5 percent of the stock. The transfers to the children were reported on a timely filed federal Gift Tax Return, Form 709. The donor's spouse consented to the gift-splitting provisions of section 2513 of the Internal Revenue Code.[10]

The ownership of the stock before and after the transfer may be summarized as follows:

Summary of Stock Holdings					
	Donor	Child 1	Child 2	Child 3	Spouse
Before	100%	0%	0%	0%	0%
After	5%	30%	30%	30%	5%

With respect to each gift, the stock was valued at approximately $50 per share representing the net asset value of Corporation, less a 25 percent discount characterized as a discount for "minority interest and marketability."

Applicable Law and Analysis

Section 2501 provides that a gift tax is imposed for each calendar year on the transfer of property by gift.

Section 2511 provides that the gift tax shall apply whether the transfer is in trust or otherwise, whether the gift is direct or indirect, and whether the property is real or personal, tangible or intangible.

---

[10]Corporation was authorized 100,000 shares of common stock, of which 36,955 were issued. Of the shares issued, 8,160 were held as treasury stock and the balance was owned by the donor.

Section 2512(a) provides that the value of the property at the date of the gift shall be considered the amount of the gift.

Section 25.2512-1 of the Gift Tax Regulations provides that, if a gift is made in property, its value at the date of the gift shall be considered the amount of the gift. The value of the property is the price at which the property would change hands between a willing buyer and a willing seller, neither being under any compulsion to buy or sell, and both having reasonable knowledge of relevant facts.

Section 25.2512-2(a) provides that the value of stocks and bonds is the fair market value per share or bond on the date of the gift. Section 25.2512-2(f) provides that all relevant factors are to betaken into account in determining fair market value including the degree of control of the business represented by the block of stock to be valued.

Rev. Rul. 59-60, 1959-1 C.B. 237, provides guidelines for valuing closely held stock. Rev. Rul. 59-60 specifically states that the size of a block of stock is a factor to be considered in determining fair market value. The revenue ruling also holds that all relevant factors must be considered and that no general formula maybe used that is applicable to different valuation situations.

In general, in determining the value of shares of stock that represent a minority interest, a discount may be allowed in appropriate circumstances to reflect the fact that the holder of a minority interest lacks control over corporate policy, and thus for example, cannot compel the payment of dividends or the liquidation of the corporation. *Ward v. Commissioner*, 87 T.C. 78, 106 (1986). Where a donor makes simultaneous gifts of multiple shares of securities to different donees, each gift is valued separately in determining fair market value for gift tax purposes. See, e.g., *Whittemore v. Fitzpatrick*, 127 F.Supp. 710 (D.C. Conn. 1954); *Avery v. Commissioner*, 3 T.C. 963 (1944); section 25.2512-2(e).

In Rev. Rul. 93-12, 1993-1 C.B. 202, a donor transferred 20 percent of the outstanding shares of a closely held corporation to each of his five children. The ruling concludes that, if a donor transfers shares in a corporation to each of the donor's children, the factor of corporate control in the family is not considered in valuing each transferred interest for purposes of section 2512. Thus, in valuing the shares, a minority discount will not be disallowed SOLELY because a transferred interest, when aggregated with interests held by other family members, would be a part of a controlling interest.

In *Estate of Winkler v. Commissioner*, TCM 1989-232, the decedent, Clara Winkler, owned 10 percent of the voting stock of a closely held corporation. Of the balance of the voting stock, 40 percent was owned by other members of the Winkler family and 50 percent was owned by members of the Simmons family. The court recognized that the decedent's block constituted a minority interest in the corporation. However, the court found that, in view of the fact that neither family possessed a controlling interest in the corporation, the decedent's minority block had special characteristics that enhanced its value. The court described these "swing vote" characteristics as follows:

> *This 10 percent voting stock could become pivotal in this closely held corporation where members of one family held 50 percent and members of another family held 40 percent. By joining with the Simmons family a minority shareholder could effect control over the corporation and by joining the Winkler family, such a minority shareholder could block action. . . . Looking at this even split between the two families, the 10 percent block of voting stock, in the hands of a third party unrelated to either family could indeed become critical. While it is difficult to put a value on this factor, we think it increases the value of the Class A voting stock by at least the 10 percent that respondent's appraiser found.*

The court went on to find that, under the facts presented, the increased value attributable to the swing vote characteristics of the stock offset any minority discount otherwise available. See also Glenn Desmond and Richard Kelley, *Business Valuation Handbook*, section 11.01 (1991) ("Likewise, if a minority block would enable another minority holder to achieve a majority with control or if the minority were needed to reach the percentage ownership needed to merge or file consolidated statements, the stock would have added value."); Shannon P. Pratt, *Valuing Small Businesses and Professional Practices*, 527 (2d ed. 1994) ("If two stockholders own 49 percent of the stock and a third owns 2 percent, the 49 percent stockholders may be on a par with each other. . . . The 2 percent stockholder may be able to command a considerable premium over the pro-rata value for that particular block because of the swing vote power."); *Estate of Bright v. United States*, 658 F.2d 999, 1007 and 1009 n.9 (5th Cir. 1981), where the court discussed swing vote analysis in detail.

In the instant case, immediately before the transfers, the donor owned 100 percent of the outstanding stock of Corporation. The donor simultaneously transferred 3 blocks of stock, each constituting 30 percent of the outstanding stock, to each of his three children. As discussed above, the three transfers are valued separately for gift tax purposes. As is evident, each gift, viewed separately, possesses the same swing vote characteristics described by the court in *Estate of Winkler*. That is, as a result of the simultaneous transfer, three individuals each owned a 30 percent block of stock. The owner of any one of the transferred blocks could join with the owner of any of the other transferred blocks and control the corporation. Thus, any one of these 30 percent blocks, whether owned by an individual related or unrelated to the family, could be critical in controlling the corporation. As the court concluded in *Estate of Winkler*, this swing vote attribute of each of the transferred blocks enhances the value of each block and is properly taken into account in determining the fair market value of each block transferred.[11]

The donor argues that attributing a swing vote value to each transferred block in this case produces an arbitrary result.

That is, if the donor had not made a simultaneous transfer, but rather had transferred each 30 percent block at different times, the valuation of each block would be different. For example, the first 30 percent block transferred might have no swing vote attributes, since after the initial transfer, the donor would continue to possess control of the corporation through his ownership of the retained 70 percent block.

However, the objection raised by the donor is inapposite. First, donor's assumption that the value of none of the three seriatim gifts would reflect swing vote attributes is incorrect. We agree that the value of the first 30 percent transfer would not reflect any swing vote value. However, the second transfer of 30 percent of the stock would possess swing vote value. Further, as a result of this second transfer, the value of the 30 percent interest held by the first transferee would increase, because that block would acquire enhanced voting control in the form of swing vote value as a result of the second transfer. After that transfer, the value of each of the three blocks would have been equalized, because no one stockholder would possess control of the corporation. This enhancement of value with respect to the first transferee's block at the time of the second transfer would constitute an indirect gift to that transferee at

---

[11]For valuation purposes, the focus is on shares actually transferred by the donor, notwithstanding that the transfers were treated as made one-half by the donor's spouse under section 2513.

the time of the second transfer. Finally, the third 30 percent block would also have swing vote value both before and after the third transfer. Thus, we believe that, even if the three transfers were made at different times, the total value of the gifts would ultimately be the same as if the three transfers were made simultaneously.

Further, under established case law, gift tax valuation results are often dependent on the nature and timing of the gift. For example, a single transfer of a large block of stock to an individual might be valued differently for gift tax purposes than several independent transfers of smaller blocks at different times. On the other hand, the result might not differ with respect to the swing value approach, or any other valuation principles, in the case of an integrated series of transfers. See, e.g., *Citizens Bank and Trust Co. v. Commissioner*, 839 F.2d 1249 (7th Cir. 1988); *Estate of Murphy v. Commissioner*, T.C.M. 1990-472. Accordingly, we do not believe the donor's objections in any way mitigate against applying swing vote analysis to the facts presented here.

As discussed above, all relevant factors are to be considered when valuing closely held stock. As the court concluded in *Estate of Winkler*, swing block potential is one such factor. In this case, each 30 percent block of stock has swing vote characteristics. The extent to which the swing vote potential enhances the value of each block transferred is a factual determination. However, all relevant factors including the minority nature of each block, any marketability concerns, and swing vote potential, should be taken into account in valuing each block.

REV. PROC. 2003-51

Section 1: Purpose

This revenue procedure sets forth guidelines for use by taxpayers and Internal Revenue Service personnel in making fair market value determinations for inventory items acquired when a taxpayer purchases the assets of a business for a lump sum or a corporation acquires the stock of another corporation and makes an election pursuant to § 338 of the Internal Revenue Code with respect to the acquisition. The Service invites public comment on issues relating to the inventory valuation methods discussed herein and to whether additional valuation methods are appropriate. This revenue procedure modifies, amplifies, and supersedes Rev. Proc. 77-12, 1977-1 C.B. 569.

Section 2: Background

If the assets of a business are purchased for a lump sum or if a corporation acquires the stock of another corporation and makes an election pursuant to § 338 with respect to the acquisition, the purchase price (actual or deemed) must be allocated among the assets acquired to determine the basis of each of the assets. In making the allocation, a taxpayer must determine the fair market value of any inventory items acquired. This revenue procedure describes methods that may be used to determine the fair market value of inventory items for purposes of the purchase price allocation.

In the situations set forth in this revenue procedure, the quantity of inventory to be valued generally would be different from the quantity usually purchased. In addition, the fair market value of the goods in process and finished goods on hand must be determined in light of what a willing purchaser would pay and a willing seller would accept for the inventory at the various stages of completion, when the former is not under any compulsion to buy and the latter is not under any compulsion to sell, both parties having reasonable knowledge of relevant facts. In making the inventory valuation determination, it is necessary to allow for a fair division between the buyer and the seller of the profit on the inventory, taking into account that the quantity of inventory purchased may be greater than the quantity of inventory usually purchased. *See Knapp King-Size Corp. v. United States*, 527 F.2d 1392 (Ct. Cl. 1975).

Section 3: Procedures for Determination of Fair Market Value

Three basic methods a taxpayer may use to determine the fair market value of inventory are the replacement cost method, the comparative sales method, and the income method.

.01 Replacement cost method. The replacement cost method generally provides a good indication of fair market value if inventory is readily replaceable in a wholesale or retail business, but generally should not be used in establishing the fair market value of the work in process or finished goods of a manufacturing concern. In valuing a bulk inventory of raw materials or goods purchased for resale under this method, the determination of the replacement cost of the individual items should be only a base or starting point. This base amount must be adjusted for factors that are generally relevant. For example, a willing purchaser might be expected to pay (and a willing seller might be expected to demand) a price for inventory that would compensate the seller not only for the current replacement cost, but also for a fair return on expenditures in accumulating and preparing the inventory for distribution. Thus, an amount equal to the fair value of the related costs that the taxpayer would have incurred in acquiring and accumulating the same quantity of goods had the goods been purchased separately (e.g., purchasing, handling, transportation, and off-site storage costs) should be added to the base amount. Additionally, in valuing a particular inventory under this method, other factors may be relevant. For example, a well balanced inventory available to fill customers' orders in the ordinary course of business may have a fair market value in excess of its cost of replacement because it provides a continuity of business, whereas an inventory containing obsolete merchandise unsuitable for customers may have a fair market value of less than the cost of replacement.

.02 Comparative sales method. The comparative sales method utilizes the actual or expected selling prices of finished goods to customers in the ordinary course of business as the base amount that must be adjusted for factors that are generally relevant in determining the fair market value of the inventory. The inventory to be valued may represent a larger quantity than the normal trading volume. The expected selling price is a valid starting point only if the inventory is expected to be used to fill customers' orders in the ordinary course of business. If the expected selling price is used as a basis for valuing finished goods inventory, the base amount must be adjusted for relevant factors, including:

- The time that would be required to dispose of this inventory;
- The expenses that would be expected to be incurred in the disposition, for example, all costs of disposition, applicable discounts (including those for quantity), sales commissions, and freight and shipping charges; and

- A profit commensurate with the amount of investment in the assets and the degree of risk. (This analysis should include (but is not limited to) an evaluation of risks of possible changes in style/design, changes in price levels, increased competition, possible adverse economic conditions, the fact that the inventory to be valued may represent a larger quantity than the normal trading volume, etc.).

.03   Income method. The income method, when applied to fair market value determinations for finished goods, recognizes that finished goods must generally be valued in a profit motivated business. As the amount of inventory may be large in relation to normal trading volume, the highest and best use of the inventory will be to provide for a continuity of the marketing operation of the going business. Additionally, the finished goods inventory will usually provide the only source of revenue of an acquired business during the period it is being used to fill customers' orders. The historical financial data of an acquired company can be used to determine the amount that could be attributed to finished goods in order to pay all costs of disposition and provide a return on the investment during the period of disposition.

.04   Work in process. The fair market value of work in process should be based on the same factors used to determine the fair market value of finished goods reduced by the expected costs of completion, including a reasonable profit allowance for the completion and selling effort of the acquiring corporation.

Section 4: Example of Replacement Cost and Comparative Sales Cost Methods

On Date 1, Manufacturer A purchased all the assets of Manufacturer B for a lump-sum payment of $31,000,000. The assets of Manufacturer B included quantities of finished goods and raw material inventory that were larger than the normal trading volume. The inventories are in good condition and the raw materials include minimal obsolete or subnormal goods. On the date of sale, Manufacturer B's books reflected finished goods inventory having a book value of $4,000,000 and raw materials having a book value of $300,000.

Manufacturer A expects to sell the acquired finished goods inventory to customers in the ordinary course of business. An appraiser hired by Manufacturer A determined that under the circumstances the expected retail selling price of the acquired finished goods inventory to customers was $6,000,000. It was also determined that the cost of disposing of the finished goods inventory, including sales commissions, freight and shipping charges, was $1,000,000. Manufacturer A calculated that it would incur a holding cost of $50,000 based on the average amount invested in holding the inventory, the period of time that would reasonably be expected to be necessary to dispose of the inventory, and the available established finance rate for the period. After taking into consideration Manufacturer A's investment in the assets of Manufacturer B, the risks Manufacturer A would incur during the time it took to dispose, in the ordinary course of its business, of the quantity of acquired inventory, and a fair division of the profit on the finished goods inventory between Manufacturer A and Manufacturer B, it was determined that the allocation of profit to Manufacturer A should be $450,000.

The appraiser determined that the replacement cost of the raw materials was $310,000. The appraiser computed a fair value of approximately $4,100 for purchasing, handling, and storage costs to acquire and accumulate the raw materials. Finally, the appraiser determined that there were minimal obsolete and subnormal goods, which would decrease the value of the inventories by approximately $100. In the ordinary course of business, Manufacturer B did not resell the raw materials without further processing. Manufacturer A also does not expect to resell in the ordinary course of business the raw materials without further processing.

Using the comparative sales method for finished goods and replacement cost method for raw materials, the fair market value of inventory for purposes of allocating the lump sum payment is computed as follows:

Fair Market Value Computation	
Gross expected selling price	$6,000,000
Disposition costs	(1,000,000)
Holding costs	(50,000)
Corporation A's profit	(450,000)
Fair Market Value of finished goods inventory	4,500,000
Current replacement cost of raw materials	310,000
Purchasing, storage, and handling costs	4,100
Obsolete and subnormal goods	(100)
Fair Market Value of raw materials inventory	314,000
Fair Market Value of acquired inventories	$4,814,000

Section 5: Conclusion

Valuing inventory is an inherently factual determination. No rigid formulas should be applied. Consequently, the three valuation methods outlined above serve only as guidelines for determining the fair market value of inventories. Similarly, the example serves only as a guideline for applying the methods.

Section 6: Request for Comments

The Service invites comments from the public on issues relating to this revenue procedure, including the current valuation methods provided herein and whether the Service should consider any additional valuation methods (for example, whether manufacturers should be permitted to apply a replacement cost method to value work in process and finished goods). Comments should be submitted by September 23, 2003, either to:

Internal Revenue Service
P.O. Box 7604
Ben Franklin Station
Washington, DC 20044
Attn: CC:PA:RU (CC:ITA:6)
Room 5525

or electronically via: *notice.comments @.irscounsel.treas.gov* (the Service comments e-mail address). All comments will be available for public inspection and copying.

Section 7: Effect on Other Documents

Rev. Proc. 77-12 is amplified, modified, and superseded.

Section 8: Effective Date

Generally, this revenue procedure is effective for taxable years ending on or after April 25, 1977. However, references in this revenue procedure to § 338 are effective for:

- Certain acquisitions occurring before September 1, 1982, if:
  1. The acquisition date with regard to an acquired corporation was after August 31, 1980, and before September 1, 1982
  2. The acquired corporation was not liquidated before September 1, 1982
  3. The acquiring corporation made an election pursuant to § 338
- Acquisitions occurring after August 31, 1982

CONCLUSION

In determining the fair market value of three 30 percent blocks of stock transferred by the donor, the swing vote attributes of each block are factors to be taken into consideration in determining the value of each block.

A copy of this technical advice memorandum is to be given to the taxpayer. Section 6110(j)(3) of the Code provides that it may not be used or cited as precedent.

Business Appraisal Reports[1]

---

[1] A checklist for reviewing a business valuation report can be found in Shannon Pratt, Robert F. Reilly, and Robert P. Schweihs, *Valuing a Business*, 4th ed. (New York: McGraw-Hill, 2000): 505–513.

SUMMARY

As noted in Chapter 2, in federal courts, the appraiser may or may not be allowed direct testimony. It is up to the judge to decide whether the appraiser will be allowed to explain or elaborate on the report submitted. In case the appraiser is not allowed direct testimony in court, the report is the direct testimony. Therefore, it is essential that all the supporting data and rationale be included within the covers of the report.

We repeat here a point emphasized in Chapter 3:

The trier of fact can only decide a case based upon the trial record. If evidence does not get into the record because it was not offered or was not admitted because of some objection, the conclusion in one trial may be different from another case where perhaps similar evidence was admitted.

To put forth a simple example, suppose that two valuation cases involving companies in the same industry are being tried at the same time; a good guideline company was presented as part of the evidence in the first case, but not in the second. Even though the guideline company presented in the first case is better than any in the second, it could not be used in the second case.

A comprehensive report can thus be outcome determinative.

In this chapter we present two widely accepted standards for business valuation report writing. In addition, the Internal Revenue Service *Business Valuation Guidelines* (see Appendix A) includes some guidelines on report writing.

The chapter then presents and discusses the elements of a thorough business valuation report. Finally, we address the organization of the report and the qualities by which one may evaluate the report.

BUSINESS VALUATION REPORT-WRITING STANDARDS

Standards for report writing are contained within the standards of all the business valuation professional organizations as well as the Internal Revenue Service *Business Valuation Guidelines*. Here we offer report-writing standards from two such organizations. As this book goes to press, the American Institute of Certified Public Accountants (AICPA) has proposed business valuation standards in draft form.

Uniform Standards of Professional Appraisal Practice (USPAP)

Exhibit 23.1 is Standard 10: Business Appraisal Reporting, from the *Uniform Standards of Professional Appraisal Practice* (USPAP). These standards are promulgated by the Appraisal Standards Board of the Appraisal Foundation. Although USPAP directly influences federally related real estate transactions, it does not dictate the standard for business appraisals. However, USPAP makes good appraisal sense, is widely respected, and is frequently referred to by courts and regulatory agencies.

American Society of Appraisers Business Valuation Standards

Exhibit 23.2 is Standard BVS-VIII, Comprehensive Written Business Valuation Reports, from the American Society of Appraisers *Business Valuation Standards*.

Exhibit 23.1   Business Valuation Report-Writing Standard of the Uniform Standards of Professional Appraisal Practice (USPAP), Standard 10

STANDARD 10: BUSINESS APPRAISAL, REPORTING

In reporting the results of a business or intangible asset appraisal, an appraiser must communicate each analysis, opinion, and conclusion in a manner that is not misleading.

> *Comment:* STANDARD 10 addresses the content and level of information required in a report that communicates the results of a business or intangible asset appraisal developed under STANDARD 9.
>
> STANDARD 10 does not dictate the form, format, or style of business or intangible asset appraisal reports, which are functions of the needs of users and providers of appraisal services. The substantive content of a report determines its compliance.

STANDARDS RULE 10-1

(This Standards Rule contains binding requirements from which departure is not permitted.)
Each written or oral business or intangible asset appraisal report must:

(a)   **clearly and accurately set forth the appraisal in a manner that will not be misleading:**

(b)   **contain sufficient information to enable the intended user(s) to understand it and note any specific limiting conditions concerning information; and**

(c)   **clearly and accurately disclose any extraordinary assumption or hypothetical condition that directly affects the appraisal and indicate its impact on value.**

> *Comment:* This requirement calls for a clear and accurate disclosure of any extraordinary assumptions or hypothetical conditions that directly affect an analysis, opinion, or conclusion. Examples might include items such as the execution of a pending agreement, atypical financing, infusion of additional working capital or making other capital additions, or compliance with regulatory authority rules. The report should indicate whether the extraordinary assumption or hypothetical condition has a positive, negative, or neutral impact on value.

STANDARDS RULE 10-2

(This Standards Rule contains binding requirements from which departure is not permitted.)

Each written business appraisal or intangible asset appraisal report must be prepared in accordance with one of the following options and prominently state which option is used: Appraisal Report or Restricted Use Appraisal Report.

> *Comment:* When the intended users include parties other than the client, an Appraisal Report must be provided. When the only intended user is the client, a Restricted Use Appraisal Report may be provided.
>
> The essential difference between these options is in the content and level of information provided.
>
> An appraiser may use any other label in addition to, but not in place of, the label set forth in this STANDARD for the type of report provided.
>
> The report content and level of information requirements set forth in this STANDARD are minimums for both types of report. An appraiser must ensure that any intended user of the appraisal is not misled and that the report complies with the applicable content requirements set forth in this Standards Rule.
>
> A party receiving a copy of an Appraisal Report or Restricted Use Appraisal Report does not become an intended user of the appraisal unless the appraiser identifies such party as an intended user as part of the assignment.

(Continued)

Exhibit 23.1   *(Continued)*

(a)   **The content of an Appraisal Report must be consistent with the intended use of the appraisal and, at a minimum:**

    (i)   **state the identity of the client and any intended users, by name or type;**

Comment : An appraiser must use care when identifying the client to ensure a clear understanding and to avoid violations of the Confidentiality section of the ETHICS RULE. In those rare instances when the client wishes to remain anonymous, an appraiser must still document the identity of the client in the workfile but may omit the client's identity in the report.

    (ii)   **state the intended use of the appraisal; (note56)**

    (iii)   **summarize information sufficient to identify the business or intangible asset appraised;**

Comment: The identification information must include property characteristics relevant to the assignment.

    (iv)   **state as relevant to the assignment, the extent to which the business interest or the interest in the intangible asset appraised contains elements of ownership control, including the basis for that determination;**

    (v)   **state the purpose of the appraisal, including the standard of value (definition) and its source;**

Comment: Stating the standard of value requires the definition itself and any comments needed to clearly indicate to the reader how the definition is being applied.

    (vi)   **state the effective date of the appraisal and the date of the report;**

Comment: The effective date of the appraisal establishes the context for the value opinion, while the date of the report indicates whether the perspective of the appraiser on the market or property use conditions as of the effective date of the appraisal was prospective, current, or retrospective.

    (vii)   **summarize sufficient information to disclose to the client and any intended users of the appraisal the scope of work used to develop the appraisal;**

Comment: This requirement is to ensure that the client and intended users whose expected reliance on an appraisal may be affected by the extent of the appraiser's investigation are properly informed and are not misled as to the scope of work. The appraiser has the burden of proof to support the scope of work decision and the level of information included in a report.

When any portion of the work involves significant business appraisal assistance, the appraiser must summarize the extent of that assistance. The signing appraiser must also state the name(s) of those providing the significant business appraisal assistance in the certification, in accordance with SR 10-3.

    (viii)   **state all assumptions, hypothetical conditions, and limiting conditions that affected the analyses, opinions, and conclusions;**

Comment: Typical or ordinary assumptions and limiting conditions may be grouped together in an identified section of the report. An extraordinary assumption or hypothetical condition must be disclosed in conjunction with statements of each opinion or conclusion that was affected.

    (ix)   **summarize the information analyzed, the appraisal procedures followed, and the reasoning that supports the analyses, opinions, and conclusions;**

Comment: The appraiser must attempt to determine that the information provided is sufficient for the client and intended users to adequately understand the rationale for the opinion and conclusions.

Exhibit 23.1 *(Continued)*

(x) **state and explain any permitted departures from specific requirements of STANDARD 9 and the reason for excluding any of the usual valuation approaches; and**

Comment: An Appraisal Report must include sufficient information to indicate that the appraiser complied with the requirements of STANDARD 9, including any permitted departures from the specific requirements. The amount of detail required will vary with the significance of the information to the appraisal.

When the DEPARTURE RULE is invoked, the assignment is deemed to be a Limited Appraisal. Use of the term "Limited Appraisal" makes clear that the assignment involved something less than or different from the work that could have and would have been completed if departure had not been invoked. The report of a Limited Appraisal must contain a prominent section that clearly identifies the extent of the appraisal process performed and the departures taken.

(xi) **include a signed certification in accordance with Standards Rule 10-3.**

(b) **The content of a Restricted Use Appraisal Report must be for client use only and consistent with the intended use of the appraisal and, at a minimum:**

(i) **state the identity of the client;**

Comment: An appraiser must use care when identifying the client to ensure a clear understanding and to avoid violations of the Confidentiality section of the ETHICS RULE.

(ii) **state the intended use of the appraisal;**

Comment: The intended use of the appraisal must be client use only.

(iii) **state information sufficient to identify the business or intangible asset appraised;**

Comment: The identification information must include property characteristics relevant to the assignment.

(iv) **state as relevant to the assignment, the extent to which the business interest or the interest in the intangible asset appraised contains elements of ownership control, including the basis for that determination;**

(v) **state the purpose of the appraisal, including the standard of value (definition) and its source;**

(vi) **state the effective date of the appraisal and the date of the report; (note58)**

Comment: The effective date of the appraisal establishes the context for the value opinion, while the date of the report indicates whether the perspective of the appraiser on the market or property use conditions as of the effective date of the appraisal was prospective, current, or retrospective.

(vii) **state the extent of the process of collecting, confirming, and reporting data or refer to an assignment agreement retained in the appraiser's workfile that describes the scope of work to be performed;**

Comment: When any portion of the work involves significant business appraisal assistance, the appraiser must state the extent of that assistance. The signing appraiser must also state the name(s) of those providing the significant business appraisal assistance in the certification, in accordance with SR 10-3.

(Continued)

Exhibit 23.1   *(Continued)*

> **(viii) state all assumptions, hypothetical conditions, and limiting conditions that affect the analyses, opinions, and conclusions;**

Comment: Typical or ordinary assumptions and limiting conditions may be grouped together in an identified section of the report. An extraordinary assumption or hypothetical condition must be disclosed in conjunction with statements of each opinion or conclusion that was affected.

> **(ix)   state the appraisal procedures followed, state the value opinion(s) and conclusion(s) reached, and reference the workfile;**

Comment: An appraiser must maintain a specific, coherent workfile in support of a Restricted Use Appraisal Report. The contents of the workfile must be sufficient for the appraiser to produce an Appraisal Report. The file must be available for inspection by the client (or the client's representatives, such as those engaged to complete an appraisal review), such third parties as may be authorized by due process of law, and a duly authorized professional peer review committee except when such disclosure to a committee would violate applicable law or regulation.

> **(x)   state and explain any permitted departures from applicable specific requirements of STANDARD 9; state the exclusion of any of the usual valuation approaches; and state a prominent use restriction that limits use of the report to the client and warns that the appraiser's opinions and conclusions set forth in the report cannot be understood properly without additional information in the appraiser's workfile; and**

Comment: When the DEPARTURE RULE is invoked, the assignment is deemed to be a Limited Appraisal. Use of the term "Limited Appraisal" makes it clear that the assignment involved something less than or different from the work that could have and would have been completed if departure had not been invoked. The report of a Limited Appraisal must contain a prominent section that clearly identifies the extent of the appraisal process performed and the departures taken.

The Restricted Use Appraisal Report is for client use only. Before entering into an agreement, the appraiser should establish with the client the situations where this type of report is to be used and should ensure that the client understands the restricted utility of the Restricted Use Appraisal Report.

> **(xi)   include a signed certification in accordance with Standards Rule 10-3.**

STANDARDS RULE 10-3

(This Standards Rule contains binding requirements from which departure is not permitted.)

Each written business or intangible asset appraisal report must contain a signed certification that is similar in content to the following form:

I certify that, to the best of my knowledge and belief:

> —   **the statements of fact contained in this report are true and correct.**
> —   **the reported analyses, opinions, and conclusions are limited only by the reported assumptions and limiting conditions and are my personal, impartial, and unbiased professional analyses, opinions, and conclusions.**
> —   **I have no (or the specified) present or prospective interest in the property that is the subject of this report, and I have no (or the specified) personal interest with respect to the parties involved.**
> —   **I have no bias with respect to the property that is the subject of this report or to the parties involved with this assignment.**

Exhibit 23.1 *(Continued)*

— my engagement in this assignment was not contingent upon developing or reporting predetermined results.

— my compensation for completing this assignment is not contingent upon the development or reporting of a predetermined value or direction in value that favors the cause of the client, the amount of the value opinion, the attainment of a stipulated result, or the occurrence of a subsequent event directly related to the intended use of this appraisal.

— my analyses, opinions, and conclusions were developed, and this report has been prepared, in conformity with the Uniform Standards of Professional Appraisal Practice.

— no one provided significant business appraisal assistance to the person signing this certification. (If there are exceptions, the name of each individual providing significant business appraisal assistance must be stated.)

Comment: A signed certification is an integral part of the appraisal report. An appraiser who signs any part of the appraisal report, including a letter of transmittal, must also sign this certification.

Any appraiser(s) who signs a certification accepts full responsibility for all elements of the certification, for the assignment results, and for the contents of the appraisal report.

When a signing appraiser(s) has relied on work done by others who do not sign the certification, the signing appraiser is responsible for the decision to rely on their work. The signing appraiser(s) is required to have a reasonable basis for believing that those individuals performing the work are competent and that their work is credible.

The names of individuals providing significant business appraisal assistance who do not sign a certification must be stated in the certification. It is not required that the description of their assistance be contained in the certification but disclosure of their assistance is required in accordance with SR 10-2(a) or (b)(vii), as applicable.

STANDARDS RULE 10-4

(This Standards Rule contains specific requirements from which departure is permitted. See DEPARTURE RULE.)

An oral business or intangible asset appraisal report must, at a minimum, address the substantive matters set forth in Standards Rule 10-2(a).

Comment: See the Record Keeping section of the ETHICS RULE for corresponding requirements.

Source: Uniform Standards of Professional Appraisal Practice (USPAP), © 2004 by The Appraisal Foundation, are reproduced with permission of The Appraisal Foundation. Additional copies of USPAP (including Advisory Opinions and Statements) are available for purchase from The Appraisal Foundation Distribution Center, P.O. Box 381, Annapolis Junction, MD 20701-0381, (800) 348-2831.

Exhibit 23.2   Business Valuation Report-Writing Standard of the American Society of Appraisers

---

AMERICAN SOCIETY OF APPRAISERS

Business Valuation Standards

BVS-VIII Comprehensive Written Business Valuation Report©

I. Preamble

A. This Standard must be followed only in the preparation of comprehensive written business valuation reports developed by all members of the American Society of Appraisers, be they Candidates, Accredited Members (AM), Accredited Senior Appraisers (ASA), or Fellows (FASA).

B. A business valuation report may be less comprehensive in content provided that the report complies with the minimum content required by Standard 10.2 of the USPAP.

C. The purpose of this Standard is to define and describe the requirements for the written communication of the results of a business valuation, analysis, or opinion, but not the conduct thereof, which may reflect the three scopes of work defined in BVS-I Section (II) B.

D. This Standard incorporates the General Preamble to the Business Valuation Standards of the American Society of Appraisers.

II. Signature and certification

A. An appraiser assumes responsibility for the statements made in the comprehensive written report and accepts that responsibility by signing the report. To comply with this Standard, a comprehensive written report must be signed by the appraiser. For the purpose of this Standard, the appraiser is the individual or entity undertaking the appraisal assignment under a contract with the client.

B. Clearly, at least one individual is responsible for the valuation conclusion(s) expressed in a report. A report must contain a certification, as required by Standard 10 of the *Uniform Standards of Professional Appraisal Practice* of The Appraisal Foundation, in which the individual(s) responsible for the valuation conclusion(s) must be identified.

III. Assumptions and limiting conditions

The following assumptions and/or limiting conditions must be stated:

A. *Pertaining to bias.* A report must contain a statement that the appraiser has no interest in the asset appraised, or other conflict that could cause a question as to the appraiser's independence or objectivity; or, if such an interest or conflict exists, it must be disclosed.

B. *Pertaining to data used.* Where appropriate, a report must indicate that an appraiser relied on data supplied by others, without further verification by the appraiser, as well as the sources that were relied on.

C. *Pertaining to validity of the valuation.* A report must contain a statement that a valuation is valid only for the valuation date indicated and for the purpose stated.

IV. Definition of the valuation assignment

The precise definition of the valuation assignment is a key aspect of the report. The following are components of such a definition and must be included in the report:

A. The business interest being valued must be clearly defined, such as "100 shares of the Class A common stock of the XYZ Corporation" or "a 20 percent limited partnership interest in the ABC Limited Partnership." The existence, rights, and/or restrictions of other classes of ownership in the subject business must also be adequately described if they are relevant to the conclusion of value.

B. The purpose and use of the valuation must be clearly stated, such as "a determination of fair market value for ESOP purposes" or "a determination of fair value for dissenters' rights purposes." If a valuation is being performed pursuant to a particular statute, the statute must be referenced.

Exhibit 23.2 *(Continued)*

C. The standard of value used in the valuation must be stated and defined. The premise or basis of value, such as the valuation of a minority interest or a controlling interest, must be stated.

D. The effective date and the report date must be stated.

V. Business description

A comprehensive written business valuation report must include a business description that covers relevant factual areas, such as:

A. Form of organization (corporation, partnership, etc.)
B. History
C. Products and/or services
D. Markets and customers
E. Management
F. Major assets, both tangible and intangible, and major liabilities
G. Outlook for the economy, industry, and business
H. Past transactional evidence of value
I. Sensitivity to seasonal or cyclical factors
J. Competition
K. Sources of information used
L. Such other factual information as may be required to present a clear description of the business, and the general context within which it operates

VI. Financial analysis

A. An analysis and discussion of a firm's financial statements is an integral part of a business valuation and must be included. Exhibits summarizing balance sheets and income statements for a period of years sufficient to the purpose of the valuation and the nature of the subject company must be included in the valuation report.

B. Any adjustments made to the reported financial data must be fully explained.

C. If projections of balance sheets or income statements were used in the valuation, key assumptions underlying those projections must be included and discussed.

D. If appropriate, the company's financial results in comparison to those of the industry in which it operates must be discussed.

VII. Valuation methodology

A. The valuation method or methods selected, and the reasons for their selection, must be discussed. The steps followed in the application of the method(s) selected must be described. The description of the methodology and the procedures followed must contain sufficient detail to allow the intended user of the report to understand how the appraiser reached the valuation conclusion.

B. The report must include an explanation of how any variables such as discount rates, capitalization rates, or valuation multiples were determined and used. The rationale and/or supporting data for any premiums or discounts must be clearly presented.

VIII. Comprehensive written business valuation report format

The comprehensive written business valuation report must clearly communicate pertinent information, valuation methods, and conclusions in a logical progression, and must incorporate the other specific requirements of this Standard, including the signature and certification provisions.

IX. Confidentiality of the report

No copies of the report may be furnished to persons other than the client without the client's specific permission or direction unless ordered by a court of competent jurisdiction.

Source: American Society of Appraisers *Business Valuation Standards.* Used with permission. All rights reserved.

ELEMENTS OF THE BUSINESS VALUATION REPORT

A full-format business valuation report prepared for tax purposes should contain the following elements:

- Identification of the property appraised
- Effective date of the appraisal
- Date of the report
- Standard of value
- Intended use of the report
- Name of client
- Name(s) of appraiser(s)
- Valuation approaches considered and used
- Assumptions and limiting conditions
- Sources of information relied on
- Description of business
- Relevant economic and industry analysis
- Financial analysis of the company
- Description of the appraisal process
- Applicable discounts and/or premiums
- Conclusion of value
- Appraiser's certification
- Qualifications of appraiser(s)
- Statement of Contingent and Limiting Conditions

Identification of Property

The appraiser should give the name of the company, the form of organization (e.g., C corporation, limited partnership), and the state of incorporation or organization. The state of incorporation is important because there could be entities of the same name in several states, and because state laws might affect value (e.g., what percentage of the voting stock is required for certain actions). The form of organization is important because owners of different types of entities have different rights and protections, and because different forms of organization are subject to different rules of taxation.

The precise ownership interest should be identified, such as 2,000 shares of common stock out of 20,000 shares outstanding. If there is more than one class of ownership interest, the other classes should be described. Any rights or restrictions applicable to the interest (e.g., arising from articles of incorporation or bylaws, contractual agreements, regulations, etc.) should be described.

The distribution of ownership interests should be described. For example, it is one thing if the other 18,000 shares are all held in a single block, another thing if the stock is widely distributed, and yet another if the balance of the stock is held in two 9,000-share blocks.

Effective Date of the Appraisal

For gift taxes and charitable contributions, the effective date is the date of the gift or contribution. For estate taxes, the taxpayer has a choice between date of death and the alternate valuation date, currently six months after the date of death.

Date of Report

For charitable contributions, the report must be prepared within 30 days before or after the date of the contribution. It must contain, at a minimum, the information required by Code section 6050L and be filed with the appropriate form in the year in which the deduction is claimed.

For gift and estate taxes, there is no requirement as to the date the report was written, except that, to start the clock on the three-year statute of limitations in accordance with Code section 6501, "credible evidence" of the value of the gift must be filed with the taxpayer's return for the year in which the gift was made, whether or not the taxpayer paid any gift tax.

Some lawyers prefer to file the estate tax valuation report with the estate tax return. Others put the report in a drawer to be brought out if the value is challenged, even if the report is available when the return is filed.

Reports prepared concurrently with the date of gift or the estate tax effective valuation date tend to be viewed as more credible than those prepared specifically for litigation. Credibility also depends on the qualifications of the appraiser and the content of the report, and it is not unusual to commission a second valuation report by a different appraiser in case of litigation.

Standard of Value

For federal tax purposes, the standard of value is fair market value, as discussed in Chapter 1. Some appraisers quote the Treasury Regulations definition of fair market value. Some even list their interpretations of fair market value as laid out in Chapter 1.

Most appraisers quote the eight factors listed in Rev. Rul. 59-60. But in many cases, one or more of the factors are not addressed in the report. It weakens the credibility of the report to list factors considered and then fail to consider one or more of them. If one or more factors listed are not commented on in the report, the implication is that they were not considered. If Rev. Rul. 59-60 is quoted in this way and the appraiser considers one or more of the factors inapplicable, the appraiser should state why.

Intended Use of the Report

The appraiser should state that the intended use of the report is to estimate fair market value for tax purposes. All too often, an appraisal prepared for some other purpose, such as a public offering or sale of the company, is subsequently used for tax purposes. Such reports usually do not adhere strictly to the Treasury's definition of fair market value and are thus not as useful for tax purposes.

Name of Client

The name of the client is the person or entity that commissioned the report, not necessarily the person or entity ultimately paying for the report. The most common example is where a law firm commissions a report for its client.

Name(s) of Appraiser(s)

Any person who had "significant involvement" in the appraisal process needs to be identified. *Significant involvement* is nowhere defined, but is usually interpreted to mean decision making, including judgment, rather than the mere collection of information.

The 2004 edition of USPAP was revised to require disclosure of the respective roles of persons listed as having significant involvement.

Valuation Approaches Considered and Used

The three recognized approaches to business valuation are the income approach, the market approach, and the asset approach. USPAP says that all three should be "considered."

The rationale for the approaches and methods used must be explained in the report. The report should also state the rationale for rejecting any of the three approaches that were not used.

Sources of Information Relied On

The report should list those information sources that were relied on in reaching the conclusion of value.

For site visits, the report should name the facilities visited and the date(s) of the visit(s). For management interviews, the report should list the names and positions of persons interviewed, and whether the interview was in person or by phone. Any other persons interviewed, such as industry experts, should also be listed.

For financial statements, the report should include the names of the statements, the period or date to which each applied, the level of preparation (i.e., audited, reviewed, or compiled), and who prepared each (i.e., name of accounting firm or "internally prepared").

For printed material or material obtained online, the report should contain sufficient bibliographic information for the reviewer of the report to be able to access the same material. Examples of these sources are economic or industry information, databases of guideline companies used in the market approach, and sources for the cost of capital used in the income approach.

The report should identify any company-specific information relied on such as articles of incorporation, shareholder agreements, customer or supplier agreements, or patents.

Description of Business

This may be very long or very short. In any case, it should be sufficient to inform the reader about lines of business, competition, market position, customer base, supplier base, management, and assets (tangible and intangible).

In most cases, either this section or a separate section has anywhere from a sentence to a few paragraphs on the history of the business.

Relevant Economic and Industry Analysis

The key word here is *relevant*. The information used should be connected to the company; that is, its implications for the company's fortunes should be addressed either in the economic and industry sections or somewhere in the valuation section.

Too many reports contain boilerplate economic and industry sections that are irrelevant to the company and are ignored in the valuation analysis. Some reports may even seem to be contradictory: The industry outlook is optimistic while the company is undergoing financial difficulties, or vice versa. Any such seeming contradictions should be explained in order to make a report credible.

Financial Analysis of the Company

Historical financial statements should be presented for a relevant number of past years, usually five. Adjustments to historical statements should be explained, as discussed in Chapter 10.

There should be some discussion as to why any historical trends observed in the past should or should not be expected to continue into the future. As Rev. Rul. 59-60 says, "Valuation is a prophecy as to the future." The only reason to review historical financial results is to provide guidance as to what to expect in the future.

The company's financial statements should be compared with industry averages and/or specific guideline companies as discussed in Chapter 11. Any departures from either industry norms or guideline company averages should be noted, along with any implications of the departures for the company's value. Too many reports have excellent financial analysis sections with little or no connection to the valuation procedures employed!

Description of the Appraisal Process

First and foremost, the description of the steps taken should be *replicable*. This means that the sources of all information used should be documented so that the reviewer can go to the same sources and get the same information. The steps followed in using the information should be spelled out so that any reviewer can duplicate the steps and reach the same conclusion.

Not far behind replicability is *rationale*. The appraiser should explain the rationale behind each step of the appraisal. What do the guideline components selected have in common with the subject company? In the income approach, how were the projected cash flows and discount or capitalization rates estimated? What were the rationale and supporting data for estimating the magnitude of any discounts or premiums that were applied?

The report should enable the reader to understand exactly what was done and why.

Applicable Discounts and/or Premiums

In most cases, values estimated by the market, income, and/or asset approaches are adjusted by one or more discounts or premiums. The base values to which each discount or premium is applied must be clearly identified. Each discount or premium should be explicitly stated, and the rationale for each explained.

Often, the discounts and/or premiums are a bigger money issue in an appraisal than the base values to which they are applied. The magnitude of the discount for lack of marketability is the most frequently encountered controversy. A serious weakness in many reports is inadequate documentation of the data used to support the magnitude of the discount or premium chosen.

Documentation of the magnitude of discounts and premiums, especially discounts for lack of marketability, is probably the weakest area in most appraisals. (See Chapter 17, Chapter 18, and Chapter 19 for suggestions on adequate documentation.)

Conclusion of Value

For federal tax purposes, the conclusion of value should be stated as a point estimate rather than a range of value. Occasionally, however, the appraiser may offer alternate conclusions, depending on the court's interpretation of legal issues or disputed facts.

When one approach dominates the conclusion of value, the report should explain why the approach dominates. When two or more approaches lead to different indications of value, the report should explain how the different indications are reconciled into a single conclusion of value. This may be done either by mathematical weighting or subjective weighting. In either case, the rationale requires explanation.

Appraiser's Certification

The report should contain a certification of the type shown in Exhibit 23.1. This is usually attached to the report as an appendix, although it may be included in the text of the report or in a letter of transmittal. In any case, the certification is an integral part of the report.

Qualifications of Appraiser(s)

The report should present the appraiser's qualifications, usually in an appendix. If two or more people are identified as having significant input, the qualifications of each should be presented.

Statement of Contingent and Limiting Conditions

There will usually be a Statement of Contingent and Limiting Conditions, most often as an appendix. One of the more important of these is whether the appraiser was accorded full access to all material requested or whether any access requested was denied (e.g., documents, site visit, management interviews).

Exhibit 23.3 Hypothetical Appraisals

A hypothetical appraisal is an appraisal based on assumed conditions which are contrary to fact or which are improbable of realization or consummation. The Society takes the position that there are legitimate uses for some hypothetical appraisals, but that it is improper and unethical to issue a hypothetical appraisal report unless (1) the value is clearly labeled as hypothetical, (2) the legitimate purpose for which the appraisal was made is stated, and (3) the conditions which were assumed contrary to fact are set forth.

Source: American Society of Appraisers, *Principles of Appraisal Practice and Code of Ethics*, Section 6.5 (July 2002). Reproduced with permission. All rights reserved.

Another important item is any extraordinary assumptions. An extraordinary assumption such as *as if* something occurred that in fact did not occur would likely lead to classification of the report as a *hypothetical appraisal*. Exhibit 23.3 is the discussion of hypothetical appraisals from the American Society of Appraisers' *Principles of Appraisal Practice and Code of Ethics*. A hypothetical appraisal would not be suitable for estimating fair market value for tax purposes.

ORGANIZATION OF THE REPORT

A typical business valuation report would be organized in the order in which the elements were listed in the preceding section. However, there is no one "correct" way to organize a business valuation report, as long as all the elements listed in the preceding section are included somewhere.

Some appraisers include a summary or executive overview at the beginning; others do not. Some appraisers include all the supporting exhibits with the main text; others place the exhibits in a separate section at the end. In either case, each exhibit should be referenced in the text.

It is a good idea to number all the pages in the report consecutively—that is, text, exhibits, and appendixes. That will facilitate finding certain references at a later date.

QUALITIES OF A GOOD APPRAISAL REPORT

There are several characteristics by which the quality of a business appraisal report may be evaluated. The more important characteristics are discussed in this section.

Does the Report Appraise the Property Identified?

The reviewer should check to be sure that the report actually appraises the property that it identifies. The most common violation of this is purporting to appraise a share of stock or a partnership interest, which consists of a bundle of rights, while actually appraising the underlying assets only.

Is the Report Understandable?

As noted earlier, the report should be understandable to the reader. This requires short sentences and clear presentation, as well as explanations of technical or difficult terms.

Comprehensiveness

A good report should cover all of the relevant bases. It should contain all of the elements listed in this chapter. Also, it should draw on enough data to provide the reader with thorough support for each conclusion (e.g., an adequate set of guideline companies for the market approach, both restricted stock and pre-IPO data in support of the discount for lack of marketability, etc.).

Internal Consistency

A good report must be *internally consistent*. Is there anything in one part of the report that appears inconsistent with anything in any other part of the report?

Cohesiveness

The report should be cohesive in the sense that it should hang together and lead the reader logically to the conclusion of value.

Incisiveness

Webster's defines *incisiveness* as follows:

- Having a cutting edge or piercing point—facilitating cutting or piercing, as sharp
- Marked by sharpness and penetration—especially in keen, clear, unmistakable resolution of matter at issue or in pointed decision effectiveness of preparation
- Clear genius that states in a flash the exact point at issue
- Keen penetration and sharp presentation that is decisive or effective—rapier quality of highly tempered steel
- Unmistakably clear outlining, analysis, and presentation that defies disbelief or question[2]

We wish that all valuation reports followed these guidelines!

IRS Guidelines

The *Internal Revenue Service Business Valuation Guidelines* (see Appendix A) include a section on what should be contained in business valuation reports. The authors heartily endorse adherence to these guidelines.

---

[2]*Webster's Third New International Dictionary*, p. 1142.

CONCLUSION

This chapter has presented two of the most widely quoted sets of standards for business valuation report writing. In addition, further directions on report writing are contained in the Internal Revenue Service *Business Valuation Guidelines* (see Appendix A).

This chapter has also presented discussions of each of the critical elements of a business appraisal report, the organization of the report, and qualities of a good report. Reports that adhere to all the factors enumerated in this chapter (as well as the business valuation principles presented elsewhere in this book) should withstand professional scrutiny and be a source of pride to their authors.

Chapter 24

Questions to Ask Business Valuation Experts

SUMMARY

This chapter consists of a partial list of questions that are useful to ask potential valuation experts. The questions are applicable in all types of valuation cases including family law, state dissenting stockholder or minority oppression actions, bankruptcy cases, ad valorem cases, and tax cases, regardless of the standard of value.

QUALIFICATIONS

Are you employed? Where?

Please describe your employment history.

Please describe your educational background.

Did your work experience allow you to get involved in _____?

Did you have occasion to focus on _____?

Since you began your career, what work have you done in the area of _____?

Do you have a copy of your curriculum vitae?

Please describe any articles you published.

Have you ever been recognized as an expert in any court on the subject of _____?

Have you previously authored articles, presented opinions in any form, or offered any testimony that is contrary to the opinion you intend to give here?

What professional designations do you hold that relate to business valuation?

American Society of Appraisers

    ❒ FASA

    ❒ ASA

    ❒ AM

Institute of Business Appraisers

    ❒ MCBA

    ❒ CBA

    ❒ BVAL

American Institute of Certified Public Accountants

    ❒ ABV

National Association of Certified Valuation Analysts

    ❒ CVA

    ❒ GVA

CFA Institute

    ❒ CFA

The Canadian Institute of Chartered Business Valuators

    ❒ FCBV

    ❒ CBV

What percentage of your time do you spend doing business valuations? If less than 100 percent, what do you do with the rest of your time?

FINANCIAL STATEMENT ADJUSTMENTS AND ANALYSIS

What adjustments to the subject company's financial statements did you make?

For each adjustment, why did you make it and how did you arrive at the amount?

Were there any adjustments you considered making, but didn't? If so, why not?

If you used the market approach, what adjustments did you make to the guideline company financial statements? (If none, why not? Analysts should be able to say that they have reviewed guideline company statements and determined that no adjustments were necessary.)

ECONOMIC AND INDUSTRY DATA

Many valuation reports have lengthy economic and industry analysis sections, but no discussion of their impact on value. The questions should establish the connection between conditions external to the company and the conclusion of value. They should also reveal inconsistencies, if any.

What industry sources did you use?

How specifically did the data in the industry sources impact your conclusion of value?

What economic information sources did you use?

How, specifically, did your economic analysis impact your conclusion of value?

SITE VISITS AND INTERVIEWS

What did you learn about the subject company on your site visits and interviews?

How did what you learned affect your methodology and/or your value conclusion?

GENERAL QUESTIONS ABOUT METHODOLOGY

For which method(s) did you use the market value of invested capital (MVIC) procedure, and for which did you use the equity procedure?

For each, why was that the best procedure to apply in this case?

DISCOUNT AND CAPITALIZATION RATES IN THE INCOME APPROACH

Note: In the income approach, the capitalization rate is a function of the discount rate. Specifically, the capitalization rate is equal to the discount rate, minus the long-term sustainable growth rate in the variable being capitalized (net cash flow, net income, pretax earnings, etc.). Therefore, to arrive at a capitalization rate in the income approach the analyst should first develop the discount rate applicable to the variable, then estimate the long-term sustainable growth rate for the variable and subtract the estimated long-term growth rate from the discount rate.

In the market approach and the excess earnings method, capitalization rates are developed differently from those in the income approach. In the market approach, the capitalization rate is the reciprocal of the valuation multiplier for the variable. In the excess earnings method, two capitalization rates are used, one a reasonable return on tangible assets and the other a capitalization rate for the excess earnings, if any. Although developed differently in the various approaches, a capitalization rate for any given economic variable developed for one approach should be reconcilable with the capitalization rate for the same variable used in the income approach.

How did you develop your equity discount rate?

Components

Source for each component

To what income variable is your equity discount rate applicable?

How did you develop your weighted average cost of capital?

What components did you include in the capital structure?

One or more classes of equity

One or more classes of debt

How did you estimate the cost for each component?

Sources

Rationale

What weight did you assign to each component?

How did you arrive at the relative weights?

There are two issues here:

1. Market values or book values. They *should* be at market value.
2. Existing capital structure or proposed capital structure.

   This is controversial, but usually should be at existing cap structure for minority interests and some industry average for controlling interests, because minority has no power to change the capitalization structure, but controlling interest does.

If the capitalization method was used, what growth rate, if any, did you subtract from the discount rate to arrive at the capitalization rate?

How did you arrive at the growth rate that you used?

If the discounting method was used, how did you arrive at the terminal value? (market multiples, Gordon Growth Model, liquidation value, etc.)

If market multiples were used, what variable did you use a multiple of? Why was that the best variable to use in this case? How did you arrive at the multiples used?

If the Gordon Growth Model was used, how did you arrive at the sustainable growth rate following the specific projection period?

If liquidation value was used, how did you arrive at the liquidation value?

PROJECTIONS USED IN THE INCOME APPROACH

What income variable did you use in the numerator of your discounting or capitalization method (net cash flow, net income, etc.)?

Why was that the best measure of economic benefits to use in this case?

What was the basis for using that (those) amount(s) in the numerator?

MARKET APPROACH

What methods did you use within the market approach?

- ❐ Guideline publicly traded method
- ❐ Guideline transaction (merger & acquisition) method
- ❐ Prior transactions or offers
- ❐ Buy/sell agreement
- ❐ Rules of thumb

What population of guideline transactions did you consider?

What databases did you use in your search for guideline transactions?

What were the criteria (parameters) for selection of guideline companies?

How (and why) did you select the variables to be used in the market approach (net cash flow, net income, book value, adjusted book value, etc.)?

For each variable, how (and why) did you select the multiple to apply to the subject company?

How (and why) did you select the weightings to apply to each variable?

ASSET-BASED APPROACH

What assets did you adjust? Why?

Did you tax-affect the adjustments? Why or why not?

For each adjustment, what was the basis for the amount of the adjustment?

Did you bring any assets onto the balance sheet that were not there before? Why or why not? What was the basis for the amount assigned to each?

What liabilities did you adjust? Why?

For each liability adjustment, did you tax-affect the adjustment? Why or why not?

Did you bring any actual or contingent liabilities onto the balance sheet that were not there before? Why or why not? What was the basis for the amount assigned to each?

ENTITY-LEVEL DISCOUNTS

If the appraiser applied any of the following discounts:

- Key person
- Contingent liability
- Portfolio (nonhomogeneous assets)
- Trapped-in capital gains

Why did you apply that particular discount?

How did you quantify the amount of the discount?

MINORITY INTEREST DISCOUNTS/CONTROL PREMIUMS

What data did you rely on to quantify the minority discount or control premium?

Why was this data appropriate in this case?

How did you quantify the amount of the minority discount/control premium?

DISCOUNTS FOR LACK OF MARKETABILITY

What data did you rely on to quantify the discount for lack of marketability?

❏ Restricted stock studies or databases (list studies or databases relied on)

❏ Pre-IPO studies or databases (list studies or databases relied on, i.e., Emory, Valuation Advisors)

❏ Partnership Profiles (state which issue, and dates of transactions covered)

Did you use averages from the studies or did you select specific transactions that most closely matched your subject?

If specific transactions were used, what were the criteria for selection of the transactions?

Why were the data on which you relied appropriate for the particular subject?

What factors affected the size of the discount? (e.g., risk factors, size of block/expected holding period)

VOTING/NONVOTING STOCK

If nonvoting stock, what data did you use to quantify the discount from the voting stock?

How did you arrive at the amount of the discount?

QUESTIONS ABOUT CONTRADICTORY PRIOR TESTIMONY

In some cases, the expert may have given prior testimony contradicting the expert's current litigation position. If so, it would be appropriate to read from the opinion or testimony in the prior case and ask something like, "Did you say this?"[1]

---

[1]The most comprehensive search of experts' testimony in business valuation cases is found at *BVLibrary.com*. Even if the experts are not named in the case opinion, the staff of Business Valuation Resources researches the names of the experts and adds them to the case opinions.

IRS Business Valuation Guidelines[1]

TABLE OF CONTENTS

INTERNAL REVENUE SERVICE BUSINESS VALUATION GUIDELINES

1.0 Introduction

The purpose of this document is to provide guidelines applicable to all IRS personnel engaged in valuation practice (herein referred to as "valuators") relating to the development, resolution and reporting of issues involving business valuations and similar valuation issues. Valuators must be able to reasonably justify any departure from these guidelines.

This document incorporates by reference, the ethical and conduct provisions, contained in the office of government ethics (OGE) standards of ethical conduct, applicable to all IRS employees.

---

[1] These Guidelines are continually updated. The latest version may be obtained by calling the IRS at (954) 423-7346.

2.0 Development Guidelines

2.1 Planning

2.1.1 Valuators will adequately plan and their managers will supervise the staff involved in the valuation process.

2.1.2 Quality planning is a continual process throughout the valuation assignment.

2.2 Identifying

2.2.1 In developing a valuation conclusion, valuators should define the assignment and determine the scope of work necessary by identifying the following:

2.2.1.1 Subject to be valued

2.2.1.2 Interest to be valued

2.2.1.3 Effective date of valuation

2.2.1.4 Purpose of valuation

2.2.1.5 Use of valuation

2.2.1.6 Statement of value

2.2.1.7 Standard and definition of value

2.2.1.8 Assumptions

2.2.1.9 Limiting conditions

2.2.1.10 Scope limitations

2.2.1.11 Restrictions, agreements and other factors that may influence value

2.2.1.12 Sources of information

2.3 Analyzing

2.3.1 In developing a valuation conclusion, valuators should obtain and analyze the relevant information necessary to accomplish the assignment, including:

2.3.1.1 The nature of the business and the history of the enterprise from its inception

2.3.1.2 The economic outlook in general and the condition and outlook of the specific industry in particular

2.3.1.3 The book value of the stock or interest and the financial condition of the business

2.3.1.4 The earning capacity of the company

2.3.1.5 The dividend-paying capacity

2.3.1.6 Whether or not the enterprise has goodwill or other intangible value

2.3.1.7 Sales of the stock or interest and the size of the block of stock to be valued

2.3.1.8 The market price of stocks or interests of corporations or entities engaged in the same or a similar line of business having their stocks or interests actively traded in a free and open market, either on an exchange or over-the-counter

2.3.1.9 Other information deemed to be relevant

2.3.2 The three generally accepted valuation approaches are the asset-based approach, the market approach and the income approach. Consideration should be given to all three approaches. Professional judgment should be used to select the approach(es) ultimately used and the method(s) within such approach(es) that best indicate the value of the business interest.

2.3.3 Historical financial statements should be analyzed and, if necessary, adjusted to reflect the appropriate asset value, income, cash flows and/or benefit stream, as applicable, to be consistent with the valuation methodologies selected by the valuator.

2.3.4 The valuator should select the appropriate benefit stream, such as pre-tax or after-tax income and/or cash flows, and select appropriate discount rates, capitalization rates or multiples consistent with the benefit stream selected within the relevant valuation methodology.

2.3.5 The valuator will determine an appropriate discount and/or capitalization rate after taking into consideration all relevant factors, such as:

    2.3.5.1 The nature of the business

    2.3.5.2 The risk involved

    2.3.5.3 The stability or irregularity of earnings

    2.3.5.4 Other relevant factors

2.3.6 As appropriate for the assignment, and if not considered in the process of determining and weighing the indications of value provided by other procedures, the valuator should separately consider the following factors in reaching a final conclusion of value:

    2.3.6.1 Marketability, or lack thereof, considering the nature of the business, business ownership interest or security, the effect of relevant contractual and legal restrictions, and the condition of the markets

    2.3.6.2 Ability of the appraised interest to control the operation, sale, or liquidation of the relevant business

    2.3.6.3 Other levels of value considerations (consistent with the standard of value in section 2.2.1.6) such as the impact of strategic or synergistic contributions to value

    2.3.6.4 Such other factors which, in the opinion of the valuator, are appropriate for consideration

2.4 Workpapers

2.4.1 Workpapers should document the steps taken, techniques used, and provide the evidence to support the facts and conclusions in the final report.

2.4.2 Valuators will maintain a detailed case activity record (form 9984) which:

    2.4.2.1 Identifies actions taken and indicates time charged

    2.4.2.2 Identifies contacts including name, phone number, subject, commitments, etc.

    2.4.2.3 Documents delays in the examination

2.4.3 The case activity record, along with the supporting workpapers, should justify time spent is commensurate with work performed.

2.5 Reviewing

2.5.1 In reviewing a business valuation and reporting the results of that review, a valuator should form an opinion as to the adequacy and appropriateness of the report being reviewed and should clearly disclose the scope of work of the review process undertaken.

2.5.2 In reviewing a business valuation, a valuator should:

    2.5.2.1 Identify the taxpayer and intended use of the valuator's opinions and conclusions, and the purpose of the review assignment

    2.5.2.2 Identify the report under review, the property interest being valued, the effective date of the valuation, and the date of the review

2.5.2.3   Identify the scope of work of the review process conducted

2.5.2.4   Form an opinion as to the completeness of the report under review within the scope of work applicable in the review assignment

2.5.2.5   Form an opinion as to the apparent adequacy and relevance of the data and the propriety of any adjustments to the data

2.5.2.6   Form an opinion as to the appropriateness of the valuation methods and techniques used and develop the reasons for any disagreement

2.5.2.7   Form an opinion as to whether the analyses, opinions and conclusions in the report under review are appropriate and reasonable, and develop the reasons for any disagreement

2.5.2.8   In the event of a disagreement with the report's factual representations, underlying assumptions, methodology or conclusions, conduct additional fact-finding, research and/or analyses necessary to make corrections or revisions to arrive at an appropriate value for the property.

3.0   Resolution Guidelines

3.1   Objective

3.1.1   The objective is to resolve the issue as early in the examination as possible. Credible and compelling work by the valuator will facilitate resolution of issues without litigation.

3.1.2   The valuator will work in concert with the internal customer and taxpayer to resolve all outstanding issues.

3.2   Arriving at conclusions

3.2.1   Once the valuator has all the information to be considered in resolving the issue, the valuator will use his/her professional judgment in considering this information to arrive at a conclusion.

3.2.2   Valuators may not have all of the information they would like to have to definitively resolve an issue. Valuators, therefore, should decide when they have substantially enough information to make a proper determination.

3.2.3   Valuators will employ independent and objective judgment in reaching conclusions and will decide all matters on their merits, free from bias, advocacy and conflicts of interest.

4.0   Reporting Guidelines

4.1   Overview

4.1.1   The primary objective of a valuation report is to provide convincing and compelling support for the conclusions reached.

4.1.2   Valuation reports should contain all the information necessary to allow a clear understanding of the valuation analyses and demonstrate how the conclusions were reached.

4.2   Report contents

4.2.1   The extent and content of the report prepared depends on the needs of each case.

4.2.2   Valuation reports should clearly communicate the results and identify the information relied upon in the valuation process. The valuation report should effectively communicate the methodology and reasoning, as well as identify the supporting documentation.

4.2.3   Subject to the type of report being written, valuation reports should generally contain sufficient information relating to the items in sections 2.2 and 2.3, above, to ensure consistency and quality of valuation reports issued by IRS valuators.

4.2.4   Reports written with respect to section 2.5.2.8, above, shall contain, at a minimum, information relating to those items in sections 2.2 and 2.3 necessary to support the revised assumptions, analyses, and/or conclusions of the valuator.

4.3   Statement

4.3.1   Each written valuation report should contain a signed statement that is similar in content to the following:

To the best of my knowledge and belief:

- The statements of fact contained in this report are true and correct.
- The reported analyses, opinions, and conclusions are limited only by the reported assumptions and limiting conditions.
- I have no present or prospective interest in the property that is the subject of this report, and I have no personal interest with respect to the parties involved.
- I have no bias with respect to the subject of this report or to the parties involved with this assignment.
- My compensation is not contingent on an action or event resulting from the analyses, opinions or conclusions in, or the use of, this report.
- My analyses, opinions, and conclusions were developed, and this report has been prepared in conformity with the applicable Internal Revenue Service Valuation Guidelines.

International Glossary of Business Valuation Terms[1]

Adjusted book value method   A method within the asset approach whereby all assets and liabilities (including off-balance-sheet, intangible, and contingent) are adjusted to their fair market values. [*NOTE:* In Canada on a going-concern basis.]

Adjusted net asset method   See Adjusted book value method.

Appraisal   See Valuation.

Appraisal approach   See Valuation approach.

Appraisal date   See Valuation date.

Appraisal method   See Valuation method.

Appraisal procedure   See Valuation procedure.

Arbitrage pricing theory   A multivariate model for estimating the cost of equity capital, which incorporates several systematic risk factors.

Asset (asset-based) approach   A general way of determining a value indication of a business, business ownership interest, or security using one or more methods based on the value of the assets net of liabilities.

Beta   A measure of systematic risk of a stock; the tendency of a stock's price to correlate with changes in a specific index.

Blockage discount   An amount or percentage deducted from the current market price of a publicly traded stock to reflect the decrease in the per-share value of a block of stock that is of a size that could not be sold in a reasonable period of time given normal trading volume.

Book value   See Net book value.

Business   See Business enterprise.

Business enterprise   A commercial, industrial, service, or investment entity (or a combination thereof) pursuing an economic activity.

Business risk   The degree of uncertainty of realizing expected future returns of the business resulting from factors other than financial leverage. See Financial risk.

Business valuation   The act or process of determining the value of a business enterprise or ownership interest therein.

---

[1]Compiled by American Institute of Certified Public Accountants, American Society of Appraisers, Canadian Institute of Chartered Business Valuators, National Association of Certified Valuation Analysts, and The Institute of Business Appraisers. Used with permission.

Capital asset pricing model (CAPM)   A model in which the cost of capital for any stock or portfolio of stocks equals a risk-free rate plus a risk premium that is proportionate to the systematic risk of the stock or portfolio.

Capitalization   A conversion of a single period of economic benefits into value.

Capitalization factor   Any multiple or divisor used to convert anticipated economic benefits of a single period into value.

Capitalization of earnings method   A method within the income approach whereby economic benefits for a representative single period are converted to value through division by a capitalization rate.

Capitalization rate   Any divisor (usually expressed as a percentage) used to convert anticipated economic benefits of a single period into value.

Capital structure   The composition of the invested capital of a business enterprise, the mix of debt and equity financing.

Cash flow   Cash that is generated over a period of time by an asset, group of assets, or business enterprise. It may be used in a general sense to encompass various levels of specifically defined cash flows. When the term is used, it should be supplemented by a qualifier (for example, "discretionary" or "operating") and a specific definition in the given valuation context.

Common size statements   Financial statements in which each line is expressed as a percentage of the total. On the balance sheet, each line item is shown as a percentage of total assets, and on the income statement, each item is expressed as a percentage of sales.

Control   The power to direct the management and policies of a business enterprise.

Control premium   An amount or a percentage by which the pro rata value of a controlling interest exceeds the pro rata value of a noncontrolling interest in a business enterprise, to reflect the power of control.

Cost approach   A general way of determining a value indication of an individual asset by quantifying the amount of money required to replace the future service capability of that asset.

Cost of capital   The expected rate of return that the market requires in order to attract funds to a particular investment.

Debt-free   We discourage the use of this term. See Invested capital.

Discount for lack of control   An amount or percentage deducted from the pro rata share of value of 100 percent of an equity interest in a business to reflect the absence of some or all of the powers of control.

Discount for lack of marketability   An amount or percentage deducted from the value of an ownership interest to reflect the relative absence of marketability.

Discount for lack of voting rights   An amount or percentage deducted from the per-share value of a minority interest voting share to reflect the absence of voting rights.

Discount rate   A rate of return used to convert a future monetary sum into present value.

Discounted cash flow method   A method within the income approach whereby the present value of future expected net cash flows is calculated using a discount rate.

Discounted future earnings method   A method within the income approach whereby the present value of future expected economic benefits is calculated using a discount rate.

Economic benefits   Inflows such as revenues, net income, and net cash flows.

Economic life   The period of time over which property may generate economic benefits.

Effective date   See Valuation date.

Enterprise   See Business enterprise.

Equity   The owner's interest in property after deduction of all liabilities.

Equity net cash flows   Those cash flows available to pay out to equity holders (in the form of dividends) after funding operations of the business enterprise, making necessary capital investments, and increasing or decreasing debt financing.

Equity risk premium   A rate of return added to a risk-free rate to reflect the additional risk of equity instruments over risk-free instruments (a component of the cost of equity capital or equity discount rate).

Excess earnings   That amount of anticipated economic benefits that exceeds an appropriate rate of return on the value of a selected asset base (often net tangible assets) used to generate those anticipated economic benefits.

Excess earnings method   A specific way of determining a value indication of a business, business ownership interest, or security determined as the sum of (a) the value of the assets derived by capitalizing excess earnings and (b) the value of the selected asset base. Also frequently used to value intangible assts. See Excess earnings.

Fair market value   The price, expressed in terms of cash equivalents, at which property would change hands between a hypothetical willing and able buyer and a hypothetical willing and able seller, acting at arm's length in an open and unrestricted market, when neither is under compulsion to buy or sell and when both have reasonable knowledge of the relevant facts. [*NOTE:* In Canada, the term *price* should be replaced with the term *highest price.*]

Fairness opinion   An opinion as to whether the consideration in a transaction is fair from a financial point of view.

Financial risk   The degree of uncertainty of realizing expected future returns of the business resulting from financial leverage. See Business risk.

Forced liquidation value   Liquidation value, at which the asset or assets are sold as quickly as possible, such as at an auction.

Free cash flow   We discourage the use of this term. See Net cash flow.

Going concern   An ongoing operating business enterprise.

Going-concern value   The value of a business enterprise that is expected to continue to operate into the future. The intangible elements of going concern value result from factors such as having a trained workforce, an operational plant, and the necessary licenses, systems, and procedures in place.

Goodwill   That intangible asset arising as a result of name, reputation, customer loyalty, location, products, and similar factors not separating identified.

Goodwill value   The value attributable to goodwill.

Guideline public company method   A method within the market approach whereby market multiples are derived from market prices of stocks of companies that are engaged in the same or similar lines of business, and that are actively traded on a free and open market.

Income (income-based) approach   A general way of determining a value indication of a business, business ownership interest, security, or intangible asset using one or more methods that convert anticipated economic benefits into a present single amount.

Intangible assets   Nonphysical assets such as franchises, trademarks, patents, copyrights, goodwill, equities, mineral rights, securities and contracts (as distinguished from physical assets) that grant rights and privileges, and have value for the owner.

Internal rate of return   A discount rate at which the present value of the future cash flows of the investment equals the cost of the investment.

Intrinsic value   The value that an investor considers, on the basis of an evaluation or available facts, to be the "true" or "real" value that will become the market value when other investors reach the same conclusion. When the term applies to options, it is the difference between the exercise price or strike price of an option and the market value of the underlying security.

Invested capital   The sum of equity and debt in a business enterprise. Debt is typically (a) all interest-bearing debt or (b) long-term interest-bearing debt. When the term is used, it should be supplemented by a specific definition in the given valuation context.

Invested capital net cash flows   Those cash flows available to pay out to equity holders (in the form of dividends) and debt investors (in the form of principal and interest) after funding operations of the business enterprise and making necessary capital investment.

Investment risk   The degree of uncertainty as to the realization of expected returns.

Investment value   The value to a particular investor based on individual investment requirements and expectations. [*NOTE:* In Canada, the term used is *value to the owner.*]

Key person discount   An amount or percentage deducted from the value of an ownership interest to reflect the reduction in value resulting from the actual or potential loss of a key person in a business enterprise.

Levered beta   The beta reflecting a capital structure that includes debt.

Limited appraisal   The act or process of determining the value of a business, business ownership interest, security, or intangible asset with limitations in analyses, procedures, or scope.

Liquidity   The ability to quickly convert property to cash or pay a liability.

Liquidation value   The net amount that would be realized if the business is terminated and the assets are sold piecemeal. Liquidation can be either "orderly" or "forced."

Majority control   The degree of control provided by a majority position.

Majority interest   An ownership interest greater than 50 percent of the voting interest in a business enterprise.

Market (market-based) approach   A general way of determining a value indication of a business, business ownership interest, security, or intangible asset by using one or more methods that compare the subject to similar businesses, business ownership interests, securities, or intangible assets that have been sold.

Market capitalization of equity   The share price of a publicly traded stock multiplied by the number of shares outstanding.

Market capitalization of invested capital   The market capitalization of equity plus the market value of the debt component of invested capital.

Market multiple   The market value of a company's stock or invested capital divided by a company measure (such as economic benefits, number of customers).

Marketability   The ability to quickly convert property to cash at minimal cost.

Marketability discount   See Discount for lack of marketability.

Merger and acquisition method   A method within the market approach whereby pricing multiples are derived from transactions of significant interests in companies engaged in the same or similar lines of business.

Midyear discounting   A convention used in the discounted future earnings method that reflects economic benefits being generated at midyear, approximating the effect of economic benefits being generated evenly throughout the year.

Minority discount   A discount for lack of control applicable to a minority interest.

Minority interest   An ownership interest less than 50 percent of the voting interest in a business enterprise.

Multiple   The inverse of the capitalization rate.

Net book value   With respect to a business enterprise, the difference between total assets (net of accumulated depreciation, depletion, and amortization) and total liabilities as they appear on the balance sheet (synonymous with Shareholder's Equity). With respect to a specific asset, the capitalized cost less accumulated amortization or depreciation as it appears on the books of account of the business enterprise.

Net cash flows   When the term is used, it should be supplemented by a qualifier. See Equity net cash flows and Invested capital net cash flows.

Net present value   The value, as of a specified date, of future cash inflows less all cash outflows (including the cost of investment) calculated using an appropriate discount rate.

Net tangible asset value   The value of the business enterprise's tangible assets (excluding excess assets and non-operating assets) minus the value of its liabilities.

Nonoperating assets   Assets not necessary to ongoing operations of the business enterprise. [*NOTE:* In Canada, the term used is *redundant assets.*]

Normalized earnings   Economic benefits adjusted for nonrecurring, noneconomic, or other unusual items to eliminate anomalies and/or facilitate comparisons.

Normalized financial statements   Financial statements adjusted for nonoperating assets and liabilities and/or for nonrecurring, noneconomic, or other unusual items to eliminate anomalies and/or facilitate comparisons.

Orderly liquidation value   Liquidation value at which the asset or assets are sold over a reasonable period of time to maximize proceeds received.

Premise of value   An assumption regarding the most likely set of transactional circumstances that may be applicable to the subject valuation (e.g., going concern, liquidation).

Present value   The value, as of a specified date, of future economic benefits and/or proceeds from sale, calculated using an appropriate discount rate.

Portfolio discount   An amount or percentage deducted from the value of a business enterprise to reflect the fact that it owns dissimilar operations or assets that do not fit well together.

Price/earnings multiple   The price of a share of stock divided by its earnings per share.

Rate of return   An amount of income (loss) and/or change in value realized or anticipated on an investment, expressed as a percentage of that investment.

Redundant assets   See Nonoperating assets.

Report date   The date conclusions are transmitted to the client.

Replacement cost new   The current cost of a similar new property having the nearest equivalent utility to the property being valued.

Reproduction cost new   The current cost of an identical new property.

Required rate of return   The minimum rate of return acceptable by investors before they will commit money to an investment at a given level of risk.

Residual value   The value as of the end of the discrete projection period in a discounted future earnings model.

Return on equity   The amount, expressed as a percentage, earned on a company's common equity for a given period.

Return on investment   See Return on invested capital and Return on equity.

Return on invested capital   The amount, expressed as a percentage, earned on a company's total capital for a given period.

Risk-free rate   A rate of return available in the market on an investment free of default risk.

Risk premium   A rate of return added to a risk-free rate to reflect risk.

Rule of thumb   A mathematical formula developed from the relationship between price and certain variables based on experience, observation, hearsay, or a combination of these; usually industry specific.

Special interest purchasers   Acquirers who believe they can enjoy post-acquisition economies of scale, synergies, or strategic advantages by combining the acquired business interest with their own.

Standard of value   The identification of the type of value being used in a specific engagement (e.g., fair market value, fair value, investment value).

Sustaining capital reinvestment   The periodic capital outlay required to maintain operations at existing levels, net of the tax shield available from such outlays.

Systematic risk   The risk that is common to all risky securities and cannot be eliminated through diversification. The measure of systematic risk in stocks is the beta coefficient.

Tangible assets   Physical assets (such as cash, accounts receivable, inventory, property plant and equipment, etc.).

Terminal value   See Residual value.

Transaction method   See merger and acquisition method.

Unlevered beta   The beta reflecting a capital structure without debt.

Unsystematic risk   The portion of total risk specific to an individual security that can be avoided through diversification.

Valuation   The act or process of determining the value of a business, business ownership interest, security, or intangible asset.

Valuation approach   A general way of determining a value indication of a business, business ownership interest, security, or intangible asset using one or more valuation methods.

Valuation date   The specific point in time as of which the valuator's opinion of value applies (also referred to as *effective date* or *appraisal date*).

Valuation method   Within approaches, a specific way to determine value.

Valuation procedure   The act, manner, and technique of performing the steps of an appraisal method.

Valuation ratio   A fraction in which a value or price serves as the numerator and financial, operating, or physical data serve as the denominator.

Value to the owner   [*NOTE:* In Canada, see Investment value.]

Voting control   De jure control of a business enterprise.

Weighted average cost of capital (WACC)   The cost of capital (discount rate) determined by the weighted average, at market value, of the cost of all financing sources in the business enterprise's capital structure.

Bibliography

BOOKS

Babitsky, Steven, and James J. Mangraviti Jr. *Cross-Examination: The Comprehensive Guide for Experts.* Falmouth, MA: SEAK, 2003.

_____. *How to Excel During Cross Examination: Techniques for Experts that Work.* Falmouth, MA: SEAK, 1997.

_____. *How to Excel During Depositions: Techniques for Experts that Work.* Falmouth, MA: SEAK, 1999.

_____. *Writing and Defending Your Expert Report: The Step-by-Step Guide with Models.* Falmouth, MA: SEAK, 2002.

Babitsky, Steven, James J. Mangraviti Jr., and Christopher J. Todd. *The Comprehensive Forensic Services Manual.* Falmouth, MA.: SEAK, 2002.

Bogdanski, John A. *Federal Tax Valuation.* New York: Warren, Gorham & Lamont, 1996. Supplemented semiannually.

Brealey, Richard A., and Stewart C. Myers. *Principles of Corporate Finance*, 7th ed. New York: McGraw-Hill/Irwin, 2003.

Business Valuation Guidelines. Internal Revenue Service, 2004.

Desmond, Glenn. *Handbook of Small Business Valuation Formulas and Rules of Thumb*, 3rd ed. Camden, ME: Valuation Press, 1993.

Estabrook, Joseph S. "Blockage Discounts." Chapter 7, Reilly, Robert F. and Robert P. Schweihs. *The Handbook for Advanced Business Valuation.* New York: McGraw-Hill, 2000: 139–153.

Feder, Harold A. *Succeeding as an Expert Witness: Increasing Your Impact and Income*, 3rd ed. Glenwood Springs, CO: Tageh Press, 2000.

Federal Tax Valuation Digest. New York: Thomson/RIA. Updated annually.

Fishman, Jay E., Shannon P. Pratt, J. Clifford Griffith, and D. Keith Wilson, et al. *PPC's Guide to Business Valuations.* Fort Worth, TX: Practitioners Publishing. Published annually.

Grabowski, Roger J., and William P. McFadden. "Applying the Income Approach to S Corporation and Other Pas-Through Entity Valuations." Robert F. Reilly and Robert P. Schweihs, eds. *The Handbook of Business Valuation and Intellectual Property Analysis.* New York: McGraw-Hill, 2004. Chapter 5: 89–125.

Hitchner, James R. *Financial Valuation: Applications and Models and Financial Valuation Workbook.* Hoboken, NJ: John Wiley & Sons, Inc., 2003.

Ibbotson, Roger, and Jay R. Ritter. "Initial Public Offerings." Chapter 30, R .A. Jarrow, V. Maksimovic and W. T. Ziemba, eds. *North-Holland Handbooks of Operations Research and Management Science*, Volume 9. Amsterdam: Elsevier, 1995: 993–1016.

Industry Valuation Update Volume 1: Wholesale Trade. Business Valuation Resources, 7412 S.W. Beaverton-Hillsdale Hwy, Suite 106, Portland, OR 97225; ph: 888/BUS-VALU (888/287-8258) or 503/291-7963; fax: 800/846-2291 or 503/291-9755; *www.BVResources.com.*

Industry Valuation Update Volume 2: Eating and Drinking Places. Business Valuation Resources, 7412 S.W. Beaverton-Hillsdale Hwy, Suite 106, Portland, OR 97225; ph: 888/BUS-VALU (888/287-8258) or 503/291-7963; fax: 800/846-2291 or 503/291-9755; *www.BVResources.com.*

Industry Valuation Update Volume 3: Construction. Business Valuation Resources, 7412 S.W. Beaverton-Hillsdale Hwy, Suite 106, Portland, OR 97225; ph: 888/BUS-VALU (888/287-8258) or 503/291-7963; fax: 800/846-2291 or 503/291-9755; *www.BVResources.com.*

Industry Valuation Update Volume 4: Software and Computer Industries. Business Valuation Resources, 7412 S.W. Beaverton-Hillsdale Hwy, Suite 106, Portland, OR 97225; ph: 888/BUS-VALU (888/287-8258) or 503/291-7963; fax: 800/846-2291 or 503/291-9755; *www.BVResources.com.*

Internal Revenue Service. *IRS Valuation Training for Appeals Officers Coursebook.* Chicago: Commerce Clearing House Incorporated, 1998.

Jefferies, Spencer, Bruce A. Johnson, ASA, and James R. Park, ASA. *A Comprehensive Guide for the Valuation of Family Limited Partnerships*, 2nd ed. Dallas: Partnership Profiles, 2003.

Lang, Eva M. and Jan Davis Tudor. *Best Websites for Financial Professionals, Business Appraisers, and Accountants*, 2nd ed. Hoboken, NJ: John Wiley & Sons, Inc., 2003.

Marlow, Jerry. *Option Pricing.* New York: John Wiley & Sons, Inc., 2001.

Matthews, Gilbert E., Sutter Securities Incorporated. "Transactions Involving Premiums for Control Blocks." Pratt, Shannon P. *Business Valuation Discounts and Premiums.* New York: John Wiley & Sons, Inc., 2001: 211–219.

Mercer, Z. Christopher. *Quantifying Marketability Discounts.* Memphis, TN: Peabody Publishing, 2001.

_____. *Valuing Enterprise and Shareholder Cash Flows: The Integrated Theory of Business Valuation.* Memphis, TN: Peabody Publishing, 2004.

Much, Paul J., and Timothy J. Fagan. "The Value of Voting Rights." Zukin, James H., ed. *Financial Valuation: Business and Business Interests.* New York: Warren Gorham & Lamont, 1996 Update: U9B-1.

Pratt, Shannon P. *Business Valuation Body of Knowledge*, 2nd ed., with Workbook. New York: John Wiley & Sons, Inc., 2003.

_____. *Business Valuation Discounts and Premiums.* New York: John Wiley & Sons, Inc., 2001.

_____. *Cost of Capital: Estimation and Applications*, 2nd ed., with Workbook. New York: John Wiley & Sons, Inc., 2002.

_____. *The Lawyer's Business Valuation Handbook: Understanding Financial Statements, Appraisal Reports and Expert Testimony.* Chicago: American Bar Association, 2000.

_____. *The Market Approach to Valuing Businesses.* New York: John Wiley & Sons, Inc., 2001.

Pratt, Shannon P., Robert F. Reilly, and Robert P. Schweihs. *Valuing a Business: The Analysis and Appraisal of Closely Held Companies*, 4th ed. New York: McGraw-Hill, 2000.

_____. *Valuing Small Businesses and Professional Practices*, 3rd ed. New York: McGraw-Hill, 1998.

Reilly, Frank K., and Keith C. Brown. *Investment Analysis and Portfolio Management*, 7th ed. Mason, OH: South-Western, 2003.

Reilly, Robert F., and Robert P. Schweihs, eds. *The Handbook for Advanced Business Valuation.* New York: McGraw-Hill, 2000.

_____. *Handbook of Business Valuation and Intellectual Property Analysis.* New York: McGraw-Hill, 2004.

_____. *Valuing Intangible Assets.* New York: McGraw-Hill, 1998.

Stocks, Bonds, Bills & Inflation, Valuation Edition. Chicago: Ibbotson Associates. Published annually.

Trugman, Gary R. *Understanding Business Valuation: A Practical Guide to Valuing Small to Medium-Sized Businesses.* New York: American Institute of Certified Public Accountants, 2001.

Van Vleet, Daniel R. "Premium and Discount Issues as Undivided Interest Valuations." Chapter 19, Shannon Pratt. *Business Valuation Discounts and Premiums.* New York: John Wiley & Sons, Inc., 2001: 292–315.

Van Vleet, Daniel R. "The S Corporation Economic Adjustment." Robert F. Reilly and Robert P. Schweihs, eds. *The Handbook of Business Valuation and Intellectual Property Analysis.* New York: McGraw-Hill, 2004. Chapter 4: 71–88.

West, Tom. *The Business Reference Guide.* Concord, MA: Business Brokerage Press. Published annually.

Zukin, James H., ed. *Financial Valuation: Businesses and Business Interests.* New York: WG&L/RIA Group, 1998.

ARTICLES AND PAPERS[1]

Abrams, Jay B., ASA, CPA. "Problems in the QMDM and Comparison to Economic Components Model: A Response to Chris Mercer." *Business Valuation Review* (June 2002): 83–91.

Aschwald, Kathryn F. "Restricted Stock Discounts Decline as Result of One-Year Holding Period." *Shannon Pratt's Business Valuation Update* (May 2000): 1–5.

Bajaj, Mukesh, Denis J. David, et al. "Firm Value and Marketability Discounts." *The Journal of Corporation Law* (Fall 2001): 89–115.

Bajaj, Mukesh, Z. Christopher Mercer, and George Hawkins. "Tax-Affecting S Corporation Earnings for the Purpose of Valuing Stock." Audio Conference. Business Valuation Resources, LLC, August 13, 2002.

Barber, Gregory A. "Valuation of Pass-Through Entities." *Valuation Strategies* (March/April 2001): 4–11, 44–45.

Bogdanski, John A. "Further Adventures with the Lack of Marketability Discount." *Estate Planning* (June 1999): 235.

Burke, Brian H. "The Impact of S Corporation Status." *Business Valuation Review* (June 2001): 15–24.

Carmen, Paul, and Melanie Gnazzo. "FMV, Mark-to-Market, and Clear Reflection of Income: The Tax Court Takes a Middle Road in Bank One." *Journal of Taxation* (August 2003): 98.

"Court Rejects All Experts; Articulates Tax Valuation Principles." *Shannon Pratt's Business Valuation Update* (January 1997): 7.

"Court Uses Raw Data from Bajaj Study to Determine DLOM." *Shannon Pratt's Business Valuation Update* (November 2003): 8–9.

Crimm, Nina J. "A Role for 'Expert Arbitrators' in Resolving Valuation Issues before the United States Tax Court: A Remedy to Plaguing Problems." *Indiana Law Review* 26, (1992): 41, 44.

Crow, Matthew R., and Brent A. McDade. "The Hypothetical Willing Seller: Maybe C Corporations Are Worth More Than S Corporations." *Mercer Capital's Value Matters*, November 26, 2003.

Denis, David J., and Atulya Sarin. "Taxes and the Relative Valuation of S Corporations and C Corporations." *Journal of Applied Finance* (Fall/Winter 2002): 5–14.

Dietrich, Mark O. "Computing Premium for S Status Based on Buyer's Benefit. *Valuation Strategies* (May/June 2003): 24–32.

Erickson, Merle (University of Chicago), and Shiing-wu Wang (University of Southern California). "The Effect of Organizational Form on Acquisition Price." *Study* (May 16, 2002).

Finkel, Sidney R. "Is There an S Corporation Premium?" *Valuation Strategies* (July/August 2001): 14–27.

---

[1]Presentations listed are available at *www.BVLibrary.com*, unless otherwise noted.

Fiore, Owen. "1998 IRS Restructuring and Reform Act Begs Timely, High-Quality Appraisals." *Shannon Pratt's Business Valuation Update* (January 1999): 1, 3–4.

Giardina, Edward. "The *Gross* Decision—Where Do We Go From Here?" *Valuation Strategies* (May/June 2002): 2–9, 46.

Goldberg, Leonard M., Esq., Denice P. Gilchrist, Esq., Goldberg, Mufson & Spar, 200 Executive Drive, Suite 355, West Orange, NJ 07052; 973/736-0100. "Income Tax and Transfer Tax Structuring Issues in the Use of Family Limited Partnerships and Family Limited Liability Companies." © 1998, Leonard M. Goldberg. November 1, 1998.

Grabowski, Rogert J. "S Corporation Valuations in a Post-Gross World—Updated." *Business Valuation Review* (September 2004): 139.

Hall, Lance. "The Value of Restricted Stock." American Society of Appraisers Annual International Conference, August 26-28, 2002, San Diego, CA. Available at *BVResources.com*.

Institutional Investor Study Report of the Securities and Exchange Commission. H.R. Doc. No. 64, Part 5, 92nd Congress, 1st Session (1971).

Jankowske, Wayne. "Second-Stage Adjustments to Value." American Society of Appraisers International Appraisal Conference. Toronto, Canada, 1996. Available at *BVLibrary.com*.

Johnson, Bruce. "Restricted Stock Discounts 1991–1995," *Shannon Pratt's Business Valuation Update* (March 1999): 1–3.

Julius, J. Michael. "Converting Distributions from S Corporations and Partnerships to a C Corporation Dividend Equivalent Basis." *Business Valuation Review* (June 1997): 65–67.

Lease, Ronald C., John J. McConnell and Wayne H. Mikkelson. "The Market Value of Control in Publicly-Traded Corporations." *Journal of Financial Economics* (1983): 439–471.

Lerch, Mary Ann. "Pretax/After Conversion Formula for Capitalization Rates and Cash Flow Discount Rates." *Business Valuation Review* (March 1990): 18–22.

Marketability Discounts in the Courts, 1991–1Q2002. Business Valuation Resources, 7412 S.W. Beaverton-Hillsdale Hwy, Suite 106, Portland, OR 97225; ph: 888/BUS-VALU (888/287-8258) or 503/291-7963; fax: 800/846-2291 or 503/291-9755 (2002). *www.BVResources.com*.

Mattson, Michael J., Donald S. Shannon, and David E. Upton. "Empirical Research Concludes S Corporation Values Same as C Corporations, Part 1 and Part 2." *Shannon Pratt's Business Valuation Update* (November and December 2002): 1, 3–5 and 1–4, respectively.

McNulty, Mary, and Michelle M. Kwon. "Tax Considerations in Choice of Entity Decisions." *Business Entities* (November/December 2002): 1.

Melone, Matthew A. "Hypothetical Valuation of Partnership Interests in Sales or Exchanges Required by New Final Regulations." *Valuation Strategies* (May/June 2000): 12–19, 43–44.

Mercer, Z. Christopher, and Joseph D. Vinso, "S Corporation Valuation." 2002 International Appraisal Conference. American Society of Appraisers, August 27, 2002.

Mercer, Z. Christopher. "Tax Court Accords Superpremium to Small Voting Block; Allows Deduction of 100% of Trapped-in Capital Gains Tax." *Judges & Lawyers Business Valuation Update* (April 1999): 1, 6–7.

Mercer, Z. Christopher. "Are S Corporations Worth More Than C Corporations?" *Business Valuation Review* (September 2004): 117.

O'Shea, Kevin C., and Robert M. Siwicki. "Stock Price Premiums for Voting Rights Attributable to Minority Interests." *Business Valuation Review* (December 1991): 165–171.

Oliver, Robert P. "Court Accepts Taxpayer's 76% Discount on Farm Corporation." *Shannon Pratt's Business Valuation Update* (December 1999): 10–13.

"Panel on Burden of Proof." 1999 Mid Year Meeting, ABA Section of Taxation, Court Procedure & Practice Committee, Orlando, FL, January 15, 1999.

Park, James R. and Bruce A. Johnson. "S Corporation Tax Treatment for Minority Interests: Suggested Treatment for a Controversial Issue." *CCH Business Valuation Alert* 4, Issue 2 (Fall 2002): 3, 6–8.

Pittock, William F., and Charles H. Stryker. "Revenue Ruling 77-276 Revisited. *SRC Quarterly Reports* (Spring 1983): 1–3.

Pratt, Shannon P. "Discounts for Lack of Marketability: Documentation, Critique, and Defense." American Society of Appraisers International Appraisal Conference, Tampa, FL, July 14, 2003.

Reilly, Robert F. "S Corporation Commercial Bank Valuation Methods and Issues." *Valuation Strategies* (May/June 2002): 29–33, 48.

Robinson, Chris, John Rumsey, and Alan White. "The Value of a Vote in the Market for Corporate Control." York University Faculty of Administrative Studies, February 1996.

Rosenthal, Lloyd L. "The Development of the Use of Expert Testimony." *Law & Contemporary Problems* (January 1935): 403.

Scherrer, Phillip S. "Why REITs Face a Merger-Driven Consolidation Wave." *Mergers & Acquisition, The Dealmaker's Journal* (July/August 1995): 42.

Silber, William L. "Discounts on Restricted Stock: The Impact of Illiquidity on Stock Prices. *Financial Analysts Journal* (July–August 1991): 60–64.

Treharne, Chris D. "Comparing Three Payout Assumptions' Impact on Values of S Versus C Corps." *Shannon Pratt's Business Valuation Update* (September 2002): 1.

Treharne, Chris D. "Valuation of Minority Interests in Pas-Through-Tax Entities." *Business Valuation Review* (September 2004): 105.

Treharne, Chris D., James Hitchner, and Nancy J. Fannon. "Valuation of Pass-Through Entities." Advanced Business Valuation Conference. American Society of Appraisers, October 8, 2004.

Treharne, Chris D., and Nancy J. Fannon. "Valuation of Pass-Through-Tax Entities: Minority and Controlling Interests." Department of the Treasury presentation, January 2003.

"Valuation 'Experts' Excluded as Unreliable Based on Numerous Errors in Methodology and Inability to Explain Conclusions." *Shannon Pratt's Business Valuation Update* (May 2003): 6–7.

Van Vleet, Daniel R. "A New Way to Value S Corporation Securities." *Trusts & Estates Magazine* (March 2003).

Van Vleet, Daniel R. "The S Corporation Economic Adjustment Model." *Business Valuation Review* (September 2004): 167.

Van Vleet, Daniel R. "The S Corporation Economic Adjustment Model Revisited." Willamette Management Associates' *Insights* (Wiinter 2004). *www.willametteinsights.com/04/Winter04article3.pdf.*

Van Vleet, Daniel R. "The Valuation of S Corporation Stock: The Equity Adjustment Multiple." *Pennsylvania Family Lawyer* (May-June 2003).

Williams, James L. (Butch), CPA, CVA, Williams, Taylor & Associates, P.C., now Dixon, Odom, PLLC, 2140 Eleventh Ave. South, Suite 400, Birmingham, AL 34205. "The 'Limitations' of Family Limited Partnerships." Prepared for The Institute of Business Appraisers 1998 National Conference, San Antonio, TX, January 30, 1998.

PERIODICALS

Business Entities. Warren, Gorman & Lamont, division of RIA, 395 Hudson St., New York, NY 10014; 800/950-1216, Ext. 1, or 800/431-9025, option 1; *www.riahome.com.* Published bimonthly.

Business Valuation Data and Publications Directory. Business Valuation Resources, 7412 S.W. Beaverton-Hillsdale Hwy, Suite 106, Portland, OR 97225; ph: 888/BUS-VALU (888/287-8258) or 503/291-7963; fax: 800/846-2291 or 503/291-9755; *www.BVResources.com.* Published annually.

Business Valuation Review. Business Valuation Committee of the American Society of Appraisers, P.O. Box 101896, Denver, CO 80250; ph: 303/744-7866; fax: 303/744-7796. Published quarterly.

Direct Investments Spectrum (formerly *Partnership Spectrum*). Partnership Profiles, Inc., P.O. Box 7938, Dallas, TX 75209; 800/634-4614; *www.dispectrum.com.* Published bimonthly.

Estate Planning. Warren, Gorman & Lamont, division of RIA, 395 Hudson St., New York, NY 10014; 800/950-1216, Ext. 1, or 800/431-9025, option 1; *www.riahome.com.* Published monthly.

Financial Analysts Journal. CFA Institute (formerly Association for Investment Management and Research), 560 Ray C. Hunt Dr., Charlottesville, VA 22903-2981; ph: 800/247-8132 or 434/951-5442; fax: 434/951-5262; *www.aimrpubs.org/shared/PubsSubscription.html.* Bimonthly publication.

Indiana Law Review. Indiana University School of Law—Indianapolis, Lawrence W. Inlow Hall, 530 W. New York St., Indianapolis, IN 46202-3225; ph: 317/274-4440 or 317/274-4039; *www.indylaw.indiana.edu/ilr/.* Published quarterly.

Journal of Applied Finance. Financial Management Association International, University of South Florida, College of Business Administration, 4202 E. Fowler Ave., Tampa, FL 33620; ph: 813/974-2084; fax: 813/974-3318; *www.fma.org.* Published semi-annually (Spring/Summer and Fall/Winter).

Journal of Financial Economics. Elsevier Science, Customer Service Dept., 6277 Sea Harbor Dr., Orlando, FL 32887-4800; ph: 877/839-7126 or 407/345-4020; fax: 407/363-1354; *www.else vier.com/wps/find/journalbibliographicinfo.cws_home/505576/description#bibliographicinfo.* Published quarterly.

Journal of Taxation. Warren, Gorman & Lamont, division of RIA, 395 Hudson St., New York, NY 10014; 800/950-1216, Ext. 1, or 800/431-9025, option 1; *www.riahome.com.* Published monthly.

Judges & Lawyers Business Valuation Update. No longer being published. Back issues available from Business Valuation Resources, 7412 S.W. Beaverton-Hillsdale Hwy, Suite 106, Portland, OR 97225; ph: 888/BUS-VALU (888/287-8258) or 503/291-7963; fax: 800/846-2291 or 503/291-9755; *www.BVResources.com.*

Law & Contemporary Problems. Duke University School of Law, Duke Law Publications, Box 90364, Science Drive/Towerview Rd., Durham, NC 27708; ph: 919/613-7101; *www.law.duke.edu/journals/lcp/.* Published quarterly.

Mergerstat Review. FactSet Mergerstat, 2150 Colorado Avenue, Suite 150, Santa Monica, CA 90404; ph: 800/455-8871; fax: 310/829-4855; *www.Mergerstat.com.* Published annually.

Shannon Pratt's Business Valuation Update, monthly, Business Valuation Resources, 7412 S.W. Beaverton-Hillsdale Hwy, Suite 106, Portland, OR 97225; ph: 888/BUS-VALU (888/287-8258) or 503/291-7963; fax: 800/846-2291 or 503/291-9755; *www.BVResources.com.*

The Tax Magazine. CCH, 4025 W. Peterson Ave., Chicago, Ill. 60646; 800/449-8114. *www.cch.com.* Published monthly.

The Journal of Corporation Law. University of Iowa, College of Law, Iowa City, IA 52242; ph: 319/335-9061; fax: 319/335-9019; *www.uiowa.edu/~lawjcl/.* Published quarterly.

Trust and Estates. Primedia, 249 W. 17th St., 3rd floor, New York, NY 10011; 212/462-3586. *www.trustsandestates.com.* Published monthly.

Valuation Case Digest. Valuation Information, Inc., 8898 Commercial Rd., Suite 3C, Commerce, Michigan 48382. 248/366-8518. Published quarterly.

Valuation Strategies. Warren, Gorham & Lamont, a division of RIA, 395 Hudson St., New York, NY 10014; ph: 800/950-1216, Ext. 1, or 800/431-9025, option 1; *www.riahome.com.* Published bimonthly.

Value Matters. Mercer Capital, 5860 Ridgeway Center Parkway, Suite 400, Memphis, Tenn. 38120; ph: 901/685-2120; fax: 901/685-2199; *www.mercercapital.com/Publications/ValueMatters/archive /Default.htm.* New postings continuously.

MERGERS AND ACQUISITIONS DATABASES

BIZCOMPS®. Business Valuation Resources, 7412 S.W. Beaverton-Hillsdale Hwy, Suite 106, Portland, OR 97225; ph: 888/BUS-VALU (888/287-8258) or 503/291-7963; fax: 800/846-2291 or 503/291-9755; *www.BVResources.com.*

Done Deals. Practitioners Publishing Company, 3221 Collinsworth, Ft. Worth, TX, 76107; ph: 800/323-8724, option 6; *www.donedeals.com.*

IBA's "Market Database." Institute of Business Appraisers; P.O. Box 17410 Plantation, FL 33318; (954) 584-1144 phone, (954) 584-1184 fax; *www.go-iba.org.*

Mergerstat®/Shannon Pratt's Control Premium Study. Business Valuation Resources, 7412 S.W. Beaverton-Hillsdale Hwy, Suite 106, Portland, OR 97225; ph: 888/BUS-VALU (888/287-8258) or 503/291-7963; fax: 800/846-2291 or 503/291-9755; *www.BVResources.com.*

Pratt's Public. Business Valuation Resources, LLC, 7412 S.W. Beaverton-Hillsdale Hwy, Suite 106, Portland, OR. 97225; ph: 888/BUS-VAL (888/287-8258) or 503/291-7963; fax: 800/846-2291 or 503/291-9755; *www.BVResources.com.*

Pratt's Stats. Business Valuation Resources, 7412 S.W. Beaverton-Hillsdale Hwy, Suite 106, Portland, OR 97225; ph: 888/BUS-VALU (888/287-8258) or 503/291-7963; fax: 800/846-2291 or 503/291-9755; *www.BVResources.com.*

DISCOUNT FOR LACK OF MARKETABILITY DATABASES

Emory Pre-PO Transaction Database, Emory Business Advisors, LLC, 611 North Broadway, Suite 210, Milwaukee, WI 53202; (800) 252-5984 or (414) 273-9991 phone, (414) 273-9992 fax; *www.emory-bizval.com.*

FMV Opinions Restricted Stock Database, Business Valuation Resources, 7412 SW Beaverton-Hillsdale Hwy, Suite 106, Portland, OR 97225; (888) BUS-VALU or (503) 291-7963 phone; (800) 846-2291 or (503) 291-7955 fax; *www.BVRsources.com.*

Valuation Advisors Pre-IPO Transaction Database, Business Valuation Resources, 7412 SW Beaverton-Hillsdale Hwy, Suite 106, Portland, OR 97225; (888) BUS-VALU or (503) 291-7963 phone; (800) 846-2291 or (503) 291-7955 fax; *www.BVRsources.com.*

Table of Cases

Estate of Williams v. Comm'r, T.C. Memo 1998-59, 75 T.C.M. (CCH) 1276

Estate of Winkler v. Comm'r, T.C. Memo 1989-231, 57 T.C.M. (CCH) 382

Estate of Wright v. Comm'r, T.C. Memo 1997-53, ¶ 67,257, 73 T.C.M. (CCH) 1863

Estate of Yaeger v. Comm'r, T.C. Memo 1986-48, 52 T.C.M. (CCH) 524

Estate of Young v. Comm'r, 110 T.C. 297 (1998)

Eyler v. Comm'r, 88 F.3d 445 (7th Cir. 1996), *aff'g* T.C. Memo 1995-123, 69 T.C.M. (CCH) 2000

First Nat'l Bank v. United States, 763 F.2d 891 (7th Cir. 1985)

Frank v. Comm'r, 447 F.2d 552 (7th Cir. 1971)

Frymire-Brinati v. KPMG Peat Marwick, 2 F.3d 183, 186 (7th Cir. 1993)

General Utilities & Operating Co. v. Comm'r, 296 U.S. 200 (1935)

Gillespie v. United States, 23 F.3d 36 (2d Cir. 1994)

Grill v. United States, 303 F.3d 922 (Ct. Cl. 1962)

Grimes v. Vitalink Comm. Corp., 1997 Del. Ch. LEXIS 124 (Del. Ch. 1997)

Gross v. Comm'r, 272 F.3d 333 (6th Cir. 2001), *aff'g* T.C. Memo 1999-254, 78 T.C.M. (CCH) 201

Gross v. Comm'r, T.C. Memo 1999-254, 78 T.C.M. (CCH) 201 (1999), *aff'd* 272 F.3d 333 (6th Cir. 2001)

Hardy v. Comm'r, 181 F.3d 1002 (9th Cir. 1999)

Heffley v. Comm'r, 884 F.2d 279 (7th Cir. 1989), *aff'g* 89 T.C. 265 (1987)

Helvering v. Walbridge, 70 F.2d 683, 684 (2d Cir. 1934), *cert. denied* 293 U.S. 594 (1934)

Hilbron v. Comm'r, 85 T.C. 677 (1985)

Holland v. Comm'r, 835 F.2d 675 (6th Cir. 1987), *aff'g*. T.C. Memo 1985-627

Howard v. Shay, 1993 U.S. Dist. LEXIS 20153 (C.D. Cal. 1993), *rev'd and remanded* 100 F.3d 1484 (9th Cir. 1996), *cert. denied* 520 U.S. 1237 (1997)

Hudson River Woolen Mills v. Comm'r, 9 B.T.A. 862, 868 (1927)

In re Jackson Nat'l Life Ins. Co., 2000 WL 33654070 (W.D. Mich. 2000), 2000 U.S. Dist. LEXIS 1318

Independence Tube Corp v. Levine, 535 N.E.2d 927, 930 (Ill. 1988)

Institutional Equipment & Interiors, Inc. v. Hughes, 562 N.E.2d 662 (Ill. 1990)

Ithaca Trust Co. v. United States, 279 U.S. 151 (1929)

J.C. Shepard v. Comm'r, 115 T.C. 30 (2000)

Knight v. Comm'r, 115 T.C. 506 (2000)

Krapf v. United States, 977 F.2d 1454 (1992)

Krapf v. United States, 35 Fed. Cl. 286 (1996)

Kumho Tire Co., Ltd. v. Carmichael, 526 U.S. 137 (1999)

Langdon v. Comm'r, 2003 U.S. App. LEXIS 2714 (8th Cir. 2003)

Laserage Tech. Corp. v. Laserage Lab., Inc., 972 F.2d 799, 805 (7th Cir. 1992)

Laureys v. Comm'r, 92 T.C. 101, 129 (1989)

Leonard Pipeline Contractors, Ltd. v. Comm'r, T.C. Memo 1996-316, 72 T.C.M. (CCH) 83, *rev'd and remanded* 142 F.3d 1133 (9th Cir. 1998)

Lightning Lube, Inc. v. Witco Corp., 4 F.3d 1153 (3d Cir. 1993)

Local Finance Corp. v. Comm'r, 407 F.2d 629 (7th Cir. 1969)

Mandelbaum et. al. v. Comm'r, T.C. Memo 1995-255, 69 T.C.M. (CCH) 2852, *aff'd* 91 F.3d 124 (1996)

Matter of Express, Inc., Nos. 812330, 812331, 812332 (N.Y. Division of Tax Appeals)

Index